PLEASE DON'T WISH ME A MERRY CHRISTMAS

CRITICAL AMERICA

General Editors: RICHARD DELGADO and JEAN STEFANCIC

PLEASE DON'T WISH ME A MERRY CHRISTMAS

A Critical History of the Separation of Church and State

Stephen M. Feldman

NEW YORK UNIVERSITY PRESS
New York and London

NEW YORK UNIVERSITY PRESS
New York and London

Library of Congress Cataloging-in-Publication Data

Feldman, Stephen M., 1955–
    Please don't wish me a merry Christmas : A critical history of the
separation of church and state / Stephen M. Feldman.
        p.   cm. — (Critical America)
    Includes bibliographical references and index.
    ISBN 0-8147-2637-2 (alk. paper)
    1. Church and state—United States—Controversial literature.
2. Christianity and antisemitism—United States.   3. Christianity
and antisemitism—History.   4. United States—Church history—20th
century.   5. United States—Politics and government—20th century.
I. Title.   II. Series. .
BR516.F44   1997
322'.1'09—dc20   96-35601
                                      CIP

New York University Press books are printed on acid-free paper,
and their binding materials are chosen for strength and durability.

Manufactured in the United States of America
10 9 8 7 6 5 4 3 2 1

To my parents, Isaac and Frances,
for the love and education they gave me

Yes, Virginia, there is a Santa Claus. . . . Alas, how dreary would be the world if there were no Santa Claus. . . . There would be no childlike faith, then, no poetry, no romance to make tolerable this existence. We should have no enjoyment, except in sense and sight. The Eternal light with which childhood fills the world would be extinguished.

—Francis Church

Speak truth to power.   —Elie Wiesel

Contents

Preface

Many people have helped me in different ways during the writing of this book. I thank the numerous individuals who commented on various parts of the manuscript: Richard Delgado, Daniel Farber, John Garvey, Gary Minda, Mark Tushnet, Tom Wartenberg, Larry Backer, Morris Bernstein, Bill Hollingsworth, Lundy Langston, Marla Mansfield, Nick Rostow, Mark Brauner, Laura Feldman, and Virginia Lockman. I appreciate also the comments received from the participants at the 1994 Mid-South Philosophy Conference, where I presented some of my ideas on the postmodern concept of power. I especially thank Richard Delgado, Jean Stefancic, and Niko Pfund for including this project in the Critical America series from New York University Press. The financial support of the Faculty Summer Research Grant Program of the University of Tulsa College of Law helped create the time needed to work on the book. The librarians at the University of Tulsa College of Law—particularly Nanette Hjelm, Carol Arnold, and Rich Ducey—helped me enormously in obtaining resources needed for research. Finally, I thank my family, Laura, Mollie, and Samuel, for always being so wonderful, loving, and supportive.

An earlier version of chapter 10 appeared in the Iowa Law Review.

CHAPTER I

Introduction

Different Stories

A STORY ABOUT THE WAYS OF POWER

I am Jewish.

In the fall of 1993, my four-year-old daughter began a prekindergarten program in an experimental public school in Tulsa, Oklahoma. That October, when my wife and I learned that the school, called the Mayo Demonstration School, had displayed and decorated a Christmas tree during the previous year, we sent the following letter to the principal:

Dear Ms. Erling:

As parents of a Mayo student, we request that the Mayo School refrain from celebrating any religious holidays. We realize that many public schools routinely celebrate religious holidays, particularly the Christian holidays of Christmas and Easter. Nonetheless, we hope that Mayo, because of its commitment to diversity and its status as a flagship institution of the public school system, will assume a position of leadership in this regard. Public school celebrations of holidays inevitably place children who belong to minority (non-Christian) religions in a dilemma. The children must choose between, on the one hand, conforming to the celebratory practices of the majority religion or, on the other hand, refusing to participate in an activity that most if not all of the other children perform. An adult facing such a dilemma might feel uncomfortable; a young child will likely suffer more intense injury. Such a child will, at a minimum, feel a distance and exclusion from the Mayo community, or worse, the child might risk overt ostracism from peers and a loss of self-esteem.

We believe that this unfortunate situation can be avoided simply by not celebrating any religious holidays. We understand that many individuals believe that certain activities—such as singing Christmas songs, participating in a Christmas play, telling Christmas stories, hunting for Easter eggs, and constructing or displaying symbols or ornaments, including a Christmas tree, Christmas tree decorations, a Santa Claus, or Easter eggs—are secular and merely recognize our American traditions. But from the perspective of a religious minority, these activities and symbols clearly denote Christian holidays; Christmas and Easter are most assuredly not secular and are not holidays for Judaism, Islam, Buddhism, or any other non-Christian religion. To us, the American traditions that should be recognized in the public schools are diversity, respect for difference, and the separation of religion from governmental institutions (including the public schools).

Possibly, many who sympathize with our concerns might respond by proposing that Mayo recognize the activities and symbols of minority religions as well as those of Christianity. For example, in December, it might be suggested that a Chanukah Menorah (candle holder) and a Kwanzaa Kinara (candle holder) be placed alongside a Christmas tree. Unfortunately, such pluralistic displays—however well-intentioned—fail to alleviate the difficulties generated by any celebrations of religious holidays in the public schools. Pluralistic holiday displays are unlikely to protect children of minority religions from the psychological and educational injuries discussed above. Any religious activities or displays inevitably will strain the Mayo community by forcing children to choose between participating in religious activities or risking exclusion and self-doubt. Moreover, such pluralistic displays, often consisting of token symbols of many religious holidays, trivialize the significance of each child's heritage. And most important, in an educational setting, these displays tend to confuse children by denigrating the important differences between religions. The celebrations of distinctive religions rarely can be equated: Chanukah is not the Jewish Christmas (Chanukah is a relatively minor Jewish holiday), just as Kwanzaa is not the African-American Christmas (Kwanzaa is not a religious holiday at all). In conclusion, a school policy sensitive simultaneously to both the importance of religion and the diversity of religious practices and beliefs should prohibit the celebration of all religious holidays.

We must emphasize that we do not wish to deny any children the joy of celebrating their religious holidays. We respect the desires of many within the Mayo community to honor their religious traditions by celebrating with family and friends in their homes and at their churches (or synagogues, mosques, or other places of religious worship). We ask only that these traditions not be observed at Mayo itself.

We thank you for your consideration of this matter.

At first, unknown to my wife and me, our letter prompted the principal to ask a Site Advisory Committee, consisting of three school personnel and five parents of Mayo students, to consider the issue of "holiday" parties.[1] When my wife eventually (though inadvertently) discovered that the Committee had placed this issue on the agenda for its next meeting, she managed to secure an invitation so that we could present our views (the principal had not given copies of our letter to the members of the committee, supposedly in an effort to protect our privacy). At the meeting, we distributed our letter to the Committee members and summarized our position orally.

In response, the Committee members informed us that this matter had been fully considered the previous year. From their perspective, the Committee and the parent-teacher association (PTA) had thoughtfully deliberated, with appropriate concern for all positions, and had decided not to display a Christmas tree, but to display instead a "holiday" tree during December. Moreover, the children had merely created (secular) art decorations that were then placed on the holiday tree; those decorations, we were told, were not Christmas ornaments. The committee members insisted that they had handled the issue with tremendous "sensitivity"; after all, they noted, unlike some other schools, Mayo had not displayed a crèche. (As Dave Barry might say: I am not making this up.) Unconvinced by the Committee's professed sensitivity, my wife emphasized that since the tree was erected only in December, its display would strongly suggest to the children that it was, in fact, a Christmas tree. In response, the one Committee member who appeared somewhat sympathetic to our position asked if the religious symbolism would be neutralized if the tree were displayed throughout the year. Hopeful for compromise, my wife agreed that she would be satisfied with this modification of the school policy (though I found it unsatisfactory). The committee then voted to present to the PTA a proposal to have the tree displayed all year long. Before the meeting ended, though, another committee member flatly declared that my wife and I were being "ridiculous."

At the next PTA meeting, the proposal was unanimously defeated.

A DOMINANT STORY ABOUT THE SEPARATION OF CHURCH AND STATE

The establishment and free exercise clauses of the first amendment to the Constitution state: "Congress shall make no law respecting an establishment of religion, or prohibiting the free exercise thereof."[2] In recent years, commentators have discussed exhaustively and have disputed vehemently the meanings of these religion clauses. Do the clauses prohibit the injection of religious values into the so-called public square of political debate? Does the establishment clause prohibit praying, moments of silence, and other religious or quasi-religious activities in public schools?

Does the free exercise clause require the government to grant religious exemptions from laws of general applicability? What doctrinal tests should courts use to determine the scope of the two clauses?[3]

Regardless of the particular topical issue, though, nearly all discussions of the religion clauses build upon one dominant or standard story of the separation of church and state. This oft-repeated and almost universally accepted story focuses on two themes. First, the separation of church and state stands as a constitutional principle that promotes democracy and equally protects the religious freedom of all Americans, especially religious outgroups, including Jews. Second, this principle emerges as a unique American contribution to political theory. Sometimes this latter theme is modified to acknowledge that the framers of the first amendment drew upon Enlightenment political thought; the principle of separation of church and state is then understood as a political idea spawned during the Enlightenment that culminated in American constitutionalism.[4] Either way, commentators assume that at some point in the history of the United States, religious freedom and equality triumphed over persecution, oppression, and injustice. Indeed, the dominant story appears in different guises only because writers disagree about *when* (and not whether) religious liberty ascended to victory: either during the late eighteenth century, after the constitutional framing and the adoption of the first amendment; during the nineteenth century, after the last official state establishments withered away; or during the twentieth century, after the Supreme Court began seriously enforcing the religion clauses against the state and federal governments.

American legal scholars and Supreme Court justices have long celebrated this dominant story of the separation of church and state. In the nineteenth century, David Dudley Field wrote: "It is the reasonable and lofty boast of this, our country, that it has made religious freedom a reality at last."[5] In the mid-twentieth century, Leo Pfeffer, the renowned church–state advocate and scholar, passionately declared:

> Before the launching of the American experiment, the concept of religious liberty and the separation of church and state was—for all practical purposes—unknown. The experiment embodied in the majestic words [of the religion clauses] was a uniquely American contribution to civilization. . . . The principle of separation and freedom was conceived as a unitary principle. Notwithstanding occasional instances of apparent conflict, separation guarantees freedom, and freedom requires separation. . . . When the constitutional fathers and the generation that adopted the Constitution formalized the concept [of separation of church and state] in the First Amendment, they thereby imposed—and intended to impose—on future generations of Americans in church and state a great moral obligation to preserve their experiment and

adhere strictly to the principle they expressed. [And] the American people have by and large been faithful to the obligation placed on them by the framers of the First Amendment; church and state have been kept separate, and religious freedom has been preserved.[6]

And again, in 1993, Stephen L. Carter wrote similarly: "The separation of church and state is one of the great gifts that American political philosophy has presented to the world."[7]

The Supreme Court too has subscribed to the dominant story. Shortly after World War II, the Court wrote: "These words [in the religion clauses] of the First Amendment reflected in the minds of early Americans a vivid mental picture of conditions and practices which they fervently wished to stamp out in order to preserve liberty for themselves and for their posterity.... The First Amendment has erected a wall between church and state. That wall must be kept high and impregnable."[8] More recently, the Court reiterated: "[The religion clauses] are recognized as guaranteeing religious liberty and equality to 'the infidel, the atheist, or the adherent of a non-Christian faith such as Islam or Judaism.'"[9]

My purpose in this book is to challenge the two themes of this dominant story of church and state. In contesting the first theme, I argue that the separation of church and state is far more (or far less) than a principle protecting democracy and religious liberty. Contrary to the dominant story, the separation of church and state stands, to a great extent, as a political and religious development that manifests and reinforces Christian domination in American society. In disputing the second theme of the dominant story, I argue that the separation of church and state, whether a principle or not, did not arise first in America, either at the time of the constitutional framing or later. Rather, as a political and religious development, the separation of church and state has slowly evolved throughout western history, beginning with the initial emergence of Christianity as it contentiously separated from Judaism. Thus, to understand the growth and transformation of the concept of separation of church and state, I follow the historical path of two institutions—the Christian church and the state—from the origins of Christianity to the present day.

In challenging the dominant story of the separation of church and state, this book offers an extended study of power in a specific context: I explain or interpret the development of Christian social power vis-à-vis the state and religious outgroups. Significantly, with regard to method, I approach the question of power in society from a postmodern perspective. Unlike a modernist approach to power, which typically locates power in some conscious or intentional center, such as an individual, a group of individuals, or a sovereign, a postmodern approach underscores that "power is everywhere and in everyone."[10] Hence, although I explore the evolution of church and state from premodernism to modernism to the current time (postmodernism or modernism/postmodernism?), I use a postmodern conception of power to understand developments throughout all of these eras. Such a postmodern approach is justified because I do not seek, particularly, to describe how individuals during the various eras subjectively understood power in a broad sense. Rather, I seek to describe (or interpret) how power operated through Christianity during the different epochs.

With this goal in mind, my precise method is to present what I call a critical social narrative of the separation of church and state. In general, a critical social narrative is a narrative re-interpretation of a series of social events and developments that is oriented toward uncovering how power operates. Roughly, in my narrative, I approach the problem of power from three perspectives: the symbolic, the structural, and the interaction of the symbolic and structural. With regard to symbolic power, I typically explore how language or discourse contributes to the orientation of power within society. With regard to structural power, I explore how power is oriented through the contingent relations of different social roles or positions in the organization of society. With regard to the interaction of symbolic and structural power, I explore how they can combine to reinforce certain societal effects such as domination. For example, a specific type of discourse might operate as an ideology that hides or legitimates particular social structures of subjugation.

I do not mean to suggest that I will describe power only in terms of symbols, structures, and their interactions. Frequently, the workings of power lie buried within layers of tradition and culture, so a critical narrative must penetrate below the surface and into history. In such a situation, the movement of power becomes evident in the sometimes intact, sometimes cracked, sometimes twisted, sometimes jumbled strata of a historical sediment. Power lies here within its *own* formations. Two points, then, bear emphasis. First, although the concepts of symbol and structure frequently help explain or interpret the formations or manifestations of power, if one follows a postmodern approach, then power should be conceptualized in multiple, flexible, and tentative ways. One should not attempt to neatly cabin power merely to facilitate simple explanations of complex social developments. Hence, in the course of my narrative of church and state, the workings of power often emerge most clearly through the details of the story rather than through any predetermined framework of analysis. Second, to be reasonably complete, a critical social narrative should consist of two parts: a critical history and a synchronic critique. A critical history explores how particular but contingent symbols and structures arose and evolved, while a synchronic critique analyzes how those symbols and structures work to orient power within society at a certain point in time, particularly the present.[11]

Therefore, I first present a critical history of the separation of church and state as it developed in western society, followed by a synchronic critique or analysis of the separation of church and state in the United States of the later twentieth century. The critical history constitutes the bulk of the book. This history begins in chapter 2 by focusing on the discourse of the New Testament in the context of the emergence of Christianity as it separated from Judaism. Most important, the New Testament for several reasons designated Jews for special religious condemnation by, for example, opposing a hellish world of Jewish carnality to a heavenly world of Christian spirituality. Throughout western history, the peculiar condemnation of "the Jews" not only has been the root source of antisemitism but also has been enormously important to the development of Christianity *and* the state. In particular, the opposition between Jewish carnality and Christian spirituality served as the symbolic framework for the development and understanding in Christendom of the secular power of the state in relation to the spiritual power of the church. Moreover, because Jews have constituted an insular and frequently despised outgroup within Christian societies, the institutions of both the church and the state often have sought to use Jews, each to its own advantage. Since, partly for this reason, Jews frequently have been manipulated and persecuted, if one is interested in accurately gauging the degree of religious freedom and equality in western societies, then the status of Jews—the prototypical religious outgroup—can serve as a convenient barometer. Consequently, whereas the twin foci of my critical social narrative are the institutions of the church and the state, the common thread weaving between the two is the treatment of Jews—in particular, the manifestations of antisemitism. Thus, while I do not intend this book to be a history of antisemitism per se, the story of antisemitism in western society necessarily plays a large role in my critical history of church and state. Of importance, then, I understand antisemitism from a postmodern perspective, consistent with my generally postmodern approach to the problem of power. Unlike someone with a more typically modernist conception of antisemitism, I do not limit the definition of antisemitism to intentional or conscious anti-Jewish actions and attitudes. Instead, in this book, "antisemitism" refers broadly to the intentional or unintentional, conscious or unconscious, hatred, dislike, oppression, persecution, domination, and subjugation of Jews qua Jews for whatever reason or motivation, whether it be religious, cultural, ethnic, racial, or political.[12]

After the initial discussion of the New Testament and the emergence of Christianity, the critical history continues in chapters 2 through 5 by following the evolution of church and state in Europe through the Roman establishment of Christianity, the Christian Middle Ages, the Christian Renaissance and Reformation in continental Europe, and the English Reformation, Civil War, and Revolution.[13] Chapters 6 through 8 follow the development of church and state in North America: from the colonial era, to the American Revolution and the framing of the Constitution, and through the nineteenth and early twentieth centuries. In chapter 9, I focus on America after World War II. During this time, the Supreme Court first became heavily embroiled in issues of church and state; much of this chapter therefore is devoted to reviewing and analyzing the Court's decisions and opinions in the particular social context of the second half of the twentieth century. Finally, chapter 10 completes the critical social narrative by presenting a synchronic critique of the separation of church and state in the postwar era. I diagnose or critically analyze how the constitutional principle of separation of church and state contributes to the current orientation of power within American society. In so doing, I elaborate the threefold perspective on power by explaining and focusing on symbolic power, structural power, and their interaction in the context of exploring church and state in late-twentieth-century America.

My conclusion, in brief, is that the dominant story of the separation of church and state is woefully simplistic and seriously misleading. The separation of church and state did not magically and suddenly appear in the United States. More important, the separation of church and state does not equally protect the religious freedom of all, including religious outgroups. To be sure, I do not argue that religious outgroups necessarily would do better without the separation of church and state. In some instances, the doctrine of separation has protected religious outgroups from oppression. But all in all, the separation of church and state provides far less shelter for religious outgroups than the dominant story would lead one to expect. Moreover, the separation of church and state imposes particular costs or disadvantages on outgroups that are not similarly borne by the Christian majority. Ultimately, the dominant story of church and state is revealed to be dominant not only because it is commonly accepted, but also because it is told from the perspective of the dominant Christian majority. And telling the story of religious freedom and equality from the perspective of the dominant religion has produced a tale that is both self-congratulatory and lacking in nuance. My critical narrative, told from the viewpoint of an American Jew, reveals the constitutional principle of the separation of church and state to be a highly complex social phenomenon that flows primarily from and helps reproduce the Christian domination of American society and culture.

CHAPTER 2

Origins of Power

The Emergence of Christianity and Antisemitism

THE NEW TESTAMENT

In 63 B.C.E., Rome conquered the Jewish homeland of Israel, and from that time through the first century C.E. and beyond, Israel remained an occupied Roman province.[1] Nevertheless, the Jewish people continued to live according to their professed covenant with God that was articulated in the Jewish laws of the Torah (the first five books of the Hebrew Bible).[2] Many Jewish sects or groups coexisted at that time, with Jesus and his followers (or disciples) constituting merely one of those sundry groups;[3] Jesus himself never imagined that he was leading or creating a religion separate from Judaism.[4] His followers, especially Paul, effectively invented Christianity only after Jesus' death when they declared that they had a new covenant with God— that is, a new testament—which supplanted the old (Jewish) one.[5]

Jesus' disciples did not write the Christian Gospels or the remainder of the New Testament until the latter part of the first century, at least one or two generations after his death.[6] Although the New Testament contained (and still contains) many inconsistencies, it decidedly condemned (and still condemns) Judaism as a religion and Jews as a people. Indeed, starting with the Gospel of Mark (written first) and culminating with the Gospel of John (written last), the four Gospels seemed to progressively intensify the condemnation of Jews and Judaism.[7] Most broadly, the New Testament directly affronted Judaism by portraying its covenant as having been superseded by the Christian one.[8] "The Jews"[9] supposedly had misunderstood their *own* laws and covenant with God.[10] Even worse, the New Testament repeatedly declared that the Jewish covenant always had been defective and that the Jews never had known God: "And the Father himself, which hath sent me, hath borne witness of me. Ye have neither heard his voice at any time, nor seen his shape. And ye have not his word abiding in you: for whom he hath sent, him ye believe not."[11] Most important, according to the New Testament, the Jews were stubbornly and tragically apostate: they not only had killed their own prophets, but ultimately they *killed their own Messiah, Jesus.*[12]

The charge of deicide against the Jews was (and still is) central to the New Testament narrative.[13] The Gospel of Mark effectively indicted the Jews, and the Gospels of Matthew, Luke, and John directly accused the Jews of "intentional murder."[14] Responsibility for Jesus' death thus was squarely placed on the Jews, who supposedly acknowledged as much by chanting, "His blood be on us, and on our children."[15] John even portrays the Jews as *insisting* that Jesus be crucified *despite* the protestations of the Roman procurator, Pilate.

> And from thenceforth Pilate sought to release [Jesus]: but the Jews cried out, saying, If thou let this man go, thou art not Caesar's friend: whosoever maketh himself a king speaketh against Caesar. When Pilate therefore heard that saying, he brought Jesus forth, and sat down in the judgment seat in a place that is called the Pavement, but in the Hebrew, Gabbatha. And it was the preparation of the passover, and about the sixth hour: and he saith unto the Jews, Behold your King! But they cried out, Away with him, away with him, crucify him. Pilate saith unto them, Shall I crucify your King? The chief priests answered, We have no king but Caesar. Then delivered he him therefore unto them to be crucified. And they took Jesus, and led him away.[16]

Not only were the Jews accused of killing Jesus, they supposedly condemned Jesus for blasphemy against Jewish law. The Jews, that is, executed Jesus for religious infractions. For instance, the Gospel of John states:

> Pilate therefore went forth again, and saith unto [the Jews], Behold, I bring him forth to you, that ye may know that I find no fault in him. Then came Jesus forth, wearing the crown of thorns, and the purple robe. And Pilate saith unto them, Behold the man! When the chief priests therefore and officers saw him, they cried out, saying, Crucify him, crucify him. Pilate saith unto them, Take ye him, and crucify him: for I find no fault in him. The Jews answered him, We have a law, and by our law he ought to die, because he made himself the Son of God.[17]

Historical evidence, however, strongly suggests that the New Testament authors intentionally fabricated this description of Jesus' death.[18] During the first century C.E., many bands of Jewish insurgents opposed Roman rule, and indeed, Jews ultimately rebelled (albeit unsuccessfully) against Rome in 66 C.E.[19] The leaders of these insurgent corps were often referred to as "kings" or "messiahs"—as many claimed to be the Jewish Messiah. In Judaism, the Messiah often was (and is) understood to be a political leader who will usher in Jewish sovereignty and world peace (Christians later transformed this Jewish concept so that the Messiah became God incarnate).[20] Hence, from the Roman standpoint, Jesus was merely another troublesome political agitator (or Messiah), a "dangerous peasant nuisance."[21] Moreover, Pilate was a vicious ruler who brutally massacred countless victims (perhaps thousands); he would not have sympathized with Jesus or any other insurgent.[22] Most likely, then, the ruling Romans, under Pilate's command, were solely responsible for killing Jesus: the Romans arrested Jesus, summarily tried him in a military-type proceeding, sentenced him to death, and executed him by crucifixion as they did similarly with hundreds, and perhaps thousands, of other Jewish insurgents.[23] Under an alternative and weaker reading of the sparse evidence, some Jews might have played, at most, a subsidiary role in Jesus' death. Two of the major Jewish sects of the time were the rival Sadducees and Pharisees—with the Pharisees being the direct ancestors of modern Jews.[24] The Romans allowed the Jews to maintain a governing institution, the Sanhedrin, which was divided into two separate bodies, one political and the other religious. The Romans occasionally ordered the political Sanhedrin, drawn from the Sadducean aristocracy, to examine and surrender Jews charged with sedition against Rome, with the Romans then passing and executing final judgment. The political Sanhedrin thus might have cooperated in the Romans' condemnation of Jesus as one of many political agitators. Even if this were the case, however, neither the Pharisees nor the religious Sanhedrin contributed to Jesus' death.[25]

Why then did Jesus' followers and the New Testament disingenuously accuse the Jews of killing Jesus, and of doing so for religious reasons? Apparently, Jesus' disciples were motivated chiefly by political self-interest; in the words of John Dominic Crossan, a Catholic theologian, the passion narratives of the New Testament were, quite simply, "Christian propaganda."[26] Once the disciples realized that few Jews were willing to convert to Christianity, the disciples focused their energies on converting the Roman gentiles. With that goal in mind, the disciples recognized that—regardless of history—they might further their cause by blaming the Jews instead of the Romans for Jesus' death. Moreover, by blaming the Jews, the

Christians could minimize their antagonization of the powerful and poten-tially oppressive Roman government. And the Jews were an obvious scape-goat: in an era of Jewish uprisings against the Romans, the disciples could conveniently accuse the Jews of defying the entreaties of the Roman agent, Pilate, even while they pressed for Jesus' death. Finally, by blaming the Jewish religion itself instead of the political Sanhedrin, the disciples were able to accentuate the differences between Christianity and Judaism.[27]

To understand the significance of this final point, one must recognize that Jesus' sudden death presented his followers with potential ruin. They were compelled either to somehow explain this violent turn of events or to admit that they *mistakenly* had believed Jesus was the Messiah prophesied in the Hebrew Scriptures (since Jesus had *failed* to usher in Jewish sover-eignty and world peace). The latter choice—admitting a mistake—would ensure humiliation and collapse for the disciples. Not only would they be acknowledging their own fallibility, but, perhaps more important, they would be implicitly conceding that they inadvertently had contributed to Jesus' death. The Romans executed Jesus because they feared him as a political insurgent, and their fears were based largely on his followers' own messianic expectations of him. If those messianic expectations were mis-placed, then his followers had contributed to Jesus' death by futilely and falsely calling him a Messiah.[28]

The disciples, borrowing concepts from other (non-Judaic) religions and philosophies, responded to this possible personal catastrophe with two inconsistent assertions. First, they insisted that Jesus had died for a specific reason: to atone for humanity's collective or original sin.[29] Second, they maintained that Jesus was not truly dead: he was resurrected and had ascended to Heaven.[30] These two assertions suggested, then, that Jesus' execution did not mark his failure and defeat, but rather represented one episode in a continuing cosmic struggle between good and evil, between God and Satan.[31] And even in that one episode featuring Jesus' death, Jesus emerged victorious because he had atoned for human sin. Moreover, the two assertions grounded the professed *universalism* of Christianity. According to this Christian dogma, *all* humans inherited the stain of origi-nal sin, and Jesus became incarnate so that he could die in atonement for the sin of *all* humanity. Christianity therefore insisted (and still insists) that it alone provides the sole and universal path to salvation.[32] To reinforce these central assertions regarding Jesus' death, the Christians searched the *Hebrew* Scriptures for historical passages which they could interpret to show that Jesus' life and death as the Messiah had been prophesied.[33] Most

Jews, of course, rejected this re-interpretation of their own history and Bible. Consequently, the disciples sought to negate the Jews' insistently Judaic understanding of the Hebrew Bible; indeed, the disciples sought, in effect, to negate Judaism itself in their effort to bolster the Christian interpretation of history as leading to Jesus as the Messiah.[34]

The New Testament starkly dramatized both the reason for and the consequence of the Jewish apostasy. If Jesus were engaged in a cosmic struggle between good and evil, then the Jews refused to "believe"[35] Jesus because, supposedly, they were from the Devil:

> Jesus said unto them, If God were your Father, ye would love me: for I proceeded forth and came from God; neither came I of myself, but he sent me. Why do ye not understand my speech? even because ye cannot hear my word. Ye are of your father the devil, and the lusts of your father ye will do. He was a murderer from the beginning, and abode not in the truth, because there is no truth in him. When he speaketh a lie, he speaketh of his own: for he is a liar, and the father of it. And because I tell you the truth, ye believe me not.[36]

The Jews therefore deserve a fate of endless persecution and suffering—until one day they finally realize their apostasy and voluntarily believe that Jesus was Christ.

> O Jerusalem, Jerusalem, *thou* that killest the prophets, and stonest them which are sent unto thee, how often would I have gathered thy children together, even as a hen gathereth her chickens under *her* wings, and ye would not! Behold, your house is left unto you desolate. For I say unto you, Ye shall not see me henceforth, till ye shall say, Blessed is he that cometh in the name of the Lord.[37]

With this execration of the Jews—they are literally condemned to Hell[38] —the New Testament continually differentiated and relentlessly denounced Judaism. Once again borrowing a theme from other religions and philosophies (here, particularly, Platonist metaphysics)—a theme that eventually would become central to the development of the doctrine of the separation of church and state—the New Testament emphasized a dualism: the carnality of the body was opposed to the spirituality of the soul. The Jews were characterized and reviled as carnal, while Christians were revered as spiritual.[39] The Jews were "born after the flesh,"[40] but Christians "[w]alk in the Spirit [and] shall not fulfill the lust of the flesh."[41] Whereas Christians emphasized faith in eternal salvation, the Jews mistakenly emphasized works or conduct in this world: "But Israel, which followed after the law of righteousness, hath not attained to the law of righteousness. Wherefore? Because they sought it not by faith, but as it were by the works of the law. For they stumbled at that stumblingstone."[42] Hence, the Christian Bible repeatedly referred (and still refers) to the Jews as hypocrites, blind fools, and hard of heart because they follow empty laws bereft of spirit. The Jews aimlessly dwelled on this-worldly matters, while Christians strove for other-worldly glory.[43] The New Testament captured this opposition between Earth and Heaven—between Jewish carnality and Christian spirituality—in a metaphor that soon would become crucial to St. Augustine: "For here we have no continuing city, but we seek one to come."[44]

While the New Testament's dichotomy between Jewish carnality and Christian spirituality eventually would become important to the development of the doctrine of the separation of church and state, the New Testament more directly addressed the relation between the secular and religious realms. In the course of once again denigrating the Pharisees (Jews) for "their hypocrisy,"[45] Jesus reputedly stated: "Render to Caesar the things that are Caesar's, and to God the things that are God's."[46] This statement seemed to recognize and approve of the existence of two realms with separate authorities: the civil or political realm subject to the Roman emperor and the religious realm subject to God's authority. The Christian rejection of the Jewish Torah, which included laws for all aspects of social and civil life, facilitated this recognition and approval of the Roman civil authority. In effect, the Christian repudiation of Jewish law opened a gap where the Roman civil law could legitimately function (within the Christian worldview).[47] Thus, unsurprisingly, this New Testament passage conveniently furthered the early Christians' political interests in relation to the Roman authorities and the Jews. In particular, this passage suggested, first, that contemporary Christians willingly accepted Roman civil authority; second, that Jesus never had aspired to the secular kingship of Israel and thus never had threatened the Roman *imperium* (secular state); and third, that Jesus was an enemy of the Jews, many of whom clearly opposed the Roman authorities.[48] In one brief passage, then, the Christians were able to ingratiate themselves with the powerful Romans while simultaneously condemning the disempowered Jews. Nonetheless, one must remember that while the New Testament here acknowledged Roman civil authority, that authority was limited to *this* world—the temporal world of the carnal Jews. Jesus Christ reigned supreme in the only world that the New Testament deemed truly important, the eternal Christian Heaven of salvation.

THE CHRISTIAN DISCOURSE OF REDEFINITION:
AN EXCURSUS ON POWER

The discourse of the New Testament illustrates clearly one type of power—symbolic (especially linguistic) power. In particular, two of the central Christian themes operate imperialistically to redefine a subcultural Other, "the Jews." The first such theme is the dualism opposing Christian spirituality against Jewish carnality and the corresponding condemnation of Judaism and this-worldly affairs. This component of Christian dogma redefines Jews by excluding them from the (acceptable) community and by objectifying and denigrating them. The second Christian theme is the professed universalism of Christianity: all individuals are deemed to exist within the unity of the Christian body, so that faith in Jesus as Christ becomes the only path to salvation. This Christian dogma redefines Jews by denying the differences between Christianity and Judaism since even Jews are deemed to be within the unity of the Christian body.

Turning to the first theme, the exclusion, objectification, and denigration of the Jewish subculture within the New Testament discourse was a crucial symbolic gesture. The condemnation of the Jews helped (and still helps) demarcate the boundaries of the Christian community: Christianity defined itself *against* Judaism. St. John Chrysostom, a Church Father, wrote: "If the Jewish rites are holy and venerable, our way of life must be false. But if our way is true, as indeed it is, theirs is fraudulent."[49] Thus the New Testament effectively fueled institutionalized antisemitism.[50] To Christianity, the Jews represent apostasy—a denial of faith in Jesus as Christ[51]—and God therefore condemns them to suffer in this world and in the next. Their bitter but deserved fate is to wallow in the muck of this-worldly carnality even as they witness the blissful spirituality of Christianity. And the only salvation for the Jews is to recognize their own hardness of heart, to declare their faith in Jesus as Christ, and hence to become Christian. Indeed, according to the New Testament, the only reason that the Jews continue to exist is to witness Christian spirituality and to eventually convert.[52] According to William Nicholls, a Christian theologian, the Christian myth—of the Jewish apostate who actually killed Christ and thus suffers the wrath of God—represents the "charter" of the Christian community.[53] This myth or story "tells the members of the community who they are, giving the community its identity and distinguishing it from others."[54] For individual Christians, then, the denigration and negation of Judaism became an integral "aspect of Christian self-identity."[55]

Despite the significance of the Jewish Other to the Christian identity and community, one must remember that the New Testament authors *created* "the Jew" of the passion narratives. The New Testament condemns a Jew who is a fiction, a "conceptual Jew,"[56] a subject of scorn unconnected to historical reality who was contrived to further the political interests of the Christians. Nonetheless, Christianity has tenaciously retained this conceptual Jew throughout the ages. In fact, the conceptual Jew is so strongly and deeply ingrained in Christian dogma that Jews need not even be present to generate antisemitism or to provoke overt antisemitic outbursts. Rather, throughout history, where Christianity has gone, antisemitism has followed.[57] Nazi Germany has bequeathed several examples of relentless though barren efforts to oppress Jews when only the conceptual Jew remained: "Even when deportations and mass murder were already under way, decrees appeared in 1942 prohibiting German Jews from having pets, getting their hair cut by Aryan barbers, or receiving the Reich sport badge!"[58] Christian doctrine and institutions have so thoroughly redefined the Jewish subculture that, one might conclude, the conceptual Jew stands as the apotheosis of cultural imperialism. Hence, because the conceptual Jew is Christian dogma and does not truly exist, Christians can readily blame "it" for just about anything, including capitalism, communism, the bubonic plague, the deaths of Christian children, and even the Holocaust![59] In a prototypical statement blaming *Jews* for *antisemitism*, Bruno Bauer wrote: "[The Jews] were thus themselves to blame for the oppression they suffered, because they provoked it by their adherence to their law, their language, to their whole way of life."[60]

The second central theme, the universalism of Christianity, which denies the differences between Christianity and other religions (including Judaism), is equally important to Christian power. This theme of Christian universalism helps sustain Christian social power by providing the rhetorical legitimation for political and cultural imperialism. Since all persons are supposedly within the unified body of Christ, all persons are theoretically subject to Christian power. For example, according to the New Testament, the Christian God has the jurisdictional power to condemn the Jews to suffering and, ultimately, Hell—even though they reject Christianity. During the Middle Ages, Christian rulers enacted numerous laws that forced Jews to wear badges or other signs of identification, isolated Jews in ghettos, and exiled Jews from entire countries.[61]

A twentieth-century manifestation of the theme of Christian universalism is the oft-mentioned "Judeo-Christian tradition."[62] Once one recognizes that Christianity historically has engendered antisemitism, then this so-called tradition appears as dangerous Christian dogma (at least from a Jewish perspective).[63] For Christians, the concept of a Judeo-Christian tradition comfortably suggests that Judaism progresses into Christianity—that Judaism is somehow completed in Christianity. The concept of a Judeo-Christian tradition flows from the Christian theology of supersession, whereby the Christian covenant (or Testament) with God supersedes the Jewish one.[64] Christianity, according to this myth, reforms and replaces Judaism. The myth therefore implies, first, that Judaism needs reformation and replacement, and second, that modern Judaism remains merely as a "relic."[65] Any current vitality within Judaism is encompassed in its supposedly improved version, Christianity. To Christians, then, Jews stubbornly resist the natural progression of history: after all, why not just accept the truth of Jesus Christ?[66] To many Jews, however, Christian proselytizing is "aggressive in its perpetual nagging of others to accept salvation through Jesus Christ."[67] The many public forms of Christian preaching—such as the prominently displayed signs asserting that "Jesus is Lord," the bumper stickers declaring that "Jesus loves you," and the ostentatious Christmas displays—all constantly and annoyingly rebuke the Jew for failing to convert to Christianity.

Most important, the myth of the Judeo-Christian tradition insidiously obscures the real and significant differences between Judaism and Christianity. As already discussed, Jesus' disciples focused on a fundamental dualism—the opposition between the carnal body and the spiritual soul—and committed Christianity to one side—the spiritual soul—largely to differentiate and denigrate Judaism. This dualism corresponds with other dualisms: an opposition between the material world and an other-worldly Heaven, an opposition between temporality and eternity, and an opposition between conduct and faith. Christianity, maintaining its commitment to spirituality, consequently emphasizes faith in eternal and other-worldly salvation. (Today this emphasis on faith over conduct is especially pronounced in forms of Protestantism.) These various dualisms thus contribute to the cutting of a Christian chasm between two realms—the realm of being (in a temporal and material world) and the realm of becoming (in an eternal and other-worldly Heaven). In Christian dogma, original sin represents this chasm, this separation between God and humanity, and Jesus, as God incarnate or the Son of God, serves to bridge the gap between the realms. To be saved, then, one must have faith in Jesus as Christ, as a span to the eternal bliss of Heaven. Christian faith thus emerges as a type of spiritual belief or attitude—a conviction, a commitment of conscience, or an internal intention that remains largely unconnected to one's conduct in the temporal and material world.[68]

Among other differences, Judaism clearly rejects all of these Christian dualisms, as well as the Christian conception of faith. Most basically, Judaism perceives no opposition or conflict between body and soul: there is simply a whole person.[69] Consequently, Judaism refuses to denigrate the temporal and material world or our life in that world; to the contrary, Judaism celebrates life. According to the Hebrew Bible, God instructs: "I have set before thee this day life and good, and death and evil . . . ; therefore choose life."[70] Indeed, "Judaism is a way of life," and as such, Judaism emphasizes the performance of good and just acts in this world.[71] The Scriptures repeatedly direct Jews toward ethical conduct: "Depart from evil, and do good; Seek peace, and pursue it";[72] "Learn to do well; Seek justice, relieve the oppressed";[73] "do that which is right and good";[74] and "Justice, justice shalt thou follow."[75]

Perhaps more so than any other quality, this stress on good and just acts defines Judaism: "Judaism is a religion of deeds, of doing. . . . To be Jewish, in short, means to be as kind, compassionate, and ethical a person as you can be."[76] Therefore, Judaism encourages us to remain optimistic about life, to oppose evil in this world, and to pursue social justice and progress through our actions.[77] In Judaism, unlike Christianity, the concept of faith itself necessarily entails action; inward belief or intention without action is meaningless.[78] Sin is defined as "failure to live up, in each given situation, to the highest moral potentialities in one's self. Man must live and act always as if his life [and his actions] were tremendously significant . . . reaching distant shores and extending far into the future."[79]

The emphasis on ethical conduct underscores that Judaism is concerned with the individual's place within the community. Many forms of Christianity, on the one hand, countenance individualism because salvation is a private concern that turns primarily on one's internal conscience, faith, and choices.[80] Judaism, on the other hand, assumes a context of social relations that are needed for performing good and just acts. Indeed, in Orthodox and Conservative Judaism, many important prayers can be said only with a *minyan*, a quorum or community of at least ten Jews.[81] All in all, Judaism strives for a balance between the individual and the community. Hillel, the famed rabbi and scholar of the first century B.C.E.,[82] said: "If I am not for myself who will be? But if I am for myself only, what am I?"[83] The relationship between individual and community is complex, but unequivocally, the individual should contribute to the well-being of the community. A Talmudic parable underscores this responsibility:

> Honi, the traveler, ... met a very, very old man busily planting a carob tree. "When will you be able to eat the fruit of the tree?" asked Honi. "In seventy years," replied the old man. "Do you expect to live that long?" the traveler queried. "I did not find the world desolate when I entered it," was the reply. "So I plant for those who come after me."[84]

To summarize, the differences between Judaism and Christianity are numerous and significant. The two religions, though, do share some common elements, such as overlapping (but not identical) ethical systems. Yet, despite some similarities, the religions differ so strikingly that insistence upon a single Judeo-Christian tradition must be met with suspicion. Indeed, upon close inspection, even some of the professed similarities between the religions fracture into distinctions. Christian doctrine, for example, suggests that the two religions share the Old Testament, but as already discussed, the Judaic understanding of the Hebrew Bible differs markedly from the Christian interpretation.[85] William Nicholls underscores the significance of this contest over the Hebrew Bible: "At the root of the split between Christianity and Judaism is a struggle for possession of the Jewish Scriptures, centering on the role of the Messiah."[86] The Christian re-interpretation of the Hebrew Bible not only denies the Judaic understanding but also stands as "the real foundation of Christian theology."[87]

In conclusion, the discourse of the New Testament operated to redefine Jews as a subcultural Other. Yet, *initially*, this discourse was relatively unimportant because, like Jews, Christians were merely one disempowered religious sect within the Roman Empire. Regardless of the anti-Judaic nature of the Christian discourse, Christianity lacked the social power to seriously harm Jews—at that time. As will be discussed in the next section of this chapter, though, once the Romans adopted Christianity as the official religion of the Empire, the previously near-harmless Christian symbolism became a foundation for centuries of Jewish persecution. Yet, while the New Testament authors and Church Fathers purposely condemned Judaism for their own benefit, they could not have *intended* that Jews be persecuted, subjugated, and murdered for the next 2,000 years.[88] Such an intent could arise only if the early Christians knew that their religion eventually would become the established church of the Empire, and such knowledge was, of course, impossible. Quite simply, the early Christians could not have anticipated that the Church soon would have the social and political power to inflict serious harm upon its enemies, especially Jews.

Nonetheless, this explanation does not justify the New Testament discourse of redefinition; it merely means that, as Anthony Giddens has noted, "[h]istory is not an intentional project."[89] Hence, as history unfolded, the antisemitic discourse of the New Testament did, in reality, sustain a remarkable range of persecutions, ranging from relatively minor (though persistent) social insults to ostracism to the most heinous crimes against humanity, including the Holocaust.[90]

THE ROMAN ESTABLISHMENT OF CHRISTIANITY: THE FIRST CRYSTALLIZATION OF CHURCH AND STATE

Initially, Christianity endured as merely one of several religions within the Roman Empire.[91] To Jews, therefore, the Christian dogmatic condemnation of Judaism was insignificant when compared, for example, with the Diaspora resulting from the final Roman defeat of the Jews in 135 C.E.[92] Until the fourth century C.E., Christianity itself suffered occasional persecution under the Romans.[93] In 311, however, Emperor Galerius issued an *Edict of Toleration*, which pardoned Christians for not worshipping pagan gods.[94] Only two years later, Emperors Constantine and Licinius issued the *Edict of Milan*, which officially permitted the practice of Christianity.[95] Moreover, Constantine increasingly became interested in and supportive of Christianity until he declared himself to be a Christian in 324.[96] Although Constantine never decreed Christianity to be the official religion of the Roman Empire, his actions effectively established Christianity as the imperial religion.[97] And then finally, on February 27, 380, Christianity sealed its political triumph: the *Edict of Emperors Gratian, Valentinian II, and Theodosius I* officially established Christianity.[98]

The Roman establishment of Christianity—first unofficial and then official—had three important consequences. First, it introduced questions regarding the relationship between church and state or, more precisely, the relationship between the powers of the papacy and the emperor:[99] would the pope or the emperor direct Christianity, and would the pope influence or control imperial affairs in some manner?[100] As might be expected, emperors and popes disagreed about how to resolve these questions; consequently, two distinctly opposed positions eventually developed. The popes formed a hierocratic view, which deemed the emperor subordinate ultimately to the pope but nonetheless empowered to rule in the temporal and material world for the purpose of protecting the corporate union of Christians.[101] The emperor, it is worth noting, supposedly was relegated to governing a realm that was, at best, irrelevant to eternal salvation and, at worst, condemned as the carnal world of the Jews. In opposition to the papal hierocratic view, the emperors developed the doctrine of Caesaropapism, which declared that the emperor had divine authority to rule over religious as well as imperial affairs.[102] And in fact, in 325, Constantine asserted control over the Church by convoking at Nicaea the first ecumenical or universal council of bishops; the council's Nicaean Creed resolved a dispute regarding the divinity of Jesus as the Son of God.[103] Hence, almost immediately after converting to Christianity, Constantine effectively created and implemented the Caesaropapist approach.[104]

The second consequence of the Roman establishment of Christianity was to infuse the *Church* (and Christianity in general) with additional power. For instance, establishment enabled the papacy to begin operating as a governmental institution,[105] and Christians suddenly held positions of authority within society. Thus, establishment supplied the power needed to speed (and to enforce) the spread of Christianity throughout the empire.[106] Moreover, establishment supplied Christians with the power necessary to begin persecuting members of other religions. In fact, the *Edict of 380*, which officially established Christianity as the Roman religion, also officially condemned all other religions:

> We desire all people, whom the benign influence of our clemency rules, to turn to the religion which tradition from Peter to the present day declares to have been delivered to the Romans by blessed Peter the Apostle ... ; this faith is that we should believe, in accordance with apostolic discipline and Gospel teaching, that there is one Godhead, Father, Son and Holy Spirit, in an equal Majesty and a holy Trinity. We order those who follow this doctrine to receive the title of Catholic Christians, but others we judge to be mad and raving and worthy of incurring the disgrace of heretical teaching, nor are their assemblies to receive the name of churches. They are to be punished not only by Divine retribution but also by our own measures, which we have decided in accordance with Divine inspiration.[107]

The third consequence of the Roman establishment of Christianity was to reinforce the *emperor's* power in at least two ways. First, Christian religious doctrine encouraged ordinary people to focus on other-worldly salvation and not on this-worldly political power; indeed, as already discussed, the New Testament explicitly instructed Christians to "[r]ender to Caesar the things that are Caesar's." Civil obedience was religiously countenanced. Second, the emperor's power was solidified through the process of centralization. Previously, throughout the empire, pagan rituals and ceremonies had helped citizens to identify strongly with their respective cities as opposed to the empire itself. Constantine's embrace of Christianity and the consequent condemnation of pagan religions thus undermined the religious and cultural diversity that had fostered the independence and autonomy of these citizens and their cities.[108] The effect, whether intended or not, of the establishment of Christianity was to increase imperial political power.

For but the first of innumerable times over the next seventeen centuries, Christianity and the state—or more precisely, in this context, the Catholic Church and the emperor—effectively struck a deal for their mutual benefit that incidentally, though seriously, injured Jews. Whereas the Roman establishment of Christianity had increased the power of both the Church and the emperor, it brought disaster down upon the Jews. Because the New Testament had designated Judaism as deserving special condemnation, Christianity had emerged as antisemitic in its origins. Initially, this Christian antisemitism had been relatively unimportant because Christians lacked the societal power to harm Jews. But after establishment, as Christian discourse and culture permeated the empire, and as an increasing number of Christians came to hold positions of authority, Christianity suddenly had the power to enforce its dogmatic antisemitism. Put in different words, when Christianity became the official religion of Rome, the orientation of societal power shifted. The Christian discourse of condemnation suddenly was aligned with the official and physical (and potentially violent) power of the Roman civil authority. A new structural organization for society was forged: Christians now stood in a relation of domination to Jews. At this time, then, the conjunction of the Church and the government (or state) clearly harmed Jews: the antisemitic discourse of the New Testament was already in place, and now the structural relations of power had shifted. The Christian re-definition of the Hebrew Bible, Jewish history, and the Jewish people could be brutally enforced until it became accepted as the normal and natural way of the world. The oppression of Jews thus proceeded—generated and seemingly legitimated by the New Testament symbolism.

Indeed, Christian emperors quickly adopted a stance toward Jews that might have seemed odd but for the New Testament. The emperors largely followed New Testament doctrine in developing a position that was to influence the treatment of Jews throughout the Middle Ages.[109] In particular, by the early fifth century, Jews were burdened with a series of oppressive legal disabilities. For example, Jewish intermarriage with Christians was punishable by death,[110] Jews could not hold advantageous public offices,[111] Jews were forced to observe Christian feasts and fasts,[112] and Jews were prohibited from building synagogues.[113] Moreover, in Rosemary Ruether's words, these "laws bristle with negative and theologically loaded epithets."[114] Judaism is called "an abominable sect and ritual"[115] with "evil teachings,"[116] and Jews thus live "shameful lives"[117] and "insult our [Christian] faith."[118] Echoing the New Testament characterization of Jews as hypocrites who lack spirit, the laws castigate Jews as "detestable in their insolent maneuvering"[119] and as "slyly"[120] obtaining or "worm[ing]"[121] their way into public offices.[122]

Despite these official condemnations and legal persecutions of Jews, the emperors respected the New Testament doctrine that maintained that Jews must continue to exist as witnesses to Christian spirituality and as eventual converts. According to Christian dogma, true conversion and salvation cannot be physically coerced in this world but rather require faith—a spiritual commitment—in Jesus as Christ. Thus, no law specifically prohibited Judaism or directly forced Jews to convert. To the contrary, the laws protected Jews enough to allow them to endure their subjugated and miserable lives, excluded "from the body of society."[123] Yet, while the emperors usually respected a limited Jewish right to exist, Christian mobs often did not. As early as 388, Christian mobs began attacking synagogues. Jews therefore relied upon state or imperial officers for protection, which was often inadequate.[124] A decree from the early fifth century typifies the official or governmental position:

> Let no one who has done no harm be molested on the ground that he is a Jew, nor let any aspect of his religion result in his exposure to contumely; in no place are their synagogues or dwellings to be set afire, or wantonly damaged, for, even if the case be otherwise and some one of them is implicated in criminal activities, obviously it is for precisely this that the vigor of the judiciary and the protection of public law have been instituted among us: That no one should have the right to permit himself private vengeance. But, just as it is Our will that this be the provision for those persons who are Jews, so too do We judge it opportune to warn the Jews that, elated, it may be, by their security, they must not become insolent and admit anything which is opposed to the reverence due to Christian worship.[125]

At this early stage in the history of Jewish–Christian relations, Christian power already has neatly positioned Jews to serve Christian interests. Jews are separated and denigrated—clearly demarcated as the Other—and as such, they are allowed to survive so that they can fulfill their crucial symbolic role for Christianity. To ensure Jewish degradation, Jews are ground into subservience, desperately needing the Christian state[126] to protect them from the Christian mobs. Moreover, to Christians, the persecution and suffering of the Jews is their just desert for their apostasy and deicide. From this perspective, if Jews wish to continue refusing eternal salvation so that they can instead wallow in the muck of this-worldly carnality, then they ought to be forced to live, in effect, like pigs.[127]

Early in the fifth century, St. Augustine wrote *The City of God*,[128] a tremendously influential theological and political treatise. Augustine derived the title of his work from several Old Testament Psalms, such as Psalm 87:3, which reads: "Glorious things are spoken of Thee, O city of God."[129] As a Christian, however, Augustine interpreted the phrase "city of God" in accordance with New Testament symbolism: "For here we have no continuing city, but we seek one to come."[130] This New Testament symbolism, of course, reflects the central Christian dualism that opposes Jewish carnality to Christian spirituality. Although commentators frequently note Augustine's debt to Platonic metaphysics,[131] they rarely mention Augustine's attitude toward Judaism;[132] nonetheless, it is explicit and clearly grounded on New Testament doctrine. To Augustine, the "carnal" and "carnal-minded"[133] Jews "live after the flesh[,] which is certainly evil."[134] As God is "the witness of conscience,"[135] Jews cannot be forced to convert since God will know that true faith in Jesus is lacking. Thus, Jews survive, now in the Diaspora, only to witness the truth of Jesus as Christ, and they deserve to suffer because they committed deicide.[136] In one trenchant passage, Augustine managed to accuse the Jews of impiety, idolatry, and killing Jesus; to assert that God therefore had punished the Jews by sending them on the Diaspora; and to maintain that the Hebrew Bible foretold this Jewish apostasy and suffering:

> [If the Jews] had not sinned against Him with impious curiosity, which seduced them like magic arts, and drew them to strange gods and idols, and at last led them to kill Christ, their kingdom would have remained to them, and would have been, if not more spacious, yet more happy, than that of Rome. And now that they are dispersed through almost all lands and nations, it is through the providence of that one true God; that whereas the images, altars, groves, and temples of the false gods are everywhere overthrown, and their sacrifices prohibited, it may be shown from their books how this has been foretold by their prophets so long before.... [137]

Augustine then predicated his political theory on his conception of the city of God, and his conception manifested the opposition of Jewish carnality to Christian spirituality. Augustine argued that original sin leads to "two kinds of human society, which we may justly call two cities, according to the language of our Scriptures. The one consists of those who wish to live after the flesh, the other of those who wish to live after the spirit."[138] The earthly city is formed by love of self, while the heavenly city—the City of God or the community of Christians—is formed by love of God.[139] Augustine consequently differentiated two spheres of authority, the ecclesiastical and the civil, which corresponded to the two cities.[140] In so doing, Augustine elaborated the New Testament recognition of (Roman) civil authority by emphasizing that the emperor exercises power only in the carnal world (of the Jews).[141] The civil or political authority—which *eventually* would become the state—was, for Augustine, "rooted in human sinfulness."[142] Civil society exists as punishment for the original sin of humanity; the state must restrain evil and punish wrongdoers. Since Christians must live temporarily in the material world of carnal depravity, they should obey the laws of political society, but only while they await and prepare for eternal salvation in Heaven. Augustine, in other words, acknowledged that the two cities and the two authorities should coexist, yet the heavenly city stands supreme over its earthly counterpart. Citizens should humbly obey even unjust civil authorities, though not because of love and respect for the emperor. Rather, obedience demonstrates one's love of God and, in any event, is necessary to contain the disorder and conflict inherent in the carnal world of original sin.[143]

Despite the prominence of *The City of God*, Augustine's conception of the two cities remains notoriously ambiguous. In fact, Augustine himself began the treatise by expressing ambivalence about his central concept, the heavenly city:

> [A] city surpassingly glorious, whether we view it as it still lives by faith in this fleeting course of time, and sojourns as a stranger in the midst of the ungodly, or as it shall dwell in the fixed stability of its eternal seat, which it now with patience waits for. . . .[144]

Quite simply, Augustine did not unequivocally define either the heavenly or the earthly city; moreover, he used the terms in various ways throughout his treatise. For example, at certain points, Augustine seemed to equate the city of God with the Church, but at other points the two are differentiated.[145] Regardless of this imprecision, Augustine's dichotomy of the two cities appeared to focus on two related distinctions. According to the first distinction, the heavenly and earthly cities referred to "two communities:"[146] the saved and the damned. These two communities are "eschatological realities"[147]—they will fulfill themselves only in their ends. One community "is predestined to reign eternally with God, and the other to suffer eternal punishment with the devil."[148] Although they are unfulfilled eschatological entities, both cities nonetheless presently exist; Augustine stated that they have begun "to run their course."[149] Here, then, Augustine edged over into the second distinction. He differentiated two measures of time or history: the sacred (eschatological time) and the *saeculum* (secular or temporal history).[150] The two cities, as eschatological realities, must be understood in *sacred* history as revealed in the Scriptures. Yet, within *secular* time, the two cities currently exist together in unfulfilled (or impure) forms. Augustine wrote: "In truth, these two cities are entangled together in this world, and intermixed until the last judgment effect their separation."[151] Because of Augustine's personal place in secular history—he lived when the Roman Empire was collapsing—he sought to disentangle the future of Christianity from the fate of the empire. Augustine posited, therefore, that the Christian city of God was progressing toward its fulfillment in sacred time, even though empires and kingdoms might rise and fall throughout secular history.[152]

In sum, Augustine was the political theorist who began developing a doctrine of separation of church and state.[153] Without doubt, he did not formulate "any specific conception" of this doctrine, and thus he did not attempt to elaborate the details of the relationship between church and state.[154] Nonetheless, his conceptions of the heavenly city and the earthly city, of the sacred and the secular, implied that the institutions of church and state should not be intimately linked.[155] Moreover, regardless of Augustine's specific intentions when writing *The City of God,* his symbolic division of the heavenly and earthly cities has grounded the subsequent development of the doctrine of the separation of church and state.[156] It bears repeating, then, that Augustine's political theory related closely to his attitude toward Jews, which echoed the already standardized Christian antisemitic dogma. The civil sphere manifested, in effect, the carnal world of Judaism; Jews were doomed to the earthly city and relegated to the protection of the state. Finally, therefore, Augustine's attitude toward the relations between church and state illustrated a truism that today is often overlooked: an individual's conception of the proper relation between church and state necessarily reflects, in part, that individual's own religious orientation.

CHAPTER 3

The Christian Middle Ages

THE EARLY MIDDLE AGES

Pope Gelasius I, pontiff from 492 to 496, drew upon Augustine to articulate a theory of church–empire (or, more loosely, church–state) relations that was ambiguous enough to be used both by popes and by emperors for at least six centuries.[1] In particular, Gelasius wrote the following letter to the emperor:

> There are indeed, most august Emperor, two powers by which this world is chiefly ruled: the sacred authority of the Popes and the royal power. Of these the priestly power is much more important, because it has to render account for the kings of men themselves at the Divine tribunal. For you know, our very clement son, that although you have the chief place in dignity over the human race, yet you must submit yourself faithfully to those who have charge of Divine things, and look to them for the means of your salvation. [But] in matters pertaining to the administration of public discipline, the bishops of the Church [know] that the Empire has been conferred on you by Divine instrumentality....[2]

Thus, Gelasius contributed to the development of the doctrine of separation of church and state by clearly delineating two distinct powers—the sacred and the royal. Each power governed within its respective sphere of action: the sacred power of the Church ruled over the spirituality of the universal body of Christianity, while the royal power of the emperor ruled over the lay affairs of the kingdom. Ecclesiastics should obey the emperor's laws related to material and temporal matters, and the emperor should obey the Church's decisions regarding religious issues such as the sacraments.

Subsequent emperors anxiously seized upon Gelasius's acknowledgment of a rightful sphere of royal or lay power together with his assertion that the emperor's power was conferred "by Divine instrumentality."[3] From the royal standpoint, Gelasius here supplied support for, if not Caesaropapism, at least a balanced dualism—power divided equally.[4] To Gelasius, however, the derivation of the emperor's power from God signified that the emperor was within the universal body of the Roman Catholic Church, not that the emperor shared power equally with the pope. Within the rigid hierarchy of the Christian universal body, only ecclesiastics were qualified to teach and decree about divine and religious matters, and only the pope stood supreme.[5]

Gelasius was, of course, thoroughly familiar with and followed the New Testament condemnation of Judaism, as demonstrated by his occasionally vituperative antisemitic statements.[6] According to the Christian antisemitic dogma revering the spiritual and reviling the carnal, the significance of the emperor's royal power in the temporal and material world naturally paled in comparison to the pope's power over eternal salvation in Heaven. Hence, Gelasius followed New Testament doctrine when he insisted that the Church's power was "much more important"[7] than the emperor's power. In sum, Gelasius articulated an unbalanced dualism in which the pope and the emperor shared power, but the pope exercised more (or more important) power than the emperor.[8]

In the next century, Emperor Justinian I largely accepted Gelasius's political theory—except for the hierocratic conclusion. In a decree issued in 535, Justinian wrote:

> The greatest gifts given by God to men from his heavenly clemency are priesthood and empire (sacerdotium et imperium). The former serves divine things, the latter rules human affairs and has care of them. Both proceed from one and the same source and provide for human life. Therefore nothing shall so preoccupy emperors as the moral wellbeing of priests, since priests pray constantly to God for the emperors themselves.[9]

Thus, Justinian endorsed the Christian dogma that all humans are within the single and universal body of Christ, and he condoned Gelasius's proposition that both the pope and the emperor derive their power from God— all of society, then, supposedly belongs to a natural and hierarchical body (or organism). But Justinian turned Gelasius's hierarchical ordering upside down: according to Justinian, the emperor, not the pope, is supreme.[10] The emperor—literally considered as "divinity on earth"[11]—condescends to ensure the suitability of the clergy because they act on his behalf by praying to God. The remainder of this decree underscored the scope of Justinian's asserted power over Church affairs: it continued by discussing the ordination of clergy and the upkeep of churches.[12]

While Justinian often is cited for his strong expression of Caesaropapism, his famous Code, "one of the most formative agencies of Europe,"[13] did not overlook the Jews. Indeed, as the emperor and professed leader of all Christianity, Justinian codified antisemitism. In the words of Rosemary Ruether, the Code held that Jews were "to present to Christian society the living proof of the social results of divine reprobation, both to testify to the truth of Christianity, and ultimately to convince the Jews themselves of this truth."[14] Thus, for example, the Code prohibited Jews from testifying in court against Christians.[15]

Gregory I, the pope from 590 to 604, looms as one of the most significant medieval figures in the development of the Church and in the treatment of the Jews. Gregory (or Gregory the Great) entertained hierocratic notions, but as an astute political realist, he realized that the emperor's strength in Constantinople and the Eastern Empire was insurmountable. Therefore, Gregory sought to expand the Church's power to the West by, for example, sending missions to England and Gaul.[16] In the East, Gregory deferred to the Caesaropapist view of the emperor, while in the West, he propagated the hierocratic notion that royal power ultimately served the Church. Gregory addressed the emperor as the "Lord Emperor" yet called the Western kings his "dearest sons."[17] Gregory's strategy proved successful: he dramatically increased the influence of the papacy and thus enabled the Church to emerge as a leading governmental institution of the Middle Ages.[18]

Meanwhile, with regard to Judaism, Gregory followed New Testament dogma, and his views became the basis for the medieval "Constitution for the Jews," which guided papal treatment of Jews throughout the Middle Ages.[19] To Gregory, Judaism "would 'pollute' Christian faith and 'deceive with sacrilegious seduction' simple Christian peasants."[20] Jews existed to be converted to Christianity even though they currently were unwilling or unable to see the truth of Jesus as Christ.[21] Nonetheless, Gregory insisted that Jews be allowed to practice their own religion and not be directly forced to convert: "Just as license ought not to be presumed for the Jews to do anything in their synagogues beyond what is permitted by law, so in those points conceded to them, they ought to suffer nothing prejudicial."[22]

Despite this seeming toleration, in reality Gregory condoned resorting to any means necessary, short of physically coercing baptism, in order to induce Jewish conversion. For example, Gregory approved of bribing Jews to convert and forcing them to attend conversion sermons.[23] Moreover, Gregory explicitly attributed his limited toleration of Jews to respect for

Christian, not Judaic, tenets. He wrote that forced baptism had "no profitable effect"[24] because true Christian faith cannot be directly coerced. Gregory continued:

> For, when any one is brought to the font of baptism, not by the sweetness of preaching but by compulsion, he returns to his former superstition, and dies the worse from having been born again.
>
> Let, therefore, your Fraternity [of Christians] stir up such men by frequent preaching, to the end that through the sweetness of their teacher they may desire the more to change their old life. For so our purpose is rightly accomplished, and the mind of the convert returns not again to his former vomit.[25]

Within Christianity, the contrast between the Western hierocratic and the Eastern Caesaropapist tendencies contributed to an eventual schism between the Roman Catholic and Eastern Orthodox churches in 1054.[26] Ultimately, though, a theological dispute culminated in this schism between East and West. The papacy had amended the Nicene Creed (which itself was a modification of the original Nicaean Creed)[27] by adding the filioque clause, which proclaimed that the Holy Spirit "'proceeds' not only 'from the Father' but also 'from the Son' (filioque)."[28] The addition of the filioque offended the Eastern Church for two reasons. First, the papacy had instituted the change unilaterally. Second, the clause transformed the conception of the Holy Trinity.[29] The papacy's commitment to the filioque underscored the increasing "Western emphasis on incarnation as the central reality of the universe."[30] Whereas Eastern Christianity inclined to the mystical—suggesting that Jesus restores humanity to its full communion with God—Western Christianity inclined to the juridical—suggesting that Jesus triumphed over original sin and atoned for human guilt. The focus of Western Christianity on God incarnate, then, legitimated and perhaps motivated the Church's efforts to seek greater temporal power in order to promote the Augustinian City of God on earth.[31]

The schism between East and West and the Western emphasis on the incarnation and temporal power precipitated the Investiture Struggle, which strained Western Christianity for close to seventy-five years.[32] During the ninth and tenth centuries, feudal authorities (lay lords) had begun appointing clerics to their positions and conferring the symbols of their religious or spiritual dignity (a ring and a staff). Such a lay investiture of ecclesiastical office often included the grant of a large fief but required that the cleric, in return, pay homage and swear fealty to the lay lord.[33] As Ernest Henderson writes: "A bishop at that time was not only a dignitary of the church, but also a prince of the realm, whose duty it was to send his contingents to the king's army, and to act as councillor at his court."[34]

The Investiture Struggle emerged because of a sustained papal challenge to this system of lay investiture. As popes and emperors vied for political dominance, the papacy sought in particular to increase the power of the Church primarily by freeing it from imperial and lay control.[35] The most dramatic and climactic events of the Struggle arose during a confrontation between Pope Gregory VII (pontiff from 1073 to 1085) and King Henry IV of Germany (the Holy Roman Emperor).[36] Gregory envisioned and attempted to implement the principles of an extreme hierocracy.[37] In developing his hierocratic themes, Gregory clearly drew upon the Christian ideology of dogmatic antisemitism, expressly condemning Jews pursuant to Christian doctrine. For example, he claimed that Jews worship Satan and therefore should be banned from holding public offices:

> We are compelled out of duty to warn Your Affection, that you ought not permit Jews in your land to be lords over Christians, or to wield any power over them any longer. For what is it to set Christians beneath Jews, and to make the former subject to the judgment of the latter, except to oppress the Church and to exalt the Synagogue of Satan, and, while you desire to please the enemies of Christ, to contemn Christ himself?[38]

Then, to facilitate his justification of a hierocracy, Gregory degraded kings and princes by symbolically placing them in the position of the Jews. For example, Gregory wrote:

> Who does not know that kings and princes are sprung from those who unmindful of God, urged on, in fact, by the devil, the prince of the world, and by pride, plunder, treachery, murders and by almost every crime, have striven with blind cupidity and intolerable presumption to dominate over their equals, that is to say, over men? [Therefore who] can doubt that the priests and Christ are to be accounted fathers and judges of kings and princes and all the faithful?[39]

Gregory thus returned to the fundamental dualism opposing Christian spirituality and Jewish carnality. Royalty springs from the temporal and material world of Jewish carnality and hence deserves condemnation. Kings and princes must bow before the Christian spirituality of the Church.

Supported by this ideological foundation, Gregory resolutely insisted that the papacy controlled royal authorities. Early in his reign, Gregory summarized his hierocratic principles as follows:

1. That the Roman Church was founded by God alone.
2. That the Roman Pontiff alone is rightly to be called universal.
3. That he alone can depose or reinstate bishops. . . .
6. That, among other things, we also ought not to stay in the same house with those excommunicated by him. . . .
9. That the Pope is the only one whose feet are to be kissed by all princes. . . .
12. That he may depose Emperors. . . .
14. That he has power to ordain a cleric of any church he may wish. . . .
16. That no synod may be called a general one without his order.
17. That no chapter or book may be regarded as canonical without his authority.
18. That no sentence of his may be retracted by any one; and that he, alone of all, can retract it.
19. That he himself may be judged by no one. . . .
22. That the Roman Church has never erred, nor ever, by the witness of Scripture, shall err to all eternity. . . .
25. That without convening a synod he can depose and reinstate bishops.
26. That he should not be considered as Catholic who is not in conformity with the Roman Church.
27. That the Pope may absolve subjects of unjust men from their fealty.[40]

Following these principles, Gregory initiated his conflict with King Henry IV by prohibiting lay investiture in February 1075. Gregory decreed:

Inasmuch as we have learned that, contrary to the establishments of the holy fathers, the investiture with churches is, in many places, performed by lay persons; and that from this cause many disturbances arise in the church by which the Christian religion is trodden under foot: we decree that no one of the clergy shall receive the investiture with a bishopric or abbey or church from the hand of an emperor or king or of any lay person, male or female. But if he shall presume to do so he shall clearly know that such investiture is bereft of apostolic authority, and that he himself shall lie under excommunication until fitting satisfaction shall have been rendered.[41]

Because lay-invested clerics provided substantial support to the empire, Gregory's actions sharply threatened Henry's power. Unsurprisingly, then, Henry initially disregarded Gregory's directives. When Henry appointed an archbishop to the see in Milan,[42] Gregory responded contentiously in a letter dated December 1075, which insisted that Henry "look more respectfully upon the master of the church—that is, St. Peter, the chief of the apostles [and hence also the pope, as St. Peter's successor]."[43] Almost immediately, Henry retorted by summoning a council that included most of the German bishops. The bishops accused Gregory of committing perjury and fornication and of usurping the papacy; they concluded by denying Gregory's authority as pope.[44]

Gregory swiftly and boldly moved to crush Henry politically. In perhaps the most famous of medieval papal decrees, Gregory excommunicated Henry and claimed to deprive him of all royal authority:

> I believe that it is and has been thy [God's] will, that the Christian people especially committed to thee should render obedience to me thy especially constituted representative. To me is given by thy grace the power of binding and loosing in Heaven and upon earth.
>
> Wherefore, relying upon this commission, and for the honor and defense of thy Church ... I deprive King Henry ... who has rebelled against thy Church with unheard-of audacity, of the government over the whole kingdom of Germany and Italy, and I release all Christian men from the allegiance which they have sworn or may swear to him, and I forbid anyone to serve him as king.
>
> And since he has refused to obey as a Christian should ... I bind him in the bonds of anathema in thy stead and I bind him thus as commissioned by thee....[45]

Henry, remaining steadfast, responded in kind. By letter, Henry addressed Gregory as "not pope but false monk"[46] and called for him to relinquish the papacy: "Descend, descend, to be damned throughout the ages."[47] Despite this adamant initial response, Henry soon realized that he lacked the political support in Germany to withstand the papal excommunication. A coalition of nobles and bishops (some of whom had previously condemned Gregory) issued Henry an ultimatum: he must either be released from excommunication within a year or be deposed from his throne. Faced with likely downfall, Henry humiliatingly submitted to Gregory. For three consecutive days during the winter of 1077, Henry stood outside in the snow of a castle courtyard, barefooted in penitence and supplicated for absolution, while Gregory waited and contemplated inside.[48]

In the end, Gregory released Henry from his excommunication, an absolution that, however reasonable, proved politically ruinous for Gregory. Many of Henry's former supporters rallied to his support, and many of those who continued to oppose Henry nonetheless felt betrayed by Gregory. Henry's adversaries soon elected a rival king and thus thrust Germany into civil war. After three years of indecision, Gregory finally decided to support the rival king, and therefore once again excommunicated and deposed Henry. This second excommunication and deposition, however, proved politically ineffective. When Henry won the civil war, he resolved to destroy Gregory, who eventually died in exile in 1085.[49]

Despite Henry's personal victory over Gregory, the Investiture Struggle effectively ended in political compromise: "royal theocracy had been defeated without papal theocracy becoming established."[50] This compromise, though, proved sufficient to facilitate a dramatic increase in papal power. The Church gained practical independence from royal authority, and the hierocratic theory holding spiritual power above temporal power was largely accepted.[51] Thus emancipated and empowered, the Church exercised unparalleled control over spiritual affairs, and as the boundary between spiritual and temporal affairs often and inevitably blurred, the Church increased its temporal power as well.[52] Indeed, the development of the Church "as an independent, corporate, political and legal entity, under the papacy"[53] suggests that it might be considered the first "modern Western state."[54]

The Church used its newfound power to relentlessly pursue the City of God on earth. And significantly for subsequent legal development, the Church viewed law as one of the most potent tools for building Western Christendom.[55] The laity were subject to the hierarchical power of the Church, which extended its juridical reach over matters such as matrimony, wills, slander, fornication, and neglect of Church festivals.[56] The already extensive yet disordered canon law was compiled and organized in the mid-twelfth century by Gratian (in his Decretum) and then in the thirteenth century by Raymond of Penaforte (first in his Summa de Poenitentia et Matrimonio and then in his papally commissioned Decretales).[57] In fact, the Church pioneered the concept of a legal system: "a distinct, integrated body of law, consciously systematized" by trained professionals.[58] Harold Berman elaborates:

[T]he church took on most of the distinctive characteristics of the modern state. It claimed to be an independent, hierarchical, public authority. Its head, the pope, had the right to legislate, and in fact Pope Gregory's successors issued a steady stream of new laws, sometimes by their own authority, sometimes with the aid of church councils summoned by them. The church also executed its laws through an administrative hierarchy, through which the pope ruled as a modern sovereign rules through his or her representatives. Further, the church interpreted its laws, and applied them, through a judicial hierarchy culminating in the papal curia in Rome. Thus the church exercised the legislative, administrative, and judicial powers of a modern state. In addition, it adhered to a rational system of jurisprudence, the canon law. It imposed taxes on its subjects in the form of tithes and other levies. Through baptismal and death certificates it kept what was in effect a kind of civil register. Baptism conferred a kind of citizenship, which was further maintained by the requirement—formalized in 1215—that every Christian confess his or her sins and take Holy Communion at least once a year at Easter. One could be deprived of citizenship, in effect, by excommunication. Occasionally, the church even raised armies.[59]

Despite the ascent of the Church, royal (and imperial) power remained vibrant: the reality of a roughly balanced dualism of power crystallized after the Investiture Struggle. The premodern idea of the political community remained grounded in the symbolic imagery of the organism, like the body of Christ. Individuals were considered to be mere subjects, not citizens empowered to participate in political affairs. As subjects, individuals fit within a rigidly hierarchical body politic that seemed natural and thus beyond the will or control of the ordinary person (or subject).[60] Yet, at this point, the shape of the modern secular state began to come into focus as emperors and kings stood at least somewhat distinct from the Church. For instance, secular legal systems emerged, though they were modeled on the preeminent canon law system. In fact, secular law was based on a foundation of Christian spirituality: the assumption was that Christians would ensure that secular law would conform to Christian purposes. All law, then—not just canon law—was "seen as a way of fulfilling the mission of Western Christendom to begin to achieve the kingdom of God on earth."[61]

The development of constitutional principles was one aspect of these burgeoning legal systems. Within the Church itself, the bureaucratic "division of functions"[62] required the formation and articulation of some constitution-like limits and checks upon the exercise of power.[63] Furthermore, because of the roughly balanced dualism of power, the emerging secular states and the Church remained "always jealous of each other's authority."[64] Thus, individuals typically lived under multiple and competing legal systems, the canon system plus one or more secular systems. The struggle to devise workable boundaries between the various competing systems spawned the formation of constitutional standards.[65]

In sum, the seeds for the doctrine of separation of church and state were the birth of Christianity and the corresponding condemnation of Judaism. Those seeds were planted in the soil of the Roman establishment of Christianity, took root in the papal–imperial political disputes of the early Middle Ages, and finally sprouted in the Investiture Struggle. As Brian Tierney writes: "[T]he overt issue of church and state that arose during the investiture contest was related to the still more fundamental problem of defining the right relationship between spiritual office and material property."[66] Equally important, the fundamental Christian dualism opposing spirituality to materiality (as well as temporality and carnality) arose from the early Christian efforts to differentiate and condemn Judaism. Thus, predictably, Gregory VII relied explicitly upon the Christian ideology of anti-semitism to support his condemnation of the temporal powers of kings and princes. Moreover, just as the early Christians effectively increased their political power by denouncing Jews, the Church of the Investiture Struggle successfully enhanced its power by denigrating the (implicitly Jewish) carnality of the temporal and material world. Even as the inchoate secular state emerged to share power with the ascendant Church, the state inherited the degraded position of Jews within the universal body of Christianity. Thus, most Christians supposedly found spiritual fulfillment in the Church but nonetheless needed protection from the potential dangers and depravities inherent in the temporal and material world—the world of the Jews and the state.

THE LATER MIDDLE AGES

Christian Power and the Persecution of Jews

Perhaps more so than any other political action, a successful declaration of war manifests supreme authority and control. Hence, soon after the Investiture Struggle, the papacy displayed its enormous strength by launching the Crusades, wars to establish the Christian City of God throughout this world. In 1095, a papal proclamation initiated the first Crusade, and the next year, bands of Christian warriors set forth.[67] The professed purpose of the first Crusade was to recapture Jerusalem and the Holy Sepulcher from the Saracens, while the avowed goal of the second Crusade (launched in 1146) was to defend the recently captured Holy Lands against potential Saracen attack. Despite these nominal objectives, however, both of these Crusades—especially the first—rapidly degenerated into a war against all heretics and infidels, particularly Jews.[68]

Throughout the Crusades, the papacy claimed to continue its earlier policy of not forcing Jewish conversion. Nonetheless, as the Crusaders crossed Europe, they slaughtered Jews in one pogrom after another. Often, Crusaders formed ill-disciplined armies, little more than Christian mobs, bent on avenging the death of Jesus.[69] These armies were unconcerned with the niceties of Christian doctrine, such as the notion that true faith cannot be coerced. Thus, the mobs repeatedly forced Jews to choose: "baptism or death."[70] During the first Crusade, the Christian armies declared:

Look you! We set out on a long road in order to reach the Burial Place, and to revenge ourselves on the Ishmaelites, and behold! here are Jews, dwelling in our midst, men whose fathers killed Him, all guiltless, and crucified Him. Let us, therefore, take our revenge first on them, and extirpate them from among the nations, so that the name of Israel will no longer be mentioned; else they must become the same as we are, and profess our faith.[71]

During this first Crusade, in particular, all of the antisemitism institutionalized within Christianity spewed forth in venomous denunciations and massacres of Jews. One Christian reported that "throughout the cities through which [the Crusaders] were passing, they wiped out completely, as enemies internal to the Church, the execrable Jewish remnants, or forced them to the refuge of baptism—but many of these later reverted, like dogs to their vomit."[72] During the first six months of 1096 alone, between one-quarter and one-third of the Jews in Germany and northern France were murdered.[73] In tragic desperation, some Jews chose suicide, as illustrated in this Christian report:

At Worms too, the Jews, flying from the persecuting Christians, hastened to the Bishop. Since he promised them rescue only on the condition that they be baptized, they begged a truce for consultation. They entered into the Bishop's chamber at that same hour, and while our people waited outside for what answer they were going to make, they, persuaded by the devil and by their own callousness, killed themselves![74]

One of the leading European Jewish communities of that time was located in Mainz, in the Rhineland of Germany. The Mainz Jews felt unusually secure, so that when reports of crusading violence reached them, they nonetheless remained confident of their own safety. Shortly afterward, however, Count Emicho of Leiningen led a crusading army to the town, thus prompting Jewish efforts to initiate negotiations.[75] Albert of Aix, a Christian, described Emicho's reaction:

Emicho and the rest of his band held a council and, after sunrise, attacked the Jews in the courtyard with arrows and lances. When the bolts and doors had been forced and the Jews had been overcome, they killed seven hundred of them, who in vain resisted the attack and assault of so many thousands. They slaughtered the women also and with the point of their swords pierced young children of whatever age and sex. The Jews, seeing that their Christian enemies were attacking them and their children and were sparing no age, fell upon one another—brothers, children, wives, mothers and sisters—and slaughtered one another. Horrible to say, mothers cut the throats of nursing children with knives and stabbed others, preferring to perish thus by their own hands rather than be killed by the weapons of the [Christians].[76]

Emicho's massacre of the Mainz Jews included the horrifying tragedy of Rachel (of Mainz) and her four children, as recorded in the Hebrew chronicles of the first Crusade:

> [Rachel of Mainz] said to her companions: "I have four children. On them as well have no mercy, lest these [Christians] come and seize them alive and they remain in their pseudo-faith. With them as well you must sanctify the Name of the holy God." One of her companions came and took the knife to slaughter her son. When the mother of the children saw the knife, she shouted loudly and bitterly and smote her face and breast and said: "Where is your steadfast love, O Lord?" Then the woman said to her companions in her bitterness: "Do not slaughter Isaac before his brother Aaron, so that he not see the death of his brother and take flight." The women took the lad and slaughtered him—he was small and exceedingly comely. The mother spread her sleeve to receive the blood; she received the blood in her sleeves instead of in the [Temple] vessel for blood. The lad Aaron, when he saw that his brother had been slaughtered, cried out: "Mother, do not slaughter me!" He went and hid under a bureau. She still had two daughters, Bella and Matrona, comely and beautiful young women the daughters of R. Judah her husband. The girls took the knife and sharpened it, so that it not be defective. They stretched forth their necks and she sacrificed them to the Lord God of Hosts, who commanded us not to renounce pure awe of him and to remain faithful to him, as it is written: "You must be wholehearted with the Lord your God." When the saintly one completed sacrificing her three children before the Creator, then she raised her voice and called to her son: "Aaron, Aaron, where are you? I shall not have mercy nor pity on you as well." She pulled him by the leg from under the bureau where he was hidden and she sacrificed him before the sublime and exalted God. She placed them under her two sleeves, two on each side, near her heart. They convulsed near her, until the enemy seized the chamber and found her sitting and mourning them. They said to her: "Show us the moneys which you have in your sleeves." When they saw the children and saw that they were slaughtered, they smote her and killed her along with them.[77]

With the papal declaration of a second Crusade in 1146, Church leaders once again provoked Christian hostility against Jews.[78] One telling episode, in particular, revealed the range and depth of Christian antisemitism. The pope appointed St. Bernard, the abbot of Clairvaux, to be the official preacher of the second Crusade. Ralph, one of the monks in Bernard's monastery, promptly began preaching vengeance against Jews for killing Christ: "Avenge the Crucified upon his enemies who live among you. Afterwards you shall journey to battle against the Muslims."[79] Partly due to Ralph, then, the horrors of the first Crusade began to recur as anti-Jewish violence quickly erupted.[80] At this point, Bernard stepped forward to rebuke Ralph and to discourage the Crusaders from killing Jews; in fact,

Bernard managed to save many Jewish lives.[81] The reasons for Bernard's actions, however, are striking. First, since Ralph was from Bernard's own monastery, Ralph was subject to Bernard's control within the Church hierarchy. By leaving the monastery to preach, Ralph had violated ecclesiastical protocol and therefore had implicitly challenged and embarrassed Bernard.[82] Second, Bernard opposed killing Jews only so that they could continue suffering in the Diaspora as witnesses to Christian spirituality unless they willingly converted. For Bernard, then, Jews were not protected because of religious toleration or simple human sympathy, but rather because, according to the New Testament, Jews had to play a crucial role in the Christian drama of eternal salvation.[83]

While the Crusades were the most deadly of the papal-initiated persecutions of the Jews, popes continued to oppress Jews in additional ways. In particular, popes relied upon the sophisticated canon law system to enforce the theologically inferior status of Jews.[84] For example, Pope Innocent III, one of the most powerful of all popes, reiterated and codified standard Christian antisemitic dogma. Innocent, who was pontiff from 1198 to 1216, expressly condemned "the carnal Jews" as "demons" who "seek only what sense perceives, who delight in the corporeal senses alone." The Jew "lies" by denying that Jesus was the Messiah, and hence God "condemned the Synagogue because of her disbelief."[85] Furthermore, Innocent, continuing previous policy, maintained (at least as an official position) that Jews should not be killed or forced to convert:

> Thus the Jews, against whom the blood of Jesus Christ calls out, although they ought not to be killed, lest the people forget the Divine Law, yet as wanderers ought they to remain upon the earth, until their countenance be filled with shame and they seek the name of Jesus Christ, the Lord. That is why blasphemers of the Christian name ought not to be aided by Christian princes to oppress the servants of the Lord [that is, Christians, especially Crusaders], but ought rather to be forced into the servitude of which they made themselves deserving when they raised their sacrilegious hands against Him Who had come to confer true liberty upon them, thus calling down His blood upon themselves and upon their children.[86]

Consequently, Innocent convoked an ecumenical council in 1215 that issued several decrees reinforcing the subjugation of Jews. One decree, for instance, was intended to increase Jewish visibility and hence vulnerability: to alert unsuspecting Christians of a Jewish presence, Jews were required to wear an identifying conical hat or yellow patch.[87] Subsequent papal decrees further contributed to the separation of Jews from the Christian social body by forcing them to live in ghettos, yet Jews were also impressed with the universalism of Christianity by being forced to attend conversion sermons.[88]

The status of Jews in the late Middle Ages reveals how the proper alignment of social forces can channel intense power into forms of cultural oppression. Christianity, at its birth, had articulated (for political expediency) a discourse of condemnation and oppression in the antisemitic doctrine of the New Testament. Then, over the millennium after Constantine, the protection of emperors and kings enabled the established Church to grow as a bureaucratic institution, thus facilitating the spread of Christianity throughout Western society. By the time of the Investiture Struggle, Christianity had become a definitive component of European culture and social organization. Finally, as the Church attained maturity, it was able to emancipate itself from the shelter and control of royal and imperial power. During the late Middle Ages, the Church thus stood at the apex of its power. Christian domination of European culture and social structure allowed the Church to control and to effectively define Jews. One of the decrees of Innocent III exemplifies the totality of Christian power by effectively forcing Jews to observe Christian holidays:

> [D]uring the last three days before Easter and especially on Good Friday, [the Jews] shall not go forth in public at all, for the reason that some of them on these very days, as we hear, do not blush to go forth better dressed and are not afraid to mock the Christians who maintain the memory of the most holy Passion by wearing signs of mourning.[89]

Still more egregiously, though, the papacy attempted to ensure "the purity of Jewish doctrine":[90] several popes, starting with Gregory IX in 1239, condemned the Jewish Talmud and ordered copies seized and burned because it did not harmonize with the Christian conception of Judaism.[91] Christians, in other words, not only condemned Judaism but also demanded that Jews "conform to the image Christians had made of them and practice what Christians told them was their religion."[92] In sum, the systemic social and legal persecutions of Jews confirmed that they were less than human—that is, less than Christian—and this social degradation of Jews bolstered Christian faith by reinforcing the truth of the Christian world view.

The Emerging Secular State

A philosophical development significant for the emerging secular state occurred early in the thirteenth century: Aristotle's writings became available to Christian philosophers and theologians.[93] To some, Aristotle's pagan philosophy dangerously threatened basic Christian tenets; yet to others, Aristotle offered potentially revolutionary insights. The radical differences between the Aristotelian and Christian concepts of the state epitomized the gulf between the two worlds of thought. In Christian theology, the emerging state was symbolically grounded on the dualism opposing Christian spirituality to Jewish carnality. In its squalid Augustinian status, the state or civil society arose as punishment for original sin, and even in the best Christian light, the state still inherited the degraded position of Judaism within the universal body of Christ.

Aristotle's concept of the state, however, contrasted dramatically with this bleak Christian view.[94] To Aristotle, the good of the state or political community and the good of the individual are inseparable. The telos or natural end of human life is eudaimonia or happiness, and one achieves happiness by living a life in accordance with virtue.[95] Most important, according to Aristotle, "man is by nature a political animal";[96] hence, one cannot live virtuously unless one lives and acts prudently and sagaciously within a political community.[97] Aristotle wrote that in "the best regime, [the citizen] is one who is capable of and intentionally chooses being ruled and ruling with a view to the life in accordance with virtue."[98] Furthermore, the government, regardless of its form or type, should pursue the satisfaction of the common good, not private interests. The political community, in short, enables individuals to be citizens and to live virtuously.[99] Contrary to Christian dogma, participation in a political community is neither punishment nor degradation, but rather the highest good. Walter Ullmann elaborates:

> The contrast between the [Christian and Aristotelian] points of view, as far as they related to government, can be expressed thus: the [Christian] governmental system, the descending, derived its substance from a principle, from a norm laid down by an a-natural organ, aiming at unity and uniformity; the [Aristotelian], ascending, started from the multiformity of natural manifestations and took them as the basis of its thesis. The one system related to the other world (life in this world was merely preparatory); the other system related to this world alone which was its goal.[100]

Within this context, St. Thomas Aquinas, who lived from 1225 to 1274, stands as the "great synthesizer."[101] He struggled to reconcile Christian faith with Aristotelian reason: according to Thomas, for example, humans can use reason to learn certain truths about God, but other truths concerning God are accessible only by faith.[102] Because he was the preeminent Christian Aristotelian of the Middle Ages, many of Thomas's ideas have had lasting importance in Western political thought, especially for the doctrine of separation of church and state. Thomas accepted many elements of Aristotle's concept of the state. For instance, Thomas wrote that "it is natural for man ... to be a social and political animal, to live in a group."[103] Furthermore, the king should attempt to promote a virtuous life for his people.[104] Thomas even wrote that "the state is a perfect community" that pursues the "common good."[105]

Largely because of these Aristotelian elements in his political thought, Thomas contributed heavily to the development of the concept of a secular state. Most important, Thomas introduced into Christendom the idea of the political. An individual no longer was merely a subject under a government descending from above; instead, one might be a citizen who participated in government.[106] Thomas helped open a "conceptual gulf" between church and state because he "showed the conceptual existence of a human body politic, the State." An individual might be a "good citizen" in a State without necessarily being a "good man."[107] This distinction, between being a good citizen and a good man, suggested that various human activities could be understood as occurring in discrete realms or spheres of action, and within these discrete spheres, different normative values might apply. Different values or standards might apply, for instance, in politics, economics, and morality.[108] Thus, political science emerged as the study or practical science of the realm of politics or good government.[109]

Nevertheless, if Thomas proved anything through his consummate efforts at synthesis, he proved that Christianity and Aristotelianism cannot be harmonized: they are incompatible. And ultimately, Thomas remained a Christian.[110] Thomas's resolute commitment to Christianity manifested itself in (among other ways) his rote expression of standard Christian anti-semitic dogma. According to Thomas, Jewish history merely prepared for the coming of Jesus,[111] and hence the New Testament perfects or fulfills the imperfect Old Testament.[112] Thomas condemned the Jews for their carnality,[113] yet consistent with Christian dogma, he maintained that they could not be forced to convert (though they certainly could be persecuted severely).[114] Jews, Thomas wrote, blasphemed against Jesus and the Holy Ghost "when [the Jews] ascribed to the prince of devils those works which Christ did by the power of His own Divine Nature and by the operation of the Holy Ghost."[115] And of course, Jews should be condemned and subjugated because they refused to accept Jesus as the Messiah and ultimately committed deicide:

> Among the Jews some were elders, and others of lesser degree.... [T]he elders, who were called rulers, knew, as did also the devils, that He [Jesus] was the Christ promised in the Law: for they saw all the signs in Him which

the prophets said would come to pass: but they did not know the mystery of His Godhead. Consequently the Apostle says: If they had known it, they would never have crucified the Lord of glory. It must, however, be understood that their ignorance did not excuse them from crime, because it was, as it were, affected ignorance. For they saw manifest signs of His Godhead; yet they perverted them out of hatred and envy of Christ; neither would they believe His words, whereby He avowed that He was the Son of God.[116]

Eventually then, as a faithful Christian and regardless of his Aristotelian bent, Thomas unsurprisingly subordinated the state to the Church. In so doing, he expressly referred to the fulfillment of the Old Testament in the New Testament:

> [S]ince in the old law earthly goods were promised to the religious people ...
> the priests of the old law ... were also subject to the kings. But in the new
> law there is a higher priesthood by which men are guided to heavenly goods.
> Consequently, in the law of Christ, kings must be subject to priests.[117]

Thus, while Thomas never degraded the state as harshly as, for example, Augustine had done, he nonetheless insisted that temporal and material affairs always must remain ancillary to eternal salvation.[118]

For this reason, according to Thomas, a king's government should be modeled on God's rule over the universe.[119] Thomas's differentiation of four types of law reflected this emphasis on God's dominion. To Thomas, eternal law manifests "the very Idea of the government of things in God the Ruler of the universe."[120] Natural law consists of a small number of principles that manifest "a participation in us of the eternal law."[121] Divine law consists of the revealed or positive law of the Christian Bible.[122] Finally, human law is the humanly created positive law that implements the general principles of the natural law.[123] Thomas believed that states could enact human (or positive) law—which he then called "civil law"—but such law always remains clearly inferior or subordinate to eternal, divine, and natural law. A purported human law that is inconsistent with divine or natural law is, according to Thomas, "no longer a law but a perversion of law."[124] Hence, contrary to the Augustinian mandate to humbly obey even unjust civil authorities, Thomas insisted that citizens should disobey unjust human laws—those positive laws that either contravene divine law or were enacted contrary to the common good.[125] In short, the state, when creating human law, should act consistently with Christian tenets.

Thomas added that the best form of government—the one most likely to pursue the common good—is a monarchy, but a monarchy in which the king is assisted by an aristocracy.[126] Thomas expressly tied this conclusion to his criticism of the Jews. He drew examples from the Old Testament to demonstrate that the power granted to a king is so great that a pure monarchy usually degenerates into tyranny. Therefore, only the most virtuous person should become king. Thomas continued:

> [P]erfect virtue is to be found in few. And, what is more, the Jews were inclined to cruelty and avarice, which vices above all turn men into tyrants. Hence from the very first the Lord did not set up the kingly authority with full power, but gave them judges and governors to rule them.[127]

Thus, Thomas supported his argument for a somewhat diluted monarchy, or a mixed form of government, by reasoning that Jewish vice had initially necessitated this governmental form. Moreover, Thomas noted, God then inflicted an absolute king on the Jews to punish them.[128]

Finally, the ultimate goal of a Christian political community is not to live virtuously in this world (as Aristotle argued), but rather to prepare for God's grace and to attain eternal heavenly salvation. Thomas wrote: "[S]ince society must have the same end as the individual man, it is not the ultimate end of an assembled multitude to live virtuously, but through virtuous living to attain to the possession of God."[129] Thomas then reasserted his hierocratic conclusion: because only the divine government of the Church could successfully lead individuals to the final goal of salvation, mere human governments must ultimately submit to papal control.[130]

In sum, Thomas helped solidify the concept of the secular state. He raised its status from the depths of Augustinian denigration so that politics in the temporal world could at least be respectably studied. Nonetheless, he remained true to his Christian roots. He not only reiterated standard Christian antisemitic doctrine, he also based much of his political theory on that dogma. Despite his Aristotelian orientation, then, Thomas subordinated the state to the Church and insisted that the state existed to help Christians prepare in this world for their blissful eternal salvation.[131]

While Thomas contributed to the theoretical concept of a state, the secular state also continued to evolve in the political hurly-burly of medieval society. Even when the Roman Catholic Church soared to the zenith of its social dominance, royal and imperial power always remained prominent. Often, the Church and the state (in the form of a royal or an imperial presence) jostled and negotiated in their efforts to impose particular structures or arrangements upon the rest of society. Unsurprisingly, as the Church and the state maneuvered for power, they each used the local Jews to further their respective interests. As already discussed, the Church issued numerous decrees during the thirteenth century to reinforce the Christian definition and subjugation of Jews. Frequently, the Church sought assistance from the civil authorities as it attempted to enforce these decrees. Sometimes the state would cooperate, and sometimes it would not—usually depending upon the state's perception of its own interests and its own power vis-à-vis the Church.[132] For example, around the twelfth century, emperors, kings, and princes began to consider and treat Jews as property: since Christian dogma effectively condemned Jews to perpetual servitude, they were defined as "serfs of the Royal (or Imperial) chamber."[133] Consequently, royal and imperial authorities gained an increased interest in encouraging the commercial activities of at least some Jews; whenever money was needed, the authorities could generate revenue by legally imposing confiscatory taxes or declaring themselves the heirs of "their" Jews. Hence, when the papal decree that required Jews to wear a conical hat or yellow badge caused some wealthier Jews to flee from Castile in 1219, the king of Castile, fearing a loss of royal income, requested the pope to suspend the decree in Castile. In this instance, the pope submitted to the royal request.[134]

Over time, though, the Church often succeeded in securing state cooperation, typically to the detriment of Jewish communities.[135] During much of the twelfth and thirteenth centuries, for example, the English kings resisted many ecclesiastical demands regarding Jews. In 1253, however, when English Jews were not generating substantial royal revenue, King Henry III issued an edict enforcing many of the antisemitic papal policies, such as the requirements that Jews wear a badge and not eat or buy meat during Lent.[136] Then, in 1290, King Edward I banished Jews from England altogether—supposedly "for the honor of the Crucified," though Edward conveniently commanded that any debts previously owed to Jews should now be paid to the state.[137]

As the thirteenth century turned toward the fourteenth, papal control of European monarchs steadily declined. States frequently complied with papal policies, but more and more often, state officials acted to further their own interests and not due to compulsion. Michael Wilks argues that, at this time, the dream of universal government—whether under an emperor or a pope—gave way to the reality of a multitude of European secular states competing with each other as well as with the Church.[138] In fact, the growing power of secular rulers led to a successful challenge of the papacy early in the 1300s. For more than a century after 1250, the popes had refused to confer the imperial crown on anyone, with the brief exception of Henry VII. Of course, this obstinacy at least appeared to doubly affirm papal political dominance. Popes not only asserted the power to designate an emperor in the first place, but also stood alone at the ostensible apex of power because no one was so designated.[139] When Louis, duke of Bavaria, was elected king of Germany and emperor in 1314, he exercised imperial power in the face of papal opposition, which led to his excommunication and deposition. But refusing to yield, Louis invaded Italy, captured Rome, and continued to defy the papacy until his death in 1347.[140] An edict, issued in 1338 by Louis and the German electors, declared that the emperor was determined through election and needed no papal confirmation. Despite the democratic tinge of this edict, it paraphrased the New Testament while tracing the emperor's secular power to God: "God has openly given the secular law to the human race through Emperors and kings.... [T]he Lord Jesus Christ Himself [ordered] that what is God's should be rendered to God and what is Caesar's to Caesar."[141]

While the rulers of the emerging secular states struggled with the popes for supremacy, the rulers simultaneously attempted to assert control over their own Christian subjects. Quite often, Jews again played an important role in these political developments. In particular, royal and imperial authorities occasionally protected or attempted to protect Jews from frenzied Christian mobs. This protective relationship, which had roots reaching back to the fourth century, surged in importance during the Crusades when Jews desperately turned to civil authorities for protection from the rampaging armies. In response, some state officials were willing to offer refuge, sometimes even issuing charters protecting Jews. Most often, though, these protective charters amounted to no more than "parchment for covering jars,"[142] as even well-intentioned state officials were unable to dissuade mobs rapt with religious fervor. In a report on a typical incident from 1096, a Jew quotes a chief municipal officer:

> "Listen to me, you Jews! At the beginning I promised you that I would shield and protect you so long as one Jew lives in this world; these promises I gave you, and so I acted, keeping my promise! But from now on, in the face of all these people, I can no longer do anything for your rescue. Consider now what you want to do. You know well that if you do not do thus and so, the city will be devastated; therefore, it is better that I deliver you to their violence than that they come upon me with a siege and level the castle."[143]

The protective relation between states and Jews continued throughout the later Middle Ages and beyond. For example, during the fourteenth century, Christians accused Jews of causing the bubonic plague by poisoning water supplies. Individual Jews were tortured until they confessed to the crime, and then entire Jewish populations were burned in retribution. In such circumstances, Jews depended upon governmental officials for protection, which, as during the Crusades, frequently proved inadequate.[144]

Again, however, state protection of Jews typically arose not from a principled commitment to religious liberty but rather from the pursuit of state interests. Occasionally, civil authorities sought to protect Jews merely to preserve public peace and order. A letter dated 1203, from King John of England to the mayor and barons of London, illustrates this view, as the king insisted upon protection for the Jews even as he compared them to dogs:

> [A]s you know that the Jews are under our special protection, we are amazed that you permit harm to be done to the Jews residing in the city of London, since this is obviously against the peace of the kingdom and the tranquility of our land. . . . We say this not only for our Jews, but also for our peace, for if we gave our peace to a dog it should be inviolably observed. Therefore, we commit henceforth the Jews residing in the city of London to your care, so that, if anyone attempts to do them harm, you shall defend them, affording them assistance by force.[145]

More often, though, governmental officials protected Jews if the officials perceived them to be useful and loyal subjects. Consequently, state protection could swiftly vanish as the governmental perception of its interests shifted.[146] If a civil official believed that opposition to a Christian mob bent on violence threatened political stability, then the government willingly sacrificed Jewish subjects to placate the mob. Or if a governmental official himself became a fanatical Christian, he would often turn on Jewish subjects and strike a blow for Jesus. At times, such as 1492 in Spain, governmental zealotry even led to the expulsion of all Jews unwilling to convert to Christianity.[147] Moreover, governmental officials readily exploited Jewish dependence by extorting money in exchange for protection. For example, in 1321, the king of France demanded 150,000 pounds from Jews accused of poisoning water supplies. In short, then, insofar as states created or recognized a legal right (however limited) for Jews to survive and practice their religion, that legal right existed to promote the interests and goals of the state, not the Jews.[148]

The medieval emergence of the secular state, together with a recognition of the relationship between governmental officials and Jews, illustrates the complex operation of power. The history of the Middle Ages reveals that the symbolism of Christian dogma provided the discursive framework for the emergence of the secular state and its separation from the Church. In particular, the dogmatic Christian dualism opposing Jewish carnality to Christian spirituality facilitated the creation of a secular sphere of action in at least two ways. First, the Christian dogma posited the existence of a temporal and carnal realm. Second, Christianity insisted that the only goal that truly matters is the spiritual attainment of eternal and other-worldly salvation; at least theoretically, then, the existence of a this-worldly secular sphere posed no threat to Christian domination. Even when Thomas's (Christianized) Aristotelianism somewhat enhanced the status of the secular state, it still remained subordinate to the Church.[149]

Within this discursive framework, political developments spurred the evolution of the state as a separate and secular entity. Unsurprisingly, the emergence of the secular state tended to benefit the two already dominant social entities or political forces of the Middle Ages—the Church, on the one hand, and royal and imperial powers, on the other. The Church sought to optimize its power. Since the Church contributed to the production of the secular state through the symbolism of its Christian dogma, the Church necessarily subordinated and often degraded the state. The state, after all, always remained tainted by its link to Jewish carnality despite being within the universal Christian body. Moreover, the creation of the secular state further empowered Christianity by reducing governmental interference in ecclesiastical affairs while still allowing the Church to occasionally enlist governmental assistance in the pursuit of Christian universalism. Hence, for example, the Church—often assisted by civil authorities, Christian mobs, or both—was able to intensify its persecution of the theologically condemned Jews.

Despite the insistent Christian denunciation of the material and temporal world, the state (royal and imperial powers) also benefited from its separation and secularization. Indeed, Thomistic theory clearly elevated the state above its degraded Augustinian status, even though Thomas continued to insist that the state was below the Church. Additionally, the burgeoning secularization allowed states to develop institutions independent of the Church. In particular, the secularization of the state facilitated the crucial development of legal systems apart from the canon law system; by the end of the thirteenth century, the idea of a public law of the state was firmly established.[150] And occasionally, the emerging states flexed their muscles, so to speak, by opposing papal decrees, such as those involving the treatment of Jews. Of course, state policies, whether regarding Jews or otherwise, typically reflected state interests. Most often, civil officials sought merely to enhance their power in relation to their subjects (or citizens) and the Church (by, for example, exploiting the social subjugation and dependence of the Jews).

CHAPTER 4

The Christian Renaissance and Reformation in Continental Europe

THE RENAISSANCE

Toward the end of the Middle Ages, certain Italian cities such as Venice and Florence, spurred by fortuitous economic prosperity, strove for independence from the Holy Roman Empire.[1] Already, in the mid-fourteenth century, Bartolus argued that the free people of the cities (or city republics) were exercising de facto merum Imperium (the highest power to make laws), so they effectively constituted sibi princeps (a prince unto themselves). During this era, though, the cities had to remain wary of papal domination, and thus many writers, such as Dante, still sided with the emperor to avoid the pope. Other writers nonetheless insisted that the Church should not interfere in the secular affairs of the cities. As early as 1324, Marsiglio of Padua anticipated a central Reformation theme when he argued that the city republics had secular jurisdiction separate from the Church. While the fate of these city republics fluctuated over the years, they provided fertile political soil for the growth of a modern theory of the state.[2]

In particular, the civic humanism of the Renaissance bloomed during the fifteenth and sixteenth centuries. Just as Thomas Aquinas previously had turned to Aristotelian theory to develop the concept of the state, the early civic humanists turned to Cicero. The humanist emphasis on the Ciceronian concept of virtus—the single or highest virtue, uniting wisdom with eloquence—contrasted sharply with the Augustinian Christian view of human nature. Whereas Augustinians saw only human depravity and sin, the humanists believed people, as citizens, could achieve excellence in political and civil society. Nonetheless, the early humanists remained fer-

50

vent Christians, struggling to force their ideas of *virtus* into a Christian framework, and the later Northern humanists even insisted that political rulers possess the godliness of a good Christian.[3]

Indeed, despite their commitment to human achievement and dignity, many humanists, both earlier and later and from all over Europe, expressed their Christian commitment in, among other ways, antisemitic tirades.[4] To these humanists, debilitative Judaic attitudes and practices had infected all aspects of society—the Church, the schools, and the city republics. This Jewish infestation had to be rooted out and eliminated. Thus, if anything, antisemitism worsened during this period. Moreover, advancing technology exacerbated the situation; the introduction and proliferation of the printing press during the fifteenth and sixteenth centuries facilitated the rapid spread of antisemitic anecdotes and accusations. For example, a scholarly and politically progressive humanist press, Hieronymous Höltzel of Nuremberg, published the following report in 1510:

> Herewith is published what formerly has been common knowledge. [A Christian stole a consecrated wafer from a Church and sold it to a Jew, Salomon.] Salomon ... laid the sacrament [the consecrated wafer] on the edge of a table and, out of congenital Jewish hatred, battered it several times over and pierced it; even then he was unable to wound the Lord's body. Finally, beside himself with rage, he yelled out, among other curses: "If you are the Christian God, then in the name of a thousand devils, show yourself!" At that moment, in reaction to the taunt, the holy body of Christ miraculously parted itself into three, just as the priest breaks it,—but with the result that the cracks took on the color of blood. The Jew carried the three parts of the wafer on his person for four weeks. [Salomon then gave two pieces of the wafer to other Jews.] The remaining piece, which was his own, he once again struck and pierced until blood flowed from it. He did everything he could to offend this last portion of the host—drowning it, burning it, and attempting in several other ways to destroy it—all to no avail. Finally it dawned on him to knead the sacrament into a scrap of matzo dough and to throw it into the oven at the Jewish Easter celebration.[5]

The Dutch monk Erasmus tersely summarized the humanist viewpoint: "If hating the Jews is the proof of a truly Christian life, then we are all excellent Christians."[6] In fact, Jews were banished from most of western and central Europe during the fifteenth and early sixteenth centuries.[7]

Nonetheless, the most renowned later humanist, Niccolo Machiavelli, did not reveal such a firm commitment to Christianity and antisemitism.[8] Writing in the early sixteenth century, Machiavelli articulated a humanist political theory remarkably limited in its Christian presuppositions. As discussed in chapter 3, Thomas had introduced into Christendom the idea

of the political. In so doing, Thomas had (re)introduced the study of politics as a practical science and had suggested that different values might
apply in different realms of action. Machiavelli deepened these Thomistic
currents in light of his own political fate.[9] As a Florentine governmental
official for almost fifteen years, Machiavelli had observed directly the political maneuvers of the various city republics as they vied for power, and in
fact, he ultimately lost his governmental position and was arrested and tortured because of a transition in Florentine rule partially due to the pope.[10]
Thus, understandably so, Machiavelli studied politics as an eminently practical topic, and he insisted, quite strikingly, that Christian values do not
apply in the political realm. To Machiavelli, the preservation and liberty of
the republic are the highest values, and the citizen and ruler should do
whatever is necessary to achieve those ends—the common good—regardless of consistency or inconsistency with Christian values.[11] Indeed,
Machiavelli argued that Christianity, at least as interpreted by the Roman
Catholic Church, undermined a people's devotion to liberty and hence
damaged a republic; Christianity rendered people humble, feeble, and too
willing to submit to tyranny.[12]

Machiavelli therefore further opened the conceptual gap between
church and state. His view of Christianity strongly suggested that the state
would do better without religion: Christianity, in effect, corrupted political
affairs. His focus on the well-being of the state contrasted starkly with the
Augustinian (and medieval) condemnation of the state to the carnal world
of the Jews. Machiavelli maintained the separation between the temporal
and spiritual worlds that the Christian execration of Judaism had introduced, but he elevated the status of the temporal state far above its lowly
Christian origins. Even so, Machiavelli argued that all secular states are
doomed to eventual ruin. Yet, whereas the traditional Christian perspective
maintained that God's will damned the secular state to its degraded position, Machiavelli instead emphasized the role of sheer fortune in the ultimate collapse of every state.[13] Indeed, subsequently, the Northern
humanists attacked Machiavelli for his supposed godlessness.[14]

Nonetheless, Machiavelli neither completely rejected Christianity nor was
he "utterly secular in his thinking."[15] Machiavelli wrote: "Princes and
republics who wish to maintain themselves free from corruption must
above all things preserve the purity of all religious observances, and treat
them with proper reverence."[16] Hence, it was the Christianity of the Roman
Catholic Church, not religion in general, that undermined liberty and republicanism; paganism was better than Catholicism for preserving a devotion to
liberty. Machiavelli, in fact, echoed the contemporaneous Reformation

attack on the Catholic Church: the Church had corrupted Christianity by giving it a "false interpretation." Properly understood, according to Machiavelli, Christianity teaches that "we ought to love and honor our country."[17]

What had prompted the Roman Catholic Church to warp Christianity so completely? Machiavelli responded decidedly: "[T]his [corruption of Christianity] arises unquestionably from the baseness of men, who have interpreted our religion according to the promptings of indolence rather than of virtue."[18] Many commentators assume that this typical Machiavellian emphasis on human baseness marked a pragmatic political realism grounded on Machiavelli's personal political experiences.[19] Undoubtedly, this assumption is at least partially valid, but a more ironic explanation harmonizes with Reformation accounts of human nature and seems just as plausible. According to this alternative (or supplemental) rationale, Machiavelli accounted for the "decadence"[20] of Christianity with a typically Christian (and non-humanist) explanation: humans are depraved and ignoble by nature,[21] and consequently, they garbled the true Christian message. Regardless of whether Machiavelli here intended a grim political realism or revealed a latent Christian world view (or both, which seems most likely), his characterization of human nature as base or sinful resonated with and was symbolically tied to the New Testament emphases on original sin and the separation of Christian spirituality from Jewish carnality. Moreover, it is worth noting, Christianity itself at least contributed to many of the historical developments that might ground a political realism (or cynicism). That is, the Christian focus on human depravity, as well as the Christian legitimation of imperialistic domination, helped shape western history for nearly 1500 years and thus provided ample evidence supporting a bleak view of political reality.[22]

Significantly, Machiavelli's (cynical and Christian) conception of human nature served as a foundation for his political thought. To Machiavelli, sheer fortune alone does not doom all secular states to ruination; rather, sheer fortune and human nature (sinfulness) together ensure the eventual collapse of all governments.[23] The tension between, on the one hand, political order and, on the other hand, fortune and human nature—and the resultant struggle to maintain the fragile political community through secular time—was a constant theme for Machiavelli. He understood virtù (virtue) as the (at least temporary) overcoming of fortune and human nature as one pursued the common good: citizens and rulers alike must seek to disregard their "own passions" and instead act for the good of the community.[24] Machiavelli thus reasoned that the best form of government—the one most likely to pursue the common good—is neither the pure monarchy, aristocracy, nor democracy, but rather the mixed republic, a mixture of government by the one, the few, and the many. This type of republic can maintain balance by drawing upon the diversity of its citizens.[25] Meanwhile, Machiavelli advised the ruler that virtù required the "judicious alternation" of Aristotelian virtue and vice: the political leader, for example, must at times exercise liberality with money, but at other times must exercise miserliness; the political leader must at times display compassion, but at other times must act cruelly; and so on.[26] A successful ruler, in short, cannot apply the same values or moral standards in public life as in personal (or private) life. Machiavellian virtù required one to do whatever was necessary to preserve the political community: "A prince . . . must imitate the fox and the lion, for the lion cannot protect himself from traps, and the fox cannot defend himself from wolves."[27] In sum, Machiavelli's civic republican theory can be understood as placing the sinful human of Christianity within the Aristotelian polis as it careens through secular time. For Machiavelli, the problem—the realpolitik problem, if one likes—necessarily was how to maintain the polis in these dire circumstances.

THE LUTHERAN REFORMATION

The Roman Catholic Church had long struggled against secular rulers for power and wealth, and the Church many times had weathered internal strife. But in 1517, a German priest and theology professor, Martin Luther, initiated an attack from within Catholicism that ultimately shattered the Church's hegemonic hold over western Christianity. Luther wrote The Ninety-Five Theses primarily to criticize the Church's practice of selling indulgences. According to Catholic doctrine, an individual was subject to divine and temporal punishment for committing a sin. The Church itself could remit the sinner's guilt through the sacrament of penance and then could bestow indulgence, a release from the temporal punishment to be due in purgatory, provided the person performed works of charity and devotion. For many years, though, the Church had been selling indulgences as a means of raising money. Luther objected to this corruption of Christian doctrine, attributing it to the Church's problematic involvement in worldly affairs. He insisted that "Christians are to be taught that the pope, in granting indulgences, needs and thus desires their devout prayer more than their money."[28]

Once Luther issued this first challenge to the Church, he began to develop theological views that increasingly distanced him from the papacy. As the controversy surrounding indulgences intensified, he claimed to discover that the New Testament did not command the performance of penance at all. To Luther, this sacrament therefore had to be abolished. Soon, Luther seemed to question most of the traditions and trappings of the medieval Church. He denounced the Church hierarchy (including the privileged status and authority of the clergy),[29] the wealth and impiety of the clergy,[30] the canon law,[31] the Church's involvement in political and military affairs, and the practice of monasticism.[32] In 1519, Luther publicly questioned papal authority, and eventually, of the Church's seven sacraments, he rejected all but two—baptism and the Eucharist.[33] In 1520, the Church issued a bull of excommunication against Luther. He responded defiantly, publicly burning the bull and several volumes of the canon law for good measure.[34]

In rejecting medieval Roman Catholic traditions, Luther sought to return to more Pauline and Augustinian notions of human nature and faith. To Luther, his Protestant theology was not revolutionary; rather, it was a return to a purer Christianity, a Christianity of the New Testament.[35] Consequently, Luther emphasized human depravity and sinfulness: humans are "full of sins, death, and damnation." But, Luther argued, if "all things in you are altogether blameworthy, sinful, and damnable," then one can never earn salvation because one's actions, one's choices, one's very will are inherently sinful.[36] Luther was especially scornful of Thomas Aquinas's Aristotelian emphasis on human reason: the notion that humans could use reason to know God (even partially) was dangerous blasphemy. One could not use reason to bring salvation any more than one could earn or cognitively choose salvation: instead, salvation was achieved through God's grace and an individual's faith. Even faith cannot be chosen; instead God chooses or predestines certain individuals for grace, though everyone is potentially open to perceiving such grace. Luther maintained:

> When you have learned [that humans are sinful and damnable] you will know that you need Christ, who suffered and rose again for you so that, if you believe in him, you may through this faith become a new man in so far as your sins are forgiven and you are justified by the merits of another, namely, of Christ alone.[37]

For the individual, then, "faith alone justifies" and enables salvation. In The Freedom of a Christian, Luther wrote: "[I]f only I believe. Yes, since faith alone suffices for salvation, I need nothing except faith exercising the power and dominion of its own liberty. Lo, this is the inestimable power and liberty of Christians." To Luther, the Christian is free because works (or conduct) are unnecessary for salvation: all that matters is faith, and faith is a purely internal matter. Faith requires that "you ascribe to [God] the glory of truthfulness and all goodness which is due him." Luther continued: "This cannot be done by works but only by the faith of the heart. Not by the doing of works but by believing do we glorify god and acknowledge that he is truthful." Likewise, "[f]aith redeems, corrects, and preserves our consciences so that we know that righteousness does not consist in works."[38]

Because justification was by faith alone, and because faith was an internal matter of conscience and heart, salvation became more direct, immediate, and individualized. An individual did not build gradually toward salvation throughout life by performing works, such as the Roman Catholic sacraments. And an individual did not need clergy—especially Catholic clergy—to intercede on his or her behalf with God. Ecclesiastics only tended to interfere with the individual's direct and immediate experience of the truth of Jesus Christ. Hence, Luther conceived of a "priesthood" of all Christians: "[A]ll of us who believe in Christ are priests and kings in Christ." Christians therefore did not need the institutional machinery of the Catholic Church; they should simply organize into congregations of the faithful. And once freed from the traditions and works of Roman Catholicism, the faithful could personally experience the primacy of "the most holy Word of God, the gospel of Christ."[39] Thus, the Scriptures, as the revealed Word, became the key to faith and a Christian life. To be clear, Luther did not suggest that each individual could idiosyncratically interpret Scripture, but rather that each person was free to receive its literal meaning.

Despite these reform teachings, Luther managed to remain somewhat conservative. He never advocated a radical individualism free of all ecclesiastical leadership. For instance, he insisted that "[a]lthough we are all equally priests, we cannot all publicly minister and teach."[40] In Church organization and governance, Luther found little direction in the Scriptures and thus often willingly accepted whatever was expedient or traditional—sometimes even surrendering control over the Church polity to the state ruler.[41] Moreover, though Luther maintained that works cannot bring salvation, he still argued that if faith is present, works can "be done to the glory of God."[42] This notion of the faithful doing "righteous deeds"[43] was the source of the idea of a calling, which would become more important in Calvinism. To Luther, "each one must attend to the duties of his own calling"[44] because, regardless of faith, we still live in the temporal and carnal world:

> Here the works begin; here a man cannot enjoy leisure; here he must indeed take care to discipline his body by fastings, watchings, labors, and other reasonable discipline and to subject it to the Spirit so that it will obey and

conform to the inner man and faith and not revolt against faith and hinder the inner man, as it is the nature of the body to do if it is other held in check.[45]

Hence, faith liberated a Christian to obey God's will, to fulfill one's duties.

As one might expect, Luther's focus on the authority of the New Testament led him to echo its antisemitic dogma. Luther repeated many (if not all) of the specific New Testament accusations against the Jews. For example, according to Luther, Jews deserve their suffering and persecution because they committed deicide and they still obstinately refuse to believe in Jesus as their savior.[46] Similarly, Luther referred to the Jews as "unyielding, stubborn ceremonialists" who continue to follow "a blind and dangerous doctrine."[47] At a broader level, the symbolic foundation of Luther's entire theology was the central New Testament dichotomy between Christian spirituality and Jewish carnality. His steadfast insistence that humans were thoroughly sinful and could be justified by faith alone directly reflected this crucial Christian dichotomy. To Luther, faith was the pathway to the Christian world of heavenly spirituality, while works (without faith) doomed one to wallowing with the Jews in this-worldly degradation. Indeed, his critique of works as a means of salvation was peppered with antisemitic references. For example, he wrote: "Human works appear attractive outwardly, but within they are filthy, as Christ says concerning the Pharisees in Matt. 23. For they appear to the doer and others good and beautiful, yet God does not judge, according to appearances but searches 'the minds and hearts.'"[48] Moreover, the New Testament condemnation of Judaism provided Luther with the symbolic imagery for his condemnation of the Roman Catholic Church. Following the lead of the humanists, Luther and other reformers believed the problem with the Church was that it was too Judaic: the Church was infected with a Jewish ethos that caused it to become overly involved in economic, legal, and other this-worldly affairs.[49] The aim of reform was to purify Christianity, to cleanse it of this Judaic infestation.

Despite this pervasive antisemitism running through Luther's theology, the early Luther enthusiastically solicited Jewish conversion. To him, the only reason that Jews had not become Christians was the corruption of Roman Catholicism. Once Jews understood the purified Christianity of Protestantism, they would willingly convert—or so Luther initially believed.[50] When Luther's efforts at conversion were thwarted, he became increasingly hostile toward Jews.[51] The reading of Scripture was central to Luther's reforms, but the Jewish reading of Scripture denied the Christian appropriation of the Hebrew Bible. In light of the Jews' stubborn refusal to convert, they must, in Luther's eyes, be condemned and persecuted; Jewish misfortune implicitly refuted the Jewish reading of Scripture.[52]

Luther's rage against the Jews drove him to advocate open violence. In 1537, Luther successfully instigated the expulsion of Jews from Saxony, and Jews were driven from other German areas over the next thirty years. A Jewish fugitive from the city of Brunswick wrote:

> We were all suddenly expelled ... on the advice of this foul priest Martin Luther and that of the rest of the council of scoundrels [that is, the council of the town]. These accursed and impecunious repudiators of this town and council have invalidated and broken everything. There was not even one among them who spoke peace. For several years they were constantly intent upon murder and destruction alone.[53]

Luther's violent turn against Jews culminated in his inflammatory essay Concerning the Jews and Their Lies. Luther began by emphasizing that the Jews were condemned because of "their lies, curses, and blasphemy." Then, in an unrelentingly truculent passage, he recommended seven ways for Christians to deal "with this damned, rejected race of Jews."[54]

> First, their synagogues or churches should be set on fire, and whatever does not burn up should be covered or spread over with dirt so that no one may ever be able to see a cinder or stone of it. And this ought to be done for the honor of God and of Christianity in order that God may see that we are Christians, and that we have not wittingly tolerated or approved of such public lying, cursing, and blaspheming of His Son and His Christians.... Secondly, their homes should likewise be broken down and destroyed. For they perpetrate the same things there that they do in their synagogues. For this reason they ought to be put under one roof or in a stable ... in order that they may realize that they are not masters in our land, as they boast, but miserable captives.... Thirdly, they should be deprived of their prayer-books and Talmuds in which such idolatry, lies, cursing, and blasphemy are taught. Fourthly, their rabbis must be forbidden under threat of death to teach any more.... Fifthly, passport and traveling privileges should be absolutely forbidden to the Jews.... Sixthly, they ought to be stopped from usury. All their cash and valuables of silver and gold ought to be taken from them and put aside for safe keeping. For this reason, as said before, everything that they possess they stole and robbed from us through their usury, for they have no other means of support.... Seventhly, let the young and strong Jews and Jewesses be given the flail, the ax, the hoe, the spade, the distaff, and spindle, and let them earn their bread by the sweat of their noses as is enjoined upon Adam's children. For it is not proper that they should want us cursed Goyyim [Gentiles] to work in the sweat of our brow and that they, pious crew, idle away their days at the fireside in laziness, feasting, and display.[55]

If there had been any doubt before, this essay erased it: Luther's reform theology did not include toleration for Jews (or Roman Catholics or any other religious group but his own).[56]

Based largely on his theology—and hence also his antisemitism—Luther developed a theory of church and state. Just as Luther longed for a return to a more Augustinian theology, he also sought to elaborate Augustine's position on church and state—colored, though, by the millennium of history that had passed, as well as by Luther's personal situation. In 1523, when Luther wrote his foremost essay on church and state, Temporal Authority: To What Extent it Should be Obeyed, he had just survived a precarious political crisis. He had, after all, alienated the two major individual bearers of political and social power: the pope and the Holy Roman Emperor. On the one hand, Luther had initiated the Reformation largely because, in his view, the papacy and the Catholic Church had become, over several centuries, excessively involved in temporal affairs. Hence, in his essay, he certainly would be expected to argue for restricted eccclesiastical involvement in secular matters. On the other hand, Luther had good reason to assert some limitations on imperial powers. After Luther had been excommunicated, the Holy Roman Emperor, Charles V, summoned Luther to appear before the Diet at Worms. Charles demanded that Luther recant his books attacking the Roman Catholic Church, and when Luther adamantly refused, Charles condemned Luther as a heretic and placed him under the ban of the Empire. Luther might soon have died a martyr if the Elector Frederick the Wise of Saxony—asserting his own power against the emperor—had not stepped forward and offered Luther refuge.[57]

Thus, in this context, Luther set forth to explicate the implications of his theology for the relations between church and state. As discussed, the central components of Luther's theology—human sinfulness and justification by faith alone—reflected the crucial New Testament dichotomy between Christian spirituality and Jewish carnality. To elaborate the relations between church and state, Luther built further on this dichotomy (and echoed Augustine's City of God). He divided humankind into two classes: those belonging to the kingdom of God and those belonging to the kingdom of the world. To rule these two classes or kingdoms, God ordained two governments: the spiritual, "by which the Holy Spirit produces Christians and righteous people under Christ," and the temporal or secular, "which restrains the un-Christian and wicked." Hence, each government operates in its own separate realm by its own appropriate means. Spiritual leaders should attend to spreading God's Word through preaching and should avoid interfering in secular affairs, while secular authorities, using reason and force if necessary, must maintain "outward peace" despite the depravity of humankind.[58] Hence, for example, only the secular government should promulgate law backed by coercion; the Roman Catholic Church's extensive canon law system should be eliminated as a this-worldly corruption.[59] Most important, then, exactly because the two governments should operate in different spheres by different means, they should not compete against each other. So long as the religious and secular rulers follow these strictures, they should complement each other's authority. Luther wrote: "For this reason one must carefully distinguish between these two governments. Both must be permitted to remain; the one to produce righteousness, the other to bring about external peace and prevent evil deeds. Neither one is sufficient in the world without the other."[60]

In order to bolster secular authority in the face of papal interference, Luther urged adherence to the New Testament behest to respect (Roman) civil authority ("Render to Caesar the things that are Caesar's, and to God the things that are God's").[61] In particular, Luther stressed the beginning of Romans 13: "Let every soul be subject unto the higher powers [of the governing authority]. For there is no power but of God: the powers that be are ordained by God. Whosoever therefore resisteth the power [of the civil authorities], resisteth the ordinance of God."[62] Consequently, Luther (more so than Augustine) emphasized the divine origin of secular authority. "[I]t is God's will that [secular authorities use] the temporal sword and law ... for the punishment of the wicked and the protection of the upright."[63] Indeed, Luther's Reformation sometimes is called "magisterial" because of his alignment with secular magistrates.[64]

At the same time, though, Luther carefully circumscribed secular power. The secular rulers rightly have authority over "life and property and external affairs on earth," but they have no authority over people's consciences. Luther here built again upon traditional antisemitic dogma. New Testament discourse emphasized that Jews cannot be forced to convert: true faith can never be coerced. Luther extended this basic doctrine regarding Jews to delineate the limits of secular authority. Secular authorities can exercise the power of the sword to regulate conduct and other external affairs, but this power cannot be used to coerce Christian faith. Citing Augustine for support, Luther declared: "[Faith] is a matter for the conscience of each individual. . . . For faith is a free act, to which no one can be forced. Indeed, it is a work of God in the spirit, not something which outward authority should compel or create." Even religious leaders, Luther added, should not coerce faith; rather, "God's word must do the fighting." Finally, Luther reinforced his position on secular and religious authority by explicitly referring to Jewish obstinence: "[E]ven if all Jews and heretics were forcibly burned no one ever has been or will be convinced or converted thereby."[65]

Thus, to Luther, so long as a secular ruler remains in the appropriate sphere of authority, subjects must obey his or her commands. Even a true Christian, who does not need worldly constraints, nonetheless should respect the secular power—if not the secular ruler. Luther emphasized that most rulers are evil fools and scoundrels, yet their authority must be respected because they are ordained by God to perform a necessary function: "to punish the wicked and to maintain peace." The rulers themselves are relegated to controlling the degraded and carnal world of the Jews. Hence, the rulers might be worthy of scorn, but their authority must be respected. Luther explicitly equated civil law with Jewish law and declared that Jewish (and hence civil) law is necessary to restrain the wicked, including the Jews, who do not belong to God's kingdom. The true "Christian submits most willingly to the rule of the sword, pays his taxes, honors those in authority, serves, helps, and does all he can to assist the governing authority, that it may continue to function and be held in honor and fear." According to Luther, a true Christian should disobey the secular ruler only if the ruler exceeds the boundaries of his or her sphere of authority—that is, only if the secular ruler attempts to command the Christian on a religious matter, such as siding with the pope or possessing Protestant books (recall Charles V's demands on Luther). Yet, even in this situation, Luther conservatively advocated only passive disobedience, not active rebellion. Punishment must be endured: "[Should the secular ruler] punish such disobedience, then blessed are you; thank God that you are worthy to suffer for the sake of the divine word."[66] In his later writings, though, Luther assumed a more assertive stance, recommending that godly princes should actively resist an ungodly emperor (again, recall Frederick the Wise's protection of Luther against Charles V).[67]

To a great extent, Luther developed his theory of church–state relations by elucidating the relationship between Jews and civil authority embodied within the New Testament discourse. On the one hand, the New Testament discourse had emphasized the dichotomy opposing Jewish carnality to Christian spirituality. God condemned the Jews to suffer in the carnal and temporal (secular) world while they witnessed the blissful salvation of Christians in their spiritual Heaven. On the other hand, the New Testament demanded that Christians respect civil authority: "Render to Caesar the things that are Caesar's, and to God the things that are God's."[68] To Luther, then, God had ordained both the secular and spiritual worlds; the secular world was degraded and sinful but nonetheless extant. God therefore had further ordained that civil authorities had the task of policing the actions of Jews and other wicked or unsaved souls in the secular world. Without the civil authorities, life in the secular world would truly be a hellish nightmare. Hence, according to Luther, Christians must respect the need for and the work of the civil or state authorities, but Christians should still recognize that those authorities themselves lived in the depraved secular world and, more important, had no power whatsoever in the spiritual world. Besides, all that truly matters is spiritual salvation in the other world, and spiritual salvation depends solely on an individual's faith and God's grace.

Luther maneuvered within this theoretical framework to suit his particular political and theological needs. His overriding initial concern, of course, was to argue for a reduced authority of religious leaders, particularly those of the Roman Catholic Church. In Luther's framework, he needed only to emphasize that religious leaders should be concerned solely with spiritual salvation—which is all that truly matters anyway—and that therefore they should refrain from interfering in the secular affairs of the carnal and temporal world. With this diminution in religious jurisdiction, though, Luther necessarily expanded the rightful authority of secular rulers, though he did so cautiously, for he feared imperial power. Hence, in the end, Luther rejected both the Caesaropapist and hierocratic positions that had echoed down through the Middle Ages. To Luther, religious and secular authorities should complement and not compete with each other.[69] Yet, while in theory neither authority was superior to the other, Luther always assumed that the secular authorities and their subjects would be Christian. He introduced Temporal Authority by writing: "I hope ... that I may instruct the princes and the temporal authorities in such a way that they will remain Christians—and Christ will remain Lord."[70] Moreover, as mentioned, Luther in no way advocated toleration of or liberty for religious outgroups, and he expressly instructed preachers to tell kings and princes to fear God and follow the commandments.[71] In fact, the later Luther expressly warned princes not to protect Jews: "You ought not, you cannot protect them, unless in the eyes of God you want to share all their abomination."[72] The secular law of the state would, in Luther's view, always be the law of a Christian ruler.[73] To be clear, then, while Luther sought to undermine the secular power of the Catholic Church, he opened the gap between the religious and secular spheres (thus further developing the concept of the separation of church and state) primarily to benefit his Protestant Church.

How do the somewhat contemporaneous political theories of Luther and Machiavelli relate to each other? Machiavelli and Luther had disparate purposes—they aimed in different directions—but interestingly, their theories weave together neatly in a complementary fashion. On the one hand, Machiavelli focused on the well-being of the state. He suggested that Christianity (that is, Roman Catholicism) corrupted political affairs by discouraging citizen involvement in this-worldly civic affairs. On the other hand, Luther focused on the religious well-being of the people. He argued that the Church interfered with the salvation of Christians because of its excessive involvement in worldly affairs. When fit together, these two arguments seem to drive toward a greater separation between church and state. Machiavelli pushed for greater separation from the state or governmental side—the Church should remain outside of civic affairs to avoid corrupting the political sphere—while Luther pushed for greater separation from the religious or spiritual side—the Church should remain outside of civic affairs so that it could concentrate on saving Christians. When combined in this manner, their arguments seem to prefigure some modern conceptions of the principle of separation of church and state in a democracy: these modern conceptions emphasize a public square of democratic debate free of religious interference and, simultaneously, a religious sphere free of political interference.

Did Luther therefore implicitly support a democratic or civic republican form of secular government, as Machiavelli did? Probably not. To be sure, Luther's concept of a congregation of the faithful, devoid of the Catholic Church's hierarchy, had populist and democratic implications in the religious sphere insofar as it suggested that all Christians are equal. His emphases on Scripture and justification by faith alone reinforced this populism because supposedly each individual could personally and directly experience the Word of God and the truth of Christ. This religious populism even resonated with the common Renaissance and civic humanist focus on human dignity in political and civil affairs. Nonetheless, Luther clearly did not intend to celebrate human dignity and excellence; to the contrary, he emphatically insisted that humans are sinful and depraved. Furthermore, as already mentioned, Luther maintained that everyone is not equally able to "publicly minister and teach" Christianity.[74] Finally, in his political theorizing, Luther never incorporated civic humanist notions of private persons as citizens. For Luther, individuals were always subjects; rulers therefore remained superiors, princes, lords, or masters, never magistrates. As ordained by God, subjects had a duty to obey and rulers had a right to command. Thus, however contrary to Luther's intentions, his political theory helped legitimate the emerging absolutist monarchies of Europe.[75]

THE CALVINIST REFORMATION

While the split between Roman Catholics and Protestants was the major division within western Christianity, Protestant reformers themselves quickly fragmented into different sects. For example, by the mid-1520s, the Anabaptists had splintered off because they insisted that baptism during infancy was invalid and that true believers therefore should be baptized as adults. These divisions between various Protestant sects could be severe. In 1524, for instance, Luther managed to have an Anabaptist opponent expelled from Saxony.[76] Luther also fell into a serious dispute during the 1520s with Huldreich Zwingli, an early leader of the Reformation in Switzerland. In particular, they disagreed about the proper interpretation of the Eucharist or Lord's Supper. Luther had accepted the Roman Catholic sacrament of the Eucharist, but only with qualifications. In Catholicism, the doctrine of transubstantiation determines the meaning of the ingestion of the bread and wine (during the Eucharist): supposedly, the words of the priest miraculously transform the bread and wine into the body and blood of Christ, thus renewing Christ's sacrifice for humanity. Although Luther accepted the Eucharist, he only partially accepted the doctrine of transubstantiation. To Luther, the bread and wine do not actually convert into the body and blood of Jesus, but nonetheless, Jesus' body and blood become present in the sacrament. Somehow, the body and blood of Jesus coexist with the bread and wine. To Zwingli, however, the bread and wine are merely symbolic: they represent the body and blood of Jesus, but the body and blood are never actually present during the sacrament. The disagreement between Luther and Zwingli led to the distinction within Protestantism between the Lutheran and Reformed movements.[77]

Jean Calvin was born in France but spent most of his adult life in Switzerland. Well educated as a humanist, Calvin was still living in France when he suddenly converted to Protestantism in 1534. Within two years, he had written the first edition of his remarkably systematic and thorough statement of reform theology, Institutes of the Christian Religion, and thus he quickly became a second-generation leader of the Reformed movement.[78] On the issue of the Eucharist, Calvin tried to reach a position midway between those of Luther and Zwingli; according to Calvin, Christ was spiritually but not physically present.[79] Nevertheless, in many ways, Calvin's theological views strongly resembled those of Luther; the differences were one of degree, not of kind. Like Luther, Calvin stressed the authority of the Scriptures: "For by his Word, God rendered faith unambiguous forever."[80] To Luther, the Old Testament was relatively unimportant because it had been superseded by the New Testament, but to Calvin, the Old and New Testaments both remained authoritative as the Word of God. The New Testament, in effect, reaffirmed the Old Testament.[81] The Calvinist notion of the covenanting community arose from Calvin's respect for the Old Testament. To Calvin, the Laws of the Old Testament represented a series of agreements between humans and God necessitated by original sin. This contractual relationship served as a model: a community of believers could reaffirm, at any time, its covenant with Christ, contractually committing itself to uphold the laws of God. As early as 1537, under Calvin's direction, all the citizens of Geneva, Switzerland, were asked to swear an oath binding them to follow God's commandments.[82]

Because Calvin, as a Christian, concentrated on the New Testament at least as much as on the Old Testament, he necessarily accentuated human depravity and sinfulness. Indeed, Calvin stressed, even more so than Luther, that original sin had condemned humans to degradation:

> [L]et us hold this as an undoubted truth which no siege engines can shake: the mind of man has been so completely estranged from God's righteousness that it conceives, desires, and undertakes, only that which is impious, perverted, foul, impure, and infamous. The heart is so steeped in the poison of sin, that it can breath out nothing but a loathsome stench. But if some men occasionally make a show of good, their minds nevertheless ever remain enveloped in hypocrisy and deceitful craft, and their hearts bound by inner perversity.[83]

Like Luther, Calvin maintained that humans are justified by faith alone. Calvin defined faith as "a firm and certain knowledge of God's benevolence toward us, founded upon the truth of the freely given promise in Christ, both revealed to our minds and sealed upon our hearts through the Holy Spirit." Because Calvin emphasized human sinfulness even more so than Luther, Calvin also tended to stress, more than Luther, that humans cannot earn faith and salvation; good works cannot bring salvation. Instead, God gives faith. In a sense, then, whereas Luther tended to focus on faith as an inward experience, Calvin concentrated on God as the objective basis of faith. Calvin underscored that because humans are so depraved, faith itself must be grounded on God and not on human capabilities or resources. Yet, Calvin also emphasized a more inward experience, which he called "conscience."

> [W]hen men have an awareness of divine judgment adjoined to them as a witness which does not let them hide their sins but arraigns them as guilty before the judgment seat—this awareness is called "conscience." It is a certain mean between God and man, for it does not allow man to suppress within himself

what he knows, but pursues him to the point of making him acknowledge his guilt.[84]

Conscience, then, is an inner awareness of one's own inescapable depravity in relation to the greatness of the truth of Jesus Christ. Hence, to Calvin, conscience does not entail human choice or free will but rather irresistible convictions. Conscience does not offer options; conscience dictates turning to Christ. Moreover, conscience, as a bridge to God, has nothing to do with works; it is unrelated to the external and carnal world. Instead, "a good conscience is nothing but an inward uprightness of heart." It is not a matter of cognitive understanding, but rather "a lively longing to worship God and a sincere intent to live a godly and holy life." Indeed, conscience is "higher than all human judgments."[85] In short, conscience is an entirely internal faculty that mediates between the individual and God.

Calvin's focus on human depravity led him to underscore (again, more so than Luther) the doctrine of predestination: God's eternal plan or decree has designated or predestined each human for salvation or damnation. Humans are so evil and God is so great that human salvation must depend entirely on God's election. "God once established by his eternal and unchangeable plan those whom he long before determined once for all to receive into salvation, and those whom, on the other hand, he would devote to destruction." Hence, the elect do not deserve salvation in any worldly sense; they simply have been chosen by God through His mercy. Meanwhile, the damned can do nothing to alter their future affliction. For both the elect and the damned, then, individual efforts and works are entirely unrelated to one's eternal fate.[86]

One might expect an emphasis on predestination to induce a grim lethargy: if one's actions have nothing to do with one's eternal future, why bother doing anything? But to Calvin, on the contrary, predestination led to the concept of the "calling" (which he also stressed more than Luther did):

> [E]ach individual has his own kind of living assigned to him by the Lord as a sort of sentry post so that he may not heedlessly wander about throughout life. . . . It is enough if we know that the Lord's calling is in everything the beginning and foundation of well-doing. And if there is anyone who will not direct himself to it, he will never hold to the straight path in his duties. For no one, impelled by his own rashness, will attempt more than his calling will permit, because he will know it is not lawful to exceed its bounds.[87]

Thus, each person should seek to fulfill his or her calling in life; one should accept one's role and perform it as well as possible. Following one's calling, though, cannot earn salvation; each individual already is predestined for salvation or damnation, and works cannot change that fate. Instead (somewhat paradoxically), one should follow his or her calling exactly because of predestination and human depravity. Because of original sin, human will and conduct are necessarily depraved and cannot bring salvation: humans cannot intend to do good, cannot pursue righteousness, and cannot choose to do godly works. Humans are emptied of even the potential for good purposes and works, so from Calvin's perspective, individuals might as well do whatever task God has assigned to them. In other words, there is no good human reason to act and no good human reason not to act. But there is a godly reason to act—namely, to fulfill God's plan as revealed in one's position and status in life.[88] Consequently, we should follow our calling with religious zeal, for it is to the glory of God. J.G.A. Pocock aptly characterizes the Calvinist predicament: "[H]aving been created to an end unfixed by him, by a being of whom he knows nothing, his first duty is to preserve himself to that end."[89] Thus, while works cannot earn salvation, works nonetheless can show one's "obedience to God" and can be a sign of salvation.[90] As Max Weber observed, the Calvinist concept of the calling spurred the so-called Protestant ethic, a rigorous asceticism combined with an insatiable drive to work—all to the greater glory of God. Weber added that this Protestant ethic strongly contributed to the development of a capitalist desire to use the earth's resources in order to acquire more and more wealth; other historians, though, question Weber's conclusions regarding the precise ties between Calvinism and capitalism.[91]

Understandably, many commentators have noted that Calvin was friendlier than Luther to Jews.[92] Such commentators often stress Calvin's insistence that the Old Testament remained authoritative; indeed, some of Calvin's opponents accused him of Judaizing because of his attitude toward the Old Testament.[93] Moreover, Calvin never wrote a virulent essay such as Luther's Concerning the Jews and Their Lies, nor did he ever advocate violence against Jews, as Luther had done. Nonetheless, Calvin's theology must be perverted beyond recognition in order to conclude, as some have done, that he was not antisemitic and instead was even philosemitic.[94] To the contrary, as one might expect from a Christian committed to the authority of the Christian Scriptures, Calvin repeatedly echoed the standard doctrinal antisemitism embodied within the New Testament.[95] Even a casual browsing through a sampling of Calvin's works reveals pervasive antisemitism. For example, Calvin wrote that Jews "had an inordinate love of themselves, and proudly despised God and his gifts."[96] Jews are hard-hearted and sottish hypocrites who "willfully deceive themselves,"[97] yet

Jews "regard the salvation of the Gentiles with envy."[98] All Jews should be blamed for killing their own prophets and Jesus Christ.[99] All Jews are guilty of sacrilege and therefore are cursed "deservedly."[100] Their suffering is warranted because they "were the cause of all their evils."[101]

Even Calvin's respect for the Old Testament as God's Word resounded with antisemitic undertones. Calvin quite clearly honored the Christian interpretation of Jewish Scripture—that is, Calvin focused on the Old Testament and not the Hebrew Bible. To Calvin, the Jewish law of the Old Testament, "unless it be directed to Christ, is a fleeting and worthless thing."[102] Calvin read the Old Testament to foretell the coming of Jesus as Christ and to condemn Jews to suffer for their apostasy and deicide.[103] Calvin's respect for the Old Testament thus did not extend to Jews themselves. His writings even vindicated the segregation of Jews in ghettoes, as well as their expulsion from entire cities and countries. Calvin wrote: "[Christian] believers must carefully avoid the society of those whom the just vengeance of God pursues, until they perish in their blind obstinacy."[104] Hence, unsurprisingly, the Calvinist Reformation invigorated the movement to exclude Jews from western and central Europe. For example, Jews had already been expelled from Geneva in 1491, but in 1582, after the Calvinist Reformation, the city council, clergy, and populace all overwhelmingly denied a Jewish request for readmission. And in Germany, the principal Calvinist state, called the Palatinate, barred Jews in 1575.[105]

At a broad level, as with Luther, the symbolic foundation of Calvin's entire theology was the antisemitic New Testament dichotomy between Christian spirituality and Jewish carnality. The central tenets of Calvin's theology—human depravity, justification by faith alone, conscience as an internal experience, and predestination—all directly reflected this crucial Christian dichotomy. Calvin stressed the opposition between outward and inward forums—a "distinction between the earthly forum and the forum of conscience."[106] The earthly forum is, of course, the carnal and temporal world of the Jews. Whereas at least some Christians can attain spiritual fulfillment in eternal salvation, all Jews fail to realize that nothing depends "on human merits," so they mistakenly continue to "glory in the flesh."[107] Hence, according to Calvin, Jews and others who focus on works as a means to salvation necessarily grovel in the human depravity of the earthly forum. Because even Christians are predestined to salvation or damnation, works cannot affect one's fate by bringing salvation. Rather, justification is by faith alone—the inward experience of conscience as a bridge to the salvation of Christian spirituality.[108]

Calvin expressed his views on the relations between church and state in the final chapter of his Institutes, which was entitled "Civil Government."[109] Like much of Calvin's theology, his views largely echoed those of Luther, though Calvin's theory of the separation of church and state emerged more as an integral part of his theology. And as such, Calvin's theory on church and state reflected the New Testament dichotomy between Christian spirituality and Jewish carnality—which, as discussed, undergirded Calvin's theology. Calvin insisted that society must have both the church and the state, but the two institutions must be kept separate: "Christ's spiritual Kingdom and the civil jurisdiction are things completely distinct." The two institutions—church and state—manifested Christian spirituality and Jewish carnality, respectively. In the very first section of "Civil Government," Calvin expressly linked the separation of church and state to the opposition between Christianity and Judaism.

> [W]hoever knows how to distinguish between body and soul, between this present fleeting life and that future eternal life, will without difficulty know that Christ's spiritual Kingdom and the civil jurisdiction are things completely distinct. Since, then, it is a Jewish vanity to seek and enclose Christ's Kingdom within the elements of this world, let us rather ponder that what Scripture clearly teaches is a spiritual fruit, which we gather from Christ's grace; and let us remember to keep within its own limits all that freedom which is promised and offered to us in him.[110]

Although the New Testament seemed to oppose Christian spirituality to Jewish carnality, when Calvin transferred this dichotomy into the realm of church–state relations, he subtly but significantly adjusted the relationship. Instead of directly opposing the state (or civil government) to the spiritual government, he maintained that they are absolutely separate but not antithetical. Calvin wrote: "[Secular] government is distinct from that spiritual and inward Kingdom of Christ, so we must know that they are not at variance."[111] Thus, to Calvin, secular and spiritual governments cannot be antagonistic exactly because they are completely separate: when two realms have no overlap, no point of contact, no interaction, then they cannot be antithetical.

Calvin continued, then, by enhancing the status of the secular state, following a trend running from Thomas Aquinas to Machiavelli to Luther. Calvin unequivocally declared that civil government is necessary and should be respected; at one point, Calvin even accorded secular government a "place of honor." Like Luther, Calvin argued that secular government is needed to maintain order and peacefulness. Humans are hopelessly depraved and sinful, and they must live (at least temporarily) in the secular world. Consequently, "to provide for the common safety and peace of all," civil government must severely punish criminals and other wicked individuals. To Calvin, the "function [of civil government] among men is no less than that of bread, water, sun, and air."[112] In light of his respect for secular government, Calvin predictably echoed Luther's conservatism by insisting that subjects should obey rulers or civil magistrates. To Calvin, resisting the magistrate is equivalent to resisting God since the civil order represents God's will. Subjects therefore should obey even unjust magistrates, who represent God's punishment for human wickedness. In short, private individuals should not "undertake anything at all politically," leaving public affairs entirely to magistrates.[113]

Yet, Calvin tempered his conservative tone with three qualifications. First, he argued that though the subject should obey even unjust commands, respect is due to the office more than to the officeholder. Extending Luther's argument that rulers themselves may be personally unworthy, Calvin wrote:

> I am not discussing the men themselves, as if a mask of dignity covered foolishness, or sloth, or cruelty, as well as wicked morals full of infamous deeds, and thus acquired for vices the praise of virtues; but I say that the order itself is worthy of such honor and reverence that those who are rulers are esteemed among us, and receive reverence out of respect for their lordship.[114]

Calvin here contributes an important component to the modern concept of sovereignty: the subject owes allegiance to the government, not to particular officials. Second, Calvin further tempered his conservative approach by reasoning that ultimate obedience must be owed to God, not to secular authorities. "If [secular rulers] command anything against him, let it go unesteemed. And here let us not be concerned about all that dignity which the magistrates possess; for no harm is done to it when it is humbled before that singular and truly supreme power of God."[115] Calvin here did not advocate active private resistance to unjust rulers, but rather a type of passive disobedience. In the event of a conflict between a civil magistrate's will and God's ordained plan, the private individual owed allegiance to God; after all, secular government always remained within the degraded temporal and carnal world of the Jews. Third, and most important with regard to the development of modern sovereignty, Calvin suggested that subjects can elect and be represented by inferior magistrates who can actively resist unjust rulers. Whereas private individuals should never directly resist a king or another secular ruler, "magistrates of the people, appointed to restrain the willfulness of kings (as in ancient times the ephors were set against the Spartan kings)," actually have a duty to resist injustice. These inferior magistrates or ephors "have been appointed protectors by God's ordinance." Therefore, if they fail to actively resist an unjust ruler, they "betray the freedom of the people" and also violate God's will. At this point, in other words, Calvin seemed to allude to some notion of citizenship. Scholars disagree about whether Calvin intended to emphasize that the ephors represented either the people, on the one hand, or God, on the other. Yet, in any event, Calvin clearly understood the ephors to be popular magistrates who should function to protect the people's freedom. It is worth noting, then, that although Calvin most often referred to "subjects" and "rulers" (which Luther always did), he nonetheless somewhat frequently talked of "magistrates" and, on occasion, explicitly mentioned "citizens." Some of Calvin's followers extended this at least implicit conception of citizenship by advocating for a right of all people—not just the ephors—to actively resist unjust rulers, thus presaging the idea of a citizen in a modern state who actively participates in the political process.[116]

In the end, Calvin's respect for the state and its magistrates arose largely from their ability to support and promote Christianity. Civil government, according to Calvin, "provides that a public manifestation of religion may exist among Christians, and that humanity be maintained among men." Indeed, Christianity is a prerequisite for good government: "[N]o government can be happily established unless piety is the first concern." Yet, simultaneously, Calvin emphasized that civil government does not have the "duty of rightly establishing religion."[117] Civil laws, in other words, should not presume to determine the religious conscience of Christians—for conscience is an internal experience beyond the realm of the external and temporal world—yet the civil laws nonetheless should provide extensive support for the flourishing of a Christian society. Moreover, again because of the need to allow Christians to experience freely the dictates of their consciences in turning to Christ, the Christian Church itself also should not attempt to coerce faith. Civil coercion (of any type or source) belongs solely in the secular and temporal (Jewish) world, while conscience and faith remain entirely distinct and within the spiritual (Christian) world. Just as the New Testament declared that Jews should not be forced to convert and have faith in Jesus Christ, so too Christians should not (and cannot) be compelled to true faith. In a manner of speaking, Calvin insisted upon the strict separation of church and state as a tenet of his reform theology.[118] The Reformed Church, without attempting to force faith, should spread Christianity throughout society. The secular government should lend its support, when possible, and otherwise should keep the depraved from turning life into an "outrageous barbarity."[119] And both church and state should leave each individual to his or her conscience, so that each person can remain free to experience inwardly Christ and Christian faith.

Despite their similarities, Calvin and Luther differed somewhat in their practical attitudes toward the separation of church and state. Whereas Luther accepted occasional state control over church polity, Calvin insisted that church organization and governance should never be surrendered to secular rulers.[120] At the same time, Calvin was willing to allow the church to intrude in secular affairs. In light of Calvin's theorizing, this position might seem paradoxical or even hypocritical; as already discussed, Calvin insisted that spiritual and secular affairs are absolutely distinct. Yet, from a Calvinist standpoint, this complete separation of the spiritual and secular actually justified church involvement in political or secular affairs. In his theory, Calvin enforced such a thorough disjunction between the spiritual and secular—based on the New Testament opposition of Christian spirituality to Jewish carnality—that the secular lacked all purpose, substance, or direction. The secular became, to Calvin, purely material. Furthermore, humans, in their degraded and sinful position, could never create or impose any legitimate purposes for secular government. Within a Christian world view, purpose and substance might possibly come from only one place, the spiritual; within Thomistic (Roman Catholic) political theory, Christian spiritual salvation provides the comprehensive good or end that determines how rulers should govern politically. But to Calvin (and contrary to Thomistic theory), Christian spirituality cannot provide the end or purpose for secular affairs because the spiritual and secular are so radically distinct. For Calvin, secular affairs can have no final end or purpose other than the glory of God: civil authorities should seek to preserve society and fulfill their callings only because it is God's plan. The only ultimate reason for any human action is that God has ordained it—the secular order, in short, is part of the divine order.[121] Thus, according to Calvin, civil magistrates act as "vicars of God" or "God's deputies," and do nothing by themselves but rather carry out "the very judgments of God."[122]

In this somewhat paradoxical sense, then, Christian spirituality—or the divine Christian order—should not only dominate the other-world, but now it should also dominate this world.[123] Consequently, not only should the secular government support the Christian Reformed Church, but the Church itself should legitimately penetrate and inform secular affairs, whether governmental or otherwise. Thus, as discussed, the concept of one's calling and the Protestant ethic in social and even economic affairs make perfect sense. And in secular government, Calvin unsurprisingly established a despotic and theocratic regime in Geneva, and once even used his political strength to ensure the conviction and burning of a theological opponent. Ultimately, Calvin seemed intent upon establishing a Christian society, nurtured by both religious and secular authorities.[124]

Despite Calvin's and Luther's attempts to minimize the enhancement of secular authority, the political reality was otherwise; many secular rulers were able to use the Reformation to enhance their powers mightily. The success of the Reformation was as much a political phenomenon as it was a religious or theological one. In particular, the religious achievements of the Protestant Reformation were, to a great extent, due to the support Calvin, Luther, and other reformers received from secular rulers, who in turn saw their own wealth and power increase. For example, not only did Frederick the Wise of Saxony protect Luther in his confrontation with the Holy Roman Emperor, Charles V, but five years later, his son, the Elector John, transformed Saxony into a Lutheran principality. Although many subjects supported their secular rulers in adopting Protestant reforms, others did not. Thus, regardless of the details of Calvin's and Luther's theories on church–state relations, secular rulers in some parts of Europe often demanded that their subjects accept the new Christian theology. On the other side, by the 1540s, Roman Catholic rulers began to suppress Protestantism with force, and religious wars lasting for many years commenced.[125] In Germany, for instance, the division between Lutheran Reformers and Catholics led eventually to outright civil war. Peace was restored in 1555 only because Charles V and his brother, King Ferdinand, determined to negotiate a settlement with the Lutherans at any cost. The Peace at Augsburg established that each prince could decide the religion to be followed in his territories. Subjects who did not like the decision of their prince would be allowed to emigrate to another territory. These concessions, however, extended only to Catholics and Lutherans, not to members of other reform sects.[126] Thus, in a practice that would become increasingly common, religious toleration (albeit limited) was born—not because of a principled theological or political commitment to toleration, but rather because harsh experience revealed that neither side in the dispute could crush the other. Toleration became a political necessity.

For many decades, though, toleration was a slippery resting point in the conflicts between Protestants and Catholics. In the latter half of the sixteenth century, France demonstrated the potential for political intrigue and recurrent war within the Reformation context.[127] In the 1550s, the number of Huguenots (or French Calvinists) increased significantly despite severe persecution. Between 1560 and 1572, Catherine de Medici, queen mother of the Holy Roman Empire, was struggling politically to preserve her power in France; for that reason, she extended a measure of religious liberty to the Huguenots.[128] French Catholics, opposed to Catherine, provoked a series of wars with the Huguenots, yet in 1572 Catherine herself, for unknown reasons, either engineered or allowed the massacre of thousands of Huguenots. Meanwhile, the French Catholics eventually divided among themselves: some sought a Catholic victory at any cost, while others (called the Politiques) supported religious toleration as a political necessity for preserving French liberty. Despite the emergence of this politique position, religious wars racked France until 1598, and they began again in 1610.

These violent events spurred the development of theoretical positions that contributed further to the modern concept of the sovereign state. In particular, after the massacres of 1572, the Huguenots sought to incite revolution, but they lacked sufficient numbers to appeal solely to coreligionists. Consequently, they sought to develop a theoretical position that appealed to moderate Roman Catholics who otherwise were disposed to oppose Catherine. Most important, following Calvin's argument regarding the Spartan ephors, the Huguenots maintained that specially chosen magistrates, representing the people, have a moral and legal right to forcefully resist a tyrant. But whereas Calvin tied the rights and duties of ephors to the will and laws of God, the Huguenots argued explicitly that magistrates have a right to resist any ruler who has failed to pursue the welfare of the people. Thus, because of political exigencies—that is, the need to appeal to Catholics as well as other Huguenots—the Huguenots articulated a theory of resistance and revolution that was political rather than religious. The Huguenots, in other words, grounded their theory on the interests of the people, not in God's order and will. Significantly, Jean Bodin, who previously had supported the Huguenots, attacked this theoretical position. In his Six Books of a Commonweal, published in 1576, Bodin articulated, perhaps for the first time, a modern theory of sovereignty. While the Huguenots sought to encourage resistance and revolution, Bodin instead advocated the pursuit of social and political order, even at the cost of liberty. To Bodin, the only means for ensuring peace and order was to accept a sovereign, an absolute monarch who commands but is never commanded.[129] Quite simply, with the temporal powers of the Roman Catholic Church significantly diminished, the idea of an absolute ruler with unshared secular power became imaginable.

During the religious wars, Jews (if they had not already been banished) could be a useful pawn. In Germany, for example, as Luther intensified his antisemitic invective, Charles V and his supporters, the loyal Catholic prince-bishops, helped save the Jewish population from total collapse. This protection of German Jewry, of course, did not mean that Catholicism suddenly had become less antisemitic. Rather, Charles and his German supporters protected Jews as "a kind of counterweight, however limited in scope, to the Protestant bourgeoisie."[130] Thus, German Jews lived through a political reality that would epitomize the position of Jews in western societies far into the future: Jews enjoyed the benefits of religious toleration because the splintering of western Christianity led to embattled and deadlocked Christian sects. While, as discussed, toleration between Christian sects eventually became a political necessity, toleration of Jews became "a matter of political expediency."[131] Outside of the Holy Roman Empire, Charles himself expelled the Jews from Naples and persuaded the papacy to initiate a Spanish-style Inquisition in Portugal. And the papacy was more than happy to support its imperial ally in this manner. Indeed, the Catholic Counter-Reformation of the mid-sixteenth century managed to intensify the usual Catholic antisemitism. In Italy, papal decrees forced Jews into ghettoes, caused some Jews to be burnt alive, and finally expelled Jews from most of the Papal States.[132] At times, Catholics and Protestants seemed locked in a competition to prove who were the better Christians by being the greatest antisemites.

In any event, why did so many secular rulers support the Protestant Reformation, even with force when necessary? For centuries, of course, monarchs had wrangled with the papacy for wealth and power. By the early sixteenth century, in some parts of Europe, eager monarchs already had found one ideological justification for questioning papal authority. A properly nurtured and growing sense of national identity tended to conflict with the Church's long-standing claim to possess supra-national jurisdictional powers. For many secular rulers, the religious Reformation provided an alternative ideological justification for challenging papal authority. In other words, from the viewpoint of many secular rulers, the Reformation primarily offered a fortuitous opportunity to enhance their wealth and power (and sometimes national identity) vis-à-vis their rival, the Roman Catholic Church.[133] A successful religious conversion meant, at the least, that the secular ruler was freed of conflict with the asserted temporal powers of the Church. The secular ruler, then, could claim to possess undivided power; as noted, during the sixteenth century, the concept of the sovereign with absolute power crystallized. To a great extent, in countries that remained predominantly Catholic, such as France and Spain, the monarchs previously had negotiated concordats (agreements) with the papacy providing for the Church to relinquish some of its power and wealth.[134] Other monarchs, unable to wrench agreements from the papacy, were now quick to seize the opportunity to undermine the Catholic Church. As Quentin Skinner succinctly observes: "[T]he price of princely avarice proved to be the endorsement of a 'full and godly' reformation."[135] Secular support for religious reform often was an incidental though ultimately significant by-product of this yearning for wealth and power.

In a sense, the Protestant Reformation of Luther and Calvin can be understood as a strategic change in the orientation of Christian power in European society. For over a millennium, the Roman Catholic Church had asserted substantial control over western society. Quite often, as during the Crusades, the papacy and the Church hierarchy had exercised enormous political strength to impose their purposes on the laity and on non-Christians. The Protestant Reformation, however, shattered the Catholic Church's monopolistic control over western religion; thus, the Church was, to some extent, forced to withdraw from secular affairs. Yet, Christianity itself did not recede: to the contrary, the Protestant churches proceeded to spread their influence throughout society. In some areas, such as Calvin's Geneva, the Protestant Church was able to impose its form of Christianity forcefully on society; as already discussed, secular rulers (for their own reasons) often played crucial roles in these imposed transformations. In any event, these forced religious changes arose from exercises of political strength that resembled the politically enforced actions of the medieval Catholic Church. But the Protestant churches also spread their influence through their congregations of the faithful. This influence was, at one and the same time, less obvious but more direct and immediate than the influence that the Catholic Church hierarchy could impose on the laity and on non-Christians. In the Protestant world, the laity effectively was the Church. Hence, Christianity could spread insidiously throughout society with no apparent imposition by a Church hierarchy or a state. From this perspective, the Reformation's separation of church and state theoretically withdrew the bureaucratized institutions of church and state from civil society, but only to allow the Protestant faithful to control civil society themselves. If the Catholic Church's greatest successes tended to be through colonization by conquest, then Protestantism's greatest successes would tend to be through colonization by infiltration and settlement.

Christianity, from its origins in the New Testament, had asserted two discourses of domination. The first discourse differentiated, objectified, and denigrated the secular world—the carnal and temporal world of the Jews. The second discourse asserted the universalism of Christianity: all individuals, including Jews, were deemed within the unity of the Christian body. Throughout the Middle Ages, the first discourse largely justified the various distinctions supporting the hierarchical organizational structure of Roman Catholicism: the distinctions between Christians and non-Christians, between clergy and laity, and between different ecclesiastics within the Church structure itself. But the second discourse—the discourse of universalism—was the primary justification for the Roman Catholic claim to exercise jurisdictional power over all of society, including secular rulers, Jews, and infidels. Asserting and maintaining the unity of the body of Christ justified, even necessitated, Catholic conquests. Whenever possible, the Catholic Church sought to impose its Christian purposes on all of western society and beyond; of course, those Christian purposes often seemed strangely temporal and carnal.

With the coming of the Reformation, however, the Christian discourse of domination shifted by intensifying the first discourse. That is, the Reformers differentiated, objectified, and denigrated the secular world with such ferocity and thoroughness that the secular became the material, bereft of any worth, substance, or purpose. Humans could neither create nor impose any legitimate reason for acting in the secular world. The second discourse—that of universalism—then became less jurisdictional and more justificatory. The only reason for the existence of anything in either the secular or spiritual world was God's own will; the difference between the spiritual and secular worlds was therefore denied. This denial of difference symbolically justified the Christian infiltration and settlement of the secular world, which otherwise lacked all meaning and purpose; in this way, the divine Christian order colonized the secular world. Most important, though, this denial of difference remained within a Christian dialectic: Christianity seemed to deny the difference between the spiritual and secular worlds while still simultaneously asserting the radical difference between those worlds. In fact, paradoxically, it was the radical difference between the worlds that enabled the denial of difference. That is, Christianity first contrasted its own spirituality with the empty materiality of the secular world, only then to assert its right to lay claim to that otherwise worthless secular realm. Ultimately, this Christian dialectic, simultaneously asserting and denying difference, helped propel a turn toward modernism by encouraging individuals to focus on this-worldly activities.[136] With roots in the New Testament condemnation of Jewish carnality, Christianity clearly placed the spiritual above the secular and temporal. Yet, Protestantism severed the two realms so completely that human activity in the secular world seemingly could not derive its purpose or meaning from the spiritual world. With spiritual salvation thus no longer an attainable goal (at least through temporal activities or works), individuals had no choice but to focus, with all their abilities, on their respective callings in the secular world—for this must then be for the greater glory of God.

In conclusion, the Reformation significantly altered the relationship between church and state in western society. Since the beginnings of Christianity, the New Testament had provided a discursive framework for the relations of church and state, with the state condemned to the carnal and temporal world of the Jews. For over a thousand years, the Roman Catholic Church and various secular rulers had struggled politically, further developing the relationship between church and state, with the Catholic Church emerging as a powerful bureaucratic institution distinct from secular rulers. The Reformation influenced this relationship in at least four ways. First, both Luther and Calvin, returning to the New Testament discourse, stressed the division between the spiritual and secular realms: the separation of church and state thus more clearly became a matter of theology (or theory). Second, Protestantism's odd modernist twist accorded a new respectability to the state. The reformers respected and even honored secular authorities insofar as the authorities fulfilled their calling, performing an important function in God's plan. Third, and most practically, the Reformation's split of Christianity almost ensured that the weakened Catholic Church would eventually lose its long-running political battle with the state for supremacy in secular and temporal affairs. Thus, insofar as the victors write history, the state became increasingly respectable within political theory despite its permanent condemnation within New Testament discourse. Fourth, despite the state's victory over the Catholic Church, the Protestant churches began to emerge as powerful social forces. Whereas the Catholic Church, as a bureaucratic and hierarchical social institution, had tended to compete with state authorities, the Protestant churches tended instead to complement and cooperate with the state in their mutual domination of society. Indeed, the term "separation of church and state," makes better sense if applied to western society before the Reformation, when the Catholic Church could be understood as a state-like organization that was clearly distinguishable from other societal institutions. After the Reformation, the Protestant churches were effectively spread throughout society—the congregations of the faithful were society (or at least, most of society). To think of society itself as embodied in the churches, as somehow completely separate from certain societal institutions, whether the state or otherwise, does not seem quite as sensible. Unsurprisingly, then, state-established or -supported churches were the norm well into the eighteenth century in Protestant as well as Catholic countries.[137]

CHAPTER 5

The English Reformation, Civil War, and Revolution

During the sixteenth and seventeenth centuries, England underwent a remarkable transformation as it passed through the Henrician Reformation, the Elizabethan Settlement, the Civil War, the Restoration of the monarchy, and finally the Glorious Revolution.[1] The causes of some of these events remain notoriously ambiguous. Different historians, for example, have attributed the Civil War of the 1640s either to religious, political, economic, or even geographical factors.[2] Those who emphasize religion tend to refer to this period as the Puritan Revolution,[3] while others insist that there was no revolution at all, Puritan or otherwise.[4] Recent scholarship tends to emphasize a multitude of causal factors. Conrad Russell, for instance, argues that three long-term causes of instability simultaneously came to a head, thus sparking the Civil War. In Russell's words, the factors were "the problem of multiple kingdoms, the problem of religious division, and the breakdown of a financial and political system in the face of inflation and the rising cost of war."[5] Nevertheless, because I am concerned with the development of church and state, I will discuss primarily the importance of religious and political factors in the English Civil War, as well as in the other major events of the sixteenth and seventeenth centuries. Indeed, the conjunction of political and religious strife in England during these two centuries, perhaps more so than any other single consideration, has shaped the current understanding of the separation of church and state in American constitutional thought. To many constitutional scholars, America needs the separation of church and state to avoid a recurrence of the English turmoil of this period.

THE ENGLISH REFORMATION

Despite the aforementioned ambiguities, most historians agree that the English Reformation began more as a political than a religious dispute.[6] In particular, the Reformation began with Henry VIII, king of England from 1509 to 1547, who was far from being a religious revolutionary. To the contrary, Henry was theologically trained and even published in 1521 an Assertion of the Seven Sacraments, which defended the seven Roman Catholic sacraments against Luther's attacks. Pope Leo X then declared Henry to be the "Defender of the Faith."[7] In any event, Henry had long been married to Catherine of Aragon. Because Catherine had been the widow of Henry's older brother, a papal dispensation had to be granted to authorize Henry and Catherine's marriage in the first place. In 1527, though, two factors prompted Henry to seek an end to his marriage with Catherine. First, he had fallen deeply in love with Anne Boleyn; second, he wished to have a male heir. Catherine was unlikely to have any more children, and to that point she had borne Henry only one surviving daughter, Mary. Since divorce as we currently know it did not then exist, Henry claimed that from a religious standpoint, the marriage had been invalid at the outset and that the pope should therefore officially annul it. At Henry's behest, his lord chancellor, Cardinal Thomas Wolsey, negotiated for two years in seeking a declaration of annulment from Pope Clement VII. Unfortunately for Wolsey, political developments on the European continent had left the pope effectively under the control of the Holy Roman Emperor, Charles V, who happened to be Catherine's nephew. Partly because of Charles's influence, the pope was not inclined to satisfy Henry, who eventually became so frustrated that he stripped Wolsey of his power and had him executed.[8]

Steadfast, Henry decided to act unilaterally. Starting in 1531, Henry took several actions designed to sever ties with the papacy. He initiated the first propaganda campaign designed to utilize the printing press to rapidly sway popular opinion, and with this popular support, he solicited parliamentary action. Henry's primary intention, of course, was to end papal jurisdiction in England, thus freeing him from papal control. By 1533, Henry had divorced Catherine, married Anne Boleyn, and had another daughter, the princess Elizabeth (later to become queen). When Clement VII threatened excommunication, Henry solidified England's break from Rome by procuring several additional key parliamentary enactments. Most important, the Act of Supremacy of 1534 declared that "the king's majesty justly and rightfully is and ought to be the supreme head of the Church of England."[9]

In effect, then, the first stage of the English Reformation consolidated church and state under Henry. Henry readily used his new power as the undisputed head of the Church of England to aggrandize power and wealth. For example, he closed and liquidated England's monasteries, raising significant sums of money and currying favor.[10] And as Christopher Hill observes, when monastic lands passed into private ownership, "the Reformation created a vested interest in Protestantism";[11] the new owners of real property formerly owned by the Roman Catholic Church would naturally oppose any return to Catholicism. Indeed, the Henrician Reformation initiated broad economic changes throughout England that would ultimately contribute to the English Civil War in the next century. Yet, under Henry, the Church of England remained in most respects largely Catholic. The Church retained its episcopal organization, being structured around bishops, and the Six Articles Act of 1539 expressly upheld many traditional Catholic beliefs and practices, including the Catholic understanding of the Eucharist, whereby the priest's words (are supposed to) miraculously transform the bread and wine into the body and blood of Christ.[12] At the same time, however, Henry had his son and heir, Prince Edward, educated by Protestant tutors.[13] Thus, while Henry successfully freed himself and England from papal control, he seemed generally ambivalent about religious doctrine.

By the time Henry died in 1547, the Church of England had undergone a strange reformation. It was no longer part of the Roman Catholic Church, but it retained much of the tradition and doctrine of Catholicism. Yet partly because of the continuing religious ferment on the continent and partly because of the lack of papal domination, the Church of England continued to be transformed. Henry's Protestant-educated son, King Edward VI, was only nine years old when he came to the throne, so England was effectively ruled by a council of regents whose chief, the duke of Somerset, was Protestant in persuasion. Hence, during Edward VI's reign, the Church of England moved more in the direction of Protestantism. The Act of Uniformity, enacted in 1549, decreed the first Book of Common Prayer, which imposed a universal set of prayers to be used throughout England. Although this Prayer Book was a mixture of Catholicism and Protestantism, perhaps its greatest significance lay in its use of English-language prayers—a Protestant innovation—as opposed to the traditional Latin prayers of Catholicism. This Prayer Book displeased almost everyone, being too Protestant for conservatives and too Catholic for Protestants, who during this time shifted their attention from Luther to Calvin. A second Act of Uniformity, passed in 1552, revised the Prayer Book and gave it a stronger Protestant orientation.[14]

Edward VI's brief reign ended with his death in 1553, when he was succeeded by Mary Tudor, the only surviving child of the marriage between Henry VIII and Catherine. Unlike Edward, Mary I was a devoted Catholic; thus, partly to remedy the unholy divorce of her parents, she sought to return England fully to the Catholic fold. Consequently, she persuaded Parliament to repeal most of the recent reform legislation and then instituted severe and unpopular persecutions, burning at the stake several Protestant-leaning bishops, including Thomas Cranmer, who had been instrumental in writing the first Book of Common Prayer. When Mary married King Philip II of Spain, the resultant fear in England of foreign influence joined with the distaste for religious violence, leading popular sentiment to turn more strongly against Roman Catholicism.[15]

Elizabeth I succeeded Mary in 1558 and remained as queen until 1603. Elizabeth was Protestant largely due to the political context of her birth: she was Henry VIII and Anne Boleyn's daughter, and the Catholic Church insistently denied the legitimacy of her parents' marriage. Regardless, Elizabeth was unconcerned with strictly enforcing either Protestantism or Catholicism, although she cared intensely about the political unity and social order of England. For that reason, Elizabeth sought to structure something of a compromise between the more extreme Protestant and Catholic positions of her predecessors, Edward and Mary. Thus, she orchestrated the so-called Elizabethan Settlement, already in place firmly by 1563, establishing the mix of Protestantism and Catholicism that came to be called Anglicanism.[16] The Act of Supremacy of 1559 recognized the Church's Catholic-like episcopal structure yet required all ecclesiastical and governmental officials to declare by oath that Elizabeth was "the only supreme governor" of England in both spiritual and temporal affairs.[17] Persons refusing to take this oath were barred from all official positions in church and state. Elizabeth herself had insisted that Parliament refer to her as the supreme governor instead of the supreme head of the Church, as Henry VIII's Act of Supremacy had proclaimed. Elizabeth's political insight was astute, as Catholics found her word ("governor") less obnoxious, even though it did not diminish her power in any practical sense. Meanwhile, the Act of Uniformity of 1559 revised and imposed the second Edwardian Book of Common Prayer (of 1552). This liturgy maintained much of its Protestant orientation but removed some of the elements that had proven most offensive to Catholics.[18] In the effort to maintain national unity, the revised Prayer Book "was a masterpiece of ambiguity where ambiguity seemed necessary."[19] Finally, the Thirty-nine Articles of Religion, issued first in 1563, established the basic faith and lasting character of the Anglican Church.[20] A common observation is that "the Church of England has Calvinist Articles alongside a Catholic liturgy," and indeed, many of the Articles were (and are) calvinistic.[21] For example, various Articles declared the following: that "Holy Scripture containeth all things necessary to salvation," that every person "deserveth God's wrath and damnation," that people can be "justified by Faith only," that good works without faith are sinful and cannot bring salvation, that God predestined some for salvation and others for damnation, and that the "visible Church of Christ is a congregation of faithful men." Finally, the dogmatic antisemitism of Reform Protestantism was (and is) evident. Of course, the Articles maintained that faith in Christ is the only means to salvation.[22] Moreover, in typical Calvinist fashion, the Articles declared that the Old Testament remained the Word of God but only insofar as it foretold of the coming of Jesus Christ— that is, the Articles emphasized the (Christianized) Old Testament and not the Hebrew Bible:

> The Old Testament is not contrary to the New: for both in the Old and New Testament everlasting life is offered to Mankind by Christ, who is the only Mediator between God and Man, being both God and Man. Wherefore they are not to be heard, which feign that the old Fathers did look only for transitory promises.[23]

Despite the strong Protestant flavor of the Articles, Elizabeth's conciliatory attitude again came into play, as ecclesiastics were not required to subscribe to the Articles until Parliament passed the Subscription Act in 1571— only after Elizabeth had been excommunicated.[24]

From the earliest days of the Elizabethan Settlement, more radical English Protestants found the Anglican Church to be too Catholic. These Calvinist (or Reformed) Protestants fruitlessly continued to seek reforms to further purify the Church—hence, they were called Puritans—but despite their frustrations, they never strongly opposed Elizabeth. Indeed, these early Puritans were known to "tarry for the magistrate," and for her part, Elizabeth tended to abide more calvinistic practices in the country parishes.[25] Nonetheless, tensions between Puritans and Anglicans continued during Elizabeth's long reign, and indeed, at around this period, the more radical Puritans pushed Calvin's theory of limited political resistance in a more populist direction. Whereas Calvin had reasoned that only an inferior magistrate or ephor can actively resist injustice, the radical Puritans argued that ordinary citizens have a right to resist.[26]

The Civil War, Restoration, and Revolution

When James I ascended the throne in 1603, matters only worsened. James, who remained king until 1625, sought greater religious uniformity throughout England and thus was less accommodating to the Puritans. For example, he demanded that clergy wear surplices (white gowns).[27] His Book of Sports, passed in 1618, explicitly encouraged recreation on Sundays and thus, from the Puritan standpoint, amounted to "a royal command to disobey the will of God."[28] Most important, James insisted that the Anglican Church retain its episcopal structure. Before becoming king of England, James had ruled Scotland, where Presbyterian Protestants had gained a foothold and thus were able to reject the organizational hierarchy of the episcopacy in favor of church governance by lay elders (or presbyters). From James's viewpoint, the lack of bishops in Scotland had severely weakened his power; in fact, he often asserted, "No bishop, no king." James's stubbornness on these religious issues caused many Puritans in England to lose their hope for continuing reform of the Anglican Church, and thus these Puritans became increasingly restive.[29]

Beyond these religious issues, James attempted to impose a more absolutist monarchy on England. As discussed, absolutist monarchies had become firmly established on the European continent during the sixteenth century, but James failed to account adequately for the significant differences between England and the continent. James's pretensions to absolute power sparked Sir Edward Coke and others to articulate the theory of the ancient constitution, which asserted that Parliament and the common law had been entrenched in England from time immemorial. Most important, then, Parliament and the common law theoretically provided certain (constitutional) rights to the English that were beyond the reach of the king.[30] Coke, therefore, implicitly began to develop a theme still needed for a theory of the modern sovereign state: the notion that sovereignty rests with the people—a theme to be elaborated more fully in English political theory later during the seventeenth century. Eventually, James's policies and miscalculations drove the Puritans into a political alliance with the parliamentarians, especially those in the House of Commons.[31]

The simmering dispute with the Puritans and Parliament, on the one side, and the monarchy, on the other, finally boiled over during the reign of James's son, Charles I, king from 1625 to 1649. Charles almost immediately managed to deepen both the religious and political disputes with the Puritans and parliamentarians. Indeed, early in Charles's monarchy, some Puritans decided to flee England and settle in North America. Nonetheless, most of Charles's opponents remained in England, and Charles quickly provoked their ire by seeking to impose taxes without parliamentary consent. Charles particularly needed funds for unpopular foreign military expeditions. Parliament responded in 1628 by enacting the Petition of Right, which declared that the English constitution mandated parliamentary action to authorize taxation. As might be expected, though, Charles ignored this Petition.[32]

Meanwhile, for religious and political support and guidance, Charles turned to William Laud, a leader of a small group within the Anglican Church strongly opposed to the Puritans. This group, soon called Laudians, rejected the Calvinist focus on Scripture alone and instead emphasized patristic writings, sacramental grace, and the episcopal organization. In actuality, Laud's personal theology was simple: he wanted the Anglican Church to be as Catholic as possible so long as the king remained its supreme head. The Puritans, for their part, accused Laud of being an Arminian heretic because he (supposedly) denied the central Calvinist doctrine of predestination. Politically, Laud could be ferocious. He thought that the Puritans were dangerously dogmatic and that the Church and government should therefore crush them by authoritatively imposing an uncompromising uniformity.[33] Thus, probably on Laud's advice, Charles issued a declaration in 1628 insisting that strict religious uniformity must be maintained, that the Church of England established the religious truth, and that the Church's episcopacy was entitled to resolve any religious disputes.[34] The House of Commons responded in kind with two actions in early 1629. A sub-committee of the House of Commons issued a set of resolutions declaring that the king's ministers had misled him on religious issues and that the spread of Roman Catholicism and Arminianism was dividing the English among themselves, as well as separating them from continental Reformed churches. Even further, the resolutions recommended "[e]xemplary punishments" of Catholics, "severe punishment" of Arminians, the burning of certain books, and the licensing of books to avoid heresy.[35] Less than a week later, the House of Commons passed a bill, dealing with both religion and taxes, that epitomized the extensive entanglement of the religious and political issues.

> 1. Whosoever shall bring in innovation of religion, or by favour or countenance seek to extend or introduce Popery or Arminianism, or other opinion disagreeing from the true and orthodox Church, shall be reputed a capital enemy to this Kingdom and Commonwealth. 2. Whosoever shall counsel or advise the taking and levying of the subsidies of Tonnage and Poundage, not being granted by Parliament, or shall be an actor or instrument therein, shall

be likewise reputed an innovator in the Government, and a capital enemy to the Kingdom and Commonwealth. 3. If any merchant or person whatsoever shall voluntarily yield, or pay the said subsidies of Tonnage and Poundage, not being granted by Parliament, he shall likewise be reputed a betrayer of the liberties of England, and an enemy to the same.[36]

The king replied by almost immediately dissolving Parliament, and remarkably, he refused to recall it for over a decade. By long-established custom in England, Parliaments had been held frequently, but the king ultimately held the power to initiate and dissolve sessions. Thus, he seemingly could rule by royal prerogative alone.[37]

In the end, though, Charles's and Laud's obstinate insistence on religious uniformity forced the king to call a Parliament again in 1640.[38] In the late 1630s, Charles tried to impose the Anglican liturgy in Scotland, thus leading the Scots to rebel openly against England. Charles needed money to fight the Scots, and when royal prerogative alone raised insufficient funds, he summoned Parliament in April 1640 to help raise further revenue. But when the old parliamentary grievances immediately resurfaced, Charles swiftly dissolved this so-called Short Parliament. The war expenses, though, continued to mount, compelling Charles again to convoke Parliament. This Parliament, which first met in November 1640, became the momentous Long Parliament,[39] controlled largely by Presbyterian Puritans.[40]

Straightaway, the Puritan-led Parliament took revenge on Charles's principal ministers. Laud, for example, was thrown into prison and eventually executed pursuant to a bill of attainder.[41] More broadly, Parliament introduced dramatic changes in religion and government. In a startling burst of action, Parliament swiftly transformed the English constitutional system.[42] The Triennial Act of 1640–1641 maintained that Parliament must meet at least once every three years; therefore, the monarch no longer could rule by royal prerogative alone.[43] The Act of May 10, 1641, declared that the king could not dissolve the Long Parliament without its consent.[44] The Tonnage and Poundage Act established that Parliament controlled all forms of taxation, whether direct or indirect.[45] Two separate acts of July 5, 1641, declared the supremacy of law and abolished the courts of the Star Chamber and the High Commission, which under Charles I had become instruments of oppression.[46]

These parliamentary actions obviously diminished the king's authority, and matters finally came to a head with the Long Parliament's passage on December 1, 1641, of the Grand Remonstrance, which extensively detailed the inequities suffered under Charles's governance and asked for extraordinary reforms. Specifically, the king would appoint only ministers that

Parliament could confide in, and Church reform would be referred to a synod of divines whose recommendations would be subject to parliamentary approval.[47] Charles responded promptly and defiantly, asserting that he would do whatever he thought "fit in prudence and honour"[48] and demanding "obedience to the laws and statutes ordained for the establishing of the true religion in this kingdom."[49] By this time, some parliamentary moderates had begun to shift their allegiance from the radicals back to the king; in short, a Royalist party had started to form. In light of this growing support, Charles crucially blundered in early January 1642, when he unilaterally attempted (and failed) to arrest five leading radical members of the House of Commons.[50] Parliament replied rebelliously by passing the Nineteen Propositions of June 1, 1642. In effect, these Propositions proposed to set aside the king's sovereignty in favor of an absolute sovereign power in Parliament.

With England on the brink of civil war, Charles's advisers persuaded him to attempt a sudden last-ditch reconciliation with Parliament. Charles therefore issued the remarkable His Majesty's Answer to the Nineteen Propositions of Both Houses of Parliament, which, in its echoing of certain Machiavellian themes, constituted an innovation in English political thought and subsequently grounded further developments in political theory.[51] His Majesty's Answer stated:

> There being three kinds of government among men, absolute monarchy, aristocracy and democracy, and all these having their particular conveniences and inconveniences, the experience and wisdom of your ancestors hath so moulded this out of a mixture of these acts as to give to this kingdom (as far as humane prudence can contrive) the conveniences of all three, without the inconveniences of any one, as long as the balance hangs even between the three estates, and they run jointly on in their proper channel (begetting verdure and fertility in the meadows on both sides) and the overflowing of either on either side raise no deluge or inundation. The ill of absolute monarchy is tyranny, the ill of aristocracy is faction and division, the ills of democracy are tumults, violence and licentiousness. The good of monarchy is uniting a nation under one head to resist invasion from abroad and insurrection at home; the good of aristocracy is the conjunction of counsel in the ablest persons of a state for the public benefit; the good of democracy is liberty, and the courage and industry which liberty begets.[52]

Thus, in the crush of political expediency, the king (or his advisers) drew upon Machiavellian political theory to justify the maintenance of public order and at least some monarchical power. In particular, His Majesty's Answer depicted England as a republic struggling to preserve itself under desperate circumstances. Moreover, England was presented as a mixed republic, a government of the one, the few, and the many. Machiavelli had suggested that this form of mixed or balanced government was best able to maintain itself because it could draw upon the diversity of all its citizens. And here, in His Majesty's Answer, the king argued that for England to preserve itself, it must maintain the proper balance in its mixed government—of monarch, lords, and commons. Thus, the king, in effect, issued a warning to Parliament: either maintain the proper balance by recognizing an appropriate degree of power in the monarch or send England plunging into anarchy. J.G.A. Pocock observes: "The theory of the mixed constitution was imported into English political rhetoric in order to naturalize there the ... Machiavellian doctrine of the republic, in which the virtues of all may neutralize the vices from which none is free, but which is historically fragile and may be overthrown at the slightest departure from balance."[53] In terms of the future of English political theory, perhaps the most important component of His Majesty's Answer is its presentation of political power. Instead of insisting that governmental power and authority descend from the king (and ultimately from God), His Majesty's Answer suggested that power lies equally in the three estates (monarch, lords, commons) and that this balanced arrangement amounted to no more than a contrivance of "humane prudence."[54] In so suggesting, His Majesty's Answer implicitly conceded that the concept of a divine right of kings was yielding to the idea of the people as sovereign. Despite these theoretical concessions by the king, both Parliament and the king moved quickly to raise armies. By the end of the summer of 1642, Civil War had erupted.[55]

At the outset of the Long Parliament, before the war began, 15,000 Londoners signed a petition regarding religion and presented it to the House of Commons, which referred it to a committee. This Root and Branch Petition of December 1640 condemned the Roman Catholic and Anglican Churches and sought to abolish the episcopacy and the Common Prayer Book.[56] Parliament never passed this specific petition, but once the Civil War began, Parliament did move in this general direction. In particular, Parliament needed to secure Scottish aid during the war, and the Scots, in return for their assistance, were thus able to demand that Parliament adopt a Presbyterian system. Hence, in 1643, Parliament passed the Solemn League and Covenant, one of the best illustrations of Presbyterian Puritan theology, both in its content and in its very use of the covenant as the (typically Calvinist) means for constituting a community.[57] This legislation began by declaring an intention to advance "the kingdom of our Lord and Saviour Jesus Christ." To overcome the religious conspiracies "against the true religion," all English people over the age of eighteen would be required to enter a solemn league and covenant. The covenant sought the preservation and reformation of religion "in doctrine, worship, discipline, and government, according to the word of God and example of the best reformed Churches." All churches throughout England would need to follow uniformly the recommended theology and organization, and the covenant left no doubt that Reformed Protestantism constituted the only true religion.

> [W]e shall ... endeavour the extirpation of popery, prelacy (that is, Church government by archbishops, bishops, their chancellors and commissaries, deans, deans and chapters, archdeacons, and all other ecclesiastical officers depending on that hierarchy), superstition, heresy, schism, profaneness, and whatsoever shall be found to be contrary to sound doctrine and the power of godliness.[58]

Finally, the covenant demanded that all English people subscribe to an archetypal Calvinist confession, emphasizing human sinfulness, a focus on the Christian Gospels, the need for faith in one's heart, and the following of God's plan in one's calling:

> [B]ecause these kingdoms are guilty of many sins and provocations against God and His Son Jesus Christ, as is too manifest by our present distresses and dangers, the fruits thereof: we profess and declare, before God and the world, our unfeigned desire to be humbled for our sins, and for the sins of these kingdoms; especially that we have not as we ought valued the inestimable benefit of the gospel; that we have not laboured for the purity and power thereof; and that we have not endeavoured to receive Christ in our hearts, nor to walk worthy of Him in our lives, which are the causes of other sins and transgressions so much abounding amongst us, and our true and unfeigned purpose, desire, and endeavour, for ourselves and all others under our power and charge, both in public and in private, in all duties we owe to God and man, to amend our lives, and each one to go before another in the example of a real reformation, that the Lord may turn away His wrath and heavy indignation, and establish these Churches and kingdoms in truth and peace.[59]

Parliament then reasserted these basic Calvinist themes in the influential Westminster Confession of Faith, which harkened back to the New Testament antagonism between Jewish carnality and Christian spirituality.[60]

Although Parliament passed the Presbyterian Solemn League and Covenant and then the Westminster Confession, not all Puritans were Presbyterians. Quite clearly, Parliament had passed the Covenant primarily because of political and military reasons—the need for Scottish aid—not because of a religious consensus. All Puritans shared certain overlapping

Reformed beliefs—and all Puritans undoubtedly opposed Laudianism—but even before the passage of the Covenant, Puritanism was somewhat divided within itself. The adoption of the Presbyterian system pursuant to the Covenant (and the later Confession) therefore tended to exacerbate these preexisting divisions among the Puritans within Parliament. In fact, Parliament split into four parties. The two major parties were the Presbyterians and the Independents, both of which originated early in the Civil War, with the more conservative Presbyterians favoring a defensive war and a negotiated peace and the Independents seeking to win the war at all costs. Thus, despite the importance of religion, the parties were not split purely along religious lines; some Independents were even Presbyterian elders. In any event, the Presbyterian party, which was in the majority, pushed Parliament to assert the authority to impose a rigid Presbyterian brand of Puritanism despite their belief in freedom of conscience. The Independents, who were mostly Congregationalists, tended to be more tolerant of different Puritan sects, and partly for that reason had the support of the parliamentary army, which consisted of Protestant enthusiasts of many persuasions. The two lesser parties were the sectaries (or the Parties of the Left) and the Erastians. The distinction between the sectaries and the Independents always remained fuzzy, with the sectaries tending to place even greater emphasis on freedom of conscience and toleration. The Erastians were the least concerned with how the religious differences were settled, so long as religious tyranny ended and civil peace was maintained.[61]

Despite the central division between the Presbyterians and Independents, Parliament's alliance with the Scots proved successful, and by 1646 the parliamentary army, led by Oliver Cromwell, had defeated the royal army. Charles I surrendered to the Scots, who eventually passed him on to the English Parliament. Nonetheless, because the Independents clearly controlled the army, the Presbyterians gradually began to shift their allegiance to Charles. Indeed, the king and the Presbyterians entered into an agreement whereby Charles's authority would be re-established in exchange for his promise to support English Presbyterianism for three years. Meanwhile, in an incredible turn of political intrigue, Charles managed to escape and to ally secretly with the Scots: in exchange for Charles's promise to support Presbyterianism, the Scottish army invaded England in August 1648. Still under Cromwell's command, however, the parliamentary army defeated the Scots, thus effectively leaving the army as the supreme power in England. In December 1648, an army detachment led by Colonel Thomas Pride expelled all Presbyterian members from Parliament. Pride's Purge left only the Independent members in Parliament, a small fraction of the original number; this remnant of the Long Parliament was known as the Rump. At the behest of the army, the Rump created a High Court of Justice for the purpose of trying Charles, who was then condemned and executed on January 30, 1649. The monarchy as well as the House of Lords soon were officially abolished. Of eventual significance, Charles died with unusual dignity, insisting that his execution amounted to unlawful violence that augured insecurity and disorder for all English people. Thus, even though Charles's monarchy had been disastrous, his death propelled him to martyrdom in the eyes of some.[62]

In any event, shortly before Charles's execution, the Council of the Army issued the Agreement of the People, a proposed constitution for England based largely on Puritan principles. Although the Agreement was never adopted, it remains significant as the first Anglo-American attempt to constitute a nation under an organic legal instrument and as a precursor of American constitutions.[63] Of particular importance for the separation of church and state, the Agreement declared Reformed Christianity to be the "public profession"; Catholicism and Anglicanism were not included in this public Christianity.[64] Furthermore, the Agreement proposed to protect freedom of conscience: the people were to be instructed in Christianity without being compelled to have faith. In this respect, the Agreement followed standard Reform doctrine, which in turn arose from the New Testament mandate to not physically force Jews to convert. The protection for freedom of conscience was explicit:

> That such as profess faith in God by Jesus Christ, however differing in judgment from the doctrine, worship or discipline publicly held forth, as aforesaid, shall not be restrained from, but shall be protected in, the profession of their faith and exercise of religion, according to their consciences, in any place except such as shall be set apart for the public worship.[65]

With this very first proposal for a national organic document, a distinctive (and persistent) vision of the relation between church and state had emerged. This vision consisted of three related parts. First, governmental support or establishment of religion was not understood to be inconsistent with freedom of conscience. The Agreement simultaneously established Reform Protestantism as the public religion and protected freedom of conscience. To some extent, Church establishment merely continued a traditional way of life. Before the Reformation, in an English society with but a single Christian Church, establishment had seemed "appropriate."[66] After the Reformation and Civil War, though, English Christianity had splintered into many sects, yet the traditional assumption—that establishment was appropriate—remained in force. Hence, the established religion itself might change, but the fact of establishment continued.

Second, freedom of conscience was protected as a matter of Puritan theology. A central component of Reform Protestantism was that conscience stands as an internal experience or faculty beyond the realm of the external and temporal world; conscience and faith cannot be compelled. Hence, when the Agreement proposed to protect freedom of conscience, it sought to protect only what Puritanism demanded for a meaningful religious (Christian) experience. In fact, the Independents' Savoy Declaration of Faith and Order, a Congregationalist religious confession that adopted a modified Westminster Confession, explicitly protected freedom of conscience.[67] To be clear, freedom of conscience did not entail human choice or discretion. Instead, freedom of conscience allowed individuals to follow the dictates of their conscience to Jesus Christ; freedom of conscience was necessary to receive the truth of Christ. Thus, the Reformed commitment to freedom of conscience did not amount to a political commitment to respect or tolerate the religious liberty of others; rather, freedom of conscience reflected a Puritan theological conviction about the preeminence of conscience and faith.[68] This second point—that freedom of conscience was protected as a matter of Puritan theology—intertwined with the first point—that religious establishment and freedom of conscience were consistent. Since freedom of conscience itself was an integral part of Reform theology, freedom of conscience would naturally be consistent with the official establishment of Reform Protestantism. Indeed, the establishment of Reform Protestantism would seem to necessitate the protection of freedom of conscience.

Third, in any particular historical context, actual toleration of different religious sects arose from political realities, not from a principled political commitment.[69] Freedom of conscience connoted toleration for only some Christian sects, with the number and identity of those sects depending upon political machinations. In this instance, the army was composed of Puritans of many different sects, so the Agreement needed to extend protection to all those sects, but protection for the defeated Catholics and Anglicans was unnecessary. Protection for other religions was, of course, totally irrelevant.[70] In short, religious toleration to a great extent amounted to no more than Christians begrudgingly accepting a disappointing political reality and attempting to put a good face on it.

With nothing but the Rump in Parliament and no new official governmental structure (since the Agreement of the People was never adopted), England operated under Cromwell as a military autocracy. In April 1653,

Cromwell finally expelled the Long Parliament by force. He then summoned a small Parliament, known as the Little or Barebones Parliament, which was dissolved on December 12. Then, on December 16, 1653, army leaders proffered a written constitution that Cromwell accepted. The Instrument of Government was the first written organic document for an entire nation, though it had no permanent constitutional significance in England. The Instrument established a government consisting of a Lord Protector, who was of course Cromwell, a single House, and a Council of State that would advise the Protector. With regard to religion, the Instrument was nearly identical to the Agreement of the People, the only difference being that the Instrument stated even more clearly than the Agreement that protection for freedom of conscience did not extend to Catholics and Prelates (Anglicans).[71] The first House elected under the Instrument in 1654 sought to enact a different constitutional scheme that would allocate greater power to Parliament, so Cromwell dissolved the House in January 1655 and ruled by military force. The short-lived English republic thus degenerated into despotism.[72]

When Cromwell died in September 1658, his son, Richard Cromwell, succeeded him as Protector. Richard, though, proved to be a weak and ineffective leader, and England thus "plunged into anarchy."[73] To many English people, already weary from years of turmoil and now facing chaos, a strong king and a national church emerged as the best course for returning to "law, order, and stability."[74] A somewhat skewed memory of Charles I reinforced this viewpoint: as mentioned, despite Charles I's many faults as king, his dignity in death led many English to view him as a martyr. Thus, in 1660, when elections produced a new Parliament, the Presbyterians combined with the Royalists (Episcopal Party) to vote for the restoration of Charles II, who had been living in exile since the execution of Charles I.[75] Just before returning to England, Charles II issued his Declaration of Breda, which proposed certain principles for governance. In language anticipating John Locke's Two Treatises of Government, the Declaration promised to protect "lives, liberties [and] estates."[76] With regard to religion, the Declaration provided that because of the plurality of religious opinions in England, there should be liberty of conscience. This provision, however, was merely precatory; it further suggested that Parliament act to fully grant "that indulgence."[77]

Thus, the Declaration offered hope at least to the Presbyterians, the most conservative of the Puritans, that they would be comprehended by a national church, but this hope soon was dashed. The first Parliament after the restoration immediately acted to reestablish a Laudian type of Anglicanism and to persecute Puritans. For example, in 1662, Parliament passed a Uniformity Act that imposed a revised Anglican Book of Common Prayer and demanded that all clergy take an oath to uphold the Anglican doctrine of the Prayer Book.[78] Hundreds of Puritan ministers sacrificed their positions rather than take the prescribed oath. In the words of Sydney Ahlstrom, "[f]or Presbyterians, Congregationalists, Baptists, and Quakers—not to mention Roman Catholics and Unitarians—social inequality, imprisonment, and legal harassment became the order of the day."[79] All Puritans, in short, were forced so far outside the establishment that they became the Dissent, and eventually, many Dissenters succumbed to the pressure and abandoned their Puritan commitment.[80]

Meanwhile, a combination of factors prompted Charles II to oppose Parliament by seeking to enforce some degree of religious toleration. In particular, Charles wanted to aid Roman Catholics largely because Louis XIV of France (a Catholic) provided Charles II with secret financial assistance. Moreover, Charles always had personally leaned toward Catholicism, though he never revealed strong religious convictions. Thus, in order to curry Dissenting (Puritan) favor for his effort to aid Catholicism, Charles issued a Declaration of Indulgence in 1673. This Declaration stated that although the Anglican Church remained the official church that all English people must support, other Christian sects were allowed to meet so long as they first received governmental approval. Parliament responded harshly with the Test Act, which effectively required all civil and military officials to be members of the Church of England.[81]

When Charles II died in 1685, his brother, James II, became king. James was Roman Catholic, and he dedicated himself to reestablishing Catholicism in England. In 1687, he issued a Declaration of Indulgence that granted to his subjects "the free exercise of their religion." The Declaration also withdrew the "oaths of supremacy and allegiance" that the Test Act had imposed, thus opening public offices to Catholics and Dissenters. Although these sections of the Declaration appeared merely to extend religious toleration, James's ultimate goal was to impose Catholicism, as the Declaration itself eventually disclosed: "We cannot but heartily wish, as it will easily be believed, that all the people of our dominions were members of the Catholic Church."[82] James's overbearing efforts to impose Catholicism galvanized English Protestants to band together: Anglicans joined Dissenters to oppose James and his Catholicism. William of Orange (from the Netherlands) was invited to invade England and depose James. William landed with a small army in November 1688, and James fled the country.

Parliament soon elected William and Mary (James's daughter) as joint monarchs; the Glorious (or Bloodless) Revolution was complete. Most important, since at least William was not entitled to the throne by heredity, the Revolution established that sovereigns were to rule "by the will of the nation—and not by any prerogative higher than the law"; the divine right of kings had yielded to the sovereignty of the people.[83] With regard to religion, Anglicanism became firmly established as the official Church of England, resting on the Thirty-nine Articles of Religion, first issued in 1563. But William and Mary, quite wisely from a political standpoint, reintroduced a degree of religious liberty. The Toleration Act of 1689 granted toleration to all Protestants (except Unitarians) who would swear an oath of allegiance to William and Mary and would reject the doctrine of transubstantiation, though Puritans remained subject to various inequities, such as paying tithes to the Anglican Church and needing governmental approval for public meetings. In fact, the Toleration Act did not stop the continuing decrease in the number of Puritans that had begun during the Restoration.[84]

By this time, nearly two centuries had passed since Henry VIII had initiated the English Reformation, and England had undergone a profound transformation. Nonetheless, once the Elizabethan Settlement had established the basic nature of the Anglican Church—as a mixture of Protestantism and Catholicism—all further religious turmoil ultimately ended with the Church of England reaffirming its Elizabethan Anglicanism. As Christopher Hill tersely declares: "'The Puritan Revolution' failed."[85] Yet, while the religious revolution may have failed, seventeenth-century England nonetheless had undergone a political and economic revolution. Christopher Hill briefly summarizes the enormous changes:

> The end of prerogative courts and of arbitrary taxation threatening security of property, sovereignty of Parliament and common law; the habit of continuous parliamentary government; effective rule of J.P.s [justices of the peace] and town corporations uncontrolled by Star Chamber or major-generals; end of monopolies; abolition of feudal tenures, but no security for copyholders; conquest of Ireland; the Navigation Act and use of sea power for an imperialist policy—these were the lasting achievements of the years 1640–60, though some were not finally confirmed until 1688.[86]

Indeed, the Puritan-generated work ethic combined with the political changes of the Civil War to help propel England into the modern capitalist world. As the lands of the Crown, the Royalists, and the Anglican Church were distributed among the people, English capital was mobilized for production where previously it had lain static, "withheld from investment." In this transformed England, a good citizen sought to accumulate wealth while remaining frugal: after 1660, "it became a social duty to get rich."[87]

Furthermore, although the Puritan Revolution may have failed, these many decades of turmoil did result in an increase in religious toleration as a political necessity. The treatment of Jews further illuminates this political development, although for several centuries, hardly any Jews lived in England. In 1290, King Edward I had expelled all Jews, and the question of officially readmitting them was not seriously discussed until the seventeenth century.[88]

During the English Civil War, the Calvinist emphasis on Scripture—both the Old and New Testaments—led many Puritans to focus on Judaism and the conceptual Jew even though real Jews were not present in meaningful numbers. For example, as already mentioned, the Westminster Confession of Faith built upon the New Testament opposition of Jewish carnality to Christian spirituality. Specifically, the Confession emphasized that God "abrogated" the earlier Jewish "covenant of works," replacing it with the Christian "covenant of grace." Because people were "utterly indisposed, disabled, and made opposite to all good, and wholly inclined to all evil," they were "incapable of life" in accordance with the Jewish covenant or testament. Yet the Jewish (or Old) testament was "all fore-signifying Christ to come"; hence, the Christian covenant of grace provided the universal means of salvation "to all nations, both Jews and Gentiles." Under the Christian or new testament, one's conscience became the bridge to God's spiritual heaven; good works could not earn salvation because of "the infinite distance between us and God," though "our duty" was to do "all we can" to fulfill our callings. The Confession even underscored the importance of honoring the Christian Sabbath of Sunday as opposed to the Jewish Sabbath of Saturday.[89]

The original Westminster Confession was largely Presbyterian, and as noted, during the Long Parliament, the Independents tended to be more tolerant than the Presbyterians of religious diversity. In fact, though, the Independents disagreed among themselves about the proper meaning and application of freedom of conscience. For this reason, together with their Calvinist respect for the Old Testament as the Word of God, the Independents expressly and extensively debated in Parliament the significance of the Old Testament and Jewish laws for determining the authority of civil magistrates over religion and conscience.[90] An anonymous essay, The Ancient Bounds, or Liberty of Conscience, Tenderly Stated, Modestly Asserted, and Mildly Vindicated, presented a typical Independent conclusion:

Whatsoever [Jewish kings and magistrates] did rightly ... yet cannot be drawn into precedent by us.... First, those were the times of the Old Testament, these of the New; therefore 'tis not a sound way of arguing from them to us in everything.... Secondly, their worship was carnal, bodily, outward, consisting much in the conformity of the outward man and practice to certain worldly ordinances.... But the worship of the New Testament is chiefly in the heart and hidden man, in spirit and in truth, which is at the beck of no human force or power. Therefore it is no good argument from that worship to this. [Consequently] kings or magistrates may not now as then compel men to religion; but that which those kings did in a typical way, Christ, the King of his Church, doth in a spiritual, antitypical way of accomplishment....[91]

Thus, ironically, even as the Independents argued for freedom of conscience, they echoed traditional New Testament antisemitic doctrine; indeed, the conception of Christian spirituality in opposition to Jewish carnality grounds the argument for freedom of conscience. According to this familiar argument, Judaism is carnal and temporal, while Christianity is spiritual. Civil authorities operate solely in the temporal sphere and therefore cannot compel true Christian faith, though Jesus will nonetheless persuade individuals to embrace Christian spirituality.

During the Civil War period, the Puritans did begin to consider the possibility of readmitting Jews to England. The primary reason that the issue arose at this time was Puritan theology, but it was not the Puritan theological commitment to freedom of conscience that prompted their support for Jewish readmission to England. Rather, some Puritans emphasized an eschatological belief in a future millennium, a period of latter-day glory on earth. To prepare for this coming millennium, most or all Jews would need to convert to Christianity. These Puritans believed that if Jews were readmitted to England, they would meet godly people who would prompt mass Jewish conversion and thus hasten the coming millennium.[92] One Puritan millenarian wrote, for instance, that Jesus Christ shall come and reign "here gloriously for a thousand years. [At that time,] there shall be a wonderful confluence of people to this church: both Jew and Gentile shall join together to flow to the beautifulness of the Lord."[93] Consequently, in 1649 and again in 1651, Parliament was petitioned to lift the ban on Jews, and in 1655, Cromwell was likewise petitioned. In each instance, no official action was taken. The 1655 petition, in particular, sparked an outburst of popular opinion against Jewish readmission, with printing presses spewing forth antisemitic propaganda, suggesting, for example, that Jews had offered half a million pounds to buy St. Paul's Cathedral in London so that they could change it into a synagogue. Even Cromwell, despite his Independent orientation, suggested that toleration should not be "stretched so far as to countenance those who denie the divinity of our Saviour."[94]

In fact, though, a small number of financially successful Marranos had begun filtering into England during the 1630s and 1640s (Marranos were Spanish Jews who at least formally had converted to Christianity). Since as a matter of practical politics Cromwell sought to promote English commerce, he was inclined to allow these Marranos to remain. The issue finally came to a head in 1656. In late 1655, England had gone to war against Spain. The Spanish Marranos thus were faced with a dilemma: either stand accused of being enemy aliens (as Spaniards) or admit to being Jews. They chose the latter, and in March 1656 they once again petitioned Cromwell. At this point, the government refused to lift the ban against Jews but nonetheless officially allowed the Marranos to remain in England as Jews. This small community of Jews continued to expand throughout the Restoration and even more so after the Glorious Revolution, as William and Mary reestablished Anglicanism but with a degree of politically inspired religious toleration. Even so, English Jews most often were treated contemptuously and were subject to legal persecution. To a great extent, then, the fate of Jews in England mirrored that of Jews in other European countries. As the various Christian sects found themselves unable to crush their opponents, a limited amount of religious toleration for different Christian groups became politically necessary. Then, when other political circumstances proved propitious, Jews managed to share in this toleration, becoming incidental beneficiaries of these Christian stalemates.[95]

ENGLISH POLITICAL THEORY

In terms of the future development of the separation of church and state, one of the most significant consequences of the English political metamorphosis was the emergence of modern political theory, particularly the writings of Thomas Hobbes, James Harrington, and John Locke.[96] Hobbes wrote most of his works during the Civil War period of the interregnum, with his most famous book, Leviathan, being published in 1651. The political and religious chaos of this period largely determined Hobbes's objectives. Leviathan—which, in Hobbes's words, was "occasioned by the disorders of the present time"[97]—appeared only two years after the regicide and before the adoption of any new official governmental structure. Thus, to Hobbes (and many of his contemporaries), the overriding concern was how to reestablish civil peace, order, and security. To some extent, then,

Hobbes followed Machiavelli as a political realist and rejected classical political philosophers, such as Aristotle, as hopeless idealists.[98] Contrary to Machiavelli, though, Hobbes's conclusion was that only an absolute sovereign could establish and maintain civil peace. Bodin had argued likewise in the previous century, but whereas Bodin had maintained that the absolute sovereign must be a monarch, Hobbes conceived of the absolute sovereign as a commonwealth or state.[99] Ultimately, Leviathan pleased neither the royalists nor the parliamentarians in the English dispute, and in fact, Hobbes himself seemed ambivalent about whom he preferred as a final victor. He favored the king in 1642 and Cromwell in the 1650s for the same reason: to Hobbes, civil peace and well-being depended upon obedience to the secular ruler.[100]

Although many political philosophers focus solely on the first half of Leviathan, a fuller understanding of Hobbes's argument requires attention to both halves.[101] In the first half, Hobbes argued from reason—he presented a science of politics—while in the second half, he argued from Scripture. Briefly, in the first half of Leviathan, Hobbes attempted to present political theory as Euclid had presented geometry, as a matter of axiomatic principles and demonstrable reasoning.[102] Hobbes posited humans as being in a state of nature where all are roughly equal physically and mentally. Furthermore, in this state of nature, a "perpetuall and restlesse desire of Power after power, that ceaseth onely in Death," places each person in constant competition with and fear of all others. The state of nature thus is equivalent to constant war, "such a warre, as is of every man, against every man." No one stands above the fray:[103] there is no personal security, no societal advancement, and no cultural development. "[T]he life of man [is] solitary, poore, nasty, brutish, and short."[104]

According to Hobbes, humans would prefer to protect themselves from the dangers inherent in the state of nature, and hence their "[r]eason suggesteth" a means to achieve security.[105] Each person must enter a covenant with all others that places all right and power in one absolute sovereign.

This is more than Consent, or Concord; it is a reall Unitie of them all, in one and the same Person, made by Covenant of every man with every man, in such manner, as if every man should say to every man, I Authorise and give up my Right of Governing my selfe, to this Man, or to this Assembly of men, on this condition, that thou give up thy Right to him, and Authorise all his Actions in like manner. This done, the Multitude so united in one Person, is called a Common-Wealth, in latine Civitas. This is the Generation of that great Leviathan, or rather (to speake more reverently) of that Mortall God, to which wee owe under the Immortall God, our peace and defence.[106]

Hence, the Leviathan maintains civil peace and order by wielding an absolute police power: each person knows that any breach of the peace or criminal action can bring swift and legitimate punishment. Finally, the sovereign itself is above the law because the sovereign's subjects covenanted only with each other; they did not covenant directly with the sovereign itself. The sovereign, Hobbes reasons, cannot breach the covenant, and subjects have relinquished all right to resist even an unjust and tyrannical sovereign, though the sovereign is obligated to protect the subjects from violence.[107]

Hobbes thus claimed to have proven that political society originated in human reason and that the state existed in order to maintain civil peace and security. Perhaps most important, then, Hobbes helped turn political theory toward modernism by arguing (in the first half of Leviathan) that sovereign power sprang from human minds and actions and did not descend directly from God;[108] here, Hobbes followed the suggestion made by Charles I in His Majesty's Answer to the Nineteen Propositions of Both Houses of Parliament, issued in 1642 just before the start of the Civil War. In fact, one might conclude that, with Hobbes, the concept of the sovereign state nearly crystallized in its full modernist form.[109] Yet, Hobbes did not conclude his book on this seemingly propitious point. For to Hobbes, his argument still stood incomplete. Because the power of the sovereign is grounded on the subjects' fear of punishment and ultimately death, the human fear of eternal damnation could potentially undermine the sovereign's absolute power. In Hobbes's words: "It is impossible a Common-wealth should stand, where any other than the Soveraign, hath a power of giving greater rewards than Life; and of inflicting greater punishments, than Death."[110] Thus, although Hobbes had demonstrated in the first half of Leviathan that reason and power could establish the commonwealth, in the second half he acknowledged that fear of any secular power pales in comparison to fear of eternal damnation. In the second half of Leviathan, then, Hobbes necessarily turned to a reading of Scripture; he insisted that Scripture must be understood to reinforce and complement his rational argument (articulated in the first half).[111] In short, the effectiveness of secular power depends upon a proper understanding of Scripture. Significantly, in the political circumstances in which Hobbes wrote, his viewpoint appears eminently sensible. Even if religious disputation was not the paramount cause of the English Civil War, religion plainly contributed heavily to the political chaos. At that time, no realistic theory of political society could possibly suggest a route to civil peace and security without accounting for religion. To attempt to do so would be to blink reality. (And this necessity may remain just as true today, despite the many political and constitutional theorists who consider religion as separate from political concerns.)

While Hobbes was not a radical Puritan, the second half of Leviathan clearly was based on a Calvinist Reformed theology, reflecting the views of many parliamentary Independents.[112] According to Hobbes, "the Kingdom of God is a Civil Common-wealth, where God himself is Soveraign"; this Kingdom, though, does not currently exist on earth.[113] Instead, Hobbes described an eschatological progression. Following in the Reformed tradition, Hobbes respected the Old Testament as the Word of God. Consequently, he emphasized the fall of Adam—the original sin that both deprived humans of eternal life and cursed them with pride. Nonetheless, according to Hobbes, "it pleased God" to covenant with the "People of Israel" (that is, Jews) through Abraham and then Moses. Then, mouthing standard New Testament and Calvinist antisemitism, Hobbes explained that the Jews were faithless and resorted to idolatry until Jesus came as the Messiah: "[t]he End of Christ's comming was to renew the Covenant of the Kingdome of God, and to perswade the Elect to imbrace it."[114] For Christians, then, the coming of Christ solved one problem emanating from original sin: the loss of eternal life. Eternal spiritual salvation became possible through faith in the truth of Christ.[115] Yet, Hobbes followed a millennialist vision: even with the coming of Christ, the Kingdom of God as a sovereign entity did not arise on this earth. Rather, life on this earth merely prepares for the future second coming of Christ, the reign of God during a latter-day glory on earth, when the Jews finally will convert. Hobbes noted that in England, Christianity had progressed from Catholicism to episcopacy to presbyteries to congregations of the faithful.[116] But more important, Hobbes understood the commonwealth or state as an intermediate point on the eschatological path to the eventual Kingdom of God. In J.G.A. Pocock's terms: "Hobbes had presented Leviathan's kingdom as occupying the present interval between the direct rule of God exercised in the Mosaic theocracy and the direct rule of God that would be exercised by the risen Christ."[117]

In sum, original sin had created two related problems: the loss of eternal life and human pride. For Christians, the coming of Jesus offered eternal salvation—solving the first problem—but until the second coming of Christ and the Kingdom of God, the problem of human pride remained. The political Leviathan, then, can be understood as solving this second problem by compelling peace and order.[118] Yet, because of the still-present fear of eternal damnation, Hobbes reasoned, if the Leviathan were to be effective—to maintain civil security—the sovereign should establish the state as a

Christian commonwealth.[119] In short, in this world, there can be but one sovereign, ruling both secular and spiritual affairs. Hobbes wrote:

> [A] Church, such a one as is capable to Command, to Judge, Absolve, Condemn, or do any other act, is the same thing with a Civil Common-wealth, consisting of Christian men; and is called a Civill State, for that the subjects of it are Men; and a Church, for that the subjects thereof are Christians. Temporall and Spirituall Government, are but two words brought into the world, to make men see double, and mistake their Lawfull Sov-eraign. It is true, that the bodies of the faithful, after the Resurrection, shall be not onely Spirituall, but Eternall: but in this life they are grosse, and cor-ruptible. There is therefore no other Government in this life, neither of State, not Religion, but Temporall; nor teaching of any doctrine, lawfull to any Subject, which the Governour both of the State, and of the Religion, forbiddeth to be taught: And that Governor must be one; or else there must needs follow Faction, and Civil war in the Common-wealth, between the Church and State; between Spiritualists, and Temporalists; between the Sword of Justice, and the Shield of Faith; and (which is more) in every Christian mans own brest, between the Christian, and the Man.[120]

Hence, in Christendom, church and state cannot be distinguished because the citizens are Christians. Eternal salvation is so unrelated to this carnal and corruptible world that the notion of separate governors over the spiritual and secular does not make sense; in attacking the Roman Catholic Church, Hobbes stressed that clergy should not exercise any independent authority over spiritual affairs.[121] At the present time, humans live only in the temporal (and not the spiritual) world, and therefore only one governor or sovereign can exist. The first half of Leviathan proved the need for an absolute sovereign in the secular commonwealth, and the second half proved a similar need from the perspective of Christian Scripture. And most important, the two halves merged together to arrive at the same con-clusion: there must be but one absolute sovereign ruling over secular and spiritual affairs. This single sovereign, moreover, should allow only one form of public worship.[122]

Even so, Hobbes maintained a semblance of the Calvinist freedom of con-science. To Hobbes, "faith is a gift of God," and only through God's grace is eternal life granted to the faithful.[123] The sovereign, as head of church and state, can regulate conduct or behavior, but true religious conscience cannot be compelled.[124] Indeed, because civil laws and commands contrary to Christ supposedly cannot affect one's salvation, Hobbes argued that one might as well obey all civil commands. Just as Hobbes had concluded in the first half of Leviathan that subjects have relinquished all right to resist even an unjust and tyrannical sovereign,[125] he likewise concluded the second half by stressing civil obedience. In fact, as Eldon Eisenach notes, for Hobbes, "obedience to civil law is righteousness."[126] Hobbes wrote:

> [T]o teach ... that Jesus was Christ, (that is to say, King,) and risen from the dead, is not to say, that men are bound after they beleeve it, to obey those that tell them so, against the laws, and commands of their Soveraigns; but that they shall doe wisely, to expect the coming of Christ hereafter, in Patience, and Faith, with Obedience to their present Magistrates.[127]

For one who is so often labeled an atheist,[128] Hobbes displayed (often albeit implicitly) a striking commitment to Calvinist Reformed theology in his political theory. To Hobbes, the anarchy of the English Civil War and the interregnum opened a rare opportunity to break the shackles of tradition and to remake society. Christians could return to a pure or Reformed Christianity, and simultaneously, individuals could reconstitute the political society, establishing an "order based on reason and justice."[129] Moreover, even Hobbes's vision of a reconstituted political society—his rationalistic argument in the first half of Leviathan—rested implicitly on a Calvinist Reformed foundation. Quite clearly, Hobbes's conception of human nature as selfish, degraded, violent, and corrupt corresponded with the Reformed emphasis on human sinfulness and depravity. Furthermore, Hobbes's entire notion of the social contract—a covenant establishing political society—reflected the Calvinist concept of the covenanting community, as manifested previously, for instance, in the Long Parliament's Solemn League and Covenant.[130] And the individualism inherent in both of these points—the selfish individual greedily pursuing his or her self-interest until choosing to agree to the covenant—mirrored the latent individualism of Calvinism, whereby each person stands alone before God, predestined for eternal salvation or damnation, with only the dictates of his or her conscience leading to the truth of Jesus.[131] Furthermore, as already mentioned, Hobbes echoed standard New Testament and Calvinist antisemitism: the Old Testament and Jewish history prepared for the coming of Jesus; the Jews refused to accept Jesus even though he was their expected savior and Messiah; the Jews questioned Jesus because they did not know of eternal salvation; Christianity renewed and thus surpassed the Jewish covenant with God; and of course, the Jews were responsible for Jesus' death.[132]

At a deeper level, Hobbes fully accepted the New Testament opposition between Christian spirituality and Jewish carnality, and used it as the implicit foundation for his theology and political theory. Indeed, Hobbes took Calvin's radical disjunction between the spiritual and secular—which flowed from the New Testament opposition—even more seriously than

Calvin himself had done. For Calvin, ultimately, the final end or purpose of secular affairs was the glory of God. For Hobbes, the glory of God might provide the eschatological end of Christian society, but neither God nor spirituality could provide any guidance or purpose for political society in this carnal and depraved world. As Perez Zagorin observes, to Hobbes, humanity is "now left solitary in a universe that is literally God-for-saken."[133] How, then, can humanity proceed in a secular world so bereft of spiritual substance and direction? The first half of Leviathan, at least, can be understood as Hobbes's effort to apply the burgeoning modern scientific techniques of his era to this theological conundrum.

James Harrington published his most important work, The Commonwealth of Oceana, in 1656, only five years after Leviathan appeared.[134] Harrington, like Hobbes, addressed the political problems of the Civil War and interregnum period, though because of the five-year interval between their respective books, Harrington wrote during the fall of the short-lived republic and the establishment of Cromwell's despotic protectorate.[135] Broadly, in a vein similar to that of Hobbes, Harrington addressed the relationship between state and subject: why might a subject owe obedience to a state, and why might a state demand obedience from its subjects? More specifically, Harrington sought to explain the collapse of the English monarchy and to recommend a form of government to replace it.[136] Oceana itself was a thinly disguised fictional representation of England. Like Hobbes, Harrington believed that he lived at a time of rare opportunity: with the confidence typical of an early modernist, he thought that the collapse of traditional governmental forms offered an occasion for humans to actively construct new (and better) forms.[137] Hence, again like Hobbes, Harrington believed that through reason, he could articulate the principles for a science of politics, though in a Machiavellian turn, Harrington emphasized that the rational study of history could best reveal those principles. Indeed, Harrington's preeminent achievement was perhaps to place the English Civil War in a broad historical context: "the collapse of the medieval political order and the emergence of the modern state."[138] Moreover, Harrington further followed in the Machiavellian tradition by articulating a civic republican political theory, and thus he strongly opposed Hobbes's political vision of Leviathan.[139] To Hobbes, rulers and citizens alike always pursue their self-preservation and self-interest, but to Harrington, a properly constructed commonwealth should encourage "participatory virtue" and pursuit of the common good.[140] In fact, Pocock argues that Harrington's Oceana, in conjunction with His Majesty's Answer to the Nineteen Propositions of Both Houses of Parliament, was crucial to the introduction and development of (Machiavellian) civic republican conceptions in Anglo-American political theory.[141] Yet, unlike Machiavelli, Harrington lived in a time of Reformed Protestantism when eschatological millennialism was prevalent. Thus, whereas Machiavelli saw all republics as doomed to the shifting fortunes of secular time, Harrington argued that a properly constructed republic could last indefinitely. While Hobbes had understood the commonwealth or state as an intermediate point on the eschatological path to the eventual Kingdom of God, Harrington envisioned the republic as "Christ's kingdom [already] returned."[142] Pocock captures this difference between Hobbes and Harrington: "Leviathan can only expect Christ's kingdom at the end of time; Oceana may be that kingdom already come."[143]

Harrington began Oceana by distinguishing between two types of government. The first is "instituted and preserved upon the foundation of common right or interest [and is called] the empire of laws and not of men." This type is the republic of Aristotle and Machiavelli. The second is ruled according to the private interests of one or a few men and is therefore called "the empire of men and not of laws."[144] Hobbes's Leviathan is of this type. For Harrington, the republic is clearly the preferred form of government, but this recognition only raises a central question: how is such an empire or government to be created and preserved?[145] Or, in other words, how can individuals be persuaded to seek the "common good or interest" instead of their own private interests?[146]

Harrington responded imaginatively to this issue by distinguishing the foundation from the superstructures of an empire. The foundation consists of the distribution of property, and this distribution (or foundation) ultimately determines the superstructures—that is, the form of government.[147] If there is but one owner of all the property, then the government will be a monarchy. If there are only a few owners—that is, a nobility—then there will be a "Gothic balance" or "mixed monarchy," as England had before the Civil War. If the property is divided among all the people, then there will be a commonwealth or republic. Harrington developed this understanding of government by following the history of England. To Harrington, the gradual dispersal of property among the English people undergirded the transfer of political power from the monarchy and nobility to the gentry and commons.[148] Throughout the later Middle Ages, the traditional mixed monarchy of England had been based on feudalism. Because Henry VII sat insecurely on the throne, however, he introduced anti-feudal measures in the hope of reducing baronial power, and then shortly afterward, Henry VIII seized and distributed the Catholic monasteries.[149] In fact, Harrington

argued that by the time of Elizabeth I, the foundation for an English republic was in place, but the superstructure or governmental form lagged
behind.[150] Hence, in the next century, with the economic foundation of
the monarchy already in ruin, Charles I was unable to build and maintain a
standing army, and thus Civil War eventually resulted. As Harrington summarized: "[T]he dissolution of this government caused the war, not the
war the dissolution of this government."[151]

To Harrington, then, the economic foundation for a republic existed
before the Civil War, but two important tasks remained. First, England
needed to construct the superstructures of republican government to fit the
contemporary foundation. Harrington suggested that the overriding purpose of Oceana was the art of political prudence, "the skill of raising such
superstructures of government as are natural to the known foundations."[152] Harrington even offered his model for republican government to
Cromwell (then, when the Restoration arrived, Harrington was thrown
into jail).[153] Second, to preserve the republic and good government, the
commonwealth needed structures that carefully delineated the daily opera-
tions of government. Harrington, like Hobbes (and Bodin), believed that an
absolute sovereign was essential to maintain civil peace and order, but as
already mentioned, Harrington insisted that the sovereign act for the common good. Consequently, the exercise of sovereign power had to be subject to constitutional limitations. Significantly, to Harrington, the structures
and not the officials make good government: "'Give us good men and they
will make us good laws' is the maxim of a demagogue, and ... exceeding
fallible. But 'give us good orders, and they will make us good men' is the
maxim of a legislator and the most infallible in the politics."[154] Consequently, Harrington painstakingly detailed the elements for his republic
of Oceana. For example, Harrington reasoned that "the senate [should be]
debating and proposing, the people resolving, and [the] magistracy executing by an equal rotation through the suffrage of the people given by the
ballot."[155] But, the most important factor for maintaining the commonwealth was a mechanism to ensure the proper distribution of property
among the people: the so-called agrarian laws. In order to establish and
preserve "the balance of dominion," the agrarian laws would prohibit pri-
mogeniture, limit ownership to lands worth not more than £2000, and
limit dowries to £1500. Of note, Harrington did not favor pure democracy,
perhaps because of his focus on property. Rather, he assumed the
supremacy of landowners; the gentry should rule over ordinary people. To
Harrington, the "people"—meaning the gentry, merchants, and yeomanry—
needed protection from the poor.[156]

With regard to religion, Harrington echoed Hobbes and the Calvinist Reformed position, insisting that both freedom of conscience and a national religion must be present. Harrington wrote:

> But as a government pretending unto liberty, and suppressing the liberty of conscience, which (because religion not according to a man's conscience can as to him be none at all) is the main, must be a contradiction; so a man that, pleading for the liberty of private conscience, refuseth liberty unto the national conscience, must be absurd. A commonwealth is nothing else but the national conscience. And if the conviction of a man's private conscience produce his private religion, the conviction of the national conscience must produce a national religion.[157]

Hence, although Harrington was not a radical Puritan,[158] he nonetheless followed the theological dictates of Reformed Protestantism. First, freedom of conscience was a theological necessity. It is worth recalling again the root of this Protestant freedom of conscience: the New Testament dogma holding that Jews cannot be forced to convert. Second, freedom of conscience and established religion were considered as being not only consistent but as intimately linked. As Harrington states, "the one cannot well consist without the other." Indeed, according to Harrington, if the commonwealth of Oceana protects liberty of conscience, it becomes "the kingdom of Christ."[159]

Since freedom of conscience was a theological requirement, Harrington quite seriously recommended the creation of a governmental council of religion (among other councils) to enforce freedom of conscience.[160] Harrington insisted, though, that the national religion should be taught and not coerced. After all, from the Reformed standpoint, regardless of governmental action, each individual's faith in Christ was a matter of the internal faculty of conscience. Harrington then added that toleration should be extended to the various Christian congregations but not to Jews.

> [T]his council [of religion], as to the protection of the liberty of conscience, shall suffer no coercive power in the matter of religion to be exercised in this nation; the teachers of the national religion being no other than such as voluntarily undertake that calling, and their auditors or hearers no other than are also voluntary. Nor shall any gathered congregation be molested or interrupted in their way of worship (being neither Jewish nor idolatrous) but vigilantly and vigorously protected and defended in the enjoyment, practice and profession of the same.[161]

Rather remarkably, Harrington thought to expressly exclude Jews even though, at that time, Jews were not officially allowed in England. In part, his thoroughness in this regard illustrates the lasting significance of the conceptual Jew of the New Testament. Furthermore, as discussed, the possibility of officially readmitting Jews was first raised during this time period; Harrington recommended that Jews settle in Ireland.[162] Hence, even as Harrington argued for liberty of conscience grounded on the New Testament prohibition of coercing Jewish conversion, he ironically denied that very liberty to (non-existent) Jews. Finally, in a subsequent essay, A System of Politics, written around 1661 but published posthumously, Harrington argued to protect the "free exercise" of religion, which he equated with liberty of conscience.[163] In this early formulation, then, the free exercise of religion—like freedom of conscience—must be understood as a theological commitment of Reformed Protestantism.

John Locke wrote later during the seventeenth century and thus in a substantially different political context. By the late 1670s in Restoration England, two opposed political groups had emerged: the Tories and the Whigs. The definitive statement of the Tory (or Court) position was by Sir Robert Filmer in his Patriarcha, which was published posthumously in 1680.[164] Filmer argued that all monarchs have inherited from (the biblical) Adam a divine right to absolute power. To Filmer, "[m]en are not born free, and therefore could never have the liberty to choose either Governors, or Forms of Government."[165] The Whig (or Country) viewpoint, meanwhile, represented an effort to inject a type of neo-Harringtonian republicanism into the political reality of Restoration England. Briefly, the Whigs rejected Filmer's absolutism and instead sought effective constitutional controls over the monarch. With the Glorious Revolution of 1688, these Whig principles triumphed as Parliament asserted the power to replace James II with William and Mary.[166]

Locke wrote in this Whig tradition. In 1689 he published his Letter Concerning Toleration, and in 1690 he published the Two Treatises of Government.[167] According to Locke's Preface to the Two Treatises, he intended "to establish the Throne of our Great Restorer, Our present King William; to make good his Title, in the Consent of the People, which being the only one of all lawful Governments, he has more fully and clearly than any Prince in Christendom."[168] Consequently, most of Locke's readers assumed that he had written the Two Treatises to defend the already completed Glorious Revolution. Nonetheless, recent scholarship has revealed that Locke began this work as early as 1679 and definitely no later than 1681. Despite the Preface, then, Locke apparently wrote most of the Two Treatises to justify a right of resistance against an unjust monarch, James II; even before James became king in 1685, Locke and others dreaded his expected attempt to reestablish Catholicism. Moreover, while many scholars have assumed that Locke wrote against Hobbes, Locke instead focused his attack primarily on Filmer—although many of Locke's ideas are in tension with Hobbesian political theory.[169]

In the First Treatise, Locke argued largely from Scripture against Filmer. In particular, Locke maintained that God gave Adam dominion over all non-human creatures "in common with the rest of Mankind."[170] Adam, that is, represented "all human beings,"[171] who then shared an equal right to rule over all other creatures. Hence, contrary to Filmer, all people are born equal; monarchs do not inherit from Adam a divine right to absolute power. Since all are one in Adam, Locke's task in the Second Treatise was to move from this (supposed) fact to the justification of constitutional government and private property.[172]

Locke began the Second Treatise by following Hobbes in positing a state of nature, but Locke and Hobbes differed in their conceptualizations of this state. Like Hobbes, Locke saw the state of nature as marked by individualistic equality: each individual enjoys "perfect freedom," an "uncontrollable liberty to dispose of his person or possessions." Whereas Hobbes, though, postulated humans to be naturally violent and aggressive, Locke wrote that "though this be a state of liberty, yet it is not a state of license."[173] Filmer had argued that adults are like children and must therefore be subject to patriarchal governmental control; Filmer denied that each individual can develop the faculty of reason.[174] Locke, in the Second Treatise, argued to the contrary: God grants all adults the ability to reason. Thus, all humans are subject to reason as the law of nature.[175] The Second Treatise, then, focused on reason as the means to "search out the laws of God as they operate in a world without visible signs of grace."[176]

> [Reason] teaches all mankind who will but consult it that, being all equal and independent, no one ought to harm another in his life, health, liberty, or possession; for men being all the workmanship of one omnipotent and infinitely wise Maker—all the servants of one sovereign master, sent into the world by his order, and about his business—they are his property whose workmanship they are, made to last during his, not one another's, pleasure; and being furnished with like faculties, sharing all in one community of nature, there cannot be supposed any such subordination among us that may authorize us to destroy another, as if we were made for one another's uses as the inferior ranks of creatures are for ours.[177]

Hence, Locke argued, while God gave the earth to all humankind to share in common, God also gave humankind the ability to reason, enabling each individual "to make use of [the earth] to the best advantage of life and convenience." Moreover, each person has a right to the "labor of his body and the work of his hands." When any individual takes an object from nature and mixes it with his or her labor, then that object or the resulting product becomes the "property of the laborer." Locke gave the following example: "He that is nourished by the acorns he picked up under an oak, or the apples he gathered from the trees in the wood, has certainly appropriated them to himself. Nobody can deny but the nourishment is his." If an individual's labor takes an object "out of the hands of nature where it was common and belonged equally to all her children," then the individual has "appropriated" the object for him or herself. According to Locke, God effectively commanded that individuals have "private possessions."[178]

For Locke, then, the state of nature is not a state of war, but it nonetheless entails fear and uncertainty.[179] Each person's possessions remain "constantly exposed to the invasion of others [and] very unsafe, very unsecure." Moreover, according to Locke, "every one has the executive power of the law of nature." Each person, that is, can punish transgressions of his or her own rights, yet as "men [are] judges in their own cases [it is apparent that] self-love will make men partial to themselves and their friends, and ... ill-nature, passion, and revenge will carry them too far in punishing others." Individuals therefore enter a social contract: they consent to join political or civil society for the "mutual preservation of their lives, liberties, and estates, which [Locke calls] by the general name 'property.'" Indeed, the "great and chief end" for political society is to protect each individual's property, including accumulated possessions. In addition, Locke maintained that "the first and fundamental natural law" of political society is "the preservation of society." To that end, each individual relinquishes his or her power to punish transgressors to the state, which settles disputes by rules or laws applied indifferently to all.[180]

Locke insisted, however, that the political power of the state was necessarily limited. Contrary to Hobbes, Locke argued that absolute sovereign power was inconsistent with self-preservation:

> Absolute arbitrary power or governing without settled standing laws can neither of them consist with the ends of society and government which men would not quit the freedom of the state of nature for, and tie themselves up under, were it not to preserve their lives, liberties, and fortunes, and by stated rules of right and property to secure their peace and quiet.[181]

Consequently, Locke recommended various mechanisms to ensure that governmental power remain limited. In the "well-ordered commonwealth," Locke argued that there should be a separation of powers. The legislative power is to make the laws, while the executive power is to enforce the law. Significantly, Locke added that the holders of the legislative power must themselves be "subject to the laws they have made." To Locke, this requirement was necessary for the rule of law, and the rule of law was the prerequisite for maintaining freedom.[182] Moreover, Locke maintained that the legislative and executive powers should be exercised in pursuit of the "public good" or "common good."[183] Any ruler who seeks to satisfy his or her "private ends" fails to act for the public good,[184] and such a ruler has "deserted the way of 'reason'"[185] and has therefore separated him or herself from the political society. In these circumstances, the people have a "right of resisting" the tyrannical governmental ruler—the ruler who has failed to act for the public good, the preservation of society.[186] Locke, it should be noted, extended the radical Calvinist position of the French Huguenots, articulated in the previous century. The Huguenots had developed a political theory of resistance: magistrates supposedly had a right to resist any ruler who failed to pursue the welfare of the people. Locke, too, asserted a political theory of resistance—the right to resist arises because of the rights and welfare of the people, not because of religious duties—but Locke accentuated the individualism inherent in Calvinist theology. For Locke, the right of resistance rests with each individual, not only with magistrates.[187]

To be sure, however, while Locke declared that the "people shall be judge"[188] of when resistance is necessary, he carefully circumscribed this right to resist. As mentioned, Locke intended to justify resistance to James II, who Locke perceived as an unjust and tyrannical monarch, but Locke readily accepted William and Mary as the new monarchs—subject to constitutional limitations. Locke, in short, was not a revolutionary egalitarian dissatisfied with anything short of democracy.[189] Hence, Locke wrote: "[S]uch revolutions happen not upon every little mismanagement in public affairs. Great mistakes in the ruling part, many wrong and inconvenient laws, and all the slips of human frailty will be born by the people without mutiny or murmur."[190]

Locke's political quietism—his advocacy of only a narrow right of resistance in the people—highlights the significance of Calvinist theology to Locke's political thought.[191] In fact, although Locke was more Anglican than radical Calvinist or Puritan, Lockean political theory has been called "political Calvinism."[192] It is worth recalling that Locke's more rational or philosophical argument in the Second Treatise was grounded in his more Scriptural argument and conclusion of the First Treatise. One of Locke's tasks was to justify moving from the universal "equality of humankind in Adam"—a conclusion of the First Treatise—to the protection in political

society of disparate property possession—a conclusion of the Second Treatise.[193] In this matter, Locke undoubtedly sought not only to support the
emergence of capitalism in seventeenth-century England but also to bolster
the Calvinist concept of the calling and the Protestant work ethic. Indeed,
Locke masterfully reconciled the emergent capitalistic and scientific (rationalistic) attitudes with the dominant Puritan theology.[194] Rational economics and politics harmonized with Christian religion: as John Dunn observes,
Locke was concerned with protecting "those freedoms which are necessary
for executing the responsibilities of the calling."[195] Dunn adds: "Locke saw
man's general political duty as simply one of conscientious subservience
[because of] its aptness for the fulfilment of God's purposes for man."[196] To
Locke, in political society, a Puritan-flavored religious liberty and toleration
coexisted with economic inequality and hence social differentiation.[197]

Locke's political theory reflected his Calvinist theology in many other
ways. For example, Locke wrote to justify resistance to James II primarily
because James attempted to force Roman Catholicism back on the English
people. Furthermore, like Hobbes, Locke retained a belief in the eschatological progress of humankind. Again, like Hobbes, he thought that a primary
means of progress was for individuals to enter into the social contract,
which reflected the Calvinist emphases on the individual and the covenanting community (and the modernist belief in human power to reorder society). The significance of Locke's theological convictions, however, emerged
most clearly in his writings that expressly focused on religion and freedom
of conscience.

For example, in Locke's Letter Concerning Toleration, his conception of
a church was distinctly calvinistic. He wrote that a church is a "free and
voluntary society," or in other words, a congregation of the faithful. Most
important, Locke derived his views both on religious toleration and on
political society from the strict Calvinist disjunction between the spiritual
and the temporal—which was grounded on the New Testament opposition
between the carnal world of the Jews and the spiritual world of the
Christians. Echoing central themes of the Second Treatise, Locke argued in
the Letter that although humans have immortal souls, they must live their
temporal lives on this earth. Thus, to provide for the protection of their
possessions, individuals consent to enter into political society. The legislative power ought therefore "to be directed [to] the temporal good and outward prosperity of the society."[198]

With regard to eternal salvation, Locke emphatically subscribed to the
Calvinist stress on the individual's inner faculty of conscience as enabling
one to receive the truth of Jesus. According to Locke, "[a]ll the life and

power of true religion consist in the inward and full persuasion of the mind; and faith is not faith without believing." Because salvation is purely a private concern of each individual's conscience, Locke reasoned that "no body ought to be compelled in matters of religion either by law or force." Despite the "outward force" that the government exercises over temporal affairs, the government cannot alter an individual's "inward persuasion of the mind." Although Locke allowed that civil magistrates, like all Christians, can attempt to persuade individuals to convert, he insisted that each person must retain complete religious liberty—freedom of conscience. "[E]very one should do what he in his conscience is persuaded to be acceptable to the Almighty." Locke's conception of freedom of conscience mirrored the New Testament doctrine regarding Jews and Christian evangelizing: Christians should seek to persuade but not coerce Jewish conversion. In fact, Locke expressly tied religious toleration and freedom of conscience to this New Testament doctrine:

> Now if we acknowledge that such an injury [baptism] may not be done unto a Jew, as to compel him against his own opinion, to practise in his religion a thing that is in its nature indifferent; how can we maintain that any thing of this kind may be done to a Christian?[199]

For Locke, then, the commitment to toleration and freedom of conscience in political society extended the New Testament toleration of the Jews writ large.

To Locke, "liberty of conscience is every man's natural right."[200] Hence, good government goes hand in hand with religious liberty: a ruler or magistrate who properly pursues the public good should not infringe on the freedom of conscience. If a ruler did not follow the public good, Locke explicitly declared that the individual's (Christian) religious conscience took priority over the laws of the political society:

> But some may ask: 'What if the magistrate should enjoin any thing 'by his authority, that appears unlawful to the conscience of a private 'person?' I answer: That if government be faithfully administered, and the counsels of the magistrate be indeed directed to the publick good, this will seldom happen. But if perhaps it do so fall out, I say, that such a private person is to abstain from the action that he judges unlawful; and he is to undergo the punishment, which it is not unlawful for him to bear.[201]

Significantly, Locke differed from his predecessors (in English political theory) by not linking freedom of conscience with the establishment of a national church. To the contrary, Locke wrote: "I affirm that the magistrate's power extends not to the establishing of any articles of faith, or forms of worship, by the force of his laws." In fact, Locke expressly and forcefully distinguished "between the church and state":

> [T]he church itself is a thing absolutely separate and distinct from the commonwealth. The boundaries on both sides are fixed and immoveable. He jumbles heaven and earth together, the things most remote and opposite, who mixes these societies; which are in their original, end, business, and in every thing, perfectly distinct, and infinitely different from each other.[202]

Locke's imagery is boundary oriented: church and state belong in separate and bounded spheres (which obviously parallel the spiritual world of Christians and the carnal world of Jews).[203] Locke argued, then, that no one but an atheist or an individual pledging allegiance to a foreign ruler should suffer civil disabilities because of religion.[204] Even Jews are tolerated: "[N]either Pagan nor Mahometan, nor Jew, ought to be excluded from the civil rights of the commonwealth, because of his religion. The Gospel commands no such thing."[205] Locke added, moreover, that the government should not restrict actions in religious rites, such as the killing of animals, that are otherwise permissible. But, he noted, generally applicable laws can restrict religious conduct: "Those things that are prejudicial to the commonweal of a people in their ordinary use, and are therefore forbidden by laws, those things ought not to be permitted to churches in their sacred rites."[206] More important, as Michael McConnell notes, Locke accepted "government financial support of state religion and never condemned the English system of supporting the church with taxes; indeed, he served as secretary to the Lord Chancellor for the presentation of benefices—that is, the dispensing of religious patronage."[207] Hence, in the end, Locke advocated only a partial disestablishment of religion: the state should not enforce any particular creeds or liturgies, but it can support a church financially.

Locke's Letter preceded the religion clauses of the U.S. Constitution by more than a century, yet his linkage of freedom of conscience with (an albeit partial) disestablishment closely foreshadowed the first amendment. For that reason, it is most important to recognize that despite Locke's willingness to tolerate Jews and other religious outgroups, he did so with the explicit assumption that the society nonetheless would remain Christian.

> Shall we suffer a Pagan to deal and trade with us, and shall we not suffer him to pray unto and worship God? If we allow the Jews to have private houses and dwellings amongst us, why should we not allow them to have synagogues? Is their doctrine more false, their worship more abominable, or is

the civil peace more endangered, by their meeting in public than in their private houses? But if these things may be granted to Jews and Pagans, surely the condition of any Christians ought not to be worse than theirs, in a Christian commonwealth.[208]

To be clear, then, toleration did not mean respect and full equality for religious outgroups. Locke reasoned that if even Jews are allowed, then surely different Christian sects also must be tolerated. In fact, in Locke's later essay The Reasonableness of Christianity, published in 1695, he repeated many of the standard antisemitic accusations of the New Testament. For example, Locke argued that all of humanity, including Jews and Gentiles, is stained by original sin. Judaism could not justify or save individuals because Jewish law was impossible to follow.[209] Hence, before the coming of Jesus, "no one then could have eternal life and bliss." After Jesus, justification could be gained only by obeying the "law of faith" of the New Testament, which "is opposed to the 'law of works'" of the Old Testament.[210] Moreover, according to Locke, Jewish law prepared for the coming of Jesus as Christ and the law of faith. Yet, the Jews failed to understand their own Scripture concerning the Messiah, and hence they stubbornly refused to accept Jesus. Jesus therefore "sharply rebuke[d] their hypocrisy, vanity, pride, malice, covetousness, and ignorance."[211] The Jews then tried desperately to destroy Jesus and ultimately were responsible for his death, crying "Crucify him."[212]

If Locke did not respect the religious views and practices of outgroups, why did he advocate disestablishment when others had not? After all, previous writers had similarly grounded freedom of conscience on the New Testament insistence that Jews must confess their error and guilt and thus convert without being coerced, yet those other writers found no inconsistency between freedom of conscience and an established church. Locke differed from his predecessors in at least one important way: his historical self-understanding and experiences.[213] Harrington previously had opened the possibility of understanding English political developments in a historical manner; for Harrington, a rational scientific attitude required attention to history. Locke thus could readily draw upon such a historical attitude, but compared with Harrington (and Hobbes too), Locke had thirty years more of significant historical experience. And based largely on that historical experience, Locke advocated (at least partial) disestablishment as a matter of political expediency: experience had revealed that a full religious establishment caused civil strife. Locke observed: "It is not the diversity of opinions, which cannot be avoided, but the refusal of toleration to those

that are of different opinions, which might have been granted, that has produced all the bustles and wars, that have been in the Christian world, upon
account of religion."[214] Disestablishment as a component of toleration was
forced upon the Christian sects as a matter of political survival. Moreover,
Locke suggested that any toleration of outgroup religions was merely incidental to the primary end of protecting Christianity. In the very first sentence of Locke's Letter, he declared that he would address the "mutual
Toleration of Christians in their different professions of religion."[215] Once
again, then, for Locke, toleration did not mean respect and full equality for
non-Christian religions.

CHURCH AND STATE AT THE
END OF THE SEVENTEENTH CENTURY

The sixteenth and seventeenth centuries significantly transformed the institutions of church and state. During the Middle Ages in western Europe,
the Roman Catholic Church had emerged as a hierarchical institution, like
a state, competing with secular rulers for political and social power. During
this period, the concept of separation of church and state could be understood readily as reflecting the differentiated (yet overlapping) spheres of
power of the respective social institutions—church and state. But with the
coming of the Reformation, the church in Protestant countries no longer
was comparable to a state. In Protestantism, the church no longer stood as
a government-like social institution competing with states for temporal
power. Instead, the church became the congregation of the faithful, spreading throughout the social body. In the Protestant era (including today) in
western society, the concept of separation of church and state became
somewhat problematic: church and state no longer clearly existed as comparable and competing societal (and temporal) institutions with separable
spheres of power. Indeed, in many instances, as in England, the ruler of the
state became the official leader of the church.[216]

Yet, the conception of separate spheres of power for church and state
did not totally disappear; rather, it metamorphosed. Whereas the notion of
separate societal (and temporal) institutions no longer seemed as apropos,
greater stress was placed on a distinction between the temporal and spiritual spheres—with this distinction arising from the New Testament antisemitic opposition between Jewish carnality and Christian spirituality.
Indeed, in Calvinist theology, the two spheres became completely dis-
jointed. So, in the temporal sphere, the state could regulate conduct and
could even impose a national church. Yet, in the spiritual sphere, freedom

of conscience had to be protected—as a Protestant theological necessity—in order to ensure the possibility of true Christian faith. Like the distinction between the temporal and spiritual spheres, this conceptualization of freedom of conscience arose from New Testament doctrinal antisemitism—the mandate that Jews should be persuaded but cannot be compelled to convert. By the end of the seventeenth century, many conceived of salvation as Locke did, as a purely private concern; the state might attend to social and political progress, but salvation was solely for the individual. Finally, while freedom of conscience (as a theological requirement) initially appeared to go hand in hand with an established church, the eventual political strife between the various Christian sects led to the proposal of disestablishment. Since the official establishment of a single Christian creed had led inevitably to resistance and turmoil, then as a matter of political expediency, official governmental disestablishment and toleration of multiple sects became imaginable—especially in a society nonetheless dominated by Christians.

Meanwhile, by the end of the seventeenth century, the modern sovereign state—a supreme and centralized political authority subject to constitutional limitations—had clearly emerged.[217] In terms of political reality, perhaps the most important factor in the development of the state was the collapse of the Roman Catholic Church's hegemonic hold over western Christendom. With the Reformation, the secular ruler (especially in Protestant countries) no longer, as a practical matter, shared political power with the Catholic Church hierarchy. Furthermore, driven by an economic expansionism that was fueled largely by the imperialistic appropriation of the Americas, absolutist states in continental Europe—particularly France and Spain—arose and solidified their power during the sixteenth and seventeenth centuries.[218] Finally, in England, the long traditions of parliamentarianism and common law combined with the eventual exhaustion of all sides in the long-running chaos of the seventeenth century to produce a political and religious compromise: a sovereign state consisting of a monarch chosen by the people and subject to clear constitutional limitations. A degree of religious liberty and toleration was granted as a political measure.

In terms of political theory, various writers added different elements to the conception of the state until, finally, the idea of the modern sovereign state was fully formed. Bodin, for example, proposed the existence of an absolute monarch with unshared power in order to ensure civil peace and order. Hobbes likewise posited an absolute sovereign, but his sovereign was a state formed by the people through a social contract. To Hobbes, the people and the rulers all acted in their own interests; the notion of a common or public good was rejected as nonsensical. Yet Harrington, writing at around the same time as Hobbes, recommended the creation of an absolute sovereign with governmental structures that would ensure the pursuit of the public good, not the private interests of the rulers. Finally, Locke conceived of the people, through a social contract, creating a sovereign state devoted to the public good—the protection and preservation of the people's lives, liberties, and possessions. Not only was Locke's sovereign state subject to constitutional limitations, but each individual subject also retained the right to resist the rulers if they became corrupt or tyrannical. Whereas Harrington had merged the pursuit of the public or common good with a conception of the subject as virtuously participating in government, Locke combined a conception of the public good with the calvinistic individualism that had appeared clearly in Hobbesian theory. To a great extent, for Locke, the public good amounted to the mutual protection of a Calvinist freedom of conscience and a capitalist economic system. Consequently, with their disparate conceptions of the common good, Harrington and Locke also understood property and its importance in different ways. Harrington stressed a wide distribution of property to promote a civic republican government, while Locke emphasized the private production and possession of property.[219]

Finally, it is worth highlighting how the theological and theoretical developments of Protestantism and the sovereign state reinforced each other. With the collapse of the Catholic Church's hegemony, the Church no longer remained as an equal and viable competitor against the state for political power. In light of this reality, the turn of Protestantism to the spiritual sphere as its own unique domain was strategically beneficial to the aggrandizement of Christian social power. In effect, Protestantism conceded a lost cause—the competition for temporal and political power—to the state and hence helped to reinforce the state's claim to absolute power in the secular sphere. The state, for its part, was more than willing to impose certain Christian creeds so long as doing so did not seriously undermine political stability. At the same time, by emphasizing spiritual salvation, the Protestant churches increased their own social power by spreading throughout the social body and developing as a new type of social institution: a congregation of the faithful. Without relying heavily on a church hierarchy imposing its power from above, the Protestant churches illustrated that a more populist symbolic imagery could generate an enormous ideological hold over a society.

CHAPTER 6

The North American Colonies

THE EARLY YEARS: CALVINIST ROOTS

For the most part, the North American colonies began as religiously and culturally Protestant, and after a brief period of slippage, they then became even more so.[1] The first European nation to gain a significant foothold in the Americas was Spain, which was Roman Catholic, but Spain predominantly influenced South and Central America. In North America, the chief long-term consequence of Spanish exploration was to spur greater efforts by the English and the French. France, also primarily Roman Catholic, initially gained a footing in North America but ultimately had little lasting effect in the colonies that eventually became the United States. Although some French came to North America inspired by a missionary zeal fueled by a desire to combat the Protestant successes in Europe, far fewer French than English were inclined to emigrate. More important, France and England repeatedly clashed in North America, sparked by both economic competition for empire and religious rivalry. Time and again, England emerged victorious from these conflicts, so that France's Roman Catholic presence dwindled. As Sydney Ahlstrom notes, because the Protestant–Catholic hostility animated these disputes between England and France, "the most enduring effect of New France on the British colonies was to intensify an already vehement hatred of 'popery.'"[2] Hence, of the major imperial powers of Europe, England emerged as the most influential in North America.

The first permanent English settlement in North America was at Jamestown, Virginia, in 1607. The initial band of 105 colonists was funded largely by a coalition of English merchants, the Virginia Company, which sought to establish a trading post and to reap substantial profits.[3] Although less important than economic profits, religious concerns also motivated the Company and the settlers. They sought to preempt Roman Catholicism in this part of the world and to spread Protestantism further by evangelizing the Native Americans. The First Charter of Virginia specified this evangelical mission:

> [S]o noble a Work [may] by the Providence of Almighty God, hereafter tend to the Glory of his Divine Majesty, in propagating of Christian Religion to such People, as yet live in Darkness and miserable Ignorance of the true Knowledge and Worship of God, and may in time bring the Infidels and Savages, living in those parts, to human Civility, and to a settled and quiet Government.[4]

While this first settlement tenaciously survived, it was initially unsuccessful. Facing numerous obstacles, the population grew slowly, and as a commercial venture, the colony lost money. By 1624, James I so distrusted the Virginia Company that he annulled its charter and transformed Virginia into a royal colony. At this point, the Anglican Church became entrenched in Virginia, and it would remain predominant there throughout the American Revolution. Church establishment in Virginia officially imposed, among other matters, the creed of the Thirty-nine Articles of Religion, the Anglican liturgy, church attendance, and a tax (or tithe) for the support of the churches and ministers.[5]

While the Jamestown, Virginia, settlement struggled, another English colony proved more successful. In 1607, a group of English Separatists—Puritans committed to establishing congregations totally apart from the Church of England—fled England for Holland. Still dissatisfied, these Separatists joined with others still in England to secure from James I a modicum of religious freedom in exchange for their settlement in North America. In 1620 they set sail on the Mayflower for America, landing (accidentally) in Plymouth, New England.[6] Before leaving the ship, the 102 Pilgrims officially constituted their community by agreeing to a typically Calvinist covenant:

> Having undertaken for the Glory of God, and Advancement of the Christian Faith, and the Honour of our King and Country, a Voyage to plant the first Colony in the northern Parts of Virginia; Do by these Presents, solemnly and mutually, in the Presence of God and one another, covenant and combine ourselves together into a civil Body Politick, for our better Ordering and Preservation, and Furtherance of the Ends aforesaid....[7]

This first English colony in New England grew slowly—by 1630, only about 300 people lived in Plymouth—but in that year, approximately 1000 settlers arrived at the Massachusetts Bay Colony, centered in the Boston area. The "Great Migration" of Puritans from England to Massachusetts had begun; by 1642, nearly 20,000 English had arrived at Massachusetts Bay. Whereas the earlier Pilgrims had been mainly Separatists, most of these later Puritan immigrants were Congregationalists—more moderate than the Separatists insofar as they were willing, at least formally, to maintain ties to the Church of England.[8]

When the Puritans moved from England to New England, they radically transformed their own social role (or structural position) in the broader society. In England, they were oppositionists—religious outsiders subject to varying degrees of oppression. The Puritan movement developed in the context of this particular social role in England. For instance, Puritanism rang with an unmistakable (albeit perverse) populism that undoubtedly appealed to many English below the level of the nobility. According to the Puritan conceptions of original sin and human depravity, all humans, regardless of their station in life, are equally depraved and have the same likelihood of either being granted grace or being doomed to damnation. Such populist, egalitarian tones perfectly suited an oppositionist group. Once in New England, however, the Puritans suddenly found themselves in a radically different social position.[9] Now they were the leaders and insiders of the society; from the outset, the American society of transplanted Europeans developed with the Puritans structurally entrenched at the apex. Predictably, they sought to maintain their newfound dominance.

Consequently, while the basic theological principles of Puritanism remained the same both inside and outside of Old England, the New Englanders began to emphasize different points. For example, upon reaching New England, freed of persecution, the Puritans experienced a burst of evangelical preaching, as one of their primary concerns "was to satisfy their long-starved appetites for sermons."[10] More important, the Massachusetts Puritans needed to develop a highly nuanced conception of the relations between church and state to (supposedly) harmonize their Congregationalism with their position of authority in New England society. In some ways, the Puritans conceived of the state as closely related to the church. Undoubtedly, the "heart of the New England Way" was the covenant.[11] To agree to the church covenant became the means for full participation in both religious and civil society.[12] Yet, in order to be able to agree to (or own) the covenant, one must first have attested to a personal conversion experience. John Winthrop, the first governor of the Massachusetts Bay

Colony, described his conversion experience, which was typical. He first came to know his own total depravity and unworthiness, and he then rose up because of Jesus: "[E]very promise I thought upon held forth Christ unto me, saying, 'I am thy salvation.'"[13] Such a conversion experience was not a sudden or immediate event; it usually required hearing sermons and conferring with ministers during "a long period of intensive and prolonged introspection."[14] A properly related or explained conversion experience signified to the church's minister and congregants that the individual had been touched by God's grace—that the person was a "visible saint"—and therefore could become a member of the church.[15] Ministers such as the early Cambridge pastor Thomas Shepard devoted many sermons to conversion, exhorting "believers to pursue diligently the divinely appointed 'means' for salvation and assurance and, for further proof, introspectively search for the 'signs' or 'evidences' that God had performed a work of grace in their lives."[16] Once an individual became a church member (usually through a vote of the congregation), he or she enjoyed significant benefits. While all residents had to attend church and pay taxes to support it, only true church members could receive the all-important Lord's Supper. More significant (politically), only male church members could attain full civil citizenship, including suffrage.[17]

Hence, whereas English Puritanism pulsed with an undercurrent of populism, New England Puritanism seemed to justify elitism (which, of course, fit the dominant social position of the New Englanders). The Massachusetts Bay Puritans reconciled their emphasis on the conversion experience with the standard Calvinist concept of predestination to legitimate the civil and religious rule of the few. Kai Erikson notes:

> The truth as seen by the Puritans was wholly clear. God had chosen an elite to represent Him on earth and to join Him in Heaven. People who belonged to this elite learned of their appointment through the agency of a deep conversion experience, giving them a special responsibility and a special competence to control the destinies of others.[18]

While, on the one hand, the New England Puritans conceived of the state as closely related to the church, on the other hand, they simultaneously understood the church and the state to be distinct institutions. As John Cotton explained, "God's institutions (such as the government of church and of commonwealth) may be close and compact, and co-ordinate one to another, and yet not confounded."[19] Hence, for example, the Puritans decided that the offices of the church and the civil government should be differentiated and that excommunication should not prompt automatic loss of civil office. More important, the New Englanders initially opposed the civil (official) imposition of Puritan religious orthodoxy. In England during the first half of the seventeenth century, neither Puritans nor Anglicans believed that the state, as a matter of political principle, should tolerate religious diversity; rather, the state should seek to impose a uniform national religion. The New England Puritans believed similarly, but for more than one reason they at first opposed the official imposition or codification of their religious orthodoxy. As Congregationalists, they were strongly committed to protecting the autonomy of each congregation.[20] Puritans should find religious truth for themselves directly from the Bible; the official imposition of a confession, noted Richard Mather, "doth seem to abridge them of that liberty."[21] John Winthrop offered a more political justification: legal codification of Puritan orthodoxy would invite unwelcome and unnecessary scrutiny from royal officials back home in England.[22]

Despite the lack of a state-imposed orthodoxy, the early Massachusetts Bay leaders never intended to tolerate religious diversity in their colony. Instead, they expected that Puritan religious hegemony could be maintained without the official imposition of orthodoxy. They sought therefore to enforce uniformity, not through state authority but through unofficial or non-governmental means: church attendance, sermons, public censure of heresy, social stigmatization, participation in (or owning) the covenant, and other non-governmental (or private) sanctions.[23] Liberty of conscience meant, in the words of Winthrop, the "liberty wherewith Christ hath made us free."[24] This early Puritan model of unofficial orthodoxy through de facto establishment would prove to be enormously important over the long term of American history.[25] Protestantism could survive and even flourish by allowing its congregational vines to spread throughout the social body without official state establishment (though the state always supported the churches).

This early New England Puritan resistance to state-imposed orthodoxy tended to highlight the typical Calvinist emphasis on the conscience of the individual. The Calvinist disjunction of the spiritual and temporal was most pronounced: civil law could not enforce religious orthodoxy because true faith arose from following one's conscience to the truth of Jesus Christ. Nevertheless, the Massachusetts Puritans themselves quickly wavered from this early commitment to de facto establishment alone. Kai Erikson observes:

> In theory, at least, each soul was left to negotiate his own way to heaven and was encouraged to act upon the promptings of his own conscience, but in

fact, an administrative machinery was slowly developing to make sure that each private conscience was rightly informed and loyal to the policies and programs of the state.[26]

Before long, this administrative machinery included civil laws that reinforced the imposed Puritan orthodoxy. In 1641, the Colony adopted a bill of rights called the Body of Liberties. While these provisions were intended mainly to control the discretion of magistrates, they also implicitly imposed Congregational Puritanism. In effect, the religious provisions protected the religious freedom to be a Congregationalist and nothing else. Section 95 was entitled "A Declaration of the Liberties the Lord Jesus hath given to the Churches." It provided in part:

> 1. All the people of god within this Jurisdiction who are not in a church way, and be orthodox in Judgement, and not scandalous in life, shall have full libertie to gather themselves into a Church Estaite. Provided they doe it in a Christian way, with due observation of the rules of Christ revealed in his word. 2. Every Church hath full liberties to exercise all the ordinances of god, according to the rules of scripture. 3. Every Church hath free libertie of Election and ordination of all their officers from time to time, provided they be able, pious and orthodox.[27]

The religious provisions of the Body of Liberties were then statutorily enacted in 1648 as part of a legal code, which also required attendance at church (absence was punishable by a fine), imposed mandatory public charges (taxes) to support the church, and provided for the punishment of contemnors of Jesus Christ and God's holy ordinances.[28]

Long before the Massachusetts Bay colonists codified their Puritan theology, they had unequivocally revealed their primary purpose for coming to America: to create a Christian society, both ecclesiastically and politically. On the ship coming from England, John Winthrop underscored the assumed coordination of church and state (as well as the importance of covenant):

> It is of the nature and essence of every society to be knit together by some covenant, either expressed or implied. . . . For the work we have in hand, it is by mutual consent, through a special over-ruling providence and a more than ordinary approbation of the churches of Christ, to seek out a place of cohabitation and consortship, under a due form of government both civil and ecclesiastical.[29]

I do not mean to suggest that religion was the sole motivation for the Puritan migration to North America. It was not. The Puritans had many reasons to leave England, including the economic opportunities of New England. It should be recognized, though, that economic and religious opportunities were intertwined.[30] The Massachusetts Bay Colony promised an opportunity to belong to a pure Reformed Church, as well as an opportunity to fulfill the Protestant work ethic. As early as 1624, for instance, a reverend in England drew upon the conjunction of Puritan religion and vigorous work to plead with James I for more royal support of the colonies. Religious conviction required greater challenges for labor:

> Our so long continued rest and peace ... our unspeakable idleness and dissolute life, have so corrupted and in manner effeminated our people generally ... that they cannot endure the hearing, much lesse the doing of any laborious attempts, of any thing that shall be troublous or any whit dangerous unto them.[31]

Hence, although religion alone did not prompt the Puritan migration, even economic opportunism was tinged with Puritan conviction. Early on, the Massachusetts Bay colonists viewed themselves as establishing a "Citty upon a Hill," a new Israel in the American wilderness.[32] They looked upon their settlement "as a little model of the glorious kingdom of Christ on earth."[33] For the Congregationalists, "the Word of God was clear and explicit," and anyone who refused to accept the Puritan understanding of God's Word was, quite simply, unwelcome in the Massachusetts Bay Colony.[34] In typical Calvinist fashion, for example, the colonists expressed great respect for the Old Testament—in their minds, after all, they constituted the new Israel—but they disdained Judaism and real Jews, who were unable to reside in Massachusetts, Connecticut, or New Hampshire throughout most of the seventeenth century.[35] In the New England Congregationalists' new Israel, they intended to enforce the Scripture and the Puritan way, not to tolerate diverse opinions. As Nathaniel Ward wrote in 1645, those individuals who disputed the Puritan lifestyle "shall have free Liberty to keep away from us, and such as will come to be gone as fast as they can, the sooner the better."[36] Perry Miller comments: "There is nothing so idle as to praise the Puritans for being in any sense conscious or deliberate pioneers of religious liberty.... To allow no dissent from the truth was exactly the reason they had come to America."[37]

While the orthodox Puritan theology was revealed in innumerable informal ways, it also was formally stated. In 1648, a Massachusetts Bay synod (or council) adopted the Cambridge Platform. The Platform began by embracing as a religious creed the Westminster Confession, excepting the sections on church governance.[38] As discussed in the previous chapter, the

Westminster Confession emphasized human sinfulness, the Christian Gospels, the need for faith in one's heart, and the following of God's plan in our callings. Moreover, the Confession built explicitly upon the New Testament's antisemitic opposition of Jewish carnality to Christian spirituality. Specifically, the Confession emphasized that God had "abrogated" the earlier Jewish "covenant of works," replacing it with the Christian "covenant of grace." Because people "are utterly indisposed, disabled, and made opposite to all good, and wholly inclined to all evil," they were "incapable of life" in accordance with the Jewish covenant or testament. Yet the Jewish (or old) testament was "all foresignifying Christ to come"; hence, the Christian covenant of grace provided the universal means of salvation "to all nations, both Jews and Gentiles." Under the Christian or new testament, one's conscience became the bridge to God's spiritual heaven; good works cannot earn salvation because of "the infinite distance between us and God," though "our duty" is to do "all we can" to fulfill our callings.[39]

To this religious creed, the Cambridge Platform added its own Congregationalist conceptions of church governance, such as the autonomy of the local churches or congregations.[40] Moreover, the Platform further elaborated the relations between church and state, stressing that civil power focuses on the outer or temporal world, not on the spiritual world of Christian salvation. Civil magistrates therefore cannot compel Christian faith or a turn of the conscience, though the civil government nonetheless should support the efforts of the churches. Consequently, for instance, civil laws should prohibit blasphemy and enforce the Christian sabbath. The Platform provided:

> The powr & authority of Magistrates is not for the restraining of churches, or any other good workes, but for helping in and furthering therof; & therefore the consent & countenance of Magistrates when it may be had, is not to be sleighted, or lightly esteemed; but on the contrary; it is part of that honour due to christian Magistrates to desire & crave their consent & approbation therin: which being obtayned, the churches may then proceed in their way with much more encouragement, & comfort.... It is not in the powr of Magistrates to compell their subjects to become church-members, & to partake at the Lords table: for the priests are reproved, that brought unworthy ones into the sanctuarie: then, as it was unlawfull for the priests, so it is unlawfull to be done by civil Magistrates.... The object of the powr of the Magistrate, are not things meerly inward, & so not subject to his cognisance & view, as in unbeliefe hardness of heart, erronious opinions not vented; but only such things as are acted by the outward man.... Idolatry, Blasphemy, Heresy, venting corrupt & pernicious opinions, that destroy the foundation, open contempt of the word preached, prophanation of the Lords day, disturbing the peaceable administration & exercise of the

worship & holy things of God, & the like, are to be restrayned, & punished by civil authority.[41]

Of course, these familiar Calvinist tenets were grounded in New Testament doctrinal antisemitism: the opposition between the carnal world of the Jews and the spiritual world of the Christians, and the prohibition against compelling Jewish conversion.

Challenges to the predominant Congregationalist orthodoxy often were met harshly.[42] For example, the Antinomian controversy of 1636–1638 began when Anne Hutchinson and her followers declared that most of the Massachusetts Bay ministers were unqualified to judge whether an individual was touched by grace. According to Hutchinson, most ministers transformed the covenant of grace into a covenant of works by searching for signs of grace that were this-worldly. Because a minister's (and congregation's) acceptance of an individual as a visible saint and church member had become the prerequisite for that person's full citizenship and participation in civil and church matters, Hutchinson effectively challenged the foundation of the Colony's religious and civil society. She questioned the authority of ministers "to use the covenant of grace as a political instrument."[43] If Hutchinson had lived a generation earlier in England, her position would have represented mainstream Puritanism. But she failed to account for the different structural position of the Massachusetts Bay Puritans: they sought to maintain their position of authority rather than to challenge the power of an established church. Hence, when Hutchinson sought to remain true to the original or English Puritanism, she rejected the modified Puritanism of the Massachusetts Bay. Ultimately, then, she was charged in a criminal prosecution with what amounted to sedition—not heresy; in the Massachusetts Bay society, church and state were woven together. Therefore, Winthrop, who served as judge and prosecutor at Hutchinson's trial, stated: "'Mrs. Hutchinson, you are called here as one of those that have troubled the peace of the commonwealth and the churches."[44] The trial concluded with Hutchinson's banishment from the Colony.

At approximately the same time, Roger Williams also challenged the leaders of the Colony, only to be banished for his oppositional views. When Williams first arrived in the Colony in 1631, he was already a committed Separatist. In fact, shortly after his arrival, Williams rejected an offer from the Boston congregation to serve as a minister because the church had not expressly renounced its tie to the Church of England. To all Puritans, the Church of England was not a true Christian church because it was insufficiently purified of this-worldly ceremonies and institutions.

While some Puritans hoped to further purify the Anglican Church, the Separatist Puritans such as Williams believed that the Anglican Church could not possibly be reformed. Therefore, to Williams, a church—even a Puritan church such as the Boston congregation—that retained any association with the Anglican Church was necessarily corrupted. Despite Williams's initial confrontation with the Boston Puritans, the nearby Salem congregation was considering him as a minister until John Winthrop and the Boston magistrates intervened. At this point, Williams wisely moved to the more Separatist-oriented Plymouth. Even there, though, Williams provoked ire. He questioned the authority of civil magistrates to intervene in church matters and declared that the Native Americans, not the colonists, were the rightful owners of the land. On this latter point, Williams reasoned that the English monarchs could not grant a patent to land in North America because the land had not been rightfully purchased from its aboriginal inhabitants. Williams left Plymouth in 1633 and accepted an offer to become an unofficial minister in Salem. Regardless of his new position, Williams continued to irritate the leaders of the Massachusetts Bay Colony. He unceasingly advocated Separatism and pressed his challenges to the civil magistrate's authority and the colonists' land ownership. Finally, in 1635, the General Court of Massachusetts Bay banished Williams. Before he could be deported to England, though, he fled from Massachusetts and founded Providence along the Narragansett bay (Williams, by the way, purchased the land from the Native Americans).[45]

As the Narragansett filled with other settlers, including many refugees from the Massachusetts Bay Colony (including Anne Hutchinson), Williams and others decided that they needed greater security for their burgeoning colony. Consequently, in 1643, Williams was chosen to go to England to obtain a charter uniting several towns into the colony of Rhode Island. In 1644—in the midst of the English Civil War period—Williams successfully secured a charter from the Long Parliament granting Rhode Island independence and liberty of conscience. Moreover, while in England, Williams published his most important book, The Bloudy Tenent of Persecution.[46]

In The Bloudy Tenent, Williams drew upon his observation of the English turmoil, as well as his experience in New England. In particular, Williams believed that the emergence of multiple Puritan sects in England— especially the somewhat opposed Presbyterians and Independents (who were mostly Congregationalists)—had undermined the possibility of having a peaceful church establishment. Williams's own experience in the Massachusetts Bay Colony reinforced this conclusion. Enforced religious uniformity brought civil strife and religious hypocrisy; only freedom of conscience and religious toleration allowed individuals to sincerely receive the truth of Christ. Hence, The Bloudy Tenent, which American constitutional scholars have hailed as a foundation for the principle of religious freedom,[47] arose in the context of religious disputes involving both New and Old England.

Williams preceded John Locke by nearly half a century, but many of Williams's themes in The Bloudy Tenent anticipated Locke's views on church and state—particularly Locke's commitment to both freedom of conscience and official disestablishment.[48] Williams emphasized the Calvinist disjunction between the spiritual and the temporal—which was grounded on the New Testament opposition between Jewish carnality and Christian spirituality. To Williams, this disjunction between the spiritual and temporal must be complete and must be taken with the utmost seriousness. Consequently, Williams reasoned that distinct institutions—the church and the state—must operate in each of these respective spheres.[49] The church should attend solely to issues of faith or conscience, while the civil state and its officers should attend solely to civil and secular matters.[50] Freedom of conscience must be strictly observed; force cannot create true faith in Christ.[51] Thus, for example, the early records of Rhode Island contain an entry withholding the right to vote from a citizen "for restraining of the libertie of conscience."[52] According to Williams, even the church cannot interfere unduly with the individual's free turn of conscience toward the truth of Jesus Christ; the church can do no more than preach the Word of God. Williams wrote:

> It is the will and command of God, that (since the comming of his Sonne the Lord Jesus) a permission of the most Paganish, Jewish, Turkish, or Antichristian consciences and worships, bee granted to all men in all Nations and Countries; and they are onely to bee fought against with that Sword which is only (in Soule matters) able to conquer, to wit, the Sword of Gods Spirit, the Word of God.[53]

Moreover, because of his experience in the Massachusetts Bay Colony, Williams (like Locke) linked his commitment to freedom of conscience with an equal commitment to formal disestablishment. To Williams, the civil imposition of a uniform national religion leads only to disaster. Church establishment undermines freedom of conscience and prompts hypocrisy because of false faith. Most important, enforced uniformity causes many individuals to become hardened in their resistance to the true (purified) Word of God. And so hardened, these wretched people thus are led to conflict and civil war in this world and to eternal damnation in the next.[54]

Williams expressly based his commitment to freedom of conscience and disestablishment on the New Testament prohibition against forcefully converting Jews. He argued that if a national church is established, then Christian hopes for converting Jews will necessarily be dashed: "In holding an inforced uniformity of Religion in a civill state, wee must necessarily disclaime our desires and hopes of the Jewes conversion to Christ." Furthermore, Williams reasoned that even a "blinde Pharisee" can be a good civil subject and should not be civilly punished for religious beliefs.

> [T]he blind-guiding seducing Pharisee shall surely pay in that dreadfull Ditch [damnation], which the Lord Jesus speakes of, but this sentence against him the Lord Jesus only pronounceth in His Church, His Spirituall judicature, and executes this Sentence in part at present and herafter to all eternity: Such a Sentence no Civill Judge can passe, such a Death no Civill Sword can inflict.[55]

Hence, to Williams's Puritan sensibilities, if the New Testament demands that even Jews must be tolerated, then surely no less must be due to Christians, regardless of their sect. To be certain, then, Williams is correctly characterized as tolerating greater religious diversity than the other New England Puritan leaders; freedom of conscience and disestablishment were religious and political cornerstones for Williams. Yet, to a great extent, Williams's religious toleration was instrumental. Toleration enabled individuals to find temporal peace and spiritual salvation in Christ instead of civil strife and spiritual doom. Williams insisted that Jews, in particular, be tolerated, but not because he respected their religion or believed in some form of religious relativism (which would mean that many different religions offered equally valid paths to salvation or to other worthy religious goals). Rather, Jews were to be tolerated because, first, the New Testament commanded no less and, second, compulsion brought only disaster. In addition, regardless of official toleration, Williams (like Locke) always expected that society would remain fully Christian; de facto establishment was assumed. Both Williams and the Massachusetts Bay Puritans agreed that Jews ought to convert to Christianity; conversion was a condition for the millennium. Unlike the Massachusetts Puritans, though, Williams believed that the most expeditious means for converting Jews was "at close range."[56] Hence, while Williams insisted that he "did profess a spiritual war against Judaism and the Turks,"[57] he tolerated them in civil society, in part, to help usher in a period of latter-day glory. The first New England Jewish community consequently formed in Newport, Rhode Island, but as Howard Sachar notes, whereas all "non-Congregationalists were second-class citizens [in Rhode Island, the] Jews were less than that."[58] In fact, Rhode Island barred Jews from enjoying full citizenship until 1842.[59] Williams himself often repeated traditional antisemitic dogma. For instance, Williams decried the Jews because they "blaspheme" the "true religion" and "stand ... for Satan against Christ." He stressed that Jews had committed the "horrible crime" of deicide: Williams lamented "the Jews killing [of] the Lord Jesus, of their cursing themselves and their posterity; of the wrath of God upon them; of their denying the Fundamentals of our Christian worship."[60]

In sum, as with Locke half a century later, Williams's conceptualization of church–state relations was boundary oriented, focusing on the symbolic imagery of separate or bounded spheres.[61] This imagery rested on a sharp distinction between a sphere of Christian spirituality and a sphere of Jewish carnality, and the related New Testament injunction against using temporal force located in the carnal sphere to compel Jewish movement to the Christian spiritual sphere. Based on this antisemitic symbolism, Williams articulated two other sets of distinctions or bounded spheres. First, he argued that the church and state operate in separate spheres: the state attends to civil matters, and the church focuses on promoting the proper orientation toward spirituality. The church and state occupied, in a sense, distinct public spheres. Second, he argued that conscience and faith must exist in a sphere protected from both the church and the state. Christian faith, in effect, can flourish only in a private sphere insulated from public coercion. Hence, Williams envisioned a "wall of separation" between the "garden" and the "wilderness"—that is, between the spiritual and carnal worlds.[62] Ultimately, in Williams's view, the state is not as degraded as in Augustinian theory, but nonetheless the state is understood as little more than a threat and a police officer. The state represents a threat because it can infringe on freedom of conscience, which is required for genuine faith in Christ. Meanwhile, the state functions as a police officer because it must control the actions of the depraved and sinful humans in the temporal world.

In light of the attitude toward and treatment of Jews in Rhode Island—known generally as the colony most tolerant of religious diversity—it is unsurprising to find that throughout the seventeenth century, extensive antisemitism predominated in all the colonies. To be sure, American colonial antisemitism often was less violent than in Europe—partly because so few Jews were actually present. Indeed, colonial antisemitism usually aimed at the conceptual Jew because hardly any real Jews lived in the colonies; by the end of the century, only about 250 Jews were in America. In all likelihood, the first group of Jewish colonial settlers arrived in 1654 in New

Netherland—that is, New York (the Newport, Rhode Island, settlement did not form until the late 1670s).[63] Peter Stuyvesant, the director of New Netherland for the Dutch West India Company, did not openly welcome these twenty-three Jewish refugees fleeing from religious persecution in Brazil. To the contrary, he petitioned the Company for permission to banish them. Stuyvesant wrote:

> The Jews who have arrived would nearly all like to remain here, but learning that they (with their customary usury and deceitful trading with the Christians) were very repugnant to the inferior magistrates, as also to the people having the most affection for you; the Deaconry also fearing that owing to their present indigence they might become a charge in the coming winter, we have, for the benefit of this weak and newly developing place and the land in general, deemed it useful to require them in a friendly way to depart; praying also most seriously in this connection, for ourselves as also for the general community of your worships, that the deceitful race—such hateful enemies and blasphemers of the name of Christ—be not allowed to further infect and trouble this new colony to the detraction of your worships and the dissatisfaction of your worships' most affectionate subjects.[64]

For economic reasons, the Company rejected Stuyvesant's request; several Jewish stockholders in the Company intervened on behalf of their co-religionists. Hence, the Jews were allowed to stay, but they could practice Judaism only in private; they were prohibited from building a synagogue.[65]

Stuyvesant's antisemitic attitude mirrored what Jews often encountered in other colonies, regardless of professions to freedom of conscience and religious toleration. For instance, in some colonies, to call a person a Jew amounted to a contemptuous insult that was cause for a lawsuit. In colonies both with and without established churches, Jews suffered legally imposed disabilities. Christianity was, quite simply, the "public religion"; it was typically considered part of the common law.[66] The legal status of Jews in the colony of Carolina is worth special note because John Locke initially framed the Fundamental Constitutions of Carolina of 1669. The Fundamental Constitutions officially established the Anglican Church even though Locke, as discussed in chapter 5, favored at least partial disestablishment; in fact, Locke claimed to oppose this establishment in Carolina.[67] In any event, in typical Calvinist fashion, the Fundamental Constitutions combined its church establishment with the protection of freedom of conscience. Specifically, the Fundamental Constitutions protected a "diversity of opinions" in religion in order to maintain "civil peace" and to remain consistent with "the true religion which we profess." Moreover, Locke explicitly tied freedom of conscience to the hope that Jews might be converted; the Fundamental Constitutions expressly included Jews within its protection for the following reason:

> [So] that Jews, heathens, and other dissenters from the purity of Christian religion may not be scared and kept at a distance from it, but, by having an opportunity of acquainting themselves with the truth and reasonableness of its doctrines, and the peaceableness and inoffensiveness of its professors, may, by good usage and persuasion, and all those convincing methods of gentleness and meekness, suitable to the rules and design of the gospel, be won ever to embrace and unfeignedly receive the truth.[68]

Maryland presents an interesting concrete illustration of how Jews occasionally fared in the face of Christian toleration. Maryland was founded in the early 1630s by George Calvert, who was the first Lord Baltimore and the secretary of state in England under James I. Calvert had become a Roman Catholic and sought to provide a refuge for his harassed co-religionists. Nonetheless, as Calvert's son implemented his father's plan, he recognized that toleration of Protestants likely would be politically expedient. Moreover, although many Roman Catholics settled in Maryland, Protestants always remained in the majority.[69] Consequently, Maryland passed the Toleration Act of 1649. Equating freedom of conscience with the free exercise of religion, the Act protected the "free exercise" of anyone "professing to believe in Jesus Christ." More specifically, it provided:

> That whatsoever person or persons within this Province . . . shall from henceforth blaspheme God, . . . or shall deny our Saviour Jesus Christ to bee the sonne of God, or shall deny the holy Trinity the father sonne and holy Ghost, or the Godhead of any of the said Three persons of the Trinity or the Unity of the Godhead . . . shall be punished with death and confiscation or forfeiture of all his or her lands.[70]

In 1658, the only Jew in the colony, Jacob Lumbrozo, was indicted for blasphemy under the act, probably after he resisted attempts to convert him. Lumbrozo avoided execution either because Richard Cromwell happened to grant a general amnesty when he became Lord Protector of England or, more likely, because Lumbrozo converted to Christianity (the facts are unclear).[71]

CHRISTIAN DECLENSION AND REVIVAL

As the seventeenth century wore on, the Christian religiosity of the colonists generally began to wane. Whereas many of the early colonists were inspired by religious zeal, the crush of daily burdens on the frontier some-times overshadowed Protestant convictions. In addition, many of the later immigrants came to the colonies more for economic than religious oppor-tunities. As Jon Butler observes, "Christian practice not only proved inse-cure but showed dangerous signs of declining rather than rising."[72] Even in Puritan Massachusetts, the percentage of residents who were active church members decreased.[73] In fact, the aging founders of New England recog-nized by the middle of the century that many of their descendants were lacking in Puritan commitment. By 1662, a Massachusetts synod had adopted the so-called Half-Way Covenant. Before this point, membership in the Puritan churches had been limited to those individuals who had attested to a conversion experience. Partly because of this stringent requirement, membership roles had been dwindling. The Half-Way Covenant was intended to help solve this problem. It provided that people who had been baptized as children were, in effect, half-members of the church. These indi-viduals still lacked the signs of grace needed to receive the Lord's Supper, but otherwise they could participate in society as church members.[74]

Although this ebb in Puritan conviction alarmed some of the early colonists, it proved to be merely temporary. As Sydney Ahlstrom observes, by the time of the American Revolution, the colonies "had become the most thoroughly Protestant, Reformed, and Puritan commonwealths in the world."[75] Approximately 90 percent of the populace had religious roots in Calvinist Protestantism. Needless to say, despite the momentary drift in Christian religiosity, antisemitism remained unabated. For example, a Calvinist theological text assigned at Yale in the late seventeenth century proclaimed that "the obstinate Jews" are "open foes of Christianity." The text continued: "[The Jews] deny the Trinity and the coming of the Messiah, and interpret carnally, what is spoken of Christ's Kingdom in the Prophets spiritually." Finally, in crucifying Christ, "the Jews drift was to sat-isfy their desire with hatred and revenge."[76]

Perhaps the most important consequence of the brief declension in Christianity in the colonies was that it facilitated the emergence of the modern sovereign state on American soil. As discussed, in the early Massachusetts Bay Colony, an individual could be a full citizen only by owning the covenant and being a church member. But when Christian con-victions temporarily diminished, the notion of a political or social compact, apart from a religious one, persisted. Perry Miller writes:

> As the religious inspiration waned, there remained no reason why all the
> people should not be held partners to the social compact; the idea that God

worked His ends through the covenant of the people grew vague and
obscure, while the notion that all the people made the covenant for their
own reason and created the state for their own purposes took on more and
more definite outlines.[77]

American political thought thus merged neatly with English political
theory of the same time period. The political state appeared as a rational
development, not merely as a consequence of God's will. For American
colonists as well as for John Locke in England, civil government seemed to
arise from laws of nature that led to the rational formation of a social contract directed to the protection of life, liberty, and possessions (or property).[78] Hence, for example, in 1717, the Massachusetts Puritan minister
John Wise wrote that in the "Natural Condition," all humans are roughly
equal. If we contemplate this Natural Condition, then we discover "the
Law of Nature to be the dictate of Right Reason." Because of their ability
to reason, then, individuals voluntarily enter into "divers Covenants" to
form civil government: "[I]t is the Produce of Mans Reason, of Humane
and Rational Combinations, and not from any direct Orders of Infinite
Wisdom, in any positive Law wherein is drawn up this or that Scheme of
Civil Government." Once in civil society, "many Great disproportions
appear, or at least many obvious distinctions are soon made amongst
Men." Moreover, in civil society, individuals often are "obliged to Sacrifice
[their] Private, for the Publick Good." Wise continued by positing a separation of powers in civil government and by suggesting that there exist three
different types of government: democracy, aristocracy, and monarchy.
Wise concluded: "The End of all good Government is to Cultivate Humanity, and Promote the happiness of all, and the good of every Man in all
his Rights, his Life, Liberty, Estate, Honour, &c." The echo of Locke in
Wise's writing is unmistakable. Unlike Locke, though, Wise strongly preferred democracy over the other possible forms of government.[79]

While the wavering of Christian religiosity facilitated the emergence of
the modern sovereign state, it had little long-term consequences for the
Protestant domination of America, though this wavering did affect the
form of American Protestantism. Partly because of the ebb in Christian
commitment, some churches sought to renew Christian vitality through
official establishments. If the Christian masses were not voluntarily flocking
to the churches, then perhaps they ought to be forced to do so.[80] Moreover, by the late seventeenth century, England had solidified its hold on the
American colonies and was threatening to establish the Church of England
on this continent. These Anglican efforts often sparked protests. The non-

Anglicans in South Carolina, for instance, complained to Parliament, though their request for toleration included an express objection to the exercise of the franchise by "aliens, Jews ... and Frenchmen."[81] In fact, during this time, the Anglican Church was revitalized in Virginia and became established in other southern colonies. Despite these successes, though, the Anglican efforts tended in many colonies only to spur the renewal and transformation of the already existing (non-Anglican) official establishments. Jon Butler writes of the late seventeenth and early eighteenth centuries: "Europeans in America did not flee their past; they embraced it. They moved toward the exercise of authority, not away from it."[82]

One result of this transformation of state establishments was the creation of what some historians call the "multiple establishment"—though Thomas Curry suggests that regardless of the political reality (of the multiple establishment), it was not understood as such during the colonial period.[83] For example, New Netherland initially had established the Dutch Reformed Church (Calvinism), but when the English conquered the colony and renamed it New York in 1664, they implemented a multiple establishment—an official yet decentralized church system that depended on local rule. Under this approach, each township could choose which church to officially support with a public tax—though every town was required to support some Protestant church.[84] Even in New England, these multiple establishments emerged. As discussed, the largely intolerant Puritan establishments originally had controlled most of New England, but by the end of the seventeenth century even Massachusetts provided for decentralized establishment, with each town choosing its Protestant denomination. An act of 1692 required every Massachusetts town to choose (by voting) an "able, learned and orthodox" minister who would be supported by revenues from a public tax levied on all residents.[85] Hence, with the threat of an Anglican establishment in the air, even the previously intolerant New England Puritans recognized the political necessity to tolerate some religious diversity—at least formally. Indeed, by the end of the seventeenth century, the original conception of New England Puritanism was dying: the churches were no longer "the voluntary communities of those who believed that they had been called to sainthood; they were churches of birthright members who were made to feel a sense of obligation."[86] And outside of New England, throughout the colonies, the pressure to tolerate multiple establishments increased in the early eighteenth century as non-English immigrants started to flow into the colonies; Scottish, German, and Swiss settlers all brought their forms of Protestantism with them.[87]

Two related points bear emphasis. First, as Locke and Roger Williams had observed, state-imposed orthodoxy did not necessarily increase Christian religiosity throughout the social body, though the institution of the multiple establishment perhaps was more successful than the traditional single establishment in this regard. Second, even in those few colonies lacking any official establishment, such as Rhode Island, the lack of governmental establishment did not equate with complete religious toleration. For instance, in Pennsylvania, known for its tolerance, the Frame of Government provided that no one shall "be compelled, at any time, to frequent or maintain any religious worship, place or ministry whatever." Yet, the Frame of Government also allowed only Christians to hold public office and expressly declared religious toleration only for those who "confess and acknowledge the one Almighty and eternal God."[88] Indeed, as Leo Pfeffer notes, religious toleration in Pennsylvania was shaped in part by the economic self-interest of its proprietor, William Penn. In particular, Penn used advertisements promising religious toleration to attract settlers, who would then help increase Penn's profits.[89]

Regardless of the existence or form of official establishment, one consistent theme remained in all colonies: civil and religious society were assumed to be Protestant. Within that context, by around 1700, most Protestants generally agreed to tolerate (Protestant) dissenters. At a minimum, the English Toleration Act of 1689 was applied to all the colonies, thus ensuring toleration to all Protestants (except Unitarians) who swore an oath of allegiance to the English monarchs and rejected the doctrine of transubstantiation.[90]

The period of Christian declension ended during the first half of the eighteenth century when the Great Awakening swept across the colonies. Although many historians place this first Protestant evangelical revival in the 1740s, it was not a discrete event that can be pinpointed in time and place.[91] Nonetheless, over the long term, the Great Awakening had an enormous effect on American society. Richard L. Bushman observes:

> [Between just 1740 and 1743] thousands were converted. People from all ranks of society, of all ages, and from every section underwent the new birth. In New England virtually every congregation was touched. It was not uncommon for ten or twenty percent of a town, having experienced grace, to join the church in a single year.... It is safe to say that most of the colonists in the 1740s, if not converted themselves, knew someone who was, or at least heard revival preaching.[92]

In many ways, the Great Awakening merely renewed traditional Calvinist Reform theological convictions. Revivalist preachers stressed the importance of Scripture, as well as the depravity and sinfulness of humanity.[93] George Whitefield, an English preacher who came to America, addressed his audiences as "O Sinners," and Jonathan Edwards, a theological leader in New England, entitled one of his sermons "Sinners in the Hands of an Angry God."[94] To most revivalists, individuals (sinners) were far too concerned with this-worldly affairs; instead, they should focus on eternal salvation, which could be attained, of course, only through faith in Jesus Christ. Whitefield stated:

> Faith is the only wedding Garment Christ requires; he does not call you because you are already, but because he intends to make you Saints.... It is for your Sakes, O Sinners, and not his own, that he thus condescends to invite you. Oh suffer him then to shew forth his Glory, even the Glory of the exceeding Riches of his free Grace, by believing on him. For we are saved by Grace thro' Faith.... It is his Spirit that must convince you of unbelief, and of the everlasting Righteousness of his dear Son—'Tis he alone must give Faith to apply his Righteousness to your Hearts.... I know of no Free-will any one hath, except a Free-will to do Evil continually—As to Spirituals we are quite dead, and have no ... Power to turn to God of ourselves.[95]

Hence, the Great Awakening renewed some central Calvinist theological themes, but it also significantly transformed American Protestantism. Indeed, some consider the Awakening to have been "a revolt against Calvinism."[96] The Puritans had long focused on the conversion experience, but with the revivalism of the eighteenth century, the notion of the conversion experience changed and became even more important. For many individuals, the conversion experience seemed to be a sudden awakening to the truth of Christ: revivalist ministers preached "a doctrine of immediate repentance from sin and immediate conversion to God."[97] In most instances, the conversion experience was somewhat communal. A minister would fervently urge a group of individuals to acknowledge their complete guilt, to face their utter despair, and, in the words of Jonathan Dickinson, a Presbyterian pastor, to see that they have "no whither else to go, and that Christ has the Words of eternal Life."[98] A conversion experience, in effect, allowed individuals to recognize God's grant of grace.

The Great Awakening also introduced a new style of preaching. Most of the revivalists were itinerants, traveling from town to town, seeking the largest possible audiences. Whitefield, for example, was reputed to preach to hundreds, even thousands, of people at once.[99] Wherever the revivalists went, their purpose remained the same: to persuade their audiences. Each preacher aimed to bring the people to the truth of Christ, regardless of their social positions. To do so, the revivalists spoke at the level of their audiences, using everyday language and often appearing to talk extemporaneously.[100] Indeed, the Great Awakening can be understood partly as a lower-class rebellion against the intellectual elite of the colonies. Many Harvard- and Yale-educated leaders were increasingly influenced by Enlightenment rationalism, yet the Christian masses found little spiritual comfort in the doctrines of Newton or rationalistic philosophy. The evangelical revivals responded to the religious hunger of "'ordinary' folk" (many of whom, not incidentally, were landowners).[101] Furthermore, this populism and anti-elitism was manifested in the revivalistic theology itself. Under the early New England Puritan theology, to own the covenant and become a full church member was somewhat difficult, but after the evangelical revival of the Great Awakening, the conversion experience and church membership became more readily available.[102]

Ultimately, the Great Awakening placed a greater emphasis on the individual's right to exercise private judgment in religious matters. With so many itinerant preachers wandering the countryside, they effectively began to compete with each other and with the more traditional ministers; the individual then could choose among the many itinerant or traditional preachers. Moreover, in stressing the personal conversion experience, the revivalists encouraged individuals "to rely on their own spiritual experiences, rather than on the authority of clergy."[103] Similarly, as a pamphlet from 1744 declared: "Every one is under an indispensable Obligation to search the Scriptures for himself."[104] Each person could personally and directly experience the literal meaning of Scripture.

To some extent, then, the Great Awakening democratized American religion (before government was democratized). The individual could listen to various preachers—who sought to cajole, to frighten, to inspire, to persuade in any way possible—and then the individual could choose to follow whatever preacher and church seemed most appealing. In this market-like atmosphere, the transformation of the conversion experience into a more sudden and immediate affair becomes understandable. A demagogic preacher might appeal more readily to the Christian masses by promising quick and easy salvation; a preacher could practically declare, "Join my church and take the shortcut to heaven!" Protestant sects, consequently, began to splinter off, creating an increasing plurality of denominations, and some of the already existing but smaller dissenting sects gained adherents and spread into new areas. The Baptists, for instance, benefited greatly from the eighteenth-century revivalism. The Baptists first arose as a sect of Puritans in England during the early seventeenth century; with difficulty, they gained a foothold in New England in the latter half of that century. In part because they long stood in the position of the dissenter or opposition-ist, both in Old England and New England, the Baptists often opposed church establishment. Yet, with the growing emphasis on a conversion experience during the Great Awakening, the central Baptist tenet of adult baptism became more appealing, and different Baptist denominations began to grow throughout the colonies.[105]

With the emergence of more and more denominations and with the developing equality (in numbers and strength) among the various denomi-nations, the pressure to have multiple establishments or disestablishment intensified. Thomas Curry writes: "The religious renewal ... lessened the status and power of existing churches. It created divisions between its sup-porters and opponents, irrevocably splitting many congregations and giv-ing rise to new churches. It strengthened the Presbyterian and Baptist denominations and propelled them into the southern colonies, disrupting and altering the religious balance."[106] Perhaps most important, in terms of the future of the separation of church and state, after the Great Awakening, no single church or denomination could ever realistically hope to dominate hegemonically an entire colony in doctrine and numbers.[107] Nonetheless, the unitary establishment of the Anglican church continued throughout the colonial period in the southern colonies.

Among the revivalists themselves, diverse views sprang forth, giving birth to new denominations. One of the most important divisions was between the revivalists who retained the Calvinist tenet of predestination and those who rejected it. The leader of the so-called Consistent Calvinists was Jonathan Edwards. According to Edwards, the eternal fate of indi-viduals—whether salvation or damnation—is "absolutely determined" by God.[108] The taint of original sin is so strong that the individual can do nothing to change his or her predestined fate; to think otherwise merely demonstrates human pride and sinfulness.[109] In opposition to Edwards and the Consistent Calvinists, some other revivalists—influenced by the general movement of Enlightenment modernism toward a more confident rational-ism—questioned the validity and implications of the dual doctrines of origi-nal sin and predestination. Though pejoratively attacked as Arminians, these revivalists gave birth to the Methodist movement. The central tenet of this movement was that grace was available to all: individuals were responsible for choosing whether to pursue salvation or damnation. From this perspective, freedom of conscience at least intimated a choice: an individual's conscience was not merely at liberty to accept the truth of Jesus Christ; rather, the individual was free to choose salvation or damnation. This Methodist approach contains an obvious potential for an anti-elitist mass appeal. Unsurprisingly, then, while Methodism first emerged as a movement during the Great Awakening and clearly defined itself as a separate denomination only in the late eighteenth century, it became the largest American denomination by 1820.[110]

During the Great Awakening, though, many revivalists tried to stake out a middle ground between the extremes of the Consistent Calvinists (Edwardseans) and the Methodists (Arminians). For example, Experience Mayhew insisted that he believed fully in original sin and "the Sovereignty of God in the Affair of Man's Salvation." Yet, simultaneously, he maintained that individuals can "go to [God for] Grace."[111] That is, even though individuals cannot save themselves, they can "strive to put themselves in the way of salvation." Insofar as this middle ground ignored the tensions or inconsistencies inherent in its theological details, it came closest to representing the mainstream of the evangelical revivalism of the seventeenth century.[112]

The Great Awakening had several important long-term consequences. Besides splintering American Protestantism into many denominations and partially democratizing American religion, the religious transformation contributed to the further emergence of the modern sovereign state in America. In particular, the evangelical revival helped fuel a stronger commitment to constitutional and democratic notions in government. Even Jonathan Edwards declared in 1748 that a ruler must be a person of "great ability for the management of public affairs." Downplaying theological convictions and qualifications, Edwards sounded remarkably like a Machiavellian political realist. According to Edwards, a person acquires "skill" in public affairs through "study, learning, observation, and experience."[113] By these means, one develops "a great understanding of men and things, a great knowledge of human nature, and of the way of accommodating themselves to it." Yet, Edwards maintained, the ruler should use this practical wisdom to promote the "public good," not to pursue his or her own "private interest."[114]

Other religious and political writers deepened the constitutional elements of American political thought. Writing in 1750, the radical Jonathan Mayhew (Experience Mayhew's son), following in the Lockean tradition, emphasized the right to resist unjust rulers. Mayhew argued that if a ruler does not pursue the "common good," then the people act reasonably if they resist and dethrone the ruler. In fact, Mayhew added, "it would be highly criminal" for a people not to resist a tyrant. Finally, Mayhew went so far as to argue that the official establishment of religion violated

Protestant theology and therefore required popular resistance. On this point, Mayhew obviously departed from the Protestant mainstream.[115]

In addition to its consequences for American Protestantism and political thought, the Great Awakening acted as a type of social cement. Although the revivalists tended to splinter American Protestantism into multiple denominations, the Great Awakening ultimately was "a great unifying force that gave to 'four-fifths' of the Christians in America 'a common understanding of the Christian life and the Christian faith.'"[116] Despite the theological disagreements among revivalists, the evangelical movement helped begin to forge a national consciousness across the boundaries of the various colonies—a national consciousness that would become crucial to the American Revolution. The later colonies, then, were marked by a unified and vigorous commitment to Protestantism, as manifested in a plurality of Protestant denominations. For the most part, the overriding goal for eighteenth-century colonial Americans strikingly resembled that of the early Puritans: to create and maintain "a Christian civilization."[117]

Because late colonial America was thoroughly Protestant in religion and culture, the colonists predictably displayed a high degree of antisemitism, though still largely against the conceptual Jew (since so few Jews were actually present). Dogmatic antisemitism was especially rampant among the Great Awakening revivalists. For example, Gilbert Tennent attacked unconverted ministers who supposedly resembled "the Old Pharisee-Teachers," who were "very proud and conceity" and "crafty as Foxes; they tried by all Means to ensnare our Lord by their captious Questions."[118] Joseph Bellamy, a student of Jonathan Edwards, condemned "the Jewish nation [for having] murdered God's own Son." In arguing that despite predestination Christian individuals are to blame for sin and bad temper, Bellamy reasoned that "[y]ou have as much power to help being of such a temper as the Scribes and Pharisees had; but Christ judged them to be wholly to blame, and altogether inexcusable."[119] Jonathan Edwards himself wrote:

> As to the Jews ... the generality of them rejected Christ and his gospel, with extreme pertinaciousness of spirit. They not only went on still in that career of corruption, which had been increasing from the time of the Maccabees; but Christ's coming, and his doctrine and miracles, and the preaching of his followers, and the glorious things that attended the same, were the occasion, through their perverse improvement, of an infinite increase of their wickedness. They crucified the Lord of Glory, with the utmost malice and cruelty, and persecuted his followers; they pleased not God, and were contrary to all men; and went on to grow worse and worse, till they filled up the measure

of their sin, and wrath came upon them to the uttermost; and they were destroyed, and cast out of God's sight, with unspeakably greater tokens of the divine abhorrence and indignation, than in the days of Nebuchadnezzar. The bigger part of the whole nation were slain, and the rest were scattered abroad through the earth, in the most abject and forlorn circumstances. And in the same spirit of unbelief and malice against Christ and the gospel, and in their miserable dispersed circumstances, do they remain to this day.[120]

This antisemitism was not limited to revivalists' pulpits. It surfaced in election day speeches, presentations of college presidents, and the civil laws of the colonies. Regardless of whether a colony had a single established church, a multiple establishment, or no establishment, Jews generally lacked political equality. Naomi Cohen summarizes:

> In all colonies statutory law reinforced the Christian character of society. Civil law prohibited blasphemy and public worship on the part of minorities; it also mandated church attendance, Sunday observance, and financial support of the colony's established church and its schools. Political rights—citizenship, voting, officeholding, service as jurors and witnesses—were usually limited, if not to church members then at least to those who took oaths of allegiance formulated in Christological terms. Since rights of trade often depended on legal citizenship, religious control penetrated the economic sphere. Christianity formally governed well nigh all aspects of life.[121]

In sum, by the late eighteenth century—the time of the American Revolution and the subsequent adoption of the Constitution—the central components of the American conception of church and state were already in place. The notion of the modern sovereign state had been firmly rooted, and the society was thoroughly Protestant. Americans believed, like the early New England Puritans, that "this was God's country with a mission to perform."[122] In colonies both with and without official establishments, church, state, and (practically) all of society worked together to support and enforce the assumed Protestant pillars of society. Not incidentally, then, church, state, and (practically) all of society also worked together to reinforce the doctrinal antisemitism of the New Testament. While most Jews in America unquestionably lived a more peaceful and secure life than their co-religionists in Europe, this state of affairs reflected more about Europe and its brand of antisemitism than about the colonies. Moreover, antisemitism in the colonies rarely reached the violent levels attained in Europe largely because so few Jews lived in North America. Without the presence of real Jews, antisemitism typically remained at the level of rhetoric aimed at the conceptual Jew. Thomas Curry describes the de facto establishment of Protestantism in eighteenth-century America: "[T]he notion of prayer and worship based on the Bible that was accepted by all Protestants . . . constituted an essential foundation of civilization. Such others as Catholics or Jews did not impinge sufficiently on their lives to challenge that assumption."[123]

CHAPTER 7

The American Revolution and Constitution

THE REVOLUTION AND ITS AFTERMATH

The American Revolution was, in the words of Gordon Wood, "the product of a complicated culmination of many diverse personal grievances and social strains, ranging from land pressures in Connecticut to increasing indebtedness in Virginia."[1] The disparate interests and occasionally antagonistic colonies fused together, though, to balk at the "remotely rooted and awkwardly imposed [British] imperial system."[2] This colonial resistance to British authority was evident in the realm of church and state. During the last few decades of the colonial period, few major controversies regarding church establishments arose. To a great extent, most Americans agreed that the colonies were Protestant in nature and that their official establishments were legitimate and beneficial. The exceptions—the major disputes—typically arose when the British and Anglicans claimed that the Church of England was, by implication, the established church of all the colonies—which were, after all, British colonies. Most non-Anglican colonists, while wholly accepting their own establishments, condemned the Church of England as a tyrannically and coercively imposed national religion. Indeed, because the British and Anglican efforts at establishment tended to spark strong opposition, those efforts tended to further "colonial solidarity."[3]

This differentiation between colonial establishments, on the one hand, and the Church of England, on the other hand, crystallized fully in the pre-Revolution debates.[4] In the midst of growing tensions between Great Britain and the colonies, particularly over the imposition and payment of taxes, Parliament passed a series of punitive enactments in 1774. These so-called Intolerable Acts (or Coercive Acts) included the Boston Port Act and the Massachusetts Government Act. The former, enacted as punishment for the Boston Tea Party (of December 16, 1773), closed the port of Boston until the town paid for the destroyed tea, while the latter attempted to eliminate the colonial government of Massachusetts. In terms of under-standing colonial attitudes toward the separation of church and state, the most important act was the Quebec Act, passed on June 22, 1774. The Quebec Act, as its name suggests, applied to Quebec and not to New England or other Atlantic seaboard colonies. Moreover, to a great extent, the Quebec Act extended religious toleration to Roman Catholics in Quebec. In effect, the act provided for something similar to an American-style multiple establishment: it extended the free exercise of religion and public financial support to Catholics and Anglicans.[5]

Throughout the colonies, the passage of the Intolerable Acts inflamed widespread alarm and forged a sense of unity against Britain. Con-sequently, the first Continental Congress was called, and on October 14, 1774, the Congress declared that the colonists were "entitled to life, lib-erty, and property, & they [had] never ceded to any sovereign power whatever, a right to dispose of either without their consent." The colonists, furthermore, were "entitled to all the rights, liberties, and immunities of free and natural-born subjects within the realm of England." As such, they sought to ensure that "their religion, laws, and liberties [would] not be subverted." The Intolerable Acts were deemed "impolitic, unjust, and cruel, as well as unconstitutional, and most dangerous and destructive of American rights." The Quebec Act, in particular, was condemned "for establishing the Roman Catholick Religion in the province of Quebec"; Parliament had erected "a tyranny there, to the great danger" of the colonies.[6] The Congress, thus, did not recognize the multiple establish-ment and religious toleration of the Quebec Act. When it came to religion, the British government was deemed tyrannical, while the colonial govern-ments supposedly supported religious liberty and freedom of conscience. Indeed, in a subsequent declaration, the Continental Congress proclaimed: "Our forefathers, inhabitants of the island of Great-Britain, left their native land, to seek on these shores a residence for civil and religious freedom."[7] Of course, as previously discussed, most of the early Puritan settlers had sought their own Christian freedom to follow the truth of Jesus. They had absolutely no intention of tolerating religious diversity.

Nonetheless, from the perspective of many Revolutionary-era colonists, the multiple establishments of the colonies protected religious liberty.[8] Yet, colonial disagreement on this issue surfaced at the first Continental Congress in 1774. The New England Baptists, led by Isaac Backus, complained that the professed multiple establishment of Massachusetts did not afford them religious freedom. Backus, influenced by Roger Williams and John Locke, reiterated the typical calvinistic disjunction between the spiritual and temporal worlds—rooted, of course, in the New Testament opposition of the Jewish world of carnality to the Christian world of spirituality. According to Backus, worldly choices and actions only tend to pollute the individual's quest for eternal salvation: true Christian freedom of conscience was therefore inconsistent with paying taxes to support a Congregationalist church. Backus forcefully made his point even as he expressed his complete support for the incipient Revolutionary cause:

> It may now be asked, What is the liberty desired? The answer is: As the kingdom of Christ is not of this world, and religion is a concern between God and the soul, with which no human authority can intermeddle, consistently with the principles of Christianity, and according to the dictates of Protestantism, we claim and expect the liberty of worshipping god according to our consciences, not being obliged to support a ministry we cannot attend.[9]

John Adams responded by acknowledging that Massachusetts had an establishment but that it did not infringe on freedom of conscience: "There is, indeed, an ecclesiastical establishment in our province; but a very slender one, hardly to be called an establishment." That is, to Adams, the Church of England was a real establishment—despotic and oppressive—while the Massachusetts establishment was a totally different breed—barely an establishment at all. The Church of England tyrannically imposed creeds and ceremonies, while the colonial establishments asked for little more than (supposedly) reasonable public support. Plus, Adams added, no one should expect the minimal establishment of Massachusetts to soon disappear.[10] Adams elsewhere managed to tie together Christianity, the common good, and a right to resist unjust rulers: "[I]f a clergyman preaches Christianity, and tells the magistrates that they were not distinguished from their brethren for their private emolument, but for the good of the people, that the people are bound in conscience to obey a good government, but are not bound to submit to one that aims at destroying all the ends of government—Oh Sedition! Treason!"[11] In short, the predominant message of this exchange between Backus and Adams was "the acknowledgement but simultaneous soft-pedaling of the Massachusetts establishment."[12] It is worth noting, though, that even Backus (predictably) viewed America as Christian, and he wanted to keep it that way. He praised a

Massachusetts constitutional provision that stated: "No man can take a seat in our legislature till he solemnly declares, 'I believe the Christian religion and have a firm persuasion of its truth.'"[13]

Less than two years after the first meeting of the Continental Congress, the American Revolution began. The elite leaders, particularly Thomas Jefferson in the Declaration of Independence, explained the necessity for rebellion in terms of a conservative Lockean right of resistance against an unjust ruler. By closely modeling the Declaration on Locke's theory of resistance, Jefferson and the other signers implicitly suggested that they, like Locke, were not anarchic revolutionaries, but rather somber, rational citizens forced by a tyrannical ruler to take extraordinary measures for the public good.[14] Hence, the intellectual elites drew heavily upon Enlightenment rationalism for succor, but most revolutionary Americans were only vaguely aware of and lacked precise knowledge of Enlightenment political philosophers. The most broadly influential political theory was perhaps the so-called Opposition Ideology, adopted from early-eighteenth-century English political thinkers. Opposition Ideology mixed together Harringtonian and Lockean themes, using Harringtonian civic republican language to articulate a Lockean notion of resistance: civic virtue seemed to demand resistance to governmental encroachments of rights and liberties.[15] While the revolutionary movement was somewhat sustained and structured by these abstract political ideas, many rebellious Americans were also driven by a (Great Awakening) revivalist fervor to continue building Christ's kingdom. Most likely, the Christian masses were impelled as much as or even more by their evangelical enthusiasm than by their appreciation for Locke, Harrington, Hume, and Rousseau. Indeed, the Continental Congress itself repeatedly invoked God and Jesus Christ, and adopted measures to promote and enforce Protestant values and practices.[16]

Nonetheless, for almost all American revolutionaries, elites and masses alike, "freedom" and "liberty" were the watchwords. These Americans were convinced that British leaders were consciously plotting to undermine colonial (and indeed English) liberty.[17] More than ever before, then, the establishment of the Church of England was condemned as tyrannical and as inconsistent with freedom of conscience. In fact, at this point, as the concept of a church establishment became associated with the rejected Anglican church, many colonials refused to acknowledge the fact of their own establishments. Whereas only two years earlier John Adams had admitted that Massachusetts had a "slender" establishment,[18] preachers in Massachusetts now maintained that "a 'legal provision' for ministers according to an 'equal and Liberal' plan did not even approach a 'political establishment' to deprive citizens of the sacred rights of conscience."[19]

Indeed, soon after the beginning of the Revolution, all of the colonies with Anglican establishments, except Virginia, eliminated the official imposition of the Church of England. Yet, even in those colonies—North Carolina, South Carolina, Georgia, and Maryland—the toppling of the Anglican establishment did not necessarily lead to complete disestablishment.[20] In South Carolina, for example, the first state Constitution, adopted in 1776, left the Anglican establishment intact.[21] Only two years later, though, a new state Constitution was being debated. Speaking before the state legislature in opposition to having any state-established church, William Tennent, a Presbyterian minister, insisted that the Anglican establishment infringed "Religious Liberty." The establishment merely tolerated Protestant dissenters without granting them full equality, as if they stood "on the same footing with the Jews." When Tennent subsequently learned, however, that a multiple establishment encompassing his own denomination was under consideration, he became an enthusiastic supporter of official establishment. Such a multiple establishment, according to Tennent, "opens the door to the equal incorporation of all denominations" because "Christianity itself [will be] the established religion of the State."[22] In fact, the new South Carolina Constitution of 1778 eliminated the Anglican establishment but imposed a broader Protestant establishment. The Constitution provided:

> That all persons and religious societies who acknowledge that there is one God, and a future state of rewards and punishments, and that God is publicly to be worshipped, shall be freely tolerated. The Christian Protestant religion shall be deemed, and is hereby constituted and declared to be, the established religion of this State. That all denominations of Christian Protestants in this State, demeaning themselves peaceably and faithfully, shall enjoy equal religious and civil privileges.[23]

In case there was any doubt, the Constitution added that "the Christian religion is the true religion."[24]

From a Protestant standpoint, the views of Tennent and other South Carolinians supporting the new establishment did not represent blatant hypocrisy. In an overwhelmingly Protestant nation with a plurality of denominations like the early America, religious liberty meant freedom to be Protestant. From early in the Reformation, freedom of conscience and official establishment seemed entirely consistent. South Carolina merely reflected this Protestant viewpoint. And because of the many denominations, a single or unitary establishment—whether of the Anglican church or any other—seemed problematic and even oppressive, while a multiple establishment closely matched the social reality. Thus, during the late eighteenth century, in those states that maintained official establishments—South Carolina, Maryland, Georgia, Massachusetts, Connecticut, and New Hampshire—the multiple establishment of Protestantism or Christianity, typically accompanied by some protection of freedom of conscience or free exercise of religion, became the norm.[25]

Meanwhile, several states—Rhode Island, Pennsylvania, New Jersey, and Delaware—inherited a colonial tradition of not having an officially established church.[26] Almost immediately, two other states—North Carolina and New York—joined this group. North Carolina repudiated its Anglican church establishment and all others as well. The North Carolina Constitution of 1776 also expressly protected freedom of conscience, yet it simultaneously limited public officeholding to those individuals who accepted "the truth of the Protestant religion."[27] The New York Constitution of 1777 expressly repudiated any official establishment, thus resolving a long-running dispute about whether a multiple establishment or an Anglican establishment existed in the state. Like states that maintained official multiple establishments as well as states without establishments, New York protected freedom of conscience, which was explicitly equated with the free exercise of religion:

> [T]he free exercise and enjoyment of religious profession and worship, without discrimination or preference, shall forever hereafter be allowed, within this State, to all mankind: Provided, That the liberty of conscience, hereby granted, shall not be so construed as to excuse acts of licentiousness, or justify practices inconsistent with the peace or safety of this State.[28]

Virginia continued its official support of the Anglican Church for a short time after the Revolution, but then during the 1780s, after a lengthy dispute, Virginia fully repudiated its establishment (without switching to an official multiple establishment). Hence, although Virginia has received enormous scholarly attention for its movement to disestablishment and its relation to the framing of the first amendment of the U.S. Constitution, this state was an anomaly. Each of the other states either, on the one hand, continued its earlier respective colonial policy by having no official establishment or by maintaining a multiple establishment, or on the other hand, switched within two years after the Revolution to disestablishment or a multiple establishment.[29] In fact, Virginia perhaps has received such enormous attention exactly because of its unusual history: there was greater debate about church establishment in Virginia than in other states and thus more information available for historical research.[30] In addition, since James Madison was prominent in the Virginia debates as well as in the development of the first amendment, his views in the state dispute often are reasonably deemed to illuminate the meaning of the first amendment.

During the Great Awakening, the number of Baptists in Virginia had increased dramatically despite the Anglican establishment. Hence, even before the Revolution, many Baptists in the state "were with good cause raising the cry of religious persecution."[31] Then, after the Revolution, when Virginia initially maintained its official establishment (through public tax support), the Baptists continued their call for religious liberty (even though dissenters were exempted from the tax).[32] To a great extent, the Virginia Baptists echoed the position of Isaac Backus: the payment of taxes to publicly support religion violated the Protestant freedom of conscience. As Backus had argued, worldly choices and actions only tend to pollute the individual's quest for eternal salvation.

Meanwhile, in 1779, Thomas Jefferson introduced in the Virginia legislature An Act for Establishing Religious Freedom. This bill provided as follows:

> That no man shall be compelled to frequent or support any religious worship, place or ministry whatsoever, nor shall be enforced, restrained, molested, or burthened in his body or goods, nor shall otherwise suffer on account of his religious opinions or belief; but that all men shall be free to profess, and by argument to maintain, their opinions in matters of religion, and that the same shall in nowise diminish, enlarge, or affect their civil capacities.[33]

As one who was heavily influenced by Enlightenment philosophy (including Locke) and deistic theology, Jefferson is renowned for insisting upon "a wall of separation between church and State," largely for the benefit of the state.[34] Jefferson, that is, is known for seeking to preserve the operation of government free of the strife that official establishments tended to propagate.[35] Nevertheless, Jefferson justified his Act for Establishing Religious Freedom with reasons that the Baptists themselves easily could have announced. For example, he wrote that an establishment tends "to corrupt the principles of that very religion it is meant to encourage, by bribing, with a monopoly of worldly honors and emoluments, those who will externally profess and conform to it."[36] Jefferson's Lockean roots help explain and illuminate his religious justifications for the act. In fact, Jefferson derived large portions of the act from Locke's Letter Concerning Toleration, and as I discussed in chapter 5, Locke's views on religion and religious toleration were distinctly Calvinist. Specifically, Locke educed his views both on religious toleration and on political society from the strict Calvinist disjunction between the spiritual and the temporal. Perhaps then, not so surprisingly, even Jefferson, the rationalistic deist who so often seemed hostile to traditional Christianity, appeared to draw implicitly upon the antisemitic imagery of the New Testament by opposing "worldly honors and emoluments" to Christian spirituality.[37] Indeed, elsewhere, Jefferson wrote that Jews' "'ideas of him [God] & of his attributes were degrading & injurious' and their '[e]thics [were] often irreconcilable with the sound dictates of reason & morality' [as well as being] 'repulsive & antisocial'.... Judaic beliefs and morality 'degraded' Jews and 'presented' the 'necessity' for their 'reformation.'"[38]

The Virginia legislature did not initially pass Jefferson's bill, though in 1779 it did repeal the statute that imposed taxes for the support of religion. Then, from 1784 to 1786, the question of state establishment once again came to the forefront in Virginia when Patrick Henry introduced in the legislature a general assessment tax to support Christianity.[39] This time, James Madison led the fight for disestablishment, articulating his views in the famous Memorial and Remonstrance. Madison expressly rejected the official establishment of Christianity: "Who does not see that the same authority which can establish Christianity, in exclusion of all other Religions, may establish with the same ease any particular sect of Christians, in exclusion of all other Sects?"[40]

In justifying disestablishment, Madison drew upon both the evangelical (Calvinist) theology of the Baptists and the more secular reasoning typically associated with Jefferson (and Locke). To Madison, experience demonstrated that the establishment of religion tended to corrupt both government and Christianity. More specifically, on the secular side, Madison argued that "[r]eligion is wholly exempt" from the cognizance of civil society as created through the social contract. Good civil government does not need the official establishment of Christianity, and in fact, civil governments more often than not have used church establishments to facilitate tyranny. In addition, as a practical matter, establishment might encourage certain (dissenting) individuals to leave the state, though they otherwise are good citizens. Most important, perhaps, experience shows that establishment cannot "extinguish Religious discord." To the contrary, establishment tends to produce civil strife, while the "true remedy [for religious discord is] equal and compleat liberty."[41] Thus, Madison followed Locke in arguing that religious liberty dampens the development of the religious hostilities that tend to destroy the state.[42]

In the Memorial and Remonstrance, Madison emphasized protecting the religious realm as much as the political realm. Madison's religious justifications echoed the standard Calvinist themes that the Baptists relied upon (and hence, of course, Madison also echoed the standard New Testament antisemitic themes). Official establishment, Madison argued, mistakenly propels this-worldly forces into the spiritual affairs of Christian salvation: "[We remonstrate against the said Bill because] the establishment proposed by the Bill is not requisite for the support of the Christian Religion. To say that it is, is a contradiction to the Christian Religion itself, for every page of it disavows a dependence on the powers of this world." Like Christians throughout the centuries, Madison wanted to spread the universal truth of Christ to non-Christians: "The first wish of those who enjoy this precious gift [of Christianity] ought to be that it may be imparted to the whole race of mankind." The use of civil force through the official establishment of religion, however, cannot create sincere converts to Christianity. According to Madison, experience reveals that official establishments undermine the "purity" of Christianity and that Christianity actually flourishes best without establishment. While Madison was far from the first to recognize that the official imposition of Christianity might impede its spread throughout the social body (for example, Roger Williams had argued the same), the importance of Madison's reiterating this point in this era of American history cannot be overstated. Madison wrote:

> [E]xperience witnesseth that ecclesiastical establishments, instead of maintaining the purity and efficacy of Religion, have had a contrary operation. During almost fifteen centuries has the legal establishment of Christianity been on trial. What have been its fruits? More or less in all places, pride and indolence in the Clergy, ignorance and servility in the laity, in both, superstition, bigotry and persecution. Enquire of the Teachers of Christianity for the ages in which it appeared in its greatest lustre; those of every sect, point to the ages prior to its incorporation with Civil policy.[43]

Hence, Madison here reproduces standard Reformation rhetoric condemning the Roman Catholic Church of the Middle Ages; Christianity ought to be restored to its "primitive State in which its Teachers depended on the voluntary rewards of their flocks." Finally, Madison added that the forced payment of taxes for a church establishment would violate "the free exercise of Religion according to the dictates of Conscience."[44]

Although Madison led the fight against the bill proposing to impose a general assessment tax for the support of Christianity, he was not alone. He was joined by many others, including, of course, the long-protesting

Baptists. Baptist petitions typically reiterated the Calvinist disjunction between the spiritual and temporal worlds: "As the Church of the Kingdom of Christ 'is not of this world' as [Jesus] declares; it appears an evident impropriety, to intrust in the management of any of its proper interests offices which relate wholly to secular matters. And cannot therefore have any proper connection with a spiritual body."[45] In the end, then, the forces in Virginia for disestablishment overwhelmed their opponents. Not only was the bill proposing the general assessment tax defeated in 1786, but Jefferson's Act for Establishing Religious Freedom was passed instead. From Jefferson's perspective, at least, this statute comprehended "within the mantle of its protection, the Jew and the Gentile, the Christian and Mohometan, the Hindoo, and Infidel of every denomination."[46]

Most important, then, regardless of Jefferson's viewpoint on the Act for Establishing Religious Freedom, the official disestablishment in Virginia and elsewhere did not diminish Christian domination of American society. Thomas Curry observes that the states "inherited the common colonial ethos that America was a Protestant country and simply assumed that Protestantism should be encouraged in non-specified ways."[47] Regardless of official establishment or disestablishment, legislative measures and even constitutional provisions continued to directly bolster Christian hegemony. Non-Christians often were burdened with civil disabilities, such as prohibitions on voting and public officeholding.[48] For instance, in Pennsylvania, which long had no official establishment, the state Constitution demanded that state legislators swear an oath that would bar Jews and atheists.[49] In 1785, Madison himself introduced in the Virginia legislature A Bill for Punishing Disturbers of Religious Worship and Sabbath Breakers, which had been drafted by Jefferson; if passed, it would have imposed a fine for working on the Christian Sabbath of Sunday.[50] And Madison introduced yet another bill providing that on certain appointed days of public fasting and thanksgiving, "ministers were to perform 'divine service and preach a sermon ... suited to the occasion' or forfeit £50."[51] In short, even with official disestablishment, de facto establishment of Christianity remained a given in American society. In the words of Forrest McDonald, "so habituated were Americans to thinking in Protestant terms that few could conceive of a civil order in any other way."[52] As Madison himself revealed, the opponents of official establishments did not intend to reduce the Christian hold on America. To the contrary, Madison and others believed that Protestantism would spread most effectively without official establishment, through the congregations of the faithful.

All in all, the period of the Revolution and early nationhood was marked by a strong movement toward disestablishment at the state level. One impetus for this movement was the influence of Enlightenment rationalism in the political thought of the elite leaders, but quite clearly, this factor paled in comparison to religious and political developments. In particular, the lingering effects of the Great Awakening fomented disestablishment. The evangelical Protestant denominations enthusiastically pressed the sharp Calvinist disjunction between the spiritual and temporal worlds to the point where the (mere) payment of a tax to support religion seemed an unacceptable intrusion of worldly matters into the realm of spiritual salvation.[53] And the increasing plurality of Protestant denominations rendered disestablishment politically expedient; with so many denominations, no single Protestant sect could long dominate any state, much less the nation. Furthermore, the Revolution itself politically propelled many states toward disestablishment. As a practical matter, in those states where the Church of England had been officially established, the continuation of an Anglican establishment seemed impolitic (or worse) after the break from Great Britain. More broadly, revolutionary Americans could no longer accept a unitary establishment. At a minimum, Americans needed to distinguish the Church of England from their own state establishments (if still extant): the former was a unitary establishment imposed from above and demanding adherence to particular creeds and ceremonies, while the latter were multiple establishments that arose directly from the people themselves and that asked only for public support. From this perspective, the movement toward multiple establishments and ultimately disestablishment arose not so much from a virtuous commitment to a principle of religious liberty for all, but rather from a political commitment to justifying American liberty vis-à-vis Britain.

And even without official establishments, Americans knew that Protestantism was established de facto anyway. As a society and culture, America was so pervasively and completely Christian that official establishments became irrelevant; de facto establishment was just there, as if it were an element of nature. Constitutional establishments were unnecessary because there always existed innumerable additional social supports for Christianity (sometimes overt and sometimes obscure). In short, official establishment had little apparent function or necessity—it almost became a redundancy. Indeed, from the perspective of Madison and others, disestablishment would facilitate the spread of Protestantism throughout the social body. Moreover, the state constitutions expressly protected freedom of conscience (or some derivation of freedom of conscience, such as the free exercise of religion).[54] Because the liberty to follow the dictates of one's conscience was, of course, a central element of Protestantism, the explicit constitutional protection of freedom of conscience amounted to an implicit governmental recognition of Protestantism. And thus somewhat ironically, many Americans at this point in history began to link disestablishment with freedom of conscience. Both Jefferson and Madison, for example, believed that the Virginia Act for Establishing Religious Freedom not only prohibited an official establishment but also protected a private or inner realm of conscience. As the act proclaimed, no one should "suffer on account of his religious opinions or belief."[55] Based on this language, Madison declared that the act protected the "human mind,"[56] and Jefferson wrote similarly, emphasizing that the act protected the individual's formation of "opinions" (not just religious opinions).[57] Thus, significantly for the future of American constitutional law in general, Madison and Jefferson both seemed to suggest that the protected private realm should include even more than religious convictions—though without doubt, the private realm encompassed at least the Protestant religious conscience.[58]

Finally, with regard to the conceptualization of the state or government, many Revolutionary-era Americans understood the state in civic republican terms—arising from the traditions of Machiavelli and Harrington.[59] This republican vision manifested itself in several ways. Having rejected the English monarchy and having no nobility, most Americans assumed that the state governments would naturally and necessarily be democratic republics—though the scope of democracy was disputed. The people—or at least some of the people—were to be sovereign. Gordon Wood argues that the American Revolution was radical exactly because it transformed America from a "monarchical, hierarchy-ridden" society into a democratic nation (regardless of the staggering disenfranchisement of more than half of the population, including the African American slaves).[60] In a sense, just as the Great Awakening had partially democratized American Protestantism over the previous forty or so years, the Revolution now partially democratized American government. Indeed, without doubt, the previous (though partial) democratization of American Protestantism contributed to the early national commitment to some form of governmental democracy; Revolutionary-era Americans already had grown accustomed to democratic notions. Moreover, this democratic drive was impelled by the relatively widespread ownership of property, which Edmund S. Morgan has called "perhaps the most important single fact about the Americans of the Revolutionary period." Yet despite the early commitment to (albeit limited) governmental democracy, Americans were distinctly aware of the fragility of republics, especially democratic ones. For most Americans, the key to creating and preserving a republic was civic virtue: because of civic virtue, ordinary citizens and governmental officials would pursue the common good and not their private interests.[61]

Two central problems emerged. First, without a preexisting royalty or nobility, where would the governmental leaders come from? And second, how could civic virtue be imbued in the people? With regard to the first question, the assumption was that the most virtuous citizens would naturally emerge to become governmental leaders, and because of their great civic commitment, they would act for the public good. With regard to the second problem, many Americans placed great stock in education and religion (Christianity) as means for teaching civic virtue to the ordinary people (from whom the natural leaders would eventually emerge). Even in colonial times, Puritan-dominated areas often offered public education, to ensure that the population was literate enough to read the Bible.[62] This desire for public education spread to other areas of the country after the Revolution; some of the early state constitutions explicitly addressed the need to create and maintain public schools and to otherwise further education. The Pennsylvania Constitution of 1776, for instance, proclaimed that a "school or schools shall be established in each county by the legislature, for the convenient instruction of youth."[63] The Massachusetts Constitution of 1780 stated that "it shall be the duty of legislatures and magistrates ... to cherish the interests of literature and the sciences, and all seminaries of them; especially the university at Cambridge, public schools, and grammar-schools in the towns."[64]

Meanwhile, many Americans viewed Protestantism as a "major adhesive force," especially for ordinary people.[65] The widespread commitment to Protestantism supposedly provided the people with the common background and the civic (Christian) virtue that enabled them to engage in republican deliberations about the public good. For this reason, Gordon Wood suggests that "to some Americans," religious freedom, denominational pluralism, and disestablishment seemed incompatible with civic republicanism.[66] That is, from Wood's perspective, these Americans believed that the official establishment of Protestantism was required to bolster the Christian supports supposedly needed for republican government. While undoubtedly some Americans held this view, Wood fails to acknowledge that many others willingly accepted de facto establishment as the best means for facilitating the spread of Protestantism throughout the American social body. From this viewpoint, de facto establishment, more so than

official establishment, could provide the strong Christian foundation supposedly so vital for civil government.[67] Either way, though—with or without official establishment—most Americans sensed that the promotion and
spread of Protestantism was crucial to the health of the state republics.

The Constitution

To a great extent, the framers of the U.S. Constitution merely followed the
trends of the time, already emergent at the state level. For the framers, the
general movement toward multiple establishments and official disestablishment meant that the new federal government would not become deeply
involved in religion. Even without the subsequently adopted first amendment religion clauses, the assumption was that the national government
under the new Constitution would lack power over religious affairs: the
national government would not infringe on freedom of conscience and
would not officially establish any religion or religions. Insofar as any official
establishments would exist in the new nation, they would follow the
American model of the multiple establishment as opposed to the English
model of the national church. Official establishments therefore would arise
from sundry choices made at the local or state level—not at the national
level. The colonial and post-Revolutionary experiences already had
revealed that Protestantism flourished sufficiently without the official imposition of a church establishment at the national level.[68]

Consequently, the Constitutional Convention of 1787 remained remarkably free of debate concerning religious matters. Preexisting consensus
rendered discussion unnecessary. The possibility of explicitly prohibiting a
religious test or oath for holding national public office was raised only
toward the end of the Convention. With little discussion, the framers
decided to include article VI, clause 3: "[N]o religious Test shall ever be
required as a Qualification to any Office or public Trust under the United
States."[69]

In the ensuing debates over whether to ratify the proposed Constitution, the question of a Bill of Rights became a central issue.[70] The Anti-
Federalists charged that the Constitution was seriously deficient because it
lacked a Bill of Rights, while the Federalists maintained that a Bill of Rights
would be superfluous and even dangerous. To the Anti-Federalists, the
proposed Constitution, if adopted, would vest enormous power in the
centralized national government, which therefore would be able to trod
upon many important individual rights and liberties. For that reason, a Bill
of Rights, protecting those rights and liberties, was deemed essential to

prevent governmental tyranny.[71] The Federalists countered by arguing that the proposed federal government would be one of limited powers; Congress, for example, would have only those powers specifically enumerated in article II, such as the powers to regulate interstate commerce and to tax the people. The federal government, in other words, would not have a broad or open-ended police power to regulate for the general health and welfare of the people. Since the expressly enumerated powers of the federal government did not include a power to infringe important individual rights, such as the right to free speech or to freedom of conscience, the Federalists maintained that a Bill of Rights was unnecessary. The new federal government simply would lack the power to violate important individual rights and liberties, whether or not a Bill of Rights was added to the Constitution.[72] Moreover, as Alexander Hamilton contended in The Federalist, Number 84, a Bill of Rights could actually undermine the protection of individual rights and liberties. If a Bill of Rights were included in the new Constitution, then at some point in the future, someone might argue that only those rights and liberties expressly protected stand beyond the reach of the federal government's power. The federal government, in other words, might tyrannize the people by trampling upon any rights and liberties not expressly delineated in the Bill of Rights. According to this argument by Hamilton, a Bill of Rights would actually serve to expand—not limit—the powers of the national government.[73]

The dispute about a Bill of Rights often focused on religious freedom. Broadly, the Anti-Federalists claimed that without a Bill of Rights, the federal government would be able to infringe on freedom of conscience and on the prerogative of the state governments to regulate religious affairs.[74] Nevertheless, the Federalists, no less so than the Anti-Federalists, sought to protect freedom of conscience—which was, after all, a crucial component of Protestantism. Also, the Federalists, again like the Anti-Federalists, sought to ensure that insofar as any governments were to have power over religious affairs, it would be the states and not the federal government. Contrary to the Anti-Federalists, however, the Federalists denied that a Bill of Rights was needed to achieve these results.

James Madison articulated the most important Federalist defenses of the proposed Constitution against the Anti-Federalist attacks. From the time of the previous disestablishment battle in Virginia, Madison was on record as strongly supporting religious liberty. In his Memorial and Remonstrance, as already discussed, Madison had argued that religious liberty was the best means for avoiding civil strife due to religious differences. For Madison, then, his defense of the proposed federal Constitution required him not to advocate for religious liberty but rather to explain that the Constitution would provide the best means for protecting such liberty. In doing so, Madison grounded his argument regarding religious liberty on his broader argument concerning civil liberty. In The Federalist, Number 10, Madison argued that a multiplicity of political factions in the United States would help protect civil rights and liberties.[75] With a multitude of factions, no single faction or political group would be able to seize sufficient power to tyrannize the people (or the states); too many other factions would oppose any particular faction bent on tyranny. In The Federalist, Number 51, Madison applied a similar argument to the protection of religious liberty. He reasoned that a "multiplicity of sects" would protect freedom of religion even without a Bill of Rights.[76] At the Virginia ratifying convention, Madison elaborated this argument:

> Is a bill of rights a security for religion? ... If there were a majority of one sect, a bill of rights would be a poor protection for liberty. Happily for the states, they enjoy the utmost freedom of religion. This freedom arises from that multiplicity of sects which pervades America, and which is the best and only security for religious liberty in any society; for where there is such a variety of sects, there cannot be a majority of any one sect to oppress and persecute the rest.... [T]he United States abound in such a variety of sects, that it is a strong security against religious persecution; and it is sufficient to authorize a conclusion, that no one sect will ever be able to outnumber or depress the rest.[77]

Hence, according to Madison, a multiplicity of sects not only is the best means for protecting religious liberty—better than a Bill of Rights—it is the only means. Even the explicit protection of religious liberty in a Bill of Rights could not protect against the political reality of religious domination that would ensue if the membership of one Protestant sect ever sufficiently outnumbered that of the other sects. Two points here bear special emphasis. First, for Madison, a constitution could structure the American governmental scheme, but such a constitution apparently could alter American society only to a limited extent. A constitutional Bill of Rights would not stop a Protestant sect that was otherwise able to dominate American society from doing so. Second, Madison viewed religious liberty from his own perspective—that is, as a Protestant. From that Protestant viewpoint, Madison saw an America that was split among diverse and sometimes opposed denominations. If, however, Madison could have seen America from a Jewish viewpoint (highly unlikely), he would have seen a radically different nation: America was hegemonically Protestant. The similarities of the Protestant denominations were far more significant than their differences, which mattered little to a true religious outsider. With or without official establishment, America was a Protestant nation.

Indeed, the central thrust of Madison's argument on religion was that Protestant factionalism would protect the religious status quo—and the status quo amounted to the de facto establishment of Protestantism. According to Madison, Protestant factionalism—more so than the Constitution—would disempower the federal government in the realm of religious affairs. Because of the multiplicity of denominations, no one Protestant sect would ever be able to use the national governmental apparatus to impose its own creeds, ceremonies, and beliefs on the other sects. The federal government, then, could not alter the religious makeup of the nation (any more than a Bill of Rights could have prevented religious domination). In fact, many of the other Federalist framers who strongly advocated for article VI, clause 3—prohibiting a religious test for federal public office—nonetheless simultaneously supported Protestant (or Christian) religious tests and establishments in their home states. For example, Oliver Ellsworth (a future chief justice of the U.S. Supreme Court) eventually chaired a committee that considered whether the state of Connecticut should continue to provide tax support for ministers and church-run schools. The committee, appointed by the state legislature, recommended to continue this form of official establishment, reasoning that "institutions for the promotion of good morals, are [proper] objects of legislative provision and support: and among these, in the opinion of the committee, religious institutions are eminently useful and important."[78]

To be clear, the de facto establishment of Protestantism did not mean that most Americans were necessarily church members, even after the Great Awakening. Nonetheless, while historians disagree about the level of church membership and attendance in the framers' generation, the number of church members was (and is) totally beside the point. As Martin Marty observes: "Church people and the unchurched alike thought of the new republic as a Protestant domain."[79] De facto establishment existed because the American culture and society were thoroughly Protestant. Protestantism and Protestant views shaped the ways that most individuals understood religion, politics, economics, and even their own individuality, regardless of who or how many belonged to churches. Perhaps the depth of Protestant hegemony was revealed less by the percentage of people attending church and more by the widespread and passionate opposition to fully accepting Jews and other non-Christians into American political life. "The vast majority of Americans assumed," according to Thomas Curry, "that theirs was a Christian, i.e. Protestant, country [that would] uphold the commonly agreed on Protestant ethos and morality."[80] Like the early colonists, most Americans believed that "this was God's country with a mission to perform."[81] Unsurprisingly, then, during the ratification debates, many participants complained that the Constitution did not expressly acknowledge Jesus Christ.[82]

In this context of de facto Protestant establishment, antisemitism predictably surfaced on both the Federalist and Anti-Federalist sides in the debates concerning religion in the proposed Constitution. While the Anti-Federalists typically claimed to seek protection for freedom of conscience, they also expressed a bizarre fear that a Jew might become president. For example, one Anti-Federalist wrote:

> 1st. There is no bill of rights in [the proposed Constitution]. 2d. Although different religions are allowed to set in Congress, yet there is no liberty given to the people to perform religious worship according to the dictates of their consciences. 3d. There is a door opened for the Jews, Turks, and Heathen to enter into publick office, and be seated at the head of the government of the United States.[83]

The Anti-Federalists, that is, demanded explicit protection for freedom of conscience, but quite clearly, this was the freedom to be Protestant. Freedom of conscience did not entail full political rights for Jews or other non-Christians, whom the Anti-Federalists wanted to bar from public office. Most important, though, the Federalists did not depart far from the Anti-Federalists' basic attitude: neither group would welcome a Jew into the presidency or into any other high public office.

The Federalist view crystallized during the ratifying debates in North Carolina. As the Convention members debated the merits of the proposed Constitution, James Iredell, a Federalist (and another future Supreme Court justice), voiced a realpolitik argument with echoes reaching back to Roger Williams, John Locke, and Madison's Memorial and Remonstrance. The federal government would not impose religious tests or persecutions because history had proven that such "intolerant spirit [had led to] wars of the most implacable and bloody nature." The proposed article VI, clause 3, would "establish a general religious liberty." Congress, according to Iredell, would "certainly have no authority to interfere in the establishment of any religion whatsoever." Finally, in response to the Anti-Federalist fear that members of religious outgroups might be elected to high public offices, Iredell candidly relied on the de facto establishment of Christianity as assurance against such a threat: "But it is never to be supposed that the people of America will trust their dearest rights to persons who have no religion at all, or a religion materially different from their own."[84] Governor Johnston then replied to an Anti-Federalist claim that the lack of a religious test for high public office would serve as an "invitation for Jews and pagans of every kind to come" to America, thus endangering "the character of the United States."

> [Governor Johnston] admitted a possibility of Jews, pagans, &c., emigrating to the United States; yet, he said, they could not be in proportion to the emigration of Christians who should come from other countries; that, in all probability, the children even of such people would be Christians; and that this, with the rapid population of the United States, their zeal for religion, and love of liberty, would, he trusted, add to the progress of the Christian religion among us.[85]

That is, while Jews and other non-Christians might come to America seeking religious freedom, they (or their children) would soon convert to Christianity.

Ultimately, of course, the states ratified and adopted the Constitution, but only after some Federalist leaders, including Madison, promised to soon add a Bill of Rights.[86] Despite the occasional expressions of antisemitism during the ratification debates and despite the de facto establishment of Protestantism, American Jews (albeit still few in number) welcomed the new Constitution. Quite simply, it placed no official limitations on their political standing; at least under the federal Constitution, Jews were full citizens.[87] Indeed, on July 4, 1788, a parade marched through Philadelphia celebrating the recent adoption of the Constitution. Included in the parade were seventeen clergy, one of whom was a rabbi. In no place outside of America would a rabbi have participated in such an event (and in fact, in many other places in America, a rabbi never would have been included).[88] Naomi Cohen summarizes the reasons for the (seeming) political emancipation of American Jews under the federal Constitution: "the small numbers of Jews in the country, the work force required for a new society, the absence of a feudal heritage, the plurality of religious sects, new ideologies, and the consignment of jurisdiction over religion to the state governments."[89] The last-mentioned reason—the assignment of jurisdictional power over religion to the states—was perhaps the most important. As discussed, with article VI, clause 3, the framers did not intend to lessen or undermine the Protestant nature of the country. Almost everyone assumed that de facto establishment would continue, with state governments supplying various kinds of supports, sometimes even officially sustaining multiple establishments with public taxes. "The American future," according to Morton Borden, "[was envisioned] as a federation of Christian states ... and the state governments—where real power would reside—would be controlled by Protestants only." For American Jews, then, the adoption of the Constitution brought little real change.[90]

The subsequent adoption of the first amendment did not alter this reality. As the Federalists had promised, Madison (who had become a member of the House of Representatives) introduced a Bill of Rights to the first Congress on June 8, 1789. The Federalists' primary concern was political: they wanted to defuse any potential Anti-Federalist charges that the Federalists were not fulfilling their promises or were attempting to aggrandize power and threaten liberty. To a great extent, the first Congress, following the Federalist position, understood the Bill of Rights as a redundancy. The amendments merely would reiterate what already was understood—that the national government had no power to infringe on religious liberty and other individual rights. The national government, in other words, could not violate freedom of conscience and could not officially establish a religion. Since, in Thomas Curry's words, "Congress was not trying to resolve concrete disputes," Congress did not give special attention to the language and substance of the Bill of Rights, including the religion clauses of the first amendment. Indeed, with regard to the adoption of the amendments, commentators have described the first Congress as being inattentive, listless, hasty, and absentminded, as affirming what was taken for granted, and as choosing merely the most felicitous-sounding provisions.[91]

Madison's initial provision regarding religion read as follows: "The civil rights of none shall be abridged on account of religious belief or worship, nor shall any national religion be established, nor shall the full and equal rights of conscience be in any manner, or on any pretext, infringed." Madison, at this time, also introduced a provision limiting state governmental power to infringe on freedom of conscience: "No State shall violate the equal rights of conscience, or the freedom of the press, or the trial by jury in criminal cases." In support of his proposed religion clauses, Madison referred to "freedom of the press and rights of conscience [as] those choicest privileges of the people." Then, in a significant acknowledgment, Madison reformulated a theme that he had introduced earlier in the Federalist Papers and in the Virginia ratifying debates. At those previous times, he had argued that a Bill of Rights could not prevent a dominant Protestant sect from tyrannizing other sects. Now, in introducing the proposed Bill of Rights, he expanded his point:

But I confess that I do conceive, that in a Government modified like this of the United States, the great danger lies rather in the abuse of the community than in the Legislative body. The prescriptions in favor of liberty ought to be levelled against that quarter where the greatest danger lies, namely, that which possesses the highest prerogative of power. But this is not found in either the Executive or Legislative departments of Government, but in the body of the people, operating by the majority against the minority.[92]

Madison asserted, in other words, that in a democracy with a national government of limited powers, the principal power and hence the predominant threat to liberty rests, ironically, with the people themselves. In a Christian nation such as the United States, then, the Christian masses represent the greatest threat to the liberty of religious outgroups. A Bill of Rights, restricting governmental action in religious affairs, cannot fully protect religious outgroups from tyranny because it does not protect against the power of the Christian masses that is spread throughout the social body.

A select committee of the House of Representatives took up consideration of Madison's proposed Bill of Rights. With regard to the proposals concerning religion, the committee eliminated Madison's second provision, which referred explicitly to state governments, and recommended a more concise formulation of his first provision. The committee's recommendation read as follows: "No religion shall be established by law, nor shall the equal rights of conscience be infringed."[93] Although this proposed text was unclear, the brief House debates following its introduction revealed a consensus that the provision would apply only against the federal government.[94] During these debates, Daniel Carroll captured the mood of the Congress. He recognized that the adoption of any provisions protecting religious liberty would allay the fears of many, but the specific words of the provisions were relatively unimportant:

He thought it would tend more towards conciliating the minds of the people to the Government than almost any other amendment he had heard proposed. He would not contend with gentlemen about the phraseology, his object was to secure the substance in such a manner as to satisfy the wishes of the honest part of the community.[95]

On August 20, 1789, the House of Representatives adopted the following language: "Congress shall make no law establishing religion, or to prevent the free exercise thereof, or to infringe the rights of conscience."[96] At this point, the provision already had come close to the final version that was eventually adopted. Four days later, the House approved its final version of the Bill of Rights, which contained the following on religion: "Congress shall make no law establishing religion or prohibiting the free exercise thereof, nor shall the rights of Conscience be infringed."[97] This provision, with its three clauses, contained only minor stylistic changes from the previous House version.

The final House resolution then went to the Senate, which considered several changes from the House language, eventually dropping the reference to rights of conscience.[98] The Senate agreed on the following language: "Congress shall make no law establishing articles of faith, or a mode of worship, or prohibiting the free exercise of religion."[99] Ultimately, a conference committee reached the final adopted version of the religion clauses of the first amendment: "Congress shall make no law respecting an establishment of religion, or prohibiting the free exercise thereof."[100] Within six months, the requisite number of states had ratified the Bill of Rights, including the religion clauses, "with little debate or controversy."[101] The first amendment religion clauses—the establishment and free exercise clauses—became effective on December 15, 1791.

Hence, Madison and the Federalists fulfilled their promise to adopt a Bill of Rights promptly after the new Constitution was implemented. In adopting the religion clauses, they rendered "explicit a point on which the entire nation agreed," as Leonard Levy notes. "The United States had no power to legislate on the subject of religion."[102] The establishment and free exercise clauses ensured that the national government would not directly infringe upon religious freedom; any governmental regulations of religious affairs were to remain a matter of state law. The failure to include an explicit reference in the first amendment to freedom of conscience was apparently insignificant. As I have mentioned several times, Protestant reformers long had equated the free exercise of religion with freedom of conscience. The framers' generation was no different. Freedom of conscience connoted the liberty to follow the dictates of one's conscience to the truth of Jesus Christ, and free exercise meant the same. For example, when approving the original Constitution, the Virginia ratifying convention had recommended the adoption of a Bill of Rights. The proposed religion clause proclaimed that "all men have an equal, natural and unalienable right to the free exercise of religion according to the dictates of conscience."[103] Like their contemporaries, then, Madison and the other members of the first Congress used the terms "free exercise" and "freedom of conscience" interchangeably.[104] I do not mean to suggest that every member of the framers' generation agreed about the implications of freedom of conscience. They did not. For example, most citizens in Massachusetts apparently believed that a general assessment to support Christianity did not violate freedom of conscience, while most Virginians thought otherwise (as revealed during the Virginia disestablishment battle). Despite disagreements about such details, however, almost all Americans broadly understood freedom of conscience (and hence free exercise) as most Protestant reformers since Calvin had understood it: the liberty to follow one's conscience to the truth of Christ.[105]

Quite clearly, then, the adoption of the first amendment religion clauses in no way altered the de facto establishment of Protestantism in America. The first amendment merely reaffirmed the preexisting social, religious, and political arrangements. In protecting the free exercise of religion (that is, freedom of conscience), the first amendment expressly protected the ability of Americans to be Protestant; freedom of conscience was, of course, the central religious orientation of all Protestant denominations. Meanwhile, the establishment clause was rooted largely in four political and religious considerations. First, a national establishment would appear too similar to the repudiated British establishment of the Church of England. Second, contrary to the English approach, the American model of the multiple establishment presumed that local control and choice were appropriate. Hence, insofar as any governments were to impose religious tests or officially impose establishments, the state and local governments—but not the federal government—should do so. Third, Madison and the other framers acknowledged a political reality that Roger Williams and John Locke had stressed long before; the official establishment of religion tends to produce civil strife. In a nation with a plurality of denominations, religious liberty was the means most likely to preserve peace. Finally, the colonial and post-Revolutionary experiences had revealed that Protestantism flourished sufficiently without the official imposition of a church establishment at the national level. To a great extent, Protestantism spread throughout society due to the diffuse social pressure to belong to the faithful. In sum, the free exercise and establishment clauses were intended primarily to reaffirm federal protection of the religious and political well-being of Protestants and their City Upon a Hill (the United States).[106] Any benefit that flowed to non-Protestant religions was merely incidental to the protection of Protestantism; religious toleration of outgroups was, for the most part, a by-product of the predominant thrust of the religion clauses. As Joseph Story, a constitutional scholar and Supreme Court justice, observed early in the nineteenth century, the first amendment was not intended to countenance or advance non-Christian religions such as Judaism.[107]

Hence, in this context of de facto establishment, Congress predictably enacted legislation bolstering Protestant hegemony. The first Congress appointed Protestant chaplains for both the House and the Senate, as well as for the army.[108] Then, in anticipation of George Washington's inauguration as president, both houses of Congress resolved that after the oath of office had been administered, congressional members would accompany Washington "to St. Paul's [Episcopal] Chapel, to hear divine service, performed by the Chaplain of Congress."[109] In addition, Congress resolved that "a Joint Committee of both Houses be directed to wait upon the President ... to request that he would recommend ... a day of Thanksgiving and Prayer, to be observed by acknowledging with grateful hearts the many signal favours of Almighty God."[110] The president complied with Congress's request by "issuing a proclamation breathing a deeply religious spirit."[111] The first Congress also reenacted the Northwest Ordinance of 1787, which contained a type of free exercise provision but simultaneously declared: "Religion, morality, and knowledge being necessary to good government and the happiness of mankind, schools and the means of education shall forever be encouraged."[112] Early Congresses even opened the hall of the House of Representatives for use in Christian services.[113]

To be clear, I do not mean to argue that Congress acted inconsistently or hypocritically by adopting the religion clauses of the first amendment while contemporaneously passing these various measures to bolster Christianity. Rather, most congressional members, as well as other Americans, understood the religious liberty embodied in the free exercise and establishment clauses within the context of the de facto establishment of Protestantism. And within this Protestant-oriented context, the various congressional actions in support of Christianity seemed neither to be extraordinary nor to constitute an official establishment. It bears repeating, then, that Protestantism, of course, remained (and remains) grounded on the New Testament, with its pervasive anti-Jewish imagery. The major American Protestant denominations—the Congregationalists, Baptists, Presbyterians, Methodists, and Episcopalians (derived from the Anglicans)—all followed creeds and confessions based on either the Westminster Confession or the Thirty-nine Articles of Religion, both of which, as already discussed, abounded in antisemitic symbolism.[114] On the whole, then, the framers' generation simply did not make a principled commitment to accord equal respect and freedom to all religions, non-Christian and Christian alike.[115] Yet, on rare occasions, there were exceptional expressions of openness. Most notably, George Washington sent the following message to the Jewish congregation in Newport, Rhode Island:

All [in the United States] possess alike liberty of conscience and immunities of citizenship. It is now no more that toleration is spoken of, as if it was by the indulgence of one class of people, that another enjoyed the exercise of their inherent natural rights. For happily the government of the United States, which gives to bigotry no sanction, to persecution no assistance, requires only that they who live under its protection should demean themselves as good citizens, in giving it on all occasions their effectual support.[116]

Nonetheless, during the late eighteenth century, the de facto Protestant establishment exerted an enormous and persistent pressure to convert on the few Jews living in America, who numbered approximately 1300 to 2000.[117] While early American Jews usually lived more peaceful and free lives than their European co-religionists, American Jews often lost their distinctive religious identity as they "were all but engulfed by their environment."[118] Some Jews drifted to Christianity because of "the sheer weight of [the] majority culture," and many others were subject to intentional (and often unrelenting) proselytization. In fact, for devout Protestant millenarians seeking to usher in the period of latter-day glory, "proselytization of the Jews became something of a social crusade."[119]

All in all, the religion clauses of the first amendment looked radically different when viewed from the position of a religious outgroup, such as the Jews, instead of from the viewpoint of the Protestant majority. From the Protestant perspective, on the one hand, the free exercise clause protected the individual faculty—conscience—needed for a meaningful religious (Christian) experience, and the establishment clause protected against the traditional nemesis (in England) of Protestant freedom of conscience—the national established church. From the Jewish standpoint, on the other hand, the religion clauses failed either to protect the central component of orthodox Judaism or to confront the traditional hazards to Jewish life. The orthodox Jew must follow the mitzvot (which translates as commandments, laws, or good deeds) of the Torah because, with the ethical, social, and ritual injunctions of the mitzvot, God (supposedly) has specified a comprehensive way and content for human fulfillment in this world.[120] But freedom of conscience is primarily an orientation toward other-worldly Christian salvation; hence freedom of conscience, as protected by the free exercise clause, is a Protestant concept that is largely unrelated to a Jewish understanding of a religious life. Meanwhile, the religion clauses offered little protection against the traditional threats to Jewish existence: the Christian masses (or mob) and organized proselytization. Moreover, these threats appeared even more pronounced in a society such as America, where evangelical fervor rippled through the social body, spreading the congregations of the faithful across the land.

Paradoxically, then, the religion clauses of the first amendment may have undermined the ability of American Jews to maintain their religious identity in comparison with, for example, medieval European Jews. As previously discussed, European Jews occasionally turned to the state for protection from the enmity and overreaching of the Christian masses (who often resorted to physical violence). In the United States, Jews less often faced physical violence, but the pressure to convert was nonetheless intense. Yet, with the adoption of the religion clauses, Jews could not turn to the national government for protection from the imperialistic actions of the Christian masses (such as proselytizing). The national government, quite simply, was supposed to remain aloof from religious affairs. The early American Jews, then, had to swallow the bitter irony when the national government itself occasionally acted to reinforce Christian hegemony, regardless of the religion clauses. Indeed, in a democratic republic such as the United States, where the national government theoretically represented the will of "the people," and the people were for the most part the Christian masses themselves, the Jews should have expected no better. With some state governments still restricting voting and public officeholding to Christians and sometimes going further to establish Protestantism or Christianity officially, and with the national government supposedly incapacitated in religious affairs (except for its occasional support for Christianity), the American Jews, a prototypical religious minority, literally had no significant institutional authority to which they could turn for assistance or protection.

With regard to the conceptualization of the state or government, American attitudes had changed in the brief period between the Revolution and the framing of the Constitution. While the elite leaders of the Revolution relied on a Lockean theory of resistance to justify the break from Great Britain, they tended to envision the new American state governments as arising in the civic republican tradition. A decade later, the constitutional framers (many of whom, of course, had been Revolutionary leaders) no longer needed to worry about justifying political resistance against the British monarchy. Furthermore, for uncertain reasons, the framers' vision of government had shifted to a mixture of civic republican and Lockean conceptions. It is worth noting, then, that many civic republican and Lockean themes are not mutually exclusive; instead, they often overlap (as the Opposition Ideology, which had influenced the revolutionaries, had underscored).[121]

To the framers, sovereignty was grounded in the people, as Locke had argued, but the Lockean vision of political society and government arising naturally from some state of nature was unimportant. Rather, the framers maintained the Revolutionary-era concern with the fragility of the democratic republic. In fact, this Machiavellian theme became even more important for the framers. Specifically, the framers retained their devotion to the civic republican motifs of civic virtue and the common good, which became the ideals for the new national government (recall that Locke also had stressed the pursuit of a common good).[122] But from the perspective of the framers, the governmental experiences in the states during the 1780s had revealed that, too often, citizens and officials lacked a virtuous commitment to the common good. Thus, while acknowledging that Americans were virtuous enough to have self-government,[123] Publius (the pseudonym of the authors of the Federalist Papers) often characterized humans as base and greedy creatures who tend to band into factions that constantly threaten the ends and security of republican government.[124] As with Machiavelli, then, the framers' conception of human nature can be understood as marking a pragmatic political realism, but simultaneously, it resonated with the Christian emphases on original sin and human depravity. Following in this Machiavellian tradition, the framers sought to construct a constitutional government that would strain toward the civic republican ideals of virtue and the common good but would simultaneously protect against the self-interested political machinations of factional groups. The purpose of the Constitution, in other words, became the structuring of a stable government that would act for the public good despite the (supposed) ignobleness of human nature and the resultant fragility of the republic.[125] Madison captured the framers' strained conjunction of hope and cynicism in The Federalist, Number 57:

> The aim of every political constitution is, or ought to be, first to obtain for rulers men who possess most wisdom to discern, and most virtue to pursue, the common good of the society; and in the next place, to take the most effectual precautions for keeping them virtuous whilst they continue to hold their public trust.[126]

The framers' Machiavellian concern with the fragility of the new republic actually led them to stress certain Lockean (and also Harringtonian) themes. Whereas the Revolutionaries had emphasized a civic republican form of liberty that stressed citizen participation in government, the framers were more wary of potential democratic excesses and governmental corruptions.[127] Thus, the new Constitution shifted power from the democratic republican state governments to the new national government, but then the Constitution attempted to limit the ability of the national government to exercise its potential power. Many of the structural provisions of the Constitution—separation of powers, checks and balances, bicameralism, federalism—tended to encumber the exercise of power by the national government. The framers, in this sense, had shifted toward a more Lockean vision (recall, though, that Harrington also had argued that sovereign power should be constitutionally limited): the framers sought to preserve preexisting individual rights from governmental infringement by limiting governmental power. Whereas the revolutionaries stressed individual liberty within the context of governmental participation, the framers generally understood individual liberty as freedom from governmental interference.[128] And, not coincidentally, the framers followed Locke by stressing the protection of an individual's right to accumulate property and wealth (once again, though, Harrington also sought to prevent supposed overreaching by the poor). Thus, the framers sought to prevent the enactment of extreme debtor relief laws, as well as the eruption of popular economically spurred insurrections such as Shays's Rebellion. More broadly, the framers also intended the new interstate commerce clause to spur business activity and boost the national economy.[129]

At least four additional elements of the Harringtonian (civic republican) tradition were significant in this context. First, while the framers sought to protect the accumulation of wealth, one reason democracy worked in America was that land ownership was widespread. Over a century earlier, Harrington had argued that a wide distribution of property would support a republic, and, in fact, widespread land ownership in America fostered a level of equality and democracy then unattainable in other parts of the world.[130] Second, with regard to democracy, the framers agreed with Harrington that not all individuals belonged to the "people." According to the framers, many individuals—particularly women and African American slaves—were barred justifiably from participating in democracy.[131] Third, the framers followed Harringtonian thought by positing that the way to ensure good government—that is, government that would supposedly pursue the common good and not seek to violate individual rights, including the right to accumulate wealth—was by building proper constitutional structures, not by relying on the virtue of governmental officials.[132] Fourth, some of the framers undoubtedly believed that they were "founding a republic in an extra-historical and legislative moment."[133] Despite the fragility of most republics, these framers (like Harrington) thought that a properly constructed republic could escape the shifting fortunes of secular time. The United States, from this viewpoint, was "the righteous empire," the Christian City of God on Earth.[134] It is worth noting, then, that the framers can be understood as conservative modernists: they believed in a human ability to structure human relations in government (through a constitution), but they certainly did not intend to transform American society radically (and as mentioned, Madison himself doubted the likely efficacy of a constitutional effort to do so).

The adoption of the Constitution, as already discussed, did not significantly alter the understanding of the relation between church and state, regardless of the changes in the conceptualization of American government. Indeed, in terms of the separation of church and state, the framers merely continued a combination of civic republican and Lockean themes that had long dominated American thought. Similar to Locke, the framers sought to protect freedom of conscience and to enforce official disestablishment (at the national level).[135] Yet, also like Locke, the framers and other Americans assumed the de facto establishment of Protestantism. Indeed, most Americans still believed that Protestantism would help imbue individuals with civic virtue, thus making them good republican citizens. To be sure, individuals disagreed about whether official church establishments at the state level would foster or hinder Christianity. Nonetheless, almost all (Protestant) Americans assumed that the spread of Protestantism, whether through de facto or official establishment, was healthy for the republic. George Washington's farewell address underscored this common assumption: "Of all the dispositions and habits which lead to political prosperity, religion and morality are indispensable supports. . . . And let us with caution indulge the supposition that morality can be maintained without religion."[136]

Finally, the framers' acceptance of (at a minimum) the de facto establishment of Protestantism suggests that they implicitly followed the boundary-oriented imagery that flows from Calvinist theology and that emerged so distinctly in Locke's and Roger Williams's writings. As previously discussed, this imagery rested on a sharp distinction between a sphere of Christian spirituality and a sphere of Jewish carnality, and the related New Testament injunction against using temporal force located in the carnal sphere to compel Jewish movement to the Christian spiritual sphere. In light of this implicit antisemitic symbolism, as well as the framers' advocacy of the free exercise and establishment clauses, two sets of boundaries seemed important to the framers as they understood the national government. First, the Protestant faculty of conscience existed in a private realm that needed to remain free of federal governmental interference. Christian faith, in effect, can flourish only in a private sphere insulated from public (including national governmental) coercion. This first boundary orientation—distinguishing between the private realm of Protestant conscience and the public realm of national governmental action—was grounded most clearly in the antisemitic imagery of the New Testament. Second, and more a matter of mere political expediency, the national government was to avoid the state-controlled realm of official establishments; the federal government was to remain aloof from decisions regarding the legal establishment of Protestantism or Christianity (though the national government could act occasionally to bolster Christian hegemony).

CHAPTER 8

The Fruits of the Framing

Church and State in Nineteenth- and Early-Twentieth-Century America

THE NINETEENTH CENTURY

The Development of Church and State

If the American Revolution took a "monarchical, hierarchy-ridden" society and propelled it toward democracy, then the Constitution at least partially altered the national route.[1] The framers, while not repudiating democracy, sought to protect against its supposed excesses. Hence, as already discussed, the Constitution shifted power from the states to the federal government but simultaneously introduced various mechanisms intended to encumber the national government. Even with the Constitution in place, however, several factors combined to keep the United States moving in its generally democratic direction, albeit along an adjusted pathway. Regardless of the new constitutional scheme and regardless of the economic class structures in American society, many Americans accepted the idea of democracy in government that had emerged so strongly during the Revolution. Thus, even though America was not truly or fully democratic, many Americans seemed to accept a democratic ideology. And in the end, the social reality began (at least) to move closer to the ideology. Gordon Wood argues (perhaps overzealously) that the new Constitution may have been "meant to temper popular majoritarianism, but no constitution, no institutional arrangements, no judicial prohibitions could have restrained the popular social forces unleashed by the Revolution." The decades of the late eighteenth and early nineteenth centuries saw "the rise of ordinary people."[2]

One important factor driving the further democratization of America was the pursuit of wealth. Economic self-interest was richly mixed into the glue that held Americans together: quite simply, most Americans united in their overwhelming commitment to commerce and the rapid accumulation of personal wealth. This burst of self-interested economic activity coincided, not incidentally, with the coming of the Industrial Revolution to America (particularly to the Northeast). The transition in the American economy was startling: in 1800, 83 percent of the labor force was in agriculture, but by 1860, only 53 percent remained similarly occupied. By 1850, the value of manufactured goods surpassed for the first time that of agricultural production. Significantly, this economic development was linked intimately to governmental democracy: on the one hand, government supported economic development; on the other hand, economic opportunism seemed to reinforce democratic government.[3]

Governmental support for commercial development in the early nineteenth century rarely took the forms of direct cash subsidies or legislative programs administered through the state and federal executive branches. Indeed, during this period, the legislative and executive governmental institutions frequently remained stagnant and sometimes even receded, but significant exceptions existed, often in the building of the infrastructure (roads, canals, railroads, docks, and so on). Most notably, in 1817, the New York legislature authorized the building of the Erie Canal, connecting the Atlantic Ocean with the Great Lakes; after the completion of the canal, freight rates between New York and Buffalo dropped by over 90 percent, sharply spurring the economy. Overall, however, direct taxes and overt governmental cash outlays were extremely unpopular. In Massachusetts, for example, the state budget remained constant at approximately $133,000 from 1795 to 1820.[4] More broadly, "American governmental expenditures in relation to gross national product ran five or six times less than those of European nations."[5]

Nevertheless, the federal and state governments found other ways to promote economic development. For instance, starting in the late eighteenth century, legislatures often granted franchises to encourage capital investments in risky commercial ventures. These franchises were initially understood to protect against competition, but as the nineteenth century wore on, the courts recognized that economic conditions were changing significantly. In response, the courts began to interpret the franchises as little more than grants to compete against other grantees.[6] More broadly, the state and federal courts developed other policies in the form of common law rules that sparked commercial activity and economic development. For instance, during the nineteenth century, the courts transformed the common law conception of property: whereas the earlier conception of property allowed owners to prevent others from injuring their property, the later conception allowed owners to do with their property whatever they desired, regardless of the effects on others. The courts, in other words, developed rules that protected property owners from potential liabilities for damages caused by efforts to develop their property for commercial purposes. Property became, in effect, an "institution of growth."[7] In another example, in the well-known case of *Swift v. Tyson*, decided in 1842, the U.S. Supreme Court held that the federal courts should decide commercial cases based on a general federal common law that implicitly would be directed toward promoting economic activity.[8]

The advance of commercial activity, supported by these and other governmental actions, seemed in turn to reinforce democratic government. Indeed, to many Americans, the pursuit of self-interest and money making was understood as "egalitarian and democratic." "If everyone in the society was involved in moneymaking and exchanging," Gordon Wood writes, "then to that extent they were all alike, all seeking their own individual interests and happiness."[9] And throughout the early nineteenth century, democratic government and political equality unquestionably expanded to some extent. At the time of the constitutional framing, most states allowed only white males who owned property to vote, but by 1825, every state but three had extended the franchise to all white males. Equally important, the first half of the nineteenth century saw the dramatic growth of populist mass politics. Beginning roughly with the Jacksonian Democrats in the late 1820s, political parties started to organize and develop systematic methods for appealing to the common "man" for the purpose of turning out the vote. In fact, the participation rate of those eligible to vote increased dramatically: between 1824 and 1840, the population grew by 57 percent, but the number of eligible voters casting a ballot in the presidential elections in those years increased by 700 percent![10]

Moreover, for the growing number of enfranchised white males, there existed at least an abstract or formal right to pursue wealth on an equal basis with other white males. In fact, between 1800 and 1860, the standard of living of the average family improved meaningfully as the gross national product per capita more than doubled. In the industrializing states of the Northeast, for example, "the range of goods and services available to ordinary consumers increased strikingly," and the economy expanded sufficiently so that the poor actually had greater purchasing power in 1860 than at the turn of the nineteenth century. In the middle of the century, the ordinary white male could choose to purchase items—clothes, books, food, newspapers—that were unavailable in such variety or quality fifty years earlier.[11]

Yet, at the same time, inequalities in American society were sharp and deep. Suffrage was still limited to white males—no women, no African Americans, and no Native Americans. Even among white males, the right to vote did not necessarily translate into effective political power, particularly because economic inequalities were increasing. An abstract right of equal opportunity to pursue wealth did not lead to even remotely egalitarian economic consequences. As Morton Horwitz observes, the legal changes promoting commercial activity did not randomly or neutrally spur economic development, but rather distributed wealth and resources in a particular and systematic manner. Namely, the legal transformation "enabled emergent entrepreneurial and commercial groups to win a disproportionate share of wealth and power in American society."[12] Thus, somewhat predictably, the largest share of the burden for economic development fell upon the already disenfranchised, enslaved, and otherwise disempowered members of society. Hence, although the poor gained greater wealth as the nineteenth century progressed, the gap between the rich and the poor was rapidly widening as the richest 10 percent of American society reaped a constantly increasing share of the wealth.[13] In sum, even though many early-nineteenth-century Americans believed that equality reigned, the unequal distribution of wealth in American society actually increased after the Revolution. The idea (or imagery) of equality and democracy did not match the (albeit) complex social reality.[14]

The economic and democratic drives of the early nineteenth century were intimately linked with the further development of American Protestantism—particularly in the Second Great Awakening. Just as in the eighteenth century, when the movement toward democracy spread from evangelical Protestantism to government, during the nineteenth century the democratic movement in government spread to Protestantism. The first Great Awakening had partially democratized Protestantism, and the Second Great Awakening, in the first half of the 1800s, continued this populist movement, significantly deepening the democratization of American Christianity. In so doing, American society—rather remarkably—became even more Christian. Nathan Hatch argues that the "wave of popular religious movements that broke upon the United States in the half century after independence did more to Christianize American society than anything before or since."[15] Indeed, by including African Americans and women, these religious movements surpassed the populism then present in American government.[16] Between 1800 and 1835, church membership nearly doubled, and if we account for the Americans who were churchgoers but not official members, then fully 75 percent of the population was attending church.[17]

In a sense, the idea and culture of American democracy drove the common people to infuse Protestantism with their populist ideology. In particular, the Calvinist concept of predestination—the pre-selection of a chosen few for salvation—appeared inconsistent with the prevalent idea of democracy. In nineteenth-century America, salvation seemingly had to be readily available to the common person; in this important way, then, Arminianism prevailed over Calvinism.[18] Nonetheless, American Protestantism remained committed to many traditional Calvinist concepts: a focus on Scripture, faith in Christ, freedom of conscience, and the notion that good works alone could not earn salvation.[19] This last point—diminishing the value of good works—was rooted, of course, in the dogmatic New Testament opposition of Christian spirituality to Jewish carnality. If salvation, though, could not be attained through good works yet was nevertheless to be readily available, then *how* was salvation to be achieved? The answer was populist and individualist: the ordinary individual can *choose* salvation.

Hence, whereas early Protestant creeds and confessions did not advert to an individual's freedom to choose salvation,[20] nineteenth-century American confessions started to do so explicitly and implicitly. For example, a Baptist Confession from 1833 declared that "all mankind are now sinners, not by constraint, but choice." That Confession continued: "[N]othing prevents the salvation of the greatest sinner on earth but his own inherent depravity and voluntary rejection of the gospel."[21] Another Baptist Confession maintained that "God has endowed man with power of free choice ... and this power of free choice is the exact measure of his responsibility." This latter Confession added that "salvation is rendered equally possible to all; and if any fail of eternal life, the fault is wholly their own."[22] The Presbyterians' *Auburn Declaration* of 1837 stated that "all such as reject the Gospel of Christ do it, not by coercion, but freely, and all who embrace it do it not by coercion, but freely."[23]

This evangelical focus on the individual's freedom to choose salvation implicitly changed the Protestant concept of freedom of conscience. Before the 1800s, freedom of conscience had denoted the freedom of individuals to follow the dictates of their conscience to the truth of Jesus Christ. Conscience did not connote choice but rather conviction, so individual religious freedom entailed no more than following one's convictions; it did not include any notion of choosing freely among various options. But as the democratized American Protestantism of the nineteenth century increasingly emphasized individual freedom of choice as a central component in a Christian life, the conception of freedom of conscience was necessarily transformed to include individual choice. To be sure, freedom of conscience still encompassed the original Protestant notion of following the dictates of one's conscience to Christ, but now, it seemed, the individual also must be free to choose whether to have faith in Christ—free to choose eternal salvation. As William G. McLoughlin observes, the evangelicals believed that "[a]ll men share a common sense or consciousness of their freedom to choose, and it is this feeling that we are free which constitutes our sense of moral responsibility."[24]

The choice to be saved by having faith in Jesus was, by many accounts, accompanied by a sudden Christian conversion experience. Whereas early American Puritans understood the conversion experience to be the culmination of a long and arduous process, the evangelical Protestants of the Second Awakening viewed the conversion experience as within easy reach. Conversion, in a sense, "became a shared act, a complementary relationship" between God and the individual: conversion ultimately remained supposedly the work of God, but the evangelicals' focus was on the individual's contribution.[25] And the individual was required to do little more than declare a belief in Christ. For example, the *Reformed Episcopal Articles of Religion* declared that the "sinner comes to Christ through no labored process of repenting and sorrowing; but he comes to Christ and repentance both at once, by means of simply believing."[26] Meanwhile, a Presbyterian minister, Barton W. Stone, stated: "We urged upon the sinner to believe now, and receive salvation—that in vain they looked for the Spirit to be given them, while they remained in unbelief … that no previous qualification was required, or necessary in order to believe in Jesus, and come to him."[27] The Methodists and Baptists—rapidly expanding to become the dominant Protestant sects—especially underscored that each individual could choose salvation, which was promised to be "imminently accessible and immediately available."[28] Indeed, one could fairly conclude that the salvation of each individual soul through a conversion experience became the be-all and end-all of Protestantism in the nineteenth century.[29]

Consequently, evangelical ministers of the Second Great Awakening were populist leaders seeking to appeal to the common people, hoping to provoke conversions by any means possible. Revivals in camp meetings, for instance, were a successful instrument for recruiting large numbers of ordinary people.[30] Revivalist preachers often sought to appeal to the raw religious emotions of their audiences. One Methodist minister, for example, declared that "the power of God was strong upon me. I turned ... and losing sight of fear of man, I went through the house shouting and exhorting with all possible ecstacy and energy."[31] The evangelical preachers also encouraged individuals to seek inspiration for themselves through the Scriptures. Indeed, the Second Awakening was broadly infused with an anti-intellectual and anti-elitist spirit. Ordinary Christians did not want university-trained clergy to lead the flock or to question the significance of their religious experiences. Common sense seemed more reliable "than the judgment of an educated few."[32] Thus, according to this viewpoint, ordinary people could read the Christian Bible without the benefit of officially sanctioned interpretation. One preacher declared that the "scriptures ... were designed for the great mass of mankind and are in general adapted to their capacities."[33] The doctrinal articles of the Evangelical Alliance, a cross-denominational association of Protestants, emphasized the "right and duty of private judgment in the interpretation of the Holy Scriptures."[34] Yet, many Americans still were illiterate, especially in the western states, such as Kentucky and Tennessee. Hence the crucial Christian experience always was the individual's conversion—the sudden and immediate burst of Christian faith. Hatch summarizes the populist element of the Second Awakening:

> America's nonrestrictive environment permitted an unexpected and often explosive conjunction of evangelical fervor and popular sovereignty. It was this engine that accelerated the process of Christianization within American popular culture, allowing indigenous expressions of faith to take hold among ordinary people, white and black. This expansion of evangelical Christianity did not proceed primarily from the nimble response of religious elites meeting the challenge before them. Rather, Christianity was effectively reshaped by common people who molded it in their own image and who threw themselves into expanding its influence. Increasingly assertive common people wanted their leaders unpretentious, their doctrines self-evident and down-to-earth, their music lively and singable, and their churches in local hands. It was this upsurge of democratic hope that characterized so many religious cultures in the early republic and brought Baptists, Methodists, Disciples of Christ, and a host of other insurgent groups to the fore. The rise of evangelical Christianity in the early republic is, in some measure, a story of the success of common people in shaping the culture after their own priorities rather than the priorities outlined by gentlemen such as the framers of the Constitution.[35]

One of the central figures in the Second Awakening was Charles Grandison Finney. Finney initially brought the Awakening to upstate New

York in the 1820s, starting the three decades of revivalism in the so-called burned-over district of New York, but even more important, he brought the revivals to major urban centers. A former lawyer, he appealed not only to the common person but also to the upper class and the growing middle class, including "lawyers, real-estate magnates, millers, manufacturers, and commercial tycoons."[36] To a great extent, Finney's views epitomized the central themes of the Second Awakening. In describing his own Christian experiences, he emphasized reading the Bible and his own mind or conscience.[37] To Finney, holiness was "voluntary and conversion a matter of personal choice more than divine action."[38] Salvation, in other words, was a simple matter: the individual chooses to accept Christ. Finney wrote:

> Gospel salvation seemed to me to be an offer of something to be accepted: and that it was full and complete; and that all that was necessary on my part, was to get my own consent to give up my sins, and accept Christ. Salvation, it seemed to me, instead of being a thing wrought out, by my own works, was a thing to be found entirely in the Lord Jesus Christ, who presented himself before me as my god and Saviour.[39]

As salvation appeared to become little more than a matter of individual choice, churches were forced increasingly to compete for converts and adherents. The individual not only could choose whether or not to believe in Christ and achieve salvation, but also could choose to join the most appealing denomination. Jon Butler observes that "to be religious in America was not only to make choices, but to choose among astonishing varieties of religion created in America and duplicated nowhere else."[40] With individuals freely switching churches, the already fragmented American Protestantism splintered into even more denominations. For instance, in his 1844 book *Religion in America,* Robert Baird mentioned, among others, Protestant Episcopalians, Moravians, Orthodox Congregational churches, Regular Baptists, Free-Will Baptists, Seventh Day Baptists, Disciples of Christ (or Campbellites), Winebrennarians, Old School Presbyterians, New School Presbyterians, Cumberland Presbyterians, Dutch Reformed Presbyterians, Reformed Presbyterians, Associate Synod Presbyterians, Associate Reformed Presbyterians, Lutherans, Methodist Episcopalians, Protestant Methodists, and Welsh Calvinistic Methodists.[41] The religious field resembled a bustling marketplace, with revivalists and churches competing for adherents, looking for the quick sale, and seeking to build memberships. In this atmosphere, the advantage of offering fast and easy salvation was obvious. Preachers, furthermore, were not above denouncing their competitors, and some groups even attacked and destroyed the meeting houses of others.[42]

The significance of these Protestant sectarian divisions, however, can be easily misunderstood. While Protestant denominations competed against each other for adherents, in so doing they often developed methods that ultimately left them stronger, more resilient, and even larger. While some of these methods were populist, such as camp meetings and offers of quick salvation, other methods were undemocratic and inegalitarian. Within particular sects, the entire church or movement sometimes arose from and rested on the charismatic authority of one individual.[43] More broadly, within American society at large, the pressure to be Protestant was intense, coercive, and institutionalized. Butler writes:

> [Denominational leaders] were concerned to shape American society and culture, not merely to manage the mundane day-to-day behavior of individuals. They were not egalitarians. They were more willing and eager to change the fundamental beliefs and behavior of whole peoples than to question their own assumptions and actions. They were frequently intolerant. They spread the desire for authority and power to unprecedented numbers of people through religious institutions whose sophistication and prowess matched and probably exceeded that of medieval Catholicism.[44]

As much as anyone, Finney exemplified this authoritative and coercive attitude: "[M]ultitudes will never yield, until the friends of God and man can form a public sentiment so strong as to crush the character of every man who will not give it up. [Many individuals will not change] until you can form a public sentiment so powerful as to force them to it."[45]

Consequently, the American culture, society, and people became even more heavily Christianized than they had been before. Within this context, freedom of religious choice existed, but it was a freedom to choose among the various Protestant denominations. To be non-Protestant—atheist, agnostic, Jewish, or even Roman Catholic—was not a choice, or at least not a choice easily made or readily accessible. Among the competing Protestant sects, one goal was universally accepted and pursued: to further Christianize America. In 1847, Horace Bushnell wrote:

> The wilderness shall bud and blossom as the rose before us; and we will not cease till a christian nation throws up its temples of worship on every hill and plain; till knowledge, virtue and religion, blending their dignity and their healthful power, have filled our great country with a manly and happy race of people, and the bands of a complete christian commonwealth are seen to span the continent.[46]

Throughout the nineteenth century, Protestants developed a variety of techniques to advance the Christianization of America. Significantly, one technique that was *not* used was the official establishment of religion. To the contrary, the movement toward eliminating the official establishment of Christianity—characteristic of the Revolutionary and early national periods—continued at the state level during the late eighteenth and early nineteenth centuries. For example, the 1790 South Carolina Constitution allowed the state to continue to incorporate churches but provided no public tax support for them. The 1798 Georgia Constitution completely erased the state's multiple establishment. The New England states of Massachusetts, Connecticut, New Hampshire, and Vermont clung most tenaciously to their official establishments, with Massachusetts being the final state to eliminate its official establishment in 1833.[47]

Thus, the revivalism of the Second Great Awakening spread across America even as states repudiated the official establishment of religion. The movement toward official disestablishment, in other words, occurred within the context of the continuing and deepening de facto establishment of Protestantism. Protestant hegemony reigned. Unsurprisingly, then, despite the elimination of governmental financial support for churches, the states continued to support Christianity explicitly and implicitly in many other ways. Joseph Story, a constitutional scholar and Supreme Court justice, considered himself a strong advocate for the separation of church and state, yet in 1833 he observed:

> [I]t is impossible for those, who believe in the truth of Christianity, as a divine revelation, to doubt, that it is the especial duty of government to foster, and encourage it among all the citizens and subjects. This is a point wholly distinct from that of the right of private judgment in matters of religion, and of the freedom of public worship according to the dictates of one's conscience.[48]

The North Carolina Constitution of 1776, for instance, had repudiated the official state establishment but simultaneously had limited public office-holding to those individuals who accepted "the truth of the Protestant religion."[49] This provision, as amended in 1835 to allow all Christians to hold public office, remained in effect until 1868.[50] Meanwhile, in Connecticut, the Constitution of 1818 ended state-coerced financial support for churches but at the same time declared that "each and every society or denomination of *Christians* shall have and enjoy the same and equal powers, rights, and privileges." The explicit preference for Christianity was included only after extensive debate during the state constitutional convention. This constitutional provision added, moreover, that the Christian denominations themselves could "tax" their members.[51]

In New Hampshire, political advantage, not principled commitment to religious liberty and toleration, led to the passage in 1819 of a *Toleration Act* that terminated public tax support for churches. At that point, though, the state constitution still retained its restriction on public officeholding; only Protestants could serve as legislators or as the governor. In fact, the state lifted this restriction by constitutional amendment only in 1877.[52] Even at that date, the New Hampshire Constitution retained explicit preferences for Protestants and Christians. The state's Bill of Rights provided as follows: first, the legislature could authorize local "support and maintenance of public protestant teachers of piety, religion, and morality"; second, "every denomination of Christians ... shall be equally under the protection of the law." These provisions were not amended until 1968 (that's right, 1968; this is not a misprint)![53]

A telling incident occurred in South Carolina in 1844. The governor, James H. Hammond, issued a Thanksgiving proclamation that referred to the United States as one of the "christian nations" and that invited "our Citizens of all denominations to Assemble at their respective places of worship to offer up their devotions to God the Creator, and his Son Jesus Christ, the redeemer of the world." Over 100 Jews from Charleston, South Carolina, signed a letter to the governor protesting the Christian bias of his proclamation. Hammond responded bluntly:

> The simple truth is, that at the time of writing my Proclamation it did not occur to me, that there might be Israelites [Jews], Deists, Atheists, or any other class of persons in the State who denied the divinity of Jesus Christ. [But] as you force me to speak, it is due to candour to say, that had I been fully on my guard, I do not think I should have changed the language of my Proclamation! and that I have no apology to make for it now.... I must say that up to this time, I have always thought it a settled matter that I lived in a Christian land! And that I was the temporary chief magistrate of a Christian people.... And whatever may be the language of Proclamation and of Constitution, I know that the civilization of the age is derived from Christianity, that the institutions of this country are instinct with the same spirit, and that it pervades the laws of the State as it does the manners and I trust the hearts of our people.... But if, inheriting the same scorn for Jesus Christ which instigated their ancestors to crucify him, they [that is, the Jews of Charleston] would have felt themselves degraded and disgraced in obeying my exhortation to worship their 'Creator,' because I had also recommended the adoration of his 'Son the Redeemer,' still I would not have hesitated to appoint for them, had it been requested, a special day of Thanksgiving according to their own creed. This, however, was not, I imagine, what the Israelites desired. They wished to be included in the same invitation to public devotion with the Christians! And to make that invitation acceptable to them,

I must strike out the corner-stone of the Christian creed, and reduce the whole to entire conformity with that of the Israelites; I must exhort a Christian People to worship after the manner of the Jews.[54]

Hammond's candid response neatly epitomized the Protestant hegemony in America. First, he admitted that he initially had not realized that any non-Christians lived in the state. Second, once he learned that some Jews lived there, Hammond adamantly reasserted that America and South Carolina were Christian lands. Third, he reiterated standard New Testament anti-semitism: the Jews were responsible for Jesus' death. Fourth, he assumed that if he had failed to favor Christianity explicitly in his proclamation, he would have been discriminating against Christians and favoring Jews. In other words, to Hammond, the notion that America was a Christian nation was normal and natural—the baseline from which to measure. Hence, a fail-ure to favor Christianity expressly amounted to a drop below the baseline, a strike against Christians, a discriminatory act in favor of Jews. Hammond understood his original proclamation, then, as neutral and non-discrimina-tory exactly because it favored Christianity.

Jewish rights per se became a controversial political issue in Maryland early in the nineteenth century.[55] The state constitution of 1776 had imposed a test oath for public office, restricting officeholders to those individuals declaring their "belief in the Christian religion."[56] As early as 1797, a Jewish resident, petitioning the state legislature, had requested that this state-imposed restriction be lifted. That request and subsequent ones were rejected until the matter came to a head in 1818. A new so-called Jew bill had been introduced in the state legislature, and when that bill was defeated, another was introduced at the very next legislative session. These bills sparked a major political dispute. Some Jeffersonians (Democratic Republicans) argued that the state Constitution should not expressly discriminate against Jews and instead should parallel the national Constitution.[57] But, simultaneously, the bills provoked a loud Protestant reactionary outburst. Protestant journals and legislators warned that passage of the Jew bill "would cause a massive influx of Jews as well as the establishment of Judaism as the state religion."[58] When Thomas Kennedy, the main sponsor of the bills, ran for reelection to the legislature in 1823, his opponent, Benjamin Galloway, labeled Kennedy the head of the "Jewish ticket." Galloway, calling himself the head of the "Christian ticket," issued a handbill that declared:

I hold [the Jew bill] to be no more nor less than an attempt to undervalue, and by so doing, to bring into popular contempt, the Christian religion.

Preferring, as I do, Christianity to Judaism, Deism, Unitarianism, or any other sort of new fangled ism, I deprecate any change in our State government, calculated to afford the least chance to the enemies of Christianity.[59]

Galloway's tactics worked: although Kennedy was a Jeffersonian running in a Jeffersonian stronghold, Galloway won the election. In fact, fifteen other candidates opposing passage of the Jew bill also defeated incumbents. In any event, Kennedy was reelected for the next legislative session, and in 1826 he finally was able to get the Jew bill enacted.[60] Pursuant to this final bill, the state Constitution retained its explicitly Christian test oath, but Jews now would be excepted. Jews would be allowed to hold office so long as they declared a "belief in a future state of rewards and punishments."[61]

Even when a state no longer had any official Christian establishment and had purged its constitution of religious restrictions on voting and public officeholding, state common law and statutes usually continued to impose legal liabilities on Jews and other non-Christians and to otherwise bolster Christian hegemony. Indeed, Martin E. Marty notes that Protestants yielded rather easily on issues such as public officeholding exactly because "they had so much else working in their favor."[62] In the early nineteenth century, for example, Jews could practice law in only four states (Pennsylvania, Virginia, South Carolina, and New York), and in Georgia only judges and Christian ministers could perform marriage ceremonies.[63] More broadly, throughout the nineteenth century (and indeed into the twentieth), leading jurists, such as Joseph Story and James Kent, and many others considered Christianity to be part of the common law.[64] Thus, numerous states enforced the Christian sabbath of Sunday as part of the common law (some states enacted blue laws). This imperialistic practice was bothersome for most Jews but particularly burdensome for those who were in business and also observed the Jewish sabbath on Saturday; unlike their Christian neighbors (and competitors), these Jews needed to close their businesses for two days instead of one.[65] In an 1846 case, a state court rather typically upheld the conviction of a Jew for selling gloves on Sunday. The court wrote:

> The Lord's day, the day of the Resurrection, is to us who are called Christians, the day of rest after finishing a new creation. It is the day of the first visible triumph over death, hell and the grave.... On that day we rest and to us it is the Sabbath of the Lord—its decent observance in a Christian community, is that which ought to be expected.[66]

The court then gratuitously added that religious freedom was due to Christian mercy and love.[67]

State courts also consistently upheld laws prohibiting blasphemy against Christianity.[68] In the New York case of *People v. Ruggles,* decided in 1811, the state's highest court upheld the constitutionality of a common law criminal conviction of Ruggles for committing blasphemy. Ruggles had said that "Jesus Christ was a bastard, and his mother must be a whore." Chancellor Kent, writing the opinion in the case, maintained "that we are a christian people, and the morality of the country is deeply ingrafted upon christianity." Thus, Kent reasoned, the state could punish blasphemy against Christ without similarly punishing blasphemies under other religions.[69] Ruggles "was sentenced to three months in jail and fined $500." Ten years later, the members of a New York State constitutional convention voted to confirm the propriety of the *Ruggles* decision and Kent's reasoning.[70]

State governments were not alone in bolstering Christian hegemony. The federal government also continued occasionally throughout the nineteenth century to directly support Christianity. For example, the government negotiated several treaties that expressly recognized and protected Christianity. An 1850 commercial treaty with Switzerland contained the following provision: "Christians alone are entitled to the enjoyment of privileges guaranteed by the present Article in the Swiss Cantons."[71] An 1858 treaty with China provided:

> The principles of the Christian religion as professed by the Protestant and Roman Catholic churches, are recognized as teaching men to do good; and to do to others as they would have others do to them. Hereafter, those who quietly profess and teach these doctrines shall not be harassed or persecuted on account of their faith. Any person [in China], whether citizen of the United States or Chinese convert, who according to these tenets peaceably teach and practise the principles of Christianity, shall in no case be interfered with or molested.[72]

Meanwhile, the U.S. Supreme Court decided *Vidal v. Girard's Executors* in 1844. This case focused on the will of Girard, who bequeathed his sizable estate for the purpose of creating a school for orphans and impoverished scholars. The will included the following limitation: "[N]o ecclesiastic, missionary, or minister of any sect whatsoever, shall ever hold or exercise any station or duty whatever in the said college; nor shall any such person ever be admitted for any purpose ... within the premises ... of the said college." The will was challenged as being hostile to Christianity and therefore contrary to the common law of Pennsylvania, where Girard had resided. In upholding the validity of the will, the Court acknowledged that "Christianity [is] a part of the common law of the state [of Pennsylvania in the sense] that its divine origin and truth are admitted, and therefore it is not to be maliciously and openly reviled and blasphemed against, to the annoyance of believers or the injury of the public." Significantly, the Court did not see any tension between, on the one hand, having the state common law encompass Christianity and, on the other hand, having a state constitution that included disestablishment and free exercise clauses. Not yet satisfied, the Court added that Judaism is a form of "infidelity"; therefore, a devise in support of Judaism might contravene the common law. The Court, however, did not conclusively decide this question because it was not raised by the facts of the case and, in the words of Justice Story, "[s]uch a case is not to be presumed to exist in a Christian country."[73]

In another nineteenth-century case, *Church of the Holy Trinity v. United States,* decided in 1892, the Supreme Court broadly declared in a unanimous opinion that "this is a Christian nation." In this case, a church had contracted for an English citizen to come to America as the church's rector and pastor, but a federal statute prohibited entering into contracts with aliens to encourage their immigration. The issue was whether this particular contract contravened the federal statute. The Court held that the statute did not prohibit the contract because the Congress of the United States, a Christian nation, could not have intended to prohibit contracting with Christian ministers. Congressional intent was to prohibit the importation of cheap, unskilled laborers—many of whom were non-Christians—because they were disrupting the American labor market. Thus, the Court concluded with an incredulous rhetorical question: "[S]hall it be believed that a congress of the United States intended to make it a misdemeanor for a church of this country to contract for the services of a Christian minister residing in another nation?"[74]

Protestant domination of America was furthered in many ways beyond state and federal governmental actions. One of the most important methods was through the creation and action of cross-denominational voluntary societies. For example, the American Temperance Society, formed in 1826, initially promoted temperate drinking but soon demanded abstinence. The American Sunday School Union, created in 1824, devoted itself to establishing a Sunday school in every town in America for the purpose of indoctrinating children in the ways of American Protestantism. Such voluntary societies, with most members drawn from the mainstream Protestant denominations, typically sought to impose Protestant values and to encourage capitalist economic activities—which seemed to go hand in hand. The imposition of Protestant values was equated with the eradication of Protestant vices, like gambling and the drinking of alcohol, which interfered with more worthy pursuits, such as the accumulation of wealth. Dwight L. Moody, a post–Civil War evangelist, stated that "men and women saved by the blood of Jesus rarely remain subjects of charity, but rise at once to comfort and respectability."[75] Hence, as Gordon Wood writes, the evangelical reformers "wanted to awaken the moral sense of the people, and they hoped to do this by rewarding industry and good behavior and punishing laziness and bad habits."[76]

The proliferation of voluntary societies eventually combined with other factors—particularly immigration and the Civil War—to lead to an organized Protestant effort to amend the Constitution. Throughout the nineteenth century, most Americans were satisfied with the de facto establishment of Protestantism, although preachers occasionally lamented the lack of an explicit constitutional acknowledgment of Jesus Christ. Yet, the makeup of the national population began to change during the middle decades of the century. Whereas in the 1820s fewer than 5000 immigrants per year entered the United States, over the next three decades the numbers dramatically increased, so that by the 1850s more than 280,000 immigrants per year arrived. So many of these immigrants settled in Northeastern cities that Americans dating back to the so-called colonial stock fell into the minority in a few urban centers.[77] It was during these decades that Jews first started emigrating to the United States in substantial numbers. In 1820, fewer than 4000 Jews lived in this country; Jews were so scarce that in 1817 a farm woman journeyed two days to see the supposed horns and tail on the first Jew to come to Cincinnati, Ohio. But because of changing fortunes in Germany, German Jews began to flow into America in 1830. Nonetheless, by 1840, there were still only approximately 15,000 American Jews.[78] The most numerous group of immigrants were Irish, most of whom were Roman Catholic. American anti-Catholicism, which always had been strong, became even more pervasive and bitter as American Protestants began to feel their hegemonic position somewhat threatened. Indeed, this sense of Protestant insecurity motivated many of the voluntary societies to press their Protestant agendas ever more intensely. In its annual report for 1855, the Bible Society of Essex County, New Jersey, proclaimed:

> At a time when a vast foreign population is rushing in on us like a flood—when infidelity on the one hand, in its protean forms, and Romanism on the other, with its determined and deadly hostility to God's truth and our free institutions—are assailing those truths, and endeavoring day and night to undermine those interests which are dear to our hearts, shall we be idle?[79]

The Civil War plainly had enormous consequences for the United States. Most obviously, the war resulted in the eradication of slavery and led to the eventual enfranchisement of African Americans. In terms of religion, the war further splintered American Protestantism, as many denominations split between Northern and Southern sects, and then after the war, many sects divided between black and white churches.[80] Moreover, as is often true of a major national crisis, the war tended to provoke additional nativist sentiments. Northerners and Southerners often interpreted the war in religious terms; Christian visions of the apocalypse and millennium abounded. Many Northerners believed that God was punishing the American people for their insufficient devotion to Jesus. Indeed, some believed that the war was a "baptism of blood" needed to cleanse and regenerate the nation in its Christian mission.[81] In 1861, Senator Charles Sumner of Pennsylvania submitted to Congress a petition from a Presbyterian synod that called for a constitutional amendment expressly acknowledging that America was a Christian nation. Within two years, voluntary societies were forming to help push for the amendment. In 1864, the leading organization, the National Association to Secure the Religious Amendment to the Constitution, formulated a petition for Congress that sought to modify the constitutional Preamble as follows:

> We, the people of the United States, humbly acknowledging Almighty God as the source of all authority and power in civil government, the Lord Jesus Christ as the Ruler among the nations, his revealed will as the supreme law of the land, in order to constitute a Christian government and, in order to form a more perfect union … do ordain and establish this Constitution for the United States of America.[82]

Unsurprisingly, this organization nonetheless insisted that it favored freedom of conscience and separation of church and state.[83]

After the war, the movement to amend the Constitution progressed into a second phase when it considerably expanded its goals and reorganized under the name the National Reform Association (NRA). Besides advocating for a Christian constitutional amendment, the NRA pledged to promote Protestant values regarding "the Sabbath, the institution of the family, the religious element in education, the oath, and public morality as affected by the liquor traffic and other kindred evils."[84] In particular, the NRA emphasized anti-liquor laws, Protestant Bible reading in the public schools (which already was a fact of life), and the enforcement of Sunday laws to symbolically underscore that Jesus Christ was "the nation's ruler." Significantly, the

NRA was not a reactionary fringe group; its president, William Strong, was appointed to the Supreme Court in 1870.[85]

These societies, such as the NRA, while constituted initially with voluntary members, nonetheless operated to a great extent as coercive institutions. They sought to impose particular values and practices and to convert individuals with intense and pervasive pressure—not with gentle persuasion or rational discourse. "They distributed books, tracts, and newspapers by the millions, and these only added to those already published by the denominations," reports Jon Butler. "If the religious and reform societies could not reshape America, they could at least drown it in a sea of paper and ink."[86] The constitutional concept of separation of church and state, present at both the federal and state levels, paved the way for the coercive actions of these societies. On the one hand, these societies were non-governmental (or private) institutions and therefore supposedly free of any constitutional constraints imposed by the separation of church and state. And on the other hand, the government could not interfere with the activities of these societies, even if it had wanted to (which it did not), because such interference would amount, after all, to a governmental infringement of the protected religious sphere (that is, a governmental violation of the separation of church and state). So all Americans, including Jews, were subject to the coercive pressures inflicted by these societies.

While American Jews always were implicitly pressured to convert by merely living in a Christian nation, Christian efforts to proselytize Jews became more formal and organized in the early nineteenth century. In 1816, the Female Society of Boston and Vicinity for Promoting Christianity Amongst the Jews was created, largely because of Hannah Adams, the nation's first female littérateur. Adams previously had written a history of the Jews maintaining that Jesus "was ignominiously rejected and put to death by the Jewish nation." She had added that the "tremendous calamities which befell [the Jews] after perpetrating this horrid crime [were] the fulfillment of our Saviour's predictions, respecting the destruction of their city and temple, and their consequent dispersion and sufferings."[87] That same year, 1816, another proselytizing organization began, the American Society for Evangelizing the Jews. This society officially lasted only into 1817, but it led to the eventual creation of the American Society for Meliorating the Conditions of the Jews (ASMCJ), which was incorporated under New York State law in 1820. The ASMCJ was well organized—for several years it published a monthly magazine—and it was led by American dignitaries. The first board of directors included John Quincy Adams (then the secretary of state and a future U.S. president), Stephen Van Rensselaer (a member of

Congress), the president of Yale College, the president of Queens College (Rutgers), a professor from Columbia College, and even former President John Adams (who was, however, not an active participant). At first, the ASMCJ devoted itself to creating a colony for Jewish immigrants who already had converted or who wanted to convert, but in 1842 the society amended its constitution to emphasize missionary work in America—that is, the proselytization of American Jews.[88] Indeed, at around this time, Robert Baird's book *Religion in America* mirrored the smug assuredness reminiscent of a young Martin Luther. To Baird, American Jews had not yet all converted only because of a lack of effort by Christians. He wrote: "A few instances of conversion to Christianity have taken place, but only a few, the attention of Christians, we may truly say, not having been sufficiently turned to that subject."[89]

In this atmosphere of Protestant hegemony, antisemitism predictably appeared as an unremarkable occurrence. In the 1790s, the Federalists often grouped "Jews, Jeffersonians, and Jacobins in an imagined plot against America."[90] For example, in 1795, a Federalist publisher and newspaper editor wrote that the Anti-Federalists and Jeffersonians were like "the tribe of Shylock [Jews]: they have that leering underlook and malicious grin, that seem to say to the honest man approach me not."[91] John Quincy Adams, then also a Federalist, declared that the "word filth conveys an ideal of spotless purity in comparison with Jewish nastiness" and that Jewish "hatred of all Christians is rancorous beyond description."[92] Jeffersonian Republicans also used antisemitic rhetoric. During the national economic crisis of the 1790s, they accused speculators of "Israeltish avarice"; declared that Federalist policies enriched "British riders, Amsterdam Jews, American Tories, and speculating lawyers and doctors"; and maintained that nine-tenths of the national debt was held by "brokers, speculators, Jews, members of congress and foreigners." During the early nineteenth century, the most prominent American Jew was Mordecai Noah, who served as the American consul to Tunis from 1813 to 1815. Newspapers constantly referred to Noah with antisemitic epithets, such as "Hooked Nose" and "Shylock."[93] The secretary of state, James Monroe, finally removed Noah from his post because "the Religion which you profess [is] an obstacle to the exercise of your consular functions."[94]

Throughout the Second Great Awakening, antisemitism was common. Leaders such as Charles Grandison Finney drew upon New Testament dogma. In 1835, for example, he wrote: "When Christ came, the ceremonial or typical [Jewish] dispensation was abrogated, because the design of those forms was fulfilled, and therefore themselves of no further use."

Finney added: "The Jews accused [Jesus] of disregarding their forms. His object was to preach and teach mankind the true religion."[95] These antisemitic attitudes were directly and overtly taught to children. The main tract of the American Sunday School Union was called *Union Questions*. Published initially in 1827 as a guide for Bible class teachers, it sold 1.6 million copies within seven years. In setting forth the Union's position on scriptural matters, it included numerous examples of standard New Testament doctrinal antisemitism, such as the accusation that Jews killed Jesus. Secular schools also used texts containing numerous examples of antisemitism. For example, *American Popular Lessons,* first published in 1820 and in its tenth edition by 1848, declared that "Jesus Christ was killed by the Jews at Jerusalem." *The National Pronouncing Speller,* aimed at primary classes and republished seven times by 1874, included a dictation or spelling exercise that required students to copy the following: "The selfish Jew, in his splendor, would not give a shekel to the starving shepherd." Even a geography book, John L. Blake's *A Geography for Children,* stated that when the Jews "became disobedient and wicked, He abandoned them, and they have been subject to reproach and derision for nearly eighteen hundred years.... [W]icked people soon become unhappy, while the virtuous and good usually live in peace and happiness." Blake continued by writing that Christians "consider [Jews and other infidels] exceedingly wicked to reject a religion given to them in so much mercy."[96]

Magazines, newspapers, and other popular literature naturally offered up their share of antisemitic rhetoric. *Harper's Magazine,* for example, ran an article that declared: "You know people who 'Jew you down.' [The] children of Abraham have always been, and still are, notorious for jewing folks down—hence they are called Jews."[97] In one telling editorial in the *Washington Sentinel,* the author sought to *praise* Jews in the following manner: "Denied citizenship in most of the countries of Christendom, debarred from the pursuits of ambition, incapable of holding offices of honor and profit, kicked and cuffed by all mankind, they have bent all their energies to one object, and that the accumulation of money."[98] Even Daniel Webster, the renowned orator and lawyer, when arguing before the Supreme Court in 1844, stated:

> When little children were brought into the presence of the Son of God, his disciples proposed to send them away; but he said, 'Suffer little children to come unto me.' Unto *me*; he did not send them first for lessons in morals to the schools of the Pharisees or to the unbelieving Sadducees, nor to read the precepts and lessons phylacteried on the garments of the Jewish priesthood.[99]

Governmental officials occasionally acted upon their antisemitic notions. For instance, in 1840, in the midst of an international crisis in the Middle East, the American consol in Beirut supported a charge of blood libel against Jews in Syria (this charge accuses Jews of killing Christians and using their blood for ritual purposes during Passover).[100] During the Civil War, Northern *and* Southern officials took turns denouncing Jews. In the South, President Jefferson Davis and several members of the Confederate Congress blamed Jews for high prices and for depreciating the Southern currency. The Union's General Ulysses S. Grant, though, was not to be outdone. As Grant prepared to attack Vicksburg, Tennessee, he sought to cut off all trade with the Confederacy because speculators were trying to take advantage of rising cotton prices. Grant, rather remarkably, claimed that all of the speculators were Jews, and thus he issued an order prohibiting Jews from traveling in the area. President Abraham Lincoln, to his credit, revoked Grant's order. More broadly, the Civil War Congress required all Army chaplains to be Christian, and then even after Congress repealed that legislation, no Jews were admitted as chaplains—even in largely Jewish companies.[101] Shortly before the War, Rabbi Isaac Leeser, the editor of *The Occident,* an antebellum Jewish periodical, astutely observed: "We have our theoretical rights, but practically they are dependent on the will of those who have numbers on their side; and if we make all the noise in the world, and brag aloud after our heart's content, we are yet strangers in stranger lands." In 1853, *The Occident* even speculated that if the Constitution were then being written, American Jews probably would be denied civil rights expressly.[102]

After the Civil War, overt expressions of antisemitism increased, mainly because of two factors. First, a few of the antebellum German-Jewish immigrants rose to prominence in banking and commercial enterprises as America entered its Gilded Age. Opponents of industrialization and of the nouveau riche industrialists—these opponents largely were New England patricians from colonial stock, as well as agrarian Populists from the South and West— quickly adverted to antisemitic themes in their efforts to gain political advantage. In fact, as the New England patricians themselves gained a stronger interest in industrialization, American Jews were largely driven out of the movement. More broadly, although many Protestants of this era considered wealth to be "a sign of divine approval," those same Protestants typically condemned any Jews who became wealthy as greedy and deceitful.[103]

Second, and perhaps more important, overt antisemitism intensified when Jewish immigration soared. Overall, in the fifty years after the Civil War, 35 million people moved to the United States, "the largest wave of immigration in American history."[104] Interestingly, despite this influx of immigrants, the percentage of foreign-born Americans changed only minimally between 1860 and 1910—going from 13 to 15 percent of the total population (but this percentage becomes much higher if one includes with the immigrants their American-born children). The largest change, though, was in the place of origin of the majority of the immigrants. Instead of arriving from Ireland, Germany, Scandinavia, and Britain—which was mostly the case before the Civil War—immigrants in the later nineteenth century arrived from Italy, Russia, and the Balkans. Significantly, during these years, "the lower class became more conspicuous, more ethnic, more poor and more separated from the rest of society."[105]

Of the approximately 3 million Russians who came to America, over 2 million were Jews, most of whom arrived between 1880 and 1915.[106] American Jews of the late nineteenth century had political equality insofar as they could vote and (at least theoretically) hold public office, but the possibility of social equality seemed to decrease inversely as the number of Jews in the country increased. Thus, whereas American antisemitism previously had been directed largely at the conceptual Jew (since few Jews were actually present), now it frequently was directed against real Jews, quite often the Jewish immigrants. Indeed, at this point, antisemitism frequently moved beyond New Testament dogma. In the early nineteenth century, discrimination against Jews in economic affairs had been somewhat rare, but by the late nineteenth century it was the norm. For example, restrictive covenants prohibiting the sale of homes to Jews became common in urban residential areas, and insurance companies discriminated against Jews by refusing to issue policies.[107]

Jews were routinely excluded from public (though usually non-governmental) institutions—social clubs (especially elite clubs), many schools and universities, recreational facilities, and even the state militia.[108] The developer of Coney Island, for instance, publicly denounced Jews and pledged to close his beach to them:

> I don't want to speak too strongly, as it might be mistaken for something entirely different from its intended sense. Personally I am opposed to Jews. They are a pretentious class, who expect three times as much for their money as other people. [And] they are driving away the class of people who are beginning to make Coney Island the most fashionable and magnificent watering place in the world.[109]

In a much-publicized incident in 1877, the financier Joseph Seligman, the most prominent American Jew of his era, arrived with his family for their annual vacation at the Grand Hotel in Saratoga Springs, New York. The Seligmans expected their usual suite to be waiting, but the desk clerk instead read them a prepared statement: "I am required to inform you that Judge [Henry] Hilton [administrator of the Grand Union] has given instructions that no Israelites shall be permitted in the future to stop at this hotel."[110] As Irving Howe observes, the Jew was "treated as a stranger not merely to the American experience or the Protestant imagination, but to the whole of the Western tradition; and thereby he comes to seem a source of possible infection, a carrier of unwanted complications."[111] In 1882, the *New York Tribune* typified American Christian attitudes when it wrote that "Hebrew immigrants [were] obstructing the walks and sitting on chairs (!) [at the Battery Park]." The paper continued: "Their filthy condition has caused many of the people who are accustomed to go to the park to seek a little recreation and fresh air to give up this practice."[112] Another newspaper reported that Jews "were accustomed to taking only one bath a year.... [That] they are utter strangers to soap and water [and that they] are on social terms with parasitic vermin, was apparent to the most casual observer."[113]

The Separation of Church and State in the Nineteenth Century: An Assessment

If official disestablishment was initially an "experiment," as Thomas Jefferson had suggested, then the nineteenth century proved the experiment to be an extraordinary success—at least from the perspective of American Protestants.[114] The last state establishments withered away early in the century, largely for two reasons: official establishment was unnecessary and politically problematic. Protestantism was flourishing in those states that already had eliminated official establishments, and the increasing plurality of Protestant denominations rendered the official establishment of religion politically difficult. All in all, during the nineteenth century, Protestantism proved that it could dominate American society without any legal establishment. Through a variety of mechanisms—both populist and coercive—Protestantism tightened its imperialistic grip on American culture and social structures.

The hegemonic hold of Protestantism on American society was evident to non-American observers. In 1835, Alexis de Tocqueville commented that "there is no country in the world where the Christian religion retains a greater influence over the souls of men than in America." He emphasized, moreover, that American government and Protestantism seemed to flow together "in one undivided current." More particularly, de Tocqueville ascribed the strength of Protestantism to the very fact that America lacked official establishments, and he added, Americans recognized as much:

> [The clergy] all attributed the peaceful dominion of religion in their country mainly to the separation of church and state. I do not hesitate to affirm that during my stay in America I did not meet a single individual, of the clergy or the laity, who was not of the same opinion on this point.[115]

More than fifty years later, in 1888, James Bryce offered similar observations:

> The matter may be summed up by saying that Christianity is in fact understood to be, though not the legally established religion, yet the national religion. So far from thinking their commonwealth godless, the Americans conceive that the religious character of a government consists in nothing but the religious belief of the individual citizens, and the conformity of their conduct to that belief. They deem the general acceptance of Christianity to be one of the main sources of their national prosperity and their nation a special object of the Divine favour.[116]

While the de facto establishment of Protestantism continued, the conceptualization of the relation between religion and government nonetheless shifted during the 1800s. As had been true previously for Roger Williams, John Locke, and the constitutional framers, the nineteenth-century relation between church and state was predicated on the antisemitic imagery of the New Testament—the opposition between Christian spirituality and Jewish carnality and the related injunction against forcing Jewish conversion. Based on this imagery, the notion of separate or bounded spheres for church and state arose, as de Tocqueville expressly recognized: "In America religion is a distinct sphere."[117] Hence, on the one hand, the nineteenth-century conceptualization of church and state as boundary oriented had deep historical roots, but on the other hand, the century contributed an important new element to the content of the religious sphere because of the transformation in the Protestant concept of freedom of conscience. Freedom of conscience previously had denoted a freedom for individuals to follow the dictates of their conscience, but as American Protestantism became increasingly democratized during the nineteenth century, the conception of freedom of conscience implicitly changed to include individual choice. The individual must be free to make important religious choices: free to choose whether to believe in Christ and also free to choose among the plurality of Protestant denominations. Conscience was intensely individualized, and individuals were the democratic subjects who could choose salvation for themselves, supposedly unfettered by educated clergy, traditions, or other authorities.[118] From the perspective of constitutional law, it is worth noting that since the religion clauses of the first amendment protected a conception of religious liberty that mirrored the Protestant freedom of conscience, as the Protestant freedom of conscience changed, so too would the conception of religious liberty embedded within the first amendment.

In any event, based partly on this transformed conception of freedom of conscience, the religious sphere (as separated from the governmental sphere) implicitly contained two components: a private realm and an institutional realm. The private realm itself encompassed two elements. First, it included the traditional Protestant notions of conscience and faith: the individual had to remain free of state coercion in order to achieve sincere Christian faith by following the dictates of conscience to Jesus. Second, based on the democratized understanding of freedom of conscience in nineteenth-century American Protestantism, the private realm included individual choice in religious matters: the individual had to remain free to make important religious choices (choosing, for example, whether to be saved). Government was not to infringe on either element of this private realm of religion; otherwise, Christians could neither sincerely follow the dictates of conscience to Jesus nor make the important choices integral to a Protestant life. This apparent privatization of religion was intensified in late-nineteenth-century America by a growing commitment to a scientific world view, spurred by the increasing acceptance of Charles Darwin's theory of evolution. Indeed, at this point, even some Bible scholars began to argue that "scientific" studies of Scripture revealed disturbing inconsistencies in the text.[119] Many Protestants responded by attempting to harmonize religion and science in accordance with their boundary-oriented views. From this standpoint, science dealt with the external world, while religion focused on the internal or private world. This division of the world followed rather easily, of course, from the traditional Christian opposition between the spiritual and the carnal (or secular).

The second component of the religious sphere was the institutional realm, which included religious institutions such as churches and voluntary societies. In one sense, these religious institutions were private because they were not governmental, but in another sense, they were *public*. The voluntary societies, in particular, were most often devoted to publicly imposing Protestant values and practices—that is, imposing them on all of the American people. These Protestant values and practices sometimes were matters of supposedly private morality, such as drinking alcohol, but the societies nonetheless sought to enforce them on the American public. The public nature of American Protestantism became even more explicit when some societies began to pursue a "Social Gospel," which included causes such as urban renewal and women's rights (though the term "Social Gospel" did not come into vogue until the early twentieth century).[120] Most broadly, the churches and societies acted publicly by seeking to define American culture as Protestant. Martin Marty's comparative study of religion in nineteenth-century America and England underscores the public power of American Protestantism. Marty writes:

> The program of the disestablished national churches in America was almost identical with that proposed by leaders of the established national church in England. They would serve as educators, providers of a moral foundation, preservers of order, and inculcators of virtue and piety and would provide a network of voluntary associations which became, said critic-from-within Calvin Colton, "so numerous, so great, so active and influential, that, as a whole, they now constitute the great school of public education, in the formation of those practical opinions, religious, social, and political, which lead the public mind and govern the country."[121]

In other words, churches and voluntary societies in America performed many of the same functions performed by the officially established Church of England (and perhaps, the American churches and voluntary societies performed them more effectively). The lack of a governmentally established church in America did not diminish the power of Christianity pulsing through the social body. Moreover, despite the public nature and public power of the American Protestant churches and societies, they were insulated from constitutional constraints on the exercise of their power. Because these Protestant institutions were considered to be private in the sense that they were not governmental, constitutional limitations on governmental actions simply did not apply. Protestants therefore were free to discriminate, to harass, and to proselytize by any means imaginable—coercive or otherwise. Significantly, as James Bryce noted, each religious community or denomination was free to "raise and apply its funds at its uncontrolled discretion."[122]

Indeed, although American religion and government both seemed to become increasingly democratized during the 1800s, it is important to recognize that democratization did not correlate with egalitarianism. Not only was freedom of conscience a Protestant theological concept, but the nineteenth-century conceptualization of religious choice always assumed a Protestant orientation. In fact, partly because of Protestant hegemony, this century revealed that the combination in America of official disestablishment and the protection of freedom of conscience did not lead to religious or social equality for members of religious outgroups, particularly American Jews (and also, most prominently, Roman Catholics). To the contrary, even as state establishments disappeared, antisemitism surged, especially when the number of Jews in America increased to the point where they became a visible minority.

Besides facing many overt antisemitic expressions and actions, American Jews were subject to organized Christian efforts at proselytization throughout the 1800s. Indeed, as the number of Jews in America increased sharply during the last two decades of the century, the number of Christian conversion societies also grew. Literally hundreds of cross-denominational societies formed for the purpose of encouraging (and coercing) Jewish conversion, and twenty-nine Christian denominations established Jewish missionary enterprises. Around 1910, however, these institutionalized conversion efforts began to fade away, largely because of failure and frustration.[123] Nevertheless, while few American Jews actively converted, many Jews found themselves losing a large part of their Jewish identities. America was de facto a Christian nation, so becoming American necessarily entailed adopting or at least acquiescing in many elements of Christian culture. Irving Howe comments that America was "resistant to Jewish conceptions [so] that ambitions realized might mean visions abandoned."[124] In short, American culture and social structures effectively *forced* American Jews to Christianize to some extent: "Moving into an environment with a Christian conception of the place of religion in society, leaving behind the public and social aspects of the Torah, and adopting for themselves this new conception of religion, in subtle ways heavily Christianized even the most Orthodox of Jews."[125]

In a sense, American Jews found themselves in a structured predicament: a dilemma produced in part by the Jewish position or role in American society. On the one hand, in any society dominated by Christians, including America, Jews occasionally needed protection from Christian overreaching, coercion, and even violence. Throughout history, when Jews needed such protection, they had turned to state or governmental officials for refuge from the Christian mobs. For this reason, then, American Jews would have been wise to renounce the separation of church and state. The separation of church and state would prevent governmental officials from lending any assistance to Jews when they opposed Christian overreaching; any such governmental assistance to Jews qua Jews presumably would be an impermissible state intrusion into religious affairs. In short, the enforcement of the separation of church and state would tend to reinforce and even strengthen the Protestant status quo since the government could never prevent Protestant institutions from exercising their excessive social power vis-à-vis American Jews. On the other hand, in an America that was overwhelmingly Christian and also increasingly democratic, Jews knew that any governmental succor for religion would almost certainly translate into support for Protestantism. Quite simply, in American democracy—however imperfect it might be—the overwhelming Christian majority would use the governmental apparatus to satisfy and reinforce its own interests and values. The government represented the Christian masses. In fact, as discussed, regardless of the separation of church and state, the state and federal governments repeatedly acted throughout the nineteenth century to bolster Christian domination.

Hence, over time, many American Jews became strong advocates for the separation of church and state. Yet, ironically, in order for American Jews even to argue for the separation of church and state, they had to adopt Protestant terms and concepts. When seeking religious liberty and equality in America, Jews needed to argue for freedom of conscience and the separation of church and state, even though those concepts were foreign to any previous Jewish world view.[126] As already discussed, freedom of conscience, in particular, was a Protestant theological concept with roots in New Testament antisemitic imagery. Further, it was this Protestant theology and Protestant interests that eventually led to the *constitutional* protection of freedom of conscience and ultimately to disestablishment. Jews thus struggled to forge the Protestant theology and interests into some type of principle of religious freedom and equality that might accord at least minimal protection to Jews, not just to Protestants. Naomi Cohen maintains that many American Jews of the nineteenth century, almost by necessity, "equated their demands with true Americanism." As a small minority, Jews needed to argue that "the inequities they suffered called for remediation primarily because they betrayed American principles rather than Jewish rights."[127] Nonetheless, as the nineteenth century illustrated, any principle of religious freedom and equality—insofar as it existed at all— did not stray far from the Protestant interests that lay in its foundation. Regardless of any such principle, the de facto establishment of Protestantism continued unabated, even with the influx of immigrants throughout the century.

The position of Jews in American society during the nineteenth century (and beyond) revealed an *ideological* quality within the constitutional protection of freedom of conscience and official disestablishment. These constitutional notions (together with Protestant theology) prompted Americans

to assert that the nation was devoted to religious liberty, yet simultaneously, a multitude of measures—many of which were coercive—operated to
ensure Protestant domination. The symbol or idea of religious liberty did
not correspond with the social reality of domination and coercion—at least
as experienced by Jews and members of other religious outgroups (including Roman Catholics). A statement by Bela Bates Edwards in 1853 epitomized the ideological relation between religious liberty and the Protestant
control over American society:

> *Perfect religious liberty* does not imply that government of the country is not a
> Christian government. The Christian Sabbath is here recognized by the civil
> authorities in a great variety of forms. Most, if not all, of our constitutions of
> government proceed on the basis of the truth of the Christian religion.
> Christianity has been affirmed to be part and parcel of the law of the land.
> The Bible is ... read daily, in one form or another, in a large proportion of the
> common schools supported by the State. There is convincing evidence to
> show that this real, though indirect, connection between the State and
> Christianity is every year acquiring additional strength, is attended with less
> and less of exception and remonstrance.[128]

CHURCH AND STATE IN THE EARLY TWENTIETH CENTURY

The relation between church and state during the early twentieth century
is best understood in the context of immigration—and the American
Protestant reactions to immigration. For the most part, the massive migrations of the late nineteenth century continued unabated during the first two
decades of the twentieth century. This influx of immigrants eventually led
to a reactionary backlash from conservative and middle-class Protestants
that emerged most clearly in changes rent upon the immigration laws.[129]

Although a movement to change the nation's largely open immigration
policy arose as early as the 1890s, the first major restriction on immigration
was not enacted until 1917.[130] An important factor leading to this and future
restrictions was the increasing acceptance of certain overtly racist beliefs:
eastern and southern Europeans were deemed racially inferior to the Nordic
and Anglo-Saxon peoples who previously had come to America. A United
States Immigration Commission report from 1910, for instance, supposedly
"proved" that Jews, Slavs, and Italians were of lower morality and intelli-
gence than white Anglo-Saxon Protestants. Calvin Coolidge, when he was
vice-president, wrote a magazine article maintaining that "biological laws
show us that Nordics deteriorate when mixed with other races."[131] In line
with this thinking, many Americans accepted the late-nineteenth-century

argument that Jews constituted a distinctive and inferior race; antisemitism was thus recast as a unique form of racism. In fact, the 1903 and 1907 immigration laws required that the country of origin be specified for each immigrant, except for Jews, who were designated as Hebrews (this practice continued into the 1930s).[132] The resident anthropologist of the American Museum of Natural History published an influential book in 1916 that condemned Jews for their "dwarf stature, peculiar mentality, and ruthless concentration on self-interest [which were then] being engrafted upon the stock of the nation."[133] Consequently, in 1917, the federal government took its first major step toward restricting immigration, imposing a literacy requirement on immigrants, with an exception for individuals seeking to escape religious persecution. The advocates of this legislation, however, were soon dismayed when they recognized that many of the immigrants were able, in fact, to pass the literacy test.

This recognition combined with the Red Scare after World War I to lead to more potent constraints. In the wake of the Russian Revolution, American manufacturers who traditionally had supported open immigration—as a source of cheap labor—suddenly feared the communist tendencies of radical immigrants. Furthermore, many Americans associated Jews with communism, so the fight to further restrict immigration focused predominantly on Jews, mostly from eastern Europe. A House of Representatives committee report on immigration from 1920 thus lamented the large number of recent Jewish immigrants and called for a two-year suspension on immigration. A leader of this movement to ban Jewish immigration was the committee chair, Albert Johnson, who relied on a report from the head of the United States Consular Service (in the State Department), Wilbur J. Carr, stating as follows: "[The Jews hoping to come to America were] of the usual ghetto type. Most of them are ... filthy, un-American and often dangerous in their habits." Carr added that potential Jewish immigrants are "[p]hysically deficient ... [m]entally deficient ... [e]conomically undesirable [and] [s]ocially undesirable: Eighty-five to ninety per cent lack any conception of patriotic or national spirit. And the majority of this percentage is mentally incapable of acquiring it."[134] Finally, in 1921, a new immigration law imposed a quota system: immigration would be limited to 3 percent of the number of the foreign-born of each nationality present in the United States as of 1910, the last census year. The undisputed purpose of the legislation was to favor potential immigrants from northwestern Europe. Then in 1924, the quota was tightened: immigration now would be limited to only 2 percent of the number of the foreign-born of each nationality present in the United States as of *1890,* when there were far fewer southern and eastern Europeans in the United States. Under this legislation, fewer than 10,000 individuals would be admitted each year from Poland, Russia, and Romania combined—countries with large numbers of Jews desperate to escape political turmoil and pogroms—while over 100,000 individuals from Great Britain, Ireland, and Germany could still come to America. This type of racist immigration policy continued into the mid-1960s.[135]

During the first half of the twentieth century, the racist and antisemitic restrictions on immigration represented but one of many instances of Protestant domination—many of which were implemented through governmental institutions. For example, as the American Jewish population grew in the late nineteenth and early twentieth centuries, the Sunday laws became increasingly problematic for many Jews. These laws were not dead letters by any means. Supported by labor unions as well as Christian ministers and preachers, Sunday laws were zealously enforced: in the early twentieth century, tens of thousands of Jews were arrested for violating them. As Supreme Court Justice David Brewer insisted in 1905 during a series of lectures, America was and would remain a Christian nation.[136]

Several important Protestant actions of the early twentieth century arose out of the interrelated Social Gospel and Progressive movements. While the Protestantism of this era remained fragmented among a multitude of denominations, the major division within Protestantism at this time was between those who focused on the individual and those who focused on the society. The former group tended to emphasize the attainment of eternal salvation for each individual soul. The latter group, in the minority, tended to stress certain broad social and economic issues. They preached the so-called Social Gospel, which was concerned primarily with the social problems arising from laissez-faire capitalism, as revealed during America's Gilded Age.[137] One of the early leaders, Josiah Strong, underscored this central concern for the relationship between money and Christianity:

> Property is one of the cardinal facts of our civilization. It is the great object of endeavor, the great spring of power, the great occasion of discontent, and one of the great sources of danger. For Christians to apprehend their true relations to money, and the relations of money to the kingdom of Christ and its progress in the world, is to find the key to many of the great problems now pressing for solution.[138]

Another Social Gospel leader, Walter Rauschenbusch, published in 1907 his most famous book, *Christianity and the Social Crisis*. Rauschenbusch saw America as engaged in a battle between the Kingdom of God and the Kingdom of Evil. As a millennialist, he believed that true Christian faith would bring victory to the Kingdom of God. He urged Americans to "rally sufficient religious faith and moral strength to snap the bonds of evil and turn the present unparalleled economic and intellectual resources of humanity to the harmonious development of a true social life."[139] Hence, according to the Social Gospel leaders, America faced enormous social and economic problems, but those problems could be overcome by applying (supposedly) true Protestant values—as prescribed by the Social Gospel. In short, almost all participants in the Social Gospel movement agreed that the United States must be the Christian Kingdom of God on earth: the Social Gospel combined its concern for the economic inequities of laissez-faire capitalism with traditional American Protestant imperialism. In 1908, for instance, the General Conference of the Methodist Episcopal Church declared that it stood for, among other things, the following: "[1] the protection of the worker from dangerous machinery, occupational disease, injuries and mortality. [2] the abolition of child labor. [3] a living wage in every industry. [4] the recognition of the Golden Rule, and the mind of Christ as the supreme law of society and the sure remedy for all social ills."[140] Significantly, many of the impoverished individuals working within the grips of the capitalist industrial order were the recent non-Protestant immigrants. The Social Gospel leaders thus sought not only to enact protections for these workers, but also to impose Protestant values on them (hopefully converting them in the process). Josiah Strong tersely sounded this imperialistic theme: "Christianize the immigrant and he will be easily Americanized."[141]

In any event, the Social Gospel movement petered out in the 1920s because many Americans, Protestant and otherwise, viewed it as challenging fundamental assumptions of the capitalist economic system. Some of the individuals involved in the movement, however, were also committed to a broader political movement: Progressivism. Indeed, Protestant values and motivations strongly colored much of the Progressive movement, and unlike the Social Gospel, Progressivism had wide support throughout Protestant America. When the short-lived Progressive political party held its presidential convention in 1912, the theme song was "Onward, Christian Soldiers," and the eventual party nominee, Theodore Roosevelt, announced, "We stand at Armageddon and we battle for the Lord."[142]

The Progressive political agenda was diverse and loosely defined. Like the Social Gospel movement, Progressivism sought to protect against the social inequities generated by laissez-faire capitalism and mass industrialization. Hence, for example, Progressives tended to support anti-trust actions and restrictions on child labor. To a great extent, though, Progressivism reflected a Protestant reactionary fear of the mass immigration of the late nineteenth and early twentieth centuries. With so many immigrants settling in the growing cities, the traditional Protestant values of rural (Anglo-Saxon) America seemed under siege from the poor and non-Protestant (mostly Roman Catholic and Jewish) urban class. Yet, almost two-thirds of America's 75 million people still remained in rural areas at the turn of the twentieth century, when Josiah Strong declared that "[It]he first city was built by the first murderer, and crime and vice and wretchedness have festered in it ever since."[143] The loosely united Progressives reacted to the perceived immigrant and urban threat in a variety of ways, ranging from activities to promote the Americanization (that is, Protestantization) of the immigrants to the aforementioned political movements to restrict immigration.[144]

The temperance movement provides another prominent illustration of the relation between Progressivism and anti-immigrant attitudes. While temperance long had been a Protestant cause, the massive influx of Roman Catholic immigrants transformed the issue in the late nineteenth and early twentieth centuries. Temperance or abstinence became more than an important Protestant value; it now was necessary to preserve the character of America in the face of an alien invasion. The Anti-Saloon League, formed in 1895, sought to generate public (that is, Protestant) support, to press for prohibition legislation (first locally and then nationally), and to ensure that any such prohibition laws were fully enforced. The League was based primarily on local churches; indeed, by 1915, 40,000 churches were cooperating with the League, which could mobilize an enormous bloc of Protestant voters in political elections. Finally, nativist and patriotic sentiments were exacerbated during World War I, with Prohibitionists emphasizing the *Germanic* names of major brewers of beer, such as Busch and Pabst. With this boost, the long temperance battle concluded with the ratification in early 1919 of the eighteenth amendment and the imposition of national Prohibition. As Joseph Gusfield succinctly states, Prohibition "established the victory of Protestant over Catholic [and] rural over urban."[145]

Women's suffrage was another long-running political movement that finally attained victory partly because of anti-immigrant sentiments. Many American Protestants initially had opposed women's suffrage as contrary to the supposedly traditional Protestant role of women in the family. The suffrage cause eventually gained respectability, however, especially when the enfranchisement of white Protestant women was deemed necessary to offset the potential votes of African Americans and non-Protestant immigrants. The ratification of the nineteenth amendment in 1920, extending the right to vote to women, can thus be understood in part as an effort to maintain

Protestant domination.[146] America had become further democratized, but not necessarily for democratic or egalitarian reasons.

Although Progressivism faded in the 1920s, Protestant (or Christian) domination of America did not. For instance, the reading of the King James (Protestant) Bible remained a staple in the public schools of most states throughout the first half of the twentieth century. In 1933, twelve states legally required reading the Bible in the public schools; eleven states prohibited it; and twenty-five states permitted it, often expressly granting local school boards the option of deciding. In one of the optional states, Ohio, 85 percent of the schools required Bible reading.[147] In 1941 the number of states legally requiring and prohibiting Bible reading remained unchanged, but by 1949 even *fewer* states legally *prohibited* Bible reading, with only eight states doing so.[148] Moreover, in those states that legally prohibited Bible reading, the practice often continued de facto.

Apart from Bible reading, the recitation of prayers was common. The memoirs of a Jewish writer who attended Virginia public schools after World War II reveal the profound confusion that such Christianizing could inflict on Jewish children:

> Every morning the principal, after reading announcements over the loudspeaker, said a prayer while students dutifully bowed their heads over their desks. [The prayer always ended with the words] "In the name of Jesus Christ our Lord, Amen." I didn't know what to do. As a Jew, I prayed straight to God, not in anyone else's name. To accept the prayer as mine was more of a sin, according to what I had been taught, than not praying at all. My sister and I talked it over. She was as upset about the prayers as I was. But we didn't see a solution. We would have jumped in front of our school bus sooner than ask to be excused. . . . During that year neither of us told a single person that we were Jewish. I don't think we were cowardly. We were simply children. "Jesus Christ our Lord" coming over the loudspeaker every morning didn't leave room for any other belief being normal. It built a wall, with my sister and me standing on the outside.[149]

Any Jewish protests of Christian prayers or Bible reading in the public schools evoked, at best, "strong irritation" from Christian-dominated school boards.[150] Rabbi Arthur Gilbert described the more dire consequences that sometimes followed Jewish complaints: "Jewish parents . . . endured cross burnings on their lawns, harassing phone calls, the threat of economic boycott, and the mass distribution of anti-Semitic hate literature."[151] Jewish objections to the ubiquitous school Christmas celebrations triggered typically harsh reactions: shortly after World War II, a "family in Chelsea, Massachusetts, was forced to go into hiding in a nearby community [and in] Hamden, Connecticut, there were swastikas, threats of boycotts, and a sign in the high school that read: 'What Eichmann started, we'll finish.'"[152]

As is evident, Christian domination of twentieth-century America often has been manifested through antisemitic rhetoric and actions. Again, the severe restrictions on Jewish immigration first imposed during the 1920s provide but one striking example. Indeed, the 1920s and 1930s saw probably the worst overt antisemitism in American history.[153] As the Anti-Defamation League noted in 1918, an "unconscious" prejudice was attached to the word "Jew."[154] Depending upon the context, Jews were assumed to be greedy capitalists, dangerous communists, dirty, pushy, deceitful, immoral, and criminal. A public school principal said of his Jewish pupils: "Their progress in studies is simply another manifestation of the acquisitiveness of the race." Such comments were typical; the progressive reformer and reporter Jacob Riis declared that Jewish children with an aptitude for mathematics showed "how strong the instinct of dollars and cents is in them."[155] More broadly, Riis wrote: "Thrift is the watchword of Jewtown, as of this people the world over. . . . Money is their God. Life itself is of little value compared with even the leanest bank account." Many Christian Americans, in other words, objectified Jews to fit stereotyped roles—roles that pictured Jews as repulsive, often as barely human, and rarely as individuals deserving respect.[156]

Unsurprisingly, then, Jews encountered economic and social discrimination and even occasional violence. On the streets, Jews constantly faced hostility and antisemitic epithets, being called "kikes" and "sheenies." As in the late nineteenth century, institutionalized social ostracism was typical. Hotels and summer resorts throughout the country were limited to Christians. In Minneapolis, Jews were excluded not only from all social, fraternal, and service clubs but also from the American Automobile Association! Through a variety of mechanisms, such as restrictive covenants and "gentlemen's agreements," Jews were banned from apartment houses and residential neighborhoods. Henry Ford, the manufacturer, accused the "Bolshevik Jew" of conspiring to overthrow the Christian nation, and at the same time, Ford published an American edition of the notorious *Protocols of the Elders of Zion*. According to the *Protocols,* supposedly written by Jewish "elders," Jews were conspiring to take over the world by controlling capital and the press through hypocrisy, bribery, fraud, and so forth. Most likely, the *Protocols* had been written in the 1890s by an author working for the Russian secret police, attempting to influence the policies of the czar.[157] Nevertheless, the myth of the *Protocols* perfectly suited Ford's antisemitic paranoia: Ford apparently was comfortable about condemning Jews for being communists (Bolsheviks) *and* capitalists (elders taking over the world).

Despite similar frequent charges that Jews were deceitful and greedy capitalists—that Jews controlled banking, finance, and Wall Street, that Jews caused farmers to lose their farms during the Depression—most American Jews in the 1920s and 1930s lived in impoverished urban ghettos. Moreover, many paths of economic opportunity were closed to Jews. They were de facto banned from banking, from insurance company management, and from the steel, coal, and automobile industries. Before the 1920s, major universities and colleges, including the Ivy League schools, admitted Jews, but when Jewish numbers increased, admission quotas were imposed, limiting Jews to as little as 3 percent of the entering classes. Some schools disguised these quotas by, for example, adopting regional instead of explicit religious quotas. A regional quota required that certain proportions of an entering class originate from specific geographical regions of the country—thus limiting the number of students from the large eastern cities where Jews were concentrated. Medical schools followed suit by also imposing near-exclusionary quotas, and those few Jews who managed to graduate (sometimes from European medical schools) then faced employment quotas at hospitals.[158] Universities deemed Jews to be aliens incapable of teaching a variety of subjects, including English literature, American history, sociology, and even mathematics. When Lionel Trilling was dismissed after teaching for four years in the Columbia English department, he was informed that "as a Freudian, a Marxist, and [a] Jew," he would not be happy there.[159]

Major law schools and law firms routinely discriminated against Jews and other outgroups.[160] In a prominent example, Felix Frankfurter, who had come to the United States at the age of twelve, graduated first in his class from Harvard Law School early in the century, yet he had difficulty finding a job with the major New York firms.[161] Three decades later, in the spring of 1936, eight *Harvard Law Review* editors lacked employment for the following year; all were Jewish.[162] In a broader vein, elite Protestant attorneys sought to protect their status and prestige during the first decades of the twentieth century by claiming that Jewish and Catholic immigrant attorneys were undermining professional morals. Harlan Stone, the progressive dean of Columbia Law School and a future Supreme Court chief justice, referred to "'the influx to the bar of greater numbers of the unfit,' who 'exhibit racial tendencies toward study by memorization' and display 'a mind almost Oriental in its fidelity to the minutiae of the subject without regard to any controlling rule or reason.'"[163] During this era, the American Bar Association (ABA) and the Association of American Law Schools (AALS) introduced professional standards partly to maintain white Anglo-Saxon Protestant domination of the legal profession. For example, the first ABA canons of professional ethics prohibited lawyer advertising, mostly hurting Jewish and Catholic solo practitioners who lacked extensive social connections and who thus necessarily relied on transient clients (such as personal injury plaintiffs).[164] State bars intentionally and overtly discriminated against non-Protestants. In 1927, the Pennsylvania state bar adopted an elaborate registration system that supposedly provided for character examinations of potential students before they began law school. Each prospective law student needed to secure a preceptor who had at least five years of experience and was willing to guarantee the student a six-month clerkship upon graduation (three years away). Furthermore, the prospective student needed to find three sponsors, including two current members of the bar. And finally, still before beginning law school, the prospective student had to be interviewed by a board of bar examiners to determine the applicant's "fitness" to practice law. Needless to say, this system facilitated the acceptance of white Protestants while successfully blocking large numbers of Jewish immigrants—referred to as "Russian Jew boys" by the chair of the Philadelphia Law Association Grievance Committee.[165]

Despite such pervasive antisemitism, President Franklin Roosevelt's New Deal significantly changed the lives of most Americans, including Jews, during the 1930s. The national government effectively became more democratic as it recognized and encompassed many previously ignored and unrepresented social groups: the government, for example, provided assistance or protection to industrial workers, staple farmers, the unemployed, and small bank depositors. In hiring governmental employees, the Roosevelt administration initiated something of a meritocratic system: educational accomplishments became more important than family lineage.[166] Moreover, the New Deal largely detached economic reform from Protestant sermonizing. Whereas the Progressives had combined their economic concerns with moralizing about sins such as drinking and prostitution, the New Dealers focused almost exclusively on economic issues. In the words of William E. Leuchtenburg, "[r]eform in the 1930s meant *economic* reform." Unlike the Progressives, the New Dealers sought to change American economic institutions without changing the people—to make life more tolerable and maybe even comfortable without necessarily imposing particular religious or moral values.[167]

And in fact, the New Deal radically altered the way government interacts with the economic marketplace. Throughout most of the nineteenth century, the national and state governments together influenced and coordinated the development of the economy. During that time, though, many governmental regulations of the economy were barely noticeable, emerging gradually and obscurely from the courts as common law rules instead of being openly and purposefully enacted by the legislatures. With the coming of the New Deal, by contrast, the national government highlighted and intensified its efforts to direct the economy. Through legislation, including the creation and expansion of administrative agencies, the New Deal government openly and affirmatively attempted to change the American economy. While laissez-faire capitalism had produced economic collapse, privation, and injustice, the increasingly bureaucratic national government of the New Deal sought to overtly control the economy in a concerted effort to end the Great Depression. Hence, although Roosevelt's critics labeled him an enemy of capitalism, most Americans understood the New Deal as the "savior of capitalism." To prevent capitalist ruin, the New Dealers enacted numerous statutes such as the National Industrial Recovery Act, the Social Security Act, and the National Labor Relations Act, which aimed "to make the industrial system more humane and to protect workers and their families from exploitation."[168]

In sum, the New Dealers sought to restructure economic relations to promote social welfare. Predictably, the New Deal program provoked conservative backlashes along several fronts. One of the most prominent and serious reactions emerged from the Supreme Court: during the early 1930s, the Court repeatedly thwarted New Deal efforts by striking down recent enactments as unconstitutional. In these cases, the Court typically reasoned that Congress had exceeded its constitutional powers by infringing upon the liberty of individuals to make contracts and control their property.[169] Nonetheless, commentators long had been arguing otherwise: without legislative protection, individuals were not free but rather were entangled in the common law rules of contracts and property skewed by the inequities of the economic marketplace. From this perspective, governmental regulation of the economy could *promote* individual liberty that was otherwise threatened by the disparities of the market.[170] Finally, in 1937, the Court capitulated under enormous political pressure and began regularly to uphold economic regulations.[171] From that point on, the legal landscape of America was radically altered: the common law no longer was the predominant governmental and legal mechanism for societal control and regulation. Instead, legislative and administrative regulation frequently and openly directed and transformed economic and social relations. The era of the national welfare state had arrived. Leuchtenburg observes:

By the end of the Roosevelt years, few questioned the right of the government to pay the farmer millions in subsidies not to grow crops, to enter plants to conduct union elections, to regulate business enterprises from utility companies to air lines, or even to compete directly with business by generating and distributing hydroelectric power.[172]

Largely because of the relative openness of the Roosevelt administration during the 1930s, American Jews for the first time experienced the Jewish "embrace of the state" that had been common throughout previous Jewish history (in Europe).[173] That is, Jews turned to the state, in particular the federal government, for refuge from the pervasive antisemitism running throughout American society. In effect, Roosevelt and American Jews entered into a cooperative arrangement. Young Jewish attorneys, many of them top graduates, could not find professionally rewarding careers in the private sector because major law firms discriminated so severely. Meanwhile, Roosevelt needed talented attorneys to staff his New Deal agencies, but many elite lawyers remained conservative and opposed the social and economic liberalism of the early New Deal. Roosevelt, when governor of New York, had already developed close working relationships with several Jews, including Jewish lawyers. Consequently, he readily turned to the pool of unemployed or underemployed Jewish attorneys to fill many of his administrative positions; many of Roosevelt's opponents disparagingly called the New Deal the "Jew Deal."[174]

The Roosevelt administration's hiring of Jews had significance beyond the New Deal. Toward the end of the New Deal, some Jews and other minorities from Roosevelt's administration were able to enter the Protestant corporate professional establishment. For the most part, these Jews (and others) had gained important knowledge during their years in governmental service; hence, they became extremely valuable sources of expertise for corporate America. Nonetheless, many of the older law firms continued to discriminate, and the power structure of the legal profession remained largely intact.[175] Moreover, those Jews who worked for the federal government and eventually for corporate America did so at a cost. These Jews were acceptable to the Protestant elite because, in Frankfurter's words, they were "bred in the same tradition."[176] In order to gain access to positions of authority and importance, Jews needed to become Americanized—that is, Christianized—at least to some significant extent. Quite clearly, if for no other reason than their status as a small numerical minority, American Jews were under enormous pressure to assimilate into the Christian culture. Moreover, from the Christian American viewpoint, Jews had freely chosen to come to America; thus, they ought to accept and adapt to the American (Christian) way of life. This view, though, was based on an odd conception of freedom—insofar as it ignored the fact that most Jews had emigrated to escape exceedingly harsh and antisemitic conditions in Europe. Regardless, Protestant Americans expected Jews to assimilate to some degree for another reason: Jews were Jewish by choice. That is, from the American Protestant perspective, anybody—even a Jew—could voluntarily choose Christian salvation. Hence, it was only fair—or so it seemed—for Jews to accept or adapt to the Christian American culture even if they continued to refuse to accept the truth of Christ.

Thus, for a Jew to become a successful American, obvious signs of Jewishness typically had to be washed away in a "kind of cultural bleaching."[177] For example, in the 1930s, the partner in a large New York law firm acknowledged that opportunities for Jews were limited, but asserted nonetheless that his firm was different. He boasted that the firm had one Jewish attorney, who was "devoid of every known quality which we in New York mean when we call a man 'Jewy.'" Similarly, when Thurman Arnold recommended a particular *Yale Law Journal* editor for a job, Arnold acknowledged that the applicant's Jewishness was his only handicap but reassuringly noted that "he was devoid of 'Jewish characteristics.'"[178] As G. Edward White bluntly observes, "a non-WASP could achieve prominence by exhibiting WASP behavioral patterns."[179] Felix Frankfurter provides the prototypical example of this phenomenon: despite the early difficulties in his legal career, Frankfurter capitalized on his extraordinary abilities to become a Harvard law professor, a confidant of Roosevelt, and finally a Supreme Court justice only because he submerged his Jewish identity to "pass" into Christian society.[180]

Hence, despite Roosevelt's willingness to hire Jews in the New Deal, the liberal openness of his administration should not be overstated. To be sure, because the administration chose employees based more on merit than lineage, Jews were able to gain positions of authority never before available to them. Yet, to gain such positions, Jews needed to act largely Christian. Furthermore, the Roosevelt administration overtly discriminated to some degree against Jews; in particular, administration officials were concerned that they not hire *too many* Jews.[181] However, by far the most important manifestation of antisemitism in the Roosevelt administration arose around the Second World War.

The primary charge of antisemitism leveled against the Roosevelt administration is that it remained largely indifferent to Jewish suffering and death during the Holocaust. To fully understand this charge, it is best to remember that Roosevelt and his administration acted within the context of an America that was pervasively antisemitic. Early in the 1930s, public opinion polls suggested that one-third of all Americans thought that "Jews had too much power," and one-fifth of Americans wanted to restrict the role of Jews in politics and business. These statistics, albeit bad, became even worse later in the decade: at that point, 41 percent of Americans believed that "Jews had too much power"; almost one-half thought that Jews were partly to blame for their own persecution in Europe; and 35–40 percent would have supported anti-Jewish laws.[182] In fact, Jews who fled Germany for America during the 1930s thought that antisemitism was worse in America than it had been in pre-Nazi Germany![183]

Antisemitism simmered at all levels of American society. Hundreds of thousands of listeners, mostly low-income Irish Catholics, tuned in to Father Charles E. Coughlin's weekly radio shows, which spouted Nazi-like accusations of Jewish world domination. Richard Wright, the famed African American author, wrote: "To hold an attitude of antagonism or distrust toward Jews was bred in us from childhood; it was not merely racial prejudice, it was a part of our cultural heritage." Antisemitism was especially strong among the educated and the affluent. Thomas Wolfe regarded Jews as "beak-nosed Shylocks from Yankeedom," and H.L. Mencken suggested that they were "the most unpleasant race ever heard of." William Faulkner called New York the "land of the kike and home of the wop," while Theodore Dreiser called it "a Kyke's dream of a ghetto."[184] In 1939, a professor at Princeton, Otto Piper, wrote a book echoing standard New Testament antisemitic dogma:

> [Jewish and Christian] views differ when they turn to the destruction of Jerusalem in 70 A.D. and to the subsequent dispersion of the Jews. From the Christian point of view there is a direct causal connection between these events and the crucifixion of Jesus. The fate of the Jews is the divine punishment for their rejection of the promised Messiah. The Jews, however, find fault with everyone except themselves. [Nonetheless] all Jews were responsible for His death. This is the reason they all have to endure the divine punishment.[185]

In 1941, a Harvard professor wrote in the *Atlantic Monthly* that Jews desired "chemical mixture, miscegenation," instead of remaining true to their "Oriental tradition." Because of this problem, the professor concluded: "I think that it is not impossible that I shall live to see the [Nazis' antisemitic] Nuremberg Laws reenacted in this country and enforced with vigor."[186]

Unsurprisingly, then, the Roosevelt administration included many anti-semites, especially (and tragically) in the State Department. Largely because of officials in the State Department, the administration provided inadequate leadership in the struggle to save European Jewish refugees during the 1930s and early 1940s.[187] In Germany, Hitler came to power in 1933, and by 1935 the antisemitic Nuremberg racial laws were in effect. Life for Jews in Germany became increasingly harsh, so emigration became paramount. Yet throughout the 1930s, not only did the American State Department officials zealously enforce the stringent quotas for immigrants from Eastern Europe (where Polish Jews were starving and being killed in pogroms), but they refused even to fill the legally permissible quotas for immigrants from Germany and the rest of central Europe. For a five-year period during the mid-1930s, less than half of the quota for German immigration was filled. As conditions in Europe worsened, a bill was introduced in 1939 in Congress to allow the admission of 20,000 refugee *children*. The secretary of state, Cordell Hull, privately opposed the bill, and Roosevelt himself never publicly supported it—perhaps partly because of the potential political fallout (a poll suggested that only 26 percent of the population supported this bill)—and the bill died in committee. By comparison, during the Battle of Britain in 1940, Congress approved almost unanimously the admission of 10,000 British children. Throughout the war years, the restrictions on Jewish immigration were never relaxed, and incredibly, the State Department manipulated the nation's visa policies from 1939 to 1941 in order to cut Jewish immigration. Then, by October 1941, the question had become moot: Germany decided to refuse any further Jewish emigration.[188] Hence, the Roosevelt administration—mirroring the sentiments of many Christian Americans—ultimately displayed remarkable indifference and even hostility toward the displacement, suffering, and death of millions of Jewish people. In fact, by the middle of 1943, the administration unquestionably knew of the mass murder of European Jews, yet beyond trying to win the war, the administration took no direct military action (such as bombing the German railroad lines) that might have saved Jewish lives.[189]

All in all, though, the Roosevelt administration displayed far less anti-semitism than most of American society. This fact, however, might say less about the administration than about American society at large. On the one hand, the New Deal always included an undercurrent of conservatism. Without minimizing the economic transformation wrought by the New Dealers, one can fairly conclude that most of them did not seek to regulate the economy for the mere sake of redistributing resources from the haves to the have-nots. Rather, Roosevelt and others sincerely believed that the

New Deal economic measures were necessary to save capitalism, or in Roosevelt's words, "to energize private enterprise." The New Dealers, in other words, were not all radicals seeking to completely remake American society. Unsurprisingly, then, the Roosevelt administration frequently tolerated antisemitism, sometimes with tragic results. In short, the administration chiefly focused first on economic reforms and then on the war effort: political calculations related to these more primary concerns forcefully shaped the administration's attitudes and actions toward both Jews and antisemites. On the other hand, regardless of motivations, Roosevelt unprecedentedly opened the government and positions of authority to American Jews, thus facilitating the integration of Jews into some previously closed segments of American society and business. More broadly, the New Deal tended to recognize and promote the interests of outgroups, even at the occasional expense of the Protestant elite. Indeed, while most New Dealers did not aim to remake American society for the mere sake of radical change, few doubted their ability to do so. At this point, then, the American national government evolved, in a sense, into the ultimate modern sovereign state. The government exuded modernist confidence: governmental experts firmly believed that they could analyze any social problem, consider various solutions, and then choose and execute the best one. If for some reason that solution did not work as planned, then another could be quickly devised and implemented. To the New Dealers, the sovereign state could control and reorder economic and social structures for the greater good of society.[190]

CHAPTER 9

The Fruits of the Framing

Church and State in Late-Twentieth-Century America

THE SUPREME COURT INTERVENES

The dominant story of the first amendment religion clauses suggests that the separation of church and state is a constitutional principle that equally protects the religious freedom of all, including religious outgroups. Most evidently, this dominant story did not fit the social reality of America through at least the end of World War II. At that time, America remained a de facto Christian nation, albeit with a small Jewish population and some other religious outgroups. American Jews often experienced Christian domination through the prism of antisemitism, sometimes expressed through governmental and sometimes through non-governmental actors. Thus, from an American Jewish perspective, the assertion that the separation of church and state preserved religious equality and freedom seems a cruel joke at best.

Despite the severe restrictions on immigration first implemented in the 1920s, the extensive migrations of the nineteenth and early twentieth centuries did, in fact, change America. Many historians argue that the long era of Protestant hegemony in America ended by the 1930s.[1] With that said, though, two qualifications bear emphasis. First, whereas the *hegemonic* hold of Protestantism on America very well may have ended, Protestant *domination* was not (and is not) over. In other words, Protestantism might not have maintained its total and pervasive control over American culture, yet it still remained (and remains) a predominant religious and cultural force in American society. Hence, emblematic of their continuing position of power, Protestant churches seeking to expand during the mid-twentieth century often agreed among themselves to divide and allocate new territories (such as a suburban development). These self-conscious divisions of territory were not arbitrary, but rather were based on strategic decisions flowing from "the use of census data, real estate and demographic projections, as well as survey data gathered by the research department of the denominational bureaucracies."[2] The avowed purpose of this Protestant church comity was to create "a dynamic program of positive church cooperation to provide an efficient and inclusive pattern of religious service in every community."[3] Furthermore, in some areas of the country, particularly the South, Protestant hegemony barely wavered.[4]

Second, while *Protestant* hegemony did in fact wane in many areas, *Christian* hegemony did not. As Protestant power declined, Roman Catholic power increased: despite the restrictions on immigration imposed during the 1920s, a large Roman Catholic population developed in America. As early as 1920, one in six Americans and one in three church members were Catholic. The political ramifications of this large Catholic population were evident immediately. In the 1920s, Catholics did not need to seek judicial intervention to protect their sacramental use of wine during Prohibition because Congress readily created a legislative exception for such use.[5] And significantly, the relative proportion of Protestant and Catholic church members would hold close to steady throughout the century. In 1958, 66.2 percent of the population considered themselves Protestant, while 25.7 percent regarded themselves as Roman Catholic. Of those individuals, though, a higher proportion of Catholics were actually church members: 56 percent of church members were Protestant, and 36 percent were Catholic. Protestants at that time still far outnumbered Roman Catholics, but Catholics had become the largest Christian group in America, outnumbering the largest Protestant denomination (the Baptists) by almost two to one. These proportions have gone roughly unchanged. In the 1990s, nine out of ten Americans claimed a specific religious affiliation, with 86.5 of them being Christians. Of those Christians, Protestants outnumbered Catholics approximately two to one, but Catholics were the largest Christian group, at 26 percent of the population (with Baptists second). Less than 2 percent of the American population is Jewish, and only 0.5 percent is Muslim.[6]

Quite clearly, then, throughout the twentieth century, Christians have remained the overwhelming religious majority in America. Protestants, taken together, are still the majority, though their numerical superiority has diminished to the point where Roman Catholics are the largest Christian group. And regardless of the proportional relations between Protestants and Catholics, because Protestantism and Catholicism both are Christ-centered religions that accept the New Testament as Scripture, they obviously have far more in common with each other than with Judaism. Most simply, Protestants and Catholics are Christians; Jews are not. Moreover, tensions between Protestants and Catholics diminished significantly after the meeting of the Second Vatican Council from 1962 to 1965.[7] I do not mean to suggest that the differences between Protestantism and Catholicism are trivial; they are not. Indeed, for a brief period in mid-century (starting at around the 1950s), Protestants sought to help maintain their dominant position vis-à-vis the burgeoning Catholic population by courting American Jews as political allies. Many Protestants thus began to invoke the so-called Judeo-Christian tradition in an effort to persuade American Jews that true Christians (that is, Protestants) and Jews were natural allies. According to this argument, then, American Jews should align politically with Protestants rather than with Catholics. In fact, Jews occasionally joined with Protestants to form political coalitions—helping, for instance, to defeat Senator Joseph McCarthy and the House Un-American Activities Committee during the Red Scare. Nonetheless, from a Jewish standpoint, the Protestant assertion of a shared Judeo-Christian tradition was self-evidently problematic: in light of the persistent antisemitism running throughout European and American history, the Judeo-Christian tradition appeared quite clearly as an invention, a myth.[8] The recent vintage of this supposed tradition was underscored by the fact that the Supreme Court mentioned it for the first time only in 1961.[9] Indeed, as already discussed in chapter 2, the concept of a Judeo-Christian tradition is not merely a harmless or even misleading myth; rather, it is an antisemitic lie that suggests that Christianity necessarily reforms and replaces Judaism.

Regardless of the invidious antisemitism manifested in the assertion of a Judeo-Christian tradition, the nature of American antisemitism changed after World War II. And the single event that perhaps most changed the character of American antisemitism was the Holocaust. As discussed in chapter 8, overt antisemitism was socially respectable and quite common in America before the Holocaust. After World War II, however, overt antisemitism and racism resounded too closely with the violence of the Holocaust and thus became socially embarrassing; for their own well-being, (Christian) Americans needed to differentiate themselves sharply from the Germans. In the words of Jerome A. Chanes, "Adolf Hitler gave antisemitism a bad name." The Germans thus were racist monsters, but Americans were different: Americans were exceptional. Americans were committed to equality and liberty for all—or so, at least, they wanted to believe.[10]

This need for Americans to distance themselves from the Nazis—the antisemitic murderers—combined with at least two other factors to help significantly reduce overt antisemitism. First, the restrictive immigration laws implemented during the 1920s severely curtailed the number of immigrant Jews coming to America. Consequently, the 1940 census for the first time marked a population with more native-born than foreign-born American Jews. Then, as these Jews increasingly assimilated into the Christian culture during the 1950s, they provoked less of the open hostility characteristic of earlier eras. Put bluntly, many Jews learned to "pass" in Christian America.[11] Second, as Derrick Bell and Mary Dudziak have argued, several factors contributed to a postwar reduction in racism against African Americans. Most important, overt racism hindered the nation's efforts to woo Third World countries during the Cold War and also interfered with national economic development, especially in the South.[12] Insofar as antisemitism had become a form of racism, the reduction in racism against African Americans implicitly undermined antisemitism; if overt racism had become socially problematic, then so apparently did overt antisemitism.

Thus, by the late 1950s, *overt* antisemitism became a social faux pas: antisemitism went underground and became secretive, tacit, and unconscious.[13] Two points require clarification. First, overt antisemitism remained strong in the years immediately after the war. Antisemitism was deeply engrained in American culture, so the ameliorative effects of the various factors—the Holocaust reaction, Jewish assimilation, and the reduction in racism—were gradual, not sudden. Second, overt antisemitism never disappeared completely, but it certainly became far less common.[14] Antisemitism became less of the normal and natural experience of daily American life. An Anti-Defamation League survey immediately after World War II revealed that 56 percent of Americans believed that Jews had too much power in the United States. By 1964 this figure had dropped to 13 percent, and in 1981 10 percent.[15] During the 1950s, Jews entered realms of the economy previously closed to them. Jews secured numerous positions at colleges and universities, including the most prestigious institutions, and successfully entered other semiacademic areas, such as publishing. Religious discrimination diminished at law firms and law schools so that, by the 1970s, it was practically eliminated. Jews also made strides in retail businesses, though major corporations continued to discriminate. In particular, with regard to the major corporations, business often was done at elite country clubs, and these clubs continued to exclude or limit Jews. In 1966, an Anti-Defamation League survey reported that of 1152 clubs, 665 discriminated against Jews: 513 barred Jews, and 152 had quotas.[16] Yet, in 1964, the federal government enacted the Civil Rights Act, which prohibited discrimination in employment and in places of public accommodation (such as hotels and restaurants) based on religion (as well as race, color, and national origin).[17]

Despite these advances, America remained a de facto Christian nation, and implicit and unconscious antisemitism always remained a prominent part of American Jewish life. Postwar America experienced waves of religiosity: a period of religious fervor, followed by a declension, followed by a time of fervor, and so forth. The 1950s was a time of Christian fervor. Hence, for example, efforts to add a Christian amendment to the Constitution were renewed at around this time. The Christian Amendment Movement, closely resembling the National Reform Association of the late nineteenth century, spearheaded this drive, annually seeking members of Congress to submit an amendment for debate. And more than once, Congress did consider proposing a constitutional amendment; in 1959, seven congressional members, more than ever before, sponsored such an action. Although no suggested amendment ever received sufficiently broad-based support to make it out of Congress, this failure revealed more about Protestant disagreement concerning the proper relation between church and state than about the degree of Christian religiosity prevalent during the 1950s.[18] Winthrop S. Hudson and John Corrigan write of this period:

> Seldom had religion been held in greater public esteem. The pledge of allegiance was amended to include the phrase "under God," prayer breakfasts were attended by the president and members of his cabinet, a prayer room was installed in the national Capitol, and both the American Legion and the National Advertising Council launched "Back to God" and "Go to Church" campaigns.[19]

Both old and novel practices that intermingled religion and government were the norm. The Supreme Court opened its daily sessions with the invocation "God save the United States and this honorable Court," legislatures at the federal and state levels began daily proceedings with prayers from publicly paid chaplains, and currency was stamped with the national motto, "In God We Trust."[20] After World War II, the practice of granting released time from the public schools for religious (Christian) education became firmly established. Under these released-time programs, which were adopted in forty-six states, children were allowed to leave their public school classes early if (and only if) they were to attend a religious class instead. The symbolic effect of these programs was to provide a governmental stamp of approval for Christian religious education.[21] Sometimes the religious classes were conducted in the public schools themselves, and the programs provided a means for proselytizing. Teachers would approach Jewish school children and ask, "Why don't you want to listen to these pretty Bible stories? We just talked today about King David; you know he was a Jew." Classmates would occasionally taunt Jewish children, calling them "Christ killer" and "dirty Jew" because they refused to participate.[22]

Throughout the 1950s, Bible reading, prayers, and Christmas and Easter celebrations continued as typical activities in the public schools. In fact, during this time, many of these religious and quasi-religious (Christian) practices were recast as part of the "American civil religion." Some Christian Americans now claimed that matters such as Sunday laws and Christmas celebrations in the public schools were part of a distinctly American civil life. These practices, in other words, were no longer characterized purely as Christian concerns, but rather were supposedly justified in secular terms. Moreover, in the late 1950s, Christian efforts to display their religious symbols publicly seemingly intensified. These displays—including crucifixes, crèches, Easter pageants, and so forth—were funded sometimes publicly and sometimes privately, and were presented sometimes on governmental and sometimes on non-governmental property.[23]

In this post–World War II context, the Supreme Court began to enforce seriously the religion clauses of the first amendment against the state and federal governments. The Holocaust and the reduction in overt antisemitism undoubtedly influenced the Court to move in this direction, but at least four other factors contributed to the transition. First, as already discussed, by the 1950s, Roman Catholicism had become the largest Christian group in America: while Protestants still far outnumbered Catholics, Catholics outnumbered the largest Protestant denomination by almost two to one. As Roman Catholics thus had become a potent political force in American democracy, the Supreme Court's judicial enforcement of the separation of church and state can be understood as another Protestant reaction to a perceived Catholic threat.[24] Significantly, the Supreme Court always remained overwhelmingly Protestant; from the 1940s through the 1970s, no more than one Catholic and one Jew ever sat on the Court at any time.[25] Hence, insofar as Roman Catholic and Protestant values and practices diverged to some extent, the separation of church and state became in part a mechanism that could prevent Catholics from imposing their views on their Protestant rivals. Many Protestants were especially opposed to the public subsidization of the Roman Catholic educational mission; Protestants frequently favored religious practices in the public schools but opposed governmental aid to Catholic schools. I do not wish, however, to overstate the significance of the Protestant–Catholic division for understanding the judicial enforcement of the separation of church and state. Positions on issues of church and state did not (and still do not) neatly divide, with Protestants on one side of the line and Catholics on the other. Indeed, during the 1950s, many Roman Catholics joined Protestants in strongly supporting practices such as the Sunday laws and religion in the public schools.[26] Nonetheless, the fact remains: the Supreme Court began to question the constitutionality of some of these activities only when Roman Catholics, with their burgeoning political power, began to strongly support such practices. Even more telling, in cases challenging governmental aid to nonpublic schools (overwhelmingly Roman Catholic), the Court has struck down the governmental action as unconstitutional nearly twice as often as it has upheld the action.[27] In light of the strong Protestant sentiments against Catholicism expressed often throughout American history, the concurrence of these judicial and social developments does not appear to be a matter of mere chance.

The second additional factor contributing to the Court's increasing solicitude for religious freedom during the postwar era was that Jews and Jewish organizations—especially the American Jewish Committee, the Anti-Defamation League, and the American Jewish Congress—stepped forward to press for the separation of church and state in the courts. In particular, the American Jewish Congress (with its general counsel, Leo Pfeffer) strongly advocated the strict separation of church and state. These organizations were buoyed by the reduction of overt antisemitism in America and spurred by a post-Holocaust sense of urgency; many Jews (though certainly not all) were determined to no longer readily allow overt antisemitism and Christianizing to go unchallenged. Consequently, in a significant number of the most important religion-clause cases, these organizations either instituted the action or participated as amicus curiae.[28]

The third factor was the Court's tendency during this period to become more protective of many civil rights: the Court's movement in religion-clause cases, that is, paralleled its movement in other cases involving individual rights. While the Court no longer was willing to grant constitutional protection to economic interests, as it had before 1937, the Court began during the 1940s and 1950s to reason that certain civil liberties stood in a "preferred position."[29] The Court increasingly granted protection to these so-called preferred freedoms, which included freedom of speech, freedom of the press, and equal protection, as well as religious liberty. Hence, the

Court's growing concern with the separation of church and state was part of a larger judicial trend to safeguard individual rights.

The fourth factor was an ever-increasing emphasis on the importance of democracy, especially in American intellectual circles. America's ideology of democracy and its tendency toward populism (in government and religion)—combining with other causes—influenced America to gradually grow more democratic through its history. At least as a formal matter (but not necessarily as a social reality), the fifteenth amendment, ratified in 1870, extended the right to vote to African Americans, and the nineteenth amendment, ratified in 1920, extended suffrage to women. But it was only in the 1930s that democracy, as a *theory* of government, became a predominant *intellectual* concern (with the possible exception of the constitutional framing period). The earlier part of the twentieth century had seen the rise of scientific empiricism and its apparent corollary, ethical relativism. The appeal of scientific empiricism became most evident in the increasingly important social sciences. In particular, by the 1920s and 1930s, social scientists had rejected formal reasoning and abstract theorizing as means to knowledge and instead turned insistently to the empirical study of individual human actions and social functions. But from this perspective, the discovery of ethical values became problematic because experience and empirical studies provided the only means to knowledge. More precisely, since a knowledge of ethical values could not be grounded clearly on empirical evidence, such values seemed to be merely relative. By the 1930s, intellectuals found it difficult to justify any set of moral values or cultural tenets over any others: all values and cultures had equal claims to validity (and invalidity).[30]

International events during the 1930s transformed this seemingly inevitable acceptance of ethical relativism into an unexpected intellectual crisis. Specifically, for many American intellectuals, the international ascent of totalitarianism (including Nazism) rendered a firm belief in American democracy and the rule of law a necessity. Yet the rise of ethical relativism forced intellectuals to contemplate a disconcerting question: if all values are relative, then why is American democracy better than totalitarianism? In sum, the conjunction of intellectual currents and international events thrust the theoretical justification of democracy to the forefront of American thought.[31]

John Dewey was one of the first to respond to this challenge. In *Freedom and Culture*, published in 1939, Dewey asked what type of culture promotes the political freedoms of democracy. To Dewey, democracy had flourished in America because the culture had produced "a basic consensus and community of beliefs" that is, a commitment to democracy.

Yet, Dewey queried, how can we ensure that democracy will not degener-
ate into totalitarianism, as it had in other parts of the world? He concluded
that the political methods of democracy—such as consultation, persuasion,
negotiation, and communication—need to be extended to the cultural
realm in order to ensure the development and preservation of a culture
that would, in turn, promote political democracy. In short, for Dewey, the
key to democracy lay in democratic procedures: "democratic ends demand
democratic methods for their realization."[32]

The need to justify democracy remained prominent after World War II
as America became enmeshed in the Cold War. Two of Dewey's themes—
the commitment to procedures or processes and the belief in an American
social consensus—became central components in the development of a relativist theory of democracy. While only a few years earlier the relativity of
values threatened to disarm democracy, the same relativism now became
the theoretical foundation for free government. According to relativist
democratic theory, a society must constantly choose what substantive values to endorse and thus what ends to pursue, but since values are relative,
the only legitimate means for choosing among disparate values is the
democratic process. Each individual supposedly brings preexisting values
to the political arena; then, through the democratic process, the community chooses to promote and pursue particular values and goals. At the
communal level, the democratic process itself provides the only criterion
for validating normative choices; there is no standard of validity higher
than acceptance by the people in the political arena. Democracy thus
resembles capitalism: the marketplace (democracy) provides a forum for
the expression of individual preferences and values, and production (the
government) responds accordingly.[33] Moreover, many political theorists
believed that American culture produced a needed consensus regarding
democratic processes. Although various individuals and interest groups
might clash in political struggles, they shared certain elementary cultural
norms that prevented the society from splintering into embittered frag-
ments. Thus, these theorists saw an American society fundamentally and
harmoniously joined in a cultural consensus celebrating the processes of
democracy: individuals freely express diverse viewpoints, they negotiate,
they disagree, and they compromise.[34]

During this postwar era, democracy not only was a predominant concern for American intellectuals, but it also became a central judicial and
political issue. Before the 1940s, the Supreme Court rarely even mentioned
democracy, but from that time on, the Court gave increasing attention
to it.[35] Besides continually referring to democracy, the Court decided a

number of cases that were explicitly intended to promote it—striking down, for example, *some* of the mechanisms that different states had designed to impede African American participation in the democratic process (despite the fifteenth amendment). To illustrate, the Court held in two of the cases that poll taxes in state elections and racially discriminatory gerrymandering were unconstitutional.[36] More broadly, the Court held that no person's vote should be worth more or less than another's: one person, one vote.[37] Meanwhile, Congress enacted legislation—the Voting Rights Act of 1965 and parts of the Civil Rights Act of 1964—designed to guarantee the right to vote by eradicating literacy, educational, and character tests that had been used to discourage minority participation.[38] Also in 1964, the twenty-fourth amendment was ratified, prohibiting poll taxes in federal elections, and in 1971, the twenty-sixth amendment guaranteed the right to vote for anyone eighteen years of age or older.

This postwar emphasis on democracy and the related rise of ethical relativism combined to help push the Court toward its more active enforcement of the separation of church and state. As value relativism had become intellectually acceptable and even in vogue, the governmental imposition of religious values and practices (or any other particular values, for that matter) seemed less justifiable than it had been in previous eras. Indeed, the Court's solicitude for all of the preferred freedoms, discussed above, can be better understood in this context. In an age of value relativism, what mattered most was protecting the ability of each individual both to formulate his or her own values and to participate in the democratic process. Hence, the Court tended to safeguard those constitutional rights that appeared integral to the formation of values—such as freedom of speech and religion—and crucial to the proper functioning of democracy—such as free speech, voting, and equal protection.[39]

In addition, this relation between religion and value relativism helps further to explain the diminution of overt antisemitism, as well as the increasingly common references to the Judeo-Christian tradition during this postwar period. Basically, the prevalence of ethical relativism rendered Judaism somewhat more acceptable to many Americans. In the words of Daniel Silver: "How could anyone claim title to The Truth in an age which had learned the truth of relativity? Whatever Heaven was, if there was a Heaven, entrance was not restricted to one set of believers."[40] Thus, to many Christian Americans (especially Protestants), Judaism came to be understood as a type of quirky Christian sect: why quibble about the details of sectarian differences when "we" all belong to the same Judeo-Christian tradition anyway? To become legitimate in America, then,

Judaism had to be transformed (at least apparently) into a *mere* religion, a matter of individual choice (in the American Protestant tradition); Judaism could no longer (appear to) be an ethnic identity or a way of life. In fact, as already mentioned, many Jews had become deeply assimilated into Christian American culture: these Jews were effectively forced to trade their distinctiveness, their religious and cultural identities, for the opportunity to succeed as Americans.[41] Jews to a great extent had moved from a period (in the early twentieth century) when their differences from Christians were accentuated and objectified and when overt antisemitism was respectable to a period (during the 1950s and later) when their differences from Christians were largely denied or ignored and when overt antisemitism became socially unacceptable.

In sum, the Supreme Court tended to become more receptive to arguments concerning the separation of church and state because of the temporary alignment of a variety of factors: Protestant reaction to Roman Catholic political strength, the advocacy of Jewish organizations, the emergence of a preferred freedoms doctrine, an increased concern for democracy, and post-Holocaust sentiments including opposition to overt antisemitism. In a sense, because of the conjunction of these factors, Jews briefly and partially solved the puzzle of American democracy. During the New Deal, American Jews had "embraced the state" by gaining positions in the Roosevelt administration, but this tie between Jews and the federal government was exceedingly brief and due largely to the unique convergence of interests between Roosevelt and unemployed and underemployed Jewish professionals. Jews thus remained in a structured predicament in American society. On the one hand, Jews occasionally needed protection from Christian overreaching, and throughout (European) history Jews had turned to governmental officials for such refuge in times of crisis. For this reason, the sharp separation of religion and government would be detrimental to Jewish interests, as Jews (qua Jews) would be unable to align with governmental officials. On the other hand, because America was a democracy and overwhelmingly Christian, any governmental support for religion inevitably reinforced Christian values and interests. For this reason, the sharp separation of church and state might, in fact, provide some protection for American Jews.

Postwar American Jews discovered a partial solution to this predicament: the Supreme Court's power of judicial review. So long as the Court remained open to Jewish arguments for the separation of church and state, Jews could (paradoxically) look to the state—that is, the Court—for protection from the state itself—that is, from the Christian masses acting through the instrumentality of the state. More precisely, Jews sought the protection of the state through the institution of the judiciary, with the courts protecting Jews from the reach of the more political branches of government (which were largely controlled by the Christian majority). And the means used by the courts to protect Jews from political overreaching was, of course, the constitutional principle of separation of church and state. So, in other words, Jews embraced the state—as embodied in the courts, especially the Supreme Court—to enforce the principle of separation of church and state in order to be protected from the Christian masses who democratically controlled the state—as embodied in the legislative and executive branches of the national, state, and local governments.

The role of American Jews in the postwar judicial evolution of the separation of church and state is highly complex. Without doubt, the major Jewish organizations played important roles in the litigated cases. Indeed, my critical narrative suggests that many Jews overestimated the benefit of a strict separation of church and state, partly because they oversimplified the relation between religion and government. Nonetheless, as I mentioned when discussing the nineteenth century, American Jews as a small numerical minority were forced to accept certain parameters of the Christian American world. Namely, when seeking religious liberty and equality in America, Jews needed to argue for freedom of conscience and the separation of church and state, even though those concepts were Christian (especially Protestant) and thus foreign to any previous Jewish world view. It was the burden of the prototypical religious outgroup—Jews—to re-articulate the Christian-Protestant theology and interests, as expressed in the religion clauses, to represent some type of principle of religious freedom and equality that might accord at least minimal protection to Jews and not just to Christians. As mentioned, a variety of factors led the Supreme Court to accept at least briefly some of the Jewish arguments concerning church and state, but insofar as any principle of religious freedom and equality developed in the courts, it never strayed far from the Christian-Protestant interests that lay at its foundation.

Before the post–World War II era, the Supreme Court infrequently decided cases under the free exercise and establishment clauses. Furthermore, even in those rare cases, the Court had interpreted the religion clauses as having little bite. Indeed, in *Permoli v. City of New Orleans*, decided in 1845, the Court held that the religion clauses did not apply against the *state* governments at all.[42] And in those cases challenging *federal* activities—typically brought under the free exercise clause—the governmental actions inevitably were upheld as constitutional. For example, in *Reynolds v.*

United States, decided in 1878, Reynolds challenged his criminal conviction for committing polygamy in a federal territory. Reynolds, a Mormon, contended that he was religiously obligated to follow polygamy, and thus he claimed that the conviction violated the free exercise clause. The Court rejected the free exercise claim and upheld Reynolds's conviction. In reaching this conclusion, the Court emphasized a distinction between beliefs and actions: Congress could not constitutionally pass laws that would infringe on religious beliefs and opinions, but Congress could restrict actions for the good of society, even if those actions were supposedly related to religious beliefs. Furthermore, the Court for the first time quoted Thomas Jefferson's gloss on the religion clauses: in an 1802 letter to the Danbury Baptist Association, Jefferson had declared that the first amendment had built "a wall of separation between church and State."[43]

The first key step in the transition of the Supreme Court's approach to the separation of church and state was the application of the free exercise and establishment clauses against the states. The mechanism for this change was the incorporation doctrine: starting in the early twentieth century, the Court held that the due process clause of the fourteenth amendment, adopted during Reconstruction in 1868, incorporated or implicitly included various provisions of the Bill of Rights. These provisions then applied against the state governments, just as they applied against the federal government. In 1940, in *Cantwell v. Connecticut*, the Court held that the free exercise clause was incorporated and applied against the states, and in 1947, in *Everson v. Board of Education*, the Court held that the establishment clause was incorporated.[44] As was somewhat common during the 1940s, *Cantwell* involved a free exercise claim combined with a free speech claim.[45] The Court held that a state violated the first amendment when it demanded that a member of the Jehovah's Witnesses obtain a permit before soliciting money on the street. Beyond the incorporation of the free exercise clause, the case had little precedential value because the Court relied on the free exercise clause only in conjunction with the free speech clause. Meanwhile, in *Everson*, as in *Reynolds*, the Court again drew upon Jefferson's metaphorical wall of separation between church and state to explicate the meaning of the religion clauses, particularly the establishment clause.[46] The Court wrote:

> The "establishment of religion" clause of the First Amendment means at least this: Neither a state nor the Federal Government can set up a church. Neither can pass laws which aid one religion, aid all religions, or prefer one religion over another. Neither can force nor influence a person to go to or to remain away from church against his will or force him to profess a belief or

disbelief in any religion. No person can be punished for entertaining or professing religious beliefs or disbeliefs, for church attendance or non-attendance. No tax in any amount, large or small, can be levied to support any religious activities or institutions, whatever they may be called, or whatever form they may adopt to teach or practice religion. Neither a state nor the Federal Government can, openly or secretly, participate in the affairs of any religious organizations or groups and vice versa. In the words of Jefferson, the clause against establishment of religion by law was intended to erect "a wall of separation between Church and State."[47]

Despite then insisting that the wall between church and state "must be kept high and impregnable," the Court nonetheless rejected the establishment clause challenge, holding that the public reimbursement of transportation costs for children attending either public or Catholic schools was constitutional.[48]

Everson, though, merely inaugurated a series of cases involving the conjunction of religion and education. In the next one, *McCollum v. Board of Education*, decided in 1948, the Court for the first time struck down a governmental action as unconstitutional under the establishment clause. *McCollum* involved a challenge to a released-time program. In this particular program, children were released early from their public school classes once each week so that they could attend religious classes, which were held in the public school buildings. Other children, not seeking religious instruction, were not similarly released from their regular classes. The Court, again emphasizing the wall of separation between church and state, held that this type of released-time program was unconstitutional: "This is beyond all question a utilization of the tax-established and tax-supported public school system to aid religious groups to spread their faith. And it falls squarely under the ban of the First Amendment."[49]

Although *McCollum* was a significant decision, it was not a harbinger of radical change: the Court did not embark on a purge of religion (Christianity) from public life, whether in the schools or elsewhere. *Zorach v. Clauson*, decided in 1952, involved another establishment clause challenge to a released-time program. In this program, unlike the one in *McCollum*, the religious instruction occurred off the public school grounds. Emphasizing this fact, the Court upheld this program as constitutional. In so doing, the Court declared:

> We are a religious people whose institutions presuppose a Supreme Being.... When the state encourages religious instruction or cooperates with religious authorities by adjusting the schedule of public events to sectarian needs, it follows the best of our traditions. For it then respects the

religious nature of our people and accommodates the public service to their spiritual needs.[50]

This declaration strongly resonated with the assertion that America is a Christian nation, which the Court had reiterated numerous times in the past.[51] Moreover, despite evidence showing that Jewish children and other nonparticipants in the released-time program were taunted, ostracized, and proselytized, the Court concluded that the state did not coerce students to participate.[52]

The next important cases arose from several different challenges to a long-standing Protestant tradition in America, the Sunday laws. In a set of four cases, the Court held that these laws violated neither the free exercise nor the establishment clause.[53] The Court downplayed the fact that the Sunday laws undisputably were historically rooted in Christianity. According to the Court, the Sunday laws now were justified by purely secular reasons, such as ensuring a day of rest.[54] Even Orthodox Jews, whose religious convictions demand that they observe the Sabbath on Saturday, were not exempted from the Sunday laws. One case was most remarkable because the Sunday law included an incredible list of exemptions:

[The Massachusetts Sunday law forbids] under penalty of a fine of up to fifty dollars, the keeping open of shops and the doing of any labor, business or work on Sunday. Works of necessity and charity are excepted as is the operation of certain public utilities. There are also exemptions for the retail sale of drugs, the retail sale of tobacco by certain vendors, the retail sale and making of bread at given hours by certain dealers, and the retail sale of frozen desserts, confectioneries and fruits by various listed sellers. The statutes under attack further permit the Sunday sale of live bait for noncommercial fishing; the sale of meals to be consumed off the premises; the operation and letting of motor vehicles and the sale of items and emergency services necessary thereto; the letting of horses, carriages, boats and bicycles; unpaid work on pleasure boats and about private gardens and grounds if it does not cause unreasonable noise; the running of trains and boats; the printing, sale and delivery of newspapers; the operation of bootblacks before 11 a.m., unless locally prohibited; the wholesale and retail sale of milk, ice and fuel; the wholesale handling and delivery of fish and perishable foodstuffs; the sale at wholesale of dressed poultry; the making of butter and cheese; general interstate truck transportation before 8 a.m. and after 8 p.m. and at all times in cases of emergency; intrastate truck transportation of petroleum products before 6 a.m. and after 10 p.m.; the transportation of livestock and farm items for participation in fairs and sporting events; the sale of fruits and vegetables on the grower's premises; the keeping open of public bathhouses; the digging of clams; the icing and dressing of fish; the sale of works of art at exhibitions; the conducting of private trade expositions between 1 p.m. and

10 p.m. . . . Permission is granted by local option for the Sunday operation after 1 p.m. of amusement parks and beach resorts, including participation in bowling and games of amusement for which prizes are awarded.[55]

And the list goes on (and on). Despite this seemingly endless litany of exemptions, the Court upheld the state's astounding refusal to grant an exemption to Orthodox Jews (would granting an exemption have undermined the purpose of the law?). In fact, many states continued to enforce Sunday laws until economic considerations forced a change: as more and more stores opened along suburban highways or in shopping malls instead of in downtown districts, Sunday became increasingly commercialized. These new stores sought to attract shoppers on the weekends, including Sundays, because urban workers could not walk (or run) conveniently into suburban stores while on workday lunch breaks or immediately after work.[56]

The next major decision, *Engel v. Vitale*, probably did more than any other to reinforce the dominant story of the separation of church and state. In 1951, the Board of Regents of the state of New York had recommended that local school boards have children recite a prayer each day in school in order to promote religious commitment and moral and spiritual values. The Regents recommended the use of a supposedly "nondenominational" prayer: "Almighty God, we acknowledge our dependence upon Thee, and we beg Thy blessings upon us, our parents, our teachers and our Country."[57] In 1958, when the school board in the town of New Hyde Park, Long Island, adopted this prayer for use in the classrooms, several parents decided to challenge its constitutionality. Early reactions to this litigation were foreboding, as the plaintiffs received numerous hate letters. One letter, for example, stated: "This looks like Jews trying to grab America as Jews grab everything they want in any nation. America is a Christian nation." Another letter declared: "If you don't like our God, then go behind the Iron Curtain where you belong, Kike, Hebe, Filth."[58] When the Supreme Court decided the case in 1962, *Engel v. Vitale* held that the daily recitation of the Regents' prayer in the public schools violated the establishment clause. The Court drew upon Protestant history to interpret the establishment clause: the Puritans, the Court recalled, had fled England for America in the seventeenth century to avoid following the governmentally imposed Book of Common Prayer for the Church of England. Daily recitation of the Regents' prayer, according to the Court, resounded too closely with the official imposition of a Prayer Book. The Court reasoned further that the first amendment prohibited any law that established an "official religion," even if the law did not coerce religious practices. Regardless, the

Court recognized that coercion existed in this particular context, although the students were allowed to remain silent or to leave the room when their classmates recited the prayer. The Court used language that buoyed the hopes of advocates of a strong separation of church and state:

> When the power, prestige and financial support of government is placed behind a particular religious belief, the indirect coercive pressure upon religious minorities to conform to the prevailing officially approved religion is plain. But the purposes underlying the Establishment Clause go much further than that. Its first and most immediate purpose rested on the belief that a union of government and religion tends to destroy government and to degrade religion.[59]

Court observers either hoped or feared—depending on their perspective—that *Engel* was a watershed decision. To many, *Engel* demonstrated the fulfillment of the dominant story of church and state: surely, the argument went, the religion clauses protected the religious freedom and equality of outgroups if even nondenominational prayers could not be recited in public school classrooms.[60] Consequently, as then described in *The New Republic*, *Engel* provoked "the most savage controversy" since 1954, when the Court held in *Brown v. Board of Education* that racially segregated public schools were unconstitutional.[61] For the most part, *Engel* unleashed a torrent of ridicule on the Court, which, according to many, "had betrayed the American way of life."[62] For example, a *Wall Street Journal* editorial lamented the likely implications of the decision: "Poor kids, if they can't even sing Christmas carols."[63] Unsurprisingly, *Engel* led to yet another spurt of proposals to add a Christian amendment to the Constitution; indeed, the 1964 platform of the Republican Party called for such an amendment. And in a particularly insidious argument, some Christians ominously observed that such judicial decisions might soon spark a wave of antisemitism. These Christians suggested, in other words, that Jews (litigating before the Court) caused antisemitism: Jews could generate a renewal of overt antisemitism if they (and other non-Christians) did not allow Christian Americans to retain those practices that stamped this nation as Christian.[64]

The Supreme Court cases decided in 1963, the year after *Engel*, supported the notion that *Engel* had been a landmark. The first case, *Abington School District v. Schempp*, also involved prayer in the public schools. A state statute required that, at the outset of each day, every public school was to read to its students ten verses from the Bible, recite the Lord's Prayer, and then recite the Pledge of Allegiance. Children could participate "voluntarily" by joining in the Bible reading and prayer recitation; during the prayer and the Pledge, students were asked to stand and speak in unison. Although the statute did not specify what Bible was to be used, the only Bible supplied by the schools was the (Protestant) King James version, which was distributed to each teacher. The Court held that voluntary Bible reading and recitation of the Lord's Prayer violate the establishment clause. In so holding, the Court acknowledged that expert evidence suggested that significant portions of the New Testament were contrary to Judaism.[65] Although the Court reiterated that "[w]e are a religious people," it continued by emphasizing that the establishment and free exercise clauses together require governmental neutrality in matters of religion.[66] Because of this demand for neutrality, the Court explicitly rejected the so-called nonpreferentialist position. According to this position, the establishment clause merely forbids the government from favoring or preferring one religion over another; it does not prohibit the government from favoring religion over non-religion. The Court reasoned that it had repudiated the nonpreferentialist position almost twenty years earlier in *Everson*: "'[N]either a state nor the Federal Government can set up a church. Neither can pass laws which aid one religion, aid all religions, or prefer one religion over another.'"[67] Based on this conception of neutrality, the Court articulated a two-pronged test—focusing on the purposes and effects of the state action—to determine whether a governmental action violated the establishment clause:

> The test may be stated as follows: what are the purpose and the primary effect of the enactment? If either is the advancement or inhibition of religion then the enactment exceeds the scope of legislative power as circumscribed by the Constitution. That is to say that to withstand the strictures of the Establishment Clause there must be a secular legislative purpose and a primary effect that neither advances nor inhibits religion.[68]

The second key religion case from 1963 was *Sherbert v. Verner*.[69] Significantly, *Sherbert* appeared to energize the free exercise clause, just as *McCollum*, *Engel*, and *Schempp* had done (or at least appeared to have done) with the establishment clause.[70] Sherbert had been discharged from her job because she refused to work on Saturday, the Sabbath of her religion, Seventh-day Adventism. When she was unable to obtain alternative employment because of her religious convictions, she applied for unemployment benefits from the state of South Carolina. The state denied Sherbert's claim for benefits, reasoning that she had refused to accept suitable work "without good cause." The Court held this state action unconstitutional under the free exercise clause. In reaching this conclusion, the Court articulated a test for adjudicating free exercise claims: a state can justify a burden on an individual's free exercise of religion only by showing that the state action is necessary to achieve a compelling state interest. Under the facts in *Sherbert*, the Court reasoned that the state's asserted interest in preventing spurious and unscrupulous unemployment claims was insufficient to justify the state action in light of this strict judicial scrutiny.[71] Most important, the compelling state interest (or strict scrutiny) test would remain as the predominant standard in free exercise actions for over two decades.

Similarly, in deciding *Lemon v. Kurtzman* in 1971, the Court articulated a test that would remain for nearly two decades as the predominant standard in establishment clause cases. The so-called *Lemon* test had three prongs: "First, the statute must have a secular legislative purpose; second, its principal or primary effect must be one that neither advances nor inhibits religion; finally, the statute must not foster 'an excessive government entanglement with religion.'"[72] This test further developed the *Schempp* standard by adding the third prong—the focus on governmental entanglement—to the previously articulated two prongs—focusing on the purposes and effects of the state action. In applying this three-pronged test, the *Lemon* Court held unconstitutional two state programs that provided financial aid to church-related schools by supplementing teachers' salaries and paying for books and other instructional materials in secular subjects.

The further development of free exercise doctrine after *Sherbert* is rather easy to summarize. In *Wisconsin v. Yoder*, decided in 1972, the Court struck down another state action as violating the free exercise clause. Members of the Old Order Amish—who are Christians—were convicted for violating a state compulsory education law because they had refused to send their children to school after the eighth grade. The Court applied the compelling state interest test and held the convictions to be unconstitutional; compulsory education did not amount to a compelling interest. In reaching this conclusion, the Court returned to the distinction between belief (or opinion) and action (or conduct) that the *Reynolds* Court had stressed in the late nineteenth century. The *Yoder* Court maintained that unlike religious beliefs, "religiously grounded conduct" can be regulated. But such conduct, the Court emphasized, is still within the ambit of the free exercise clause; therefore, contrary to the state's argument, the Amish's actions were not automatically unprotected under the first amendment.[73]

For many years after *Yoder*, the Court continued to claim that the compelling state interest test was presumptively the proper standard in free exercise cases. The Court would (at least nominally) apply the compelling state interest test unless the factual circumstances suggested that a lower level of scrutiny was appropriate.[74] In fact, regardless of the level of judicial scrutiny, between 1972 (when *Yoder* was decided) and 1990 (when the free exercise doctrine was expressly and significantly changed), the Court held that a governmental action contravened the free exercise clause in only three cases. And each of those cases closely resembled *Sherbert*: the free exercise claims were brought by Christians (belonging either to a minority sect or to no sect at all) who had been denied unemployment benefits.[75]

In all other cases, the Court upheld the governmental actions. For example, in *United States v. Lee*,[76] the Court applied strict scrutiny but nonetheless concluded that the free exercise clause did not require the federal government to exempt an Old Order Amish employer from collecting and paying Social Security taxes. In *Bob Jones University v. United States*,[77] the Internal Revenue Service (IRS) denied tax-exempt status to private schools that, for religious reasons, discriminated on the basis of race. The Court held that the IRS action survived strict scrutiny under the free exercise clause; the eradication of racial discrimination in education was deemed a compelling state interest. In *Goldman v. Weinberger*, the Court rejected the free exercise claim of an Orthodox Jewish rabbi, Goldman, who was an officer in the Air Force. Air Force regulations prohibited wearing any headgear indoors, but as an Orthodox Jew, Goldman needed to wear a yarmulke (skullcap) at all times. In evaluating Goldman's request for a free exercise exemption from the Air Force regulations, the Court reasoned that the special needs of the military for obedience and unity rendered strict scrutiny inappropriate. The Court then concluded that the regulations were reasonable, and as such, they did not violate the free exercise clause.[78] In *Bowen v. Roy* and *Lyng v. Northwest Indian Cemetery Protective Association*, the Court upheld governmental actions that were inconsistent with the religious practices of Native Americans. In both cases, strict scrutiny was deemed inappropriate: the burdens on religion supposedly were insufficient to require that the government justify its actions with compelling interests.[79] In *O'Lone v. Estate of Shabazz*, the Court held that prison regulations preventing Muslim prisoners from attending certain religious services did not violate the free exercise clause. Because of a perceived need to defer to prison officials, the Court reasoned that a level of judicial scrutiny lower than the compelling state interest test was appropriate for evaluating the free exercise claims of prisoners. The Court thus concluded that the prison regulations were constitutional because they were rationally related to a legitimate governmental interest.[80]

Finally, in *Employment Division, Department of Human Resources v. Smith*, decided in 1990, the Court expressly changed the standard for evaluating free exercise claims. Smith belonged to the Native American Church, whose members participate in religious rituals that include the supervised consumption of peyote. Smith was discharged from his job at a private drug rehabilitation clinic because his use of peyote violated the state criminal laws. The Court held that the state criminal law prohibiting the use of peyote even for religious purposes did not violate the free exercise clause. In reaching this conclusion, the Court once again emphasized a distinction between religious beliefs and conduct (or actions). The first amendment precluded all governmental regulations of religious beliefs, but it did not similarly preclude governmental restrictions on conduct—such as the use of peyote—even if the conduct arose from religious convictions. A governmental prohibition on particular religiously motivated conduct would be unconstitutional only if the government restricted that conduct exactly because of its religious foundation.[81] Consequently, and most important, the Court abandoned the strict scrutiny test for free exercise challenges to laws of general applicability. For such laws, the Court claimed that the compelling state interest test was appropriate only in cases involving the denial of unemployment compensation, such as *Sherbert*. In other situations, the Court suggested that the "political process" would effectively determine the scope of free exercise rights.[82] Remarkably, then, the *Smith* Court moved from the previous doctrine of presumptively applying strict scrutiny in free exercise cases—*supposedly* showing almost no deference to the political process—to a doctrine without meaningful judicial scrutiny of challenged governmental actions—a standard showing extraordinary deference to the legislative process. Soon after *Smith*, though, Congress attempted to reinstate the compelling state interest test by enacting the *Religious Freedom Restoration Act of 1993*, but the effects and even the constitutionality of that legislation remain in serious doubt.[83] In any event, based on the *Smith* Court's constitutional doctrine, a free exercise challenge to a governmental action has little chance of success: in all likelihood, the Court would hold a state action unconstitutional under the free exercise clause only if the government intentionally and egregiously discriminated on the basis of religion.[84]

Meanwhile, the further development of establishment clause doctrine is complex. From 1971 until the mid-1980s, the three-pronged *Lemon* test remained unequivocally the dominant standard. For example, in *Stone v. Graham*, decided in 1980, the Court considered the constitutionality of a state statute that required the biblical Ten Commandments to be posted on public classroom walls. Reasoning that the statute violated the first prong of the *Lemon* test because it had no secular purpose, the Court held that it contravened the establishment clause.[85] In *Mueller v. Allen*, decided in 1983, the Court reviewed a state statute that allowed "taxpayers to claim a deduction from gross income for certain expenses incurred in educating their children." Although the statute allowed all parents to claim this deduction—whether their children attended public or private schools—the primary beneficiaries of this statute were parents with children in private schools, which were overwhelmingly parochial (Christian).[86] Nonetheless, the Court held that the statute was constitutional because it satisfied all three prongs of the *Lemon* test, although a strong four-justice dissent argued that the statute violated the second or "primary effects" prong.[87] Significantly, the majority characterized the *Lemon* test as only a "helpful signpost," thus revealing that the justices' commitment to this standard was wavering.[88]

The weakening hold of the *Lemon* test on the Court emerged unmistakably in an opinion handed down only days after *Mueller*. In *Marsh v. Chambers*, the Court held that the practice of having a publicly paid chaplain open state legislative sessions with a prayer did not violate the establishment clause. In so holding, the Court ignored the *Lemon* test and instead reasoned that the opening of legislative sessions "with prayer is deeply embedded in the history and tradition of this country."[89] Unsurprisingly, in light of the Court's reliance on American tradition, the opinion concluded by reiterating that "[w]e are a religious people."[90] Moreover, and also unsurprisingly, the specific state involved in the dispute, Nebraska, had selected the same chaplain for sixteen straight years: he was Protestant (Presbyterian). Although the chaplain characterized his prayers as "nonsectarian," some of the prayers were distinctly Christian, such as the following:

> Father in heaven, the suffering and death of your son brought life to the whole world moving our hearts to praise your glory. The power of the cross reveals your concern for the world and the wonder of Christ crucified.
>
> The days of his life-giving death and glorious resurrection are approaching. This is the hour when he triumphed over Satan's pride; the time when we celebrate the great event of our redemption.[91]

Lynch v. Donnelly, decided in 1984, revealed that establishment clause doctrine had plunged into disarray. The city of Pawtucket, Rhode Island, erected a Christmas display in a park in the heart of the shopping district. The Court described the display as follows:

The display is essentially like those to be found in hundreds of towns or cities across the Nation—often on public grounds—during the Christmas season. The Pawtucket display comprises many of the figures and decorations traditionally associated with Christmas, including, among other things, a Santa Claus house, reindeer pulling Santa's sleigh, candy-striped poles, a Christmas tree, carolers, cutout figures representing such characters as a clown, an elephant, and a teddy bear, hundreds of colored lights, a large banner that reads "SEASONS GREETINGS," and the crèche at issue here. All components of this display are owned by the City.[92]

The sole issue was whether the governmental display of the crèche violated the establishment clause.

The Court ultimately upheld the constitutionality of the governmental action, but the Court's opinion revealed the deep ambivalence (or confusion) of the justices regarding the appropriate doctrine for adjudicating an establishment clause issue. After stating the facts, the Court began with a review of American history—echoing the *Marsh* Court's approach—to show that government and religion have often been entwined despite the establishment clause: "There is an unbroken history of official acknowledgment by all three branches of government of the role of religion in American life from at least 1789." Unlike the *Marsh* Court, however, the *Lynch* Court did not rely solely on history or tradition to uphold the governmental action. Instead, the Court noted that there is no mechanical or fixed rule for resolving establishment clause issues. Yet, the Court continued, the *Lemon* test has often been "useful" in such cases. Consequently, the Court presented the *Lemon* test, only to immediately add a caveat: "But we have repeatedly emphasized our unwillingness to be confined to any single test or criterion in this sensitive area."[93]

Finally, the Court proceeded to apply the *Lemon* test to the facts, but even when applying *Lemon*, particularly the first two prongs (the purpose and effect prongs), the Court again stressed American history in reasoning that the governmental action here satisfied the *Lemon* requirements. In determining that the display of the crèche (supposedly) had a secular purpose, the Court cast Christmas as a historical event rather than a Christian holiday: "The city, like the Congresses and Presidents, however, has principally taken note of a significant historical religious event long celebrated in the Western World. The crèche in the display depicts the historical origins of this traditional event long recognized as a National Holiday."[94] Then, in analyzing the second prong—whether the primary effect of the crèche was to advance religion—the Court again adverted to history. Specifically, the Court reasoned that if the governmental display of the crèche were to fail the primary effects prong of *Lemon*, then many other traditional forms of governmental support for religion—forms that the Court already had upheld—would have to be deemed unconstitutional. Finally, the Court concluded that the display of the crèche did not amount to excessive governmental entanglement with religion—the third prong of *Lemon*. According to the majority, administrative entanglement did not exist because governmental officials were not involved in religious affairs. Furthermore, the crèche display did not generate any political divisiveness.[95] Consequently, the Court held that the governmental display of the crèche satisfied the *Lemon* test and therefore was constitutional.

Because of dissatisfaction with the *Lemon* test, Justice Sandra Day O'Connor wrote a concurrence in *Lynch* that advocated the adoption of an alternative approach. O'Connor's so-called endorsement test had two prongs. First, does the state action create excessive governmental entanglement with religion? Second, does the state action amount to governmental endorsement or disapproval of religion?[96] The endorsement test can be read in at least two different ways. Under one reading, the endorsement test, for the most part, merely reformulated the *Lemon* test. The first prong of the endorsement test was the same as the third prong of the *Lemon* test, and the second prong of the endorsement test amounted in practice to a combination of the purpose and effects prongs (the first two prongs) of the *Lemon* test.[97] Under a second reading, the endorsement test stressed, more so than the *Lemon* test, that the establishment clause should protect an individual's connection to or standing within the political community.[98]

Over the next several years, the Court continued to apply the *Lemon* test to resolve most establishment clause issues,[99] but simultaneously, the endorsement test gathered enough support to appear likely to emerge eventually as the predominant standard. In *County of Allegheny v. American Civil Liberties Union*, decided in 1989, the constitutional question of governmental displays of religious symbols once again was raised. Two different displays were challenged: "The first is a crèche placed on the Grand Staircase of the Allegheny County Courthouse [in downtown Pittsburgh]. The second is a Chanukah menorah placed just outside the City-County Building, next to a Christmas tree and a sign saluting liberty."[100] Apparently, a majority of justices could not agree on any one test or standard for determining the constitutionality of these displays, so the majority opinion articulated both the *Lemon* and the endorsement tests, suggesting that the latter refined the former.[101] Meanwhile, a plurality opinion in the same case not only fully accepted the endorsement test but also argued that a majority of justices previously had accepted the test, though never in one majority opinion.[102] Finally, Justice Anthony Kennedy, concurring and dissenting, advocated that the Court adopt yet a different approach to establishment clause issues. Kennedy's so-called coercion test had two parts: "government may not coerce anyone to support or participate in any religion or its exercise; and it may not, in the guise of avoiding hostility or callous indifference, give direct benefits to religion in such a degree that it in fact 'establishes a [state] religion or religious faith, or tends to do so.'"[103]

Regardless of which test a majority of justices truly applied in *Allegheny County*, the case underscored that the constitutionality of governmental displays of religious symbols would be determined in an ad hoc fashion, with the result depending upon the specific facts of each case. The Court held that the display of the crèche was unconstitutional because it stood alone, unlike the crèche in *Lynch,* which had been part of a larger "Christmas display."[104] Since the *Allegheny County* crèche stood apart, "nothing in the context of the display detracts from the crèche's religious message."[105] Using similar reasoning, the Court then held that the display of the menorah was constitutional largely because it was accompanied by a Christmas tree and a sign saluting liberty. Any religious message of the menorah supposedly was dissipated since the menorah stood within the larger holiday display.[106]

In *Lee v. Weisman,* decided in 1992, the Court held that public schools violate the establishment clause by having clergy deliver invocation and benediction prayers at graduation ceremonies.[107] Daniel Weisman had challenged the constitutionality of this governmental activity after a rabbi offered prayers at his daughter's middle school graduation in Providence, Rhode Island. The series of events that led the school to have a *rabbi* deliver the prayers is illuminating.[108] The Providence school district had a policy of permitting the middle and high schools to invite clergy to give invocation and benediction prayers at graduations. When Weisman's older daughter graduated from middle school in 1986, the speakers at the ceremony included a Baptist minister who asked the audience to stand, bow their heads, and say a prayer that explicitly referred to Jesus Christ. Weisman, who was Jewish, felt "violated" and "appalled," and consequently he complained to school officials.[109] He requested that future graduation ceremonies not include prayers, but the school district refused to change its policy. Thus, when Weisman's younger daughter, Deborah, approached her graduation from middle school in 1989, Weisman twice inquired whether the principal, Robert E. Lee, planned to have prayers at the forthcoming graduation ceremony. After initially not responding to Weisman's inquiries,

Lee finally revealed that he had invited a rabbi to say the prayers. Lee and other school officials assumed that if a rabbi delivered the prayers, then Weisman would not and indeed could not complain. Weisman nonetheless was dissatisfied: he did not want any prayers and did not wish to have his religious beliefs imposed on others. Regardless of Weisman's wishes, Lee refused to revoke the invitation to the rabbi. Then, before the graduation, Lee advised the rabbi to say nonsectarian prayers and also gave the rabbi a pamphlet prepared by the National Conference of Christians and Jews that contained guidelines for public prayers at civic ceremonies.[110] Deborah Weisman and her family attended her graduation ceremony, and the rabbi did in fact deliver the invocation and benediction prayers. Subsequently, Daniel Weisman sought a permanent injunction barring Lee and other Providence public school officials from inviting clergy to say prayers at future graduations.

With a clever gambit, the Court declared that it would resolve this case without clearing the morass of establishment clause doctrine. Specifically, the Court stated that in this case it would not reconsider the vitality of the *Lemon* test,[111] but the Court did not then apply or otherwise rely upon *Lemon*. Instead, the Court wrote:

> It is beyond dispute that, at a minimum, the Constitution guarantees that government may not coerce anyone to support or participate in religion or its exercise, or otherwise act in a way which "establishes a [state] religion or religious faith, or tends to do so." The State's involvement in the school prayers challenged today violates these central principles.[112]

The majority opinion, written by Justice Kennedy, thus accepted the coercion test, first introduced in Kennedy's *Allegheny County* dissent, as a permissible method for adjudicating establishment clause claims. The *Weisman* Court seemed to suggest that of the three major establishment clause tests—the *Lemon*, coercion, and endorsement tests—the coercion test provides the least protection for religious liberty. Hence, if a governmental action contravenes the coercion test, then the action surely would violate the *Lemon* and endorsement standards and should be held unconstitutional. The Court, according to this reasoning, could decide the *Weisman* case without determining the fate of the beleaguered *Lemon* test. The implication, apparently, is that *Lemon*, at least for the time being, remains good law—an adequate if not the predominant method for adjudicating establishment clause issues.[113]

In any event, the Court focused its analysis on the issue of coercion: would the public school practice of having clergy deliver prayers at graduation coerce a student such as Deborah Weisman into participating in a religious exercise? In concluding that coercion was present in this context, the Court emphasized that the graduates were adolescents, who might be coerced more easily than adults. Thus, contrary to the argument of Justice Antonin Scalia in dissent, coercion might exist even though the government was not "by force of law and threat of penalty" imposing a religious orthodoxy or demanding financial support for religion.[114] Rather, coercion can be indirect and can arise from psychological pressure to conform to certain religious practices. The majority wrote:

> The undeniable fact is that the school district's supervision and control of a high school graduation ceremony places public pressure, as well as peer pressure, on attending students to stand as a group or, at least, maintain respectful silence during the Invocation and Benediction. This pressure, though subtle and indirect, can be as real as any overt compulsion.[115]

Having accepted a conception of coercion that included indirect and psychological pressure, the Court still needed to respond to two more governmental arguments: first, that Deborah voluntarily chose to attend the graduation, and second, that she was free to attend the graduation without participating in the prayers. If either of these arguments were accepted, then Deborah and other students seemingly would not be coerced to participate in a religious exercise. With regard to the first point, the Court reasoned that while Deborah chose or consented to attend the graduation, she did not do so voluntarily. That is, her only choices were to attend or not to attend, but a graduation ceremony is such an important event to many students and their families that Deborah's choice to attend should not have been deemed voluntary. Absence from the graduation "would require forfeiture of those intangible benefits which have motivated the student through youth and all her high school years." With regard to the second point, the Court maintained that Deborah could not have attended the graduation without feeling coerced to participate in the prayers. According to the majority opinion, a "reasonable dissenter" in the position of Deborah Weisman would have believed that her attendance at graduation "signified her own participation or approval of [the prayers]."[116]

Cases after *Weisman* have not clarified the doctrinal confusion swirling around the establishment clause. For the most part, the justices in these recent cases have avoided confronting the problematic status of the doctrine. The Court has eschewed articulating any definitive standard for adjudicating the establishment clause issues, and instead usually has emphasized a need for governmental neutrality in religious affairs. For example, in *Zobrest v. Catalina Foothills School District*, the Court held that a public school district can provide a sign-language interpreter for a student in a Roman Catholic high school without contravening the establishment clause. The Court reasoned, in typical language, that "government programs that neutrally provide benefits to a broad class of citizens defined without reference to religion are not readily subject to an Establishment Clause challenge just because sectarian institutions may also receive an attenuated financial benefit."[117] In *Rosenberger v. Rectors and Visitors of the University of Virginia*, the Court came close to articulating some type of test for resolving establishment clause issues: "[W]e must in each case inquire first into the purpose and object of the governmental action in question and then into the practical details of the program's operation."[118] Nonetheless, in holding that the University of Virginia had violated the establishment clause by withholding university financial support for a student-run Christian publication, the Court emphasized that the government must act neutrally, not treating religious organizations less favorably than secular ones.[119]

In one case, *Capitol Square Review and Advisory Board v. Pinette*, decided in 1995, the intense disagreement among the justices became manifest. In *Pinette*, the Court held that a private actor, the Ku Klux Klan, could constitutionally display a large Latin (Christian) cross on public property. In a plurality opinion, four justices explicitly rejected the endorsement test: "[T]he endorsement test does not supply an appropriate standard for the inquiry before us. It supplies no standard whatsoever."[120] In particular, the plurality emphasized that the endorsement test itself raises a difficult problem: if, following the endorsement test, any governmental action that endorses religion is to be held unconstitutional, then from whose perspective should endorsement be determined? Despite this difficulty, four other justices expressly accepted and applied the endorsement test, but they disagreed about the ultimate result. Justice O'Connor's concurrence, joined by Justices David Souter and Stephen Breyer, insisted that "the endorsement test necessarily focuses upon the perception of a reasonable, informed observer."[121] To O'Connor, this reasonable observer should be "a personification of a community ideal of reasonable behavior, determined by the [collective] social judgment."[122] Justice John Paul Stevens, who dissented, agreed that the endorsement test is the appropriate standard and that it should be applied from the perspective of a reasonable observer. But Stevens criticized O'Connor's conception of the reasonable observer as being an "ideal human [who] comes off as a well-schooled jurist." To Stevens, the reasonable observer should be a person "who may not share the particular religious belief" symbolized in the disputed public

246 PLEASE DON'T WISH ME A MERRY CHRISTMAS

display.[123] Hence, *Pinette* did not clarify the doctrine for adjudicating establishment clause issues: to the contrary, *Pinette* disclosed the depth of disagreement that exists among the justices in this field.

A BRIEF ASSESSMENT OF THE SUPREME COURT CASES

In one popular formulation of the dominant story of the separation of church and state, constitutional scholars and historians maintain that the Supreme Court decisions in the latter half of the twentieth century fulfilled the American principle of religious liberty. In this section and in the next chapter, I contest this viewpoint. To be sure, during some of the period after World War II, the Court articulated doctrine—such as the strict scrutiny test in free exercise cases—that seemed especially protective of religious minorities. Nevertheless, a study of the holdings in religion clause cases reveals far fewer victories for religious outgroups than the dominant story would lead one to expect. In this section, then, I challenge the dominant story in two ways: first, by reviewing the case holdings, and second, by discussing how the Court conceptualizes religion in distinctly Christian terms. In the next chapter, I delve deeper into the relation between the cases, the separation of church and state, and the Christian domination of American society. In the end, the dominant story seems not only false but even duplicitous.

As Mark Tushnet has trenchantly noted, only Christians ever win free exercise cases.[124] Members of small Christian sects sometimes win and sometimes lose free exercise claims, but non-Christians *never* win. The significance of Christianity to a successful free exercise claim emerged most clearly in *Wisconsin v. Yoder*. The Court there emphasized that Old Order Amish communities were devoted "to a life in harmony with nature and the soil, as exemplified by the simple life of the early Christian era that continued in America during much of our early national life." Thus, the Court seemed especially receptive to the Amish's claim for a free exercise exemption from a state compulsory-education law because they were able to appeal to the justices' romantic nostalgia for a mythological past—a simple Christian America.[125] This national past—however mythological it might be—was one that most of the justices (as Protestants) could readily understand; its meaning resonated with the religious and cultural horizons of the justices themselves. Thus, whereas members of non-Christian religious minorities have difficulty convincing the Court of the sincerity and meaningfulness of their religious convictions, the *Yoder* Court quoted the New Testament in reasoning that "the traditional way of life of the Amish is not merely a matter of personal preference, but one of deep religious conviction." Because the Amish were Christians, the Court could easily relate their way of life to Christian society and Christian history:

> Whatever their idiosyncrasies as seen by the majority, this record strongly shows that the Amish community has been a highly successful social unit within our society, even if apart from the conventional "mainstream." Its members are productive and very law-abiding members of society; they reject public welfare in any of its usual modern forms. . . . We must not forget that in the Middle Ages important values of the civilization of the Western World were preserved by members of religious orders who isolated themselves from all worldly influences against great obstacles. There can be no assumption that today's majority is "right" and the Amish and others like them are "wrong."[126]

The Court consequently sympathized with the Amish's contentions in *Yoder* far more than it ever seemed to do with those of non-Christians, whether Jews, Moslems, or others.[127] The *Yoder* Court's receptive attitude contrasts sharply with the Court's approach to the free exercise claim of the Orthodox Jewish Air Force officer in *Goldman v. Weinberger*. In rejecting Goldman's request for a free exercise exemption to allow him to wear his yarmulke despite Air Force regulations, the Court wrote: "The considered professional judgment of the Air Force is that the traditional outfitting of personnel in standardized uniforms encourages the subordination of personal preferences and identities in favor of the overall group mission."[128] Two points in this passage bear emphasis. First, the Court's stress upon "standardized uniforms" disregards the fact that the *standard* will almost always mirror the values and practices of the dominant majority—namely Christians. Put bluntly, the U.S. military is unlikely to require everyone to wear a yarmulke as part of the standard uniform. Second, and most clearly opposed to the *Yoder* Court's receptiveness, the *Goldman* Court characterized the wearing of a yarmulke as a matter of mere *personal preference*. Evidently, the majority of the justices (all of the justices at this time were Christian) were unable to comprehend the significance of the yarmulke. In Orthodox Judaism, the wearing of a yarmulke or other head covering is far from a personal preference; it is a custom going back so many centuries that it has attained the status of a religious law. For many Orthodox Jews, wearing a yarmulke is not a choice but a necessary part of being Jewish; to fail to wear one would amount to a sin. Moreover, Justice Harry Blackmun's dissent revealed that the Court was informed about the significance of the yarmulke to Orthodox Jews.[129] Apparently, the majority nevertheless could not grasp the meaning of this non-Christian religious practice.

Finally, in *Employment Division, Department of Human Resources v. Smith,* the Court repudiated the strict scrutiny test for free exercise challenges to laws of general applicability and upheld a state law prohibiting the use of peyote even for religious purposes. In so doing, the Court brushed away any semblance of doctrine that had suggested that the free exercise clause equally protects the religious freedom of all, including outgroups. If *Smith* has a virtue, it lies in the forthright manner in which the majority declared that religious outgroups will not receive judicial protection from most instances of majoritarian overreaching and insensitivity. Quite simply, when the government enacts a law of general applicability, the protection of religious liberty and equality will depend upon the political process. The Court will not attempt to enforce any particular principle of religious freedom and instead will defer to the legislative decision, so long as it is not infected by discriminatory intent. Moreover, the *Smith* Court expressly acknowledged that this judicial approach to free exercise favors the religious majority: "It may fairly be said that leaving accommodation to the political process will place at a relative disadvantage those religious practices that are not widely engaged in; but that [is an] unavoidable consequence of democratic government."[130]

While the *Smith* Court candidly admitted that it would no longer pretend to judicially protect religious outgroups under the free exercise clause, the Court was either less forthright or less aware that its very conception of religion was distinctly Christian. This Christian concept of religion was evident in at least two related ways (both of which have appeared in other cases). First, the Court emphasized a distinction between belief and conduct: the first amendment fully protects religious beliefs but does not similarly protect religiously motivated conduct.[131] This constitutional doctrine mirrors basic Christian dogma: that salvation depends largely on faith or belief in the truth of Jesus Christ and not on works or conduct in this world.[132] And this Christian dogma, stressed particularly in Protestantism, is grounded on the antisemitic imagery of the New Testament: the opposition between a world of Christian spirituality and a world of Jewish carnality, and the injunction against forcing Jewish conversion because true Christian faith cannot be compelled. Hence, from a Christian standpoint, the potential for uncoerced belief in Christ must be protected in order for salvation to be possible, but the protection of this-worldly conduct is unnecessary because such conduct is largely unrelated to salvation. Indeed, the *Smith* Court closely echoed Luther and Calvin by emphasizing that while the government cannot be allowed to coerce beliefs, the government must be able to regulate conduct to prevent social chaos or, in the Court's words, to avoid "courting anarchy."[133]

Second, the Court's Christian conception of religion was evident in the justices' assumption that only *individual choices* have religious significance sufficient to require constitutional protection. The Court wrote: "The government's ability to enforce generally applicable prohibitions of socially harmful conduct, like its ability to carry out other aspects of public policy, 'cannot depend on measuring the effects of a governmental action on a religious objector's spiritual development.'"[134] From the Court's Christian standpoint, so long as the government does not coerce religious belief, governmental activity is unlikely to seriously affect an individual's religious well-being. An individual's religious development or salvation—in the Christian world view—depends upon freedom of conscience: the individual must be able to follow the dictates of conscience to the truth of Christ. Moreover, as the concept of freedom of conscience evolved in nineteenth-century American Protestantism, the individual must remain free to choose Christian salvation, that is, free to choose to accept Christ. Governmental activities that impede the use of peyote, as in *Smith*, or that damage lands sacred to Native Americans, as in *Lyng v. Northwest Indian Cemetery Protective Association*, or that prevent an Orthodox Jew from wearing a yarmulke, as in *Goldman v. Weinberger*, do not interfere (supposedly) with the individual's freedom to make religiously significant choices. Consequently, from the Court's Christian-biased perspective, these types of governmental activities are constitutionally permissible under the free exercise clause.[135]

In establishment clause cases, too, the centrality of the Christian conception of freedom of conscience stands paramount. *Lee v. Weisman* might be considered a good case from the perspective of religious minorities: Weisman, a Jew, won the case, as the Court held that public schools violate the establishment clause by having clergy deliver invocation and benediction prayers at graduation ceremonies. Indeed, since the *Weisman* Court displayed unusual sensitivity to and empathy for the experiences of religious outgroups, the decision unquestionably stands as one of the best of the good cases, enforcing a strong wall of separation between church and state.[136] Yet, even in *Weisman*, the Court's Christian conception of religion was unmistakable, as the majority opinion emphasized the importance of freedom of conscience under both the free exercise and establishment clauses: "A state-created orthodoxy puts at grave risk that freedom of belief and conscience which are the sole assurance that religious faith is real, not imposed."[137] Similarly, in another apparently good case, *Wallace v.*

Jaffree, holding unconstitutional a statute authorizing a period of silence for "meditation or voluntary prayer," the Court underscored the significance of freedom of conscience to both religion clauses by identifying "the individual's freedom of conscience as the central liberty that unifies the various Clauses in the First Amendment." Then, in a passage dripping with unintended irony, the Court appeared to stress that first amendment protections extend equally to all religions, but in making this argument, the Court unwittingly used Christian and Protestant imagery, focusing on individual faith and voluntary choice in religious matters.

> Just as the right to speak and the right to refrain from speaking are complementary components of a broader concept of individual freedom of mind, so also the *individual's freedom to choose* his own creed is the counterpart of his right to refrain from accepting the creed established by the majority. At one time it was thought that this right merely proscribed the preference of one Christian sect over another, but would not require equal respect for the conscience of the infidel, the atheist, or the adherent of a non-Christian faith such as Islam or Judaism. But when the underlying principle has been examined in the crucible of litigation, the Court has unambiguously concluded that the individual *freedom of conscience* protected by the First Amendment embraces the right to select any *religious faith* or none at all. This conclusion derives support not only from the interest in respecting the *individual's freedom of conscience,* but also from the conviction that religious beliefs worthy of respect are the product of *free and voluntary choice by the faithful,* and from recognition of the fact that the political interest in forestalling intolerance extends beyond intolerance among Christian sects—or even intolerance among "religions"—to encompass intolerance of the disbeliever and the uncertain.[138]

Hence, the holdings in cases such as *Wallace* and *Weisman* reveal that religious outgroups, including American Jews, occasionally emerge from litigation with a victory—a decision that prohibits the Christian majority from using the instrumentality of the government to impose Christian practices or values. These victories, though, are often less pronounced than they at first appear, as suggested by the foregoing discussion. Even when upholding the rights of religious minorities, the Court conceptualizes the very notion of religion in distinctively Christian terms. While judicial victories for religious outgroups are not necessarily Pyrrhic, such victories nonetheless often come with great costs. To be clear, I am not suggesting that religious outgroups, including American Jews, would be better off without the judicial decisions striking down various governmental actions in support of Christianity. But I am arguing that the story is far more complex than the dominant story of church and state suggests.

In fact, regardless of the Christian bias embedded in many of the Court's opinions, a simple review of the establishment clause holdings reveals fewer victories than suggested by the dominant story of church and state. Most of the victories have come in cases that challenged either, on the one hand, egregious impositions of religious (usually Christian) practices and values in public schools or, on the other hand, governmental aid to religious schools (overwhelmingly Roman Catholic). In some notable victories, the Court struck down the following governmental actions as violating the establishment clause (this list is not exhaustive): voluntary Bible reading and reciting the Lord's Prayer in the public schools;[139] the daily recitation of a state-created "nondenominational" prayer in the public schools;[140] a released-time program with instruction on public school grounds;[141] a statute that prohibited public schools from teaching the theory of evolution;[142] state programs providing financial aid to church-related schools by, for instance, supplementing teachers' salaries and paying for instructional materials;[143] a tuition tax scheme providing tax credits and deductions for parents with children in nonpublic schools;[144] a statute that required the posting of the Ten Commandments on public classroom walls;[145] a state law regulating charitable solicitations that favored certain religions over others;[146] a state program providing remedial education to children in parochial schools;[147] a statute authorizing a period of silence for meditation or voluntary prayer in the public schools;[148] a statute that required public school teachers to teach creation science whenever they taught the theory of evolution;[149] the governmental display of a crèche standing alone;[150] and a public school policy to have clergy deliver invocation and benediction prayers at graduation ceremonies.[151]

These decisions are significant, but they do not justify the pervasive belief in the dominant story of church and state. Even if these cases represented genuine victories for religious outgroups seeking the strict separation of church and state, a similar number of cases represented equally significant losses. During the post–World War II era, the Court upheld the following governmental actions as not violating the establishment clause (again, this list is not exhaustive): the governmental reimbursement of transportation costs for children attending either public or Catholic schools;[152] a released-time program when religious instruction was not on public school grounds;[153] Sunday closing laws without exemptions for Jews or others with non-Sunday sabbaths;[154] a statute lending books to parochial school students;[155] the granting of property tax exemptions to churches;[156] a state university opening its facilities to registered student groups, including an evangelical Christian student group that focused on religious worship and discussion;[157] a statute providing all parents with a tax deduction for certain educational expenses, regardless of whether their children attended public or nonpublic schools;[158] having a publicly paid chaplain open state legislative sessions with a prayer;[159] the governmental exhibit of a crèche as part of a larger Christmas display;[160] a statutory exemption of religious organizations for employment discrimination on the basis of religion in connection with secular nonprofit activities;[161] governmental provision of a sign-language interpreter for a student at a Roman Catholic high school;[162] the display on public property by a private actor of a large Latin (Christian) cross;[163] and governmental financial support of an explicitly Christian student publication.[164]

One of the most remarkable *losses* for religious outgroups was *Thornton v. Caldor, Inc.*, decided in 1985.[165] In *Thornton*, the Court considered the constitutionality of a Connecticut statute that allowed employees to not work on their religious sabbath, whatever day of the week that might be. The statute, without doubt, manifested an unusual degree of legislative sensitivity to religious outgroups: the state legislature recognized that not everybody is a Christian celebrating a Sunday sabbath, so the state provided non-Sunday sabbath observers (such as Jews) with benefits similar to those enjoyed for two centuries by most Christians in states with Sunday closing laws. The Court, it should be recalled, previously had upheld the constitutionality of Sunday laws in the face of free exercise and establishment clause challenges.[166] If the dominant story of church and state were accurate—that is, if the separation of church and state truly were a constitutional principle that equally protects the religious freedom of all, including outgroups—then one would expect the Court to uphold this Connecticut statute. After all, the Court already had upheld Sunday laws, and this statute appeared merely to accommodate the religious practices of outgroups. Nonetheless, the Court held that the statute violated the establishment clause. To reach this conclusion, the Court relied on the second prong of the *Lemon* test, reasoning that the primary effect of the statute was to advance religion.[167] Consequently, despite the professions (or pretensions?) of the dominant story, the Court not only upheld (in previous cases) the constitutionality of Sunday closing laws, thus approving the legal imposition of the traditional Christian sabbath, but then the *Thornton* Court also struck down a statute designed to accommodate the sabbaths of religious outgroups, thus denying equal treatment and full religious liberty to certain minorities.

Moreover, in reaching this conclusion, the *Thornton* Court's reasoning (once again) displayed a distinctly Christian conception of religion. In particular, the Court characterized an individual's observance of the sabbath as a matter of mere choice. In fact, the Court suggested that if it upheld the statute, then an individual might designate whatever day of the week he or she chooses as the sabbath.[168] In so reasoning, the Court echoed the Christian and particularly Protestant notions that religious beliefs matter more than conduct and that religiously significant actions are a matter of individual choice. Specifically, from the Court's perspective, a person's conduct in observing the sabbath seemed relatively unimportant because (from the Christian standpoint) it could not affect salvation (which is solely a matter of belief or faith). Furthermore, according to the Court, the religious individual remains free to choose whether or not to observe the sabbath in the first place. The Court ignored (or was unaware) that for some outgroup religions, such as Judaism, conduct may be as important as or even more important than belief. Moreover, for many Jews, especially the Orthodox, following the sabbath is far from being a matter of individual choice: it is a central component of the religion. Morris N. Kertzer writes: "The Sabbath is more than an institution in Judaism. It is *the* institution of the Jewish religion."[169] Considering that the disputed statute was expressly intended to accommodate members of outgroup religions, the justices' failure to seriously heed the views of minorities revealed the incredible tenacity of the Court's Christian bias.

Moreover, the Court does not always show such indifference toward sabbath observance. Indeed, if *Thornton* is compared with another case from the 1980s, *Frazee v. Illinois Department of Employment Security*, the Court's indifference (or hostility?) toward religious outgroups (and their sabbaths) and not toward sabbath observance in general is underscored. In *Frazee*, the Court held that the state had violated the free exercise clause by denying Frazee unemployment benefits when he refused to work on Sunday because he was Christian. Most telling, in comparison with *Thornton*, the *Frazee* Court reasoned that the claimant's desire to observe Sunday as the sabbath was not a "purely personal preference," even though he was *not* a member of any particular Christian church or sect.[170] Apparently, for the *Frazee* Court, a bald assertion of Christianity was sufficient to establish the importance of the sabbath and the legitimacy of the resultant free exercise claim.

To be clear, I do not mean to suggest with this discussion that the Supreme Court justices never have been motivated, even in part, by a desire to follow their conception of the separation of church and state as a constitutional principle. Undoubtedly, some justices were so motivated (at least sometimes). Nonetheless, the justices' very conceptions of separation of church and state most often arose from their Christian backgrounds. Indeed, as I have discussed, totally apart from the *justices'* conceptions or understandings, the concept of the separation of church and state itself is rooted in Christianity. The dominant story of church and state therefore is just too simple and misleading. A constitutional principle of separation of church and state does *not* equally protect the religious liberty of all, including outgroups, and does *not* determine judicial outcomes in religion clause cases. The true story is much more complex.

CHAPTER 10

A Synchronic Analysis of the Separation of Church and State in the Late Twentieth Century

Concluding Remarks

The dominant story of the separation of church and state consists of two claims. First, the separation of church and state stands as a constitutional principle that promotes democracy and equally protects the religious liberty of all, especially religious outgroups, including Jews. Second, this principle emerges as a unique American contribution to political theory. My critical social narrative has demonstrated the bankruptcy of the second claim. The separation of church and state did not magically spring into being in America, during either the colonial or the constitutional framing period, even if the Enlightenment background of American thought is accounted for. Instead, the separation of church and state emerged as a political and religious development beginning with early Christianity and evolving over the next two millennia.

My narrative also has called into question the first claim of the dominant story. Various versions of the dominant story place the victorious ascendance of religious liberty and equality at different times: during the late eighteenth century, after the framing and the adoption of the first amendment; during the nineteenth century, after the last official state establishments withered away; or during the twentieth century, after the Supreme Court began seriously enforcing the religion clauses against the state and federal governments. Regardless of these variations, the de facto establishment of Christianity and the pervasive antisemitism throughout the nation's history render any version of the dominant story highly suspect. American social reality belies the assertion that a constitutional principle of separation of church and state promotes democracy and equally protects the religious liberty of all in America.

To bring my critical social narrative of church and state to a close, this chapter presents a synchronic critique of the separation of church and state in the latter twentieth century. I diagnose (or critically analyze) how the constitutional principle of separation of church and state contributes to the current orientation of power within American society.[1] How does the constitutional concept of separation of church and state contribute to the Christian domination of American society, including Christian cultural imperialism over religious outgroups, particularly Jews? To pursue this analysis, I approach the problem of Christian social power from three perspectives, which correspond to the first three sections of this chapter. First, I focus on how *symbolic* power—especially in the form of language—contributes to Christian domination: how does the constitutional discourse of the Supreme Court in religion clause cases sustain this domination? Second, I focus on *structural* power: how does the separation of church and state relate to the structural relations within American society? Third, I examine the *relationship between symbolic and structural* power: especially, how does the symbolism of the separation of church and state create an ideology that simultaneously masks and legitimates Christian domination?

Two related points, mentioned in chapter 1, should be underscored at this point. First, I approach the question of power in society from a postmodern perspective.[2] Unlike a modernist approach to power, which typically locates power in some conscious or intentional center, such as an individual, a group of individuals, or a sovereign, a postmodernist approach underscores that "power is everywhere and in everyone."[3] Second, my analysis of Christian power in American society entails an extensive discussion of antisemitism.[4] From a postmodern standpoint, antisemitism cannot be limited to intentional or conscious anti-Jewish actions and attitudes. Instead, antisemitism refers broadly to the intentional or unintentional, conscious or unconscious, hatred, dislike, oppression, persecution, domination, and subjugation of Jews qua Jews for whatever reason or motivation, whether it be religious, cultural, ethnic, racial, or political.

SYMBOLIC POWER

Symbolism should be understood as a technique for or a means of implementing power and, simultaneously, as a consequence or effect of power.

The most pervasive type of symbolism is language.[5] In one way, language represents a technique of power because words directly and indirectly implement power. Some words, such as those constituting a promise or a threat, amount to performative acts, while other words trigger certain feelings, actions, or both in the interpreter (the person hearing or reading the words).[6] For example, particular words can trigger specific coercive and violent social actions or practices: the legal discourse denying a petition for habeas corpus can lead to a capital defendant's execution. Yet, in a second way, language looms as an even more direct means of implementing power. As Michel Foucault says: "Discourse transmits and produces power."[7] Our "distinct ways of talking about and interpreting events" constitute the shape of our very being-in-the-world.[8] The conceptual distinctions and criteria of legitimation embedded in our discursive practices shape our understandings and perceptions of social events and reality. Hence, in this second way, language appears as a technique of power because it helps to produce and reproduce meaning and thus social reality.[9]

The philosophical hermeneutics of Hans-Georg Gadamer elucidates this power of language.[10] Gadamer explains that our prejudices and interests, derived from communal traditions (including the culture and history of our community), simultaneously enable and constrain understanding and interpretation.[11] Prejudices and interests open us to the possibility of understanding: without prejudices and interests, understanding and communication are impossible. But at the same time, our prejudices and interests necessarily constrain and direct our understanding and communication. One's life within a community and its cultural traditions always limits or distorts one's range of vision—what one can possibly perceive or understand. In short, we can never step outside the horizon of our prejudices and interests to find some firmer foundation for understanding.[12] Moreover, according to Gadamer, language is the "medium" of tradition and understanding: "Language is the fundamental mode of operation of our being-in-the-world and the all embracing form of the constitution of the world."[13] Hence, from a Gadamerian perspective, language (as tradition) appears as a technique of power insofar as it enables and constrains (or produces and limits) understanding and meaning (and hence social reality).

Simultaneously, though, language appears as a consequence or effect of power. According to Gadamer, we are historical beings who *live* in tradition, just as we live in a community: tradition is not a thing of the past; rather, it is something we constantly participate in. Thus, we constantly constitute and reconstitute our tradition and hence our language as we engage in dialogical understanding. The use of a language is recursive;

language reproduces itself. In sum, then, language can be understood as both a technique and an effect of power because, on the one hand, language helps (re)produce meaning and social reality, and on the other hand, language itself is part of the (re)produced social reality.[14]

Within any large society, different cultures or subcultures have their own distinctive (though often overlapping) languages. Different (sub)cultures therefore offer contrasting discursive interpretations of social events and reality (or, in effect, different social realities). There is, in short, a struggle between discourses. Cultural imperialism arises when one discourse or culture manages to dominate another.[15] And when one culture emerges to thoroughly dominate the competing (sub)cultures, then that dominant culture exercises hegemonic power. That is, the dominant culture so completely controls the understanding of social events and reality that its understanding becomes the normal, the neutral, and the natural. As Dick Hebdige declares, the dominant culture tends "to masquerade as nature."[16] The contingent assumptions and interpretations of the dominant culture become tacit, invisible, or appear as mere common sense; they become so neatly woven into the social fabric that they no longer are understood as cultural or as manifestations of power. In short, power hides behind its own productions.

As discussed, we constantly constitute and reconstitute our traditions: cultural traditions therefore are neither static nor permanent. Gadamer writes: "Even the most genuine and pure tradition does not persist because of the inertia of what once existed. It needs to be affirmed, embraced, cultivated."[17] Like any cultural tradition, then, an imperialistic or hegemonic culture must constantly be reproduced and sustained. For that reason, subcultural discourses or interpretations of reality represent "oppositional readings," deviant threats to the complex web of meanings enforced by the dominant culture.[18] For the imperialistic culture to maintain its dominant position, it must neutralize or subdue any such threats. One common technique for subduing a subcultural discourse is the redefinition of the subculture—the redefinition of the "Other."[19] This redefinition can occur in at least two different ways. First, the differences between the dominant culture and the subculture can be denied. That is, the difference of the Other is denied; the Other becomes the Same. The distinct elements of the subculture are ignored or obscured as the dominant culture imperialistically absorbs the subordinate group.[20] Second, the dominant culture can actively exclude and objectify the members of the subcultural group. With this latter form of redefinition, the dominant group may acknowledge the differences of the subculture, but those differences now establish the inferiority of the subcultural group.[21] In short, the dominant culture defines difference (from itself) as inferiority. In many instances, the dominant culture consigns the members of the subcultural group to a position beyond common decency, sometimes outside of humanity itself. From the perspective of members of the dominant culture, such objectification can seem to justify the most heinous emotional and physical abuses of the subcultural members (for, after all, they are barely human or even less than human). Most important, with either form of redefinition—denial of difference, or exclusion and objectification—the dominant culture attempts to define the *subculture* itself. The struggle between the dominant and subcultural discourses encompasses the very being and social identity of the subcultural group and its members.

This viewpoint partly reveals how Christian cultural domination has historically produced antisemitism. For most of the last two millennia, Christians have maintained a position of hegemonic domination in western society by, in part, implementing both forms of redefinition to subdue the threat of a Jewish subculture.[22] To some extent, the difference between Christianity and Judaism lies in the *meaning* attributed to the life and death of Jesus: to Christians, but not to Jews, Jesus was the Messiah and the Son of God.[23] Consequently, the New Testament, as Christian discourse (and dogma), seeks to subdue the threat of the Jewish counter-discourse—the Jewish refusal to accept the Christian meaning of Jesus. As discussed in chapter 2, the New Testament denies the Jewish difference by appropriating Jewish history and the Hebrew Bible (literally renamed as the Old Testament) to support the Christian interpretation of reality (the coming of Jesus as the Messiah). After Jesus' death, his followers searched the *Hebrew Bible* for historical passages that they could interpret to show that *Jesus'* life and death as the Messiah had been prophesied. They sought, in effect, to deny or negate the Jewish understanding of Judaic history in their effort to bolster the Christian interpretation of history as leading to Jesus as the Messiah. The New Testament, in short, attempts to (re)define Judaism itself to serve Christian purposes.

Furthermore, the New Testament objectifies Jews and attempts to establish their inferiority. In particular, the New Testament opposes a world of Christian spirituality to a world of Judaic carnality. Indeed, according to Christian discourse, Jews refused to accept Jesus because, supposedly, they were from the Devil. Hence, the New Testament condemns the Jewish world yet nonetheless commands that Jews not be physically coerced into converting to Christianity. The New Testament narrative therefore expressly designates the Jews as deserving a fate of endless persecution and suffering— until they finally realize their blindness and truly come to believe that Jesus was Christ.

The initial redefinition of Jews in the New Testament has generated and appeared to justify many subsequent imperialistic acts by Christians. For hundreds of years during the Middle Ages, Jews were persecuted, subjugated, and sometimes even banished from Christian society. They were forced to wear badges or other signs of identification, isolated in ghettos, and exiled from entire countries. In twentieth-century Europe, the still-persistent objectification of Jews facilitated the Holocaust. Average Germans more readily performed their jobs within the modern bureaucratic state because they felt spiritually and emotionally distant from Jews, and eventually, of course, this distance was solidified by the physical isolation of Jews in ghettos and concentration camps. In sum, for nearly 2000 years of western history, Christian hegemonic power has been remarkably complete.

In America today, the more common (though not solitary) form of antisemitic redefinition is denial of difference. Many Christians seem to consider Judaism to be merely a quirky Protestant sect: Chanukah, for example, becomes the Jewish Christmas when Jews erect Chanukah bushes (do they celebrate Easter too?). Christian hegemony and the concomitant denial of difference are so complete in America that the most egregious examples of cultural imperialism fade to invisibility. Jews must accept the public display of a crèche as representative of secular American traditions. Jews must participate (joyfully) in the annual Christmas party, play, carol singing, or whatever. Any Jew who objects is (take your pick) pushy, odd, a kill-joy, or ridiculous. Jews, after all, are (supposedly) no different from other (Christian) Americans; therefore, they should participate in the "neutral" and "secular" social activities of the school, business, and community. In short, even the most blatant, ostentatious, and public celebratory symbols of Christianity are considered neither extraordinary nor offensive; to the contrary, they usually are accepted, condoned, and sometimes even governmentally financed. From this perspective, many if not most Christians do not *intentionally* oppress or discriminate against Jews. Rather, Christian Americans (as well as members of American religious outgroups, such as Jews) are born and mature within a pervasively Christian society that acculturates them to (immediately and unconsciously) understand Christian views, symbols, and activities as the neutral, normal, and natural.[24] In Gadamerian terms, the Christian traditions of America produce Christian prejudices and interests in individuals.

In interpreting the religion clauses of the first amendment, the Supreme Court contributes to this cultural imperialism by explicitly and implicitly using Christian concepts to explicate the constitutional provisions. In Gadamerian terms, the justices understand the religion clauses from their own horizon constituted by (to a great extent) Christian prejudices and interests. Hence, as discussed in chapter 9, the Court emphasizes that the first amendment protects the individual's freedom of conscience, which is grounded firmly on Protestant and New Testament theology. Another striking example is the Court's recently developed "coercion test" in establishment clause cases. Under this test, which a majority applied in *Lee v. Weisman,* the government acts unconstitutionally if it coerces anyone "to support or participate in any religion or its exercise."[25] This prohibition against governmental coercion resonates strongly with the New Testament injunction against coercing Jews to convert to Christianity. According to this Christian theology, true Christian faith cannot be forced, so the Court must interpret the religion clauses to protect the individual's ability to willingly or voluntarily follow his or her conscience to Christ.

The Court's understanding of the first amendment in Christian terms is most broadly evident in the metaphorical wall of separation between church and state, which the Court tends to stress most strongly in those cases that appear to be victories for religious outgroups. While the Court typically attributes this concept to Thomas Jefferson, a rationalist and deist, the metaphor is firmly grounded in the Puritan symbolic imagery of separate or bounded spheres, as previously articulated by writers such as Roger Williams and John Locke. This bounded-spheres imagery, in turn, rests on the New Testament symbolic opposition between distinct worlds of Christian spirituality and Jewish carnality, and the related injunction against using temporal force to compel Jewish conversion. To a great extent, then, the Court interprets the religion clauses to create a wall of separation between church and state because of this Christian symbolism: in order for religion and government both to flourish, the church and the state must remain within their respective spheres. Thus, as suggested in the New Testament, the state must not interfere with religious affairs. Religious (Christian) faith cannot be sincere if coerced by civil or state officials; the state, in effect, represents a threat to religiosity and salvation. In addition, the flip side of this relation became increasingly significant as the modern sovereign state developed and swelled in importance: the church should not interfere in governmental affairs. In particular, advocates of a strong and high wall of separation between church and state insist that the state cannot function properly if political discourse and governmental activities are influenced or determined by religious faith. From this perspective, the modern democratic state supposedly rests upon rationality—rationality should ground public discourse and governmental actions—and religious faith is arational, if not irrational. As the Court wrote in *McCollum v. Board of Education,* "the First

Amendment rests upon the premise that both religion and government can best work to achieve their lofty aims if each is left free from the other within its respective sphere."[26]

This Christian-derived bounded-spheres imagery also grounds the public/private dichotomy that is so central to religion clause cases. In this manifestation of the bounded spheres, the carnal and temporal realm becomes the public sphere of secular governmental action. The spiritual realm of Christian faith becomes the private sphere of individual religious action and salvation. In fact, quite often, the Court's discourse in religion clause cases bolsters Christian cultural imperialism by construing or labeling oppressive Christian displays and revelries either as secular or as protected private sphere activities.[27] When, for example, a particular activity is defined or coded as private—as separate from government—then the constitutional constraints imposed upon state actors are rendered irrelevant. This public/private dichotomy was crucial in *Capitol Square Review and Advisory Board v. Pinette,* decided in 1995. The Court held that the display of a large Latin (Christian) cross on public property did not violate the establishment clause. The public property, a "state-owned plaza surrounding the Statehouse in Columbus, Ohio," qualified as a traditional public forum because "[f]or over a century the square [had] been used for public speeches, gatherings, and festivals." More important, though, the plurality opinion emphasized that a private actor, the Ku Klux Klan, and not the government had erected the cross: "[P]rivate religious expression receives *preferential* treatment under the Free Exercise Clause. It is no answer to say that the Establishment Clause tempers religious speech. By its terms that Clause applies only to the words and acts of government. It [does not impede] purely private religious speech." Thus, even when the government must grant a permit to a speaker (as in *Pinette*), the constraints of the establishment clause do not apply; private actors remain free to disseminate their Christian messages on publicly owned property. In fact, quite predictably, after the district court issued an injunction permitting the Klan to erect its cross, the state "then received, and granted, several additional applications to erect crosses on [the public plaza]."[28]

Employment Division, Oregon Department of Human Resources v. Smith, when viewed in conjunction with *Pinette,* elucidates the intimate link between the public/private dichotomy and Christian societal domination. In holding that the compelling state interest test should not be used in most instances to adjudicate the constitutionality of laws of general applicability, the Court acknowledged that the religious majority occasionally might act through the legislative process to the disadvantage of religious minorities.

Nonetheless, to the Court, this possibility was an "unavoidable consequence of democratic government."[29] Thus, while the *Pinette* Court emphasized that the free exercise clause extends preferential treatment to private religious expression, the *Smith* Court declared that the free exercise clause allows the majority, through legislation, to restrict the religious practices of minorities. If these two cases are read together in the context of American society, they suggest that the free exercise clause extends *preferential* treatment to *Christian* religious expression and beliefs. Because the overwhelming majority of Americans are Christian, most private religious expression will be Christian (and protected by *Pinette*), and most legislative actions will reflect Christian beliefs and practices (and be protected by *Smith*).[30]

In a similar vein, when a particular activity is defined or coded as *secular*, the activity supposedly has been removed from the realm of the religious and is therefore legitimated by the principle of separation of church and state. Despite the possibility that a Jew or a member of another minority religion might experience or perceive that very activity as decidedly Christian, the declaration of secularity (by the Supreme Court or some other empowered governmental actor or institution, such as a school board) justifies the activity within the dominant discourse. And quite often, constitutional rhetoric imperialistically ignores religious outgroups and the oppressive consequences of Christian activities and symbols for members of such outgroups; there is, in other words, a denial of experiences and perceptions that differ from the Christian viewpoint. In this manner, constitutional rhetoric effectively neutralizes or normalizes many common forms of Christian societal domination by declaring or coding them to be secular.[31]

For example, in *McGowan v. Maryland* and *Braunfeld v. Brown,* the Supreme Court upheld the constitutionality of Sunday closing laws in the face of establishment and free exercise clause challenges. The Court claimed to identify the general sentiments of the American people by effacing the differences between Christian Americans and other Americans (the plaintiffs in *Braunfeld,* for instance, were Orthodox Jews).

> [I]t is common knowledge that the first day of the week has come to have special significance as a rest day in this country. *People of all religions and people with no religion* regard Sunday as a time for family activity, for visiting friends and relatives, for late sleeping, for passive and active entertainments, for dining out, and the like. "*Vast masses of our people, in fact, literally millions,* go out into the countryside on fine Sunday afternoons in the Summer...." Sunday is a day apart from all others. The cause is irrelevant; *the fact exists.* It would seem unrealistic for enforcement purposes and perhaps detrimental to the general welfare to require a State to choose a common day of rest other than that which *most persons* would select of their own accord.[32]

The Court trivialized the long history of Sunday blue laws, which showed that they originated and developed to support Christian beliefs. According to the Court, the governmental choice of Sunday for a day of mandated rest was "of a secular rather than of a religious character."[33] Consequently, the Orthodox Jewish plaintiffs in *Braunfeld* were forced, in effect, to observe the Christian day of rest, Sunday, even though their own sabbath was Saturday.

Based on similar (though perhaps more outrageous) reasoning, in *Lynch v. Donnelly* the Court held that the public display of a crèche does not violate the establishment clause. The Court wrote:

> When viewed in the proper context of *the Christmas Holiday season,* it is apparent that ... there is insufficient evidence to establish that the inclusion of the crèche is a purposeful or surreptitious effort to express some kind of subtle governmental advocacy of a particular religious message. In a pluralistic society a variety of motives and purposes are implicated. The City ... has principally taken note of a *significant historical religious event* long celebrated in the Western World. The crèche in the display depicts the *historical origins* of this *traditional event* long recognized as a *National Holiday.* ... The narrow question is whether there is a secular purpose for Pawtucket's display of the crèche. The display is sponsored by the City to celebrate *the Holiday* and to depict the origins of that Holiday. These are legitimate secular purposes.[34]

This passage illustrates how the Court used legal discourse to neutralize the Christian message of a crèche for purposes of constitutional adjudication. In the Court's terms, Christmas—the Christian holiday celebrating the birth of Jesus Christ—somehow becomes secular. The Court coded (or labeled) Christmas as a traditional and historical event, and the very birth of Jesus himself becomes merely the historical origin of that event. Hence, members of religious outgroups are symbolically absorbed into the Christian mainstream so that they too must enjoy and celebrate "the" Holiday.

Regardless of how a dominant culture attempts to redefine a subculture and its members—either through denial of difference, or exclusion and objectification, or both—one symptom (and cause) of redefinition is the silence (and even invisibility) of the Other. Members of the subcultural group go unheard (and sometimes unseen) by members of the dominant cultural and other subcultural groups. Indeed, in the face of cultural imperialism, outgroup members sometimes figuratively (and sometimes literally) stop speaking, so that there is nothing to be heard.[35] In *Lynch,* for example, the Court supported its conclusion by noting that, prior to that lawsuit, nobody had complained about the crèche even though it had been publicly displayed for forty years.[36] To the Court, this silence meant that the crèche had not generated dissension; apparently, everybody happily supported the Christmas display. The Court overlooked the possibility, however, that Christian cultural imperialism had produced the silence of religious out-group members. Silence can bespeak domination, not consensus.

STRUCTURAL POWER

Although language is both a technique and an effect of power that contributes to cultural imperialism, language simultaneously floats or plays at a distance from power. For instance, when the Supreme Court denies the habeas petition of a capital defendant, the consequences that follow are unrelated to the niceties of legal reasoning in the Court's opinion. The reality of an execution does not turn on whether the legal doctrine or discourse mandated a particular conclusion. To the contrary, the justices on the Supreme Court exercise power over habeas petitioners not necessarily because of legal acumen or judicial expertise, but rather because they are Supreme Court justices. Each justice operates from a position or role of extraordinary power within the social institution of the criminal justice system.[37] From this perspective, then, we see that power frequently is structural. That is, power "exists in relationships—it has a primary location in the ongoing, habitual ways in which human beings relate to one another."[38] Individuals often exercise power not because of their personal qualities, abilities, or knowledge, but because they occupy certain relatively embedded (though contingent) social roles that endure within complex social practices and institutions. To be sure, social roles do not exist in some pure or idealistic sense; they are neither self-defining nor defined solely through language (though discourse contributes to the construction of social roles). Rather, social roles are defined in part by the relations between various institutional positions, that is, by the organizational scheme of the society.[39]

Furthermore, social roles do not merely empower individuals, such as Supreme Court justices, to perform certain actions; social roles also help *produce* perceptions, attitudes, and actions. In other words, social structures and the resultant social roles at least partly construct or constitute subjects (or persons). The very identity and being of an individual are partly constituted by the position or role that he or she holds within the organizational scheme of the society—by the set of social relations that the individual's position or role holds vis-à-vis other positions and roles. Hence, some feminists emphasize that a nurturing relationship between parent and infant can produce certain pro-social personality traits.[40] At the same time, however, this perspective underscores that cruelty, hatred, and inhumanity are also (at least partly) socially produced through the structural organization of society. An otherwise ordinary and moral person can readily perform incredible atrocities on others if placed in the appropriate social role. In one psychology experiment, for example, subjects were divided into two groups, prisoners and guards, with the guards having complete control over the prisoners. Beyond all expectations, the guards enthusiastically fulfilled their authoritarian roles by brutally mistreating the prisoners.[41] As Iris Marion Young writes:

> Oppression [including cultural imperialism] in the structural sense is part of the basic fabric of a society, not a function of a few people's choice or policies. You won't eliminate this structural oppression by getting rid of the rulers or making some new laws, because oppressions are systematically reproduced in major economic, political, and cultural institutions.[42]

From this perspective, then, we can understand Christian domination and antisemitism to be at least partly structural. Once again, then, antisemitism is revealed to be not merely a matter of intentional discrimination against Jews; rather, individuals (typically, Christians) fulfill their roles within an antisemitically structured society—a society organized in a manner to produce social relations manifesting antisemitism. Moreover, since social structures partly constitute subjects, the antisemitic structures embedded in society partly construct or constitute the Christian subject or individual to be antisemitic. To be clear, I do not mean that every Christian person intentionally discriminates against Jews, but rather that most Christians participate in cultural imperialism by assuming that certain inherently Christian symbols and interpretations of social reality represent the normal, the neutral, and the natural. And most Christians participate in cultural imperialism exactly because they are Christians. They occupy the position of Christian (whether or not they actively practice Christianity) in a society hegemonically dominated by Christian culture and religion.

It bears emphasis that the conceptualization of social structures should not be reified. Social roles and structures do not exist in some pure or idealistic sense, nor are they concrete or material objects that exist apart from social relations. Rather, structures and roles develop over time, through history, as certain social relations are repeated again and again, becoming entrenched (or habituated) in evolving social practices and institutions. In this sense, then, social structures are historically contingent: they depend in part on what has come before, on the historical development of social relations. Consequently, the structures of Christian domination in American society are historically contingent. The structures arose and exist because of the particular shape and movement of American history. That contingency, though, does not make them any less real or significant.[43]

In the previous section, I discussed how the legal discourse of the religion clauses contributes to Christian cultural imperialism. Yet, once Christian imperialism and antisemitism are revealed to be also structural, legal discourse appears in an alternative light, as but one factor affecting the strength and pervasiveness of religion (Christianity) in society. In particular, insofar as the power of Christianity is partly structural, it arises from the organization of social relations, from the daily, mundane social interactions of individuals fulfilling certain social roles or positions. Consequently, legal discourse might, in some circumstances, have little effect on the structures of Christian domination in America (or on the societal or de facto establishment of Christianity).

In a comparative study of religion in nineteenth-century America and England, Martin Marty observes that the programs and functions of the disestablished churches in America closely resembled those of the established Church of England.[44] This study suggests that the existence or non-existence of an officially (or governmentally) established church does not necessarily affect the power of Christianity pulsing through the social body; in some instances, official establishment might not alter the degree of Christian cultural imperialism. Hence, for example, during the nineteenth century, even as a growing number of states disestablished their churches, American Protestantism became stronger as the Second Great Awakening spread across the country, and overt antisemitism increased in response to Jewish immigration. Perhaps more telling, today in the late twentieth century, the United States, of course, still has no officially established churches, but it is far more religious than any other western industrialized nation. And the religion of the United States is clearly Christianity. Despite some ebb in the religiosity of Americans during the 1960s and 1970s, recent studies suggest that "nine persons in ten believe Jesus Christ actually lived, seven in ten believe he was truly God, and six in ten think one must believe in the divinity of Christ to be a Christian. [Studies also document] consistently high levels of belief in life after death, heaven, and Christ's presence in heaven."[45] Furthermore, statistics suggest that the educated are more religious than the uneducated:

> Among college graduates in this country, only 3% say they do not believe in God, while 77% report that their relationship with God is either "extremely close" or "somewhat close." The percentage of college graduates who

believe in life after death (76%) is the same as that for the general population, and the percentage of college graduates who attend church nearly every week (30%) is slightly higher than the national average.[46]

Unsurprisingly, with Christianity being so strongly if unofficially established in America, even *overt* antisemitism may be resurgent. While doubted by some, the conclusions of the Anti-Defamation League's 1992 Audit of Anti-Semitic Incidents are alarming, even with the caveat that the implications of such social science surveys are ambiguous. The ADL Audit found that approximately 50 million Americans hold "strong" antisemitic beliefs.[47] Worse still, these Americans "qualified" as strongly antisemitic by answering affirmatively at least six out of eleven questions that tested for overt antisemitism, such as whether Jews are more willing than others to use shady practices to get ahead.[48] Many more Americans answered one or more of these questions affirmatively without reaching the number needed to qualify as strongly antisemitic. For example, approximately 77.5 million Americans believe that Jews have too much power in the United States. Thus, in just over one decade, the proportion of Americans believing that Jews have too much power has *increased* from 10 percent to over 30 percent![49] Significantly, the ADL Audit does not even attempt to measure or report the number of Americans who harbor antisemitic attitudes but do not express them overtly, either because of social etiquette or because their antisemitism operates primarily at an unconscious or unintentional level. At a minimum, then, one should certainly be wary of claims that antisemitism in America is dying or dead.[50]

Specific reports of antisemitic incidents, including violence and vandalism, support the conclusion that overt antisemitism has been increasing over the last ten to fifteen years. From 1988 to 1992, the number of antisemitic episodes on college campuses, usually involving graffiti and hate speech, grew by 110 percent. Throughout the 1980s, the number of attacks on or defacements of Jewish homes, synagogues, and community centers increased relatively consistently. In a startling incident in 1992, a drama group at an Indiana high school was presenting a play about Jewish survivors of the Nazi concentration camps. When the non-Jewish cast wore the Jewish stars from their costumes, they were subjected to "flagrant antisemitism." One cast member stated: "I was in class and people were snickering 'I hate Jews' and 'Jews killed Christ'."[51]

Overt antisemitism even has begun to reemerge as a political force. Whereas less than twenty years ago an obviously antisemitic statement would have probably been fatal to a public life, in politics or otherwise, during the 1980s and 1990s, politicians and other public leaders have uttered antisemitic remarks with few negative consequences.[52] In some prominent examples, Governor Kirk Fordice of Mississippi declared that the United States was a "Christian nation," and when asked to say instead "Judeo-Christian," he explicitly refused.[53] Secretary of State James Baker, responding to American Jews who criticized his anti-Israel stance, said, "Fuck them [the Jews]. They didn't vote for us."[54] Presidential candidate Jesse Jackson referred to New York City as "Hymietown."[55] Presidential candidate and columnist Pat Buchanan charged that the Israeli Defense Ministry and its "amen corner" in the United States had promoted the Persian Gulf War; Buchanan then called Congress an "Israeli-occupied" territory.[56] Some Christian fundamentalist leaders echoed traditional antisemitic attitudes. Pat Robertson wrote that rich Jews have conspired to take over the world, and Jerry Falwell said, "A Jew can make more money accidentally than you can make on purpose."[57] As the 1992 ADL Audit concludes: "In the worlds of politics, culture, and education, Jew-baiting, anti-Semitic scapegoating and conspiracy accusations have become not only more common, but more casually tolerated and rationalized ... reflecting [an] erosion of the taboo against open bigotry."[58]

With Christian domination and antisemitism being so deeply entrenched in the structures of American society, legal discourse—even Supreme Court constitutional discourse on the religion clauses—cannot completely control the manifestation of power in the religious realm.[59] Supreme Court decisions, one might say, are not self-executing: decisions holding, for example, that prayers in the public schools are unconstitutional do not necessarily beget the eradication of public school prayers throughout the nation. The *New York Times* reported in 1994 that, despite the Court rulings, "prayer is increasingly a part of school activities from early-morning moments of silence to lunchtime prayer sessions to pre-football-game prayers for both players and fans. [P]articularly in the South, religious clubs, prayer groups and pro-prayer students and community groups are making religion and prayer part of the school day." In fact, the *Times* added, a school superintendent in a town near Austin, Texas, was removed from office after issuing a directive that prohibited prayers at football games and other school events.[60] In short, so long as the country remains pervasively Christian, the Court's ability to change the structures (and eliminate the symbols) of the de facto establishment of Christianity is highly questionable (assuming that the Court actually wants to do so, which it does not).[61]

Because Supreme Court justices are themselves embedded in the structures of Christian domination in American society, they tend to reach decisions that manifest and then reproduce those very structures. The Court, more often than not, interprets the concept of separation of church and state in a manner that remains consistent with most practices and values of the dominant Christian majority. This phenomenon is most obvious in cases where the Court explicitly relies on American history or traditions to throw light on the meaning of the religion clauses. Christian domination is deeply rooted in American history, so any judicial reliance on tradition or history inevitably will result in the constitutional approval of Christian practices and values. Predictably, then, in *Marsh v. Chambers,* the Court upheld the practice of having a publicly paid chaplain open state legislative sessions with a prayer, even though the same Protestant minister had served as chaplain for sixteen consecutive years. The Court stressed that the use of such publicly paid chaplains was a common tradition in state and federal legislatures throughout American history. Similarly, in *Lynch v. Donnelly,* the Court relied upon a history of governmental entwinement with religion (Christianity) to guide the application of the *Lemon* test. Consequently, the Court managed to conclude that the governmental display of a crèche was secular, did not advance religion, and was thus constitutional. In these and similar cases, the Court's reliance on history tends to give a constitutional imprimatur to the preexisting structures of American society—to the structures of Christian domination. Indeed, in *Marsh,* the Court stressed that it sought to acknowledge "beliefs widely held among the people of this country"; such beliefs unavoidably manifest Christian values and practices.[62]

THE INTERACTION OF SYMBOLIC AND STRUCTURAL POWER

The relation between symbolic and structural power is complex, and I do not pretend to offer here a complete analysis of that relationship. Most briefly, symbolic power helps reconstruct the social relations that generate societal structures both directly (for instance, by coding the existence of certain social roles) and indirectly (for instance, by providing rhetoric that hides the structural imposition of power). Simultaneously, structural power helps reconstruct language and other symbols because structures help produce both the individual (who uses language appropriate to his or her role) and the entire social system (which provides the environment for nurturing the symbols of that social system by, for example, partly determining what social roles carry sufficient power to strongly influence the meanings of particular symbols).[63]

In the previous chapter, I discussed how the Court consistently conceptualizes religion in Christian terms, even in cases that strongly enforce the separation of church and state. The interaction of structural and symbolic power further illuminates this phenomenon. In particular, members of the Supreme Court occupy certain structured roles in American society: they are justices, *and* they are usually Christian, most often Protestant. As *justices,* they wield tremendous power (even if they cannot alone change society), and as *Christians,* they wield their judicial power from the dominant religious and cultural position within American society. Thus, even in decisions that seem to protect religious outgroups, the justices typically understand and present religion in predominantly Christian terms.

Many commentators claim that *Engel v. Vitale* exemplifies the dominant story of the separation of church and state. *Engel,* it is argued, demonstrated that the establishment clause protects religious outgroups because the Court held that in the public schools even nondenominational prayers could not be forced on non-Christians, agnostics, and atheists. But even in *Engel,* the justices reiterated the "principle" of separation of church and state with language that unwittingly re-presented and reinforced a Christian and specifically Protestant world view: "The Establishment Clause ... stands as an expression of principle on the part of the Founders of our Constitution that religion is too personal, too sacred, too holy, to permit its 'unhallowed perversion' by a civil magistrate."[64] By contrasting the "perversions" wreaked by civil magistrates with the holiness of religion, the Court echoed the New Testament opposition between the carnal world of the condemned Jews and the spiritual world of the saved Christians. The Court's symbolic imagery implicitly suggested that a world of Christian spirituality must be protected from the poison of the carnal and temporal (Jewish) world. Moreover, by suggesting that religion is a highly "personal" matter, the justices' rhetoric resonated with the Christian focus on individual salvation and the especially Protestant emphasis on individual choice.

One of the most important ways in which symbolic and structural power can interact is to produce ideology: symbolism, usually language (discourse), that either justifies, legitimates, explains, masks, or renders uncontroversial particular structured social relations.[65] In the context of separation of church and state, the constitutional discourse of the religion clauses both masks and legitimates Christian hegemony. The dominant story of church and state maintains that the religion clauses of the Constitution protect minority religions against oppression. Supposedly, the principle of separation of church and state secures religious liberty fully and equally for all, including religious outgroups. Hence, the story continues (in its post–World War II incantation), to safeguard the all-important principle of separation of church and state, the Supreme Court stands vigil, enforcing the religion clauses by ensuring that the government does not become overly involved in religion. Yet, contrary to the rhetoric of the dominant story, the structure of American society constantly produces and reproduces Christian hegemonic domination, regardless of governmental involvement or noninvolvement in religion. In other words, constitutional discourse furnishes a façade of governmental neutrality and individual religious freedom, but behind that legitimating façade, Christian cultural imperialism pulses through the social body of America.

After *Employment Division, Oregon Department of Human Resources v. Smith*, for example, a law of general applicability that burdens religiously motivated conduct will be held unconstitutional under the free exercise clause only if the government intentionally discriminated on the basis of religion.[66] Based on this intent requirement, if the complainant cannot prove that the government has acted culpably, then the Court supposedly must conclude that the government acted neutrally and therefore constitutionally. But this intent requirement fails to account for perhaps the most pervasive manifestation of Christian imperialism in America today—namely, unconscious religious oppression, and more specifically, unconscious antisemitism. As discussed in the preceding sections on symbolic and structural power, antisemitism often is not intentional or conscious, but rather is a product of acculturation and structural relations that frequently operate at an unconscious level.[67] Hence, under the current free exercise doctrine, governmental actions manifesting unconscious antisemitism most likely will be deemed constitutional and therefore legitimate in American society. Moreover, the Court's establishment clause doctrine operates similarly. Under the *Lemon* test (and perhaps under the endorsement test as well), the Court must inquire into the purposes and effects of governmental action. Yet, the Court has been conspicuously hesitant to strike down governmental actions based solely on their effects, so the *Lemon* inquiry most often focuses on the purpose prong.[68] As with the free exercise doctrine, this judicial focus on governmental purposes or intentions will lead the Court to grant constitutional approval and legitimacy to actions that manifest unconscious antisemitism.

County of Allegheny v. American Civil Liberties Union further illustrates in an interesting fashion how constitutional discourse can legitimate Christian cultural imperialism. The Court held that the public display of a crèche violated the establishment clause. Although this holding might appear to recognize the strong Christian symbolism of Christmas and Christmas displays—including a crèche—the Court nonetheless noted: "The presence of *Santas* or other *Christmas* decorations elsewhere in the county courthouse ... fail to negate the endorsement effect of the crèche. The record demonstrates clearly that the crèche, with its floral frame, was its own display distinct from any other decorations or exhibitions in the building."[69] Hence, the Court held that a crèche standing alone is religious, but in so doing, the Court legitimated as secular the display of many other Christmas symbols, such as a Santa Claus and a Christmas tree.[70] These are, to be sure, *Christian* symbols: as Winnifred Fallers Sullivan notes, items such as a Santa, a tree, and the like are "the very stuff of ritual and of religious symbolism."[71] In fact, the Court bizarrely suggested that a crèche would be rendered secular if it were displayed *with* such other Christmas decorations. (On a personal note, I have known many Jewish children who wanted a Christmas tree or to visit with Santa Claus, but I have never known any Jew who believed that Christmas, Christmas trees, or Santa was Jewish or anything other than Christian.)

Derrick Bell's interest-convergence thesis helps to further elaborate the ideological quality of religion clause jurisprudence. According to Bell, African Americans historically have gained social justice only when their interests happened to converge with the interests of the white majority. For example, Bell argues that the Supreme Court decided *Brown v. Board of Education* not because it was morally or legally right, but because it coincided with the interests of middle- and upper-class whites.[72] If we attempt to transfer this interest-convergence thesis to the realm of religion, and specifically to the separation of church and state, then we can generalize and enhance the thesis, understanding it anew as representing a technique of power.

The doctrine of separation of church and state assumes that the government poses the greatest threat to religious liberty. This assumption, as discussed, arises largely from the New Testament dichotomy between a spiritual world and a temporal and carnal world. In pre-capitalist and pre-democratic societies, moreover, despotic states often established official religions, forced individuals to support those favored religions, and thereby frequently provoked civil strife. Nonetheless, the modern (postmodern?) democratic state represents little threat to a hegemonically dominant cultural group, such as Christians in America. Quite simply, in a democracy dominated by Christians and including a plurality of Christian sects and groups, the government rarely (if ever) can muster the despotic power to oppress Christians qua Christians (or to oppress specific groups of Christians).[73]

The modern democratic state, however, readily can muster the despotic power to oppress religious outgroups such as Jews. This realization underscores that religious outgroups benefit, at least to some degree, from the separation of church and state. In the American democracy, the overwhelming Christian majority largely controls the government, if only because of sheer numbers. To the extent that the constitutional doctrine of separation of church and state actually prevents the Christian-dominated government from actively and directly conjoining with or bolstering religion, then Christianity cannot be imposed on members of outgroup religions through the instrumentality of the government. And to be sure, the courts do occasionally interpret the religion clauses to prevent a conjuncture of Christianity and government. As discussed in chapter 9, a number of cases can be characterized as victories for religious outgroups. For example, in *Abington School District v. Schempp*, the Court held that the recitation of the Lord's Prayer in public schools is unconstitutional.[74] Likewise, in *Edwards v. Aguillard*, the Court held as unconstitutional a state statute that required public schools to teach creation science whenever they taught the theory of evolution.[75] Nevertheless, while the separation of church and state occasionally protects minority or outgroup religions, that protection often dwindles into a limited, hypothetical, or even nonexistent refuge. Thus, as noted, many cases can be characterized as losses for religious outgroups. Christianity can be imposed on members of outgroup religions through the instrumentality of the government so long as legal discourse labels or codes the governmental action as secular or private. Governmental actions conducted in the guise of secularity, for instance, can endorse, propagate, and otherwise support Christianity because, from the perspective of constitutional doctrine, the government has not impermissibly conjoined with religion (since the governmental action is considered non-religious).[76]

Recalling Derrick Bell's interest-convergence thesis, we now can understand why the separation of church and state often provides only minimal benefits to outgroup religions such as Judaism. To a great extent, outgroup religions benefit when (or because) their interests happen to converge or correspond with the interests of Christians. The benefits to outgroups, in other words, are *incidental*, while the *primary* benefits of separation of church and state flow, in fact, to Christianity, the hegemonically dominant religion in America. Furthermore, while the accrual of primary benefits to Christianity occasionally entails incidental benefits for outgroup religions, it also frequently imposes certain costs on those outgroup religions. For instance, as the discussion of ideology suggests, the principle of separation of church and state simultaneously benefits Christianity and harms minority religions by furnishing a façade of governmental neutrality and religious freedom that hides and legitimates the Christian cultural imperialism that pulses through the American social body.[77] Indeed, the concept of neutrality that lies entrenched in the Court's current understanding of the separation of church and state forestalls considering seriously that the religion clauses might prohibit governmental commingling with Christianity (the *church*) while nonetheless allowing governmental succor to outgroup religions, which are otherwise subject to the hegemonic domination of Christianity.[78]

The Court recently faced this very problem and reacted predictably. In *Board of Education of Kiryas Joel Village School District v. Grumet*, the state of New York statutorily created a special school district following the boundary lines of the Village of Kiryas Joel. All the residents of the village belonged to a small Jewish sect, the Satmar Hasidim. The Satmars sent most of their children to private religious schools, but these schools were unable to provide adequate facilities for handicapped children. When the Satmars initially sent these children to public schools in neighboring communities, the children suffered "panic, fear, and trauma ... in leaving their own community and being with people whose ways were so different."[79] New York therefore created the special public school district so that the village could operate a publicly funded school for the handicapped children.[80] The Court held, however, that the state had violated the establishment clause because the statute was not neutral: state assistance of the Satmar Hasidim offended the "principle at the heart of the Establishment Clause, that government should not prefer one religion to another, or religion to irreligion." This reasoning underscores that the Court refuses to recognize differences between the social realities of mainstream Christians and outgroup sects such as the Satmar Hasidim.[81] To the Court, neutrality is the criterion for constitutionality, yet in a hegemonically Christian society such as America, "neutrality" equals Christianity.

The link between neutrality and Christianity becomes even clearer when *Grumet* is compared with *Rosenberger v. Rectors and Visitors of the University of Virginia*, decided in 1995. Once again emphasizing governmental neutrality, the *Rosenberger* Court held that the establishment clause did not prohibit the University of Virginia from funding an explicitly Christian magazine created and run by students. The Christian nature of the magazine was undisputed: it expressly challenged "Christians to live, in word and deed, according to the faith they proclaim and to encourage students to consider what a personal relationship with Jesus Christ means."[82] In dissent, Justice Souter unequivocally characterized the magazine as evangelical proselytization.[83] Nonetheless, the majority reasoned that the governmental action was *neutral* because the university funded other student activities as well as the magazine. In fact, the Court stated that if the university failed to fund the magazine, the university "could undermine the very neutrality the Establishment Clause requires."[84] Thus, by ostensibly enforcing governmental neutrality, the Court—first in *Grumet* and then in *Rosenberger*—reinforced Christian hegemony.[85] According to the Court, neutrality prohibited New York from creating a public school for the handicapped children of a small and insular Jewish sect, yet neutrality also somehow demanded that Virginia fund a magazine devoted to Christian proselytizing.

The Court's insistence on governmental neutrality supposedly prevents the justices from expressly considering the orientation of power in American society. To the Court, the Christian domination of America should not explicitly affect the interpretation of the religion clauses—though, as I argue, the Christian domination of America implicitly or unconsciously shapes the Court's understanding of the first amendment. Yet, because the Court refuses to expressly acknowledge Christian domination, the justices readily equate Christian and Jewish symbols—for instance, deeming as constitutionally equivalent the governmental displays of a crèche and a Jewish menorah.[86] But, of course, the governmental displays of a crèche and a menorah do not carry equal symbolic weights exactly because of the orientation of power in American society—exactly because of Christian domination. Most broadly, the effect or significance of a particular symbol—as a manifestation of power—depends partly on how it aligns with other contemporaneous forces or manifestations of power. When a Jew sees a governmentally displayed crèche, he or she understands the crèche within the context of Christian imperialism. A Jew likely experiences the crèche as having significant symbolic weight because it is yet *another* affirmation of Christian power, because it stands in a consistent line with (or pointing in the same direction as) other symbols and structures establishing Christian domination. As such, the crèche might readily cause a Jew to feel humiliated, angry, speechless, excluded, or alienated. When, on the other hand, a Christian sees a governmentally displayed menorah, he or she probably experiences it quite differently.[87] The menorah is not aligned consistently with most other symbolic or structural manifestations of power in American society. To the contrary, the governmental display of a menorah conflicts with the usual symbolic and structural components of Christian domination (except insofar as the menorah serves an ideological function). Consequently, to a Christian, the potential symbolic power of the menorah is neutralized; the menorah rarely will carry significant force. Many Christians, undoubtedly, will not even know what the menorah is or what it stands for. Put in simple terms, a Christian child who occasionally sees a menorah is not going to come home and ask her parents if they can celebrate Chanukah or become Jewish. But a Jewish child who *constantly* is exposed to Christmas displays and constantly is told about Christmas is, quite possibly, going to come home at some point and ask for a Christmas tree, if not to fully celebrate Christmas. In short, in American society, there is a difference between being Christian and Jewish. Yet the Court steadfastly ignores this difference by claiming to insist upon governmental neutrality, and in so doing, the Court contributes to the reproduction of Christian domination.

Once one recognizes the relation between, on the one hand, the orientation of power in American society and, on the other hand, the interpretation of the separation of church and state, some of the Court's decisions are thrown into a different light. As mentioned, for example, *Lee v. Weisman* might be considered a good case from the perspective of religious minorities: Weisman, a Jew, won the case, as the Court held that public schools violate the establishment clause by having clergy deliver invocation and benediction prayers at graduation ceremonies. Yet, one can easily overlook that a *rabbi,* and not a Christian preacher or priest, had delivered the prayers in that case. Thus, if limited to its precise facts, *Weisman* held that a rabbi cannot constitutionally deliver graduation prayers. More significant, the Court never considered the possibility that, in America, having a rabbi deliver prayers at graduation is *not* equivalent to having a member of the Christian clergy do the same. Because a rabbi delivers graduation prayers *in the face* of Christian domination, so to speak, the rabbi's words do not have the same symbolic import that a Christian clergyman's words would have. The Christian clergyman's prayers, after all, would be delivered with the support of and not in opposition to Christian domination. Quite simply, in America, is there any *real* chance that the government would give excessive and systematic support to *Judaism*? Indeed, if one recalls the factual circumstances that led up to the case, the reason a *rabbi* was saying the graduation prayers in the first place was that the public school principal, Lee, sought to co-opt the complainant, Weisman. Weisman had been distraught because a Baptist minister had delivered distinctly Christian prayers at his older daughter's graduation. When Weisman's younger daughter approached her graduation from middle school, Weisman sought to avoid a recurrence of this humiliating situation. Consequently, Weisman asked Lee whether a clergyman would be delivering prayers. Then, only because of Weisman's inquiries, Lee decided to have a rabbi say the prayers. Lee assumed that Weisman would not and could not complain if a rabbi offered the prayers. In effect, Lee seemed to be inviting Weisman to *temporarily* join the Christian ingroup, and in so doing, Lee expected Weisman to be grateful for the opportunity. Weisman nonetheless was dissatisfied. Of course, the Court's interpretation of the separation of church and state in *Weisman* effaced these factual circumstances, as well as the potential differences between having a rabbi and a Christian clergyman deliver the prayers.[88] For the Court to do otherwise would require it to acknowledge that America is a de facto Christian nation and that governmental neutrality actually reproduces Christian hegemony. To do otherwise, that is, would require the Court to admit that the dominant story of church and state is a myth, that religious outgroups do not enjoy religious freedom equally with Christians.

The Court, of course, cannot and will not take this step. Yet, religiously charged political events consistently reveal the bankruptcy of the dominant story. For example, constitutional challenges to traditional Christian practices still provoke hostile reactions from many citizens. In *Lynch v. Donnelly*, when the American Civil Liberties Union first filed suit challenging the constitutionality of the governmentally displayed crèche in Pawtucket, Rhode Island, many citizens and officials reacted immediately and angrily. The mayor, Dennis M. Lynch, denounced the suit as "a petty attack aimed at taking Christ out of Christmas."[89] The *Pawtucket Evening Times* labeled the suit "absurd," and over 90 percent of the mail and telephone calls to the city and the ACLU supported the city and the practice of displaying the crèche.[90] At one point, Mayor Lynch defended the city's crèche with words that ironically echoed the dominant story of church and state:

> One of the reasons my ancestors came to the United States was to escape religious persecution and to live in a country where they were guaranteed freedom of speech and religion. These freedoms have made this country strong. [T]he people of Pawtucket have banded together to renew those views and to claim the rights for their children and grandchildren.[91]

Despite Lynch's rather typical views, the district court struck down the display of the crèche as unconstitutional. Unperturbed, though, Lynch proceeded to show that even the judicial enforcement of the establishment clause cannot stop public displays of Christian symbols. When no longer the mayor, Lynch helped form a non-governmental group (Citizens Committed to Continuing Christmas), which bought the crèche from the city and erected it nearby. Other communities acted similarly. These communities, of course, relied on the public/private dichotomy to insulate them from constitutional scrutiny: perhaps the government could not display a crèche at Christmas, but a private (non-governmental) actor could exhibit the same crèche in an area open to the public. Regardless, the Supreme Court, of course, eventually reversed the decision of the district court, which the court of appeals had affirmed. To the Supreme Court, Mayor Lynch had been correct: the separation of church and state embodied in the religion clauses of the first amendment did not bar even a governmental display of a crèche.

To be clear, I am not suggesting that constitutional principles such as the separation of church and state do not exist at all. Rather, constitutional principles can exist, but they necessarily arise from a cauldron of political and social interests: those interests then constitute the elemental components of the principle.[92] Even if such a principle eventually becomes a causal factor within society, the principle retains its elemental components (albeit altered in form) and thus seldom acutely contravenes the interests that engendered it. Consequently, in the context of American society, the principle of separation of church and state should be understood largely as a political and religious development that primarily benefits the dominant religion, Christianity. Benefits occasionally flow to outgroup religions, but those benefits typically are incidental, not primary. Moreover, the separation of church and state sometimes disadvantages outgroup religions in distinct ways. Before concluding, I will discuss three additional ways in which the ostensible principle of separation of church and state benefits Christianity and harms minority religions, including Judaism.

First, the principle of separation of church and state increases the likelihood that Christian-oriented governmental action will be labeled or coded as secular and therefore legitimated. That is, the very existence of the separation of church and state as a constitutional principle tends to reify the state as a secular organ or instrumentality. Because the separation of church and state supposedly stands as a foundational principle of our governmental system, it is often presumed that action taken by the government is, of course, secular (merely because it is governmental action, and the government is, by definition, secular). In other words, governmental action is presumptively secular and therefore consistent with the constitutional principle of separation of church and state exactly because it is governmental action. This presumption of secularity for governmental action becomes especially strong when the government has been performing the challenged activity for many years. In *Lynch v. Donnelly*, for example, the Court held that the governmental display of a crèche was secular because, in part, American governments had a long history of celebrating Christmas.[93]

A second way in which the ostensible principle of separation of church and state benefits Christianity and harms outgroup religions stems from the need of cultural traditions to reproduce themselves. The constitutional discourse of the religion clauses tends to constantly reconstruct and inflate the importance of the principle of separation of church and state itself, which in turn reinforces Christian cultural imperialism. In particular, whenever any incidental benefit is afforded to a religious outgroup, Americans (especially Christians) can pound their chests and either boast or rage about the significance of the first amendment. The more boastful Americans say, in effect, "Look how *great* we are! We grant religious liberty to religious minorities (even to Jews)." Meanwhile, the more enraged Americans are apt to say, in effect, "Look how *terrible* we are! We grant religious liberty to religious minorities (even to Jews). This is a *Christian* nation!" Either way, by magnifying the importance of the incidental benefits flowing to Jews and other outgroups, constitutional rhetoric sustains and even invigorates the dominant story of the separation of church and state as a principle protecting religious freedom, especially for outgroups.[94] In other words, the constitutional discourse of the dominant story bolsters the dominant story itself. If, as discussed earlier, cultural traditions need to reproduce themselves to remain vital, then the tradition of church and state assiduously gratifies this internal need.

Third, the incidental benefits flowing to religious outgroups contribute to the social construction of American Jews. In short, Christians are not the only Americans to boast about the significance of the first amendment. Although Christian domination is, to a great extent, imposed upon American Jews, Jews also frequently acquiesce in Christian cultural imperialism *because, in part, of the separation of church and state.* The first amendment appears to and occasionally does protect Jews from *governmental* oppression, which throughout history has been conspicuous, though sporadic; the Holocaust, of course, reminds us of the grim potential for state-imposed persecution. Because of this apparent protection from such egregious impositions of state power, American Jews often are seduced into supporting, advocating for, and even celebrating the separation of church and state.[95] As noted, the major American Jewish defense organizations have often played important roles in many of the post–World War II religion clause cases. But in their avid support for strict separation, many Jews fail to perceive the more insidious contemporary danger—Christian cultural imperialism—that lurks within the American social body. Thus, the American Jew is "normalized": he or she becomes an American, like any other (Christian) American, only with a different religion (which is a purely private matter, anyway). And as an American, he or she, of course, celebrates the extraordinary protection of religious liberty that all Americans enjoy.[96]

Furthermore, the Court's Christian-biased interpretation of the religion clauses contributes to this normalization or Christianization of American Jews. Basically, the Court implicitly encourages Jews to act like Christians because when Jews do so, they become more likely to win religion clause cases. Since the Supreme Court justices are themselves embedded in the structures of Christian domination, the justices usually interpret the religion clauses consistently with the practices and values of the Christian majority. Therefore, the Court's decisions tend to protect the practices and values of religious *outgroups* only insofar as they align or harmonize with Christianity (especially Protestantism)—or more precisely, only insofar as the *Court understands* the outgroup practices and values to align or harmonize with Christianity. For example, Jews are most likely to bring a successful religion clause claim if they fit comfortably within the normal (meaning Christian) structures of American society—if the Jews, that is, relate to others as Christians do. In short, Jews have their best chance of winning when they act (or seem to act) Christian. In *County of Allegheny v. American Civil Liberties Union*, the Court held that the governmental display of a Jewish menorah was constitutional largely because it was accompanied by a Christmas tree and a sign saluting liberty. In other words, the menorah could be constitutionally displayed because it was part of a *Christmas* exhibit.[97] The justices found the menorah to be constitutionally acceptable because they understood it as the Jewish equivalent of a Christmas tree; the Jewish practice seemed to parallel the Christian practice. This case contrasts starkly with *Goldman v. Weinberger*.[98] In that case, the Court rejected the free exercise claim of an Orthodox Jewish Air Force officer who sought to wear his yarmulke in contravention of Air Force regulations. Quite simply, the justices seemed unable to comprehend the religious meaning of the yarmulke because it did not easily translate into Christian terms. The justices completely mischaracterized the yarmulke by suggesting that an Orthodox Jew wears one as a matter of mere personal preference. Consequently, Jews and other religious outgroups are implicitly urged to act consistently with Christian practices and values to help bring about a convergence with Christian interests. If Jews want to belong (at least partly) to America, they largely need to conform to Christian practices (and not vice versa). Hence, although Chanukah is only a minor festival in Judaism, its significance has been magnified enormously because it falls around the same time of year as Christmas. Chanukah has become, in a sense, the Jewish Christmas. Few Christian Americans probably know that the most sacred days in Judaism are Rosh Hashanah (the Jewish New Year) and Yom Kippur (the Day of Atonement, coming nine days after Rosh Hashanah), which come early in the autumn.[99] Because these days, unlike Chanukah, do not fall near especially important Christian holidays, the Jewish holy days remain mysteries to most Americans.

Although American Jews and members of other religious outgroups acquiesce, to some extent, in Christian cultural imperialism, one should not overlook that they also resist Christian domination in many ways. For Jews, as an example, resistance can be expressed sometimes merely by remaining Jewish (that is, by not becoming Christian). In America, where Christianity is so ubiquitous and firmly embedded as the neutral and natural, separation from the normalized Christian order of the social world can produce a type of existential anxiety or even terror.[100] Yet, the only alternative for American Jews is submission to the final step of Christian hegemonic domination, the elimination of the Jewish subculture. Furthermore, although many American Jews accept and support the separation of church and state, they never *just choose* to do so; rather, they are always in part compelled.[101] Many Jews who publicly acquiesce in and even celebrate the principle of separation of church and state might harbor a "hidden transcript," a discourse of resistance and opposition expressed primarily to other Jews or outgroup members.[102] To these Jews, a more open or public statement of resistance seems impolitic or even dangerous. From this perspective, seeking judicial enforcement of the strict separation of church and state may not be ideal, but it offers the best possible means for opposing Christian cultural imperialism within the perceived political realities of America.

FINAL THOUGHTS: A POLITICAL STATEMENT

We live within an intricate and endless web of power: it surrounds and constitutes us. My critical social narrative of the separation of church and state has followed the historical spinning of a significant part of that web, tracing the development of two institutions—church and state—from the beginnings of Christianity up to the present day. Throughout this narrative, I have underscored attitudes and actions toward Jews. Largely because the New Testament designates Jews for special condemnation, the treatment of Jews in western history has often reflected the changing relations between church and state. Significantly, in late-twentieth-century America, the conceptualization of the separation of church and state reflects the symbols and structures of Christian domination—including antisemitism. These current symbols and structures still contain threads that wind back to the New Testament, medieval Roman Catholicism, and post-Reformation Protestantism. Unsurprisingly, then, despite the pretensions of the dominant story of the separation of church and state, the sticky web of Christian cultural and social power seems ever-present. The dominant story maintains that the religion clauses of the first amendment equally protect the religious liberty of all, including Jews and other religious outgroups. But the social reality is far different—far more complex.

Once one rejects or at least doubts the dominant story, then if one looks and listens, examples of Christian domination are easily found. Here, then, are some incidents that caught my attention while I was working on this book. Some involve highly personal interactions, while others focus on statements made in a public medium such as a newspaper. I hope that they communicate in some manner the experience of being an outgroup member consciously facing cultural imperialism, the experience of almost-daily small and large acts of domination, the experience of cumulative frustration in coping with these acts—the sense of being ensnared in the web of Christian domination.

My six-year-old daughter wanted to order a book about Thanksgiving from a scholastic book club. Each Thanksgiving book, though, was included in a package with a Christmas book.

The Uptown Comedy Club in New York City produced and broadcast a blatantly antisemitic rap sketch that was distributed nationally to 101 television stations, including the WGN superstation. The "sketch depicted both black and white rappers dressed as Orthodox Jews, 'rapping' mean-spirited and hateful rhetoric about Jews, such as 'Come pay your fee. I really want to sue you … I want to overcharge you … Come and pay your fee. You stupid, stupid bastard."[103]

When our daughter was born, our neighbors kindly gave her a gift. Unfortunately, it was a New Testament.

Shortly after the November 1994 elections, Chuck Gosnell, a leader of the Christian Coalition in Colorado, declared, "One-third of the votes cast nationally were from Christian conservatives. We helped elect the candidates God wants in office."[104] Republicans in the newly elected House of Representatives pledged to seek a constitutional amendment to explicitly allow prayers in the public schools, and President Bill Clinton was generally supportive of such an amendment.[105] The Republicans also wanted to shrink "government-funded welfare programs and shift the social safety net to churches and religious charities."[106] A Baptist reverend, supporting this proposed transition, said:

> Churches do what it takes to move a person to a new life. We can do it better than government. Government deals with the effects of poverty. We deal with the root cause—moral depravity. … The moral authority of the church is part of everything we do. If you come here, you'll know it. Everything we do has a Bible component.[107]

My dental hygienist asked what name my wife and I were considering for our soon-to-be-born son. When I told her, "Samuel Jacob," she replied, "I don't mean to be racist, but that sounds so Jewish."

One of the recently elected Republicans, Congresswoman Linda Smith, explained her entrance into politics by mentioning that her husband, in his political activities, brought many people to their house for debates: "Professors in the area, and liberals, and Jews."[108]

When my wife told a friend that we do not celebrate Christmas, the friend responded incredulously, asking how we could deprive our daughter of Santa Claus. Another friend asked my wife what *church* Temple Israel is affiliated with. Then the friend said she had never before met a Jew, although she had seen two television characters who (she thought) were supposed to be Jewish.

On December 8, 1994, a reader asked in the "Call the Editor" section of the *Tulsa World* (presently, the only daily newspaper published in Tulsa, Oklahoma): "I would like to know if it is true if the *Tulsa World* is owned and published by a Jewish family as are 95 percent (of other newspapers) in America." Totally ignoring the antisemitic intimations of this inquiry, the newspaper editors responded as follows:

> Most American newspapers today are owned by publicly held companies whose stock is traded on the New York Stock Exchange or similar markets. Thus anyone can own a piece of a newspaper company. The *Tulsa World* is owned by the Lorton family, which has been in Tulsa since shortly after statehood. The Lortons are members of an Episcopal church.[109]

My daughter says that some of her friends at school teased her and her one Jewish classmate for not celebrating Christmas.

In November 1994, the editors of the *Wall Street Journal* declared their support for a proposed constitutional amendment to allow public school prayers. After suggesting a specific prayer, the editors asked: "Would any serious person object? Is this an anti-Semitic utterance?"[110]

My daughter asked if she could be Christian when she grew up. "Why?" I asked. "So I can celebrate Christmas." Subsequently, we were playing at a neighborhood park when I realized that she was repeatedly singing, "Merry Christmas."

When President George Bush thanked an association of Christian radio and television station officers for their support during the Persian Gulf War, Bush said, "'I want to thank you for helping America, as Christ ordained, to be a light unto the world.'"[111]

My family attended a play at a small public playhouse in early December 1994. As an unannounced precursor to the play, one of the actors invited all of the children in the audience to come up on stage and listen to a reading of "The Night Before Christmas." My daughter decided not to go on stage. Later that day, we went to the Tulsa public zoo. The zoo was covered with Christmas lights, Christmas music was being broadcast throughout the zoo, and a large Santa Claus exhibit was displayed in the polar bear building. My daughter wanted to sit and talk about Santa. That evening, we ate dinner at a local pancake restaurant. The front entrance was adorned with several dozen drawings of Christmas stockings done by children who had eaten there. When we were seated, my daughter was handed a copy of a Christmas stocking to color in.

A federal district court held that a public school curriculum that included singing Christian songs at Christian places of worship did not violate the establishment clause. Meanwhile, a federal court of appeals held that Hawaii's designation of Good Friday as a state holiday did not violate the establishment clause. Yet, another federal court of appeals held that a city ordinance banning the sale of food mislabeled as kosher according to Orthodox Jewish dietary laws violated the establishment clause.[112]

I was reading the original story of *The 101 Dalmatians* to my daughter. Several chapters into the book, the story suddenly turned on the experience of a miracle on Christmas eve when the dalmatians found sanctuary in a Christian church.[113]

A mainstream British magazine, *The Spectator,* reported that Jews govern filmmaking in Hollywood and deny employment to non-Jews. The author, a correspondent for Britain's top conservative newspaper, described Jews as "'fiercely competitive,' clannish, vulgar, 'compulsive storytellers and talented negotiators.'"[114]

From before Thanksgiving to the end of December every year, I am bombarded by Christmas symbols and messages. One year, a national fast food restaurant had a sign announcing, "Christmas Glasses Now Here." The local public park had a sign inviting children to "Make a Christmas Tree." The major intersection near my home had a temporary Christmas tree store with large signs advertising "Merry Christmas, Christmas Trees." And I drove by a van that had a big sign (not merely the ubiquitous bumper sticker) declaring, "Jesus is Our Lord and Savior."

The president of the Southern Baptist Convention said: "It is interesting at great political rallies how you have a Protestant to pray, a Catholic to pray, and then you have a Jew to pray. With all due respect to those dear people, my friends, God Almighty does not hear the prayer of a Jew."[115]

I repeatedly am handed Christian proselytizing flyers or find them tucked under the wiper blades on my car windshield. One such flyer asked: "If you died tonight in a car wreck, where would you go? To Heaven? Or to Hell?" It then advised me to follow Jesus if I wanted to get to Heaven.

On December 8, 1992, a letter to the editor in the *Tulsa World* stated:

> How can the idiots on the Supreme Court rule you can't say a prayer in school when it isn't a law but a right. Just because some minority with a heathen religion doesn't want to pray our way doesn't give those dumb bunnies any right to ban prayer. If you want to believe heathen, go back to the country you came from. No one asked to have you over here.[116]

On September 1, 1995, I received an advertisement in the mail from an exclusive shopping center in Tulsa. The advertisement stated: "Dear Christmas shopper: Every year you're faced with the same question: what to buy your employees for Christmas."

The school superintendent of Sand Springs, a suburb of Tulsa, Oklahoma, announced that players and fans would continue to pray before football games despite the Supreme Court's decision in *Lee v. Weisman*.[117]

In 1995, my father (who lives in Arizona) received an envelope in the mail. The return address, handwritten, was, "From Some One that Loves You." Inside was an eight-page tract encouraging Jews to convert to Christianity.

The New Republic reported that the Internet has become a means for spreading antisemitic propaganda.[118]

One recent December, one of my colleagues said, "It is sure getting cold." I responded, "Yes. It's nice." My colleague replied: "That's what cold weather is all about. It makes it feel more like Christmas." I reacted by saying—nothing. Silence.

So, caught in this web of power, what's a person to do?[119]

I ask for one small political act. I request each reader to consider making a simple and direct statement questioning Christian imperialism. My idea: next year, when someone wishes you a "Merry Christmas," just say, "Please don't! Don't wish me a Merry Christmas."

Notes

Notes to the Epigraph

* Judith A. Boss, Is Santa Claus Corrupting Our Children's Morals?, 11 Free Inquiry 24 (Fall 1991) (quoting Francis Church, Yes, Virginia, There is a Santa Claus, New York Sun (1896)).

† Transcript of Remarks by Reagan and Wiesel at White House Ceremony, New York Times, Apr. 20, 1985, at §1, p. 4. (quoting Elie Wiesel).

Notes to Chapter 1

1. My description of these events is based solely on my and my wife's recollection. I have no transcript or other recording of events.

2. U.S. Const. amend. 1.

3. See, e.g., Richard John Neuhaus, The Naked Public Square (1984); William P. Marshall, In Defense of Smith and Free Exercise Revisionism, 58 U. Chi. L. Rev. 308 (1990); Michael W. McConnell, Free Exercise Revisionism and the Smith Decision, 57 U. Chi. L. Rev. 1109 (1990); Steven D. Smith, Symbols, Perceptions, and Doctrinal Illusions: Establishment Neutrality and the "No Endorsement" Test, 86 Mich. L. Rev. 266 (1987); Mark Tushnet, "Of Church and State and the Supreme Court": Kurland Revisited, 1989 S. Ct. Rev. 373; Symposium, Religion and the Public Schools After Lee v. Weisman, 43 Case W. Res. L. Rev. 699 (1993); Symposium, Religion in Public Life: Access, Accommodation, and Accountability, 60 Geo. Wash. L. Rev. 599 (1992).

4. See, e.g., Gerard V. Bradley, Church–State Relationships in America 122 (1987); James E. Wood, Jr., et al., Church and State in Scripture, History, and Constitutional Law 57 (1958).

5. David Dudley Field, The Theory of American Government, North Am. Rev. (June 1888), reprinted in 3 Speeches, Arguments, and Miscellaneous Papers of David Dudley Field 372, 385 (Titus Munson Coan ed., 1890). Field similarly wrote:

> The greatest achievement ever made in the cause of human progress is the total and final separation of church and state. If we had nothing else to boast of, we could lay claim with justice that first among the nations we of this country made it an article of organic law that the relations between man and his Maker were a private concern, into which other men have no right to intrude.

David Dudley Field, American Progress, in Jurisprudence 6 (1893), quoted in Leo Pfeffer, Church, State, and Freedom ix (1953).

6. Pfeffer, supra note 5, at 604–05; see Philip B. Kurland, The Origins of the Religion Clauses of the Constitution, 27 Wm. & Mary L. Rev. 839, 856–57, 860 (1986) (uniqueness of framers' goal of protecting individual religious liberty). Also, in the mid-twentieth century, Anson Phelps Stokes wrote a three-volume study on the separation of church and state in America in which he expressly advocated the dominant story, although he sometimes gave it a distinctly Christian twist. See Anson Phelps Stokes, 1 Church and State in the United States 6, 26, 37, 646–47 (1950). Leo Pfeffer published a revised edition of his book in 1967, but his views remained unchanged; he merely updated the discussions of precedent to account for the cases decided after 1953. See Leo Pfeffer, Church, State, and

Freedom (rev. ed. 1967). All subsequent citations to Pfeffer will be to his original 1953 edition.

7. Stephen L. Carter, The Culture of Disbelief 107 (1993).

8. Everson v. Board of Education, 330 U.S. 1, 8, 18 (1947).

9. County of Allegheny v. American Civil Liberties Union, 492 U.S. 573, 590 (1989) (quoting Wallace v. Jaffree, 472 U.S. 38, 52 (1985)).

10. Nancy Fraser, Unruly Practices: Power, Discourse, and Gender in Contemporary Social Theory 26 (1989); see Stephen M. Feldman, The Persistence of Power and the Struggle for Dialogic Standards in Postmodern Constitutional Jurisprudence: Michelman, Habermas, and Civic Republicanism, 81 Geo. L.J. 2243, 2258–66 (1993). Modernists tend to cabin (or limit the conceptualization of) power for the sake of methodological and experimental ease: it is easier to analyze and test for power if it is supposedly centered on some conscious agent. See, e.g., Peter Morriss, Power: A Philosophical Analysis 124–27 (1987) (how to test for and measure power).

11. See Pierre Bourdieu & Loïc Wacquant, The Purpose of Reflexive Sociology, in An Invitation to Reflexive Sociology 61, 90, 109 (1992) (emphasizing that sociological or synchronic analysis cannot be separated from historical study); cf. Saul Cornell, Moving Beyond the Canon of Traditional Constitutional History: Anti-Federalists, the Bill of Rights, and the Promise of Post-Modern Historiography, 12 L. & Hist. Rev. 1 (1994) (criticizing Whig histories that present inexorable progressive development and recommending a postmodern approach that emphasizes a plurality of competing discourses and concepts).

12. On the nineteenth-century origins and the current use of the term "antisemitism" to describe various manifestations of hostility toward Jews, see A Note on the Spelling and Usage of "Antisemitism," in Antisemitism in America Today xv (Jerome A. Chanes ed., 1995). Jerome Chanes gives the following definition of antisemitism: "all forms of hostility manifested toward the Jews throughout history." Jerome A. Chanes, Antisemitism and Jewish Security in America Today: Interpreting the Data. Why Can't Jews Take "Yes" for an Answer?, in Antisemitism in America Today 3, 5 (Jerome A. Chanes ed., 1995). If this conception of antisemitism includes unintentional and unconscious anti-Jewish actions and sentiments, then I can live with it. But see David A. Gerber, Anti-Semitism and Jewish–Gentile Relations in American Historiography and the American Past, in Anti-Semitism in American History 3, 3 (David A. Gerber ed., 1986) (stressing conscious attitudes and intentional behavior in defining antisemitism).

13. To be clear, I am not writing a general history of Christianity. Instead, I follow the development of Christianity insofar as it is significant to the history of separation of church and state as it culminates in American constitutionalism. Consequently, I follow Christianity as it makes its way to the North American colonies. Thus, when Christianity splits in the Middle Ages between east and west, I follow western Christianity. When Christianity splits during the Reformation, I focus more on Protestantism. In other words, I emphasize the Christian groups that were of predominant influence in shaping the American constitutional concept of separation of church and state.

NOTES TO CHAPTER 2

1. See Isidore Epstein, Judaism: A Historical Presentation 99 (1959). Another useful general historical account of Judaism is Paul Johnson, A History of the Jews (1987).

2. See Genesis, Exodus, Leviticus, Numbers, and Deuteronomy. Citations of the Hebrew Bible are to the following edition: The Holy Scriptures (Philadelphia, The Jewish Publication Society of America 1955) (according to the Masoretic Text). Books on Judaism in general include the following: Beryl D. Cohon, Judaism: In Theory and Practice (1948); David C. Gross, How to Be Jewish (1988); Louis Jacobs, The Jewish Religion (1995); Morris N. Kertzer, What Is a Jew? (1953); Roy A. Rosenberg, The Concise Guide to Judaism (1990); Milton Steinberg, Basic Judaism (1947); Joseph Telushkin, Jewish Literacy (1991). Books that focus on the differences between Judaism and Christianity include the following: Abba Hillel Silver, Where Judaism Differs (1987); Trude Weiss-Rosmarin, Judaism and Christianity: The Differences (1943).

3. See William Nicholls, Christian Antisemitism 31–32 (1993); Elaine Pagels, The Origin of Satan 3–6, 34 (1995). Some other books on antisemitism in general include the following: Edward H. Flannery, The Anguish of the Jews: Twenty-Three Centuries of Antisemitism (1985); Gavin I. Langmuir, History, Religion, and Antisemitism (1990); Harold E. Quinley & Charles Y. Glock, Anti-

Semitism in America (1979); Robert S. Wistrich, Antisemitism: The Longest Hatred (1991). A book on the Jewish internalization of antisemitic attitudes is Sander L. Gilman, Jewish Self-Hatred (1986). Books that focus on the relationship between Christianity and antisemitism include the following: John Dominic Crossan, Who Killed Jesus? Exposing the Roots of Anti-Semitism in the Gospel Story of the Death of Jesus (1995); Weddig Fricke, The Court-Martial of Jesus (Salvator Attanasio trans., 1987); Frederic Cople Jaher, A Scapegoat in the New Wilderness: The Origins and Rise of Anti-Semitism in America (1994); Jacob Neusner, Jews and Christians: The Myth of a Common Tradition (1991); James Parkes, The Conflict of the Church and the Synagogue (1934); James Parkes, Judaism and Christianity (1948) [hereinafter Parkes, Judaism]; Rosemary Ruether, Faith and Fratricide: The Theological Roots of Anti-Semitism (1974); Samuel Sandmel, Anti-Semitism in the New Testament? (1978); Antisemitism and Foundations of Christianity (Alan Davies ed., 1979). Books that focus on the Holocaust include the following: Zygmunt Bauman, Modernity and the Holocaust (1989); Lucy S. Dawidowicz, The War Against the Jews: 1933-1945 (1975); Martin Gilbert, The Holocaust (1986); Raul Hilberg, The Destruction of the European Jews (1985) (three volumes).

4. Indeed, Jesus was probably an observant Jew, or in current terms, an Orthodox Jew. See Nicholls, supra note 3, at 45-84. For Josephus's Christianized account of Jesus, see Flavius Josephus, Antiquities of the Jews, reprinted in 3 Complete Works of Josephus 94 (Bigelow, Brown edition, based on the Havercamp trans.).

5. Therefore, Christians call the Hebrew Bible the Old Testament. See Niels C. Nielsen, Jr., et al., Religions of the World 435 (1983). Most, if not all, of the New Testament probably originated during the first eighty years of the Christian movement. See Martin E. Marty, A Short History of Christianity 28-29 (1959); Robert C. Monk & Joseph D. Stamey, Exploring Christianity: An Introduction 18, 232 (2d ed. 1990). Other helpful histories of Christianity include the following: Margaret Deanesly, A History of the Medieval Church 590-1500 (8th ed. 1954); Everett Ferguson, Backgrounds of Early Christianity (2d ed. 1993); Robin Lane Fox, Pagans and Christians (1987).

6. See Nicholls, supra note 3, at 18, 31, 43-44, 83; Richard Tarnas, The Passion of the Western Mind 89, 92 (1991). The Church had adopted the Greek version of the Hebrew Bible (as the Old Testament) before the New Testament was completely written and canonized. See Nicholls, supra note 3, at 154.

To be clear, I am not using the term "disciples" to refer to Jesus' twelve selected disciples. See Monk & Stamey, supra note 5, at 23.

7. See Pagels, supra note 3, at 8, 33.

8. The New Testament states: "[Christ] is the mediator of the new testament, that by means of death, for the redemption of the transgressions that were under the first testament, they which are called might receive the promise of eternal inheritance." Hebrews 9:15 (emphasis in the original); see Nicholls, supra note 3, at 12, 172-73 (on the Christian theology of supersession). Rosemary Ruether, a Christian theologian, writes: "The heart of the conflict between Jew and Christian ... lies in the Christian claim to the 'true Israel' which defines the old Israel as apostate and 'divorced' by God. This sets Christian anti-Judaism fundamentally apart from pagan antisemitism." Rosemary Ruether, The Faith and Fratricide Discussion: Old Problems and New Dimensions, in Antisemitism and Foundations of Christianity 230, 233 (Alan Davies ed., 1979).

9. The New Testament repeatedly refers to Jews as "the Jews." See, e.g., John 5:18; 19:12. This rhetoric tends to reinforce the Christian message that Jews are different and strange—the Other. Consequently, when I discuss Christian descriptions and treatments of Jews, I often use the Christian terminology, "the Jews," to underscore Christian antisemitic attitudes. Otherwise, I shall ordinarily refer merely to Jews or Judaism.

Quotations from the New Testament are from the King James version. See Holy Bible (containing the Old and New Testaments) (King James Version 1611); see also Holy Bible (translated from the Latin Vulgate, Douay-Rheims version 1582) (Catholic Bible). For purposes of this text, the differences between the Douay-Rheims and King James versions of the Christian Bible are insignificant.

10. "Search the scriptures; for in them ye think ye have eternal life: and they are they which testify of me. And ye will not come to me, that ye might have life." John 5:39-40; see Matthew 22:34-46 (Jesus argues that Pharisees misunderstood the Hebrew Scriptures); Galatians 2:21 (attacks Jewish law).

11. John 5:37-38; accord Matthew 22:29, 34-46 (Pharisees do not understand God); Galatians 2:21 (attacks Jewish law); Acts 28:26-28 (Jews never understand God); Hebrews 8:6-13 (Jewish

covenant is defective); see Ruether, supra note 3, at 70–73 (Jesus' disciples searched the Hebrew Bible to show that it meant that Jesus was the Messiah).

12. The New Testament states:

> [T]he Jews: Who both killed the Lord Jesus, and their own prophets, and have persecuted us; and they please not God, and are contrary to all men: Forbidding us to speak to the Gentiles that they might be saved, to fill up their sins alway: for the wrath is come upon them to the uttermost.

1 Thessalonians 2:14–16; see Nicholls, supra note 3, at 84, 126–27.

13. See Nicholls, supra note 3, at 3 (the image of the Jew as Christ killer is a central element in Christian myth and is taught to all Christians).

14. See Pagels, supra note 3, at 10, 103.

15. Matthew 27:25 (emphasis omitted).

16. John 19:12–16. The official Latin title of Pilate as governor of the Roman province of Judea was praefectus, combining "prefect" (emphasizing military command) with "procurator" (emphasizing financial responsibility). Ferguson, supra note 5, at 42.

17. John 19:4–7. Likewise, the Gospel of John adds: "Therefore the Jews sought the more to kill him, because he not only had broken the sabbath, but said also that God was his Father, making himself equal with God." John 5:18. And in a similar vein:

> I [Jesus] and my Father are one. Then the Jews took up stones again to stone him. Jesus answered them, Many good works have I shewed you from my Father; for which of those works do ye stone me? The Jews answered him, saying, For a good work we stone thee not; but for blasphemy; and because that thou, being a man, makest thyself God.

John 10:30–33 (emphasis omitted).

18. John Dominic Crossan calls the passion narratives "prophecy historicized," not "history remembered." Crossan, supra note 3, at 1–8; see Pagels, supra note 3, at 3–111. But cf. Raymond E. Brown, The Death of the Messiah (1994) (arguing that the passion narratives represent historical fact). The passion narratives are the New Testament passages referring to the trial and death of Jesus. See Nicholls, supra note 3, at 21.

19. See Fricke, supra note 3, at 117–20 (many bands of insurgents); Silver, supra note 2, at 97 (many messianic movements). From 66 to 73 C.E., the Jews fought a war to free themselves from Roman rule. Rome defeated the Jews and destroyed the Jewish Temple in Jerusalem in 70 C.E. See Epstein, supra note 1, at 108–12; Johnson, supra note 1, at 127, 136–40.

20. See Nicholls, supra note 3, at 86–89; Telushkin, supra note 2, at 545–47. Rabbi Telushkin emphasizes that many Jews long have been skeptical about the coming of a Messiah. He reports that a first-century sage, Rabban Yochanan ben Zakkai, said: "If you should happen to be holding a sapling in your hand when they tell you that the Messiah has arrived, first plant the sapling and then go out and greet the Messiah." Telushkin, supra note 2, at 545.

21. Crossan, supra note 3, at 212. See Fricke, supra note 3, at 117–20; Johnson, supra note 1, at 141; Silver, supra note 2, at 97.

22. See Jaher, supra note 3, at 34–35; Nicholls, supra note 3, at 105–07; Pagels, supra note 3, at 14 (during the first century C.E., the Romans arrested and crucified thousands of Jews).

23. See Fricke, supra note 3, at 4, 109, 127–32.

24. During this period, there were at least four major groups within the Jewish community—the Sadducees, the Pharisees, the Zealots, and the Essenes—but many Jews did not officially belong to any of these groups. When Rome defeated the Jews and destroyed the Jewish Temple in Jerusalem in 70 C.E., the vitality of the Sadducees was undermined because they focused largely on Temple worship. In fact, the Pharisees were the only group to substantially survive the war. See Epstein, supra note 1, at 95–109; Johnson, supra note 1, at 127, 136–40; Monk & Stamey, supra note 5, at 6–7, 9; Ruether, supra note 3, at 45, 60, 75, 77.

25. See Epstein, supra note 1, at 95–107; Fricke, supra note 3, at 4; Johnson, supra note 3, at 100, 106, 108, 121–22, 127; Ruether, supra note 3, at 58–59, 67–69, 86–88; Wistrich, supra note 3, at 13–14. William Nicholls tersely summarizes the historical record: "The Jews did not conspire to kill [Jesus] and were not responsible for his death. He met his end on a Roman cross condemned by a

Roman official for a Roman offense." Nicholls, supra note 3, at xxvi. In 1965, the Second Vatican Council's Declaration on the Church's Attitude to Non-Christians contained a tepid repudiation of the charge of deicide against the Jews. This Declaration has had little effect on Christian education because it is contrary to the Christian Gospels. See Wistrich, supra note 3, at 235.

26. Crossan, supra note 3, at 152.

27. See Jaher, supra note 3, at 21; Nicholls, supra note 3, at 27, 107–08; Pagels, supra note 3, at 10–11, 15; Ruether, supra note 3, at 89–95; Wistrich, supra note 3, at 13–14. Everett Ferguson notes that early Christianity was in a struggle with Judaism for the allegiance of pagans. Ferguson, supra note 5, at 573. Samuel Sandmel emphasizes that the Gospel of Mark was shaped to assure the Gentile Christian community of its full validity. See Sandmel, supra note 3, at 47–48.

28. See Nicholls, supra note 3, at 16–17, 90–99.

29. Pre-Christian Gnosis emphasized a dichotomy of material and spiritual worlds, where humanity can be redeemed by the descent of a savior. See Ferguson, supra note 5, at 282–92; Nicholls, supra note 3, at 132; cf. Silver, supra note 2, at 97–98 (explaining the Christian interpretation of Jesus' death as universal atonement).

30. The concept of a dying and rising god was probably borrowed from the pagan mystery religions. See Fox, supra note 5, at 94–96, 124–26; Nicholls, supra note 3, at 132; Tarnas, supra note 6, at 109–10. But cf. Ferguson, supra note 5, at 279–82 (Christianity borrowed from mystery religions, though perhaps less than many assume).

31. See Pagels, supra note 3, at 11–13.

32. See Neusner, supra note 3, at 5–6; Nielsen, supra note 5, at 485; Silver, supra note 2, at 161; Monika K. Hellwig, From the Jesus of Story to the Christ of Dogma, in Antisemitism and Foundations of Christianity 118, 122, 126–27 (Alan Davies ed., 1979). The claimed universality of the Christian way is one reason that proselytizing is such an integral part of the religion. See Nielsen, supra note 5, at 487–88.

33. Christians therefore read the Old Testament differently from the way Jews read the Hebrew Bible: in each religion, the text (of the Hebrew Bible or Old Testament) is understood within the context of a larger canon (and each religion has a different larger canon). See Neusner, supra note 3, at ix–x; Ruether, supra note 3, at 117–82; Gregory Baum, Introduction, in Rosemary Ruether, Faith and Fratricide: The Theological Roots of Anti-Semitism 1, 11–12 (1974). In fact, the New Testament at times seems to blatantly misread the Hebrew Bible. See Ruether, supra note 3, at 86, 109; cf. Pagels, supra note 3, at 77 (giving example of Greek mistranslation of Hebrew Bible). William Nicholls writes:

> The Old Testament is not the Jewish Bible. It is an extremely novel reading of the Septuagint Greek translation of the Hebrew Scriptures. So reread, the Bible is no longer the history of covenant and Torah but a complex web of predictions of the life, death and resurrection of Jesus the Messiah.

Nicholls, supra note 3, at 114.

34. See Parkes, Judaism, supra note 3, at 107–08; Ruether, supra note 3, at 89–95; Wistrich, supra note 3, at 13–14.

35. John 8:42–47; 10:22–39.

36. John 8:42–45. Elaine Pagels emphasizes how the New Testament associated Satan with Jews (who refused to accept Jesus as the Messiah) and not with the Romans. See Pagels, supra note 3, at 13–15.

37. Matthew 23:37–39; accord 1 Thessalonians 2:14–16.

38. See Matthew 11:20–24 (Jews condemned to Hell); Luke 10:13–15; 16:19–31 (same).

39. See Ferguson, supra note 5, at 315, 367; Fox, supra note 5, at 94–96; Nicholls, supra note 3, at 33–34; Ruether, supra note 3, at 104; Wistrich, supra note 3, at 15; cf. Etienne Gilson, History of Christian Philosophy in the Middle Ages 70–81, 93–94 (1955) (Augustine and other Church Fathers were influenced by Plato through Neoplatonists, especially Plotinus). In effect, Christianity imbued Jewish eschatology, which contrasted two historical stages of time, with Platonist metaphysics, which contrasted two metaphysical realms, the material and the spiritual (or, respectively, the world of objects and the world of forms or ideas). See Plato, Phaedo, in Plato, The Republic and Other Works 487, 505–12, 534–35 (B. Jowett trans., 1973) (Anchor Books ed.); Plato, The Republic, in Plato, The Republic and Other Works 7, 169–73 (B. Jowett trans., 1973) (Anchor Books ed.); cf. Silver, supra note 2, at 184, 189–95 (on the dualism of Christianity).

40. Galatians 4:23; see Colossians 2:16–23 (Jewish practices are carnal).

41. Galatians 5:16.

42. Romans 9:31–32.

43. For references to hypocrisy, see Matthew 22:18 (on hypocrisy); Matthew 23:3 (Jews "say, and do not"); Matthew 23:28 (Jews "outwardly appear righteous unto men, but within ye are full of hypocrisy and inequity"); Luke 11:44 ("ye are as graves which appear not"). For references related to being blind fools, see Matthew 23:17 ("Ye fools and blind") (emphasis omitted). For references related to being hard of heart, see Mark 10:2–9; Matthew 19:1–9. For a reference to the Christian emphasis on spiritual glory, see Matthew 5:29–30 (prefer physical suffering to eternal suffering in Hell).

44. Hebrews 13:14. Augustine did not directly quote this passage. Instead, he derived the title of his treatise, The City of God, from several Old Testament Psalms. See St. Augustine, 2 The City of God, at bk. XI, §1 (Marcus Dods trans. & ed., 1948) (quoting Psalms 46:4; 48:1; 87:3). Nonetheless, as will be discussed later in this chapter, Augustine interpreted the phrase "city of God" in accordance with New Testament symbolism.

45. Mark 12:15.

46. Mark 12:17; accord Luke 20:25.

47. See Nicholls, supra note 3, at 278–79, 467 n.3. Nicholls notes that the word "secular" comes from a Latin word meaning a period of time. Originally, therefore, "secular" contrasted with "eternity," not with "religion." See id. at 279.

48. See Jaher, supra note 3, at 21.

49. Wistrich, supra note 3, at 16–17 (quoting from Homily 1, Against the Jews, in W.A. Meeks & R.L. Wilken, Jews and Christians in Antioch in the First Four Centuries of the Common Era 97 (1978)).

50 See Cohon, supra note 2, at 218–19 (Christianity, as developed by Paul, directly negated Judaism); Pagels, supra note 3, at 34 (the identification of Satan with Jesus' Jewish opponents would fuel antisemitism for centuries); Ruether, supra note 3, at 121 ("Christian scriptural teaching and preaching per se is based on a method in which anti-Judaic polemic exists as the left hand of its christological hermeneutic"); Baum, supra note 33, at 5–6 ("The central Christian affirmation seems to negate the possibility of a living Judaism"). Zygmunt Bauman writes:

> Christianity could not reproduce itself, and certainly could not reproduce its ecumenical domination, without guarding and reinforcing the foundations of Jewish estrangement—the view of itself as the heir and the overcoming of Israel. The self-identity of Christianity was, in fact, estrangement of the Jews. It was born of the rejection by the Jews. It drew its continuous vitality from the rejection of the Jews. Christianity could theorize its own existence only as an on-going opposition to the Jews.

Bauman, supra note 3, at 38 (emphasis in the original). But cf. Davies, supra note 3 (a collection of essays considering whether Christianity is inherently antisemitic; most essays, however, conclude that Christianity can be separated from antisemitism).

51. See, e.g., Luke 10:33; 17:16; John 4:40–42 (emphasizing Jews as faithless).

52. Ruether writes that, to Christianity, Jews are "preserved in a physical way as a witness to God's wrath upon Jewish 'unbelief.'" Ruether, supra note 3, at 56; see id. at 95–97 (Jewish practices are carnal and unrelated to salvation); id. at 105–07 (for Paul, Jews exist only to be converted to Christianity); see, e.g., Romans 9:1–11:36 (Jews exist to convert).

53. Nicholls, supra note 3, at 3.

54. Id.

55. Bauman, supra note 3, at 38.

56. Id. at 39–41.

57. Antisemitism, however, spread to non-Christian cultures and religions. See Wistrich, supra note 3, at 195–267 (on antisemitism among Moslems).

58. Bauman, supra note 3, at 17 (quoting Christopher R. Browning, The German Bureaucracy and the Holocaust, in Genocide: Critical Issues of the Holocaust 147 (Alex Grobman & Daniel Landes eds., 1983)).

59. See Johnson, supra note 1, at 207; Wistrich, supra note 3, at 26–32, 96, 164–65; see, e.g., Karl Marx, On the Jewish Question (1843), in The Marx-Engels Reader 26, 49 (Robert C. Tucker ed., 2d

ed. 1978) (blames Jews for causing Christians to become capitalists). Wistrich writes: "Austrian 'anti-semitism without Jews' (they constitute only 0.1 per cent of the total population) seemed to be illustrating the truth of Henryk Broder's remark about the Germans: that they will never forgive the Jews for Auschwitz!" Wistrich, supra note 3, at 96.

60. Bruno Bauer, The Jewish Problem (1843), reprinted in The Jew in the Modern World: A Documentary History 262, 262 (Paul R. Mendes-Flohr & Jehuda Reinharz eds., 1980).

61. See Johnson, supra note 1, at 169–310; Parkes, Judaism, supra note 3, at 135 & n.35. For an example of a decree from the thirteenth century that required Jews to wear conical hats or yellow patches, see That Jews Should be Distinguished From Christians in Dress, reprinted in The Jew in the Medieval World: A Source Book, 315–1791, at 138 (Jacob R. Marcus ed., 1938).

62. See, e.g., Marsh v. Chambers, 463 U.S. 783, 793 (1983); McGowan v. Maryland, 366 U.S. 420, 442 (1961); cf. Stephen L. Carter, The Culture of Disbelief 88 (1993) (on the origins of the rhetoric of the Judeo-Christian tradition); Robert Wuthnow, The Restructuring of American Religion 76–77 (1988) (the same).

63. See Ruether, supra note 3, at 62–63; Weiss-Rosmarin, supra note 2, at 9–10 (Judaism and Christianity are irreconcilable); Moshe Halbertal, The Scourge of Reason, New Republic, March 15, 1993, at 35, 37 (the Judeo-Christian tradition is an illusion). Jacob Neusner writes: "The conception of a Judeo-Christian tradition that Judaism and Christianity share is simply a myth in the bad old sense: a lie." Neusner, supra note 3, at ix; accord id. at 93–104.

64. Rosemary Ruether, a Christian theologian, observes that this fiction "reduces Judaism to the Scriptures of Hebrew national religion which stand as the 'Old Testament' to the Christian 'New Testament,' declared to be its universal and spiritual fulfillment." Ruether, supra note 3, at 63.

65. Neusner, supra note 3, at 18–19. Neusner refers to this mistaken characterization of Christianity as reforming Judaism as a "Protestant error" because it sees Christianity relating to Judaism as Protestantism relates to Roman Catholicism. Id. at 18.

66. See id. at 28, 103. Ruether ironically turns this argument on its head:

> [T]he Judaism which rejected Jesus as the Christ and which resisted Christian preaching was not the Judaism of the temple priesthood [the Sadducees] of Jesus' lifetime, but the Judaism of the Pharisees, which brought to full development at Jamnia that alternative to the temple which also excluded the Christian answer. This was the Judaism with which Christianity was in conflict during its early mission. If Christianity regards Judaism as "obsolete" and its continued existence as a "mystery," now that it has "rejected" its own future in Christ, it might be equally true that Judaism regards Christianity as "obsolete," a holdover from the heady apocalypticism of Jewish Palestine from the time of the Maccabees to the Sicarii of the Jewish Wars. This, from the Pharisaic perspective, had already been proven a false line of development. That Christianity could actually survive such a birth and continue to grow, not merely to adulthood but into a kind of giant, is, from the Jewish perspective, an enigma, given the self-contradiction of its religious starting point. That Christians could through the ages continue to assert that the Messiah has come, when evil demonstrably continues to reign—and, still more, to do such evil "in his name"—is, from a Jewish perspective, an unfathomable self-contradiction.

Ruether, supra note 3, at 62.

67. Neusner, supra note 3, at 28; see Monk & Stamey, supra note 5, at 212; cf. Weiss-Rosmarin, supra note 2, at 126–51 (Jews cannot accept Jesus as a prophet, teacher, or rabbi). Early Jews proselytized, but Judaism has not endorsed this practice for at least 2000 years. See Kertzer, supra note 2, at 202–03; Monk & Stamey, supra note 5, at 212; Nielson, supra note 5, at 434; Wistrich, supra note 3, at 8.

68. See Denise Lardner Carmody & John Tully Carmody, Christianity: An Introduction 40–42 (1983); Monk & Stamey, supra note 5, at 103–04, 109–17; Ruether, supra note 3, at 78; Weiss-Rosmarin, supra note 2, at 51, 54, 62. See generally Neusner, supra note 3, at 13 (differentiating being and becoming).

Different Christian theologians, of course, have different conceptions of faith. My description of faith in the text is closer to an Augustinian and Protestant definition of faith than to a Thomistic definition, which tends to be more cognitive and intellectual. See Monk & Stamey, supra note 5, at

67–68, 142. Richard Tarnas defines Christian faith as follows: "[T]he soul's active, freely willed embrace of Christ's revealed truth, with man's commitment of belief and trust working in mysterious interaction with God's freely bestowed grace." Tarnas, supra note 6, at 112.

69. See Cohon, supra note 2, at 99–100; Weiss-Rosmarin, supra note 2, at 47, 92; cf. Silver, supra note 2, at 190 ("the more dualistic the more anti-Judaistic").

70. Deuteronomy 30:15–19.

71. Kertzer, supra note 2, at 3; see Nielson, supra note 5, at 399, 444–45; Steinberg, supra note 2, at 12–15. Most Jews do not believe in an afterlife, although the Talmud can be interpreted as suggesting that there is one. See Gross, supra note 2, at 127–28; Silver, supra note 2, at 265–68.

72. Psalms 34:15.

73. Isaiah 1:17.

74. Deuteronomy 6:18.

75. Deuteronomy 16:20; accord Exodus 22:21–26 (do good; for example, care for strangers); Isaiah 16:5 (act righteously and seek justice); 51:1 (pursue righteousness); Jeremiah 5:1 (seek truth and justice).

76. Gross, supra note 2, at xxx. Maimonides, a Jewish philosopher who drew upon Aristotle, said, "[t]he reward for virtuous living … was the good life itself." Kertzer, supra note 2, at 14; see Steinberg, supra note 2, at 66, 78 (on Maimonides and virtue). Morris Kertzer writes:

> The story is told of a Gentile who asked Hillel, the great rabbi and scholar of the first century, B.C.E., if he could tell him all there was to know about Judaism while he stood on one foot! Hillel replied: 'Certainly! What is hateful to thee, do not unto thy neighbor. That is all there is in the Torah. All the rest is commentary. I suggest you study the commentary.'

Kertzer, supra note 2, at 8 (emphasis in the original).

Among Orthodox Jews particularly, Jewish law—the rules of conduct—is considered sweet and good partly because it promotes ethical conduct in this world, but in Christianity, law is necessary only because people are depraved. See Silver, supra note 2, at 136–37; Weiss-Rosmarin, supra note 2, at 84, 89. There are 613 mitzvot, or laws and regulations. See Gross, supra note 2, at 23, 53–54. The Judaic concern for this world is also evidenced by Judaism's tendency to promote and celebrate study and education, which are means to cultivate good and just conduct in this world. See Cohon, supra note 2, at 127–28; Kertzer, supra note 2, at 7.

77. See Kertzer, supra note 2, at 6; Silver, supra note 2, at 137–38, 152, 179–80, 258–59; Weiss-Rosmarin, supra note 2, at 65.

78. See Monk & Stamey, supra note 5, at 129 (the key difference between Christianity and Judaism is that the former emphasizes faith and belief, while the latter does not); Pagels, supra note 3, at 74 (the message of the New Testament is that one finds the Kingdom of God by believing in Jesus as the Messiah, even if one is otherwise lacking in spiritual self-knowledge); Silver, supra note 2, at 173–75 (on the Jewish concept of faith). Silver writes:

> [E]xtreme inwardness, which regards the act itself as of little or no account, is alien to Judaism. A meritorious act is important even without kavanah, without the correct inner intent, without its having been done li'shmah—for its own sake. By performing it the agent may ultimately come to acquire the correct inner attitude—for men learn by doing and are affected by whatever activity they are engaged in, and a moral act per se has a social utility, quite apart from the agent's intent.

Silver, supra note 2, at 139.

79. Silver, supra note 2, at 112; accord Steinberg, supra note 2, at 86 (sin is failure to be just and righteous, a failure to lead the good life). Judaism rejects the concept of original sin (see Kertzer, supra note 2, at 199–200), yet Judaism acknowledges that all people are susceptible to sin: "Perfection is not a human trait." Steinberg, supra note 2, at 89.

80. For example, Martin E. Marty describes the Christianity of Southern Protestants as "otherworldly individualism." Martin E. Marty, Protestantism in the United States: Righteous Empire 222 (2d ed. 1986).

81. See Jacobs, supra note 2, at 347–48; Telushkin, supra note 2, at 643–44.

82. See Kertzer, supra note 2, at 8.

83. The Tractate Avot 1:14, in The Talmud: Selected Writings 221 (Ben Zion Bokser trans., 1989); see Cohon, supra note 2, at 111.

84. Kertzer, supra note 2, at 115; see The Tractate Taanit 23a, in The Talmud: Selected Writings 117 (Ben Zion Bokser trans., 1989); Cohon, supra note 2, at 101, 127; Silver, supra note 2, at 115, 189–95; Weiss-Rosmarin, supra note 2, at 76.

85. See supra notes 33–34 and accompanying text.

86. Nicholls, supra note 3, at 87.

87. Id. at 122. Nicholls writes:

> The texts that the leadership of the new [Christian] movement found in the Torah, the Prophets and the Psalms, came to be known as the Testimonies. They are the real foundation of Christian theology. The texts are referred to many times in the New Testament, they are quoted and paraphrased in the Christian liturgy, and they formed the basis of Christian instruction from the first. In the following centuries they would be collected together in books called Testimonies.

Id.

Another spurious similarity between Judaism and Christianity lies in their respective understandings of monotheism. Judaism resolutely maintains the unity and oneness of God: God is absolutely incorporeal and thus has no human attributes. See Kertzer, supra note 2, at 200; Weiss-Rosmarin, supra note 2, at 15–21. Meanwhile, Christianity justifies Jesus' death by understanding him as the Son of God, as God incarnate, who upon death ascended to Heaven. To Judaism, a Holy Trinity—a God, a Son who is God incarnate, and a Holy Spirit—cannot be the incorporeal unity of a truly monotheistic religion. These radically different conceptions of monotheism lead, of course, to further differences between Judaism and Christianity. For instance, whereas many forms of Christianity abound with pictorial and sculptured images of Jesus, as God incarnate, Judaism never represents or visualizes its Deity because doing so would be inconsistent with the incorporeal unity of God: "Thou shalt not make unto thee a graven image, nor any manner of likeness, of any thing that is in heaven above." (Exodus 20:4); see Johnson, supra note 1, at 8, 63; Weiss-Rosmarin, supra note 2, at 21.

With regard to the Judaic concept of God, Judaism further maintains that God is personal (though not personified), which means that God remains near all persons so that they can all know goodness and therefore how to act justly and righteously. See Exodus 33:18–23 (humans cannot see the face of God but can learn all the goodness); Deuteronomy 30:11–14 (the word of good conduct is within all); Silver, supra note 2, at 3. Moreover, God is worshipped most genuinely through conduct, not through prayer:

> Judaism holds that man can most genuinely worship god by imitating those qualities that are godly: as God is merciful, so we must be compassionate; as God is just, so we must deal justly with our neighbor; as god is slow to anger, so we must be tolerant in our judgment.

Silver, supra note 2, at 7. Finally, even the importance of believing in God is disputed within Judaism. Some reason that one worships God adequately merely by living a just and ethical life (see Halbertal, supra note 63, at 37), while others insist that one must have "at least a modicum of belief in God" (Gross, supra note 2, at 6). See generally Steinberg, supra note 2, at 31–58 (on the Jewish concept of God).

88. Rosemary Ruether has done the most complete study of the antisemitism in the writings of the Church Fathers. This writing is called the adversus Judaeos literature. See Ruether, supra note 3. For a summary of this literature, see Nicholls, supra note 3, at 208.

89. Anthony Giddens, Profiles and Critiques in Social Theory 32 (1982).

90. Because of the eventual importance of the New Testament discourse, it should be noted that the two central themes—first, the dualism between Christian spirituality and Jewish carnality, and second, Christian universalism—stand somewhat in tension at a theoretical level. Exclusion and condemnation (the first theme) tends to undermine the openness and inclusiveness that universalism (the second theme) seems to require. This tension between the themes, however, has not weakened Christianity, but rather has introduced flexibility and thus resiliency into Christian social power.

Significantly, the relation between the themes facilitates the Christian exercise of oppressive power: Christians easily justify the subjugation and persecution of non-Christians (especially Jews), first, by claiming power over them because all are within the universal body of Jesus and, second, by condemning them for refusing to accept the spiritual fulfillment of that united and uniform Christian body. See generally Robert A. Williams, The American Indian in Western Legal Thought (1990) (explores the significance of Christian universalism for the domination of Native Americans).

91. See Monk & Stamey, supra note 5, at 33–48. Books that discuss the development of Christianity, antisemitism, or the doctrine of separation of church and state during the Roman Empire and the Middle Ages include the following: Harold J. Berman, Law and Revolution: The Formation of the Western Legal Tradition (1983); Fox, supra note 5; James Muldoon, Popes, Lawyers, and Infidels (1979); Edward A. Synan, The Popes and the Jews in the Middle Ages (1965); Brian Tierney, The Crisis of Church and State 1050–1300 (1988) [hereinafter Tierney, Crisis]; Brian Tierney, Religion, Law, and the Growth of Constitutional Thought 1150–1650 (1982) [hereinafter Tierney, Religion]; Walter Ullmann, The Growth of Papal Government in the Middle Ages (1955) [hereinafter Ullmann, Growth]; Walter Ullmann, A History of Political Thought: The Middle Ages (1965) [hereinafter Ullmann, History]; Church, State, and Jew in the Middle Ages (Robert Chazan ed., 1980) [hereinafter Chazan]; Church and State Through the Centuries: A Collection of Historic Documents With Commentaries (Sidney Z. Ehler & John B. Morrall trans. & eds., 1954) [hereinafter Ehler]; Documents of the Christian Church (Henry Bettenson ed., 2d ed. 1963) [hereinafter Bettenson]; The Jew in the Medieval World: A Source Book, 315–1791 (Jacob R. Marcus ed., 1938) [hereinafter Marcus]; Select Historical Documents of the Middle Ages (Ernest F. Henderson ed., 1892) [hereinafter Henderson]. General histories that provide useful information regarding the Roman Empire and the Middle Ages include the following: J.M. Roberts, The Penguin History of the World (1987); The Columbia History of the World (John A. Garraty & Peter Gay eds., 1972) [hereinafter Columbia].

92. See Johnson, supra note 1, at 140–43; Monk & Stamey, supra note 5, at 9.

93. See Monk & Stamey, supra note 5, at 42–43; Bettenson, supra note 91, at 7–14.

94. See Edict of Toleration (311), reprinted in Bettenson, supra note 91, at 15.

95. See Edict of Milan (313), reprinted in Bettenson, supra note 91, at 15.

96. See Monk & Stamey, supra note 5, at 43; Roberts, supra note 91, at 277–79; Bettenson, supra note 91, at 16–18.

97. A division between Eastern and Western Christianity began as early as Constantine's rule. When Constantine moved his capital from Rome to Constantinople in 330, the new imperial court and armies overshadowed the Church. Hence, the prelates of Constantinople tended to accept the Caesaropapist claims of the Eastern emperors. In the West, however, the gradual disintegration of royal and imperial authority allowed the Church to dominate. See Tierney, Crisis, supra note 91, at 8–9.

98. See Edict of the Emperors Gratian, Valentinian II, and Theodosius I establishing Catholicism as the State Religion (Feb. 27, 380), reprinted in Ehler, supra note 91, at 6–7.

99. At this point in history, the modern concept of a state did not exist. Ullman suggests that the concept of the state per se did not develop until closer to the thirteenth century (see Ullmann, History, supra note 91, at 17–18), though other commentators place the emergence of the state in the eleventh century. See Berman, supra note 91, at 113; Tierney, Religion, supra note 91, at 10. In any event, during the late stages of the Roman Empire and the early Middle Ages, the key distinction was between the clergy (ordained members of the Church) and the laity (unordained members). See Ullmann, Growth, supra note 91, at 1–2. Thus, for several hundred years, the central conflict was not so much between church and state as between priesthood (sacerdotium) and kingship (regnum), fought within the single and universal body of Christ. See Ullmann, History, supra note 91, at 17–18. Part of my argument, though, is that the rhetorical seeds of the modern state originated with the New Testament condemnation of Judaism as carnal.

100. Walter Ullmann writes:

> Who—that was the basic problem—was to govern, that is to direct and orientate the corporate union of Christians—the emperor, because he was emperor, or the pope because he was successor of St Peter? ... [W]ho was functionally qualified to define the doctrine, purpose and aim underlying the corporate union of all Christians, to direct that body according to its underlying purpose and aim—emperor or pope?

Ullmann, Growth, supra note 91, at 11; see Ehler, supra note 91, at 1–2.

101. See Ullmann, Growth, supra note 91, at 13–14; Ullmann, supra note 91, at 100.

102. See Ehler, supra note 91, at 2; Ullmann, Growth, supra note 91, at 18; Ullmann, History, supra note 91, at 35.

103. This council led to the adoption of the Nicaean Creed, which asserted belief "in one God the Father [and in] Jesus Christ, the Son of God, begotten of the Father, only-begotten, that is, of the substance of the Father." The Creed of Nicaea (325), reprinted in Bettenson, supra note 91, at 25; see Monk & Stamey, supra note 5, at 46; Columbia, supra note 91, at 232.

104. See Roberts, supra note 91, at 277–79; Ehler, supra note 91, at 2. In a sense, Constantine's Caesaropapism merely continued the approach typical of pagan states of antiquity, which combined religion and politics and which deemed the emperor divine. See Ehler, supra note 91, at 1; Ullmann, History, supra note 91, at 35. The difference, of course, was that Constantine's Caesaropapism substituted Christianity for the earlier pagan religions.

105. See Ullmann, History, supra note 91, at 20.

106. Cf. Peter Brown, Power and Persuasion in Late Antiquity: Towards a Christian Empire (1992) (on the spread of Christianity around 300–450 C.E.); Jon Butler, Awash in a Sea of Faith: Christianizing the American People 18–23 (1990) (Christianizing Europe was a problem, not a given).

107. Edict of the Emperors Gratian, Valentinian II, and Theodosius I establishing Catholicism as the State Religion (Feb. 27, 380), reprinted in Ehler, supra note 91, at 7. Robin Lane Fox underscores the link between Christianity and rising religious intolerance:

> [Christianity] changed the degree of freedom with which people could acceptably choose what to think and believe. Pagans had been intolerant of the Jews and Christians whose religions tolerated no gods except their own. Yet the rise of Christianity induced a much sharper rise in religious intolerance and the open coercion of religious belief. Christians were quick to mobilize force against [other religions].

Fox, supra note 5, at 23.

108. See Brown, supra note 106, at 19; Mark 12:17. Emperor Theodosius officially prohibited paganism by 391. See Columbia, supra note 91, at 222–23; Roberts, supra note 91, at 285; Synan, supra note 91, at 19–20.

109. See Synan, supra note 91, at 19–20, 28.

110. See Law of Constantius (Aug. 13, 339), reprinted in Marcus, supra note 91, at 4–5.

111. See A Law of Theodosius II (Novella III) (Jan. 31, 439), reprinted in Marcus, supra note 91, at 5–6. Jews could still hold public offices that entailed financial ruin. See Marcus, supra note 91, at 3–4.

112. See Ruether, supra note 3, at 190; cf. Nicholls, supra note 3, at 192 (Constantine mandated that Sunday be a day of rest).

113. See A Law of Theodosius II (Novella III) (Jan. 31, 439), reprinted in Marcus, supra note 91, at 5–6.

114. Reuther, supra note 3, at 194.

115. A Law of Theodosius II (Novella III) (Jan. 31, 439), reprinted in Marcus, supra note 91, at 6.

116. Id.

117. Law of Constantius (Aug. 13, 339), reprinted in Marcus, supra note 91, at 4–5.

118. A Law of Theodosius II (Novella III) (Jan. 31, 439), reprinted in Marcus, supra note 91, at 5.

119. Id. at 6.

120. Id. at 5.

121. Id. at 6.

122. For further legal condemnations of Jews and Judaism, see Reuther, supra note 3, at 194–95.

123. Baum, supra note 33, at 13.

124. See Nicholls, supra note 3, at 203; see, e.g., Johnson, supra note 1, at 164.

125. Synan, supra note 91, at 30.

126. I use the term "state" loosely here. See supra note 99.

127. In fact, over the years, Jews often have been portrayed as pigs. See Jaher, supra note 3, at 70.

128. St. Augustine, The City of God (Marcus Dods trans. & ed., 1948) (except where otherwise noted, all of my subsequent citations to The City of God will be to the second volume of this edition). Augustine lived from 354 to 430 and wrote The City of God around 412 to 427. For discussions of Augustine and his political thought, see Etienne Gilson, The Christian Philosophy of Saint Augustine (L.E.M. Lynch trans., 1960) [hereinafter Gilson, Augustine]; Etienne Gilson, History of Christian

Philosophy in the Middle Ages 70–81 (1955) [hereinafter Gilson, Middle Ages]; Ernest L. Fortin, St. Augustine, in History of Political Philosophy 176 (Leo Strauss & Joseph Cropsey eds., 3d ed. 1987); R.A. Markus, Marius Victorinus and Augustine, in The Cambridge History of Later Greek and Early Medieval Philosophy 327 (A.H. Armstrong ed., 1967) [hereinafter Markus, Augustine]; R.A. Markus, Refusing to Bless the State: Prophetic Church and Secular State, reprinted in Sacred and Secular 372 (1994) [hereinafter Markus, Refusing]; R.A. Markus, The Sacred and the Secular: From Augustine to Gregory the Great, reprinted in Sacred and Secular 84 (1994) [hereinafter Markus, Sacred].

129. Psalm 87:3; see Psalms 46:4; 48:1. Augustine quoted these passages in Augustine, supra note 128, at bk. XI, § 1 (vol. 1).

130. Hebrews 13:14.

131. Augustine was influenced by Platonic and Neoplatonic metaphysics even though he probably had little direct knowledge of Plato's own writings. See Gilson, Middle Ages, supra note 128, at 70–81, 93, 94; Paul Vincent Spade, Medieval Philosophy, in The Oxford History of Western Philosophy 55, 56–57, 89 (Anthony Kenny ed., 1994); Tarnas, supra note 6, at 101–08. Thomas Aquinas expressly noted that Augustine was a Platonist: "[W]henever Augustine, who was imbued with the doctrines of the Platonists, found in their teaching anything consistent with faith, he adopted it; and those things which he found contrary to faith he amended." St. Thomas Aquinas, Summa Theologica, in I Basic Writings of St. Thomas Aquinas, at pt. I, qu. 84, art. 5 (Anton C. Pegis ed., 1945).

132. See, e.g., Markus, Augustine, supra note 128, at 406–19 (in discussing Augustine's concept of two cities, Markus does not mention Augustine's view of Jews or Judaism); Fortin, supra note 128 (not discussing Augustine's attitude toward or treatment of Judaism). Etienne Gilson offers an uncritical description of a narrow part of Augustine's use of Judaism: Gilson notes that, according to Augustine, only grace can bring salvation and eliminate sin, while the Jewish law cannot do so. See Gilson, Augustine, supra note 128, at 153–54, 169. Most often, Gilson uses a rather thin euphemism, referring to the old man (Jews) as opposed to the new man (Christians). See, e.g., id. at 176.

133. St. Augustine, The Work of the Monks, in The Fathers of the Church 323, 349, 350 (Roy J. Deferrari ed., 1952).

134. Augustine, supra note 128, at bk. XIV, § 2.

135. Id. at bk. XIV, § 28.

136. See id. at bk. XVII, §§ 18, 46; Johnson, supra note 1, at 165.

137. Augustine, supra note 128, at bk. IV, § 34 (vol. 1). Augustine similarly wrote:

> [T]he Jews who slew Him, and would not believe in Him, because it behoved Him to die and rise again, were yet more miserably wasted by the Romans, and utterly rooted out from their kingdoms, where aliens had already ruled over them, and were dispersed through the lands (so that indeed there is no place where they are not), and are thus by their own Scriptures a testimony to us. . . .

Id. at bk. XVII, § 46.

138. Augustine, supra note 128, at bk. XIV, § 1; see Fortin, supra note 128, at 195–98 (on the two cities).

139. Augustine, supra note 128, at bk. XIV, § 28.

140. See Fortin, supra note 128, at 196–97.

141. "Render to Caesar the things that are Caesar's, and to God the things that are God's." Mark 12:17; accord Luke 20:25.

142. Tierney, Crisis, supra note 91, at 10.

143. See Augustine, supra note 128, at bk. XIX, § 17; Gilson, Augustine, supra note 128, at 179; Fortin, supra note 128, at 183, 195–98; Markus, Augustine, supra note 128, at 417–18; Markus, Refusing, supra note 128, at 374.

144. Augustine, supra note 128, at bk. I, § 1 (vol. 1).

145 See Fortin, supra note 128, at 96; Markus, Augustine, supra note 128, at 412; see, e.g., Augustine, supra note 128, at bk. XX, § 9 ("the Church even now is the kingdom of Christ, and the kingdom of heaven").

146. Augustine, supra note 128, at bk. XV, § 1.

147. Markus, Augustine, supra note 128, at 412.

148. Augustine, supra note 128, at bk. XV, § 1.

149. Id.; see Fortin, supra note 128, at 195.

150. See J.G.A. Pocock, The Machiavellian Moment 32, 43, 45 (1975); Eric Voegelin, The New Science of Politics 118–19 (1987 ed.); Markus, Augustine, supra note 128, at 406–12. Markus also argues that Augustine suggested a threefold conceptual scheme involving the sacred, the profane, and the secular. The profane is the opposite of the sacred, while the secular represents an intermediate realm where the sacred and profane overlap. The secular was "the realm to which the institutions of politically organized societies belong." Markus, Sacred, supra note 128, at 85.

151. Augustine, supra note 128, at bk. I, § 35 (vol. 1); accord id. at bk. XI, § 1 (vol. 1).

152. See Marcus Dods, Preface, in St. Augustine, The City of God (Marcus Dods trans. & ed., 1948). Thus, Etienne Gilson argues that Augustine's purpose was to trace a "theology of history." Gilson, Middle Ages, supra note 128, at 80. R.A. Markus argues that Augustine's denigration of civil authority marked a change in Christian attitudes. According to Markus, from the time of the Roman establishment of Christianity, Christians readily accepted the culture, values, social structure, and political institutions of the Roman Empire. "[T]he prevailing assumption was hardly questioned: the Roman Empire was God's chosen means for the social embodiment of Christianity, with a kind of messianic mission in the world, its emperor the representative of God's own authority over a society which was the image of His Kingdom." Markus, Refusing, supra note 128, at 373; accord Voegelin, supra note 150, at 109–10 (the Roman Empire was practically built into Christianity).

153. Again, I use the term "state" loosely here. See supra note 99.

154. Markus, Augustine, supra note 128, at 417; see Gilson, Augustine, supra note 128, at 180–81; Fortin, supra note 128, at 196–97.

155. Markus writes:

> The general implications of [Augustine's view] are clearly hostile to any close linking of the two institutions [of church and state], and indeed part of Augustine's purpose appears to have been to question radically the theological premises of the view of history which led to so close a linking of the Christian Church to the Roman Empire during the fourth century.

Markus, Augustine, supra note 128, at 417.

156. Richard Tarnas writes, for example, that "the doctrine of the two cities would have much influence on subsequent Western history, affirming the autonomy of the spiritual Church vis-à-vis the secular state." Tarnas, supra note 6, at 148.

NOTES TO CHAPTER 3

1. See Church and State Through the Centuries: A Collection of Historic Documents With Commentaries 2 (Sidney Z. Ehler & John B. Morrall trans. & eds., 1954) [hereinafter Ehler]; James E. Wood, Jr., et al., Church and State in Scripture, History, and Constitutional Law 61 (1958). Books that discuss the development of Christianity, antisemitism, or the doctrine of separation of church and state during the Roman Empire and the Middle Ages include the following: Harold J. Berman, Law and Revolution: The Formation of the Western Legal Tradition (1983); Margaret Deanesly, A History of the Medieval Church 590–1500 (8th ed. 1954); Robin Lane Fox, Pagans and Christians (1987); James Muldoon, Popes, Lawyers, and Infidels (1979); Martin E. Marty, A Short History of Christianity (1959); Edward A. Synan, The Popes and the Jews in the Middle Ages (1965); Brian Tierney, The Crisis of Church and State 1050–1300 (1988) [hereinafter Tierney, Crisis]; Brian Tierney, Religion, Law, and the Growth of Constitutional Thought 1150–1650 (1982) [hereinafter Tierney, Religion]; Walter Ullmann, The Growth of Papal Government in the Middle Ages (1955) [hereinafter Ullmann, Growth]; Walter Ullmann, A History of Political Thought: The Middle Ages (1965) [hereinafter Ullmann, History]; Williston Walker, A History of the Christian Church (3d ed. 1970); Church, State, and Jew in the Middle Ages (Robert Chazan ed., 1980) [hereinafter Chazan]; Ehler, supra; Documents of the Christian Church (Henry Bettenson ed., 2d ed. 1963) [hereinafter Bettenson]; The Jew in the Medieval World: A Source Book, 315–1791 (Jacob R. Marcus ed., 1938) [hereinafter Marcus]; Select Historical Documents of the Middle Ages (Ernest F. Henderson ed., 1892) [hereinafter Henderson]. General histories that provide useful information regarding the Roman Empire and the Middle Ages

include the following: J.M. Roberts, The Penguin History of the World (1987); The Columbia History of the World (John A. Garraty & Peter Gay eds., 1972) [hereinafter Columbia].

2. Letter from Pope Gelasius I to Byzantine Emperor Anastasius I (494), reprinted in Ehler, supra note 1, at 11.

3. Id.

4. Cf. Tierney, supra note 1, at 10–11 (Gelasius was ambiguous enough to be interpreted as supporting either a balanced dualism or papal superiority); David S. Clark, The Medieval Origins of Modern Legal Education: Between Church and State, 35 Am. J. Comp. L. 653, 662–63 (1987) (attributes to Gelasius a more balanced dualism).

5. See Ullmann, Growth, supra note 1, at 19, 20–23.

6. See Synan, supra note 1, at 32–35. But cf. id. (Gelasius also tolerated and perhaps befriended particular Jews).

7. Letter from Pope Gelasius I to Byzantine Emperor Anastasius I (494), reprinted in Ehler, supra note 1, at 11.

8. See Ehler, supra note 1, at 10.

9. Justinian's Novella VI (535), reprinted in Tierney, Crisis, supra note 1, at 15. On the importance of Justinian's Corpus Jurisprudence Civilis and his Novellae to the development of western legal thought, see Ullmann, History, supra note 1, at 46–47.

10. See Ullmann, Growth, supra note 1, at 31–33; Ullmann, History, supra note 1, at 47–48.

11. Ullmann, Growth, supra note 1, at 32.

12. See Ehler, supra note 1, at 9.

13. Ullmann, History, supra note 1, at 47.

14. Rosemary Ruether, Faith and Fratricide: The Theological Roots of Anti-Semitism 196 (1974). Other books on antisemitism that I cite in this chapter include the following: Zygmunt Bauman, Modernity and the Holocaust (1989); Gavin I. Langmuir, History, Religion, and Antisemitism (1990); William Nicholls, Christian Antisemitism: A History of Hate (1993); James Parkes, Judaism and Christianity (1948) [hereinafter Parkes, Judaism]; Robert S. Wistrich, Antisemitism: The Longest Hatred (1991).

15. A Law of Justinian (July 28, 531), reprinted in Marcus, supra note 1, at 6–7.

16. See Marty, supra note 1, at 125–26; Ullmann, History, supra note 1, at 49–50; Bettenson, supra note 1, at 151–53.

17. Ullmann, History, supra note 1, at 50; see Ullmann, Growth, supra note 1, at 38.

18. See Ullmann, History, supra note 1, at 49–50. Ullmann argues that the Church was "the most influential and important governmental institution in the medieval period." Ullmann, Growth, supra note 1, at 1. R.A. Markus notes that Gregory was influenced by Augustine's writings, but the reality of secular power had radically changed during the two centuries between their lives. This changed historical context affected their different views on secular power and the relation between church and state. See R.A. Markus, The Sacred and the Secular: From Augustine to Gregory the Great, reprinted in Sacred and Secular 84, 87–96 (1994).

19. See Synan, supra note 1, at 35, 81, 97–98, 229–32.

20. Id. at 37.

21. Moreover, Gregory wrote that "[t]he Old Testament is the prophecy of the New, the New is the explanation of the Old." Deanesly, supra note 1, at 27 (quoting Gregory).

22. Id. at 46 (quoting Gregory I).

23. See id. at 48–49, 120; cf. Ruether, supra note 14, at 190 (the practice of forcing Jews to listen to Christian conversion sermons began in the fifth century).

24. Letter from Gregory to Virgilius, Bishop of Arles, and Theodorus, Bishop of Marseilles, in Gaul (June 591), reprinted in Marcus, supra note 1, at 112.

25. Id.

26. See Marty, supra note 1, at 141–45.

27. Compare The Creed of Nicaea (325), reprinted in Bettenson, supra note 1, at 25 with The Nicene Creed, reprinted in Bettenson, supra note 1, at 25–26.

28. Berman, supra note 1, at 178.

29. See id. at 105, 581 n.26; Marty, supra note 1, at 152–53.

30. Berman, supra note 1, at 179.

31. See id. at 179, 521. For a discussion of the differences between the Eastern and Western Churches, see id. at 174–78; Robert C. Monk & Joseph D. Stamey, Exploring Christianity: An Introduction 48–55 (2d ed. 1990).

32. See Uta-Renate Blumenthal, The Investiture Controversy: Church and Monarch From the Ninth to the Twelfth Century (1988); Henderson, supra note 1, at 365–409; Walker, supra note 1, at 204–12. See generally Berman, supra note 1, at 1–19 (connecting the schism and the Investiture Struggle together as part of a revolution in legal thought); Tierney, Crisis, supra note 1, at 33–34 (connecting the schism with the Investiture Struggle).

33. See Deanesly, supra note 1, at 93–94; Ehler, supra note 1, at 24; Ullmann, History, supra note 1, at 82–83; Walker, supra note 1, at 204; Clark, supra note 4, at 668.

34. Henderson, supra note 1, at 352. The investiture ceremony and practice was a central component of feudalism. See Blumenthal, supra note 1, at 28–29.

35. The Church's rallying cry for the Investiture Struggle was "the freedom of the church." Berman, supra note 1, at 105; accord id. at 108. F.H. Hinsley argues that the Investiture Struggle should be understood more as a struggle for power between two theocratic authorities (the papacy and the emperor) than as a clash between secular and spiritual authorities. F.H. Hinsley, Sovereignty 58–60 (2d ed. 1986).

36. For a detailed description of the dispute between Gregory and Henry, see Blumenthal, supra note 32, at 113–27. Uta-Renate Blumenthal argues that Gregory's prohibition of lay investiture arose because of a preexisting tension between Gregory and Henry and was not the underlying cause of the dispute between them. See id. at 120–21. According to Blumenthal, the true founder of the Holy Roman Empire—the successor state to Charlemagne's empire—was an earlier Henry (919–936), although the empire was not official until the coronation of Otto I as emperor in 962. See id. at 31.

37. See Ullmann, Growth, supra note 1, at 262–63. For example, in a letter written to a bishop, Gregory quotes Pope Gelasius: "'There are indeed, most august Emperor, two powers by which this world is chiefly ruled: the sacred authority of the Popes and the royal power; of these the priestly power is much more important, because it has to render account for the kings of men themselves at the Divine tribunal.'" Letter of Pope Gregory VII to Hermann, Bishop of Metz (March 15, 1081), reprinted in Ehler, supra note 1, at 29, 33. For an excellent summary of Gregory's hierocratic principles, see Ullmann, Growth, supra note 1, at 272–309.

38. Synan, supra note 1, at 65.

39. Letter of Pope Gregory VII to Hermann, Bishop of Metz (March 15, 1081), reprinted in Ehler, supra note 1, at 29, 33. Similarly, Gregory declared that "[kings], far too much given to worldly affairs, think little of spiritual things; [pontiffs], dwelling eagerly upon heavenly subjects, despise the things of this world." Tierney, supra note 1, at 87.

40. The Dictatus Papae, reprinted in Ehler, supra note 1, at 43–44. This document was inserted in Gregory's official Register in March, 1075, but whether Gregory actually authored it is sometimes disputed. See Ehler, supra note 1, at 43; Tierney, Crisis, supra note 1, at 46.

41. Decree Forbidding Lay Investiture (Nov. 19, 1078), reprinted in Henderson, supra note 1, at 365. The decree from 1075 has not survived, but its content was similar to that of this decree from 1078. Henderson, supra note 1, at 352.

42. The dispute over the see in Milan actually had begun several years earlier under the reign of Pope Alexander II. See Tierney, supra note 1, at 53.

43. See Letter of Gregory VII to Henry IV (Dec. 1075), reprinted in Henderson, supra note 1, at 367, 368; Walker, supra note 1, at 209.

44. See Letter of the Bishops to Gregory VII (Jan. 24, 1076), reprinted in Henderson, supra note 1, at 373–76; Walker, supra note 1, at 209.

45. Deposition of Henry by Gregory (Feb. 1076), reprinted in Tierney, Crisis, supra note 1, at 60–61.

46. Henry IV's Answer to Gregory VII (Jan. 24, 1076), reprinted in Henderson, supra note 1, at 372. The date of this letter is unclear. Although Henderson dates it as January 24, 1076, which would place it before Gregory's excommunication of Henry, it is better dated just after the excommunication. See Tierney, Crisis, supra note 1, at 53–54; Walker, supra note 1, at 209 & n.5.

47. Henry IV's Answer to Gregory VII (Jan. 24, 1076), reprinted in Henderson, supra note 1, at 373.

48. See Deanesly, supra note 1, at 102; Henderson, supra note 1, at 353–54; Walker, supra note 1, at 209.

49. See Deanesly, supra note 1, at 103; Tierney, Crisis, supra note 1, at 54–55; Walker, supra note 1, at 209–10.

50. Tierney, Crisis, supra note 1, at 86; accord Blumenthal, supra note 32, at 118 ("theocratic kingship became an anachronism"); see, e.g., Concordat of Worms Between Pope Calixtus II and the Emperor Henry V (Sept. 23, 1122), reprinted in Ehler, supra note 1, at 48–49. Deanesly summarizes the Concordat of Worms as follows: "The emperor renounced investiture by ring and staff, and promised canonical election; the pope assented to election in the emperor's presence, to investiture with the 'regalia' by touching the sceptre before consecration, and to the performance of homage and fealty." Deanesly, supra note 1, at 105; see Ehler, supra note 1, at 24–25 (discussing the compromise). Whether Gregory's personal reign as pontiff should be categorized as revolutionary, reformatory, or even conservative is subject to dispute. See Clark, supra note 4, at 669 n.51.

51. See Ehler, supra note 1, at 50–51. Some clerics insisted that the pope, as the spiritual leader, ruled over both spiritual and temporal affairs. Other (though fewer) clerics maintained that although the pope was supreme, he should remain apart from the carnal degradations inherent in temporal and material affairs. See Tierney, Crisis, supra note 1, at 87–88.

52. See Ullmann, History, supra note 1, at 138–39. The increase in the Church's temporal power was central to the transformation of the doctrine of two swords. In the twelfth century, Bernard of Clairvaux interpreted the doctrine in an extremely hierocratic fashion. To Bernard, the pope possessed "both swords, the spiritual as well as the physical-material sword." Ullmann, Growth, supra note 1, at 431; see Muldoon, supra note 1, at 14–15; Tierney, Crisis, supra note 1, at 8; cf. Ullmann, Growth, supra note 1, at 345 (King Henry IV's interpretation of the doctrine of two swords was a more balanced dualism).

53. Berman, supra note 1, at 520; see id. at 51.

54. Id. at 113.

55. The Church worked "for the redemption of the laity and the reformation of the world, through law." Id. at 520; see id. at 179, 521.

56. See T.M. Parker, The English Reformation to 1558, at 4–5, 10 (2d ed. 1966).

57. See Chazan, supra note 1 at 17–42; see also Berman, supra note 1, at 86 (on the extensive laws and legal orders even before the systematization of the canon law).

58. Berman, supra note 1, at 49; see id. at 49–50, 76, 520–21; Quentin Skinner, 1 The Foundations of Modern Political Thought: The Renaissance 14 (1978).

59. Berman, supra note 1, at 113–14. Berman acknowledges, however, that calling the Church a state is somewhat paradoxical: "Yet it is a paradox to call the church a modern state, since the principal feature by which the modern state is distinguished from the ancient state, as well as from the Germanic or Frankish state, is its secular character." Id. at 114.

60. See id. at 260; Tierney, Religion, supra note 1, at 10; Michael Walzer, The Revolution of the Saints 6, 171–72 (1965). Berman writes that while one side of the Papal Revolution (the Investiture Struggle) was the enhancement of Church power, "[a]nother side of it was the enhancement of the secular political and legal authority of emperors, kings, and lords, as well as the creation of thousands of autonomous, self-governing cities." Berman, supra note 1, at 520.

61. Berman, supra note 1, at 521; see id. at 166, 195, 273. Berman writes:

> Secular law was supposed to emulate the canon law. All the various secular legal systems—feudal, manorial, mercantile, urban, royal—adapted to their own uses many basic ideas and techniques of the canon law, if only because the canon law was more highly developed and was available for imitation. This was inevitable, since in the twelfth and thirteenth centuries most lawyers, judges, and other professional advisers and officers of secular legal institutions were clerics and either had been trained in canon law or were generally familiar with its basic features. At the same time, the secular authorities resisted the encroachments of the ecclesiastical authorities upon the secular jurisdiction; and for that reason, too, they sought to achieve for secular law the cohesion and sophistication of the canon law.

Id. at 274.

62. Id. at 213.

63. See id. at 213–14; Tierney, Religion, supra note 1, at 10–12.

64. Tierney, Religion, supra note 1, at 10; accord Berman, supra note 1, at 260.

65. See Berman, supra note 1, at 225. Brian Tierney writes: "[T]he juridical culture of the twelfth century—the works of the Roman and canon lawyers, especially those of the canonists where religious and secular ideas most obviously intersected—formed a kind of seedbed from which grew the whole tangled forest of early modern constitutional thought." Tierney, Crisis, supra note 1, at 1.

66. Tierney, Crisis, supra note 1, at 87.

67. According to Jonathan Riley-Smith, a "crusade was a holy war fought against those perceived to be the external or internal foes of Christendom for the recovery of Christian property or in defence of the Church or Christian people." Jonathan Riley-Smith, The Crusades xxviii (1987). Edward Synan notes that "the Crusades were first and last a papal enterprise." Synan, supra note 1, at 69; see Robert Chazan, European Jewry and the First Crusade 171 (1987) [hereinafter Chazan, European Jewry].

68. See Deanesly, supra note 1, at 109; Marcus, supra note 1, at 115; Walker, supra note 1, at 219–21. The first massacres of Jews occurred in the spring of 1096. See Paul Johnson, A History of the Jews 208 (1987); Synan, supra note 1, at 67.

69. See Synan, supra note 1, at 66–67. Robert Chazan argues that during the first Crusade, there were three distinguishable groups of Crusaders: baronial forces, who eventually captured Jerusalem and did not engage in extensive antisemitic violence; bands led by Peter the Hermit; and other bands stirred up by Peter the Hermit. See Chazan, supra note 1, at 113; Chazan, European Jewry, supra note 67, at 50–60.

70. Id. at 71. Jewish accounts confirm that the Crusaders sought to totally destroy the Jews either by conversion or by death. According to Jewish reports, the Christians declared: "Let us take vengeance first upon them. Let us wipe them out as a nation; Israel's name will be mentioned no more. Or else let them be like us and acknowledge the son [of God]." Chazan, European Jewry, supra note 67, at 69 (quoting Hebrew First-Crusade Chronicle L).

71. Synan, supra note 1, at 71.

72. Synan, supra note 1, at 70; see Langmuir, supra note 14, at 290; Ruether, supra note 14, at 205–08; Wistrich, supra note 14, at 23.

73. See Wistrich, supra note 14, at 23.

74. Synan, supra note 1, at 73.

75. See Chazan, supra note 1, at 136–37.

76. Chazan, European Jewry, supra note 67, at 70 (quoting Albert of Aix).

77. Id. at 111–12. Chazan provides translations of the two original Hebrew First-Crusade chronicles. See id. at 223–97. This particular passage is from the Hebrew First-Crusade Chronicle L, reprinted in id. at 258–59. Incredibly, Chazan concludes that the first Crusade had only a limited overall impact on European Jewry because the Jewish community survived and continued. See id. at 8. Such a conclusion minimizes the significance of human suffering that occurred during the Crusade, as well as the loss of life. As Robert Wistrich reports, during the first six months of 1096 alone, one-quarter to one-third of the Jews in Germany and northern France were murdered. See Wistrich, supra note 14, at 23.

78. For example, Peter the Venerable, a leader of the second Crusade, wrote:

> What does it profit to track down and to persecute enemies of the Christian hope outside, indeed far beyond, the frontiers, if the evil, blaspheming Jews, far worse than Saracens, not at a distance, but in our midst, so freely and audaciously blaspheme, trample underfoot, deface with impunity Christ and all Christian mysteries?

Synan, supra note 1, at 76.

79. The Report of Ephraim, reprinted in Chazan, supra note 1, at 107, 108 (quoting the monk Ralph). Ralph is sometimes called Rudolph or Radulph. See Chazan, supra note 1, at 104; Chazan, European Jewry, supra note 67, at 169–79; Nicholls, supra note 14, at 229–32.

80. Compare The Report of Otto of Freising, reprinted in Chazan, supra note 1, at 106, 106 (reporting that with regard to the preaching of Ralph, "a large number of Jews were killed in this stormy uprising") and Nicholls, supra note 14, at 230–32 (reporting anti-Jewish violence during the second Crusade) with Chazan, European Jewry, supra note 67, at 169–79 (referring to anti-Jewish sentiment).

81. For example, Ephraim ben Jacob (who lived from 1132 to about 1200) reported that in France, a leading rabbi, Jacob ben Meir (called Rabbenu Tam—"Our master, the perfect one"), was physically assaulted, but that otherwise, the only Jewish injuries were economic (though they were severe). See Marcus, supra note 1, at 304–05.

82. Bernard wrote: "I find three things most reprehensible in him [Ralph]: unauthorized preaching, contempt for episcopal authority, and incitation to murder." Letter from Bernard to Archbishop of Mainz (1146), reprinted in Chazan, supra note 1, at 104, 105.

83. See, e.g., Bernard's Missive Calling Forth the Second Crusade, reprinted in Chazan, supra note 1, at 100, 103; see Nicholls, supra note 14, at 329–32; Synan, supra note 1, at 76, 78; cf. Chazan, European Jewry, supra note 67, at 175–79 (emphasizing Bernard's protection of Jews). Nicholls contrasts Bernard's somewhat typical attitude toward Jews with that of Peter Abelard, who managed to overcome Christian antisemitic dogma in order to compassionately understand the Jewish plight. See Nicholls, supra note 14, at 227.

84. See Synan, supra note 1, at 81; Wistrich, supra note 14, at 25–26; cf. Muldoon, supra note 1, at 4–5 (the Decretales, the second volume of the canon law, published in 1234, forbade Jews from building new synagogues and having Christian slaves). Moreover, the exercise of papal power over Jews served as the model for the exercise of power over all non-Christians. See Muldoon, supra note 1, at 27. Raul Hilberg compiled a chart showing the parallels between medieval canon law and Nazi law. See Raul Hilberg, 1 The Destruction of the European Jews 11–12 (1985) (reprinted in William Nicholls, Christian Antisemitism: A History of Hate 204–06 (1993)).

85. Synan, supra note 1, at 88–89 (quoting Innocent III).

86. Langmuir, supra note 14, at 294–95 (quoting Innocent III); accord Synan, supra note 1, at 92–93; Wistrich, supra note 14, at 33–34.

87. The decree stated:

> In some provinces a difference in dress distinguishes the Jews or Saracens from the Christians, but in certain others such a confusion has grown up that they cannot be distinguished by any difference. Thus it happens at times that through error Christians have relations with the women of Jews or Saracens, and Jews or Saracens with Christian women. Therefore, that they may not, under pretext of error of this sort, excuse themselves in the future for the excesses of such prohibited intercourse, we decree that such Jews and Saracens of both sexes in every Christian province and at all times shall be marked off in the eyes of the public from other peoples through the character of their dress....

That Jews Should be Distinguished From Christians in Dress, reprinted in Marcus, supra note 1, at 138. For discussions of other decrees, see Johnson, supra note 68, at 210–11, 214; Marcus, supra note 1, at 137–41; Synan, supra note 1, at 87, 103–06; Wistrich, supra note 14, at 25.

88. See Muldoon, supra note 1, at 51; Parkes, Judaism, supra note 14, at 132 & n.32, 135 & n.35; Wistrich, supra note 14, at 25.

89. That Jews Should be Distinguished From Christians in Dress, reprinted in Marcus, supra note 1, at 139.

90. Muldoon, supra note 1, at 51 (emphasis added).

91. See Chazan, supra note 1, at 221–24; Marcus, supra note 1, at 145–47; Synan, supra note 1, at 107–08; see also Johnson, supra note 68, at 215, 217. Pope Innocent IV, pontiff from 1243 to 1254, renewed the condemnation:

> Ungrateful to the Lord Jesus Christ who, His forebearance overflowing, patiently awaits their conversion; they manifest no shame for their guilt, nor do they reverence the dignity of the Christian faith. Omitting or contemning the Mosaic Law and the prophets, they follow certain traditions of their elders, the very ones for which the Lord took them to task in the Gospel, saying: "Why is it that you yourselves violate the commandment of God with your traditions?" [Matt. 15:3]. It is traditions of this stripe—in Hebrew they call them "Thalamuth," and an immense book it is, exceeding the text of the Bible in size, and in it are blasphemies against God and His Christ, and against the blessed Virgin, fables that are manifestly beyond all explanation, erroneous abuses and unheard-of stupidities—yet this is what they teach and feed their children ... and render them totally alien to the teaching of the Law and the prophets, fearing lest the Truth which is

understood in the same Law and Prophets, bearing patent testimony to the only-begotten Son of God, who was to come in flesh, they be converted to the faith, and return humbly to their Redeemer.

Synan, supra note 1, at 112; see Marcus, supra note 1, at 146–49.

Of course, Innocent IV asserted his universal power over all:

> [T]he pope, who is vicar of Jesus Christ, has power not only over Christians but also over all infidels, for Christ had power over all, whence it is said in the psalm, "Give to the king thy judgment O god" (Psalm 71:2), and he would not seem to have been a careful father unless he had committed full power over all to his vicar whom he left on earth. Again he gave the keys of the kingdom of heaven to Peter and his successors and said, "Whatsoever you shall bind, etc." (Matthew 16:19). And again, elsewhere, "Feed my sheep, etc." (John 21:17).... But all men, faithful and infidels, are Christ's sheep by creation even though they are not of the fold of the church and thus from the foregoing it is clear that the pope has jurisdiction and power over de iure though not de facto.

Quod Super of Innocent IV (1250), reprinted in Tierney, Crisis, supra note 1, at 155–56; see Muldoon, supra note 1, at 6–10, 22. For a discussion of the successors to Innocent IV, see Muldoon, supra note 1, at 50–51.

92. Langmuir, supra note 14, at 296.

93. Actually, Aristotle's logical writings had been translated into Latin during the fifth to sixth centuries, but they were not widely available. Virtually all of his remaining works were translated and became readily accessible in the thirteenth century. See Paul Vincent Spade, Medieval Philosophy, in The Oxford History of Western Philosophy 55, 56–57 (Anthony Kenny ed., 1994); Richard Tarnas, The Passion of the Western Mind 176–77 (1991); Ullmann, History, supra note 1, at 170.

94. Aristotle's major political writings are the following: Aristotle, Nichomachean Ethics (I. Bywater trans.), reprinted in The Complete Works of Aristotle 1729–1867 (Jonathan Barnes ed., 1984) [hereinafter Aristotle, Nichomachean Ethics]; Aristotle, The Politics (Carnes Lord trans., 1984) [hereinafter Aristotle, The Politics]. For a summary of Aristotle's political thought, see Carnes Lord, Aristotle, in History of Political Philosophy 118–54 (Leo Strauss & Joseph Cropsey eds., 3d ed. 1987).

95. See Aristotle, Nichomachean Ethics, supra note 94, at bk. I.

96. Aristotle, The Politics, supra note 94, at bk. I, ch. 2.

97. Aristotle, Nichomachean Ethics, supra note 94, at bk. VI, ch. 1–3; Aristotle, The Politics, supra note 94, at bk. I, ch. 2.

98. Aristotle, The Politics, supra note 94, at bk. III, ch. 13.

99. Id. at bk. III, ch. 7, 9. Aristotle wrote: "For the city is not any chance multitude, but one self-sufficent with a view to life." Id. at bk. VII, ch. 8. Jowett translated this passage as follows: "For a state is not a mere aggregate of persons, but ... a union of them sufficing for the purposes of life." Aristotle, Politics (B. Jowett trans.), reprinted in The Complete Works of Aristotle 2108 (Jonathan Barnes ed., 1984).

100. Ullmann, History, supra note 1, at 170. Tierney observes that during the Middle Ages, the legitimacy of the ruler was based on a hierarchy ordained from above, not consented to from below. Tierney, supra note 1, at 42–43. Yet, he continues: "The theory of government by consent (based on arguments from liberty and equality) was fully formulated by the early fourteenth century." Id. at 52 (emphasis added). That is, the theory of government by consent did not first develop in the seventeenth century, as some commentators have suggested. See id. at 52, 104–05.

101. D.W. Hamlyn, A History of Western Philosophy 104 (1987). Some of Thomas's most important works are the following: St. Thomas Aquinas, On Kingship (Gerald B. Phelan trans., 1982 ed.) [hereinafter On Kingship]; St. Thomas Aquinas, Summa Contra Gentiles: Providence (Book III) (Vernon J. Bourke trans., 1956) [hereinafter Gentiles]; St. Thomas Aquinas, Summa Theologica (Benziger Bros., 1st complete American ed. 1946) [hereinafter Theologica]. Unless otherwise noted, all of my subsequent citations to Summa Theologica will be to this Benziger Brothers edition. Where noted, I will cite St. Thomas Aquinas, Summa Theologica, in II Basic Writings of St. Thomas Aquinas (Anton C. Pegis ed., 1945) [hereinafter Theologica (Pegis ed.)]. For discussions of Thomas's philosophy, see Frederick Copleston, 2 A History of Philosophy 302–434 (1950); Brian Davies, The Thought of Thomas Aquinas (1992); Etienne Gilson, The Christian Philosophy of St. Thomas Aquinas (L.K.

Shook trans., 1956) [hereinafter Gilson, Aquinas]; Etienne Gilson, History of Christian Philosophy in the Middle Ages (1955) [hereinafter Gilson, Middle Ages]; Ernest L. Fortin, St. Thomas Aquinas, in History of Political Philosophy 248 (Leo Strauss & Joseph Cropsey eds., 3d ed. 1987).

102. See Gilson, Aquinas, supra note 101, at 16–17. Thomas's interpretation of Aristotle was heavily influenced by Maimonides. See 3 Encyclopaedia Judaica 229–30 (1971); Anton C. Pegis, Introduction, in Theologica (Pegis ed.), supra note 101, at xliv. Some other medieval Scholastic philosophers, such as William of Ockham, rejected Thomas's effort at synthesis and instead saw two realms—one of faith, and one of empiricism and reason. See Tarnas, supra note 93, at 190, 201–08; cf. Gilson, Middle Ages, supra note 101, at 382 (Augustinians objected to Thomas's incorporation of Aristotelian themes into Christian theology).

103. On Kingship, supra note 101, at bk. 1, ch. 1, ¶ 4; accord Theologica, supra note 101, at pt. I–II, qu. 72, art. 4.

104. See On Kingship, supra note 101, at bk. 2, ch. 3, ¶ 106; ch. 4, ¶¶ 116–18.

105. Theologica, supra note 101, at pt. I–II, qu. 90, art. 2.

106. See Ullmann, History, supra note 1, at 171, 175–76.

107. Id. at 179, 183. Compare Theologica, supra note 101, at pt. I, qu. 60, art. 5 (if a person is a virtuous citizen, then sometimes he or she might be required to sacrifice even his or her life for the public good) with id. at pt. II–II, qu. 31, arts. 2–3 (the amount of beneficence owed to others varies with the circumstances).

108. See Ullmann, History, supra note 1, at 176–77. Thus, for example, Thomas wrote:

> Now one man's connection with another may be measured in reference to the various matters in which men are engaged together; (thus the intercourse of kinsmen is in natural matters, that of fellow-citizens is in civic matters, that of the faithful is in spiritual matters, and so forth): and various benefits should be conferred in various ways according to these various connections, because we ought in preference to bestow on each one such benefits as pertain to the matter in which, speaking simply he is most closely connected with us.

Theologica, supra note 101, at pt. II–II, qu. 31, art. 3.

109. Theologica, supra note 101, at pt. I, qu. 1, art. 5; see Ullmann, History, supra note 1, at 177.

110. See Copleston, supra note 101, at 416–17; Hamlyn, supra note 101, at 104; Fortin, supra note 101, at 268–71. Michael Wilks writes that "a Christian Aristotelianism was itself a contradiction in terms." Michael Wilks, The Problem of Sovereignty in the Later Middle Ages 120 (1963). Copleston suggests that Thomas "did not fully realise the latent tension, in regard to certain points, between his Christian faith and his Aristotelianism." Copleston, supra note 101, at 424.

111. Thomas wrote: "[T]he worship prescribed by the [Jewish] Law foreshadowed the mystery of Christ: so that whatever they did was a figure of things pertaining to Christ." Theologica, supra note 101, at pt. I–II, qu. 102, art. 6. As is true of Augustinian scholars, few Thomistic scholars mention Thomas's antisemitic attitude, though it is explicit. See, e.g., Davies, supra note 101, at 257–60, 353–54 (an uncritical account of Thomas's discussion of the Old Law in opposition to the New Law); Gilson, Aquinas, supra note 101, at 264–70 (ignores Thomas's distinction between the Old Law and the New Law). But cf. Frederic Cople Jaher, A Scapegoat in the New Wilderness: The Origins and Rise of Anti-Semitism in America 61 (1994) (on Thomas's antisemitism).

112. Thomas wrote:

> [T]he New Law is compared to the Old as the perfect to the imperfect. Now everything perfect fulfils that which is lacking in the imperfect. And accordingly the New Law fulfils the Old by supplying that which was lacking in the Old Law. . . . [T]he New Law fulfils the Old by justifying men through the power of Christ's Passion.

Theologica, supra note 101, at pt. I–II, qu. 107, art. 2; cf. Theologica (Pegis ed.), supra note 101, at pt. I–II, qu. 107, art. 1 ("the Old Law is like a pedagogue of children . . . whereas the New Law is the law of perfection"). Thus, for Thomas, Christianity is the only and universal way to salvation. See Theologica, supra note 101, at pt. I–II, qu. 108, art. 2 ("we cannot of ourselves obtain grace, but through Christ alone").

113. See Gentiles, supra note 101, at bk. 3, part 1, ch. 27 (condemns Judaism for holding that just men receive their rewards in bodily pleasures).

114. Thomas wrote:

> [The Jews] are by no means to be compelled to the faith, in order that they may believe, because to believe depends on the will: nevertheless they should be compelled by the faithful, if it be possible to do so, so that they do not hinder the faith, by their blasphemies, or by their evil persuasions, or even by their open persecutions. It is for this reason that Christ's faithful often wage war with unbelievers, not indeed for the purpose of forcing them to believe, because even if they were to conquer them, and take them prisoners, they should still leave them free to believe, if they will, but in order to prevent them from hindering the faith of Christ.

Theologica, supra note 101, at pt. II–II, qu. 10, art. 8.

115. Id. at pt. II–II, qu. 14, art. 1.

116 Id. at pt. III, qu. 47, art. 5 (emphasis omitted); accord id. at pt. III, qu. 47, art. 6.

117. On Kingship, supra note 101, at bk. 2, ch. 3, ¶ 111.

118. Cf. id. at bk. 2, ch. 3, ¶ 110 (clearly distinguishes spiritual from earthly things). Thomas explicitly attributed secular power to God, thus placing the secular state within the universal Christian body: "The spiritual and the secular power are both derived from the divine power; and therefore the secular power is under the spiritual only in so far as it has been subjected to it by God." St. Thomas Aquinas, Commentum in IV Libros Sententiarum (1253–55), reprinted in Tierney, Crisis, supra note 1, at 171.

119. See On Kingship, supra note 101, at bk. 2, chs. 1–3, ¶¶ 93–102.

120. Theologica, supra note 101, at pt. I–II, qu. 91, art. 1. Thomas wrote: "Now it is evident, granted that the world is ruled by Divine Providence ... that the whole community of the universe is governed by Divine Reason. Wherefore the very Idea of the government of things in God the Ruler of the universe, has the nature of a law." Id. For discussions of Thomas's concept of law, see Gilson, Aquinas, supra note 101, at 264–70; Lloyd L. Weinreb, Natural Law and Justice 53–63 (1987).

121. Theologica, supra note 101, at pt. I–II, qu. 96, art. 2.

122. Id. at pt. I–II, qu. 91, arts. 4–5; see supra note 112 (on Thomas's distinction between the imperfection of the Old Law (and Testament) and the perfection of the New Law (and Testament)).

123. Id. at pt. I–II, qu. 91, art. 3. Thomas divided the human (or positive) law into two types: the law of nations and the civil law. With regard to the civil law, Thomas wrote: "[T]hose things which are derived from the law of nature by way of particular determination belong to the civil law, according as each state decides on what is best for itself." Id. at pt. I–II, qu. 95, art. 4 (Pegis ed.).

124. Id. at pt. I–II, qu. 95, art. 2.

125. See id. at pt. I–II, qu. 96, art. 4; see also Copleston, supra note 101, at 419. According to Thomas, a law contravenes the common good if it was enacted for the private and selfish ends of the legislator. A law is unjust also if the legislature acted beyond its power. Thomas qualified his recommendation to disobey unjust laws by suggesting that they should be obeyed if disobedience would produce further scandal or disturbance. See Theologica, supra note 101, at pt. I–II, qu. 96, art. 4. Finally, although a law enacted for the common good ordinarily should be obeyed, it should be disobeyed when, in a specific instance, observance would contravene the general welfare. Only individuals in positions of authority, however, should attempt to determine when these rare situations arise, and only those individuals should disobey the law. See id. at pt. I–II, qu. 96, art. 6.

It is worth noting that Thomas's recommendation to disobey unjust laws reflects his Aristotelian bent. That is, whereas Augustine emphasized human depravity because of original sin, Thomas demonstrated a commitment to human reason and its ability to discern the just and unjust. Nonetheless, despite the tension between Thomas's and Augustine's positions, Thomas did cite Augustine's discussion of law. See id. at pt. I–II, qu. 96, art. 4.

126. See Theologica, supra note 101, at pt. I–II, qu. 105, art. 1; Gilson, Aquinas, supra note 101, at 327–32.

127. Theologica (Pegis ed.), supra note 101, at pt. I–II, qu. 105, art. 1.

128. Id.

129. On Kingship, supra note 101, at bk. 2, ch. 3, ¶ 107.

130. See id. at bk. 2, ch. 3, ¶¶ 108–09. Thomas wrote:

> To [the Pope] all the kings of the Christian People are to be subject as to our Lord Jesus Christ Himself. For those to whom pertains the care of intermediate ends should be subject to him to whom pertains the care of the ultimate end, and be directed by his rule.

Id. at bk. 2, ch. 3, ¶ 110; accord id. at bk. 2, ch. 4, ¶ 114; cf. Theologica, supra note 101, at pt. I–II, qu. 72, art. 4 (the Divine Law contains and surpasses the rule of reason).

131. Hence, Copleston writes that to Thomas, the state is the "handmaid of the Church." Copleston, supra note 101, at 416.

I do not mean to suggest that Thomas was the first Christian thinker to begin enhancing the status of the temporal world. Eric Voegelin discusses how Joachim of Flora, in the late twelfth century, introduced a periodization of history that has strongly influenced the modern understanding of politics. See Eric Voegelin, The New Science of Politics 110–19 (1987 ed.).

132. See Chazan, supra note 1, at 167–238.

133. Nicholls, supra note 14, at 234. Thomas Aquinas approved of this position:

> [I]t is true, as the law declares, that Jews, in consequence of their sins, are or were destined to perpetual slavery, so that sovereigns of states may treat their goods as their own property, with the sole proviso that they do not deprive them of all that is necessary to sustain life.

From Thomas Aquinas to the Duchess of Brabant, reprinted in Chazan, supra note 1, at 199, 200.

134. See Letter from Pope Honorius III to the Archbishop of Toledo (Mar. 20, 1219), reprinted in Chazan, supra note 1, at 179; Nicholls, supra note 14, at 234.

135. See Chazan, supra note 1, at 169–70, 185–95.

136. Edict of King Henry III (Jan. 31, 1253), reprinted in Chazan, supra note 1, at 188–89.

137. Edict of King Edward I (Nov. 5, 1290), reprinted in Chazan, supra note 1, at 317, 318–19.

138. See Wilks, supra note 110, at vii–ix, 151; cf. Hinsley, supra note 35, at 60–64 (emphasizes the segmentation of Christendom into many communities or kingdoms). The dream of universal government may have ended, but this development did not prevent the Church or the emerging secular states from pursuing the City of God on earth. The Spanish Inquisition, starting in the late fifteenth century, was but one effort to purify Christendom. See Marcus, supra note 1, at 51–55, 173–78; Nicholls, supra note 14, at 261–67.

139. See, e.g., Bull "Unam sanctam" of Pope Boniface VIII on the Plenitude of the Papal Power (Nov. 18, 1302), reprinted in Ehler, supra note 1, at 89 (asserting the hierocratic power of the papacy in the context of a dispute between King Philip IV of France and Pope Boniface VIII).

140. See Ehler, supra note 1, at 93–95; Wilks, supra note 110, at 240–41.

141. Decree "Licet iuris" of the Diet of Frankfort on the Election of Emperors (Aug. 8, 1338), reprinted in Ehler, supra note 1, at 94. Louis's successor, Charles of Bohemia, negotiated a compromise with the papacy that lasted throughout the Middle Ages: the Pope would confer the imperial crown so long as the emperor promised never to go to Italy except for his coronation. See Ehler, supra note 1, at 94.

142. Johnson, supra note 68, at 208.

143. Synan, supra note 1, at 73–74.

144. See Marcus, supra note 1, at 43–47. For other examples of state protection of Jews, see Johnson, supra note 68, at 243 (during the Reformation in Germany, the Catholic emperor and princes found Jews to be useful allies against Protestants); id. at 250–51 (kings protected Jews in Poland during late sixteenth century). In 1361, King John of France stated:

> Jews have no country or place of their own in all Christendom where they can live and move and have their being, except by the purely voluntary permission and goodwill of the lord or lords under whom they wish to settle to dwell under them as their subjects, and who are willing to receive and accept them to this end.

Parkes, Judaism, supra note 14, at 125.

145. Letter from King John of England to Mayor and Barons of London (July 29, 1203), reprinted in Chazan, supra note 1, at 122, 123.

146. See Johnson, supra note 68, at 199, 243; Langmuir, supra note 14, at 304; Muldoon, supra note 1, at 32; Ruether, supra note 14, at 224.

147. See Chazan, supra note 1, at 319–22; Marcus, supra note 1, at 51; see also id. at 24 (Jews expelled from France in 1182); Wistrich, supra note 14, at 101 (England banished Jews for 400 years).

148. See Synan, supra note 1, at 129–30; cf. Bauman, supra note 14, at 50–51 (arguing that Jews served as a buffer between society and political leaders throughout premodern European history);

Stephen Holmes, Jean Bodin: The Paradox of Sovereignty and the Privatization of Religion, 30 Nomos 5, 6 (1988) (at times, such as in sixteenth-century France, "rights were created and maintained by the modern state to promote the goals of the modern state").

149. Michael Wilks argues that the basic principles undergirding the separation of church and state were established by the middle of the fourteenth century, though they were not completely formulated until developed by Locke in the seventeenth century. See Wilks, supra note 110, at 527. See generally Ullmann, History, supra note 1, at 159–65 (offering reasons why Christendom accepted some aspects of Aristotelianism).

150. See Hinsley, supra note 35, at 70–72.

NOTES TO CHAPTER 4

1. Max Lerner writes:

> What gave the city-states of Italy their Renaissance grandeur was not some mysterious flowering of the humanist spirit at the time. It was the fact that with the opening of the East by the crusades, the breakup of the manorial economy and the growth of trade and handicraft manufacture, the cities of Italy found themselves strategically placed with respect to the world trade routes.... The expansion of the economic power of these cities went on apace into the end of the fifteenth century.

Max Lerner, Introduction, in Niccolo Machiavelli, The Prince and the Discourses xxxiii (Modern Library ed. 1950); see J.M. Roberts, The Penguin History of the World 477 (1987) (emphasizing the rise of commercial wealth from the 1100s on). But cf. The Columbia History of the World 487–88 (John A. Garraty & Peter Gay eds., 1972) (arguing that the commercial status of Renaissance Italy was complex and that many historians overestimate the degree of economic prosperity) [hereinafter Columbia].

2. See Quentin Skinner, 1 The Foundations of Modern Political Thought: The Renaissance 11–22 (1978) [hereinafter Skinner I]. Skinner writes:

> The theory of popular sovereignty developed by Marsiglio and Bartolus was destined to play a major role in shaping the most radical version of early modern constitutionalism. Already they are prepared to argue that sovereignty lies with the people, that they only delegate and never alienate it, and thus that no legitimate ruler can ever enjoy a higher status than that of an official appointed by, and capable of being dismissed by, his own subjects. It was only necessary for the same arguments to be applied in the case of a regnum [kingdom] as well as a civitas [city-state] for a recognisably modern theory of popular sovereignty in a secular state to be fully articulated.

Id. at 65.

3. See id. at 87–88, 92–93, 231.

4. See Heiko A. Oberman, The Roots of Anti-Semitism: In the Age of Renaissance and Reformation (James I. Porter trans., 1984); see also Jonathan I. Israel, European Jewry in the Age of Mercantilism 1550–1750 at 13–15 (2d ed. 1989); Skinner I, supra note 2, at 92 (on the ways other than antisemitism that the humanists expressed their Christian views).

5. Oberman, supra note 4, at 97–98; see id. at 50, 80. The published report continues by turning to a related matter:

> [While all the Jews in the town of Braunschweig] were in jail, the obstinate, blind dogs confessed that in the past few years they had purchased seven Christian children, one from his own peasant mother for twenty-four groschen, another for three guilder, and a third for ten. These children they pierced with needles and knives, tortured, and finally killed them. Then they prepared the blood with pomegranates and served it for dinner.

Id. at 98–99.

6. Id. at 74. This statement is usually (mis)understood as showing Erasmus's toleration for Jews (see id. at 109), but Erasmus was "the towering exponent of Christian humanist anti-Semitism." Israel, supra note 4, at 14.

7. See Israel, supra note 4, at 6–13.

8. Machiavelli's major works include the following: Niccolo Machiavelli, Discourses on the First Ten Books of Titus Livius, reprinted in The Prince and the Discourses 99 (Christian E. Detmold trans., Modern Library ed. 1950) [hereinafter Machiavelli, Discourses]; Niccolo Machiavelli, The Prince, reprinted in The Prince and the Discourses 2 (Luigi Ricci trans., Modern Library ed. 1950) [hereinafter Machiavelli, Prince]. For discussions of Machiavelli's thought, see J.G.A. Pocock, The Machiavellian Moment (1975); Skinner I, supra note 2; Leo Strauss, Niccolo Machiavelli, in History of Political Philosophy 296 (Leo Strauss & Joseph Cropsey ed., 3d ed. 1987).

9. There is strong disagreement about the significance of scholastic thought to the development of Renaissance political theory. See Skinner I, supra note 2, at 49. For my purposes, I do not need to take a stance on how directly the line of descent runs from the scholastics to the Renaissance thinkers. I do maintain, however, that Thomas's (re)introduction of political science had lasting influence, even on writers who rejected his other arguments and themes. Hence, I argue that Machiavelli quite clearly rejected a Thomistic commitment to Christianity, yet he still wrote within a genre (political science) that had developed partly because of Thomas.

10. See Lerner, supra note 1, at xxv–xxviii.

11. See Machiavelli, Discourses, supra note 8, at bk. I, ch. 26; bk. III, ch. 41; Skinner I, supra note 2, at 183. Skinner argues that Machiavelli's separation of Christian values from politics (and the pursuit of the common good) differentiated him from his contemporaries, though Skinner also notes that Guicciardini agreed that Christianity corrupts a people. See Skinner I, supra note 2, at 167–68, 182–85. In The Prince, Machiavelli emphasized that a political leader's most important goal must be the preservation of the state or political community, and that overarching goal justifies the use of any means necessary. Machiavelli, Prince, supra note 8, at ch. 18.

12. See Machiavelli, Discourses, supra note 8, at bk. II, ch. 2; cf. id. at bk. III, ch. 1 (the orders of St. Francis and St. Dominic revived the sentiment of Christianity whereby the people do not criticize even wicked rulers, instead obeying them and leaving their punishment to God).

13. See id. at bk. I, ch. 2. Fortune stands for the random changes of the world that are, for the most part, beyond human control. See Machiavelli, Prince, supra note 8, at ch. 7, 25. In a sense, even though Machiavelli elevated the status of the state, he also destabilized the state. Within more Christian-oriented theories, the state was typically degraded but it nonetheless remained within God's plan. To Machiavelli, the fate of the state was removed from God's plan; the state rose and fell with the whims of sheer fortune. See Pocock, supra note 8, at 400.

14. See Skinner I, supra note 2, at 250–51. Nonetheless, as the sixteenth century wore on and political turmoil (due to religious hostilities) mounted, Machiavelli's views were increasingly accepted. See id. at 251–54.

15. Lerner, supra note 1, at xxxviii.

16. Machiavelli, Discourses, supra note 8, at bk. I, ch. 12.

17. See Machiavelli, Discourses, supra note 8, at bk. II, ch. 2. Machiavelli wrote:

> [I]f the Christian religion had from the beginning been maintained according to the principles of its founder, the Christian states and republics would have been much more united and happy than what they are. Nor can there be a greater proof of its decadence than to witness the fact that the nearer people are to the Church of Rome, which is the head of our religion, the less religious are they. And whoever examines the principles upon which that religion is founded, and sees how widely different from those principles its present practice and application are, will judge that her ruin or chastisement is near at hand.

Id. at bk. I, ch. 12. Despite Machiavelli's criticism of the Catholic Church, he seemed to admire its "temporal power." Machiavelli, Prince, supra note 8, at ch. 11.

18. Id.

19. See, e.g., Lerner, supra note 1, at xxxi.

20. Machiavelli, Discourses, supra note 8, at bk. I, ch. 12.

21. See id. at bk. I, ch. 3; Machiavelli, Prince, supra note 8, at ch. 18. Thus, according to Machiavelli, a prince is better to be feared than loved. See Machiavelli, Prince, supra note 8, at ch. 17.

22. I am not suggesting that the world would be all peaches and cream without Christianity, though it certainly would be different. Exactly what the world would presently be without Christianity is, of course, a matter of hopeless conjecture.

23. See Machiavelli, Discourses, supra note 8, at bk. I, ch. 2.

24. Id. (democracy fails when each individual consults "his own passions"). For a discussion of the common good, see id. at bk. III, ch. 47. Machiavelli was not the only political theorist of his time to understand virtù (virtue) in this manner, though he differed somewhat from his contemporaries in his understanding of how one can attain virtù. See Skinner I, supra note 2, at 117–38; 175–85.

25. See Machiavelli, Discourses, supra note 8, at bk. I, ch. 2, 9, 20, 59.

26. Strauss, supra note 8, at 301; see Machiavelli, Prince, supra note 8, at ch. 15–19.

27. Machiavelli, Prince, supra note 8, at ch. 18.

28. Martin Luther, The Ninety-Five Theses (1517), in Martin Luther's Basic Theological Writings 21, 25 (Timothy F. Lull ed., 1989).

29. Luther wrote: "It does not help the soul if the body is adorned with the sacred robes of priests or dwells in sacred places or is occupied with sacred duties or prays, fasts, abstains from certain kinds of food, or does any work that can be done by the body and in the body." Martin Luther, The Freedom of a Christian (1520), in 31 Luther's Works 327, 345 (Harold J. Grimm ed., 1957) [hereinafter Luther, Freedom]. In his essay, Temporal Authority, he added: "Among Christians there is no superior but Christ himself, and him alone. What kind of authority can there be where all are equal and have the same right, power, possession, and honor, and where no one desires to be the other's superior, but each the other's subordinate?" Martin Luther, Temporal Authority: To What Extent it Should be Obeyed (1523), in 45 Luther's Works 75, 117 (Walther I. Brandt ed., 1956) [hereinafter Luther, Temporal].

30. Luther wrote: "I have truly despised your [the pope's] see, the Roman Curia, which, however, neither you nor anyone else can deny is more corrupt than any Babylon or Sodom ever was, and which, as far as I can see, is characterized by a completely depraved, hopeless, and notorious godlessness." Luther, Freedom, supra note 29, at 336.

31. See, e.g., Martin Luther, Commentary on Psalm 101 (1535), in 13 Luther's Works 143, 198–99 (Jaroslav Pelikan ed., 1956).

32. See generally Robert C. Monk & Joseph D. Stamey, Exploring Christianity: An Introduction 122 (2d ed. 1990); Richard Tarnas, The Passion of the Western Mind 233–34 (1991).

33. Luther wrote:

> If the influence of custom is added and confirms this perverseness of nature [that works can bring salvation], as wicked teachers have caused it to do, it becomes an incurable evil and leads astray and destroys countless men beyond all hope of restoration. Therefore, although it is good to preach and write about penitence, confession, and satisfaction, our teaching is unquestionably deceitful and diabolical if we stop with that and and do not go on to teach about faith.

Luther, Freedom, supra note 29, at 363; see Monk & Stamey, supra note 32, at 69. The seven Catholic sacraments are as follows: baptism, confirmation, the Eucharist (or the Lord's Supper or communion), penance, holy orders, marriage, and anointing of the sick. Luther accepted the Eucharist but only with qualifications. In Catholicism, the meaningfulness of the ingestion of the bread and wine (during the Eucharist) is determined by the doctrine of transubstantiation: the words of the priest miraculously transform the bread and wine into the body and blood of Christ, thus renewing Christ's sacrifice for humanity. Luther accepted the Eucharist, but he only partially accepted the doctrine of transubstantiation. To Luther, bread and wine are not actually converted into the body and blood of Jesus; nonetheless, Jesus' body and blood are somehow present in the sacrament. Luther's position is sometimes known as "consubstantiation" because the body and blood of Jesus coexist with the bread and wine. See Monk & Stamey, supra note 32, at 58, 72.

34. See Martin Luther, Why the Books of the Pope and His Disciples Were Burned (1520), in 31 Luther's Works 379 (Harold J. Grimm ed., 1957).

35. In 1529, Charles V, emperor of the Holy Roman Empire, demanded that previous concessions to Lutheran Reformers be withdrawn. The Lutherans replied with a formal protest, which led to the designation "Protestant." See Quentin Skinner, 2 The Foundations of Modern Political Thought: The Age of Reformation (1978) [hereinafter Skinner II]. It is worth noting that Luther, during his lifetime, denied that there was a "Lutheran Church." See Sydney E. Ahlstrom, A Religious History of the American People 76 (1972).

36. Luther, Freedom, supra note 29, at 346–47, 351; see Martin Luther, Heidelberg Disputation (1518), in Martin Luther's Basic Theological Writings 30, 30–31 (Timothy F. Lull ed., 1989) (free will

to do good works cannot gain grace, and thinking so is a sin) [hereinafter Luther, Heidelberg]; Martin Luther, Disputation Against Scholastic Theology (1517), in Martin Luther's Basic Theological Writings 13, 14 (Timothy F. Lull ed., 1989) (human will is "innately and inevitably evil and corrupt") [hereinafter Luther, Disputation]; Tarnas, supra note 32, at 235.

37. Luther, Freedom, supra note 29, at 347; see Martin Luther, The Bondage of the Will (1525), in Martin Luther's Basic Theological Writings 173, 178–82 (Timothy F. Lull ed., 1989); Luther, Disputation, supra note 36; see also Joshua Mitchell, Not By Reason Alone 20–24 (1993) (on Luther's attacks on Aristotle and Thomas); Skinner II, supra note 35, at 8; Duncan B. Forrester, Martin Luther and John Calvin, in History of Political Philosophy 318, 321 (Leo Strauss & Joseph Cropsey eds., 3d ed. 1987) (Luther's attacks on reason in religion). Luther declared:

> Since human nature and natural reason, as it is called, are by nature superstitious and ready to imagine, when laws and works are prescribed, that righteousness must be obtained through laws and works; and further, since they are trained and confirmed in this opinion by the practice of all earthly lawgivers, it is impossible that they should of themselves escape from the slavery of works and come to a knowledge of the freedom of faith.

Luther, Freedom, supra note 29, at 376.

38. Luther, Freedom, supra note 29, at 346–48, 353, 355, 373; see Martin Luther, Lectures on Titus (1527), in 29 Luther's Works 4, 7 (Jaroslav Pelikan & Walter A. Hansen eds., 1968) ("nothing justifies except believing in Christ"). To Luther, faith was an "inner awareness of, need for, and dependence on God." Monk & Stamey, supra note 32, at 68. Faith cannot be a cognitive or intellectual experience, but rather is an "an innate orientation of the self as a spiritual being to its creator." Id. at 142. In the Thomistic lexicon, on the other hand, faith was "the intellectual acceptance of a belief not conclusively demonstrated by rational means." Id.

39. Luther, Freedom, supra note 29, at 345, 354, 356; see Monk & Stamey, supra note 32, at 70; Tarnas, supra note 32, at 239.

40. Luther, Freedom, supra note 29, at 356; see Monk & Stamey, supra note 32, at 68 (not a radical individualism).

41. See Forrester, supra note 37, at 328.

42. Luther, Freedom, supra note 29, at 353.

43. Luther, Disputation, supra note 36, at 16.

44. Luther, Temporal, supra note 29, at 101.

45. Luther, Freedom, supra note 29, at 358–59. In a sense, Luther not only was conservative, he was downright reactionary. As discussed, Luther sought to return to a Pauline and Augustinian Christianity. To Luther, the pagan philosophy of Aristotle, so important to Thomas, had corrupted medieval Christianity.

46. See Luther, Heidelberg, supra note 36, at 39–40. Luther wrote:

> It is known well enough that the Jews have at all times been Christ's greatest enemies, their claim to be God's most loyal friends notwithstanding. It is undeniable that this verse [of Psalm 68] chronicles their fate: their head is shattered; they no longer have a kingdom, a government, and priesthood. Soon after Christ's ascent they lost that head and never regained it, which is the result of but one crime, namely, their hostility to Christ and their refusal to let Him be God.

Martin Luther, Commentary on Psalm 68 (1521), in 13 Luther's Works 1, 23 (Jaroslav Pelikan ed., 1956).

47. Luther, Freedom, supra note 29, at 353, 373. In addition, to Luther, salvation through the Jewish law was utterly impossible, and this impossibility prepared people to believe in Jesus as Christ. See id. at 348–49.

48. Luther, Heidelberg, supra note 36, at 34.

49. See Oberman, supra note 4, at 43, 50, 105.

50. See Martin Luther, That Jesus Christ Was Born a Jew, reprinted in The Jew in the Medieval World: A Source Book, 315–1791 at 166 (Jacob R. Marcus ed., 1938); Oberman, supra note 4, at 22.

51. See, e.g., Martin Luther, Commentary on Psalm 110 (1535), in 13 Luther's Works 225 (Jaroslav Pelikan ed., 1956). In this Commentary, Luther argued that Jewish history had prepared for the coming of Jesus, that the Jews nonetheless refused to believe Jesus because he lacked the trappings of

this-worldly power, and that the Jews then committed deicide and therefore deserve to suffer. See id. at 265, 273, 284.

52. See Richard L. Rubenstein, Luther and the Roots of the Holocaust, in Persistent Prejudice: Perspectives on Anti-Semitism 11, 31–34 (Hebert Hirsch & Jack D. Spiro eds., 1988).

53. Hayim Hillel Ben-Sasson, The Reformation in Contemporary Jewish Eyes, 4 Proceedings of the Israel Academy of Sciences & Humanities 239, 289 (1969–1970) (this report was written in 1547).

54. Martin Luther, Concerning the Jews and Their Lies (1543), in The Jew in the Medieval World: A Source Book, 315–1791 at 167, 167 (Jacob R. Marcus ed., 1938).

55. Id. at 167–68. Any Jews who refused to work should be stripped of their money and banished from the country. See id. at 168–69. Richard L. Rubenstein understandably links Luther's dehumanization of Jews and his advocacy of violence to the Holocaust. Rubenstein, supra note 52.

56. As early as 1524, Luther managed to have an Anabaptist opponent, Carlstadt, expelled from Saxony. See Skinner II, supra note 35, at 74–81.

57. See Harro Höpfl, Luther and Calvin on Secular Authority vii–xvi (1991); Williston Walker, A History of the Christian Church 309–10 (3d ed. 1970).

58. Luther, Temporal, supra note 29, at 88, 91; see id. at 128–29 (secular laws should be based on reason); Luther, Psalm 101, supra note 31, at 196–99; Martin Luther, Commentary on Psalm 82 (1530), in 13 Luther's Works 41, 42–43 (Jaroslav Pelikan ed., 1956). Luther explained that even though reason is unrelated to salvation, a secular government should use reason because that government has nothing to do with attaining salvation. See Luther, Psalm 101, supra note 31, at 198. Reason alone, though, is insufficient for maintaining civil order; sometimes coercion must be used. Quentin Skinner notes that to Luther, "[a]ll coercive powers are . . . treated as temporal by definition." Skinner II, supra note 35, at 14.

A true Christian has no need of secular constraints, but without the secular authorities, "men would devour one another, seeing that the whole world is evil and that among thousands there is scarcely a single true Christian." Luther, Temporal, supra note 29, at 91.

59. See Harold J. Berman, Law and Revolution: The Formation of the Western Legal Tradition 30 (1983).

60. Luther, Temporal, supra note 29, at 92.

61. Mark 12:17. Luther cited several New Testament passages echoing this sentiment. See, e.g., Luther, Temporal, supra note 29, at 77, 85–86, 111.

62. Rom. 13:1–2; see Luther, Temporal, supra note 29, at 77. According to Quentin Skinner, "Luther's influence helped to make this the most cited of all texts on the foundations of political life throughout the age of the Reformation." Skinner II, supra note 35, at 15.

63. Luther, Temporal, supra note 29, at 87 (emphasis added).

64. See Höpfl, supra note 57, at viii; Skinner II, supra note 35, at 77.

65. Luther, Temporal, supra note 29, at 105–08, 114–15.

66. Id. at 94, 102, 110–13. Luther added: "Outrage is not to be resisted but endured." Id. Luther also wrote: "Although tyrants do violence or injustice in making their demands, yet it will do no harm as long as they demand nothing contrary to God." Luther, Freedom, supra note 29, at 370.

67. See Höpfl, supra note 57, at xiii–xv; Skinner II, supra note 35, at 74.

68. Mark 12:17.

69. See Skinner II, supra note 35, at 14–15; Forrester, supra note 37, at 325.

70. See Luther, Temporal, supra note 29, at 83.

71. See Luther, Psalm 101, supra note 31, at 195.

72. Luther, supra note 54, at 168.

73. See Berman, supra note 59, at 30, 197; Mitchell, supra note 37, at 38 (to Luther, the political realm was not disenchanted).

74. Luther, Freedom, supra note 29, at 356; see Monk & Stamey, supra note 32, at 68 (not a radical individualism).

75. See Höpfl, supra note 57, at xiii–xv; Skinner II, supra note 35, at 73. Machiavelli had already discussed citizens and magistrates. See, e.g., Machiavelli, Discourses, supra note 8, at bk. III, ch. 34, 47.

76. The opponent was named Carlstadt. See Skinner II, supra note 35, at 74–81; Walker, supra note 57, at 326–32.

77. See Ahlstrom, supra note 35, at 72–81; Monk & Stamey, supra note 32, at 58, 72; Walker, supra note 57, at 324–25. Luther's position is sometimes known as "consubstantiation" because the body and blood of Jesus coexist with the bread and wine.

78. See Jean Calvin, Institutes of the Christian Religion (Ford Lewis Battles trans., John T. McNeill ed., 1960) (first published 1536) [hereinafter Calvin, Institutes]; Walker, supra note 57, at 348–49. Williston Walker notes: "The Institutes ... were, as published in 1536, far from the extensive treatise into which they were to grow in Calvin's final edition of 1559; but they were already the most orderly and systematic popular presentation of doctrine and of the Christian life that the Reformation produced." Walker, supra note 57, at 350. Two excellent works on Calvin's political thought and the political implications of his theology are the following: Ralph C. Hancock, Calvin and the Foundations of Modern Politics (1989); Skinner II, supra note 35.

79. See Walker, supra note 57, at 352. Like Luther, Calvin accepted only two sacraments: baptism and the Lord's Supper. See id.

80. Calvin, Institutes, supra note 78, at bk. 1, ch. VI, § 2. Walker suggests that "Calvin's mind was formulative rather than creative." Walker, supra note 57, at 350. Calvin's main ideas were drawn from Luther and Butzer. See id.

81. Calvin wrote:

> What then? You will ask: will no difference remain between the Old and New Testaments? What is to become of the many passages of Scripture wherein they are contrasted as utterly different? I freely admit the differences in Scripture, to which attention is called, but in such a way as not to detract from its established unity.

Calvin, Institutes, supra note 78, at bk. 2, ch. XI, § 1; see Skinner II, supra note 35, at 236 (on reaffirmation of the Old Testament).

82. See Skinner II, supra note 35, at 236; Walker, supra note 57, at 352–53.

83. Calvin, Institutes, supra note 78, at bk. 2, ch. V, § 19.

84. Calvin, Institutes, supra note 78, at bk. 3, ch. II, § 7; bk. 3, ch. XI, § 19; bk. 3, ch. XIII, § 5; bk. 3, ch. XVII, § 1; bk. 3, ch. XVIII, § 9; bk. 4, ch. X, § 3; see Hancock, supra note 78, at 128–29, 132.

85. Calvin, Institutes, supra note 78, at bk. 4, ch. X, § 4; bk. 4, ch. XX, § 5; see id. at bk. 3, ch. XIX, § 16 ("A good conscience ... is nothing but inward integrity of heart"). See generally Michael J. Sandel, Freedom of Conscience or Freedom of Choice?, in Articles of Faith, Articles of Peace 74, 88 (James Davison Hunter & Os Guinness eds., 1990) ("conscience dictates, choice decides").

86. Calvin, Institutes, supra note 78, at bk. 3, ch. XXI, §§ 1, 5, 7. Calvin added: "We assert that, with respect to the elect, this plan was founded upon his freely given mercy, without regard to human worth; but by his just and irreprehensible judgment he has barred the door of life to those whom he has given over to damnation." Id. at bk. 3, ch. XXI, § 7; see David C. Williams & Susan H. Williams, Volitionalism and Religious Liberty, 76 Cornell L. Rev. 769, 867–68 (1991).

87. Calvin, Institutes, supra note 78, at bk. 3, ch. X, § 6.

88. See Hancock, supra note 78, at 98–99, 108–09, 133.

89. Pocock, supra note 8, at 370.

90. Calvin, Institutes, supra note 78, at bk. 3, ch. XI, § 20; bk. 3, ch. XVII, § 6; see Hancock, supra note 78, at 134.

91. Max Weber, The Protestant Ethic and the Spirit of Capitalism (Talcott Parsons trans., 1958); see Michael Walzer, The Revolution of the Saints 304–07 (1965).

92. See, e.g., William Nicholls, Christian Antisemitism: A History of Hate 273–74 (1993); Oberman, supra note 4, at 139–41; Robert S. Wistrich, Antisemitism: The Longest Hatred 38 (1991).

93. See Paul Johnson, A History of the Jews 242–43 (1987); 5 Encyclopaedia Judaica 66–67 (1971).

94. See, e.g., Nicholls, supra note 92, at 273–74, 261, 465 n.1; Oberman, supra note 4, at 139–43.

95. See 5 Encyclopaedia Judaica 67 (1971); cf. Eugene J. Fisher, Anti-Semitism and Christianity: Theories and Revisions of Theories, in Persistent Prejudice: Perspectives on Anti-Semitism 11, 23 (Hebert Hirsch & Jack D. Spiro eds., 1988) (almost all major reformers, including Luther and Calvin, were united as anti-Jewish). Calvin even accused some of his opponents of Judaizing. See 5 Encyclopaedia Judaica 66 (1971).

96. Jean Calvin, 1 Commentary on a Harmony of the Evangelists, Matthew, Mark, and Luke 361 (William Pringle trans., 1956) [hereinafter Calvin, Harmony].

97. Jean Calvin, 3 Commentaries on the Twelve Minor Prophets 338, 345 (John Owen trans., 1950); accord Jean Calvin, 4 Commentaries on the Twelve Minor Prophets 202 (John Owen trans., 1950) (Jewish practices are "all hypocrisy and deception").

98 Jean Calvin, Commentaries on the Epistles of Paul the Apostle to the Philippians, Colossians, and Thessalonians 260 (John Pringle trans., 1957) [hereinafter Calvin, Epistles of Paul].

99. Id. at 259.

100. Jean Calvin, 5 Commentaries on the Twelve Minor Prophets 587 (John Owen trans., 1950); see Jean Calvin, 4 Commentaries on the Twelve Minor Prophets 202 (John Owen trans., 1950) (Jews are guilty of "false worship").

101. Jean Calvin, 5 Commentaries on the Twelve Minor Prophets 587 (John Owen trans., 1950); see Jean Calvin, 3 Commentaries on the Twelve Minor Prophets 356–59 (John Owen trans., 1950).

102. Calvin, Institutes, supra note 78, at bk. 4, ch. XIV, § 25; see id. at bk. 2, ch. X, § 23. Calvin wrote that Jews worship "an idol instead of the true God. . . . Whosoever, then, seeks really to know the only true God, must regard him as the Father of Christ." Jean Calvin, Commentaries on the Catholic Epistles 28 (John Owen trans., 1959).

103. See Calvin, Institutes, supra note 78, at bk. 2, ch. X, § 23; Jean Calvin, 3 Commentaries on the Twelve Minor Prophets 338, 345, 356–59 (John Owen trans., 1950); cf. Jean Calvin, 4 Commentaries on the Twelve Minor Prophets 202 (John Owen trans., 1950); Jean Calvin, 5 Commentaries on the Twelve Minor Prophets 587 (John Owen trans., 1950) (these commentaries on Jewish prophets repeat standard antisemitic accusations against Jews). In another essay, Calvin declared that the Jewish prophets gave testimony to the coming salvation in Jesus Christ, but Jews "wander wretchedly" because they misread Scripture. Calvin, Harmony, supra note 96, at 69–70.

104. Calvin, Epistles of Paul, supra note 98, at 261.

105. See Israel, supra note 4, at 13; Johnson, supra note 93, at 243. In fact, Calvin himself had little actual contact with Jews because, during the first twenty-five years of his life, he lived in parts of France from which Jews had long since been expelled. Then, for his last twenty-five years, he lived mostly in Geneva, from which Jews had been expelled in 1491. 5 Encyclopaedia Judaica 66 (1971).

106. Calvin, Institutes, supra note 78, at bk. 4, ch. X, § 5; accord id. at bk. 4, ch. X, § 3.

107. Calvin, Harmony, supra note 96, at 91.

108. Cf. Calvin, Institutes, supra note 78, at bk. 3, ch. XIX (on Christian liberty).

109. See id. at bk. 4, ch. XX, §§ 1–32.

110. Id. at bk. 4, ch. XX, § 1.

111. Id. at bk. 4, ch. XX, § 2.

112. Id. at bk. 4, ch. XX, §§ 2, 3, 9. In one of his Commentaries, Calvin wrote:

> It would, indeed, be better for us to be wild beasts, and to wander in forests, than to live without government and laws; for we know how furious human passions are. Unless, therefore, there be some restraint, the condition of wild beasts would be better and more desirable than ours.

John Calvin, Commentary on Jeremiah 30:9, in A Calvin Reader 66, 66 (William F. Keesecker ed., 1985)

113. Calvin, Institutes, supra note 78, at bk. 4, ch. XX, §§ 22–23. Calvin wrote: "[T]hey who rule unjustly and incompetently have been raised up by him to punish the wickedness of the people; that all equally have been endowed with that holy majesty with which he has invested lawful power." Id. at bk. 4, ch. XX, § 25.

114. Id. at bk. 4, ch. XX, § 22; see Höpfl, supra note 57, at xliii. .

115. Calvin, Institutes, supra note 78, at bk. 4, ch. XX, § 32.

116. Id. at bk 4, ch. XX, § 31; see id. at bk 4, ch XX, §§22–31 (using terms: rulers, subjects, magistrates, and citizens); see also Skinner II, supra note 35, at 231–34 (discussing conflicting scholarly interpretations of Calvin); Walzer supra note 91, at 60 (arguing that the ephors should not be understood as true representatives of the people because ordained by God and not the people); Höpfl, supra note 57, at xiv (suggesting that Calvin, unlike Luther, qualified the notion of subjects and ruler with civic humanist ideas of citizenship).

117. Calvin, Institutes, supra note 78, at bk. 4, ch. XX, §§ 3, 9.

118. See id. at bk. 4, ch. X, § 5; bk. 4, ch. XI, § 16; cf. Forrester, supra note 37, at 328–29.

119. Calvin, Institutes, supra note 78, at bk. 4, ch. XX, § 3. Calvin wrote:

> [C]ivil government has as its appointed end, so long as we live among men, to cherish and protect the outward worship of God, to defend sound doctrine of piety and the

position of the church, to adjust our life to the society of men, to form our social behavior to civil righteousness, to reconcile us with one another, and to promote general peace and tranquillity.

Id. at bk. 4, ch. XX, § 2.

120. See Forrester, supra note 37, at 328.

121. See Hancock, supra note 78, at 98–99, 108–09, 133. As Ralph Hancock notes, "Calvin is very much concerned to ground human institutions by establishing the political order as part of the divine order." Id. at 34. Hancock emphasizes that Calvin rejected the effectiveness of classical reason in the natural world. Classical (or natural) reason was significant to Catholicism because of Aristotle's influence on Thomas. Moreover, Hancock argues that Calvin's reform theology has much in common with modern rationalism. Unlike classical (or natural) reason, modern rationalism views the world as bereft of purpose and substance. See, e.g., id. at 20.

122. Calvin, Institutes, supra note 78, at bk. 4, ch. XX, § § 6, 10.

123. See Hancock, supra note 78, at 25–35.

124. See Walker, supra note 57, at 355–56; 5 Encyclopaedia Judaica 67 (1971); see also Anson Phelps Stokes, 1 Church and State in the United States 107 (1950).

125. See Skinner II, supra note 35, at 20, 81–89, 189–91.

126. See Religious Peace of Augsburg (Sept. 25, 1555), reprinted in Church and State Through the Centuries: A Collection of Historic Documents With Commentaries 164 (Sidney Z. Ehler & John B. Morrall trans. & eds., 1954) [hereinafter Ehler].

127. I draw most of the information regarding the Huguenots and the French religious wars from Skinner II, supra note 35, at 242–55, 332–39; Walker, supra note 57, at 380–85; Columbia, supra note 1, at 564–66.

128. Catherine was the virtual ruler of France for two decades after the death of Henry II in 1559. See Columbia, supra note 1, at 564.

129. Jean Bodin, Six Bookes of a Commonweale, at bk. I, ch. 8 (Harv. Univ. Press ed. 1962, a facsimile of the English translation of 1606) (originally published in French in 1576). Bodin wrote: "Sovereignty is the most high, absolute, and perpetual power over the citizens and subjects in a Commonweale." Id.; see Skinner II, supra note 35, at 284–88. According to F.H. Hinsley, sovereignty entails "the idea that there is a final and absolute political authority in the community," F.H. Hinsley, Sovereignty 17 (2d ed. 1986), while to Charles Tilly, a theory of sovereignty appears to be "a set of coherent justifications which could be widely used in the consolidation of power." Charles Tilly, Reflections on the History of European State-Making, in The Formation of National States in Western Europe 21 (Charles Tilly ed., 1975). Hinsley argues that the concept of sovereignty was first formulated in ancient Rome and then again in sixteenth-century Europe, probably first by Bodin. See Hinsley, supra, at 70, 126, 140–41. Michael Wilks, on the other hand, argues that a theory of the absolute sovereignty of monarchs existed during the Middle Ages, though it was articulated most often by the papacy. See Michael Wilks, The Problem of Sovereignty in the Later Middle Ages viii (1963).

130. Israel, supra note 4, at 15; see Ben-Sasson, supra note 53, at 291–92.

131. Israel, supra note 4, at 16 (emphasis added).

132. See id. at 16–23; Ben-Sasson, supra note 53, at 307–12.

133. See Skinner II, supra note 35, at 54–64; Columbia, supra note 1, at 535–37.

134. See, e.g., Pragmatic Sanction of Bourges enacted by Charles VII, King of France (July 7, 1438), reprinted in Ehler, supra note 59, at 112; see Skinner II, supra note 35, at 59–60.

135. Skinner II, supra note 35, at 64.

136. See generally Tarnas, supra note 32, at 285–86 (modernity inverts the Christian priority of the spiritual over the material world).

137. See Jon Butler, Awash in a Sea of Faith: Christianizing the American People 10–12 (1990).

NOTES TO CHAPTER 5

1. Books that provide useful information about these events include the following: John Adair, Founding Fathers: The Puritans in England and America (1982); George Burton Adams, Constitutional History of England (1934 ed.) [hereinafter Adams, Constitutional History]; Sydney E. Ahlstrom,

A Religious History of the American People (1972); A.G. Dickens, The English Reformation (1964); Christopher Hill, The Century of Revolution, 1603–1714 (1961) [hereinafter Hill, Revolution]; Christopher Hill, Puritanism and Revolution (1958) [hereinafter Hill, Puritanism]; F.W. Maitland, The Constitutional History of England (1908); Edmund S. Morgan, Inventing the People (1988); T. M. Parker, The English Reformation to 1558 (2d ed. 1966); J.G.A. Pocock, The Machiavellian Moment (1975); Stuart Prall, The Bloodless Revolution: England, 1688 (1972) [hereinafter Prall, Bloodless]; Cecil Roth, A History of the Jews in England (1941); Conrad Russell, The Causes of the English Civil War (1990); Bernard Schwartz, The Roots of Freedom: A Constitutional History of England (1967); Paul Seaward, The Restoration (1991); Quentin Skinner, 2 The Foundations of Modern Political Thought: The Age of Reformation (1978) [hereinafter Skinner II]; Goldwin Smith, A Constitutional and Legal History of England (1955); Williston Walker, A History of the Christian Church (3d ed. 1970); Michael Walzer, The Revolution of the Saints (1965); Select Documents of English Constitutional History (George Burton Adams & H. Morse Stephens eds., 1929) [hereinafter Adams, Documents]; Documents of the Christian Church (Henry Bettenson ed., 2d ed. 1963) [hereinafter Bettenson]; The Constitutional Documents of the Puritan Revolution 1625–1660 (Samuel R. Gardiner ed., 3d ed. 1906) [hereinafter Gardiner]; Documents Illustrative of English Church History (Henry Gee & William John Hardy eds., 1921) [hereinafter Gee]; The Puritan Revolution: A Documentary History (Stuart E. Prall ed., 1968) [hereinafter Prall]; 3 The Creeds of Christendom (Philip Schaff ed., 3d ed. 1877) [hereinafter Schaff]; Puritanism and Liberty (A.S.P. Woodhouse ed., 1938) [hereinafter Woodhouse].

2. For a survey of different approaches, see I Hill, Puritanism, supra note 1, at 3–31.

3. See, e.g., Gardiner, supra note 1; Prall, supra note 1.

4. See, e.g., Russell, supra note 1, at 7. Christopher Hill, meanwhile, calls the English Civil War a revolution, but not a Puritan revolution. Moreover, even without referring to the revolution as Puritan, Hill argues that religion was an important causal factor. See, e.g., Hill, Puritanism, supra note 1, at 23–25, 29–30.

5. Russell, supra note 1, at 213. Christopher Hill also attributes the Civil War to a combination of factors. See Hill, Puritanism, supra note 1; Hill, Revolution, supra note 1, at 111–92.

6. Christopher Hill writes: "The Reformation in England was an act of state." Hill, Puritanism, supra note 1, at 32.

7. See Adair, supra note 1, at 62–63; Parker, supra note 1, at 35–37; Walker, supra note 1, at 358.

8. See Ahlstrom, supra note 1, at 84–86; Parker, supra note 1, at 33–37; Walker, supra note 1, at 358–59.

9. Act of Supremacy of Henry VIII (1534), reprinted in Adams, Documents, supra note 1, at 239, 239; see Adams, Documents, supra note 1, at 226–39 (on several of Henry's actions); Skinner II, supra note 1, at 93–107 (Thomas Cromwell, Henry's chief minister during the 1530s, engineered the propaganda campaign).

10. See Act for the Dissolution of the Lesser Monasteries (1536); reprinted in Adams, Documents, supra note 1, at 243; Act for the Dissolution of the Greater Monasteries (1539); reprinted in Adams, Documents, supra note 1, at 251; see also Ahlstrom, supra note 1, at 85; Hill, Puritanism, supra note 1, at 32–33; Parker, supra note 1, at 77–78.

11. Hill, Puritanism, supra note 1, at 44.

12. See The Six Articles Act (1539), reprinted in Adams, Documents, supra note 1, at 253; Gardiner, supra note 1, at xv–xvi; Hill, Puritanism, supra note 1, at 32–49.

13. See Parker, supra note 1, at 93–95.

14. See First Act of Uniformity of Edward VI (1549), reprinted in Adams, Documents, supra note 1, at 272; Second Act of Uniformity (1552), reprinted in Adams, Documents, supra note 1, at 278; Adair, supra note 1, at 65; Ahlstrom, supra note 1, at 86–87; Gardiner, supra note 1, at xv–xvi; Walker, supra note 1, at 362–64; The Puritans in America: A Narrative Anthology 2–3 (Alan Heimert & Andrew Delbanco eds., 1985).

15. See Ahlstrom, supra note 1, at 87–88; Walker, supra note 1, at 365–66.

16. Cf. Adair, supra note 1, at 89–90 (the Church of England was not called Anglican until the seventeenth century).

17. The Act of Supremacy (1559), reprinted in Adams, Documents, supra note 1, at 296, 299; cf. Maitland, supra note 1, at 364–66, 514–16 (on religious oaths and declarations).

18. See The Act of Uniformity (1559), reprinted in Adams, Documents, supra note 1, at 302; Walker, supra note 1, at 367. .

19. Smith, supra note 1, at 284. Smith adds: "Roman Catholic and Protestant doctrines were merged together in a chameleon communion service that could mean different things to different individuals." Id.

20. The Thirty-nine Articles of Religion of the Church of England (1571), reprinted in Schaff, supra note 1, at 486. The Articles were first adopted in 1562 in Latin and printed and issued in 1563. The Latin Articles were revised and translated into English in 1571. The Articles are sometimes referred to as the Articles of 1562. See Schaff, supra note 1, at 486.

21. Dickens, supra note 1, at 251; see W.R. Matthews, The Thirty-nine Articles 8 (1961). The General Convention of the Protestant Episcopal Church in the United States adopted the Articles in 1801. See Schaff, supra note 1, at 486.

22. The Thirty-nine Articles of Religion of the Church of England, at arts. VI, IX, XI, XIII, XVII, XIX, XVIII (1571), reprinted in Schaff, supra note 1, at 489, 493–95, 497–99. To facilitate comprehension, I quote from the 1801 American revision instead of the 1571 English edition.

23. Id. at art. VII, reprinted in Schaff, supra note 1, at 491–92.

24. The Subscription (Thirty-nine Articles) Act (1571); reprinted in Gee, supra note 1, at 477; see Ahlstrom, supra note 1, at 88–90; Smith, supra note 1, at 284–85; Walker, supra note 1, at 367–68.

25. Ahlstrom, supra note 1, at 93; see Ahlstrom, supra note 1, at 88–90; Gardiner, supra note 1, at xvi; Walker, supra note 1, at 402-03. The Puritans themselves divided during Elizabeth's reign into those who were willing to wait for governmental reforms of the Anglican Church and the more radical Separatists, who found the Roman practices of the Church unpalatable. See Walker, supra note 1, at 404–05.

26. See Skinner II, supra note 1, at 210–38; Walker, supra note 1, at 406–07; cf. Duncan B. Forrester, Richard Hooker, in History of Political Philosophy 356, 357–58 (Leo Strauss & Joseph Cropsey eds., 3d ed. 1987) (Hooker wrote against this radical right of resistance); see also Richard Hooker, The Laws of Ecclesiastical Polity, in Hooker's Works (John Keble ed., 7th ed. 1888).

27. See Gardiner, supra note 1, at xv–xvi.

28. Walker, supra note 1, at 410. The Book of Sports was reissued in 1633 under Charles I. The King's Majesty's Declaration to His Subjects Concerning Lawful Sports to be Used (1633), reprinted in Gee, supra note 1, at 528.

29. Walker, supra note 1, at 407; see Ahlstrom, supra note 1, at 93; Martin E. Marty, Protestantism in the United States: Righteous Empire 10–11 (2d ed. 1986) (on Presbyterianism); Prall, supra note 1, at xv–xvi; Walker, supra note 1, at 407–10.

30. Pocock opposes the ancient constitution to a conception of feudal law. According to this latter conception, English medieval history revealed that the common law was not an unchanging standard and thus was subject to royal transformation. See J.G.A. Pocock, The Ancient Constitution and the Feudal Law (1967). Bernard Schwartz contrasts Coke's position with that of Francis Bacon. According to Bacon, tradition alone could not render the common law authoritative, and thus the king must be above the common law. See Schwartz, supra note 1, at 111–15.

31. See Gardiner, supra note 1, at xvi–xvii; Morgan, supra note 1, at 11–233; Prall, supra note 1, at xvi; Walker, supra note 1, at 410. The common lawyers were also part of the alliance with the parliamentarians and Puritans.

32. The Petition of Right (June 7, 1628), reprinted in Gardiner, supra note 1, at 66; see Schwartz, supra note 1, at 130–52.

33. Laud rejected the Arminian label, though he refused to take a clear stance on predestination. See Gardiner, supra note 1, at xi–xxiii. The term "Arminian" arose from the Dutch theologian Arminius. See Prall, supra note 1, at 312. Richard Hooker expressed views similar to those of Laud, though Hooker tended to be more open and opposed to persecution than Laud was. Contrary to the ancient constitution, Hooker argued that law is changeable, and contrary to Calvinism, he argued that reason as well as Scripture should play an important role in moral and political affairs. See Hooker, supra note 26; Forrester, supra note 26, at 358–64.

Charles also married a Roman Catholic, who of course became queen, thus further offending the Puritans. See Ahlstrom, supra note 1, at 93.

34. The declaration stated: "[T]he Articles of the Church of England ... do contain the true doctrine ... agreeable to God's Word ... requiring all our loving subjects to continue in the uniform profession thereof, and prohibiting the least difference from the said Articles." The King's Declaration Prefixed to the Articles of Religion (Nov. 1628) (commonly printed with the Book of Common Prayer), reprinted in Gardiner, supra note 1, at 75, 75; see also Schaff, supra note 1, at 486–87.

35. The resolutions, however, accepted the appointing of bishops but requested better appointments in the future. Resolutions on Religion Drawn by a Sub-Committee of the House of Commons (Feb. 24, 1629), reprinted in Gardiner, supra note 1, at 77.

36. Protestation of the House of Commons (Mar. 2, 1629), reprinted in Gardiner, supra note 1, at 82, 82–83.

37. See The King's Declaration Showing the Causes of the Late Dissolution (Mar. 10, 1629), reprinted in Gardiner, supra note 1, at 83; Schwartz, supra note 1, at 144.

38. See Russell, supra note 1, at 217 (Charles's efforts to enforce English religion in Scotland was a major precipitating cause of the English Civil War).

39. See Walker, supra note 1, at 412–13.

40. See Walker, supra note 1, at 413.

41. See id. The same fate fell upon Thomas Wentworth, the earl of Strafford, who had vigorously advocated the king's prerogative (complete authority to rule without Parliament). See The Act for the Attainder of the Earl of Strafford (May 10, 1641), reprinted in Gardiner, supra note 1, at 156; Schwartz, supra note 1, at 154–61.

42. See Schwartz, supra note 1, at 161–66.

43. See The Triennial Act (Feb. 15, 1640–1641), reprinted in Adams, Documents, supra note 1, at 350.

44. The Act Against Dissolving the Long Parliament Without its Own Consent (May 10, 1641), reprinted in Gardiner, supra note 1, at 158.

45. The Tonnage and Poundage Act (June 22, 1641), reprinted in Gardiner, supra note 1, at 159.

46. See The Act for the Abolition of the Court of Star Chamber (July 5, 1641), reprinted in Gardiner, supra note 1, at 179; The Act for the Abolition of the Court of High Commission (July 5, 1641), reprinted in Gardiner, supra note 1, at 186. On the significance of the rule of law for the Civil War, see Russell, supra note 1, at 136–60.

47. See The Grand Remonstrance, With the Petition Accompanying It (Dec. 1, 1641), reprinted in Gardiner, supra note 1, at 202.

48. The King's Answer to the Petition Accompanying the Grand Remonstrance (Dec. 23, 1641), reprinted in Gardiner, supra note 1, at 233, 234.

49. The King's Proclamation on Religion (Dec. 10, 1641), reprinted in Gardiner, supra note 1, at 232, 232.

50. See Gardiner, supra note 1, at xxxvi; Schwartz, supra note 1, at 167–73.

51. See Pocock, supra note 1, at 361–71.

52. His Majesty's Answer to the Nineteen Propositions of Both Houses of Parliament (June 1642), quoted in Pocock, supra note 1, at 362.

53. Pocock, supra note 1, at 365; see id. at 364.

54. His Majesty's Answer to the Nineteen Propositions of Both Houses of Parliament (June 1642), quoted in Pocock, supra note 1, at 362; see Pocock, supra note 1, at 362.

55. See Gardiner, supra note 1, at xxxvii–viii, 258–61; Morgan, supra note 1, at 55–70. .

56. The Root and Branch Petition (Dec. 11, 1640), reprinted in Gardiner, supra note 1, at 137; see Gee, supra note 1, at 537.

57. The Solemn League and Covenant (1643), reprinted in Gee, supra note 1, at 569. This application of Reformed theology through a covenant was sometimes called a "federal theology." See Ahlstrom, supra note 130.

58. See Gee, supra note 1, at 570–71.

59. Id. at 573.

60. The Westminster Confession of Faith (1647), reprinted in Schaff, supra note 1, at 600. Sydney E. Ahlstrom notes that the Reformed confessions of the Solemn League and Covenant and the Westminster Confession remain important, especially in the United States. He writes: "Nor were these

formulations forgotten amid wars and violence; they remain normative in Scotland and their immense influence on the thought and practice of American Congregationalists, Presbyterians, and Baptists makes them by far the most important confessional witness in American colonial history." Ahlstrom, supra note 1, at 94. Ahlstrom adds that "the Westminster Confession would become by far the most influential doctrinal symbol in American religious history." Id. at 131.

61. See Bettenson, supra note 1, at 250; Hill, Puritanism, supra note 1, at 6; Hill Revolution, supra note 1, at 126–29, 165; Prall, supra note 1, at 81; Woodhouse, supra note 1, at 14–19 & n.1.

In 1642, at the outset of the Civil War, there was a remarkable lack of "any principled defence of resistance." Russell, supra note 1, at 132. This lack of radical theory helps explain the moderate Presbyterian position. See id. at 132–36. While the Independents included many Congregationalists, the sectaries included more Anabaptists and Separatists. See Woodhouse, supra note 1, at 18. Roger Williams, who already had gained notoriety in the American colonies, stood in the sectary tradition. See id. at 18 n.1.

62. See Adams, Constitutional History, supra note 1, at 322–26; Gardiner, supra note 1, at xliii–lii; Hill, Revolution, supra note 1, at 111–18, 141–42; Walker, supra note 1, at 414–15; cf. Prall, supra note 1, at 108–47 (on the opposing armies).

63. The Agreement of the People (Jan. 15, 1649), reprinted in Gardiner, supra note 1, at 359; see Schwartz, supra note 1, at 175–77. The General Council of the Army was "composed of the Generals and representatives of other officers and of the rank and file." Hill, Revolution, supra note 1, at 113. Edmund S. Morgan argues that Parliament refused to adopt the Agreement because the Agreement suggested that the "people" existed outside of Parliament. Morgan, supra note 1, at 72–74.

64. The Agreement stated: "It is intended that the Christian Religion be held forth and recommended as the public profession in this nation, which we desire may, by the grace of God, be reformed to the greatest purity in doctrine, worship and discipline, according to the Word of God." The Agreement of the People (Jan. 15, 1649), reprinted in Gardiner, supra note 1, at 359, 369–70. Moreover, the Agreement explicitly added "that Popery or Prelacy be not held forth as the public way or profession in this nation." Id. at 370.

65. Id.

66. Russell, supra note 1, at 214.

67. See The Savoy Declaration of the Congregational Churches (1658), reprinted in Schaff, supra note 1, at 707, 710 (Preface), 719 (ch. XXI), 720 (ch. XXIV). The Savoy Declaration stated:

> Although the magistrate is bound to encourage, promote, and protect the professors and profession of the gospel, and to manage and order civil administrations in a due subserviency to the interest of Christ in the world, and to that end to take care that men of corrupt minds and conversations do not licentiously publish and divulge blasphemy and errors, in their own nature subverting the faith and inevitably destroying the souls of them that receive them; yet in such differences about the doctrines of the gospel, or ways of the worship of God, as may befall men exercising a good conscience, manifesting it in their conversation, and holding the foundation, not disturbing others in their ways or worship that differ from them, there is no warrant for the magistrate under the gospel to abridge them of their liberty.

Id. at ch. XXIV, reprinted in Schaff, supra note 1, at 720.

The Savoy Declaration, as a Congregationalist statement, extended a greater degree of toleration than the original Presbyterian Westminster Confession. A few Independent divines had sat at the Westminster Assembly, which drafted the Confession that was then adopted by Parliament, but the Independents were known as the "Dissenting Brethren." See Bettenson, supra note 1, at 250. The Westminster Confession stated:

> The civil magistrate may not assume to himself the administration of the Word and Sacraments, or the power of the keys of the kingdom of heaven: yet he hath authority, and it is his duty to take order, that unity and peace be preserved in the Church, that the truth of God be kept pure and entire, that all blasphemies and heresies be suppressed, all corruptions and abuses in worship and discipline prevented or reformed, and all the ordinances of God duly settled, administered, and observed. For the better effecting whereof

he hath power to call synods, to be present at them, and to provide that whatsoever is
transacted in them be according to the mind of God.

The Westminster Confession of Faith (1647), at ch. XXIII, reprinted in Schaff, supra note 1, at 653.
    68. For example, the Independent position was reflected in the following statement:

There are two things contended for in this liberty of conscience: first to instate every
Christian in his right of free, yet modest, judging and accepting what he holds; secondly,
to vindicate a necessary advantage to the truth, and this is the main end and respect of
this liberty. I contend not for variety of opinions; I know there is but one truth. But this
truth cannot be so easliy brought forth without this liberty. . . .

The Ancient Bounds, or Liberty of Conscience, Tenderly Stated, Modestly Asserted, and Mildly Vindicated (1645), reprinted in Woodhouse, supra note 1, at 247, 247.
    69. Christopher Hill notes: "Religious toleration, which has come to be thought of as the hall-
mark of 'Independency', was forced upon the 'Independent' members of Parliament by political necessity." Hill, Revolution, supra note 1, at 166.
    70. The Council of Mechanics passed and the Council of War endorsed a resolution that would
have added a clause to the Agreement favoring toleration for all religions, "'not excepting Turkes, nor
Papists, nor Jewes.'" Roth, supra note 1, at 153 (quoting Mercurius Pragmaticus (Dec. 19–26, 1648)).
When opposition appeared, the resolution was dropped; instead Parliament was petitioned to readmit
Jews into England. See Roth, supra note 1, at 153.
    71. The Instrument of Government (Dec. 16, 1653), reprinted in Gardiner, supra note 1, at 405.
The Instrument stated:

[Those who] profess faith in God by Jesus Christ . . . shall not be restrained from, but
shall be protected in, the profession of the faith and exercise of their religion . . . provided
this liberty be not extended to Popery or Prelacy, nor to such as, under the profession of
Christ, hold forth and practise licentiousness.

Id. at 416; see Gardiner, supra note 1, at lvi.
    72. See Adams, Constitutional History, supra note 1, at 325–27; Hill, Revolution, supra note 1, at
115–16, 133–39; Schwartz, supra note 1, at 177.
    73. Hill, Revolution, supra note 1, at 139.
    74. Id. at 142.
    75. In 1659 the Rump Parliament returned to power, and in 1660 it acceded to popular pressure to
readmit the members expelled in 1648. This Parliament immediately dissolved itself and called for a
parliamentary election. The result was the so-called Cavalier Parliament, which voted to restore
Charles II. See Ahlstrom, supra note 1, at 94; Prall, Bloodless, supra note 1, at 21; Seaward, supra note
1, at 1; Walker, supra note 1, at 415.
    76. Id. at 466.
    77. See The Declaration of Breda (Apr. 4, 1660), reprinted in Gardiner, supra note 1, at 465, 466.
The Declaration provided:

And because the passion and uncharitableness of the times have produced several opinions in religion, by which men are engaged in parties and animosities against each other
(which, when they shall hereafter unite in a freedom of conversation, will be composed or
better understood), we do declare a liberty to tender consciences, and that no man shall
be disquieted or called in question for differences of opinion in matter of religion, which
do not disturb the peace of the kingdom; and that we shall be ready to consent to such
an Act of Parliament, as, upon mature deliberation, shall be offered to us, for the full
granting that indulgence.

Id. at 466.
    78. Last Act of Uniformity (May 19, 1662), reprinted in Adams, Documents, supra note 1, at 427;
see Hill, Revolution, supra note 1, at 245; Walker, supra note 1, at 415.
    79. Ahlstrom, supra note 1, at 95; see Walker, supra note 1, at 416; see, e.g., The Clarendon Code,
reprinted in Bettenson, supra note 1, at 293 (three acts aimed at abolishing nonconformity).

80. See Jon Butler, Awash in a Sea of Faith: Christianizing the American People 27 (1990); Walker, supra note 1, at 416.

81. Charles II's Declaration of Indulgence (Feb. 1, 1673), reprinted in Adams, Documents, supra note 1, at 434; Test Act (Mar. 29, 1673), reprinted in Adams, Documents, supra note 1, at 436; see Hill, Revolution, supra note 1, at 194–95; Walker, supra note 1, at 416–17.

82. James II's Declaration of Indulgence (Apr. 4, 1687), reprinted in Adams, Documents, supra note 1, at 451, 452–53.

83. Schwartz, supra note 1, at 197; see Morgan, supra note 1, at 94–121; Prall, Bloodless, supra note 1, at 89–165, 202, 273–77; Hill, Revolution, supra note 1, at 199; Schwartz, supra note 1, at 188–93; Walker, supra note 1, at 417. Mary would have been next in line for the throne but for the birth of a son to James II on June 10, 1688. Morgan, supra note 1, at 106–7.

84. The Toleration Act (May 24, 1689), reprinted in Adams, Documents, supra note 1, at 459; see Adams, Constitutional History, supra note 1, at 376; Ahlstrom, supra note 1, at 96; Butler, supra note 80, at 27; Walker, supra note 1, at 418; Hugh Trevor-Roper, Toleration and Religion After 1688, in From Persecution to Toleration: The Glorious Revolution and Religion in England 389 (Ole Peter Grell et al. eds., 1991); Introduction, in From Persecution to Toleration: The Glorious Revolution and Religion in England 1, 10–16 (Ole Peter Grell et al. eds., 1991); see also The Bill of Rights (Dec. 16, 1689), reprinted in Adams, Documents, supra note 1, at 462.

85. Hill, Puritanism, supra note 1, at 30.

86. Id. at 30.

87. Id. at 155, 195; see id. at 75, 155–56; Hill, Revolution, supra note 1, at 146–47; Pocock, supra note 1, at 445–46, 462–63.

88. See Peter Toon, The Question of Jewish Immigration, in Puritans, the Millennium and the Future of Israel: Puritan Eschatology 1600 to 1660, at 115, 115–16 (Peter Toon ed., 1970) [hereinafter Toon, Question]. Before the expulsion, England had regulated Jewish life with laws modeled on Roman and canon law. See Shael Herman, Legacy and Legend: The Continuity of Roman and English Regulation of the Jews, 66 Tul. L. Rev. 1781, 1801–15 (1992). Other sources providing useful information regarding the treatment of Jews in England are the following: Roth, supra note 1; Puritans, the Millennium and the Future of Israel: Puritan Eschatology 1600 to 1660 (Peter Toon ed., 1970) [hereinafter Toon]; Robert M. Healey, The Jew in Seventeenth-Century Protestant Thought, 46 Am. Soc'y of Church History 63 (1977); David S. Katz, The Jews of England and 1688, in From Persecution to Toleration: The Glorious Revolution and Religion in England 217 (Ole Peter Grell et al. eds., 1991).

A very small number of Jews somehow managed to survive in England over the centuries. For example, during the sixteenth century, a negligible number of financially successful Marranos, fleeing the Spanish Inquisition, filtered into England to form a small community in London. By the early seventeenth century, however, the community was almost completely dissipated. See Roth, supra note 1, at 135–44.

89. The Westminster Confession of Faith, at ch. VI, VII, XI, XIV, XVI, XVIII–XXI (1647), reprinted in Schaff, supra note 1, at 600, 615, 617–18, 626, 630–31, 634–35, 637–41, 643–45, 648–49; see id. at ch. XIX, reprinted in Schaff, supra note 1, at 641 (Old Testament "prefiguring Christ"); id. at ch. XX, reprinted in Schaff, supra note 1, at 643–44 (on the superiority of the New Testament to the Jewish laws); id. at ch. XXV, reprinted in Schaff, supra note 1, at 657 (the "universal" Church of Christianity); id. at ch. XXXIII, reprinted in Schaff, supra note 1, at 671–73 (on the day of the last judgment, all persons "shall appear before the tribunal of Christ"); Walker, supra note 1, at 413–14.

90. See, e.g., The Whitehall Debates (Dec. 14, 1648), reprinted in Woodhouse, supra note 1, at 125, 155–66.

91. The Ancient Bounds, or Liberty of Conscience, Tenderly Stated, Modestly Asserted, and Mildly Vindicated (1645), reprinted in Woodhouse, supra note 1, at 247, 264–65.

92. The Puritan concept of postmillennialism became respectable only during the seventeenth century. See Hill, Puritanism, at 141–42; Healey, supra note 88, at 74–78; Peter Toon, Introduction, in Toon, supra note 88, at 8, 18–19; Toon, Question, supra note 88, at 116–17.

93. A Glimpse of Sion's Glory (1641), reprinted in Prall, supra note 1, at 90–91.

94. Roth, supra note 1, at 157 (quoting Oliver Cromwell); see id. at 152–53, 156–57, 160–62.

95. See Jonathan I. Israel, European Jewry in the Age of Mercantilism 1550–1750, at 1–3 (2d ed. 1989); Paul Johnson, A History of the Jews 276–78 (1987); William Nicholls, Christian Antisemitism:

A History of Hate 271–72 (1993); 14 Encyclopaedia Judaica 19–20 (1971); Roth, supra note 1, at 135–39, 154–61, 164–66, 173–95; Healey, supra note 88, at 70–71; Katz, supra note 88, at 230–48; Toon, Question, supra note 88, at 121, 125.

96. In particular, I shall focus on the following works: James Harrington, The Commonwealth of Oceana (1656), in The Commonwealth of Oceana and A System of Politics 1 (J.G.A. Pocock ed., 1992) [hereinafter Harrington, Oceana]; James Harrington, A System of Politics (written around 1661 but published posthumously), in The Commonwealth of Oceana and A System of Politics 267 (J.G.A. Pocock ed., 1992) [hereinafter Harrington, System]; Thomas Hobbes, Leviathan (C.B. Macpherson ed., 1968) (first published 1651); John Locke, Two Treatises of Government (Peter Laslett ed., rev. ed. 1963) [hereinafter Locke, Two Treatises]; John Locke, The Second Treatise of Government (Liberal Arts Press ed. 1952) [hereinafter Locke, Second Treatise]; John Locke, The Reasonableness of Christianity (George W. Ewing ed., 1965) (first published in 1695) [hereinafter Locke, Christianity]; John Locke, A Letter Concerning Toleration (1689), in Four Letters on Toleration 2 (London 1870; reprint of 7th ed. 1758) [hereinafter Locke, Toleration]. For helpful discussions of Hobbes's, Harrington's, and Locke's writings, see John Dunn, The Political Thought of John Locke (1969); Eldon Eisenach, Two Worlds of Liberalism: Religion and Politics in Hobbes, Locke, and Mill (1981); Hill, Puritanism, supra note 1; Hill, Revolution, supra note 1; Joshua Mitchell, Not By Reason Alone (1993); Pocock, supra note 1; Perez Zagorin, A History of Political Thought in the English Revolution (1954); Laurence Berns, Thomas Hobbes, in History of Political Philosophy 396 (Leo Strauss & Joseph Cropsey eds., 3d ed. 1987); Charles Blitzer, Introduction, in James Harrington, The Political Writings of James Harrington (1955); Robert A. Goldwin, John Locke, in History of Political Philosophy 476 (Leo Strauss & Joseph Cropsey eds., 3d ed. 1987); Peter Laslett, Introduction, in John Locke, Two Treatises of Government 15 (Peter Laslett ed., rev. ed. 1963); C.B. Macpherson, Introduction, in Thomas Hobbes, Leviathan (C.B. Macpherson ed., 1968) (first published 1651); J.G.A. Pocock, Introduction, in James Harrington, The Commonwealth of Oceana and A System of Politics (J.G.A. Pocock ed., 1992) [hereinafter Pocock, Introduction].

97. Hobbes, supra note 96, at 728.

98. See Pocock, supra note 1, at 378 (though Hobbes differs from Machiavelli, they both start with a de facto argument); Berns, supra note 96, at 396–97.

99. See Hobbes, supra note 96, at 227, 498–99; see also Zagorin, supra note 96, at 181–82.

100. See Macpherson, supra note 96, at 13–14; Prall, supra note 1, at 1–2.

101. See Eisenach, supra note 96, at 13–72; Mitchell, supra note 96, at 46–72.

102. See Hill, Revolution, supra note 1, at 181–82; Berns, supra note 96, at 407. Christopher Hill notes that Hobbes followed in the wake of Francis Bacon's revolutionary approach to science. See Hill, Revolution, supra note 1, at 179–81; see, e.g., Francis Bacon, Novum Organum, reprinted in The English Philosophers From Bacon to Mill 24–123 (Edwin A. Burtt ed., 1939).

103. See id. at 183.

104. See Hobbes, supra note 96, at 161, 183, 185–86.

105. Id. at 188; see id. at 223–27.

106. Id. at 227 (emphasis in the original).

107. See id. at 230; Berns, supra note 96, at 408; see also Hobbes, supra note 96, at 272, 375 (the commonwealth can dissolve if the sovereign fails to protect the subjects); cf. Hobbes, supra note 96, at 192, 199 (individuals cannot renounce their right to resist assault by force).

108. See Hill, Puritanism, supra note 1, at 277–78; Pocock, supra note 1, at 378. Hill writes: "Paradoxically, it is the absolutist Hobbes who demonstrated that the state exists for man, that it is the product of human reason, and therefore that political theory is a rational science." Hill, Puritanism, supra note 1, at 278. For a discussion of the importance of human control and instrumentalism to the concept of modernism, see Stephen M. Feldman, From Modernism to Postmodernism in American Legal Thought: The Significance of the Warren Court, in The Warren Court: A Retrospective (Bernard Schwartz ed., Oxford University Press, forthcoming).

109. See Skinner II, supra note 1, at 349–54. F.H. Hinsley notes that while Bodin was perhaps the first theorist to articulate the modern concept of sovereignty, Hobbes was the first English theorist to do so. See F.H. Hinsley, Sovereignty 140–41 (2d ed. 1986). See generally Charles Tilly, Reflections on the History of European State-Making, in The Formation of National States in Western Europe 21 (Charles Tilly ed., 1975) (on the conceptions of state and sovereignty).

110. Hobbes, supra note 96, at 478.

111. See id. at 478–79; see also Eisenach, supra note 96, at 49, 57; Mitchell, supra note 96, at 47.

112. See Pocock, supra note 1, at 397. Christopher Hill writes: "Hobbes had no love for Puritanism, for he held that the logical conclusion of its belief in the rights of the individual conscience was complete anarchy." Hill, Puritanism, supra note 1, at 284.

113. Hobbes, supra note 96, at 484; see id. at 525–26, 629.

114. Id. at 515; see id. at 442–45, 501. Hobbes noted that "[with] the planting of Christian religion . . . the number of Christians encreased wonderfully every day, and in every place. Id. at 181.

115. See Mitchell, supra note 96, at 56–58.

116. See Hobbes, supra note 96, at 482, 710–11.

117. Pocock, supra note 1, at 398.

118. See Mitchell, supra note 96, at 53–58.

119. See Hobbes, supra note 96, at 409–626; Berns, supra note 96, at 418.

120. Hobbes, supra note 96, at 498–99 (emphasis in the original); see also id. at 575.

121. See id. at 627–715; Pocock, supra note 1, at 397–98.

122. See Hobbes, supra note 96, at 405.

123. Id. at 527; see id. at 483; see also id. at 195–96 (salvation is by "the Free Grace of God onely").

124. Hobbes wrote:

> [A] true and unfeigned Christian is not liable to Excommunication: Nor he also that is a professed Christian, till his Hypocrisy appear in his Manners, that is, till his behaviour bee contrary to the law of his Soveraign, which is the rule of Manners, and which Christ and his Apostles have commanded us to be subject to. For the Church cannot judge of Manners but by externall Actions, which Actions can never bee unlawfull, but when they are against the Law of the Common-wealth.

Id. at 541; see Eisenach, supra note 96, at 58.

125. See Hobbes, supra note 96, at 230, 527.

126. Eisenach, supra note 96, at 57.

127. Hobbes, supra note 96, at 532.

128. See Berns, supra note 96, at 419; D.W. Hamlyn, A History of Western Philosophy 130 (1987). According to Hill: "It is quite clear, in fact, that Hobbes does not really believe in Christianity, in any normal sense of the word 'belief', and merely accepts it as the creed authorized in the state in which he lived." Hill, Puritanism, supra note 96, at 286. But Hill adds that Hobbes believed in God. See id. at 293–94.

129. Eisenach, supra note 96, at 66. On both accounts—religious and political—Englishmen could see themselves as attempting to return to an idyllic past. Religiously, of course, the parliamentarian Puritans saw themselves as overcoming Catholicism and Anglicanism and returning to the pure form of early Christianity. Politically, they saw themselves as shaking off the Norman yoke. That is, many English thought that their traditional institutions of liberty and freedom had been corrupted after the Norman conquest in the eleventh century. See id. at 50; Hill, Puritanism, supra note 1, at 57–58.

130. Hill writes: "The contract idea which [Hobbes] adopts was almost the private property of the Puritan and revolutionary opposition." Hill, Puritanism, supra note 1, at 278.

131. See id. Daniel Bell emphasizes the importance of the Reformation development of individualism for the emergence of modernity. See Daniel Bell, The Cultural Contradictions of Capitalism 16, 257–58 (1978).

132. See Hobbes, supra note 96, at 413, 425, 481, 513–15, 517.

133. Zagorin, supra note 96, at 169. Ralph Hancock notes that "Calvin's understanding of this [carnal] world reveals his profound affinities with the rationalistic materialism commonly associated with such authors as Hobbes and Locke." Ralph C. Hancock, Calvin and the Foundations of Modern Politics 20 (1989).

134. See Harrington, Oceana, supra note 96.

135. See Pocock, Introduction, supra note 96, at ix. Harrington scholars disagree about when Harrington began working on Oceana. See, e.g., Hill, Puritanism, supra note 1, at 299–300 (began around 1649–1650); Blitzer, supra note 96, at xxi (began around 1653); Pocock, Introduction, supra note 96, at xxv (began around 1654). It is worth noting that both Hobbes and Harrington were more observers than participants in the Civil War. See Hill, Puritanism, supra note 1, at 300.

136. See Pocock, Introduction, supra note 96, at ix, xii, xv.

137. Pocock writes: "Oceana is not a utopia so much as an occasione, a moment of revolutionary opportunity at which old historical forms have destroyed themselves and there is a chance to construct new forms immune from the contingencies of history (known as fortuna)." Id. at xviii.

138. Blitzer, supra note 96, at xxxv; see Zagorin, supra note 96, at 133–35; Blitzer, supra note 96, at xxvii. Blitzer notes, however, that Harrington criticized Hobbes for analogizing a science of politics to geometry. To Harrington, the science of politics should be more like "anatomy, the study of complex living organisms." Blitzer, supra note 96, at xxviii. Blitzer also observes that Harrington believed his empirically (or scientifically) derived principles of government did not depend ultimately "on Scriptural authority for their validity." Id. at xxxi. Nevertheless, Harrington further believed his principles could be proven from Scripture as well. See id.

139. See Harrington, Oceana, supra note 96, at 9–14; Zagorin, supra note 96, at 133–34; Pocock, Introduction, supra note 96, at xv.

140. Pocock, supra note 1, at 397; see Hobbes, supra note 96, at 225–26 (ants can pursue the common good, but humans cannot); Berns, supra note 96, at 409–10.

141. See Pocock, supra note 1, at 383–400.

142. Id. at 399; see Zagorin, supra note 96, at 135.

143. Pocock, supra note 1, at 399.

144. Harrington, Occana, supra note 96, at 8–9.

145. Harrington writes:

> But seeing they that make the laws in commonwealths are but men, the main question seems to be how a commonwealth comes to be an empire of laws and not of men? or how the debate or result of a commonwealth is so sure to be according unto reason, seeing they who debate and they who resolve be but men.

Id. at 20–21.

146. Id. at 21–22.

147. Harrington wrote:

> Domestic empire is founded upon dominion. Dominion is property real or personal; that is to say in lands, or in money and goods. Land, or the parts and parcels of a territory, are held by the proprietor or proprietors, lord or lords of it, in some proportion; and such ... as is the proportion or balance of dominion or property in land, such is the nature of the empire.

Id. at 11.

148. Id. at 11–12, 55–57.

149. In Oceana, Harrington referred to Henry VII as Panurgus and to Henry VIII as Coraunus. See, e.g., id. at 55, 60; see also Prall, supra note 1, at 25–26.

150. See Harrington, Oceana, supra note 96, at 56; Hill, Puritanism, supra note 1, at 301–02. Harrington referred to Elizabeth as Parthenia. See, e.g., Harrington, Oceana, supra note 96, at 56; see also Prall, supra note 1, at 25.

151. Harrington, Oceana, supra note 96, at 56 (emphasis omitted); see Hill, Puritanism, supra note 1, at 302. Perez Zagorin writes:

> The balance of property, therefore, is the foundation, and upon it is reared the form of government as the superstructure. The root cause of political disturbance lies in a discord between the two. For as landed property gradually passes to new social groups, the existing superstructure ceases to be stable and can be maintained only by force. It is the violent preservation of the superstructure against a new balance which brings on civil war. The essence of political prudence, consequently, consists in the raising of such superstructures as will be compatible with the distribution of property.

Zagorin, supra note 96, at 136.

152. Harrington, Oceana, supra note 96, at 60.

153. See Hill, Puritanism, supra note 1, at 300, 309.

154. Harrington, Oceana, supra note 96, at 64; see Zagorin, supra note 96, at 140; Blitzer, supra note 96, at xxxvii.

155. Harrington, Oceana, supra note 96, at 34; see id. at 69–243 (explaining the details of Oceana). Charles Blitzer summarizes Harrington's various constitutional mechanisms: "Indirect elections, bicameralism, rotation in office, guarantees of religious liberty and liberty of conscience, the 'agrarian law,' the secret ballot, universal military training, free public education—all of these devices and many others, contained in the proposed constitution of the equal commonwealth of Oceana." Blitzer, supra note 96, at xxxviii.

156. Harrington, Oceana, supra note 96, at 33, 100–01; see Hill, Puritanism, supra note 1, at 306–07.

157. Harrington, Oceana, supra note 96, at 39.

158. See Hill, Puritanism, supra note 1, at 146.

159. Harrington, Oceana, supra note 96, at 63, 232.

160. Harrington wrote:

> The council of religion as the arbiter of this commonwealth in cases of conscience more peculiarly appertaining unto religion, Christian charity, and a pious life, shall have the care of the national religion and the protection of the liberty of conscience, with the cognizance of all causes relating unto either of them.

Id. at 126.

161. Id. at 127.

162. See id. at 5–6; Roth, supra note 1, at 167.

163. Harrington wrote: "Liberty of conscience entire, or in the whole, is where a man according to the dictates of his own conscience may have the free exercise of his religion, without impediment to his preferment or employment in the state." Harrington, System, supra note 96, at 282.

164. Robert Filmer, Patriarcha, or the Natural Power of Kings (1680).

165. Locke, Two Treatises, supra note 96, at 178; see Dunn, supra note 96, at 44, 47, 50, 58–76.

166. See Dunn, supra note 96, at 43–45; Pocock, supra note 1, at 406–08; Prall, Bloodless, supra note 1, at 253–54. Some Whig (or country) demands, though, were never satisfied, such as the exclusion of officeholders from the House of Commons and having short, frequently elected Parliaments. See Pocock, supra note 1, at 406–08. Also, by the next century, the affiliation of the Whigs and Tories with country and court had shifted. See Prall, Bloodless, supra note 1, at 291–92.

167. Locke's First Letter Concerning Toleration was actually published in Latin in 1685 and then in English in 1689. See Locke, Second Treatise, supra note 96, at xxiii.

168. Locke, Two Treatises, supra note 96, at 171.

169. See Dunn, supra note 96, at 48, 77–83; Laslett, supra note 96, at 58–79, 80–92. Locke, though, clearly was fully aware of Hobbes's Leviathan. See, e.g., Locke, Two Treatises, supra note 96, at 185 (mentioning Leviathan).

170. Locke, Two Treatises, supra note 96, at 196.

171. Mitchell, supra note 96, at 80 (emphasis omitted in part).

172. See id. at 74, 82, 90.

173. Locke, Second Treatise, supra note 96, at 4–5. Locke also wrote that people are "by nature, all free, equal, and independent." Id. at 54.

174. See id. at 86–87.

175. See Locke, Two Treatises, supra note 96, at 311; cf. id. at 347–48 (Adam had reason initially, but subsequent humans must develop their faculty to reason as they mature).

176. Eisenach, supra note 96, at 92.

177. Locke, Second Treatise, supra note 96, at 5–6. Here, then, Locke's state of nature appeared to be prepolitical. But in other places, Locke offered a definition of a state of nature that is not prepolitical: "Men living together according to reason, without a common superior on earth with authority to judge between them, is properly the state of nature." Id. at 13.

178. Id. at 17–18, 21. For a summary of Locke's argument justifying the differentiation of property ownership, see Mitchell, supra note 96, at 82–85.

179. See Locke, Second Treatise, supra note 96, at 12–13; see also Goldwin, supra note 96, at 478–79.

180. Locke, Second Treatise, supra note 96, at 9, 70–71, 75; see id. at 6–7, 48–49, 54–55, 65, 79–80, 98–99, 123–24. Although unclear, in some passages, "property" appears to mean primarily possessions, while in other passages it appears to mean life, liberty, and estates (possessions). Also, in Locke's terms, the state of nature and political society have different natural laws.

181. Id. at 78; see Goldwin, supra note 96, at 497.

182. Id. at 82–83; see Goldwin, supra note 96, at 509. Locke distinguished political society from government in theory but not in practice. That is, the action of consenting to the formation of political society theoretically preceded the formation of a specific form of government. But once a people agreed to form political or civil society (which had to be done unanimously), the first order of business was necessarily to form a specific government (which was by majority decision). See Locke, Second Treatise, supra note 96, at 119, 139; Goldwin, supra note 96, at 500.

Locke also wrote of a federative power—focused on the relations of the political society to other societies and individuals—but he maintained that the executive and federative powers should not be separated. See Locke, Second Treatise, supra note 96, at 82–84.

183. See Locke, Second Treatise, supra note 96, at 8, 50, 63–64, 73, 75, 76, 81–83, 88–95, 112–13, 118, 124–25, 136. Locke also wrote that "the end of government [is] the good of the community." Id. at 93.

184. Locke, Second Treatise, supra note 96, at 92; accord id. at 112.

185. Dunn, supra note 96, at 179.

186. Locke, Second Treatise, supra note 96, at 117. As many recent political theorists have stressed, Locke emphasized strong doses of individualism and natural rights preexisting the state—the hallmarks of liberalism—but many of these theorists have overlooked a perhaps equally strong measure of the civic republican common good in Locke's writing. See Stephen M. Feldman, Republican Revival/Interpretive Turn, 1992 Wis. L. Rev. 679, 687–89; cf. Stephen Holmes, The Secret History of Self-Interest, in Beyond Self-Interest 285 (J. Mansbridge ed. 1990) (according to Locke, "[p]roper interests are those that are compatible with 'the general Good' of all"). Compare Louis Hartz, The Liberal Tradition in America 46 (1955) (which abruptly dismisses the importance of republican theory to American Revolutionaries), with Pocock, supra note 1 (which emphasizes the importance of civic republican thought to American Revolutionaries and constitutional framers).

187. See Skinner II, supra note 1, at 238–40, 338–39; cf. Dunn, supra note 96, at 51 (on Locke's individualism being rooted in Calvinistic theology).

188. Locke, Second Treatise, supra note 96, at 138.

189. Locke argued that once political society is formed, a majority can choose a particular form of government. But among the forms of democracy, oligarchy, and monarchy, Locke did not express a strong preference. See id. at 73–74; Goldwin, supra note 96, at 500.

190. Locke, Second Treatise, supra note 96, at 126. In the Two Treatises, Locke revealed that he was heavily influenced by the writing of Richard Hooker. See, e.g., Locke, Second Treatise, supra note 96, at 50 n.1, 51 n.2, 53 n.3. Hooker, writing near the end of Elizabeth's reign, argued against the radical Calvinist position that the people themselves possessed a general right of resistance. See Hooker, supra note 26; Skinner II, supra note 1, at 107; Forrester, supra note 26, at 356.

191. See Dunn, supra note 96, at 250; Eisenach, supra note 96, at 3, 6, 73–114; Mitchell, supra note 96, at 73–97; cf. Dunn, supra note 96, at 265 (links Locke's right of resistance to his theology); Hancock, supra note 133, at 20 (linking Hobbes and Locke with Calvin). John Dunn writes that "the Lockean social and political theory is to be seen as the elaboration of Calvinist social values." Dunn, supra note 96, at 259.

192. See Winthrop S. Hudson & John Corrigan, Religion in America 95 (5th ed. 1992). In the editor's Introduction to Locke's The Reasonableness of Christianity, George W. Ewing observes that Locke intended in that later essay (published in 1695) to oppose deism, but some Calvinists nonetheless believed that Locke's position, harmonizing reason and Christianity, was too dangerous and too near a deistic world view. Ewing adds that although Locke did not consider himself to be a strict Calvinist, he echoed certain Calvinist themes, especially the focus on Scripture. George W. Ewing, Introduction, in Locke, Christianity, supra note 96, at vii, xii–xvi. Sydney Ahlstrom notes that Locke follows in the tradition of normative Anglicanism. Ahlstrom, supra note 1, at 96. But, as noted earlier in the text, Anglicanism combines Calvinist articles with more Catholic liturgies.

193. Mitchell, supra note 96, at 82.

194. See Hill, Puritanism, supra note 1, at 298. Douglas Hay calls Locke the apologist for the deification of property in the seventeenth century. Douglas Hay, Property, Authority and the Criminal Law, in Albion's Fatal Tree 17, 18–19 (Douglas Hay et al., eds., 1975).

195. Dunn, supra note 96, at 245.

196. Id. at 93.

197. See id. at 250. To Locke, final redemption is possible only with the future second coming of Christ. Hence, in Joshua Mitchell's words: "The task of human beings who dwell in this present moment of history is to make sure that the integrity of the self is maintained." Mitchell, supra note 96, at 96. In other words, for Locke, the City of God does not presently exist on earth.

198. Locke, Toleration, supra note 96 at 7, 11, 28.

199. Id. at 6, 20, 28, 32; see id. at 6–7 (force cannot bring salvation); id. at 18 (individuals "must be left to their own consciences"); id. at 27 ("the care of each man's salvation belongs only to himself").

200. Id. at 32.

201. Id. at 29.

202. Id. at 6, 13, 36. Likewise, Locke wrote: "For churches have neither any jurisdiction in worldly matters, nor are fire and sword any proper instruments wherewith to convince mens minds of error, and inform them of the truth." Id. at 12.

203. See generally Duncan Kennedy, Toward an Historical Understanding of Legal Consciousness: The Case of Classical Legal Thought in America, 1850–1940, 3 Research in Law & Sociology 3 (1980) (on the imagery of bounded spheres in American legal thought).

204. See Locke, Toleration, supra note 96, at 10, 31–32, 35. Locke wrote:

> [N]o private person has any right in any manner to prejudice another person in his civil enjoyments because he is of another church or religion. All the rights and franchises that belong to him as a man, or as a denison, are inviolably to be preserved to him. These are not the business of religion. No violence nor injury is to be offered him, whether he be Christian or Pagan.

Id. at 10.

205. Id. at 35.

206. See id. at 22–23.

207. Michael W. McConnell, The Origins and Historical Understanding of Free Exercise of Religion, 103 Harv. L. Rev. 1409, 1433 (1990).

208. Locke, Toleration, supra note 96, at 35 (emphasis added); see id. at 2.

209. See Locke, Christianity, supra note 96, at 1–3, 9, 12–13. Locke wrote:

> The difference between the law of works and the law of faith is only this: that the law of works makes no allowance for failing on any occasion. Those that obey are righteous; those that in any part disobey, are unrighteous, and must not expect [eternal] life, the reward of righteousness.

Id. at 13.

210. Id. at 9–10. At other points, Locke wrote more in the Calvinist tradition by suggesting that Jesus and the New Testament fulfilled but did not "dissolve the [Jewish] law." Id. at 13–14.

211. Id. at 12–13, 89.

212. Id. at 92–95 (citing Luke 23:22).

213. Cf. Pocock, supra note 1, at 401–02 (emphasizing the emergence of historical self-understanding during seventeenth and eighteenth centuries).

214. Locke, Toleration, supra note 96, at 36; see Mitchell, supra note 96, at 78; John Dunn, The Claim to Freedom of Conscience: Freedom of Speech, Freedom of Thought, Freedom of Worship?, in From Persecution to Toleration: The Glorious Revolution and Religion in England 171, 174–75 (Ole Peter Grell et al. eds., 1991); David A.J. Richards, Religion, Public Morality, and Constitutional Law, 30 Nomos 152, 154–55 (1988). Skinner traces this politique position regarding religion and the state back to Bodin:

> For as soon as the protagonists of the rival religious creeds showed that they were willing to fight each other to the death, it began to seem obvious to a number of politique theorists that, if there were to be any prospect of achieving civic peace, the powers of the

State would have to be divorced from the duty to uphold any particular faith. With Bodin's insistence in his Six Books that it ought to be obvious to any prince that 'wars made for matters of religion' are not in fact 'grounded upon matters directly touching his estate', we hear for the first time the authentic tones of the modern theorist of the State

Skinner II, supra note 1, at 352.

215. Locke, Toleration, supra note 96, at 2.

216. See Butler, supra note 80, at 10–12 (after the Reformation, in Protestant and Catholic nations, state-supported churches were the norm).

217. At one point, Skinner characterizes the modern sovereign state as follows: "[T]he distinctively modern idea of the State [is] a form of public power separate from both the ruler and the ruled [that constitutes] the supreme political authority within a certain defined territory." Skinner II, supra note 1, at 353; see Hinsley, supra note 109, at 7, 17–18. Of course, any definitions of sovereignty and state are controversial.

218. See Tilly, supra note 109, at 27.

219. See Pocock, supra note 1, at 424, 435–36.

NOTES TO CHAPTER 6

1. I used the following sources of information on religious and political developments during the colonial period: John Adair, Founding Fathers: The Puritans in England and America (1982); Sydney E. Ahlstrom, A Religious History of the American People (1972); Jon Butler, Awash in a Sea of Faith: Christianizing the American People (1990); Naomi W. Cohen, Jews in Christian America: The Pursuit of Religious Equality (1992); Thomas J. Curry, The First Freedoms: Church and State in America to the Passage of the First Amendment (1986); Jonathan Edwards: Representative Selections (Clarence H. Faust & Thomas H. Johnson eds., 1962) [hereinafter Faust & Johnson]; Everett Emerson, Puritanism in America, 1620–1750 (1977); Kai T. Erikson, Wayward Puritans (1966); Mark DeWolfe Howe, The Garden and the Wilderness (1965); Winthrop S. Hudson & John Corrigan, Religion in America (5th ed. 1992); Frederic Cople Jaher, A Scapegoat in the New Wilderness: The Origins and Rise of Anti-Semitism in America (1994); Leonard W. Levy, The Establishment Clause: Religion and the First Amendment (1986); Martin E. Marty, Protestantism in the United States: Righteous Empire (2d ed. 1986); Perry Miller, Errand Into the Wilderness (1956) [hereinafter Miller, Errand]; Perry Miller, The New England Mind: From Colony to Province (1953) [hereinafter Miller, New England Mind]; Perry Miller, Roger Williams: His Contribution to the American Tradition (1953) [hereinafter Miller, Roger Williams]; Perry Miller, Orthodoxy in Massachusetts, 1630–1650 (1933) [hereinafter Miller, Orthodoxy]; Leo Pfeffer, Church, State, and Freedom (1953); Irwin H. Polishook, Roger Williams, John Cotton and Religious Freedom: A Controversy in New and Old England (1967); Williston Walker, The Creeds and Platforms of Congregationalism (1960); Timothy L. Hall, Roger Williams and the Foundations of Religious Liberty, 71 B.U. L. Rev. 455 (1991); Michael W. McConnell, The Origins and Historical Understanding of Free Exercise of Religion, 103 Harv. L. Rev. 1409 (1990); William G. McLoughlin, 'Enthusiasm for Liberty': The Great Awakening as the Key to the Revolution, 87 Proceedings of the Am. Antiquarian Soc. 69 (1977); Harry S. Stout, Religion, Communications, and the Ideological Origins of the American Revolution, 34 Wm. & Mary Q. 519 (1977); The Great Awakening: Documents on the Revival of Religion, 1740–1745 (Richard L. Bushman ed., 1969) [hereinafter Bushman]; Documents of American History (Henry Steele Commager ed., 3d ed. 1947) (in 2 volumes) [hereinafter 1 Commager and 2 Commager]; The Puritans (Perry Miller & Thomas H. Johnson eds., 1963 ed.) (all citations will be to the first volume of this two-volume set) [hereinafter Miller & Johnson]; The Federal and State Constitutions, Colonial Charters, and Other Organic Laws of the United States (Ben Perley Poore ed., 2d ed. 1924) (in 2 volumes) [hereinafter 1 Poore and 2 Poore]; 3 The Creeds of Christendom (Philip Schaff ed., 3d ed. 1877) [hereinafter Schaff]; The Puritan Tradition in America, 1620–1730 (Alden T. Vaughan ed., 1972) [hereinafter Vaughan]; Church and State in American History (John F. Wilson & Donald L. Drakeman eds., 2d ed. 1987) [hereinafter Wilson & Drakeman].

2. Ahlstrom, supra note 1, at 67; see id. at 36–69.

3. See id. at 104–05, 184–85. The primary concern for profit is apparent in The First Charter of Virginia. See The First Charter of Virginia (1606), reprinted in 2 Poore, supra note 1, at 1888–93.

4. The First Charter of Virginia (1606), reprinted in 2 Poore, supra note 1, at 1888 (emphasis in the original); see Ahlstrom, supra note 1, at 184–85. For an excellent discussion of the importance of Christianity in the conquest of Native Americans, see Robert A. Williams, The American Indian in Western Legal Thought (1990).

5. See Ahlstrom, supra note 1, at 104–05, 184–85, 188–89; Levy, supra note 1, at 3–4. The Church of England was established in Virginia by law in 1626. See Butler, supra note 1, at 99. Even before that time, though, laws required everyone to attend church and observe the Christian Sabbath, and punished religious transgressions such as blasphemy, sacrilege, and criticizing the doctrine of the Trinity. See Articles, Lawes, and Orders, Divine, Politic, and Martiall for the Colony in Virginia (1610–1611), reprinted in Wilson & Drakeman, supra note 1, at 11–12; Levy, supra note 1, at 3. I discuss the Thirty-nine Articles and the Book of Common Prayer in chapter 5.

6. See Ahlstrom, supra note 1, at 105–06, 135–39; Emerson, supra note 1, at 33; Marty, supra note 1, at 11–12.

7. Agreement Between the Settlers at New Plymouth (1620), reprinted in 2 Poore, supra note 1, at 931 (emphasis omitted).

8. See Ahlstrom, supra note 1, at 105–06; Emerson, supra note 1, at 17, 33, 37. For an extensive discussion of the differences between Separatist and Non-Separatist Congregationalists, see Miller, Orthodoxy, supra note 1, at 53–101.

9. Kai Erikson writes: "By virtue of one long sea voyage, the New England Puritans had been transformed from an opposition party into a ruling elite." Erikson, supra note 1, at 72; see Miller, Orthodoxy, supra note 1, at 172–86; Walker, supra note 1, at 166–67.

10. Miller, Orthodoxy, supra note 1, at 149.

11. Emerson, supra note 1, at 49; see, e.g., Covenant of the Charlestown-Boston Church (1630), reprinted in Walker, supra note 1, at 131.

12. John Cotton stated: "[It is] by the light of nature that all civil relations are founded in covenant." Emerson, supra note 1, at 49 (quoting John Cotton).

13. Id. at 35 (quoting John Winthrop); see id. at 47–50. For many other examples of similar conversion experiences, see Thomas Shepard's Confessions, 58 Publications of the Colonial Society of Massachusetts (George Selement & Bruce C. Woolley eds., 1981) [hereinafter Confessions].

14. Introduction, in Confessions, supra note 13, at 1, 2.

15. Erikson, supra note 1, at 40; Miller, Errand, supra note 1, at 147.

16. Introduction, in Confessions, supra note 13, at 15.

17. See Emerson, supra note 1, at 49–51, 67; Erikson, supra note 1, at 60; Miller, Errand, supra note 1, at 147; Vaughan, supra note 1, at 92–93.

18. Erikson, supra note 1, at 48.

19. Emerson, supra note 1, at 51 (quoting John Cotton).

20. See Erikson, supra note 1, at 61; Hall, supra note 1, at 463.

21. Miller, Orthodoxy, supra note 1, at 148 (quoting Richard Mather).

22. See id. at 148–49.

23. For example, Perry Miller notes that "discipline was unobtrusively set up and started on its career" by a "barrage of . . . pulpit oratory." Miller, Orthodoxy, supra note 1, at 149; see id. at 166–85; see also Erikson, supra note 1, at 61; see, e.g., The Records of the First Church in Boston, 1630–1868, 39 Publications of the Colonial Society of Massachusetts (1961) (includes records of church memberships, discipline, and dismissals).

24. Curry, supra note 1, at 6 (quoting John Winthrop, 2 The History of New England from 1630–1649, at 229–30 (James Savage ed., Boston 1825, New York reprint ed. 1972)).

25. In American jurisprudence, Mark DeWolfe Howe introduced the notion of de facto establishment. See Howe, supra note 1, at 11.

26. Erikson, supra note 1, at 73.

27. The Body of Liberties of the Massachusetts Collonie in New England (1641), reprinted in 5 The Founders' Constitution 46, 47 (Philip B. Kurland & Ralph Lerner eds., 1987).

28. See The Laws and Liberties of Massachusetts 9, 18–20 (Harvard University Press 1929) (reprint of the 1648 edition). For discussions of the development of civil law supporting Puritanism, see Erikson, supra note 1, at 62; Miller, Orthodoxy, supra note 1, at 233–34.

29. I quote this passage as modified by Sydney Ahlstrom to facilitate comprehension. Ahlstrom, supra note 1, at 146 (quoting John Winthrop, A Modell of Christian Charity, reprinted in Miller & Johnson, supra note 1, at 195–99).

30. See Ahlstrom, supra note 1, at 114–16; Emerson, supra note 1, at 32–35.

31. Ahlstrom, supra note 1, at 117 (quoting A Plain Path-Way to Plantations (1624), quoted in Louis B. Wright, Religion and Empire: The Alliance Between Piety and Commerce in English Expansion, 1558–1625, at 149 (1943)).

32. John Winthrop, A Modell of Christian Charity (1630), reprinted in Miller & Johnson, supra note 1, at 195, 199. Compare Jaher, supra note 1, at 92 (emphasizing this element of New England Puritan thought) with Emerson, supra note 1, at 45 (suggesting that at first, the New England Puritans did not think of themselves as the new Israel, though this idea soon emerged).

33. Ahlstrom, supra note 1, at 149 (quoting Urian Oakes, New England Pleaded With 49 (1673)).

34. Miller, Errand, supra note 1, at 145; see id. at 143–45.

35. See Arthur Hertzberg, The Jews in America 33 (1989); Jaher, supra note 1, at 92; Jacob R. Marcus, The Colonial American Jew, 1492–1776, at 297–305, 412–26 (1970) (all citations in this chapter are from the first volume of this three-volume set); Howard M. Sachar, A History of the Jews in America 18 (1992). In 1740, Great Britain enacted a law that allowed Jews to be naturalized in the American colonies. Before that time, however, some colonies had taken initiatives to allow Jewish naturalization. See An Act for Naturalizing Such Foreign Protestants, and Others Therein Mentioned, As Are Settled or Shall Settle, in any of His Majesty's Colonies in America (1740), reprinted in A Documentary History of the Jews in the United States, 1654–1875, at 26 (Morris U. Schappes ed., 1950) [hereinafter Schappes].

36. Nathaniel Ward, The Simple Cobler of Aggawam (printed in 1647 but written in 1645), reprinted in Miller & Johnson, supra note 1, at 226, 227.

37. Miller, Errand, supra note 1,. at 144–45; accord Emerson, supra note 1, at 38. In 1681, Samuel Willard, a minister in Boston, wrote in response to Anabaptists who claimed that the Massachusetts Bay Colony should be committed to toleration: "I perceive they are mistaken in the design of our first Planters, whose business was not Toleration; but were professed Enemies of it, and could leave the World professing they died no Libertines. Their business was to settle, and (as much as in them lay) secure Religion to Posterity, according to that way which they believed was of God." Miller, Errand, supra note 1, at 145 (quoting Samuel Willard) (emphasis omitted).

38. See The Cambridge Platform (1648), reprinted in Walker, supra note 1, at 194–95 (excepting some sections on "church-discipline" in chapters XXV, XXX, and XXXI of the Westminster Confession); see Walker, supra note 1, at 182–85 (on the Cambridge synod's adoption of the Confession); see also Emerson, supra note 1, at 47, 79–82.

39. The Westminster Confession of Faith, at ch. VI, VII, XVI, XIX (1647), reprinted in Schaff, supra note 1, at 600, 615, 617–18, 634–35, 641; see id. at ch. XI, XIV, XVIII, XX, reprinted in Schaff, supra note 1, at 626, 630–31, 637–40, 643–45; cf. id. at ch. XIX, reprinted in Schaff, supra note 1, at 641 (Old Testament "prefiguring Christ"); id. at ch. XX, reprinted in Schaff, supra note 1, at 643–44 (on the superiority of the New Testament to the Jewish laws); id. at ch. XXXIII, reprinted in Schaff, supra note 1, at 671–73 (on the day of the last judgment, all persons "shall appear before the tribunal of Christ").

40. See The Cambridge Platform (1648), reprinted in Walker, supra note 1, at 203–17. Williston Walker writes: "[The Cambridge Platform] affirms the permanent principles of Congregationalism with . . . clearness and insistence. The autonomy of the local church, the dependence of the churches upon one another for counsel, the representative character of the ministry, are all plainly taught and have given to the Platform a lasting value and influence." Walker, supra note 1, at 186.

41. I quoted this passage from a slightly edited version in 1 Commager, supra note 1; see The Cambridge Platform (1648), reprinted in 1 Commager, supra note 1, at 29. For Walker's presentation of the unedited version, see The Cambridge Platform (1648), reprinted in Walker, supra note 1, at 235–37.

42. Janice Knight argues that the Massachusetts Bay Puritans were not dominated by a single univocal orthodoxy. That is, disagreement occurred not just at the margins but also at the center. Janice Knight, Orthodoxies in Massachusetts: Rereading American Puritanism (1994).

43. Erikson, supra note 1, at 86 (emphasis added); see id. at 71–107.

44. Id. at 93 (quoting John Winthrop) (emphasis added).

45. See Ahlstrom, supra note 1, at 166; Miller, Roger Williams, supra note 1, at 19–20; Polishook, supra note 1, at 4–18; The Puritans in America: A Narrative Anthology 196–99 (Alan Heimert & Andrew Delbanco eds., 1985); Hall, supra note 1, at 465–69. The records of the land purchase are contained in 1 Records of the Colony of Rhode Island and Providence Plantations, in New England, 1636–1663 (for 1637–1638), at 18–20 (John Russell Bartlett ed., A. Crawford Greene and Brothers, State Printers 1856) [hereinafter Records]. Some of the early Providence settlers signed a covenant in 1636 that limited the state to dealing only with civil (not religious) matters:

> We whose names are hereunder, desirous to inhabit in the town of Providence, do promise to subject ourselves in active and passive obedience to all such orders or agreements as shall be made for public good of the body in an orderly way, by the major consent of the present inhabitants, masters of families—incorporated together in a Towne fellowship, and others whom they shall admit unto them only in civil things.

Id. at 14 (Aug. 20, 1636).

46. Roger Williams, The Bloudy Tenent of Persecution, for Cause of Conscience, Discussed (1644), in 3 The Complete Writings of Roger Williams (1963); see Ahlstrom, supra note 1, at 168; Miller, Roger Williams, supra note 1, at 101; Polishook, supra note 1, at 19–23; Hall, supra note 1, at 469–73.

47. Mark DeWolfe Howe wrote in 1965 the seminal work regarding Williams's importance to the religion clauses of the first amendment, The Garden and the Wilderness. See Howe, supra note 1.

48. Locke, however, apparently did not directly follow Williams. See Hall, supra note 1, at 488–89.

49. See Williams, supra note 46, at 73 (emphasizing how a city should operate independently of religious sects).

50. For example, Williams wrote: "All Civill States with their Officers of justice ... are proved essentially Civill, and therefore not Judges, Governours or Defendours of the Spirituall or Christian State and Worship." Id. at 3 (emphasis omitted).

51. Williams wrote:

> True it is, the Sword may make ... a whole Nation of Hypocrites: But to recover a Soule from Sathan by repentance, and to bring them from Antichristian doctrine or worship, to the doctrine or worship Christ, in the least true internall or externall submission, that only works the All-powerfull God, by the Sword of the Spirit in the hand of his Spirituall officers.

Id. at 136 (emphasis omitted).

52. Records, supra note 45, at 16 (May 21, 1637). In 1637, thirty-seven families agreed "to hould forth liberty of Conscience." Id. at 28 (1637); see Winnifred Fallers Sullivan, Paying the Words Extra: Religious Discourse in the Supreme Court of the United States 74 (1994).

53. Williams, supra note 46, at 3 (emphasis omitted).

54. Williams wrote: "God requireth not an uniformity of Religion to be inacted and inforced in any civill State; which inforced uniformity (sooner or later) is the greatest occasion of civill Warre, ravishing of conscience, persecution of Christ Jesus in his servants, and of the hypocrisie and destruction of millions of souls." Id. at 3–4 (emphasis omitted).

55. Id. at 4, 124–25 (emphasis omitted).

56. Hertzberg, supra note 35, at 38; see Howe, supra note 1, at 11 (on de facto establishment in early America); Jaher, supra note 1, at 92; Peter Toon, Preface, in Puritans, the Millennium and the Future of Israel: Puritan Eschatology 1600 to 1660, at 6, 6–7 (Peter Toon ed., 1970) (on the Puritan beliefs about the millennium). Although the Massachusetts Bay Puritans were intolerant of Jews, they believed firmly in the importance of Jewish conversion. In the 1690s, in fact, Cotton Mather declared that the "conversion of the Jewish nation" was his primary task. Hertzberg, supra note 35, at 41 (quoting Cotton Mather).

57. Hertzberg, supra note 35, at 38 (quoting Roger Williams).

58. Sachar, supra note 35, at 18; see Hertzberg, supra note 35, at 39.

59. See Cohen, supra note 1, at 17–18; McConnell, supra note 1, at 1425.

60. Jaher, supra note 1, at 93–94 (quoting Roger Williams).

61. See generally Duncan Kennedy, Toward an Historical Understanding of Legal Consciousness: The Case of Classical Legal Thought in America, 1850–1940, 3 Research in Law & Sociology 3 (1980) (on the imagery of bounded spheres in American legal thought).

62. Roger Williams, Mr. Cottons Letter Lately Printed, Examined and Answered (1644), reprinted in Miller, Roger Williams, supra note 1, at 89, 98; cf. Howe, supra note 1, at 6 (Williams sought to erect a wall of separation to protect religion); Hall, supra note 1, at 481–82 (disagreeing with Howe, Hall argues that Williams sought to protect both religion and the state).

63. See Cohen, supra note 1, at 16, 18; Jaher, supra note 1, at 94, 109–10; cf. Cohen, supra note 1, at 16–17 (on antisemitism against a "mythical Jew"). Marcus and Sachar both note that other isolated Jews preceded this group in New Netherlands. See Marcus, supra note 35, at 215–16; Sachar, supra note 35, at 13.

64. Peter Stuyvesant, Petition to Expel the Jews from New Amsterdam (1654), reprinted in The Jew in the Modern World: A Documentary History 357 (Paul R. Mendes-Flohr & Jehuda Reinharz eds., 1980).

65. See Dutch West India Company, Reply to Stuyvesant's Petition (1655), reprinted in The Jew in the Modern World: A Documentary History 358 (Paul R. Mendes-Flohr & Jehuda Reinharz eds., 1980); Sachar, supra note 35, at 14. Marcus notes that although very few Jews were stockholders in the Company, the Company was nearly bankrupt and needed all of the support and good will that it could muster. Marcus, supra note 35, at 220. In subsequent correspondence, though, the Company referred to Judaism as an "abominable religion." Dutch West India Company, Rights of the Jews of New Amsterdam (1656), reprinted in The Jew in the Modern World: A Documentary History 358, 359 (Paul R. Mendes-Flohr & Jehuda Reinharz eds., 1980).

Jews in New Netherland faced additional difficulties. For example, the sale of a house from a Christian to a Jew was disallowed "for pregnant reasons." See Petition to Keep a House Bought at Auction (Dec. 17, 1655) (denied, Dec. 23, 1655), reprinted in Schappes, supra note 35, at 8, 9. Conditions improved slightly when the English took control of New York in 1664, but by that time, almost all of the original Jewish settlers had left. See Paul Johnson, A History of the Jews 278–79 (1987); Sachar, supra note 35, at 15–17.

66. Cohen, supra note 1, at 3; see id. at 18; Jaher, supra note 1, at 96; Marcus, supra note 35, at 229–30.

67. See The Fundamental Constitutions of Carolina (1669), reprinted in 2 Poore, supra note 1, at 1397, 1406 [hereinafter Fundamental Constitutions]; Cohen, supra note 1, at 17.

68. Fundamental Constitutions, supra note 67, at 1406–07. I must note that for Locke to seek to advise Jews of "the peaceableness and inoffensiveness" of Christians seems a cruel joke after the centuries of antisemitic persecution, both before and after the Reformation.

69. See Ahlstrom, supra note 1, at 109.

70. Maryland Toleration Act (Apr. 21, 1649), reprinted in 1 Commager, supra note 1, at 31, 31.

71. See The Indictment of Dr. Jacob Lumbrozo in Maryland (Feb. 23, 1658), reprinted in Schappes, supra note 35, at 13; Cohen, supra note 1, at 16; Jaher, supra note 1, at 88; Marcus, supra note 35, at 449–50; Sachar, supra note 35, at 19.

72. Butler, supra note 1, at 38; see Miller, New England Mind, supra note 1, at 15; Vaughan, supra note 1, at 298.

73. See Butler, supra note 1, at 62–63. Not all historians agree that New England Puritanism went through a period of decline. See Vaughan, supra note 1, at 297.

74. Miller, New England Mind, supra note 1, at 95; see Emerson, supra note 1, at 85–88. Jon Butler writes:

> The Half-Way Covenant of 1662 confirmed new, complex, and incomplete church membership patterns. Some residents were "full" church members who had "owned the covenant" by testifying to God's work in their lives; some were baptized adults who had not yet owned the covenant and therefore were "half-way" members; and some were unbaptized sons and daughters of the baptized "half-way" members.

Butler, supra note 1, at 60.

75. Ahlstrom, supra note 1, at 124; see id. at 124 n.1.

76. Jaher, supra note 1, at 107 (quoting Johannes Wollebious, The Abridgement of Christian Divinitie 24, 59, 231 (Alexander Ross trans., 2d ed. London: John Saywell 1656)).

77. Miller, Errand, supra note 1, at 151.

78. See id.; Miller & Johnson, supra note 1, at 193–94.

79. John Wise, Vindication of the Government of New-England Churches (1717), reprinted in Miller & Johnson, supra note 1, at 257, 258–60, 263–64, 269; see id. at 265–69. Wise wrote:

> That it seems to me as though Wise and Provident Nature by the Dictates of Right
> Reason excited by the moving Suggestions of Humanity; and awed with the just demands
> of Natural Libertie, Equity, Equality, and Principles of Self-Preservation, Originally drew
> up the Scheme [of civil government], and then obtained the Royal Approbation.

Id. at 257.

80. See Butler, supra note 1, at 98–128.

81. Curry, supra note 1, at 58; see Miller, Errand, supra note 1, at 145.

82. Butler, supra note 1, at 128; see id. at 101–06. The Anglican Church was established in Maryland, Georgia, and the Carolinas, as well as in Virginia. See id. at 99–102; Curry, supra note 1, at 58; Levy, supra note 1, at 5.

83. See Curry, supra note 1, at 197–98, 208–20; cf. Levy, supra note 1, at 6–10 (the multiple establishment was a distinctly American phenomenon).

84. See Curry, supra note 1, at 62–63; Levy, supra note 1, at 9–11. Leonard Levy traces in some detail the evolution of the multiple establishment in New York. See Levy, supra note 1, at 10–15 (in towns with a heterogeneous religious population, several different established Protestant churches were likely to exist, each supported by the taxes of its own communicants).

85. Levy, supra note 1, at 15 (quoting the act of the General Court). This act did contain exceptions; Boston, for example, was outside the scope of its coverage. See id. The Charter of Massachusetts Bay of 1691 provided that "there shall be a liberty of Conscience allowed in the Worshipp of God to all Christians (Except Papists)." The Charter of Massachusetts Bay (1691), reprinted in 1 Poore, supra note 1, at 942, 950; see Butler, supra note 1, at 105–06; Levy, supra note 1, at 15.

86. Emerson, supra note 1, at 87; see Miller, Errand, supra note 1, at 145 (on the death of New England Puritanism).

87. See Wilson & Drakeman, supra note 1, at 32–33.

88. Frame of Government of Pennsylvania (1682), reprinted in 2 Poore, supra note 1, at 1518, 1526. The colonies that did not have an official establishment were Rhode Island, Pennsylvania, Delaware, and New Jersey. See Curry, supra note 1, at 72, 76, 106.

89. See Pfeffer, supra note 1, at 78–80. Pfeffer argues that the same held true in other proprietary colonies such as Maryland.

90. See Curry, supra note 1, at 78–79, 83.

91. See Butler, supra note 1, at 164–65. Butler notes that the term "Great Awakening," referring to the 1730s and 1740s, was coined only in the 1840s. Id.

92. Bushman, supra note 1, at xii.

93. See Curry, supra note 1, at 95–96. Bushman writes that the thrust of the Great Awakening was "to strengthen traditional Calvinism and to tailor it to evangelistic purposes." Bushman, supra note 1, at xiv.

94. Jonathan Edwards, Sinners in the Hands of an Angry God, reprinted in Faust & Johnson, supra note 1, at 155; George Whitefield, Marriage of Cana (1742), reprinted in Bushman, supra note 1, at 33, 34; see Nathan Cole, The Spiritual Travels of Nathan Cole, reprinted in Bushman, supra note 1, at 67, 67–69; Jonathan Dickinson, True Scripture-Doctrine, reprinted in Bushman, supra note 1, at 77, 77–78; see also Miller, Errand, supra note 1, at 155.

95. Whitefield, supra note 94, at 34–35 (emphasis in the original); see Dickinson, supra note 94, at 81–82; cf. Jonathan Edwards, Freedom of the Will, reprinted in Faust & Johnson, supra note 1, at 263 (rejecting the Arminian notion of human free will); see also McLoughlin, supra note 1, at 73–74.

96. Hudson & Corrigan, supra note 1, at 80.

97. McLoughlin, supra note 1, at 80. McLoughlin writes: "The central feature of the great revivals of the 1730s and 1740s was the experience of individual conversion." Id. at 79.

98. Dickinson, supra note 94, at 82 (emphasis omitted); see id. at 81–82; Bushman, supra note 94, at 67. One person described his conversion experience as follows:

> God appeared unto me and made me Skringe: before whose face the heavens and the
> earth fled away; and I was Shrinked into nothing; I knew not whether I was in the body
> or out, I seemed to hang in open Air before God, and he seemed to Speak to me in an
> angry and Sovereign way what won't you trust your Soul with God; My heart answered
> O yes, yes, yes; before I could stir my tongue or lips.... When God appeared to me

every thing vanished and was gone in the twinkling of an Eye, as quick as A flash of light-ning; But when God disappeared or in some measure withdrew, every thing was in its place again and I was on my Bed. My heart was broken; my burden was fallen of my mind; I was set free, my distress was gone, and I was filled with pineing desire to see Christs own words in the bible.

Cole, supra note 94, at 69–70. This particular conversion experience was somewhat atypical because it was largely private and included a vision of God. See Bushman, supra note 1, at 66–67.

99. See A Report on Whitefield in New York, in The New England Weekly Journal (Dec. 4, 1739), reprinted in Bushman, supra note 94, at 22, 22–23.

100. See McLoughlin, supra note 1, at 91; Stout, supra note 1, at 525–27.

101. Miller, Errand, supra note 1, at 156; cf. Richard Tarnas, The Passion of the Western Mind 302 (1991) (can explain the frequent outbursts of intense Christian revivals as reactions to the abstract, mechanistic scientism of modernity). But Hudson and Corrigan emphasize that the Great Awakening ultimately touched "every class—rich and poor, educated and uneducated." Hudson & Corrigan, supra note 1, at 69. On landowning, see Gordon S. Wood, The Creation of the American Republic, 1776–1787, at 100 (1969) ("'the people of America, are a people of property; almost every man is a freeholder'").

102. See Miller, Errand, supra note 1, at 160. Hudson and Corrigan note, however, that the requirement of any conversion experience at all for church membership could be more burdensome than the approach of the Half-Way Covenant. See Hudson & Corrigan, supra note 1, at 75.

103. Curry, supra note 1, at 96; see id. at 99.

104. Id. at 97 (quoting a pamphlet published anonymously but written by Elisha Williams, a Congregationalist minister and former president of Yale). To be clear, this focus on the individual experience of Scripture did not mean that each person could interpret the Bible idiosyncratically. Rather, each person could personally and directly experience the literal meaning of Scripture.

105. See Ahlstrom, supra note 1, at 170–76, 292–93; Hudson & Corrigan, supra note 1, at 18–19, 45–46, 75; McLoughlin, supra note 1, at 91; cf. Miller, Errand, supra note 1, at 161–62 (early New England Puritans were not democratic).

106. Curry, supra note 1, at 96. Jon Butler writes: "A striking pluralism of Christian expression soon supplemented the state churches of eighteenth-century America." Butler, supra note 1, at 174. Robert T. Handy argues that while the Great Awakening tended to benefit some established churches, especially in New England, overall the increase in denominations weakened the establishments. Handy, supra note 1, at 17–19. Bernard Bailyn argues that the Great Awakening weakened already weak establishments. Bernard Bailyn, The Ideological Origins of the American Revolution 249–50 (1967).

107. See Curry, supra note 1, at 103; cf. Hudson & Corrigan, supra note 1, at 28–59 (on the diversity of denominations).

108. Faust & Johnson, supra note 1, at xciii (quoting Edwards, Decrees and Elections).

109. See Faust & Johnson, supra note 1, at xciii–xcvi; Hudson & Corrigan, supra note 1, at 80–81. For Edwards's extensive defense of the doctrine of original sin, see Jonathan Edwards, Doctrine of Original Sin Defended (1758), reprinted in 3 The Works of Jonathan Edwards (1970) [hereinafter Edwards, Original Sin].

110. See Ahlstrom, supra note 1, at 288–89, 326; Hudson & Corrigan, supra note 1, at 71, 81, 122–26, 138; Anson Phelps Stokes, 1 Church and State in the United States 149, 723 (1950). McLoughlin writes:

God . . . was speaking to individuals directly. He was expressing directly his personal con-cern with each and every person as an individual, not as a member of a community or a church or a parish but as a man who was wholly responsible for his own salvation and who would have no one to blame but himself if he did not answer God's call and obey his commands.

McLoughlin, supra note 1, at 83.

111. Experience Mayhew, Grace Defended (1744), reprinted in Bushman, supra note 1, at 136, 137, 143 (emphasis omitted).

112. Clyde A. Holbrook, Introduction, in Jonathan Edwards, Doctrine of Original Sin Defended (1758), reprinted in 3 The Works of Jonathan Edwards 1, 8 (1970); see Hudson & Corrigan, supra note 1, at 81.

113. Miller, Errand, supra note 1, at 164 (quoting Jonathan Edwards's funeral sermon for John Stoddard in 1648, except for the last quoted phrase, which is in Perry Miller's and not Jonathan Edwards's words) (emphasis omitted).

114. Id. at 164–65 (these words are again quoted from Jonathan Edwards) (emphasis omitted). Only after articulating these practical political points did Edwards add that a ruler should be pious. See id. at 165–66.

115. Jonathan Mayhew, A Discourse Concerning Unlimited Submission (Jan. 30, 1750), reprinted in Miller & Johnson, supra note 1, at 277, 279–80 & n.*. Mayhew wrote:

> [N]o civil rulers are to be obeyed when they enjoin things that are inconsistent with the commands of God: All such disobedience is lawful and glorious; particularly, if persons refuse to comply with any legal establishment of religion, because it is a gross perversion and corruption (as to doctrine, worship and discipline) of a pure and divine religion, brought from heaven to earth by the Son of God, (the only King and Head of the christian church) and propagated through the world by his inspired apostles. All commands running counter to the declared will of the supreme legislator of heaven and earth, are null and void: And therefore disobedience to them is a duty, not a crime.

Id. at 279 n.* (emphasis in the original). For a discussion of Mayhew's radical views in relation to traditional Calvinism, see Curry, supra note 1, at 100–01. For another but earlier argument for a right of resistance, see John Barnard, The Throne Established by Righteousness, reprinted in Miller & Johnson, supra note 1, at 270.

116. Hudson & Corrigan, supra note 1, at 82 (quoting L.J. Trinterud, The Forming of an American Tradition 197 (1949)); see Ahlstrom, supra note 1, at 293–94.

117. Handy, supra note 1, at 19; see Hudson & Corrigan, supra note 1, at 83, 111.

118. Gilbert Tennent, The Danger of an Unconverted Ministry (1740), reprinted in Bushman, supra note 1, at 87, 88. Similarly, Whitefield used the term "Self-righteous Pharisees" as an appellation of contempt. Whitefield, supra note 94, at 33.

119. Joseph Bellamy, True Religion Delineated (1750), reprinted in Bushman, supra note 1, at 144, 149.

120. Edwards, Original Sin, supra note 109, at 182. For some other antisemitic passages from Edwards (and others), see Jaher, supra note 1, at 108; see, e.g., Dickinson, supra note 94, at 79 ("Israel doth not know") (emphasis omitted).

121. Cohen, supra note 1, at 15–16; see Jaher, supra note 1, at 99–12; Cohen, supra note 1, at 18.

122. Hudson & Corrigan, supra note 1, at 26.

123. Curry, supra note 1, at 124; see Leonard Dinnerstein, Antisemitism in America 10–11 (1994).

NOTES TO CHAPTER 7

1. Gordon S. Wood, The Creation of the American Republic, 1776–1787, at 75 (1969) [hereinafter Wood, Creation]; see id. at 28–29. Other sources that are helpful in understanding the era of the American Revolution and the constitutional framing are as follows: Sydney E. Ahlstrom, A Religious History of the American People (1972); Bernard Bailyn, The Ideological Origins of the American Revolution (1967); Morton Borden, Jews, Turks, and Infidels (1984); Jon Butler, Awash in a Sea of Faith: Christianizing the American People (1990); Naomi W. Cohen, Jews in Christian America: The Pursuit of Religious Equality (1992); Thomas J. Curry, The First Freedoms: Church and State in America to the Passage of the First Amendment (1986); Robert T. Handy, A Christian America (2d ed. 1984); Louis Hartz, The Liberal Tradition in America (1955); Winthrop S. Hudson & John Corrigan, Religion in America (5th ed. 1992); Frederic Cople Jaher, A Scapegoat in the New Wilderness: The Origins and Rise of Anti-Semitism in America (1994); Leonard W. Levy, The Establishment Clause: Religion and the First Amendment (1986); Martin E. Marty, Protestantism in the United States: Righteous Empire (2d ed. 1986); Forrest McDonald, Novus Ordo Seclorum (1985); Edmund S. Morgan, Birth of the Republic, 1763–1789 (rev. ed. 1977) [hereinafter Morgan, Birth]; Edmund S.

Morgan, Inventing the People (1988) [hereinafter Morgan, Inventing]; Leo Pfeffer, Church, State, and Freedom (1953); J.G.A. Pocock, The Machiavellian Moment (1975); Howard M. Sachar, A History of the Jews in America (1992); Gordon S. Wood, The Radicalism of the American Revolution (1991) [hereinafter Wood, Radicalism]; Harold J. Berman, Religion and Law: The First Amendment in Historical Perspective, 35 Emory L.J. 777 (1986); Timothy L. Hall, Roger Williams and the Foundations of Religious Liberty, 71 B.U. L. Rev. 455 (1991); Michael W. McConnell, The Origins and Historical Understanding of Free Exercise of Religion, 103 Harv. L. Rev. 1409 (1990); Frank Michelman, Foreword: Traces of Self-Government, 100 Harv. L. Rev. 4 (1986); Harry S. Stout, Religion, Communications, and the Ideological Origins of the American Revolution, 34 Wm. & Mary Q. 519 (1977); Documents of American History (Henry Steele Commager ed., 3d ed. 1947) (in 2 volumes) [hereinafter 1 Commager and 2 Commager]; 5 The Founders' Constitution (Philip B. Kurland & Ralph Lerner eds., 1987) [hereinafter Kurland]; The Federal and State Constitutions, Colonial Charters, and other Organic Laws of the United States (Ben Perley Poore ed., 2d ed. 1924) (in 2 volumes) [hereinafter 1 Poore and 2 Poore]; A Documentary History of the Jews in the United States, 1654–1875 (Morris U. Schappes ed., 1950) [hereinafter Schappes]; Church and State in American History (John F. Wilson & Donald L. Drakeman eds., 2d ed. 1987) [hereinafter Wilson & Drakeman].

2. Wood, Creation, supra note 1, at 75. Pauline Maier argues that the arrogance of British officials added an "emotional element" to a revolution that was "otherwise carried on in the language of law and right." Pauline Maier, Popular Uprisings and Civil Authority in Eighteenth-Century America, in American Law and the Constitutional Order 69, 75 (Lawrence Friedman & Harry Scheiber eds., 1978).

3. Wilson & Drakeman, supra note 1, at 52; see Curry, supra note 1, at 109–12 (on Massachusetts in the early eighteenth century); Levy, supra note 1, at 10–15 (on New York from the late seventeenth through the mid-eighteenth century); see also Ahlstrom, supra note 1, at 361–62. Thomas Curry writes: "Massachusetts and Connecticut . . . together with New York, the colonies that experienced the sharpest controversies between Anglicans and non-Anglicans, produced the most discussion of 'establishment' in its American context. Elsewhere, frequent use of the term went unaccompanied by argument as to its definition." Curry, supra note 1, at 106.

4. General historical information on the Revolutionary period can be found in the following sources: Stephan Thernstrom, 1 A History of the American People 149–207 (2d ed. 1989); Howard Zinn, A People's History of the United States 59–75 (1980).

5. The Intolerable Acts (1774), reprinted in 1 Commager, supra note 1, at 71–76; see The Boston Port Act (Mar. 31, 1774), reprinted in 1 Commager, supra note 1, at 71; Massachusetts Government Act (May 20, 1774), reprinted in 1 Commager, supra note 1, at 72; The Quebec Act (June 22, 1774), reprinted in 1 Commager, supra note 1, at 74–75; cf. Levy, supra note 1, at 7 (on the Quebec Act). The Administration of Justice Act allowed criminal trials to be transferred from Massachusetts to Great Britain. Administration of Justice Act (May 20, 1774), reprinted in 1 Commager, supra note 1, at 73. See generally Morgan, Birth, supra note 1, at 58–59 (discussing the Coercive Acts).

6. Declaration and Resolves of the First Continental Congress (Oct. 14, 1774), reprinted in 1 Commager, supra note 1, at 82, 82–84.

7. Declaration of the Causes and Necessity of Taking Up Arms (July 6, 1775), reprinted in 1 Commager, supra note 1, at 92, 92–93 (emphasis added).

8. As mentioned in the previous chapter, the colonists did not themselves use the term "multiple establishment." See Curry, supra note 1, at 210.

9. Isaac Backus, A History of New England (1774–1775), reprinted in Kurland, supra note 1, at 65, 65. Backus stated that Baptists, "as a distinct denomination of Protestants [had] long been denied the free and full enjoyment of those rights, as to the support of religious worship." Id. With regard to his refusal to pay taxes to support a church, Backus wrote: "I cannot give in the certificates they require without implicitly acknowledging that power in man which I believe belongs only to God." Backus, supra note 9, at 65; see Hall, supra note 1, at 488–89; McConnell, supra note 1, at 1431; David C. Williams & Susan H. Williams, Volitionalism and Religious Liberty, 76 Cornell L. Rev. 769, 873 (1991).

10. Backus, supra note 9, at 65 (quoting John Adams). Adams stated: "[W]e might as well expect a change in the solar system, as to expect they would give up their establishment." Id. (quoting John Adams); see Curry, supra note 1, at 133.

11. John Adams, Novanglus, No. 4 (Feb. 13, 1775), reprinted in Kurland, supra note 1, at 66.

12. Curry, supra note 1, at 132.

13. Robert T. Handy, The Magna Charta of Religious Freedom in America, in Wilson & Drakeman, supra note 1, at 85, 89 [hereinafter Handy, Magna Charta].

14. See The Declaration of Independence (July 4, 1776), reprinted in 1 Commager, supra note 1, at 100. I do not mean to suggest that the Revolution itself was conservative, but rather that, at its outset, the elite leaders justified their actions in largely conservative (and rational) terms. See Wood, Radicalism, supra note 1, at 4–8 (summarizing how the Revolution was radical, not conservative, in terms of social change). In the words of Edmund Randolph, the Revolution was "'the result of reason.'" Wood, Creation, supra note 1, at 4.

15. See Bailyn, supra note 1, at 22–54; Michelman, supra note 1, at 47–55; cf. Bailyn, supra note 1, at 26–30 (Americans on both sides of the dispute would loosely cite many different Enlightenment thinkers).

16. See Nathan O. Hatch, The Democratization of American Christianity 221 (1989); Ellis Sandoz, A Government of Laws: Political Theory, Religion, and the American Founding 99–101, 110–13, 134–36 (1990); William G. McLoughlin, 'Enthusiasm for Liberty': The Great Awakening as the Key to the Revolution, 87 Proceedings of the Am. Antiquarian Soc. 69, 70–73, 77–78, 93–94 (1977); cf. Hudson & Corrigan, supra note 1, at 92, 131–32 (some elite leaders were deists, but the dominant religious influence of the framers' generation was Puritanism recast by evangelicalism); Pfeffer, supra note 1, at 106–09 (discussing the Continental Congress); Wood, Radicalism, supra note 1, at 329–30 (Protestantism was "a major adhesive force for ordinary Americans," but many founding fathers disdained traditional Christianity).

17. See Bailyn, supra note 1, at 94–95; Thernstrom, supra note 4, at 172–73.

18. Backus, supra note 9, at 65 (quoting John Adams).

19. Curry, supra note 1, at 174 (quoting various sermons from that period).

20. See Hudson & Corrigan, supra note 1, at 99. The colonies that clearly had Anglican establishments were Virginia, North Carolina, South Carolina, Georgia, and Maryland. In New York, there was a long-running dispute over whether there was a multiple establishment or an Anglican establishment. Compare id. (characterizing New York as having an Anglican establishment) with Levy, supra note 1, at 10–15 (a detailed account of the New York dispute). See also Curry, supra note 1, at 161–62 (on the New York dispute).

21. See Constitution of South Carolina (1776), reprinted in 2 Poore, supra note 1, at 1615; Curry, supra note 1, at 148.

22. Butler, supra note 1, at 260 (quoting William Tennent); Levy, supra note 1, at 5 (quoting William Tennent); see Curry, supra note 1, at 150; Levy, supra note 1, at 8.

23 Constitution of South Carolina (1778), reprinted in 2 Poore, supra note 1, at 1620, 1626.

24. Id. The 1778 Constitution also provided that no one "be obliged to pay towards the maintenance and support of a religious worship that he does not freely join in." Id. at 1627.

25. See Butler, supra note 1, at 258–61; Curry, supra note 1, at 134–92. For example, the Maryland Constitution of 1776 provided as follows:

> [A]ll persons, professing the Christian religion, are equally entitled to protection in their religious liberty. . . . [T]he Legislature may, in their discretion, lay a general and equal tax, for the support of the Christian religion; leaving to each individual the power of appointing the payment over of the money, collected from him, to the support of any particular place of worship or minister, or for the benefit of the poor of his own denomination, or the poor in general of any particular county.

Constitution of Maryland (1776), reprinted in 1 Poore, supra note 1, at 817, 819.

26. Rhode Island actually did not adopt a Constitution in the immediate aftermath of the Revolution and thus did not expressly address the question of establishment. See Levy, supra note 1, at 25.

27. Constitution of North Carolina (1776), reprinted in 2 Poore, supra note 1, at 1409, 1410, 1413–14; see Curry, supra note 1, at 151–52.

28. Constitution of New York (1777), reprinted in 2 Poore, supra note 1, at 1328, 1338 (emphasis omitted). Compare Hudson & Corrigan, supra note 1, at 99 (characterizing New York as having an Anglican establishment) with Levy, supra note 1, at 10–15, 26 (detailed account of the New York dispute). See also Curry, supra note 1, at 161–62 (on the New York dispute).

29. Levy notes that some states switched from dual to (broader) multiple establishments. See Levy, supra note 1, at 26.

30. In Everson v. Board of Education, 330 U.S. 1, 8–13 (1947), the Supreme Court relied heavily on the so-called Virginia experience. See also Pfeffer, supra note 1, at 93–102 (emphasizing the transition in Virginia as revolutionary).

31. Curry, supra note 1, at 134.

32. See id. at 135–37; Levy, supra note 1, at 51–52; 56–57; Handy, Magna Charta, supra note 13, at 88.

33. Thomas Jefferson, An Act for Establishing Religious Freedom (1779) (passed in the Assembly of Virginia in 1786), in Social and Political Philosophy 247, 248 (John Somerville & Ronald E. Santoni eds., 1963).

34. Thomas Jefferson, Letter to Danbury Baptist Assocation (Jan. 1, 1802), in Wilson & Drakeman, supra note 1, at 78, 79 [hereinafter Jefferson, Danbury] (Jefferson here stated that the first amendment religion clauses built "a wall of separation between church and State"); see Ahlstrom, supra note 1, at 367–68.

35. See, e.g., Curry, supra note 1, at 137–38.

36. Jefferson, supra note 33, at 248. Likewise, Jefferson wrote:

> [A]ll attempts to influence [the mind] by temporal punishments or burdens, or by civil incapacitations, tend only to beget habits of hypocrisy and meanness, and are a departure from the plan of the Holy Author of our religion, who being Lord both of body and mind, yet chose not to propagate it by coercions on either, as was in his Almighty power to do.

Id. at 247.

37. See McConnell, supra note 1, at 1430–31, 1449–50. While Jefferson often seemed hostile to traditional forms of Christianity, he also was hostile to Judaism. He called Judaism "degrading and injurious" and Jewish ethics "repulsive." Id. at 1450 (quoting Letter from Thomas Jefferson to Dr. Benjamin Rush (Apr. 21, 1803)).

38. Jaher, supra note 1, at 130 (quoting Jefferson's letters).

39. See Levy, supra note 1, at 53–54.

40. James Madison, To the Honorable General Assembly of the Commonwealth of Virginia: A Memorial and Remonstrance (June 20, 1785), in James Madison on Religious Liberty 55, 57 (Robert S. Alley ed., 1985).

41. Id. at 56–59; see Curry, supra note 1, at 142–43; Berman, supra note 1, at 786–87.

42. Roger Williams made this same point, but Madison apparently was not directly influenced by Williams's writing. See Berman, supra note 1, at 787 n.32; Hall, supra note 1, at 488–89.

43. Madison, supra note 40, at 57–59. Madison wrote:

> Compare the number of those who have as yet received [Christianity] with the number still remaining under the dominion of false Religions; and how small is the former! Does the policy of the Bill tend to lessen the disproportion? No; it at once discourages those who are strangers to the light of revelation from coming into the Region of it; and countenances by example the nations who continue in darkness, in shutting out those who might convey it to them. Instead of Levelling as far as possible, every obstacle to the victorious progress of Truth, the Bill with an ignoble and unchristian timidity would circumscribe it with a wall of defence against the encroachments of error.

Id. at 59.

44. Id. at 57–58 (Madison quoted the latter passage from the Virginia Bill of Rights (1776), reprinted in 2 Poore, supra note 1, at 1908, 1909).

45. Levy, supra note 1, at 57 (quoting a Baptist petition from 1785). Another petition stated as follows:

> But religion and all its duties being of divine origin and of a nature wholly distinct from the secular affairs of the public society ought not to be made the object of human legislation.

For the discharge of the duties of religion every man is to account for himself as an individual in a future state and ought not to be under the direction of influence of any human laws.

Id.; cf. McConnell, supra note 1, at 1437–40 (emphasizing the Baptists in the drive for religious freedom in Virginia).

46. Thomas Jefferson, From His "Autobiography," in Social and Political Philosophy 250, 250 (John Somerville & Ronald E. Santoni eds., 1963); see Levy, supra note 1, at 59–60. Jefferson wrote this passage when discussing the enactment of the act and the rejection of an amendment to the preamble that would have added an explicit reference to Jesus Christ. To Jefferson, the overwhelming defeat of this amendment proved the broad scope of protection given by his statute. See Borden, supra note 1, at 14–15.

47. Curry, supra note 1, at 162.

48. See Hudson & Corrigan, supra note 1, at 102; McDonald, supra note 1, at 42–43; James E. Wood, Jr., Introduction: Religion and the Constitution, in The First Freedom: Religion and the Bill of Rights 1, 8–9 (James E. Wood, Jr., ed., 1990). For a discussion of all of the state constitutional restrictions on voting and public officeholding based on religion, see Borden, supra note 1, at 11–15.

49. Constitution of Pennsylvania (1776), reprinted in 2 Poore, supra note 1, at 1540, 1543. For the protection of freedom of conscience and the prohibition on official establishment, see id. at 1541.

50. See Handy, Magna Charta, supra note 13, at 89.

51. Curry, supra note 1, at 148 (quoting a legislative bill). Curry writes that "there can be little doubt that Madison personally disapproved of it; but the fact that he included it in the collection was significant." Id. Why Curry concludes that Madison disapproved of this bill that he introduced is unclear; Curry does not suggest that he is aware that Madison also introduced the 1785 bill imposing a fine on Christian Sabbath breakers.

52. McDonald, supra note 1, at 42.

53. See McConnell, supra note 1, at 1438–40. McConnell writes: "The greatest support for disestablishment and free exercise therefore came from evangelical Protestant denominations, especially Baptists and Quakers, but also Presbyterians, Lutherans, and others." Id. at 1439.

54. By 1789, every state had a constitutional provision protecting religious freedom. See id. at 1455.

55. Jefferson, supra note 33, at 248.

56. After the passage of the act, Madison wrote a letter to Jefferson, stating: "I flatter myself [that] this Country extinguished for ever the ambitious hope of making laws for the human mind." James Madison, Letter to Thomas Jefferson (Jan. 22, 1786), in James Madison on Religious Liberty 61, 62 (Robert S. Alley ed., 1985).

57. After receiving a letter from Madison regarding the passage of the act, Jefferson wrote back to Madison, stating:

In fact, it is comfortable to see the standard of reason at length erected, after so many ages, during which the human mind has been held in vassalage by kings, priests, and nobles; and it is honorable for us, to have produced the first legislature who had the courage to declare, that the reason of man may be trusted with the formation of his own opinions.

Thomas Jefferson, Letter to James Madison (Dec. 16, 1786), in Social and Political Philosophy 249, 250 (John Somerville & Ronald E. Santoni eds., 1963) (emphasis added); cf. Jefferson, Danbury, supra note 34, at 79 ("the legislative powers of government reach actions only, and not opinions").

58. I do not mean to suggest that the act protected only a private realm of conscience, mind, or opinion, as opposed to religious conduct. Yet, the act clearly focused on protecting the conscience, and to the extent that the state legislature contemplated any protection of religious conduct, the legislature obviously would have understood that conduct as arising from Christian practices. Cf. McConnell, supra note 1, at 1451–55 (argues that Jefferson's view was to protect only beliefs, while Madison's view—which was more typical of Americans—was to protect beliefs and conduct).

59. See Bailyn, supra note 1, at 280–301; Morgan, Inventing, supra note 1, at 291; Pocock, supra note 1, at 462–552; Wood, Creation, supra note 1, at 46–90; Michelman, supra 1. In terms of English

civic republican theory, commentators disagree about whether Harringtonian concepts (from the seventeenth century) or neo-Harringtonian Opposition Ideology (from the eighteenth century) had more influence on the Revolutionary-era Americans. While Harringtonian theory tended to emphasize virtuous participation in republican government, Opposition Ideology tended to emphasize the virtuous protection of rights and liberties from governmental encroachment. See Bailyn, supra note 1, at 35–54; Michelman, supra note 1, at 47–55.

60. Wood, Radicalism, supra note 1, at 4–8; see id. at 169–89; see also Morgan, Birth, supra note 1 (arguing that equality was the principle grounding the American Revolution); Morgan, Inventing, supra note 1 (discussing the development of the idea of the sovereignty of the people in England and America). But see Hartz, supra note 1, at 35, 97 (emphasizes the democratic nature of America and suggests that in America, democracy was not revolutionary). Wood argues that the Revolutionary rejection of a natural social hierarchy led to the questioning of slavery. That is, according to Wood, before the Revolution, slavery had seemed noncontroversial, but with the democratic impulse of the early nation, slavery became anomalous. See Wood, Radicalism, supra note 1, at 186–87.

61. Morgan, Birth, supra note 1, at 7; see Bailyn, supra note 1, at 281–82, 300–01; Wood, Creation, supra note 1, at 53–59, 65–66, 93.

62. See Pfeffer, supra note 1, 15 275–90 (discussing the development of public education); Wood, Creation, supra note 1, at 72 (on the importance of public education); Wood, Radicalism, supra note 1, at 190–91 (the Revolutionary generation was preoccupied with education and its relation to virtue).

63. Constitution of Pennsylvania (1776), reprinted in 2 Poore, supra note 1, at 1540, 1547.

64. Constitution of Massachusetts (1780), reprinted in 1 Poore, supra note 1, at 956, 970.

65. Wood, Radicalism, supra note 1, at 329.

66. Wood, Creation, supra note 1, at 427.

67. See McConnell, supra note 1, at 1442. Indeed, Wood elsewhere discusses Chancellor James Kent's opinion in The People of New York v. Ruggles, decided in 1811, as underscoring the lingering connection between Christianity and civic republicanism. As Wood acknowledges, New York did not have an officially established church at this time. My point, then, is that official establishment was not a prerequisite for Americans who believed that Christianity was necessary for civic republican government. See Wood, Radicalism, supra note 1, at 331; see also People v. Ruggles, 8 Johns. R. 290 (N.Y. 1811), reprinted in Kurland, supra note 1, at 101.

68. See Pfeffer, supra note 1, at 110, 115. Thomas Jefferson wrote:

> Our sister States of Pennsylvania and New-York . . . have long situated without any establishment at all. The experiment was new and doubtful when they made it. It has answered beyond conception. They flourish infinitely. Religion is well supported; of various kinds, indeed, but all good enough; all sufficient to preserve peace and order. . . . Let us too give this experiment fair play.

Thomas Jefferson, Notes on the State of Virginia 315–16 (1801), quoted in Berman, supra note 1, at 786 n.30.

69. U.S. Const. art. VI, cl. 3; see Cohen, supra note 1, at 30–31.

70. See Levy, supra note 1, at 66. Some critics of the proposed Constitution undoubtedly used the lack of a Bill of Rights as a convenient excuse for attacking the proposed governmental scheme, even though they had broader and deeper concerns regarding the expanded powers of the national government. See Curry, supra note 1, at 194–95. Besides those sources previously cited in this chapter, the following sources provided helpful information regarding the framing and adoption of the Constitution: The Debates in the Several State Conventions on the Adoption of the Federal Constitution (Jonathan Elliot ed., 1836) [hereinafter Elliot's Debates]; Daniel A. Farber & Suzanna Sherry, A History of the American Constitution (1990) [hereinafter Farber & Sherry]; The Federalist (C. Rossiter ed. 1961); The Complete Anti-Federalist (Herbert J. Storing ed., 1981) [hereinafter Storing].

71. See Herbert J. Storing, What the Anti-Federalists Were For 64–70 (1981).

72. The Federalist No. 84, at 510–15 (Alexander Hamilton) (C. Rossiter ed., 1961).

73. Id. at 513–15.

74. According to the Anti-Federalists, "[t]he right of conscience shall be held inviolable; and neither the legislative, executive nor judicial powers of the United States shall have authority to alter,

abrogate, or infringe any part of the constitution of the several states, which provide for the preservation of liberty in matters of religion." The Address and Reasons of Dissent of the Minority of the Convention of Pennsylvania To Their Constituents (Dec. 18, 1787), in Storing, supra note 70, at 201.

75. The Federalist No. 10, at 82–84 (J. Madison) (C. Rossiter ed. 1961).

76. The Federalist No. 51, at 324–25 (J. Madison) (C. Rossiter ed. 1961). Madison's ideas on factions arose from his observations of the post-Revolutionary state governments, as well as from his reading of David Hume on factions. See Marc M. Arkin, "The Intractable Principle": David Hume, James Madison, Religion, and the Tenth Federalist, 39 Am. J. Legal Hist. 148 (1995); see, e.g., David Hume, Of Parties in General, reprinted in Essays: Moral, Political and Literary 54 (Oxford University Press ed. 1963).

77. 3 Elliot's Debates, supra note 70, at 330 (emphasis added).

78. William Casto, Oliver Ellsworth's Calvinism: A Biographical Essay on Religion and Political Psychology in the Early Republic, 36 J. Church & State 507, 525 (1994) (quoting Ellsworth's committee); see Borden, supra note 1, at 17–20.

79. Marty, supra note 1, at 22; cf. Borden, supra note 1, at 3 (noting the disagreement between historians); Butler, supra note 1, at 223 (Christianity "emerged with renewed vigor in the 1780s"); Marty, supra note 1, at 41–42, 48 (suggesting that the majority of Americans were unchurched).

80. Curry, supra note 1, at 219; see Borden, supra note 1, at 3, 9; cf. Marty, supra note 1, at 41 (America had de facto establishment even though the majority in the new nation were "unchurched").

81. Hudson & Corrigan, supra note 1, at 26; see id. at 112.

82. See Borden, supra note 1, at 58.

83. A Watchman, Letter From a Bostonian (Feb. 4, 1788), in 4 Storing, supra note 70, at 229, 232. Another writer suggested that a Jewish president "might order the rebuilding of Jerusalem." Cohen, supra note 1, at 31.

84. 4 Elliot's Debates, supra note 70, at 192–94. Governor Johnston echoed this view: "I leave it to gentlemen's candor to judge what probability there is of the people's choosing men of different sentiments from themselves." Id. at 199.

85. Id. at 199–200.

86. See Levy, supra note 1, at 66; McConnell, supra note 1, at 1480. Several states ratified the Constitution with a recommendation to add a Bill of Rights. See McConnell, supra note 1, at 1480–81.

87. The Jewish congregation of Newport, Rhode Island, expressed their gratitude for this turn of events to George Washington:

> Deprived as we have hitherto been of the invaluable rights of free citizens, we now (with a deep sense of gratitude to the Almighty Disposer of all events), behold a Government . . . which to bigotry gives no sanction, to persecution no assistance—but generously affording to All liberty of conscience, and immunities of citizenship—deeming every one, of whatever nation, tongue, or language equal parts of the great governmental machine.

From the Newport Congregation to the President of the United States (Aug. 17, 1790), reprinted in Schappes, supra note 1, at 79, 79.

88. See Borden, supra note 1, at 4–6; Sachar, supra note 1, at 32. "At the feast following the parade a kosher table was laid for Jewish citizens." Jaher, supra note 1, at 124.

89. Cohen, supra note 1, at 33; cf. Borden, supra note 1, at 10 (this constitutional provision arose from a "combination of principle and necessity").

90. Borden, supra note 1, at 17. Frederic Cople Jaher writes that "[i]ndependence and nationhood thus brought little departure from the customary experience of American Jewry." Jaher, supra note 1, at 113.

91. See Gerard V. Bradley, Church–State Relationships in America 70 (1987); Curry, supra note 1, at 194, 198–99, 216; Levy, supra note 1, at 74, 79, 108–09.

92. House of Representatives, Amendments to the Constitution (June 8, July 21, Aug. 13, 18–19, 1789), 1 Annals of Cong. 424–50, 661–65, 707–17, 757–59, 766 (Joseph Gales ed., 1789), reprinted in Kurland, supra note 1, at 20, 25–27.

93. House Select Committee Draft (July 28, 1789), reprinted in Farber & Sherry, supra note 70, at 433. At least one Jew, Jonas Phillips, was on record as requesting the original Constitutional Convention to bar states from imposing political disabilities on Jews. See Letter from Jonas Phillips to

the Federal Constitutional Convention (Sept. 7, 1787), reprinted in Schappes, supra note 1, at 68 (a petition from Jonas Phillips to the Constitutional Convention asking for constitutional protection against state constitutional provisions such as the one in Pennsylvania, which demanded that a governmental official acknowledge that the Old and New Testaments are given by divine inspiration, thus precluding Jews from holding office). Previously, a group of Jews had petitioned for a change of the Pennsylvania state constitutional provision. See Extract from the Journal of the Council of Censors, Philadelphia (Dec. 23, 1783), and a Newspaper Comment (Jan. 21, 1784), reprinted in Schappes, supra note 1, at 63. Of note, Jonas Phillips was subsequently fined for refusing to be a witness in court on a Saturday because of his observance of the Jewish Sabbath. See Schappes, supra note 1, at 584 n.2 (citing John Samuel, Some Cases in Pennsylvania Wherein Rights Claimed by Jews are Affected, 5 Am. Jewish Hist. Soc'y Publications 35 (1897)).

94. See House of Representatives, Amendments to the Constitution (Aug. 15, 17, 20, 1789), 1 Annals of Cong. 729–31, 755, 766 (Joseph Gales ed., 1789), reprinted in Kurland, supra note 1, at 92, 92–93; Curry, supra note 1, at 200–04 (quoting House debates from Aug. 15, 1789).

95. House of Representatives, Amendments to the Constitution (Aug. 15, 17, 20, 1789), 1 Annals of Cong. 729–31, 755, 766 (Joseph Gales ed., 1789), reprinted in Kurland, supra note 1, at 92, 93.

96. Id. at 94.

97. House Resolution (Aug. 24, 1789), reprinted in Farber & Sherry, supra note 70, at 435, 435.

98. Senate Journal (Sept. 3, 1789), reprinted in Wilson & Drakeman, supra note 1, at 77, 77; see Farber & Sherry, supra note 70, at 242; McConnell, supra note 1, at 1483–84.

99. Senate Journal (Sept. 3, 1789), reprinted in Wilson & Drakeman, supra note 1, at 77, 77.

100. U.S. Const. amend. I. Virtually no records of the Conference Committee proceedings exist. See Proposed Amendments and Ratification (1789), 1 Elliot 338–40, reprinted in Kurland, supra note 1, at 40; see also Farber & Sherry, supra note 70, at 243.

101. McConnell, supra note 1, at 1485; see Levy, supra note 1, at 85.

102. Levy, supra note 1, at 89.

103. Virginia Ratifying Convention, Proposed Amendments (June 27, 1788), reprinted in Kurland, supra note 1, at 89, 89; cf. Michael J. Sandel, Freedom of Conscience or Freedom of Choice?, in Articles of Faith, Articles of Peace 74 (James Davison Hunter & Os Guinness eds., 1990) (distinguishes freedom of conscience as understood by the framers' generation with the twentieth-century concept of freedom of choice in religion).

104. McConnell, supra note 1, at 1494. In subsequently explaining the meaning of the first amendment, Madison freely substituted one phrase for the other. See James Madison, Report on the Virginia Resolutions (Jan. 1800), reprinted in Kurland, supra note 1, at 141, 146–47. McConnell acknowledges that the framers' generation often used "free exercise" and "freedom of conscience" interchangeably, but then he argues that the terms significantly differ from each other. See McConnell, supra note 1, at 1488–1500. McConnell argues that in contemporary dictionaries, "exercise" connoted action, while "conscience" connoted belief or thought. McConnell's argument has two weaknesses. First, a dictionary definition of "exercise" does not necessarily explain the meaning of "free exercise," which was a political and religious term of art. Second, McConnell ignores the fact that the first Congress did not carefully consider the precise meanings of the terms in adopting the first amendment. That is, Congress did not apparently believe that its various proposed versions of the first amendment communicated significantly different meanings, but rather that the different versions were more or less "felicitous-sounding." Curry, supra note 1, at 216; cf. id. at 213 (in the early drafts of the first amendment, the protection of freedom of conscience was redundant with free exercise).

105. See Curry, supra note 1, at 202; cf. Samuel Adams, The Rights of the Colonists (Nov. 20, 1772), reprinted in Kurland, supra note 1, at 60 ("every Man living in or out of a state of civil society, has a right peaceably and quietly to worship God according to the dictates of his conscience").

106. According to Steven D. Smith, "[t]he religion clauses [were] simply an assignment of jurisdiction over matters of religion to the states—no more, no less." Steven D. Smith, Foreordained Failure: The Quest for a Constitutional Principle of Religious Freedom 18 (1995). I agree with Smith, but only partially. That is, to me, the religion clauses were jurisdictional, but not solely so. Even though the Constitution largely left power to officially establish religion with the states, it affirmed a particular substantive religious world view (that of Protestantism).

Philip B. Kurland writes: "De facto establishment was not an evil at which the first amendment was directed." Philip B. Kurland, The Origins of the Religion Clauses of the Constitution, 27 Wm. & Mary L. Rev. 839, 860 (1986). Thomas Curry notes that liberty of conscience included freedom from "'popish' ceremonies" of the Roman Catholic tradition, and that "liberty of conscience [was] for everyone 'whose religious Principles are not incompatible with a Protestant Country, or destructive to the Community.'" Curry, supra note 1, at 88, 103.

107. Joseph Story, 3 Commentaries on the Constitution of the United States 728 (1991; originally published in 1833). See generally Derrick A. Bell, Race, Racism, and American Law 39 (2d ed. 1980); Derrick A. Bell, Brown v. Board of Education and the Interest-Convergence Dilemma, 93 Harv. L. Rev. 518 (1980). According to Bell's interest-convergence thesis, African Americans historically have gained social justice only when their interests happened to converge with the interests of the white majority.

108. See Curry, supra note 1, at 218; 1 Stokes, supra note 1, at 484–85.

109. Journal of the First Session of the House of Representatives (Apr. 29, 1789), reprinted in 1 Stokes, supra note 1, at 485. The Senate version differed only slightly from this House version. See 1 Stokes, supra note 1, at 485.

110. Annals of Congress (Sept. 25, 1789), reprinted in 1 Stokes, supra note 1, at 486.

111. 1 Stokes, supra note 1, at 487; see id. at 487–88 (Washington's presidential proclamation).

112. The Northwest Territorial Government (July 13, 1787), reprinted in 1 Poore, supra note 1, at 429, 431; see Curry, supra note 1, at 218; McConnell, supra note 1, at 1458.

113. See 1 Stokes, supra note 1, at 499. At the state level, of course, similar laws bolstering Christianity were common. Laws enforcing the Christian Sabbath, for example, "enjoyed widespread support." Curry, supra note 1, at 218. Anson Stokes notes that the Senate ratified a treaty with Tripoli in 1797 stating that "the government of the United States of America is not, in any sense, founded on the Christian religion." Nonetheless, as Stokes emphasizes, this treaty was superseded by another within a decade, and the new treaty omitted this language, suggesting that America was indeed a Christian nation. 1 Stokes, supra note 1, at 497–98.

114. See, e.g., The Baptist Confession (1688), reprinted in 3 The Creeds of Christendom 738 (Philip Schaff ed., 3d ed. 1877) [hereinafter Schaff] (based on Westminster Confession); Methodist Articles of Religion (1784), reprinted in Schaff, supra, at 807 (based on Thirty-nine Articles); The Confession of the Cumberland Presbyterian Church (1813), reprinted in Schaff, supra, at 771 (based on Westminster Confession). For my discussion of antisemitism in the Westminster Confession and the Thirty-nine Articles of Religion, see chapter 5.

115. Jaher writes: "[M]ost Americans remained uncommitted to equality for Jews and Catholics, wanted to be governed by Protestants, and were willing in some states and on some issues to legalize this preference." Jaher, supra note 1, at 121.

116. George Washington, To the Hebrew Congregation in New Port, Rhode Island (1790), reprinted in Schappes, supra note 1, at 80, 80.

117. See Borden, supra note 1, at 6–7; Jaher, supra note 1, at 120; McConnell, supra note 1, at 1466. Jews constituted approximately one-twentieth to one-tenth of 1 percent of the American population. See Marty, supra note 1, at 41; Michael A. Meyer, Response to Modernity: A History of the Reform Movement in Judaism 228 (1988).

118. Meyer, supra note 117, at 228; see Jaher, supra note 1, at 98–99, 119–22; Sachar, supra note 1, at 36–37.

119. Sachar, supra note 1, at 35, 37.

120. See David C. Gross, How to Be Jewish 53–54 (1988); Roy A. Rosenberg, The Concise Guide to Judaism 120 (1990); Joseph Telushkin, Jewish Literacy 495–96 (1991).

121. While Harringtonian theory tended to stress virtuous participation in republican government, Opposition Ideology tended to emphasize the virtuous protection of rights and liberties from governmental encroachment. See Bailyn, supra note 1, at 35–54; Michelman, supra 1, at 47–55.

For discussions of the combination of Lockean and civic republican themes in the framers' thought, see Pocock, supra note 1, at 506–52; Wood, Creation, supra note 1, at 391–564. Cf. Thomas Pangle, The Spirit of Modern Republicanism (1988) (arguing that framing represented a mix of Lockean and civic republican themes but ultimately emphasizing Locke). I state in the text that the framers' vision of government arose "for uncertain reasons" because historians disagree so strongly as to the motivations of the framers. Explanations range from a virtuous commitment to preserve democracy to a selfish attempt to preserve wealth in the face of democratic threats. Compare Charles Beard, An Economic Interpretation of the Constitution of the United States (1913) (the Constitution reflects the property interests of the framers) with Essays on the Making of the Constitution (Leonard W. Levy ed., 2d ed. 1987) (essays reacting to Beard's thesis).

122. See Pocock, supra note 1, at 527, 545; Wood, Creation, supra note 1, at 283, 290; see also supra chapter 5, third section (on Locke). I do not mean to suggest that the concept of the common good has meant the same thing to all individuals. It has not.

123. See The Federalist No. 55, at 346 (James Madison) (Clinton Rossiter ed., 1961).

124. See The Federalist No. 6, at 54 (Alexander Hamilton) (Clinton Rossiter ed., 1961) (factions occur because "men are ambitious, vindictive, and rapacious"); The Federalist No. 10, at 79 (James Madison) (Clinton Rossiter ed., 1961) (factionalism is normal to the operation of government); The Federalist No. 85, at 523–24 (Alexander Hamilton) (Clinton Rossiter ed., 1961) (people are imperfect).

125. See The Federalist No. 10 (James Madison) (Clinton Rossiter ed., 1961); The Federalist No. 51, at 322 (James Madison) (Clinton Rossiter ed., 1961) ("Ambition must be made to counteract ambition."); Pocock, supra note 1, at 462–552. For Publius's emphasis on the public or common good, see The Federalist No. 1, at 33–35 (Alexander Hamilton) (Clinton Rossiter ed., 1961); The Federalist No. 10 (James Madison) (Clinton Rossiter ed., 1961); The Federalist No. 31, at 194 (Alexander Hamilton) (Clinton Rossiter ed., 1961); The Federalist No. 45, at 289 (James Madison) (Clinton Rossiter ed., 1961). A faction was characterized as any group, whether a minority or a majority, that opposed the public good. The Federalist No. 10, at 78 (James Madison) (Clinton Rossiter ed., 1961); see The Federalist No. 73, at 443 (Alexander Hamilton) (Clinton Rossiter ed., 1961). Madison wrote: "To secure the public good and private rights against the danger of such a faction, and at the same time to preserve the spirit and the form of popular government, is then the great object to which our inquiries are directed." The Federalist No. 10, at 80 (James Madison) (Clinton Rossiter ed., 1961).

126. The Federalist No. 57, at 350 (James Madison) (Clinton Rossiter ed., 1961).

127. See Wood, Creation, supra note 1, at 24 (on the Revolutionary-era conception of liberty).

128. Cf. Hartz, supra note 1, at 59–62 (placing enormous emphasis on the Lockean impulses of the framers in seeking to limit governmental power). Pocock and others in the "civic republican revival" have criticized Hartz for overemphasizing Locke's importance. See, e.g., Pocock, supra note 1, at 509, 527; see also Stephen M. Feldman, Republican Revival/Interpretive Turn, 1992 Wis. L. Rev. 679, 682–701 (on civic republican revival). As already discussed, this emphasis on protection from government also was characteristic of neo-Harringtonian Opposition Ideology, which tended to emphasize the virtuous protection of rights and liberties from governmental encroachment. See Bailyn, supra note 1, at 35–54; Michelman, supra 1, at 47–55.

129. See U.S. Const. art. II, § 8, cl. 3. Shays's Rebellion was named after Daniel Shays, a former militia captain and one of the leaders of the insurrection. In 1785 and 1786, a commercial depression struck Massachusetts, leading to foreclosures on many tracts of land. Town meetings led to demands for legislative action to protect the vulnerable landowners, but no legislative relief was granted. Finally, in the autumn of 1786, Shays led a rebellion in central and western Massachusetts, breaking up meetings at courts and threatening the armory at Springfield. In the end, the insurrection was suppressed, but the state legislature enacted many of the reforms and protections sought by the protestors. See Shays's Rebellion (1786), in 1 Commager, supra note 1, at 126; Thernstrom, supra note 1, at 196–98; Wood, Creation, supra note 1, at 410–13.

130. Gordon Wood writes: "American society with its high proportion of freeholders seemed naturally made for republicanism." Wood, Radicalism, supra note 1, at 169. Likewise, "'the people of America, are a people of property; almost every man is a freeholder.'" Wood, Creation, supra note 1, at 100.

131. The Federalist No. 54, at 336–41 (James Madison) (Clinton Rossiter ed., 1961); cf. Morton White, Philosophy, The Federalist, and the Constitution 125–27 (1987) (on the elitism of the framers); Morton White, The Philosophy of the American Revolution 266–67 (1978) (elitism was an important element leading to disenfranchisement of many groups under the Constitution).

132. See, e.g., The Federalist No. 57, at 350 (James Madison) (Clinton Rossiter ed., 1961).

133. Pocock, supra note 1, at 525.

134. See Marty, supra note 1. Perhaps the leading proponent of Harringtonian thought during this period was John Adams. See Christopher Hill, Puritanism and Revolution 311 (1958).

135. Recall that Locke had advocated only partial disestablishment. See supra Chapter 5, third section.
136. George Washington, Farewell Address (Sept. 17, 1796), reprinted in 1 Commager, supra note 1, at 169, 173; see Butler, supra note 1, at 213–14; Bradley, supra note 91, at 123; McConnell, supra note 1, at 1440–43.

NOTES TO CHAPTER 8

1. Gordon S. Wood, The Radicalism of the American Revolution 6 (1991) [hereinafter Wood, Radicalism]; see id. at 229–31. Other sources that proved helpful in writing this chapter were the following: Sydney E. Ahlstrom, A Religious History of the American People (1972); Jerold S. Auerbach, Unequal Justice: Lawyers and Social Change in Modern America (1976); Morton Borden, Jews, Turks, and Infidels (1984); Jon Butler, Awash in a Sea of Faith: Christianizing the American People (1990); Naomi W. Cohen, Jews in Christian America: The Pursuit of Religious Equality (1992); Thomas J. Curry, The First Freedoms: Church and State in America to the Passage of the First Amendment (1986); David Max Eichhorn, Evangelizing the American Jew (1978); Lawrence M. Friedman, A History of American Law (2d ed. 1985); Benjamin Ginsberg, The Fatal Embrace: Jews and the State (1993); Kermit L. Hall, The Magic Mirror (1989); Robert T. Handy, A Christian America (2d ed. 1984); Nathan O. Hatch, The Democratization of American Christianity (1989); Arthur Hertzberg, The Jews in America (1989); Morton J. Horwitz, The Transformation of American Law, 1780–1860 (1977); Irving Howe, World of Our Fathers (1976); Winthrop S. Hudson & John Corrigan, Religion in America (5th ed. 1992); James Willard Hurst, Law and the Conditions of Freedom in the Nineteenth-Century United States (1956); Frederic Cople Jaher, A Scapegoat in the New Wilderness: The Origins and Rise of Anti-Semitism in America (1994); Paul Johnson, A History of the Jews (1987); William E. Leuchtenberg, Franklin D. Roosevelt and the New Deal (1963); Leonard W. Levy, The Establishment Clause: Religion and the First Amendment (1986); Martin E. Marty, Protestantism in the United States: Righteous Empire (2d ed. 1986); William G. McLoughlin, The American Evangelicals, 1800–1900 (1968); William Nicholls, Christian Antisemitism: A History of Hate (1993); Leo Pfeffer, Church, State, and Freedom (1953); Howard M. Sachar, A History of the Jews in America (1992); Anson Phelps Stokes, 3 Church and State in the United States (1950); Stephan Thernstrom, A History of the American People (2d ed. 1989) (in 2 volumes [hereinafter 1 Thernstrom and 2 Thernstrom]; Howard Zinn, A People's History of the United States (1980); G. Edward White, Revisiting the New Deal Legal Generation, reprinted in Intervention and Detachment 132 (1994) [hereinafter White, Revisiting]; Harold J. Berman, Religion and Law: The First Amendment in Historical Perspective, 35 Emory L.J. 777 (1986); Michael W. McConnell, The Origins and Historical Understanding of Free Exercise of Religion, 103 Harv. L. Rev. 1409 (1990); The Jews of the United States, 1790–1840, A Documentary History (Joseph L. Blau & Salo W. Barron eds., 1963) (in 3 volumes) [hereinafter 1 Blau & Barron, 2 Blau & Barron, and 3 Blau & Barron]; Documents of American History (Henry Steele Commager ed., 3d ed. 1947) (in 2 volumes) [hereinafter 1 Commager and 2 Commager]; Religious Liberty in the Supreme Court (Terry Eastland ed. 1993) [hereinafter Eastland]; 5 The Founders' Constitution (Philip B. Kurland & Ralph Lerner eds., 1987) [hereinafter Kurland]; The Jew in the Modern World: A Documentary History (Paul R. Mendes-Flohr & Jehuda Reinharz eds., 1980) [hereinafter Mendes-Flohr & Reinharz]; The Federal and State Constitutions, Colonial Charters, and Other Organic Laws of the United States (Ben Perley Poore ed., 2d ed. 1924) (in 2 volumes) [hereinafter 1 Poore and 2 Poore]; 3 The Creeds of Christendom (Philip Schaff ed., 3d ed. 1877) [hereinafter Schaff]; A Documentary History of the Jews in the United States, 1654–1875 (Morris U. Schappes ed., 1950) [hereinafter Schappes]; Church and State in American History (John F. Wilson & Donald L. Drakeman eds., 2d ed. 1987) [hereinafter Wilson & Drakeman].
2. Wood, Radicalism, supra note 1, at 230, 330; see id. at 229–43.
3. Id. at 325–47; see Hall, supra note 1, at 88 (giving statistics); Hurst supra note 1, at 3–32 (criticizing the view of the nineteenth century as a time of laissez faire); 1 Thernstrom, supra note 1, at 238 (giving statistics); cf. Daniel Bell, The Cultural Contradictions of Capitalism 54–80 (1978) (emphasizing the Protestant ethic).
4. See Horwitz, supra note 1, at 100; 1 Thernstrom, supra note 1, at 243, 250–51; cf. Friedman, supra note 1, at 177–201 (discussing law and the economy in the early nineteenth century).

5. Gordon S. Wood, Faux Populism, New Republic, Oct. 23, 1995, at 39, 40 (reviewing Robert H. Wiebe, Self-Rule: A Cultural History of American Democracy (1995)) [hereinafter Wood, Populism]; see Friedman, supra note 1, at 185–86 (discussing limited taxing and spending); 1 Thernstrom, supra note 1, at 223–24 (on the Jeffersonian revolution in the federal government, cutting back federal taxing and spending).

6. Compare Trustees of Dartmouth College v. Woodward, 17 U.S. (4 Wheat.) 518 (1819) (the contract clause of the U.S. Constitution protected private vested interests in a corporate charter) with Charles River Bridge Co. v. Warren Bridge Co., 36 U.S. (11 Pet.) 420 (1837) (the grant of a charter should be construed narrowly in favor of the state so that the state can grant a subsequent charter to a competing company). See Hall, supra note 1, at 96–97; Horwitz, supra note 1, at 109–39.

7. Hurst, supra note 1, at 28; see Horwitz, supra note 1, at 99–102, 211–52.

8. 41 U.S. (16 Pet.) 1 (1842), overruled by Erie R. Co. v. Tompkins, 304 U.S. 64 (1938); see Grant Gilmore, The Ages of American Law 30–36 (1977); Horwitz, supra note 1, at 245–52.

9. Wood, Radicalism, supra note 1, at 337, 340.

10. See 1 Thernstrom, supra note 1, at 324–27; Wood, Radicalism, supra note 1, at 294; Zinn, supra note 1, at 95. The three states that did not by 1825 extend the franchise to all white males were Rhode Island, Virginia, and Louisiana.

11. See Thernstrom, supra note 1, at 251–53.

12. Horwitz, supra note 1, at xvi.

13. See id. at 101; 1 Thernstrom, supra note 1, at 252–53. These disparities of wealth were a national phenomenon, but in the South they were most pronounced. See 1 Thernstrom, supra note 1, at 283–84.

14. See Wood, Radicalism, supra note 1, at 340. Insofar as the idea (or imagery) of equality and democracy did not match the social reality, the idea (of equality and democracy) itself helped justify the contemporary inequitable social arrangements and the further pursuit of wealth. In general, the idea that equality already exists (when in fact it does not) tends to legitimate the maintenance of actual inequalities. Moreover, in this specific context, the largely judicial (as opposed to legislative or executive) promotion of economic development tended to obscure and mystify the growing inequalities of wealth and power. In general, when a court issues a common law decision, supposedly grounded on the rule of law, the political and economic implications of that action are less obvious than, for example, those of an overt legislative enactment to increase taxes to fund a public subsidy. See Horwitz, supra note 1, at 100–01.

15. Hatch, supra note 1, at 3.

16. The Christianization of African Americans occurred largely in two stages. In the first, during the colonial era, slaveholders destroyed significant elements of the traditional African religious systems. In the second, starting in the late eighteenth century and continuing into the nineteenth century, Christianity filled the spiritual void left by the first-stage destruction. African American slaves were thus active participants in the Second Great Awakening. See Butler, supra note 1, at 129–63; Hatch, supra note 1, at 102–13.

17. See Hudson & Corrigan, supra note 1, at 129–30; see also Marty, supra note 1, at 169.

18. See McLoughlin, supra note 1, at 4, 10; cf. Hatch, supra note 1, at 69–70 (on the Christian movement).

19. See Ahlstrom, supra note 1, at 441–42 (emphasizes Calvinist views of the Baptists).

20. See, e.g., The Westminster Confession of Faith (1647), reprinted in Schaff, supra note 1, at 600, 614 (individuals cannot escape their sinful nature), 623 (the individual, as sinful, cannot will or do anything to gain salvation).

21. The New Hampshire Baptist Confession (1833), reprinted in Schaff, supra note 1, at 742, 743–44.

22. Confession of the Free-Will Baptists (1834, 1868), reprinted in Schaff, supra note 1, at 749, 749–50, 753 (emphasis omitted).

23. The Auburn Declaration (1837), reprinted in Schaff, supra note 1, at 777, 780.

24. McLoughlin, supra note 1, at 8.

25. Id. at 10.

26. Articles of Religion of the Reformed Episcopal Church in America (1875), reprinted in Schaff, supra note 1, at 814, 818.

27. Hatch, supra note 1, at 172–73 (quoting Barton W. Stone).

28. Hatch, supra note 1, at 172; see Hudson & Corrigan, supra note 1, at 138; Wood, Radicalism, supra note 1, at 332. By 1844, the Methodist Episcopal Church "was nearly one-half size larger than any other Protestant body." Hatch, supra note 1, at 220; see Hudson & Corrigan, supra note 1, at 28 (by 1820, Methodists and Baptists were the leading denominations).

29. See Hatch, supra note 1, at 40–43; Wood, Radicalism, supra note 1, at 333.

30. See Hatch, supra note 1, at 55; Hudson & Corrigan, supra note 1, at 135–38.

31. Hudson & Corrigan, supra note 1, at 136 (quoting John McGee).

32. Id. at 162.

33. Id. at 182 (quoting the Unitarian Noah Worcester). Another preacher stated: "[T]he Bible, the whole Bible, and nothing but the Bible," id. (quoting Charles Beecher, The Bible a Sufficient Creed 26 (1850)).

34. The Doctrinal Basis of the Evangelical Alliance (1846), reprinted in Schaff, supra note 1, at 827, 827 (adopted by the Organization of the American Branch of the Evangelical Alliance in Jan. 1867).

35. Hatch, supra note 1, at 9. Martin Marty writes: "The accent on conversion was so strong that through much of the nineteenth century many southerners saw the act of turning to faith as the be-all and end-all of religion." Marty, supra note 1, at 62; see Hudson & Corrigan, supra note 1, at 135.

36. Hudson & Corrigan, supra note 1, at 140; see Butler, supra note 1, at 283; Hatch, supra note 1, at 199–200; Hudson & Corrigan, supra note 1, at 139–40.

37. Finney wrote:

> I would go to my room and spend a long time on my knees over my Bible. Indeed I read my Bible on my knees a great deal during those days of conflict, beseeching the Lord to teach me his own mind on those points. I had nowhere to go but directly to the Bible, and to the philosophy or workings of my own mind. I gradually formed a view of my own mind, as revealed in consciousness.

Hatch, supra note 1, at 199 (quoting Charles G. Finney, Memoirs 54 (1876)).

38. Mary Jo Weaver, Introduction to Christianity 147 (2d ed. 1991).

39. Charles G. Finney, Memoirs of Rev. Charles G. Finney 20 (1876) (quoted in Robert C. Monk & Joseph D. Stamey, Exploring Christianity: An Introduction 94 (2d ed. 1990)).

40. Butler, supra note 1, at 256.

41. See Robert Baird, Religion in America (1844), reprinted in McLoughlin, supra note 1, at 30, 32–33.

42. See Wood, Radicalism, supra note 1, at 332.

43. See id. at 9.

44. Butler, supra note 1, at 287–88. Butler adds that the "Christian contribution to a developing American democracy rested as fully on its pursuit of coercive authority and power as on its concern for individualism or its elusive antiauthoritarian rhetoric." Id. at 287.

45. Handy, supra note 1, at 50 (quoting Charles G. Finney, Lectures to Professing Christians 90 (New York 1837)) (Finney was here advocating temperance).

46. Handy, supra note 1, at 56 (quoting Horace Bushnell, Barbarism the First Danger: A Discourse for Home Missions 32 (1847)); see Handy, supra note 1, at 27. Besides the Roman Catholics, the Christian denominations that were least connected to mainstream American Protestantism were the Mormons and the Jehovah's Witnesses. See Marty, supra note 1, at 71.

47. See Constitution of Georgia (1798), reprinted in 1 Poore, supra note 1, at 388, 395; Constitution of South Carolina (1790), reprinted in 2 Poore, supra note 1, at 1628, 1632–33; Curry, supra note 1, at 150; Levy, supra note 1, at 38, 48–51. Michael McConnell observes that during the late eighteenth century, "[o]utside of New England, only Maryland, South Carolina, and Georgia retained some form of establishment, and in none of these states did actual financial or other material support go into effect." McConnell, supra note 1, at 1437.

48. Joseph Story, 3 Commentaries on the Constitution of the United States 723 (1991; originally published in 1833). Story added: "[T]here will probably be found few persons in this, or any other Christian country, who would deliberately contend, that it was unreasonable, or unjust to foster and encourage the Christian religion generally, as a matter of sound policy, as well as of revealed truth." Id. at 724; see Borden, supra note 1, at 102.

49. Constitution of North Carolina (1776), reprinted in 2 Poore, supra note 1, at 1409, 1413–14.

50. See Amendments to the Constitution of 1776, reprinted in 2 Poore, supra note 1, at 1415, 1418 (allowing all Christians to hold office); Constitution of North Carolina (1868), reprinted in 2 Poore, supra note 1, at 1419, 1430 (this Constitution still barred "all persons who shall deny the being of Almighty God"); Borden, supra note 1, at 42–50. Borden notes that Jacob Henry, who was Jewish, served in the state legislature in 1808 without any objections. When he was reelected, however, another delegate protested that Henry "denies the divine authority of the New Testament." Borden, supra note 1, at 43. Ultimately, the legislature allowed Henry to retain his seat, reasoning that the constitutional provision barred non-Protestants from holding offices within a "civil department" of the state and that the legislature was not technically a civil department. Id. at 44.

51. Constitution of Connecticut (1818), reprinted in 1 Poore, supra note 1, at 258, 264; see Borden, supra note 1, at 28. In 1843, the Connecticut state legislature passed a special enactment providing "that Jews who may desire to unite and form religious societies, shall have the same rights, power and privileges which are given to Christians." Borden, supra note 1, at 29.

52. Constitution of New Hampshire (1792), reprinted in 2 Poore, supra note 1, at 1298–1301, 1308–09 (the amendments were framed by a convention in 1876 and ratified by the people on Mar. 13, 1877); see Borden, supra note 1, at 33–34; Levy, supra note 1, at 40. New Hampshire was the last state to eliminate its religious test or restriction on public officeholding. See Borden, supra note 1, at 32. Frederic Cople Jaher writes: "Between the 1780s and 1830s these restraints [on public officeholding] were eliminated except in New Jersey, North Carolina, Rhode Island, and New Hampshire, and were absent from the fundamental charters of newly admitted states. From 1789 to 1792, for example, Delaware, Pennsylvania, South Carolina, and Georgia . . . enfranchised Jews." Jaher, supra note 1, at 121.

53. Constitution of New Hampshire (1792), reprinted in 2 Poore, supra note 1, at 1294; see Borden, supra note 1, at 35–36.

54. Correspondence Between the Jews of Charleston, S.C. and the Governor of South Carolina, and other documents (Nov. 1844), reprinted in Schappes, supra note 1, at 235, 236–37, 240–42.

55. Information on the so-called Jew bill of Maryland can be found in 1 Blau & Barron, supra note 1, at 33–55; Borden, supra note , at 36–42; Cohen, supra note 1, at 40–42.

56. Constitution of Maryland (1776), reprinted in 1 Poore, supra note 1, at 817, 820.

57. See Report of the Select Committee (1818), reprinted in 1 Blau & Barron, supra note 1, at 37.

58. Cohen, supra note 1, at 41.

59. Election Handbill (1823), reprinted in 1 Blau & Barron, supra note 1, at 48, 49.

60. See 1 Blau & Barron, supra note 1, at 48; Jaher, supra note 1, at 132. Jaher notes that the bill probably passed more for economic reasons than for a principled commitment to religious liberty. See Jaher, supra note 1, at 132–33.

61. Final Form of the "Jew Bill" (1826), reprinted in Blau & Barron, supra note 1, at 53, 53. This bill was incorporated in the Maryland Constitution of 1851. See Constitution of Maryland (1851), reprinted in 1 Poore, supra note 1, at 837, 839.

62. Marty, supra note 1, at 47; see Cohen, supra note 1, at 28 (arguing that state laws lagged behind state constitutions); Curry, supra note 1, at 220 (regardless of the elimination of tax support for religion, "Americans inherited traditions of government interference in religious matters"); Stokes, supra note 1, at 143–58 (on various state laws supporting Christianity).

63. See Jaher, supra note 1, at 121.

64. See Borden, supra note 1, at 31, 98–103; Cohen, supra note 1, at 55–56; Jaher, supra note 1, at 139; cf. B.H. Hartogensis, Denial of Equal Rights to Religious Minorities and Non-Believers in the United States, 39 Yale L.J. 659 (1930) (tracing the notion that Christianity is part of the common law to Lord Coke).

65. See Cohen, supra note 1, at 58–61; Jaher, supra note 1, at 138–39. Although not all American Jews opposed Sunday laws (see Borden, supra note 1, at 110), many did. For example, "Rabbi Isaac Leeser wrote before the Civil War that compulsory observance of Sunday was no different in kind from mandatory church attendance or involuntary baptism." Cohen, supra note 1, at 5.

66. Borden, supra note 1, at 113 (quoting City Council of Charleston v. Benjamin (1846)). For discussions of additional cases, see Blau & Barron, supra note 1, at 21–27; Borden, supra note 1, at 111–25; see, e.g., Updegraph v. Commonwealth, 11 Serg. & Rawl. 393 (Pa. 1822) (cited and discussed in Berman, supra note 1, at 781).

67. See Borden, supra note 1, at 113–14 (discussing City Council of Charleston v. Benjamin (1846)); Cohen, supra note 1, at 61–62 (same). For an editorial commenting on this case, see Editorial Article, "Sunday Laws," in Sunday Times and Noah's Weekly Messenger (Feb. 13, 1848), reprinted in Schappes, supra note 1, at 279.

68. See, e.g., State v. Ambs, 20 Mo. 214 (1854) (cited and discussed in Berman, supra note 1, at 781).

69. People v. Ruggles, 8 Johns. R. 290 (N.Y. 1811), reprinted in Kurland, supra note 1, at 101, 101.

70. See Borden, supra note 1, at 31–32; Berman, supra note 1, at 780–81. In 1838, Chief Justice Lemuel Shaw agreed with Kent's general reasoning and decision and thus upheld a blasphemy conviction in Massachusetts. See Borden, supra note 1, at 100; Stokes, supra note 1, at 150–51.

71. Cohen, supra note 1, at 53; see Borden, supra note 1, at 75–94 (discussing various treaties).

72. Borden, supra note 1, at 79 (quoting article 29 of the China Treaty of 1858).

73. 43 U.S. (2 How.) 127, 133, 198 (1844).

74. 143 U.S. 457, 463–71 (1892).

75. McLoughlin, supra note 1, at 13 (quoting Dwight L. Moody); see Butler, supra note 1, at 278–79; Cohen, supra note 1, at 146–50; Marty, supra note 1, at 74–75.

76. Wood, Radicalism, supra note 1, at 335; see Marty, supra note 1, at 86–95, 107–15; Wood, Radicalism, supra note 1, at 331–34.

77. See Borden, supra note 1, at 58–60; 1 Thernstrom, supra note 1, at 257–58.

78. See Cohen, supra note 1, at 43; Hertzberg, supra note 1, at 120; Johnson, supra note 1, at 365–66; Sachar, supra note 1, at 41.

79. 1 Thernstrom, supra note 1, at 258 (quoting the 1855 annual report of the Bible Society of Essex County, New Jersey); see Levy, supra note 1, at 170; Marty, supra note 1, at 131–34; 1 Thernstrom, supra note 1, at 258–59.

80. See Hudson & Corrigan, supra note 1, at 213–16; Marty, supra note 1, at 139–40, 144–46.

81. Hudson & Corrigan, supra note 1, at 211; see Borden, supra note 1, at 60–62; Cohen, supra note 1, at 66; cf. Hertzberg, supra note 1, at 134–35 (on overt antisemitism during the Civil War).

82. Stokes, supra note 1, at 584–85 (emphasis omitted); see Cohen, supra note 1, at 66; Borden, supra note 1, at 62–63.

83. See Cohen, supra note 1, at 66; Stokes, supra note 1, at 585–86.

84. Stokes, supra note 1, at 584; see Cohen, supra note 1, at 69.

85. Cohen, supra note 1, at 72; see id. at 69.

86. Butler, supra note 1, at 280; see Cohen, supra note 1, at 38.

87. Jaher, supra note 1, at 144 (quoting Hannah Adams, 1 The History of the Jews from the Destruction of Jerusalem to the Nineteenth Century 64–65 (1812)); see Eichhorn, supra note 1, at 28–30; Jaher, supra note 1, at 127, 144.

88. See Eichhorn, supra note 1, at 33–34, 43–50, 78–79; Jaher, supra note 1, at 145.

89. Handy, supra note 1, at 52 (quoting Robert Baird, Religion in America; or, An Account of the Origin, Progress, Relation to The State and Present Condition of the Evangelical Churches in the United States 283 (New York 1844)).

90. Jaher, supra note 1, at 133.

91. Id. (quoting James Rivington, Preface to the American Edition, in Henry James Pye, 1 The Democrat; or, Intrigues and Adventures of Jean Le Noir vii (New York: James Rivington 1795)) (emphasis omitted).

92. Eichhorn, supra note 1, at 52 (quoting John Quincy Adams, 10 Memoirs of John Quincy Adams 90–91); Jaher, supra note 1, at 135 (quoting John Quincy Adams, 1 Memoirs of John Quincy Adams 58) (emphasis omitted). Adams later became a Democratic-Republican.

93. Jaher, supra note 1, at 135–36.

94. Johnson, supra note 1, at 367 (quoting James Monroe); see Sachar, supra note 1, at 45–46.

95. Jaher, supra note 1, at 143 (quoting Finney, Lectures on Revivals of Religions (1835)).

96. See Jaher, supra note 1, at 146–47; id. at 150 (quoting Eliza Robbins, American Popular Lessons 148 (1820, 1829)); id. at 151 (quoting John L. Blake, A Geography for Children 28, 56 (1831)); id. at 207.

97. Jaher, supra note 1, at 239 (quoting Harper's Magazine, vol. 22, at 404 (1866)); see id. at 154–69.

98.   Editorial, "The Jews as Citizens," in Washington Sentinel, Washington, D.C. (May 21, 1854), reprinted in Schappes, supra note 1, at 342, 342.

99.   Borden, supra note 1, at 27–28 (emphasis omitted) (quoting Daniel Webster, 6 The Works of Daniel Webster 153 (Boston 1854)). Webster was arguing in the case of Vidal v. Girard's Executors, 43 U.S. (2 How.) 127 (1844).

100.   Consular Report to the Department of State (Mar. 24, 1840), reprinted in Schappes, supra note 1, at 200. The secretary of state did not support this charge of blood libel. See Letter from Secretary of State to American Minister in Turkey (Aug. 17, 1840), reprinted in Schappes, supra note 1, at 209.

101.   See Hertzberg, supra note 1, at 143; Jaher, supra note 1, at 196–99; Letter to President Abraham Lincoln, from Jews in Paducah, Kentucky (Dec. 29, 1862), reprinted in Schappes, supra note 1, at 472.

102.   Cohen, supra note 1, at 54 (emphasis omitted); see id. at 39.

103.   Marty, supra note 1, at 152; see Ginsberg, supra note 1, at 59–61, 76–83.

104.   Hertzberg, supra note 1, at 152; see 1 Thernstrom, supra note 1, at 469.

105.   Wood, Populism, supra note 5, at 41; see Hertzberg, supra note 1, at 152–53; Sachar, supra note 1, at 116–17; 1 Thernstrom, supra note 1, at 470; cf. Hudson & Corrigan, supra note 1, at 206 (by 1900, one-third of the 75 million Americans were foreign born or the children of foreign born).

106.   See Hertzberg, supra note 1, at 152–53; Sachar, supra note , at 116–17.

107.   See Howe, supra note , at 410; Editorial, "The Insurance Companies and the Jews," Sunday Dispatch, Philadelphia (Apr. 21, 1867), reprinted in Schappes, supra note 1, at 510; see also Editorial, New York Sun (Mar. 17, 1849), reprinted in Schappes, supra note 1, at 286 (example of antebellum economic discrimination; the newspaper ran advertisements for shade painters that stated, "No Jews wanted here"); Marty, supra note 1, at 129 (discussing increased antisemitism). Also, at this time, anti-semitism became more racial, not merely a matter of religion. See Nicholls, supra note 1, at 313–25.

108.   See Howe, supra note 1, at 409–10; Sachar, supra note 1, at 98–104; B.F. Waterman, Letter to the Editor, The Jewish Times, New York (Oct. 25, 1872), reprinted in Schappes, supra note 1, at 559 (Jews not allowed in the state militia).

109.   Stanley McKenna, Reviving a Prejudice: Jewish Patronage Not Welcomed at Manhattan Beach, New York Herald, July 22, 1879, reprinted in Mendes-Flohr & Reinharz, supra note 1, at 368.

110.   See Sachar, supra note 1, at 98.

111.   Howe, supra note 1, at 396.

112.   Id. at 396 (quoting New York Tribune, June 13 & Aug. 6, 1882).

113.   Id. at 396 (quoting New York Herald, June 23, 1882; New York Tribune, June 20, 1882).

114.   Thomas Jefferson, Notes on the State of Virginia 315–16 (1801), quoted in Berman, supra note 1, at 786.

115.   Alexis de Tocqueville, 1 Democracy in America 302–03, 308 (Henry Reeve text, revised by Francis Bowen, edited by Phillips Bradley; Alfred A. Knopf 1945) (first published in French in 1835); cf. id. at 311 (when religion and the state join, religion can only be hurt because the inevitable anger at the state is transferred to religion). De Tocqueville added that in America, "from the beginning, politics and religion contracted an alliance which has never been dissolved." Id. at 300.

116.   James Bryce, 2 The American Commonwealth 698–704 (3d ed. 1894), reprinted in Wilson & Drakemen, supra note 1, at 154, 156.

117.   Alexis de Tocqueville, 2 Democracy in America 27 (Henry Reeve text, revised by Francis Bowen, edited by Phillips Bradley; Alfred A. Knopf 1945) (first published in French in 1840).

118.   See Hatch, supra note 1, at 35, 40–43.

119.   See Hudson & Corrigan, supra note 1, at 256–61.

120.   See id. at 196, 299–303; Marty, supra note 1, at 151–52.

121.   Martin E. Marty, Living With Establishment and Disestablishment in Nineteenth Century Anglo-America, in Readings on Church and State 55, 67 (James E. Wood, Jr., ed., 1989) (quoting Calvin Colton, A Voice from America to England: By an American Gentleman 97 (1839)); see B.H. Hartogensis, Denial of Equal Rights to Religious Minorities and Non-Believers in the United States, 39 Yale L.J. 659, 665–66 (1930) (the institution of Christianity in America is similar to the established Church of England).

122.   Bryce, supra note 116, at 154.

123. See Eichhorn, supra note 1, at 141.

124. Howe, supra note 1, at 251–52.

125. Nicholls, supra note 1, at 288. Nicholls adds:

> Indeed, perhaps the effect on the most traditional Jews ... was the most profound, inasmuch as they now focused their intense loyalty to tradition on the details of religious observance that differentiated them from other Jews whose observance was laxer or more adjusted to modern conditions. Thus their dedication to being Jewish became focused on religion to a degree Jews had hardly known before, and indeed was not characteristic of the tradition.

Id.

126. See Pfeffer, supra note 1, at 8.

127. Cohen, supra note 1, at 8.

128. Handy, supra note 1, at 49 (quoting Bela Bates Edwards, 1 Writings of Bela Bates Edwards 490 (Boston 1853)) (emphasis omitted and added); accord Philip Schaff, Church and State in the United States (1888), reprinted in Wilson & Drakeman, supra note 1, at 151.

129. See Hertzberg, supra note 1, at 237–45; Marty, supra note 1, at 224; Sachar, supra note 1, at 319–24; 2 Thernstrom 1 supra note 1, at 633–38.

130. Previous restrictions had been directed against Chinese immigrants in the 1880s and Japanese immigrants in the early twentieth century. See U.S. Bureau of Immigration, Annual Report of the Commissioner-General of Immigration (1923), reprinted in 2 Commager, supra note 1, at 315; 2 Thernstrom, supra note 1, at 633.

131. Sachar, supra note 1, at 324 (quoting Calvin Coolidge, Whose Country Is This?, Good Housekeeping).

132. See Cohen, supra note 1, at 94–99.

133. Sachar, supra note 1, at 321 (quoting Madison Grant, The Passing of the Great Race (1916)).

134. Congressional Committee on Immigration, Temporary Suspension of Immigration (1920), reprinted in Mendes-Flohr & Reinharz, supra note 1, at 405, 406–07; see Hertzberg, supra note 1, at 237–45; Sachar, supra note 1, at 319–324; 2 Thernstrom, supra note 1, at 633–38. Carr was a virulent antisemite, as revealed by his diary. After taking a boat trip to Albany, he wrote: "Most of the passengers were Jews of one kind or another. [It was] appalling to observe the lack of appreciation of the privilege they are having." After visiting Detroit, Carr wrote that it was laden with "dust, smoke, dirt, Jews." Richard D. Breitman & Alan M. Kraut, Anti-Semitism in the State Department, 1933–44: Four Case Studies, in Anti-Semitism in American History 167, 171 (David A. Gerber ed., 1986).

135. See Immigration Act of 1924, reprinted in 2 Commager supra note 1, at 372; Hertzberg, supra note 1, at 242; Sachar, supra note 1, at 323–24; 2 Thernstrom, supra note 1, at 637. Between 1919 and 1921, approximately 60,000 Jews were killed in fighting along the Russian-Polish border. See Hertzberg, supra note 1, at 298.

136. Cohen, supra note 1, at 100–01 (citing David J. Brewer, The United States a Christian Nation (1905)); see Cohen, supra note 1, at 110–11; Friedman, supra note 1, at 587; Howe, supra note 1, at 362.

137. See Ahlstrom, supra note 1, at 785–804; Hudson & Corrigan, supra note 1, at 299–303; Marty, supra note 1, at 177–78, 197–206.

138. Josiah Strong, Our Country (1886), reprinted in McLoughlin, supra note 1, at 194, 195.

139. Walter Rauschenbusch, Christianity and the Social Crisis 422 (1907), quoted in Ahlstrom, supra note 1, at 785–86. Rauschenbusch made the point about the Kingdom of Evil clearer in a book published in 1917, A Theology for the Social Gospel. See Ahlstrom, supra note 1, at 801–02.

140. The Social Creed of the Churches, Statement Adopted by the General Conference of the Methodist Episcopal Church (May 1908), reprinted in 2 Commager, supra note 1, at 232, 232.

141. Strong, supra note 138, at 205; See Hudson & Corrigan, supra note 1, at 302.

142. Hudson & Corrigan, supra note 1, at 303; see Richard Hofstadter, The Age of Reform (1955); Marty, supra note 1, at 205; 2 Thernstrom, supra note 1, at 586–611.

143. Josiah Strong, The Twentieth Century City 181 (1898), quoted in Hofstadter, supra note 142, at 176; see Handy, supra note 1, at 103; Hofstadter, supra note 142, at 9; Marty, supra note 1, at 202–04; 2 Thernstrom, supra note 1, at 600–03.

144. See Hofstadter, supra note 142, at 176–82.

145. Joseph R. Gusfield, Symbolic Crusade: Status Politics and the American Temperance Movement 7 (1966); see Friedman, supra note 1, at 586; Hall, supra note 1, at 250–51; Handy, supra note 1, at 128–30; Hofstadter, supra note 142, at 289–93; Hudson & Corrigan, supra note 1, at 238, 303–05; 2 Thernstrom, supra note 1, at 638–40.

146. See Auerbach, supra note 1, at 20–21; Handy, supra note 1, at 80–81; Marty, supra note 1, at 201; 2 Thernstrom, supra note 1, at 705–09.

147. See Alvin W. Johnson, The Legal Status of Church–State Relationships in the United States with Special Reference to the Public Schools 28–29, 60 (1934), cited in Schappes, supra note 1, at 722 n.24.

148. See National Education Association, The Status of Religious Education in the Public Schools (1949), cited in Schappes, supra note 1, at 722–23 n.24; Cohen, supra note 1, at 108 (giving statistics from 1941 and arguing that between the world wars, the movement to require Bible reading intensified).

149. Kenneth Karst, Belonging to America 102 (1989) (quoting Pat Arnow, The Year We Hid Our Religion, 1985 Liberty 3 (May–June)).

150. See Howe, supra note 1, at 379–380.

151. Cohen, supra note 1, at 138 (quoting Arthur Gilbert, A Jew in Christian America 137 (1966)).

152. Cohen, supra note 1, at 163.

153. I do not mean to suggest that all American Christians overtly and consciously discriminated on the basis of religion. See, e.g., A Protest Against Antisemitism, New York Times, Jan. 16, 1921, reprinted in Mendes-Flohr & Reinharz, supra note 1, at 409 (over 100 prominent Christians protesting antisemitism).

154. See Nathan Perlmutter & Ruth Ann Perlmutter, The Real Anti-Semitism in America 29 (1982).

155. Howe, supra note 1, at 273.

156. Sachar, supra note 1, at 155 (quoting Jacob Riis, How the Other Half Lives (1902)); see Michael N. Dobkowski, A Historical Survey of Anti-Semitism in America Prior to World War II, In Persistent Prejudice: Perspectives on Anti-Semitism 63, 70 (Hebert Hirsch & Jack D. Spiro eds., 1988).

157. Protocols of the Elders of Zion, reprinted in Mendes-Flohr & Reinharz, supra note 1, at 296–99; Cohen, supra note 1, at 93; Ginsberg, supra note 1, at 8; Hertzberg, supra note 1, at 203; Sachar, supra note 1, at 326–27.

158. See Ginsberg, supra note 1, at 96; Hertzberg, supra note 1, at 245–47; Howe, supra note 1, at 411–12; Sachar, supra note 1, at 330–34.

159. See Hertzberg, supra note 1, at 247; Sachar, supra note 1, at 331–32. Three years later, Trilling was reappointed when the university president intervened.

160. See Hall, supra note 1, at 258; Hertzberg, supra note 1, at 245–47.

161. See G. Edward White, Felix Frankfurter, the Old Boy Network, and the New Deal: The Placement of Elite Lawyers in Public Service in the 1930s, reprinted in Intervention and Detachment 149, 155–56 (1994) (these events occurred in 1905) [hereinafter White, Frankfurter]. Frankfurter eventually became the first Jewish associate at the New York firm of Hornblower, Byrne, Miller and Potter. See Sachar, supra note 1, at 447.

162. See Auerbach, supra note 1, at 186.

163. Id. at 107; see id. at 74–129; Sachar, supra note 1, at 332–33.

164. See Auerbach, supra note 1, at 49–52; Hall, supra note 1, at 259. The American Law Institute and the Restatement movement of the 1920s also manifested antisemitism. See Robert Stevens, Two Cheers for 1870: The American Law School, 5 Persp. Am. Hist. 405, 463–64 (1971).

165. See Auerbach, supra note 1, at 127; Sachar, supra note 1, at 333.

166. See Leuchtenburg, supra note 1, at 61, 347; 2 Thernstrom, supra note 1, at 725–45; G. Edward White, Recapturing New Deal Lawyers, 102 Harv. L. Rev. 489, 514–15 (1988) [hereinafter White, Recapturing]; White, Revisiting, supra note 1, at 134–35. I thank G. Edward White for emphasizing to me the connection between the transformation of democracy and the transformation of the economy.

167. Leuchtenburg, supra note 1, at 339 (emphasis in the original); see id. at 338–39, 344.

168. Id. at 333, 336.

169. See, e.g., Carter v. Carter Coal Co., 298 U.S. 238 (1936); A.L.A. Schechter Poultry Corp. v. United States, 295 U.S. 495 (1935).

170. See, e.g., Morris R. Cohen, The Basis of Contract, 46 Harv. L. Rev. 553 (1933); Morris R. Cohen, Property and Sovereignty, 13 Cornell L.Q. 8 (1927); Robert Hale, Coercion and Distribution in

a Supposedly Non-Coercive State, 33 Pol. Sci. Q. 470 (1923). Roosevelt himself clearly subscribed to this view. See Leuchtenburg, supra note 1, at 333.

171. See, e.g., West Coast Hotel Co. v. Parrish, 300 U.S. 379 (1937). For a discussion of the political circumstances surrounding Roosevelt's Court-packing plan, see William E. Leuchtenburg, The Origins of Franklin D. Roosevelt's Court-Packing Plan, 1966 Sup. Ct. Rev. 347. Documents related to the Court-packing plan can be found in Reform of the Federal Judiciary (1937), reprinted in 2 Commager, supra note 1, at 562–73.

172. Leuchtenburg, supra note 1, at 335; see Bruce A. Ackerman, Reconstructing American Law (1984); Bruce A. Ackerman, Constitutional Politics/Constitutional Law, 99 Yale L.J. 453 (1989) (arguing that the New Deal amounted to a significant constitutional amendment outside of the official article five amendment process).

173. See Ginsberg, supra note 1.

174. See Auerbach, supra note 1, at 184–97; Ginsberg, supra note 1, at 104, 113; Hertzberg, supra note 1, at 252–53; Sachar, supra note 1, at 446–50.

175. See Auerbach, supra note 1, at 224–32.

176. Id. at 224.

177. Howe, supra note 1, at 228; see Robert Wuthnow, The Restructuring of American Religion 76–77 (1988).

178. Auerbach, supra note 1, at 186. Derrick Bell writes similarly of a Hobson's choice for African Americans: accept white culture in order to be successful or be black and face failure. See Derrick Bell, Faces at the Bottom of the Well: The Permanence of Racism 78, 140 (1992).

179. White, Recapturing, supra note 166, at 512–13.

180. See Robert A. Burt, Two Jewish Justices: Outcasts in the Promised Land 39 (1988); Sanford Levinson, Who Is a Jew(ish Justice)?, 10 Cardozo L. Rev. 2359, 2367 (1989); White, Frankfurter, supra note 161, at 154–56.

181. See Auerbach, supra note 1, at 187–88; White, Recapturing, supra note 166 at 512–15; White, Revisiting, supra note 1, at 134–35.

182. See Hertzberg, supra note 1, at 286, 289; Johnson, supra note 1, at 503–04; Sachar, supra note 1, at 478.

183. See Martin Jay, The Dialectical Imagination: A History of the Frankfurt School and the Institute of Social Research, 1923–1950, at 34 (1973); Gunnar Myrdal, An American Dilemma 53, 1186 n.4 (1944).

184. See Sachar, supra note 1, at 325, 452–55; Richard Wright, Black Boy 54 (1937).

185. Otto Piper, God in History 90–91 (1939).

186. Sachar, supra note 1, at 457.

187. See Howe, supra note 1, at 392–94 n.*; Johnson, supra note 1, at 503–04; Sachar, supra note 1, at 468–95; Richard D. Breitman & Alan M. Kraut, Anti-Semitism in the State Department, 1933–44: Four Case Studies, in Anti-Semitism in American History 167 (David A. Gerber ed., 1986).

188. See Sachar, supra note 1, at 533–35, 552.

189. See Department of State Bulletin, Bermuda Conference Joint Communique (May 1, 1943), reprinted in Mendes-Flohr & Reinharz, supra note 1, at 511; Shmuel Zygelboym, Where Is the World's Conscience?, New York Times (June 4, 1943), reprinted in Mendes-Flohr & Reinharz, supra note 1, at 512 (a suicide letter). In 1943, the Treasury Department (the secretary was Henry Morgenthau) prepared a report, entitled "Report to the Secretary on the Acquiescence of This Government in the Murder of the Jews," which detailed the State Department's subversion of rescue efforts. Confronted in 1944 with this report, Roosevelt finally took refugee policy away from the State Department and gave it to a newly formed War Refugee Board. Using only non-governmental funds, the Board did manage to help save about 200,000 Jews from the fate suffered by their 6 million murdered co-religionists. Only 1000 of these refugees were allowed to come to the United States. See Sachar, supra note 1, at 544–46.

190. See Leuchtenburg, supra note 1, at 332, 336; cf. id. at 344–46 (on the pragmatism of the New Dealers in attempting to improve on the lives of Americans); Zygmunt Bauman, Modernity and the Holocaust 65, 70, 73, 91–92, 113–14 (1989) (emphasizes that in modernity, humans assume that they can improve social conditions by reorganizing society on a rational basis); Feldman, From Modernism, supra note 1 (on the development of this component of modernism).

Notes to Chapter 9

1. See Jerold S. Auerbach, Unequal Justice: Lawyers and Social Change in Modern America 108 (1976); Robert T. Handy, A Christian America 181–84 (2d ed. 1984); Martin E. Marty, Protestantism in the United States: Righteous Empire 127–28 (2d ed. 1986). Other sources that proved helpful in this chapter were the following: Sydney E. Ahlstrom, A Religious History of the American People (1972); Naomi W. Cohen, Jews in Christian America: The Pursuit of Religious Equality (1992); Leonard Dinnerstein, Antisemitism in America (1994); Benjamin Ginsberg, The Fatal Embrace: Jews and the State (1993); Kermit L. Hall, The Magic Mirror (1989); Arthur Hertzberg, The Jews in America (1989); Irving Howe, World of Our Fathers (1976); Winthrop S. Hudson & John Corrigan, Religion in America (5th ed. 1992); Leonard W. Levy, The Establishment Clause: Religion and the First Amendment (1986); Edward A. Purcell, Jr., The Crisis of Democratic Theory (1973); Howard M. Sachar, A History of the Jews in America (1992); Laurence H. Tribe, American Constitutional Law (2d ed. 1988); Robert Wuthnow, The Restructuring of American Religion (1988); Stephen M. Feldman, From Modernism to Postmodernism in American Legal Thought: The Significance of the Warren Court, in The Warren Court: A Retrospective (Bernard Schwartz ed., Oxford University Press, forthcoming) [hereinafter Feldman, From Modernism]; Michael J. Sandel, Freedom of Conscience or Freedom of Choice?, in Articles of Faith, Articles of Peace 74 (James Davison Hunter & Os Guinness eds., 1990); Morton J. Horwitz, Foreword: The Constitution of Change: Legal Fundamentality Without Fundamentalism, 107 Harv. L. Rev. 30 (1993); Michael W. McConnell, Religious Freedom at a Crossroads, 59 U. Chi. L. Rev. 115 (1992); Kathleen M. Sullivan, Religion and Liberal Democracy, 59 U. Chi. L. Rev. 195 (1992); David C. Williams & Susan H. Williams, Volitionalism and Religious Liberty, 76 Cornell L. Rev. 769 (1991); Documents of American History (Henry Steele Commager ed., 3d ed. 1947) (in 2 volumes) [hereinafter 1 Commager and 2 Commager]; Religious Liberty in the Supreme Court (Terry Eastland ed. 1993) [hereinafter Eastland]; Church and State in American History (John F. Wilson & Donald L. Drakeman eds., 2d ed. 1987) [hereinafter Wilson & Drakeman].

2. Peter L. Berger, The Sacred Canopy 143 (1967); see Robert Lee, The Social Sources of Church Unity 169–86 (1960).

3. Lee, supra note 2, at 170 (quoting a Statement of Department of Field Administration, National Council of Churches).

4. See Marty, supra note 1, at 141–42, 217–18.

5. See Volstead Act of Oct. 28, 1919, 41 Stat. 305, codified at 27 USC § 16, repealed by Act of Aug. 27, 1935, 49 Stat 872; see also Sullivan, supra note 1, at 216.

6. See Ahlstrom, supra note 1, at 1002; Hudson & Corrigan, supra note 1, at 241, 340–41 & n.35, 425; Marty, supra note 1, at 3, 208.

7. See Wuthnow, supra note 1, at 94–95. As Arthur Hertzberg observes, some Protestants in the early twentieth century might have become less religious than they had been in the past, "but they knew that they were Christian, at least in relation to Jews." Hertzberg, supra note 1, at 174; cf. Wuthnow, supra note 1, at 77 (on Protestant and Catholic antisemitism after World War II).

8. See, e.g., Arthur A. Cohen, The Myth of the Judeo-Christian Tradition, Commentary 74 (Nov. 1969); see also Stephen L. Carter, The Culture of Disbelief 88 (1993) (on the origins of the rhetoric of the Judeo-Christian tradition); Wuthnow, supra note 1, at 75–76 (to Protestants, Catholicism was fatally flawed because of the need to defer to papal authority, so many Protestants viewed Jews as potential allies in the battle against Catholic power). During the Red Scare of the 1950s, Joseph McCarthy and the Senate openly attacked elite WASPs as well as the entertainment industry. While the Senate did not seem antisemitic in these attacks, the House Un-American Activities Committee (HUAC) revealed antisemitic attitudes. In its investigation of the movie industry, HUAC considered it important to reveal that certain actors had changed their names and were really Jewish. See Ginsberg, supra note 1, at 120–25; Sachar, supra note 1, at 625–27.

9. See McGowan v. Maryland, 366 U.S. 420, 442 (1961).

10. Jerome A. Chanes, Antisemitism and Jewish Security in America Today: Interpreting the Data. Why Can't Jews Take "Yes" for an Answer?, in Antisemitism in America Today 3, 24 (Jerome A. Chanes ed., 1995); cf. Ginsberg, supra note 1, at 141 (by 1960, the news media declared overtly antisemitic expressions to be extremist and un-American); Howe, supra note 1, at 630 (the Holocaust provoked "widespread shame" among non-Jews, thus rendering overt antisemitism socially unacceptable);

Marty, supra note 1, at 244–46 (the Holocaust built sympathy for Jews); Gerald N. Rosenberg, The Hollow Hope: Can Courts Bring About Social Change? 163 (1991) (the rhetoric of World War II associated Nazism with racism, and the cold war continued this relation).

While still in America after the war, several Frankfurt School scholars published a five-volume series, Studies in Prejudice, commissioned by the American Jewish Committee. One important argument asserted that antisemitism was a disease associated with an "authoritarian personality." The suggestion was that Americans were healthy, that is, uninfected with the disease. See Hertzberg, supra note 1, at 310; Sachar, supra note 1, at 751.

11. Many Christians assumed that antisemitism would (and should) continue until Jews became more like Christians—if not actually becoming Christians. See Wuthnow, supra note 1, at 76–77.

12. See Bell, Brown v. Board of Education and the Interest-Convergence Dilemma, 93 Harv. L. Rev. 518 (1980); see also Mary L. Dudziak, Desegregation as a Cold War Imperative, 41 Stan. L. Rev. 61 (1988).

13. See Dinnerstein, supra note 1, at 162–66; Wuthnow, supra note 1, at 95, 221–22.

14. See Wuthnow, supra note 1, at 76 (immediately after World War II, Protestant religious leaders still took it for granted that antisemitism was part of American culture). A 1963 study of Sunday School literature revealed persistent antisemitism. See Marty, supra note 1, at 245.

15. See Sachar, supra note 1, at 791; see also Hertzberg, supra note 1, at 380. Renae Cohen reports slightly different statistics. According to Cohen, a 1964 survey indicated that 11 percent of Americans thought Jews had too much power, and a 1981 survey reported a 20 percent figure. Cohen notes that these surveys asked the "Jewish power" question in different ways and that the different forms of the question may have affected the results. See Renae Cohen, What We Know, What We Don't Know About Antisemitism: A Research Perpsective, in Antisemitism in America Today 59, 64–68, 74, 76, 80 n.9 (Jerome A. Chanes ed., 1995).

16. See Hertzberg, supra note 1, at 308–10, 350; Howe, supra note 1, at 608–11; Robert Stevens, Law School: Legal Education in America from the 1850s to the 1980s 246 (1983).

17. The section on employment discrimination (Title VII) also prohibited sexual discrimination. See Civil Rights Act of 1964, 78 Stat. 243, 42 U.S.C. §§ 2000e et. seq. The 1972 amendments to the Civil Rights Act underscored that employers had to make reasonable efforts to accommodate religious practices as well as religious beliefs.

18. See Cohen, supra note 1, at 127–28, 269 n.16; Marty, supra note 1, at 241.

19. Hudson & Corrigan, supra note 1, at 363; see Handy, supra note 1, at 187–90; Marty, supra note 1, at 242.

20. See Levy, supra note 1, at 126–27; cf. Yehudah Mirsky, Civil Religion and the Establishment Clause, 95 Yale L.J. 1237, 1238 (1986) (discussing continuing practices and citing 36 U.S.C. §§ 169 (h), 172, 186 (1985)).

21. A released-time program differs from a dismissed-time program. In the latter, all children are dismissed from school early so that whoever desires to attend religious school can do so. In a sense, a dismissed-time program involves less governmental approval than a released-time program because the public schools do not give children attending religious school any special treatment (early dismissal). See Cohen, supra note 1, at 131–58; cf. Zorach v. Clauson, 343 U.S. 306, 320 (1952) (Frankfurter, J., dissenting) (dismissed time would be constitutional but released time should not be).

22. Cohen, supra note 1, at 132–33, 148; see Levy, supra note 1, at 171 (quoting the affidavit of Leah Cunn in the trial proceedings of Zorach v. Clausen, 343 U.S. 306 (1952)).

23. See Cohen, supra note 1, at 128, 233–34; Sachar, supra note 1, at 795; Mirsky, supra note 20.

24. Cf. Wuthnow, supra note 1, at 72–74 (on Protestant perceptions of a Roman Catholic threat).

25. Through 1990, 91 of 104 Supreme Court justices came from Protestant backgrounds. Eight justices were Roman Catholic: Roger Taney (appointed in 1835), Edward D. White (1894), Joseph McKenna (1897), Pierce Butler (1922), Frank Murphy (1939), William Brennan (1956), Antonin Scalia (1986), and Anthony Kennedy (1987). Five justices were Jewish: Louis Brandeis (1916), Benjamin Cardozo (1932), Felix Frankfurter (1939), Arthur Goldberg (1962), and Abe Fortas (1965). See Congressional Quarterly, Guide to the U.S. Supreme Court 794 (2d ed. 1990). James F. Byrnes, who served as an associate justice for only the 1941–1942 term, was born into a Roman Catholic family but converted to Episcopalianism when he married in 1906. More recently, two more Jewish justices have been appointed: Ruth Bader Ginsburg and Stephen G. Breyer.

26. See Cohen, supra note 1, at 129, 138–39, 222; Ira C. Lupu, The Lingering Death of Separationism, 62 Geo. Wash. L. Rev. 230, 231 (1994); cf. Wuthnow, supra note 1, at 73 (many court cases found Protestants and Catholics on opposite sides of the fence).

27. See Geoffrey R. Stone, Louis M. Seidman, Cass R. Sunstein, & Mark V. Tushnet, Constitutional Law 1494–1503 (2d ed. 1991) (listing cases); McConnell, supra note 1, at 134 (characterizes the Warren Court as deeply suspicious of Catholicism). Laurence Tribe argues that this pattern is based on a consistent application of coherent constitutional considerations. See Tribe, supra note 1, at 1219–21.

28. Naomi Cohen does an outstanding job of tracing the role of the major Jewish organizations in advocating for the separation of church and state. See Cohen, supra note 1, at 123–246; see also Robert F. Drinan, Mending the Wall, 38 Stan. L. Rev. 615 (1986) (on Leo Pfeffer).

29. Murdock v. Pennsylvania, 319 U.S. 105, 115 (1943) (free speech, press, and religion are in preferred position); see Alpheus Thomas Mason, The Core of Free Government, 1938–1940: Mr. Justice Stone and "Preferred Freedoms," 65 Yale L.J. 597 (1956); see also Feldman, From Modernism, supra note 1.

30. See Purcell, supra note 1, at 3–94; Feldman, From Modernism, supra note 1; Stephen M. Feldman, Republican Revival/Interpretive Turn, 1992 Wis. L. Rev. 679, 683–84; cf. Morton White, Social Thought in America (1976) (on the rejection of formalism in the early twentieth century).

31. See Purcell, supra note 1, at 138; Feldman, From Modernism, supra note 1. As the United States approached intervention in World War II, Roosevelt's speeches underscored the need to protect democracy. See, e.g., F.D. Roosevelt's Address at Charlottesville, Virginia (June 10, 1940), reprinted in 2 Commager, supra note 1, at 614.

32. John Dewey, Freedom and Culture 134, 175 (1939). Dewey used the term "culture" in a broad sense so that it would include economic and other social institutions. See id. at 6–12.

33. See Purcell, supra note 1, at 235–66; Jane Mansbridge, The Rise and Fall of Self-Interest in the Explanation of Political Life, in Beyond Self-Interest 3, 8–9 (Jane Mansbridge ed., 1990); see Daniel Bell, The Cultural Contradictions of Capitalism 20–24 (1978) (discussing capitalism and democracy).

34. See Purcell, supra note 1, at 235–66. Robert Dahl wrote: "To assume that this country has remained democratic because of its Constitution seems to me an obvious reversal of the relation; it is much more plausible to suppose that the Constitution has remained because our society is essentially democratic." Robert Dahl, A Preface to Democratic Theory 143 (1956). Likewise, Louis Hartz argued that America was marked by a moral unanimity that simultaneously allowed or included conflict. Louis Hartz, The Liberal Tradition in America 14–20 (1955).

35. See Horwitz, supra note 1, at 56–57.

36. Harper v. Virginia Board of Elections, 383 U.S. 663 (1966) (poll taxes); Gomillion v. Lightfoot, 364 U.S. 339 (1960) (racial gerrymandering).

37. Reynolds v. Sims, 377 U.S. 533 (1964). I do not mean to suggest that the Court and the process theorists totally agreed on the proper judicial methods for promoting democracy. To the contrary, the Court and the "legal process" theorists of the legal academy strongly disagreed about a number of important matters. See Feldman, From Modernism, supra note 1.

38. Voting Rights Act of 1965, 79 Stat. 437, 42 U.S.C. §§ 1973 et seq.; Civil Rights Act of 1964, 78 Stat. 241, 42 U.S.C. §§ 1971, 1975(a)–(d), 2000(a)–(h)(4). Congress had previously enacted the Civil Rights Acts of 1957 and 1960, both of which included inadequate sections on voting rights. See Derrick Bell, Race, Racism, and American Law 145–46 (2d ed. 1980). The Voting Rights Act was amended in 1970, 1975, and 1982. See Hall, supra note 1, at 325–26; see, e.g., Voting Rights Act Amendment of 1970, 84 Stat. 314, 42 U.S.C. § 1973aa.

39. See Brown v. Board of Education, 347 U.S. 483, 493 (1954) (emphasizing a connection between education, good citizenship, and democracy); Horwitz, supra note 1, at 64 (discussing the relation between democracy and Brown).

40. Daniel Jeremy Silver, Foreword, in Abba Hillel Silver, Where Judaism Differs vii (1987).

41. Arthur Hertzberg writes that during the 1950s, for Jews to be accepted in America, they had to sacrifice much of their Jewishness. For those Jews, "Jewishness [was] best forgotten." Hertzberg, supra note 1, at 305; see The Jew in the Modern World: A Documentary History 399 (Paul R. Mendes-Flohr & Jehuda Reinharz eds., 1980); cf. Wuthnow, supra note 1, at 221–22 (a large proportion of Jews came to identify themselves as "just Jews" rather than as Jews in a deep religious sense).

42. 44 U.S. (3 How.) 589 (1845); see also Barron v. Baltimore, 32 U.S. (7 Pet.) 243 (1833) (the fifth amendment takings clause does not apply against states).

43. See 98 U.S. 145, 164–67 (1878); see also Thomas Jefferson, Letter to Danbury Baptist Assocation (Jan. 1, 1802), in Wilson & Drakeman, supra note 1, at 78, 79. I discussed Jefferson's attitudes in the first section of chapter 7. For another case upholding a restriction against polygamy, see Davis v. Beason, 133 U.S. 333 (1890). The Court there wrote: "Bigamy and polygamy are crimes by the laws of all civilized and Christian countries. They are crimes by the laws of the United States." Id. at 341.

44. See Everson v. Board of Education, 330 U.S. 1 (1947); Cantwell v. Connecticut, 310 U.S. 296 (1940). In Cantwell, the Court wrote: "The fundamental concept of liberty embodied in [the fourteenth amendment] embraces the liberties guaranteed by the First Amendment." 310 U.S. at 303.

45. See, e.g., West Virginia State Board of Education v. Barnette, 319 U.S. 624 (1943), overruling Minersville v. Gobitis, 310 U.S. 586 (1940) (both cases involved free exercise and free speech claims by Jehovah's Witnesses challenging compulsory flag salute statutes; Barnette struck down the statute by relying on the free speech clause).

46. See Everson, 330 U.S. at 15–16 (citing Reynolds v. United States, 98 U.S. 145, 164 (1878)). The Everson Court emphasized that the rejection of official establishment in Virginia during the 1780s provided special guidance for the understanding of the first amendment. See Everson, 330 U.S. at 8–13.

47. Everson, 330 U.S. at 15–16.

48. Id. at 18.

49. 333 U.S. 203, 210 (1948).

50. 343 U.S. 306, 313–14 (1952).

51. See, e.g., United States v. MacIntosh, 283 U.S. 605, 625 (1931) ("We are a Christian people."); Church of the Holy Trinity v. United States, 143 U.S. 457, 465–71 (1892) ("this is a religious people," "a religious nation," and a "Christian nation"); Davis v. Beason, 133 U.S. 333, 341 (1890) (the United States is one of the "Christian countries").

52. See Zorach, 343 U.S. at 311; Cohen, supra note 1, at 147–49. Justice Black, dissenting in Zorach, wrote:

> Here the sole question is whether New York can use its compulsory education laws to help religious sects get attendants presumably too unenthusiastic to go unless moved to do so by the pressure of this state machinery. That this is the plan, purpose, design and consequence of the New York program cannot be denied. The state thus makes religious sects beneficiaries of its power to compel children to attend secular schools.

343 U.S. at 318.

53. See Gallagher v. Crown Kosher Super Market of Massachusetts, Inc., 366 U.S. 617 (1961) (emphasizing the establishment clause claim); Braunfeld v. Brown, 366 U.S. 599 (1961) (emphasizing the free exercise claim); Two Guys from Harrison-Allentown, Inc. v. McGinley, 366 U.S. 582 (1961) (emphasizing the establishment clause claim); McGowan v. Maryland, 366 U.S. 420 (1961) (emphasizing the establishment clause claim).

54. See McGowan, 366 U.S. at 431–45.

55. Gallagher, 366 U.S. at 619–21; see also Braunfeld v. Brown, 366 U.S. 599 (1961).

56. See Cohen, supra note 1, at 219–22.

57. 370 U.S. 421, 422, 430 (1962). I draw background information on this case from Cohen, supra note 1, at 165–77.

58. See Cohen, supra note 1, at 168.

59. Engel, 370 U.S. at 425–26, 430–31.

60. See Cohen, supra note 1, at vii, 244 (arguing that by the mid-1960s, Christianity no longer was the American public religion).

61. Engel v. Vitale, The New Republic (July 9, 1962), reprinted in Eastland, supra note 1, at 142, 142; see Brown v. Board of Education, 347 U.S. 483 (1954).

62. Cohen, supra note 1, at 171.

63. In the Name of Freedom, Wall Street Journal (June 27, 1962), reprinted in Eastland, supra note 1, at 138, 138. But cf. Prayer Is Personal, New York Times (June 27, 1962), reprinted in Eastland, supra note 1, at 137 (supporting the decision despite the critical public reaction).

64. See Cohen, supra note 1, at 171–77, 211. Sachar writes: "In 1962 alone, a group of Southern and Republican congressmen sponsored forty-nine separate constitutional amendments to permit school prayer." Sachar, supra note 1, at 796.

65. See 374 U.S. 203, 206–10 (1963) (Schempp was a companion case with Murray v. Curlett; see id. at 203 n.*, 211).

66. Id. at 213 (quoting Zorach v. Clauson, 343 U.S. 306, 313 (1952)).

67. Schempp, 374 U.S. at 216 (quoting Everson v. Board of Education, 330 U.S. 1, 15 (1947)).

68. Schempp, 374 U.S. at 222.

69. 374 U.S. 398 (1963).

70. Before Sherbert, the Court had not held any governmental action to be unconstitutional solely under the free exercise clause. Previous cases that found governmental actions inconsistent with the free exercise clause always involved free speech claims as well. See, e.g., Cantwell v. Connecticut, 310 U.S. 296 (1940).

71. See Sherbert, 374 U.S. at 399–401, 403, 406–09.

72. 403 U.S. 602, 612–13 (1971) (quoting Walz v. Tax Commission, 397 U.S. 664, 674 (1970)).

73. 406 U.S. 205, 220 (1972); see id. at 221–29. The Court wrote: "But to agree that religiously grounded conduct must often be subject to the broad police power of the State is not to deny that there are areas of conduct protected by the Free Exercise Clause of the First Amendment and thus beyond the power of the State to control, even under regulations of general applicability." Id. at 220.

74. See Sullivan, supra note 1, at 215; see also McConnell, supra note 1, at 127–28 (summarizing free exercise cases from 1963 to 1990).

75. See Frazee v. Illinois Department of Employment Security, 489 U.S. 829 (1989) (holding unconstitutional the denial of unemployment benefits to a Christian who refused to work on Sundays but did not belong to an established church or sect); Hobbie v. Unemployment Appeals Commission of Florida, 480 U.S. 136 (1987) (holding unconstitutional the denial of unemployment benefits to a convert to Seventh-day Adventism); Thomas v. Review Board of the Indiana Employment Security Division, 450 U.S. 707 (1981) (holding unconstitutional the denial of unemployment benefits to a Jehovah's Witness who refused to continue to work in a munitions factory because of his religious objections to war).

76. 455 U.S. 252 (1982).

77. 461 U.S. 574 (1983).

78. See 475 U.S. 503, 507–10 (1986). After the Court decided Goldman, Congress passed a law that effectively set aside the Air Force regulation at issue. See Pub. L. 100–180, 100th Cong., 1st Sess. (1987); Kenneth L. Karst, The First Amendment, The Politics of Religion and the Symbols of Government, 27 Harv. C.R.-C.L. L. Rev. 503, 507 (1992).

79. Lyng, 485 U.S. 439 (1988); Bowen, 476 U.S. 693 (1986). In Bowen, a Native American contended that according to his religious beliefs, the assignment of a Social Security number to his daughter would rob her of spiritual power. The Court held that a federal mandate to have a Social Security number before receiving certain federal benefits did not violate the free exercise clause. In Lyng, the Court held that timber harvesting and road building on national forest lands that had been used for Native American religious practices did not violate the free exercise clause. With regard to doctrine, in Bowen a plurality applied a reasonableness test, and in Lyng a majority held that the compelling state interest test was inappropriate. See Lyng, 485 U.S. at 450–51.

80. See 482 U.S. 342, 349–50 (1987). For a discussion (including analyses of lower court cases) of the rights of Jewish prisoners to wear beards and yarmulkes and to eat kosher food, see Abraham Abramovsky, First Amendment Rights of Jewish Prisoners: Kosher Food, Skullcaps, and Beards, 21 Am. J. Crim. L. 241 (1994).

81. See 494 U.S. 872, 877–79 (1990). The Smith Court wrote:

> [A] State would be "prohibiting the free exercise [of religion]" if it sought to ban such acts or abstentions only when they are engaged in for religious reasons, or only because of the religious belief that they display. It would doubtless be unconstitutional, for example, to ban the casting of "statues that are to be used for worship purposes," or to prohibit bowing down before a golden calf.

Id. at 877–78; see Williams & Williams, supra note 1, at 847–48 (commenting on the Smith Court's emphasis on governmental intent).

82. 494 U.S. at 890; see id. at 883.

83. Religious Freedom Restoration Act of 1993, Pub. L. 103–141, Nov. 16, 1993, 107 Stat. 1488 (codified at 42 U.S.C. §§ 2000bb to 2000bb-4 (1994)) (reinstating the compelling state interest test for laws of general applicability infringing free exercise rights); see Jay S. Bybee, Taking Liberties With the First Amendment: Congress, Section 5, and the Religious Freedom Restoration Act, 48 Vand. L. Rev. 1539 (1995). Just recently, the Fifth Circuit Court of Appeals held that the act (RFRA) is constitutional. See Flores v. City of Boerne, 1996 WL 23205 (5th Cir. Jan. 23, 1996). This case certainly will not be the only or the last word on the subject.

84. In Church of the Lukumi Babalu Aye, Inc. v. City of Hialeah, 113 S.Ct. 2217 (1993), the Court held that the compelling state interest test still applied to a governmental action (city ordinances) that was intended to discriminate against a particular religion, Santeria. Santeria is a fusion of Roman Catholicism and the traditional African religion of the Yoruba people. The Court concluded that the state action violated the free exercise clause. In two other subsequent cases raising free exercise claims, the Court held governmental actions unconstitutional but not specifically under the free exercise clause. In Lamb's Chapel v. Center Moriches Union Free School District, 113 S.Ct. 2141 (1993), a school district denied a Christian church access to school premises. The church sought to show a film, for religious purposes, dealing with family and child-rearing issues. Although the church raised free speech and free exercise claims, the Court focused on free speech in holding the governmental action unconstitutional. In Rosenberger v. Rectors and Visitors of the University of Virginia, 115 S.Ct. 2510 (1995), the Court held that the University of Virginia had violated the first amendment by withholding payment for a student publication because it was Christian. As in Lamb's Chapel, though, a free exercise claim was intermingled with a free speech claim, and the Court focused on free speech in holding the state action unconstitutional.

85. See 449 U.S. 39, 41–42 (1980). The state had asserted a secular purpose in the text of the statute itself, but the Court concluded that such an avowal could not overcome the plainly religious purpose behind the posting of the Ten Commandments.

86. See 463 U.S. 388, 391 (1983); see also id. at 408–11 (Marshall, J., dissenting). In distinguishing this case from Committee for Public Education & Religious Liberty v. Nyquist, 413 U.S. 756 (1973), the Mueller majority emphasized that the disputed statute allowed all parents to claim the deduction, while the statute in Nyquist allowed only parents with children in nonpublic schools to claim an otherwise similar tax deduction. Mueller, 463 U.S. at 398–99.

87. See Mueller, 463 U.S. at 405, 408–09 (Marshall, J., dissenting).

88. See id. at 394.

89 463 U.S. 783, 786 (1983). In dissent, Justice Brennan wrote that "if the Court were to judge legislative prayer through the unsentimental eye of our settled doctrine, it would have to strike it down as a clear violation of the Establishment Clause." Id. at 796 (Brennan, J., dissenting). For a case decided before Lemon in which the Court emphasized history or tradition, see Walz v. Tax Commission, 397 U.S. 664 (1970) (upholding the constitutionality of granting churches exemptions from property taxes).

90. Marsh, 463 U.S. at 792 (quoting Zorach v. Clauson, 343 U.S. 306, 313 (1952)).

91. Marsh, 463 U.S. at 823 n.2 (Stevens, J., dissenting). This particular prayer was given to the legislature in 1978. According to the majority, the chaplain stopped referring explicitly to Jesus Christ after a Jewish legislator complained in 1980. See id. at 793 n.14.

92. 465 U.S. 668, 671 (1984).

93. Id. at 674, 679.

94. Id. at 680–81. The Court also added confusion to the precise meaning of the purpose prong in the Lemon test. The Court insisted that a governmental action failed this prong only if it was "motivated wholly by religious considerations." Id. at 680 (emphasis added). In cases both before and after Lynch, the Court interpreted the purpose prong differently. For example, in Stone v. Graham, 449 U.S. 39 (1980), the legislature had explicitly articulated a secular purpose for the disputed statute, but the Court nonetheless held that the statute had no secular purpose. The Court took a similar approach, disregarding the legislature's stated purpose, in Edwards v. Aguillard, 482 U.S. 578 (1987).

95. See Lynch, 465 U.S. at 683–85.

96. O'Connor wrote:

The Establishment Clause prohibits government from making adherence to a religion relevant in any way to a person's standing in the political community. Government can run afoul of that prohibition in two principal ways. One is excessive entanglement with religious institutions, which may interfere with the independence of the institutions, give the institutions access to government or governmental powers not fully shared by non-adherents of the religion, and foster the creation of political constituencies defined along religious lines. The second and more direct infringement is government endorsement or disapproval of religion. Endorsement sends a message to nonadherents that they are outsiders, not full members of the political community, and an accompanying message to adherents that they are insiders, favored members of the political community. Disapproval sends the opposite message.

Id. at 687–88 (O'Connor, J., concurring).

97. See, e.g., id. at 690 (O'Connor, J., concurring).

98. See, e.g., Lee v. Weisman, 112 S.Ct. 2649, 2665 n.9 (1992) (Blackmun, J., concurring); id. at 2676 (Souter, J., concurring). Regardless of the correct interpretation of the endorsement test, Justice O'Connor rather remarkably concluded in Lynch that the "display of the creche ... cannot fairly be understood to convey a message of government endorsement of religion." Lynch, 465 U.S. at 693 (O'Connor, J., concurring).

99. See, e.g., Corporation of the Presiding Bishop of the Church of Jesus Christ of Latter-day Saints v. Amos, 483 U.S. 327 (1987) (under the Lemon test, the Court upheld the Title VII exemption of religious organizations for employment discrimination on the basis of religion in connection with secular nonprofit activities); Edwards v. Aguillard, 482 U.S. 578 (1987) (under the Lemon test, the Court held unconstitutional a statute requiring the teaching of creation science whenever evolution is taught).

100. 492 U.S. 573, 578 (1989).

101. See id. at 592–94.

102. The plurality argued that the four dissenters in Lynch actually had accepted the endorsement test, as articulated in O'Connor's Lynch concurrence. See Allegheny County, 492 U.S. at 595–97 (plurality).

103. Id. at 659 (Kennedy, J., concurring and dissenting) (quoting Lynch, 465 U.S. at 678).

104. Lynch, 465 U.S. at 671; see Allegheny County, 492 U.S. at 598–602.

105. Allegheny County, 492 U.S. at 598.

106. See id. at 613–21.

107. 112 S.Ct. 2649 (1992).

108. I drew these facts from four sources: Weisman, 112 S.Ct. at 2652–54; Henry J. Reske, And May God Bless, 78 A.B.A. J. 47 (Feb. 1992); telephone interview with Daniel Weisman (Feb. 8, 1996); telephone interview with Henry J. Reske, reporter with the A.B.A. J. (Aug. 17, 1993). The Weisman Court raised the question of why the principal chose a rabbi, but the Court then stated that the record did not resolve this matter. Weisman, 112 S.Ct. at 2655.

109. Telephone interview with Daniel Weisman (Feb. 8, 1996).

110. The pamphlet, entitled Guidelines for Civic Occasions, recommended that "public prayers at nonsectarian civic ceremonies be composed with 'inclusiveness and sensitivity.'" Weisman, 112 S.Ct. at 2652.

111. The Court wrote: "We can decide the case without reconsidering the general constitutional framework by which public schools' efforts to accommodate religion are measured. Thus we do not accept the invitation ... to reconsider our decision in Lemon." Id. at 2655.

112. Id. (quoting Lynch, 465 U.S. at 678).

113. Justice Blackmun's concurrence supports this reading of the majority opinion:

> The Court holds that the graduation prayer is unconstitutional because the State "in effect required participation in a religious exercise." Although our precedents make clear that proof of government coercion is not necessary to prove an Establishment Clause violation, it is sufficient. Government pressure to participate in a religious activity is an obvious indication that the government is endorsing or promoting religion.

Weisman, 112 S.Ct. at 2664 (Blackmun, J., concurring).

114. Id. at 2683 (Scalia, J., dissenting).

115. Id. at 2658; see id. at 2659 (discussing peer pressure among adolescents).

116. Id. at 2658–59.

117. 113 S.Ct. 2462, 2466 (1993). In Board of Education of Kiryas Joel Village School District v. Grumet, 114 S. Ct. 2481, 2491 (1994), the Court emphasized that governmental power "must be exercised in a manner neutral to religion." Indeed, at one point, the Court wrote that the statute was unconstitutional because it failed "the test of neutrality." Id. at 2494.

118. 115 S.Ct. 2510, 2521 (1995).

119. See id. at 2521–22; cf. Ira C. Lupu, The Lingering Death of Separationism, 62 Geo. Wash. L. Rev. 230, 256 (1994) (recent cases reveal the triumph of the neutrality-based view of religion clauses).

120. 115 S.Ct. 2440, 2450 n.3 (1995).

121. Id. at 2452 (O'Connor, J., concurring).

122. Id. at 2455 (quoting W. Keeton et al., Prosser and Keeton on The Law of Torts 175 (5th ed. 1984)).

123. Pinette, 115 S.Ct. at 2466 & n.5 (Stevens, J., dissenting).

124. Mark Tushnet, "Of Church and State and the Supreme Court": Kurland Revisited, 1989 S. Ct. Rev. 373, 381.

125. Wisconsin v. Yoder, 406 U.S. 205, 210 (1972). The Court added that "the Amish communities singularly parallel and reflect many of the virtues of Jefferson's ideal of the 'sturdy yeoman' who would form the basis of what he considered as the ideal of a democratic society." Id. at 225–26. But cf. id. at 246–47 (Douglas, J., dissenting) (questions the majority's reliance on idyllic agrarianism).

126. Id. at 216, 222–24. Moreover, the Court explicitly stressed the long history of the Amish (as Christians) as significant to the decision: "It cannot be overemphasized that we are not dealing with a way of life and mode of education by a group claiming to have recently discovered some 'progressive' or more enlightened process for rearing children for modern life." Id. at 235. The Court emphasized that "the Amish community has been a highly successful social unit within our society." Id. at 222.

127. The Amish, however, do not always win. See, e.g., United States v. Lee, 455 U.S. 252 (1982).

128. 475 U.S. 503, 508 (1986).

129. See id. at 525 (Blackmun, J., dissenting); Roy A. Rosenberg, The Concise Guide to Judaism 124–25 (1990) (discussing the importance of a yarmulke).

130. 494 U.S. 872, 890 (1990). After Smith, Congress acted to statutorily reinstate the compelling state interest test for laws of general applicability infringing free exercise rights. See Religious Freedom Restoration Act of 1993, Pub. L. 103–141, Nov. 16, 1993, 107 Stat. 1488 (codified at 42 U.S.C. §§ 2000bb to 2000bb-4 (1994)).

131. The Court wrote: "The free exercise of religion means, first and foremost, the right to believe and profess whatever religious doctrine one desires. Thus, the First Amendment obviously excludes all 'governmental regulation of religious beliefs as such.'" Smith, 494 U.S. at 877 (quoting Sherbert v. Verner, 374 U.S. 398, 402 (1963)).

132. See Marci A. Hamilton, The Belief/Conduct Paradigm in the Supreme Court's Free Exercise Jurisprudence: A Theological Account of the Failure to Protect Religious Conduct, 54 Ohio St. L.J. 713 (1993). Hamilton notes that many other commentators attempt to downplay the importance of the belief/conduct dichotomy. See id. at 721 & n.30.

133. Smith, 494 U.S. at 888.

134. Id. at 885 (quoting Lyng v. Northwest Indian Cemetery Protective Assn., 485 U.S. 439, 451 (1988)).

135. See Lyng, 485 U.S. 439 (1988); Goldman, 475 U.S. 503 (1986); Williams & Williams, supra note 1, at 811–13, 828–34, 846–47 (emphasizing the Court's protection of volitionalist religions); see also Tribe, supra note 1, at 1160–61 (the most fundamental principle that the Court has discovered in the religion clauses is voluntarism: religious beliefs and practices should be based on voluntary choices, not governmental influence); Sandel, supra note 1, at 85–86 (the Court and commentators rely on a voluntarist justification for religious liberty). While the Smith Court stressed the religious significance of individual choice—which is especially important in American Protestantism—it is worth noting that the author of the majority opinion (Justice Scalia) and another member of the majority (Justice Kennedy) are Roman Catholic.

136. For example, the Court wrote:

> Assuming, as we must, that the prayers were offensive to the student and the parent who now object, the intrusion was both real and, in the context of a secondary school, a violation of the objectors' rights. That the intrusion was in the course of promulgating religion that sought to be civic or nonsectarian rather than pertaining to one sect does not lessen the offense or isolation to the objectors. At best it narrows their number, at worst increases their sense of isolation and affront.

Weisman, 112 S.Ct. 2649, 2659 (1992).

137. Id. at 2658; see id. at 2656 (religious beliefs and choices are within the private sphere); see also id. at 2657–58 (a fuller discussion of the free exercise and establishment clauses).

138. 472 U.S. 38, 41–42, 50, 52–54 (1985) (emphasis added in the indented quotation).

139. Abington School District v. Schempp, 374 U.S. 203 (1963).

140. Engel v. Vitale, 370 U.S. 421 (1962).

141. McCollum v. Board of Education, 333 U.S. 203 (1948).

142. Epperson v. Arkansas, 393 U.S. 97 (1968).

143 Lemon v. Kurtzman, 403 U.S. 602 (1971).

144. Committee for Public Education & Religious Liberty v. Nyquist, 413 U.S. 756 (1973).

145 Stone v. Graham, 449 U.S. 39 (1980).

146. Larson v. Valente, 456 U.S. 228 (1982).

147. Aguilar v. Felton, 473 U.S. 402 (1985).

148. Wallace v. Jaffree, 472 U.S. 38 (1985).

149. Edwards v. Aguillard, 482 U.S. 578 (1987).

150. County of Allegheny v. American Civil Liberties Union, 492 U.S. 573 (1989).

151. Lee v. Weisman, 112 S.Ct. 2649 (1992).

152. Everson v. Board of Education, 330 U.S. 1 (1947).

153. Zorach v. Clauson, 343 U.S. 306 (1952).

154. Gallagher v. Crown Kosher Super Market of Massachusetts, Inc., 366 U.S. 617 (1961); Two Guys from Harrison-Allentown, Inc. v. McGinley, 366 U.S. 582 (1961); McGowan v. Maryland, 366 U.S. 420 (1961).

155. Board of Education v. Allen, 392 U.S. 236 (1968).

156. Walz v. Tax Commission, 397 U.S. 664 (1970).

157. Widmar v. Vincent, 454 U.S. 263 (1981).

158. Mueller v. Allen, 463 U.S. 388 (1983).

159. Marsh v. Chambers, 463 U.S. 783 (1983).

160. Lynch v. Donnelly, 465 U.S. 668 (1984).

161. Corporation of the Presiding Bishop of the Church of Jesus Christ of Latter-day Saints v. Amos, 483 U.S. 327 (1987).

162. Zobrest v. Catalina Foothills School District, 113 S.Ct. 2462 (1993).

163. Capitol Square Review and Advisory Board v. Pinette, 115 S.Ct. 2440 (1995).

164. Rosenberger v. Rectors and Visitors of the University of Virginia, 115 S.Ct. 2510 (1995).

165. 472 U.S. 703 (1985).

166. See Gallagher v. Crown Kosher Super Market of Massachusetts, Inc., 366 U.S. 617 (1961) (emphasizing the establishment clause claim); Braunfeld v. Brown, 366 U.S. 599 (1961) (emphasizing the free exercise claim); Two Guys from Harrison-Allentown, Inc. v. McGinley, 366 U.S. 582 (1961) (emphasizing the establishment clause claim); McGowan v. Maryland, 366 U.S. 420 (1961) (emphasizing the establishment clause claim).

167. See Thornton, 472 U.S. at 709–10.

168. The Court wrote that the issue was "whether a state statute that provides employees with the absolute right not to work on their chosen Sabbath violates the Establishment Clause of the First Amendment." Id. at 704–05 (emphasis added). Then, in (mis)describing the statute, the Court wrote: "The statute arms Sabbath observers with an absolute and unqualified right not to work on whatever day they designate as their Sabbath." Id. at 708–09 (emphasis added).

169. Morris N. Kertzer, What Is a Jew? 151 (1953) (emphasis in the original); see Rosenberg, supra note 129, at 13, 126 (on the Jewish Sabbath); Sandel, supra note 1, at 89 (criticizes Thornton for its conception of the Sabbath); cf. McConnell, supra note 1, at 125 (criticizes Justice O'Connor's concurrence in Thornton for its conception of the Sabbath).

170. 489 U.S. 829, 833 (1989).

NOTES TO CHAPTER 10

1. My approach to power is heavily influenced by the works of Michel Foucault and Pierre Bourdieu. See, e.g., Michel Foucault, Discipline and Punish (Alan Sheridan trans., 1977) [hereinafter Foucault, Discipline and Punish]; Michel Foucault, The History of Sexuality (Robert Hurley trans., 1978) [hereinafter Foucault, History of Sexuality]; Michel Foucault, Truth and Power, in The Foucault Reader 51 (Paul Rabinow ed., 1984); Michel Foucault, Two Lectures, in Power/Knowledge 78 (1980) [hereinafter Foucault, Two Lectures]; Michel Foucault, How Is Power Exercised?, reprinted in Hubert L. Dreyfus & Paul Rabinow, Michel Foucault: Beyond Structuralism and Hermeneutics 216 (2d ed. 1983) [hereinafter Foucault, How Is]; Michel Foucault, Why Study Power: The Question of the Subject, reprinted in Hubert L. Dreyfus & Paul Rabinow, Michel Foucault: Beyond Structuralism and Hermeneutics 208 (2d ed. 1983) [hereinafter Foucault, Why Study Power]. For an outstanding synthesis of Foucault's work, see Hubert L. Dreyfus & Paul Rabinow, Michel Foucault: Beyond Structuralism and Hermeneutics (2d ed. 1983), and for an excellent collection of essays critiquing Foucault, see Foucault: A Critical Reader (David Couzens Hoy ed., 1986). On Bourdieu, see Pierre Bourdieu, In Other Words: Essays Towards a Reflexive Sociology (Matthew Adamson trans., 1990) [hereinafter Bourdieu, In Other]; Pierre Bourdieu, Language and Symbolic Power (Gino Raymond & Matthew Adamson trans., 1991) [hereinafter Bourdieu, Language]; Pierre Bourdieu, The Logic of Practice (Richard Nice trans., 1990) [hereinafter Bourdieu, Logic]; Pierre Bourdieu & Loïc Wacquant, The Purpose of Reflexive Sociology, in An Invitation to Reflexive Sociology 61 (1992). For useful introductions to Bourdieu, see John B. Thompson, Introduction, in Bourdieu, Language, supra, at 1; Loïc J.D. Wacquant, Toward a Social Praxeology: The Structure and Logic of Bourdieu's Sociology, in Pierre Bourdieu & Loïc J.D. Wacquant, An Invitation to Reflexive Sociology 1 (1992). For a collection of essays on Bourdieu, see Bourdieu: Critical Perspectives (Craig Calhoun et al. eds., 1993). Some other helpful sources on understanding the postmodern concept of power include the following: John Brenkman, Culture and Domination (1987); Nancy Fraser, Unruly Practices: Power, Discourse, and Gender in Contemporary Social Theory (1989); Allan C. Hutchinson, Dwelling on the Threshold: Critical Essays on Modern Legal Thought (1988); Duncan Kennedy, Sexy Dressing Etc. (1993); Jana Sawicki, Disciplining Foucault: Feminism, Power, and the Body (1991); Thomas E. Wartenberg, The Forms of Power (1990); Rethinking Power (Thomas E. Wartenberg ed., 1992).

Some social and legal theorists studying subcultures, including legal culture, have produced some interesting recent works on power. See Dick Hebdige, Subculture: The Meaning of Style (1979); James C. Scott, Domination and the Arts of Resistance: Hidden Transcripts (1990); Patricia Ewick & Susan S. Silbey, Conformity, Contestation, and Resistance: An Account of Legal Consciousness, 26 New Eng. L. Rev. 731 (1992); Sally Engle Merry, Culture, Power, and the Discourse of Law, 37 N.Y.L. Sch. L. Rev. 209 (1992); Susan Silbey, Making a Place for Cultural Analyses of Law, 17 Law & Soc. Inquiry 39 (1992).

The study and theory of power is sometimes referred to as "cratology." See J.M. Balkin, Understanding Legal Understanding: The Legal Subject and the Problem of Legal Coherence, 103 Yale L.J. 105, 167 n.126 (1993).

2. Helpful sources on postmodernism include the following: Zygmunt Bauman, Intimations of Postmodernity (1992); Steven Connor, Postmodernist Culture (1989); David Harvey, The Condition of Postmodernity (1989); Fredric Jameson, Postmodernism, or, The Cultural Logic of Late Capitalism (1991); Jean-François Lyotard, The Postmodern Condition: A Report on Knowledge (Geoff Bennington & Brian Massumi trans., 1984); Feminism/Postmodernism (Linda J. Nicholson ed., 1990); Roy Boyne & Ali Rattansi, The Theory and Politics of Postmodernism: By Way of an Introduction, in Postmodernism and Society 1 (Roy Boyne & Ali Rattansi eds., 1990); Stephen Crook, The End of Radical Social Theory? Notes on Radicalism, Modernism and Postmodernism, in Postmodernism and Society 46 (Roy Boyne & Ali Rattansi eds., 1990).

3. Fraser, supra note 1, at 26; see Stephen M. Feldman, Diagnosing Power: Postmodernism in Legal Scholarship and Judicial Practice (With an Emphasis on the Teague Rule Against New Rules in Habeas Corpus Cases), 88 Nw. U. L. Rev. 1046 (1994) [hereinafter Feldman, Diagnosing Power]; Stephen M. Feldman, The Persistence of Power and the Struggle for Dialogic Standards in Postmodern Constitutional Jurisprudence: Michelman, Habermas, and Civic Republicanism, 81 Geo. L.J. 2243, 2258–66 (1993) [hereinafter Feldman, The Persistence of Power].

4. Some books on antisemitism and Jewish history that I rely upon in this chapter include the following: Zygmunt Bauman, Modernity and the Holocaust (1989); Naomi W. Cohen, Jews in Christian America: The Pursuit of Religious Equality (1992); Leonard Dinnerstein, Antisemitism in America (1994); Benjamin Ginsberg, The Fatal Embrace: Jews and the State (1993); Arthur Hertzberg, The Jews in America (1989); Paul Johnson, A History of the Jews (1987); William Nicholls, Christian Antisemitism (1993); Nathan Perlmutter & Ruth Ann Perlmutter, The Real Anti-Semitism in America (1982); Harold E. Quinley & Charles Y. Glock, Anti-Semitism in America (1979); Howard M. Sachar, A History of the Jews in America (1992); Charles E. Silberman, A Certain People: American Jews and Their Lives Today (1985); Antisemitism in America Today (Jerome A. Chanes ed., 1995) [hereinafter Chanes].

5. See Bourdieu, Language, supra note 1 (language is a means of communication and a medium of power). Foucault writes:

> [I]n any society, there are manifold relations of power which permeate, characterise and constitute the social body, and these relations of power cannot themselves be established, consolidated nor implemented without the production, accumulation, circulation and functioning of a discourse.

Foucault, Two Lectures, supra note 1, at 93. Another type of symbolic power is art. See Bourdieu, Language, supra note 1, at 164.

6. In Austinian terms, utterances (or speech acts) are performatives because they have illocutionary and perlocutionary force. Illocutionary force arises from an act done in uttering—for example, a promise or a threat. Perlocutionary force arises when an utterance has an effect on others—for example, embarrassment or fright. See J.L. Austin, Performative-Constative, in The Philosophy of Language 13 (John Searle ed., 1971); John Searle, Introduction, in The Philosophy of Language 1 (John Searle ed., 1971).

7. Foucault, History of Sexuality, supra note 1, at 101. Foucault adds: "[Discourse] reinforces [power], but also undermines and exposes it, renders it fragile and makes it possible to thwart it." Id.; see Richard J. Bernstein, Foucault: Critique as a Philosophic Ethos, in The New Constellation 142, 160 (1991). Critical race theorists emphasize the significant power of speech. For example, Charles Lawrence writes: "[R]acist speech constructs the social reality that constrains the liberty of non-whites because of their race." Charles R. Lawrence, If He Hollers Let Him Go: Regulating Racist Speech on Campus, 1990 Duke L.J. 431, 444; cf. Patricia J. Williams, The Alchemy of Race and Rights 61 (1991) (the legacy of slavery and Jim Crow exists in the "powerful and invisibly reinforcing structures of thought, language, and law").

8. Merry, supra note 1, at 217; see id. at 217–18. To be clear, I do not mean to suggest that all words or forms of language are equally constraining or coercive. Without suggesting that words have force totally apart from the context of their use, we can still recognize that different linguistic practices may be more coercive and violent than others. For example, hate speech is usually more violent and harmful than saying "Hello." See Richard Delgado, Words That Wound: A Tort Action for Racial Insults, Epithets, and Name-calling, 17 Harv. C.R.-C.L. L. Rev. 133 (1982); Mari Matsuda, Public Response to Racist Speech: Considering the Victim's Story, 87 Mich. L. Rev. 2320 (1989). But cf. R.A.V. v. City of St. Paul, 112 S. Ct. 2538 (1992) (holds unconstitutional an ordinance punishing hate speech). Moreover, different linguistic practices are associated with different social practices, some of which also are more coercive and violent than others. For example, the Supreme Court's linguistic practices sometimes are associated with social practices—such as capital punishment—that are of the more violent variety.

9. See Linda J. Nicholson, Introduction, in Feminism/Postmodernism 1, 11 (Linda J. Nicholson ed., 1990); see also Wartenberg, supra note , at 135. Adam Thurschwell focuses on two forms of violence inherent in legal discourse: direct violence triggered by legal rhetoric and the destruction of

meaning. See Adam Thurschwell, Reading the Law, in The Rhetoric of Law 275 (Austin Sarat & Thomas R. Kearns eds., 1994); see also Kennedy, supra note 1, at 181 ("The stage for the play of signifiers is sometimes a killing field"). The legal theorist who perhaps has most clearly focused on the violence of language is Robert Cover. See, e.g., Robert M. Cover, Foreword: Nomos and Narrative, 97 Harv. L. Rev. 4 (1983); Robert M. Cover, Violence and the Word, 95 Yale L.J. 1601 (1986).

10.   See Hans-Georg Gadamer, Truth and Method (Joel Weinsheimer & Donald G. Marshall trans., 2d rev. ed. 1989); Feldman, Diagnosing Power, supra note 3, at 1060–65; Stephen M. Feldman, The New Metaphysics: The Interpretive Turn in Jurisprudence, 76 Iowa L. Rev. 661, 681–90 (1991).

11.   With regard to how prejudices enable understanding, Gadamer writes: "[T]he historicity of our existence entails that prejudices, in the literal sense of the word, constitute the initial directedness of our whole ability to experience. Prejudices are biases of our openness to the world." Hans-Georg Gadamer, The Universality of the Hermeneutical Problem, in Josef Bleicher, Contemporary Hermeneutics 133 (1980) [hereinafter Gadamer, The Universality]. Stanley Fish writes similarly that "already-in-place interpretive constructs are a condition of consciousness." Stanley Fish, Dennis Martinez and the Uses of Theory, 96 Yale L.J. 1773, 1795 (1987); see Fish, Change, 86 S. Atlantic Q. 423, 424, 433 (1987).

12.   See Gadamer, The Universality, supra note 11, at 133; see also Stanley Fish, Critical Self-Consciousness, Or Can We Know What We're Doing?, in Doing What Comes Naturally 436, 450–55 (1989). Gadamer uses the metaphor of the "horizon" to communicate the notion that one's possibilities for understanding are limited. The horizon is "the range of vision that includes everything that can be seen from a particular vantage point." Gadamer, Truth and Method, supra note 10, at 302; see id. at 306.

13.   Gadamer, Truth and Method, supra note 10, at 384; Gadamer, The Universality, supra note 11, at 128.

14.   Gadamer writes: "Tradition is not simply a permanent precondition; rather, we produce it ourselves inasmuch as we understand, participate in the evolution of tradition, and hence further determine it ourselves." Gadamer, Truth and Method, supra note 10, at 293; see James B. White, Judicial Criticism, 20 Ga. L. Rev. 835, 867 (1986); cf. Anthony Giddens, Profiles and Critiques in Social Theory 10 (1982) (social structuration is recursive because structure is both the medium and the outcome of the practices it organizes); Niklas Luhmann, Operational Closure and Structural Coupling: The Differentiation of the Legal System, 13 Cardozo L. Rev. 1419, 1422–34 (1992) (the social theory of autopoiesis focuses attention on communication as a central operation in the reproduction of the legal system).

To clarify a point that Gadamer leaves somewhat ambiguous, prejudices and interests should not be understood as mere mental forms or ideas that can be replaced by merely imagining different forms or ideas. Rather, prejudices and interests are learned or absorbed in a deep sense; they become embodied in individuals. That is, prejudices and interests are not like a pair of rose-colored glasses that can be removed and replaced with a pair of green-tinted glasses. To the contrary, once entrenched or learned, particular prejudices and interests are not easily changed or shaken, though they always remain contingent and potentially alterable.

Bourdieu's notion of the embodiment of a practice suggests that prejudices and interests should be understood not merely as a "state of mind" but also as a "state of body." See Bourdieu, Logic, supra note 1, at 68. In fact, Bourdieu writes that "[l]anguage is a body technique." Bourdieu, Language, supra note , at 86. Thus, we might understand language and tradition as also being, in the words of Julia Annas, "socially embodied" or "embodied in various forms of social life." Julia Annas, MacIntyre on Traditions, 18 Phil. & Pub. Aff. 388, 388–89 (1989) (discussing Alasdair MacIntyre's notion of tradition); see Feldman, The Persistence of Power, supra note 3, at 2258–61 (criticizing Habermas's argument that we can separate symbolic reproduction in a lifeworld from material reproduction).

15.   See Bourdieu, In Other, supra note 1, at 133–35. "[T]he social world is the site of continual struggles to define what the social world is." Bourdieu & Wacquant, supra note 1, at 70. James Scott writes:

> [I]t is clear that the frontier between the public [transcript of a dominant group] and the hidden [transcript of an oppressed group] is a zone of constant struggle between dominant and subordinate—not a solid wall. The capacity of dominant groups to prevail—though never totally—in defining and constituting what counts as the public transcript and

what as offstage is ... no small measure of their power. The unremitting struggle over such boundaries is perhaps the most vital arena for ordinary conflict. . . .

Scott, supra note 1, at 14; see Hebdige, supra note 1, at 17.

16. Hebdige, supra note 1, at 102; see Fraser, supra note 1, at 181.

17. Gadamer, supra note 10, at 281.

18. Hebdige, supra note 1, at 102; see id. at 16–17.

19. My conception of the "Other" is heavily influenced by Derridean deconstruction. See, e.g., Jacques Derrida, Of Grammatology 31, 47, 62 (Gayatri Chakravorty Spivak trans., 1976); see also Jacques Derrida, Positions (Alan Bass trans., 1981); Jacques Derrida, Différance, in Margins of Philosophy 3 (Alan Bass trans., 1982); Jacques Derrida, Force of Law: The "Mystical Foundation of Authority," 11 Cardozo L. Rev. 919 (1990).

20. See Hebdige, supra note 1, at 94–99; cf. Roy Boyne, Foucault and Derrida: The Other Side of Reason 124 (1990) (there are two responses to difference: exclusion, and neutralization and incorporation); Richard J. Bernstein, Incommensurability and Otherness Revisited, in The New Constellation 57, 68 (1991) ("the primary thrust of Western tradition has always been to reduce, absorb, or appropriate what is taken to be 'the Other' to 'the Same'").

21. See Boyne, supra note 20, at 124; Drucilla Cornell, Beyond Accommodation 136 (1991); Hebdige, supra note 1, at 94–99. Another technique for subduing the subcultural discourse is to coopt the subcultural signs by converting them into marketable and mass-produced commodities. See Hebdige, supra note 1, at 94–99.

22. Religious discourse is one of the most significant means for producing meaning and social reality. Its significance is magnified, moreover, because it typically denies the meaning-producing role of humans in society. See Peter L. Berger, The Sacred Canopy 100–01 (1967).

23. This definition of difference is itself oriented toward Christianity. That is, from a Jewish perspective unconcerned with Christianity, no special meaning is attributed to the life and death of Jesus because he is of no importance in Judaism. Jesus becomes important to Jews only because they live in a pervasively Christian world.

24. See John M. Hartenstein, Comment, A Christmas Issue: Christian Holiday Celebration in the Public Elementary Schools Is an Establishment of Religion, 80 Cal. L. Rev. 981, 999 (1992) (discussing the pervasiveness of Christmas symbols and celebrations). The theologian James Parkes writes:

> [D]ay by day, week by week, year by year, century by century, the New Testament is read "as the word of God" without omission or comment. Is not this the reason why Jews are treated differently from others, why protest is not made which would be made for any other people? It has sunk into the sub-conscious—or unconscious—of Christians that "after all, Jews ought to have become Christians, and, if they don't see it, they can fairly be expected to take the consequences." Their conduct two thousand years ago is constantly brought before us: they are never shown as a normal, contemporary people with a normal contemporary religion.

James Parkes, Preface, in Antisemitism and Foundations of Christianity v, x–xi (Alan Davies ed., 1979); cf. Hartenstein, supra, at 997 (discussing how schools educate children about Christmas).

25. County of Allegheny v. American Civil Liberties Union, 492 U.S. 573, 659 (1989) (Kennedy, J., concurring and dissenting); see Lee v. Weisman, 112 S.Ct. 2649 (1992).

26. 333 U.S. 203, 212 (1948); see Weisman, 112 S.Ct. 2649, 2656 (1992).

27. Mark Tushnet observes that "where the Justices feel pressure to validate a religious activity, they are likely to respond by treating it as essentially nonreligious." Mark Tushnet, "Of Church and State and the Supreme Court": Kurland Revisited, 1989 S. Ct. Rev. 373, 399. The conception of a public/private dichotomy has been criticized in other contexts. See, e.g., Morris R. Cohen, Property and Sovereignty, 13 Cornell L.Q. 8 (1927); Jennifer Nedelsky, Law, Boundaries, and the Bounded Self, 30 Representations 162 (1990); cf. Linda R. Hirshman, The Rape of the Locke: Race, Gender, and the Loss of Liberal Virtue, 44 Stan. L. Rev. 1133, 1157–58 (1992) (feminists emphasize that liberalism and social contract theory leave intact private exercises of power).

28. 115 S.Ct. 2440, 2444–45, 2449 (1995) (emphasis added); see id. at 2447–49.

29. 494 U.S. 872, 890 (1990).

30. In O'Connor's Pinette concurrence, she at least recognizes the possibility of majority domination: "At some point, for example, a private religious group may so dominate a public forum that a formal policy of equal access is transformed into a demonstration of approval." Pinette, 115 S.Ct. at 2454 (O'Connor, J., concurring).

The Christian majority might express its toleration for outgroup religions by occasionally extending protection to the outgroups' religious practices. See, e.g., Religious Freedom Restoration Act of 1993, 42 U.S.C. §§ 2000bb to 2000bb-4 (1994) (statutorily restoring the compelling state interest test for laws of general applicability that infringe free exercise rights). As is evident, though, when these acts of toleration occur, they usually benefit the majority (sometimes more so than the minority) and almost never harm the majority.

The public/private dichotomy also was supposedly decisive in Corporation of the Presiding Bishop of the Church of Jesus Christ of Latter-day Saints v. Amos, 483 U.S. 327 (1987). In Amos, the Court upheld a Title VII exemption allowing religious organizations to discriminate in employment on the basis of religion, even though, in this instance, the Mormon Church had discriminated in connection with secular nonprofit activities as opposed to specifically religious activities. The Court emphasized that the Church (a private actor), not the government, had forced the employee to choose whether to change his religious practices or lose his job. See, e.g., id. at 337 n.15 (distinguishing Amos from Thornton v. Caldor, Inc., 472 U.S. 703 (1985)).

31. For a discussion of the concept of secularity, see Berger, supra note 22, at 107.

32. McGowan v. Maryland, 366 U.S. 420, 451–52 (1961) (citations omitted; emphasis added); see Braunfeld v. Brown, 366 U.S. 599 (1961).

33. McGowan, 366 U.S. at 444. In Braunfeld, the plurality reasoned that keeping one's business open or closed is merely a secular activity. 366 U.S. at 605. While that assertion may be correct, it is certainly not true that keeping one's business open or closed on Sunday is secular. Rather, the choice of Sunday obviously reflects the religious preferences of the dominant Christian majority. See id. at 614 (Brennan, J., dissenting); Cohen, supra note 4, at 55–56, 61–62; cf. McGowan, 366 U.S. at 431–35 (on the history of the Sunday laws).

34. 465 U.S. 668, 680–81 (1984) (emphasis added).

35. Cf. Bourdieu, Language, supra note 1, at 52 (arguing that dominated speakers can become speechless); Scott, supra note 1, at 3 (the greater the domination of a subordinate group, the more likely the subordinated will say, if anything, what the dominant want to hear); Robin West, Feminism, Critical Social Theory and Law, 1989 U. Chi. Legal F. 59, 66–78 (arguing that patriarchal power produces silence in women). William Nicholls writes: "A well-known and authoritative manual of Christian doctrine, used as a textbook in many colleges, has no section at all devoted to the Jews, or to what Christian theologians have said about them. There has been a kind of conspiracy, conscious or unconscious, to render the Jews invisible." Nicholls, supra note 4, at 15.

36. 465 U.S. at 684–85; see id. at 693 (O'Connor, J., concurring).

37. See Feldman, Diagnosing Power, supra note 3, at 1071–72 (focusing on structural power in the context of habeas petitions); cf. Douglas Hay, Property, Authority and the Criminal Law, in Albion's Fatal Tree 17, 44–45 (Douglas Hay et al., eds., 1975) (in eighteenth-century England, the rule of law did not determine which criminal defendants were executed; more broadly, the rule of law did not control the exercise of power).

38. Wartenberg, supra note 1, at 165 (emphasis omitted); see Margaret A. Coulson & Carol Riddell, Approaching Sociology: A Critical Introduction 44–45 (1970); cf. Peter L. Berger, Invitation to Sociology: A Humanistic Perspective 86–98 (1963) (emphasizing how social institutions pattern human conduct, as if individuals were playing various roles).

39. The meaning or significance of social roles also varies with the context. Cf. Anthony Giddens, Central Problems in Social Theory 12–18 (1979) (suggesting that a social role should be understood, in part, as the product of the differences or oppositions from other such roles and, in part, as a matter of interpretive context). Wartenberg writes that "power ... accrues to individuals when they occupy certain social roles." Wartenberg, supra note 1, at 157. He adds that an "expert may be an authority about certain subject matters, [but] this authority is distinguishable from the authority she comes to have as a result of being situated as an empowered agent." Id. at 154 (emphasis in the original).

One should not, however, overestimate the stability of social roles, which are always contingent. See Coulson & Riddell, supra note 38, at 17–18, 39, 41, 46–47 (emphasizing that social roles or "positions" change).

40. See Sawicki, supra note 1, at 63; see also Carol Gilligan, In a Different Voice (1982) (on the psychology of an ethic of care); Nel Noddings, Caring (1984) (on the philosophy of an ethic of care). Pierre Bourdieu argues that personal dispositions adjust to the logic of societal positions. See Bourdieu, In Other, supra note 1, at 130; Bourdieu & Wacquant, supra note 1, at 74, 81. Foucault has focused extensively on the social and historical constitution of the subject. See, e.g., Foucault, Discipline and Punish, supra note 1; Foucault, Why Study Power, supra note 1. In legal theory, Pierre Schlag has consistently focused on the social construction of the subject. See, e.g., Pierre Schlag, Normative and Nowhere to Go, 43 Stan. L. Rev. 167 (1990) [hereinafter Schlag, Normative]; Pierre Schlag, The Problem of the Subject, 69 Tex. L. Rev. 1627 (1991). I discuss Schlag's work in Diagnosing Power, supra note 3, at 1084–1104.

41. Craig Haney, Curtis Banks, & Philip Zimbardo, Interpersonal Dynamics in a Simulated Prison, 1 International J. Criminology & Penology 69 (1973); see Stanley Milgram, Obedience to Authority: An Experimental View (1974) (psychology experiments suggesting that social roles produce inhumanity); see also Bauman, supra note , at 152–67 (discussing the implications of Milgram and Zimbardo's experiments).

42. Iris Marion Young, Five Faces of Oppression, in Rethinking Power 174, 176 (Thomas E. Wartenberg ed., 1992).

43. Cf. Bourdieu & Wacquant, supra note 1, at 143–44 (suggesting that structures of power and subjugation develop historically).

44. Martin E. Marty, Living with Establishment and Disestablishment in Nineteenth Century Anglo-America, in Readings on Church and State 55, 67 (James E. Wood, Jr., ed., 1989). In a similar vein, Richard S. Kay notes that in 1982, Canada adopted the equivalent of a free exercise clause but did not adopt an establishment clause. To Kay, before that time, Canada already had a liberal, tolerant society, and since that time, the Canadian record on religious tolerance appears to be as good as that of the United States. On the other hand, Kay argues that Canada does not prohibit the types of non-coercive injuries that the American establishment clause prevents. See Richard S. Kay, The Canadian Constitution and the Dangers of Establishment, 42 DePaul L. Rev. 361 (1992). Meanwhile, Susan M. Gilles argues that the church establishment in England has both advantages and disadvantages. She underscores, however, that mainstream religions are favored in government funding and that out-group religions occasionally encounter free exercise problems. Susan M. Gilles, "Worldly Corruptions" and "Ecclesiastical Depedations": How Bad Is an Established Church?, 42 DePaul L. Rev. 349 (1992).

45. Robert Wuthnow, The Restructuring of American Religion 300 (1988); see Jon Butler, Awash in a Sea of Faith: Christianizing the American People 1 (1990); Nathan O. Hatch, The Democratization of American Christianity 210–11 (1989); Winthrop S. Hudson & John Corrigan, Religion in America 390–91, 408–14 (5th ed. 1992); Martin E. Marty, Protestantism in the United States: Righteous Empire 250–58 (2d ed. 1986); Michael M. Maddigan, The Establishment Clause, Civil Religion, and the Public Church, 81 Cal. L. Rev. 293, 294–95 (1993).

46. Steven D. Smith, The Rise and Fall of Religious Freedom in Constitutional Discourse, 140 U. Pa. L. Rev. 149, 174–75 (1991) (citing Unsecular America 142 (Richard J. Neuhaus ed., 1986) (appendix at 142, tbl. 20)).

47. See Anti-Defamation League (ADL), 1992 Audit of Anti-Semitic Incidents 1 (1993) [hereinafter Audit]; cf. Ginsberg, supra note 4, at 2–8 (arguing that antisemitism runs in cycles and that there are currently signs of an upturn); Nicholls, supra note 4, at xxviii, 282 (emphasizing that antisemitism continues and that more virulent forms seem to be breaking out again). In a review of several studies of attitudinal (as opposed to behavorial) antisemitism, including the 1992 ADL Audit, Jerome A. Chanes warns that such social science studies must be viewed warily. With that in mind, he concludes that the data are unclear. Chanes adds, however, that there is a strong argument that antisemitism still is decreasing, but at the same time, he acknowledges that the ADL Audit reported a clear increase in the percentage of Americans who believe that Jews have too much power (the "Jewish power" question). Jerome A. Chanes, Antisemitism and Jewish Security in America Today: Interpreting the Data. Why Can't Jews Take "Yes" for an Answer?, in Chanes, supra note 4, at 3, 7–14. Renae Cohen compares the techniques and conclusions of studies of antisemitism conducted in 1964, 1981, and 1992 (the ADL Audit). She argues that "the results of the three surveys point to a lessening of expressed negativity toward Jews over the twenty-eight years between the first and last studies, with the notable exception of the stereotypes of Jewish power and, to a lesser extent, dual loyalty [that is, the belief that American Jews are more loyal to Israel than to the United States]." Renae Cohen, What We

Know, What We Don't Know About Antisemitism: A Research Perspective, in Chanes, supra note 4, at 59, 77–78.

48. Telephone interview with Alan Schwartz, director of research, ADL, New York office (Apr. 5, 1994); see Quinley & Glock, supra note 4, at 1–20 (on the method of testing for antisemitism).

49. See Audit, supra note 47, at 1 (77.5 million Americans works out to approximately 31 percent). Both Howard Sachar and Arthur Hertzberg report the 10 percent figure from 1981; see Hertzberg, supra note 4, at 380; Sachar, supra note 4, at 791. Renae Cohen, however, reports slightly different statistics. According to Cohen, a 1964 survey indicated that 11 percent of Americans thought Jews had too much power, while a 1981 survey reported a 20 percent figure. In comparing these surveys with the 1992 ADL Audit, Cohen notes that each of the surveys asked the "Jewish power" question in different ways and therefore may have affected the results. See Cohen, supra note 47, at 64–68, 74, 76, 80 n.9.

The responses to the "Jewish power" question may vary depending on the area of the country. For example, a Roper Organization poll "revealed that nearly half of all New Yorkers say Jews have too much influence in the life and politics of the city. Among Hispanics, 66% said Jews had too much influence, and 63% of Blacks indicated the same beliefs." Some Jurors Rejoice as Antisemitic Murder Goes Unpunished, Response (The Wiesenthal Center World Report), Winter 1992, at 2.

50. See, e.g., Silberman, supra note 4, at 337–42, 366; cf. Johnson, supra note 4, at 458 (in France in 1906, antisemitism was pronounced dead, but only two years laters, virulent antisemitism was evident); Mortimer Ostow, Myth and Madness: The Psychodynamics of Antisemitism 1–2 (1996) (noting that historically antisemitism has ebbed and flowed, and now it seems to be on the upswing); Perlmutter & Perlmutter, supra note 4, at 93 (arguing that on surveys, many Christians answer to "pass the test"); Tom W. Smith, Anti-Semitism in Contemporary America 19–22 (1994) (discussing the difficulty in empirically ascertaining the existence and extent of hidden, latent, and new antisemitism); Cohen, supra note 47, at 60 (noting that unexpressed antisemitism will not show up in surveys).

51. See Audit, supra note 47, at 3–6; Sachar, supra note 4, at 793–94; see also Center for Democratic Renewal, They Don't All Wear Sheets: A Chronology of Racist and Far Right Violence—1980–1986, at 24, 45, 50, 61, 64 (compiled by Chris Lutz) (reporting many hate crimes committed against Jews during this period of the 1980s).

52. See William F. Buckley, Jr., In Search of Anti-Semitism (1992); Ginsberg, supra note 4, at 224, 235–36; Chanes, supra note 47, at 24; Ruth Wisse, The Unchosen, The New Republic, June 15, 1992, at 15 (discussing the resurfacing of antisemitism in American politics).

53. See Ginsberg, supra note 4, at 234–35.

54. See id. at 223 (quoting Marianne Goldstein et al., Baker's 4-Letter Slam at U.S. Jews, New York Post, Mar. 6, 1992, at 2). When President Ronald Reagan was criticized for planning to visit a military cemetery in Bittburg, Germany, because it contained the graves of forty-seven members of the Nazi SS, Reagan responded by arguing that the Nazi soldiers "were victims, just as surely as the victims in the concentration camps." See Silberman, supra note 4, at 361. During the Reagan years, "a White House staffer named Fred Malek was assigned the task of counting the number of Jewish employees in the Bureau of Labor Statistics, an office within the Labor Department, after the agency released economic data that displeased the president." Ginsberg, supra note 4, at 187.

55. See Dinnerstein, supra note 4, at 219. Jackson used the terms "Hymie" and "Hymietown" at other times as well. See id.; Sachar, supra note 4, at 820.

56. See Ginsberg, supra note 4, at 232–33; Chanes, supra note 47, at 15.

57. See Ginsberg, supra note 4, at 212, 234. Politicians also began invoking distinctly Christian or Protestant symbols for political advantage (recall George Bush's thousand points of light). See Marty, supra note 45, at 257–58; John 1:9 (including the symbolism of lights).

58. Audit, supra note 47, at 12. In 1993, the Sixth Circuit Court of Appeals issued an opinion suggesting that Jews had improperly influenced a Justice Department investigation. The Court wrote: "It is obvious from the record that the prevailing mindset at OSI [Office of Special Investigations] was that the office must try to please and maintain very close relationships with various interest groups [previously identified as Jewish organizations] because their continued existence depended upon it." Demjanjuk v. Petrovsky, 10 F.3d 338, 355 (6th Cir. 1993); see Steven Lubet, That's Funny, You Don't Look Like You Control the Government: The Sixth Circuit's Narrative on Jewish Power, 45 Hastings L.J. 1527 (1994).

59. Cf. Gerald N. Rosenberg, The Hollow Hope: Can Courts Bring About Social Change? (1991) (the Supreme Court generally does not cause significant social change).

60. Peter Applebome, Prayer in Public Schools? It's Nothing New for Many, New York Times, Nov. 22, 1994, at A1, A13.

61. See Rosenberg, supra note 59 (questions the power of courts to institute serious social change); Jerry Fink, School Prayer Bill Praised in Poteau, Tulsa World, Mar. 17, 1995 (in response to the nearly unanimous approval by the Oklahoma House of Representatives of a school prayer bill, a spokesperson for the Poteau Ministerial Alliance said that the bill, if it became law, merely would reaffirm the current practices of the Poteau school district). In 1962, The New Republic reported that more than a decade after McCollum v. Board of Education, 333 U.S. 203 (1948), held that the Illinois released-time program violated the establishment clause, this program in Illinois "continued relatively unabated." Engel v. Vitale, The New Republic (July 9, 1962), reprinted in Religious Liberty in the Supreme Court 142, 143 (Terry Eastland ed. 1993). Daniel Weisman (from Lee v. Weisman, 112 S.Ct. 2649 (1992)) reports that after the district court had held in 1989 that public schools violated the establishment clause by having prayers at graduation, the local archbishop appealed to schools to continue having prayers. And in fact, many Rhode Island schools did offer graduation prayers in 1990. Moreover, even after the Supreme Court held in 1992 that this practice was unconstitutional, some schools continued offering graduation prayers. Telephone interview with Daniel Weisman (Feb. 8, 1996).

Legislation can be as ineffective as Court decisions in bringing about social change. For example, a 1968 statute that banned racial discrimination in most housing sales and rentals has produced little change in the pattern of residential segregation. See Nathan Glazer, A Tale of Two Cities, New Republic, Aug. 2, 1993, at 39–41 (reviewing Douglas S. Massey & Nancy A. Denten, American Apartheid: Segregation and the Making of the Underclass (1993)).

62. Marsh, 463 U.S. 783, 792 (1983); see Lynch, 465 U.S. 668 (1984).

63. See Bourdieu, In Other, supra note 1, at 135 (arguing that social structures produce the symbols or language that, in turn, reproduce the social structures); Hutchinson, supra note 1, at 159–61 (arguing that the social orientation of power influences what meanings are accepted); Scott, supra note 1, at ix–x, 4 (arguing that power relations affect discourse); Bourdieu & Wacquant, supra note 1, at 148 (arguing that symbolic power varies with the position of the speaker); Austin Sarat & William L.F. Felstiner, Law and Social Relations: Vocabularies of Motive in Lawyer/Client Interaction, 22 Law & Soc'y Rev. 737 (1988) (arguing that the attorney's dominant position influences the struggle between attorney and client to interpret the social events surrounding the client's divorce). Zygmunt Bauman writes: "'[S]tructure' is culture sedimented, the petrification of the cultural products of cultural activity.... Cultural activity never starts in any generation, in any particular place, from scratch. It always has to reckon with what has already been accomplished by previous generations." Bauman, supra note 2, at 210.

64. 370 U.S. 421, 431–32 (1962) (quoting James Madison, To the Honorable General Assembly of the Commonwealth of Virginia: A Memorial and Remonstrance (1785)). In Abington School District v. Schempp, 374 U.S. 203, 226 (1963), the Court made a similar statement: "The place of religion in our society is an exalted one, achieved through a long tradition of reliance on the home, the church and the inviolable citadel of the individual heart and mind."

65. See Bourdieu, Language, supra note 1, at 169; Hebdige, supra note 1, at 11–15; David Held, Introduction to Critical Theory: Horkheimer to Habermas 186 (1980); Robert W. Gordon, Legal Thought and Legal Practice in the Age of American Enterprise, 1870–1920, in Professions and Professional Ideologies in America 70, 71–72 (1983). I do not mean to suggest that my conception of ideology is the only possible one. Indeed, in different contexts, I might prefer a broader or narrower definition. In a Law and Society Review symposium devoted to law and ideology, the Special Issue editors emphasized the ambiguity of the term "ideology." They suggested at least six different possible meanings:

> (1) false consciousness associated with and produced by particular structures of domination; (2) systems of belief of a group or class; (3) coherent meanings encoded in social relations and institutions; (4) consciousness linked to material conditions; (5) contested areas of social life as opposed to those that are taken for granted; and (6) the processes by which meanings and ideas are produced.

From the Special Issue Editors, 22 Law & Soc'y Rev. 629, 629 (1988) (in Symposium on Law and Ideology).

66. 494 U.S. 872 (1990).

67. Cf. Charles Lawrence, The Id, the Ego, and Equal Protection: Reckoning with Unconscious Racism, 39 Stan. L. Rev. 317 (1987) (arguing that the intent requirement in equal protection doctrine does not account for unconscious racism).

68. See Laurence H. Tribe, American Constitutional Law 1216 (2d ed. 1988) (the effects prong does not always lead to a searching judicial inquiry); see, e.g., Lynch v. Donnelly, 465 U.S. 668 (1984); Mueller v. Allen, 463 U.S. 388 (1983).

69. 492 U.S. 573, 598–99 n.48 (1989) (emphasis added).

70. Indeed, Justice Blackmun explicitly stated that a "Christmas tree … is not itself a religious symbol." Id. at 616 (opinion of Blackmun, J.); see id. at 632–33 (O'Connor, J., concurring).

71. Winnifred Fallers Sullivan, Paying the Words Extra: Religious Discourse in the Supreme Court of the United States 53 (1994); cf. Allegheny County, 492 U.S. at 639–43 (Brennan, J., dissenting) (a Christmas tree is not secular).

72. See Bell, Brown v. Board of Education and the Interest-Convergence Dilemma, 93 Harv. L. Rev. 518 (1980); see also Mary L. Dudziak, Desegregation as a Cold War Imperative, 41 Stan. L. Rev. 61 (1988) (Brown resulted, at least in part, from the white majority's interest in improving the image of the United States in foreign affairs); see also Brown v. Board of Education, 347 U.S. 483 (1954). Bell writes: "[T]he degree of progress blacks have made away from slavery and toward equality has depended on whether allowing blacks more or less opportunity best served the interests and aims of white society." Derrick Bell, Race, Racism and American Law 39 (2d ed. 1980).

73. See Michael Mann, The Autonomous Power of the State, reprinted in Power in Modern Societies 314, 315–16 (Marvin E. Olsen & Martin N. Marger eds., 1993) (distinguishing despotic from infra-structural power and arguing that in many capitalist democracies, such as the United States, the state's great infrastructural power gives it great despotic power over marginal and minority groups but little despotic power over dominant groups). According to Foucault, an "ideology of right" is an ineffective protection against state power because it developed to protect against a king's (juridical) power, not to protect against the disciplinary and pastoral power of the modern/postmodern state. See Foucault, Two Lectures, supra note 1, at 105–08.

74. 374 U.S. 203 (1963). Naomi Cohen argues that Schempp was one of the key cases in legitimat-ing the secular public schools. See Cohen, supra note 4, at 213.

75. 482 U.S. 578 (1987).

76. In Foucauldian terms, the juridical-political theory of sovereignty tends to conceal power. See Barry Smart, Foucault, Marxism and Critique 85 (1983).

77. Bourdieu writes: "[I]deologies serve particular interests which they tend to present as universal interests, shared by the group as a whole." Bourdieu, Language, supra note 1, at 167; see Ruti Teitel, A Critique of Religion as Politics in the Public Sphere, 78 Cornell L. Rev. 747, 809–10 (1993) (allowing all religions equal access to public facilities favors those religions that seek to proselytize; nonevangelizing religions, such as Hinduism, do not want public access).

78. See Christopher L. Eisgruber, Madison's Wager: Religious Liberty in the Constitutional Order, 89 Nw. U. L. Rev. 347, 409 (1995) (recommending legislation to sustain minority religions because they contribute alternative perspectives to the political order). Without governmental protection and assistance, a religious outgroup in America resembles an unprotected individual confronted by the overwhelming power of a cartel in the economic marketplace. Cf. Berger, supra note 22, at 140–44 (on cartelization in religion). Daniel Conkle argues that the Supreme Court should focus on the mes-sage or effect of governmental actions on religious outsiders because insiders already are strongly embraced by the community. Nonetheless, he simultaneously defends traditional or long-standing governmental practices despite their offense to religious outsiders. See Daniel O. Conkle, Toward a General Theory of the Establishment Clause, 82 Nw. U. L. Rev. 1113, 1178–84 (1988); cf. Kenneth L. Karst, The First Amendment, The Politics of Religion and the Symbols of Government, 27 Harv. C.R.-C.L. L. Rev. 503, 516 (1992) (if using the endorsement test to adjudicate establishment clause claims, the Court should determine endorsement from the perspective of the outsider). Steven D. Smith criti-cizes Conkle's (albeit weak) suggestion that the Court emphasize the inclusion of religious outsiders. See Steven D. Smith, Foreordained Failure: The Quest for a Constitutional Principle of Religious Freedom 114–15 (1995).

79. 114 S.Ct. 2481, 2485 (1994).

80. Aguilar v. Felton, 473 U.S. 402 (1985), and School Dist. of Grand Rapids v. Ball, 473 U.S. 373 (1985), previously had held that publicly funded classes on religious school premises violate the establishment clause.

81. 114 S.Ct. at 2491; see id. at 2494. The Court wrote: "Here the benefit flows only to a single sect, but aiding this single, small religious group causes no less a constitutional problem than would follow from aiding a sect with more members or religion as a whole." Id. at 2492. Jeffrey Rosen argues, however, that the Satmar Hasidim used coercive measures to maintain their own hegemonic position within their small community. See Jeffrey Rosen, Village People, The New Republic, Apr. 11, 1994, at 11.

82. 115 S.Ct. 2510, 2515 (1995); see id. at 2521–24.

83. See id. at 2535, 2539 (Souter, J., dissenting).

84. Id. at 2525; see id. at 2524–25.

85. In his concurrence in Grumet, Justice Kennedy almost seems to understand this outsider viewpoint. He writes:

> The Satmars' way of life, which springs out of their strict religious beliefs, conflicts in many respects with mainstream American culture. . . . [B]y creating the district, New York did not impose or increase any burden on non-Satmars, compared to the burden it lifted from the Satmars, that might disqualify the District as a genuine accommodation.

114 S.Ct. at 2502 (Kennedy J., concurring). Of course, Kennedy nonetheless concludes that the statute ultimately violates the establishment clause.

86. See, e.g., County of Allegheny v. American Civil Liberties Union, 492 U.S. 573 (1989) (never acknowledging that the government displays of a crèche and a menorah might be constitutionally distinct exactly because one symbol is Christian and one is Jewish); cf. Sullivan, supra note 71, at 144–45 (suggesting that to many American Protestants, a crèche is a vague Christmas symbol of more importance to Roman Catholics). Even in his dissent in Pinette, Justice Stevens goes so far as to equate a Latin (Christian) cross with a menorah. See Capitol Square Review and Advisory Board v. Pinette, 115 S.Ct. 2440, 2470 (1995) (Stevens, J., dissenting).

87. After the Supreme Court's decision upholding the governmental display of a crèche in Lynch v. Donnelly, 465 U.S. 668 (1984), Norman Redlich, the dean of the New York University Law School, wrote: "When I see a government-supported creche, I suddenly feel as if I have become a stranger in my own home, to be tolerated only as long as I accept dominant religious values." Wayne R. Swanson, The Christ Child Goes to Court 173 (1990) (quoting Norman Redlich, Nativity Ruling Insults Jews, New York Times, Mar. 26, 1984, sec. A); cf. Hartenstein, supra note 24, at 1020–21 (emphasizing the difference between how a Christian and a non-Christian perceive a Christmas display). Bourdieu talks of power as operating on a field that is the locus of various relations of force. See Bourdieu & Wacquant, supra note 1, at 96–104.

88. The Weisman Court raised the question of why the principal chose a rabbi, but the Court then stated that the record did not resolve this matter. Weisman, 112 S.Ct. at 2655.

89. Swanson, supra note 87, at 19–20 (quoting Mayor Lynch).

90. See id. at 20 (quoting the editorial, Pawtucket Evening Times, Dec. 18, 1980)).

91. Id. at 31–32 (quoting Mayor Lynch). More forthrightly, a Baptist reverend unabashedly declared that religious outgroups need to conform to Christian practices:

> [W]hen anybody attacks Christianity and nibbles away, eventually the whole structure of American society is threatened. This is a Christian country. We invite all men to take residence here. But one condition of that residency is that they respect our traditions. These are a part of America and we feel that whoever comes in has an obligation to respect them, to become familiar with them, and to abide by them.

Id. at 22 (quoting Barbara Carton, Nativity Scene Participants Speak Out, Providence Journal, Dec. 6, 1981, sec. A). Not all Christians attacked the ACLU position; 31 Protestant ministers issued a public statement supporting the ACLU. See id. at 22–23.

92. To be clear, I do not mean to suggest that individuals feel motivated only by the pursuit of self-interest. Individual motivations are much more complex. See Stephen M. Feldman, Whose Common

Good? Racism in the Political Community, 80 Geo. L.J. 1835 (1992) (contrasting self-interest with other motivations).

93. See Lynch v. Donnelly, 465 U.S. 668, 679–81 (1984).

94. "[T]he privileged of culture tend to perpetuate their monopoly, very often under the appearance of sacrificing it." Bourdieu & Wacquant, supra note 1, at 88.

95. See Bauman, supra note 2, at 51 (on the concept of seduction as a form of social control); Bourdieu & Wacquant, supra note 1, at 81 (suggesting that the dominated participate in their own domination by adjusting their expectations to their limited social possibilities).

96. Cf. Sawicki, supra note 1, at 64 (a disciplinary technology can subjugate more readily because it also enhances power by developing competencies and skills). In effect, then, American Jews acquiesce to an exchange: the threat of overt, flagrant governmental conjunction with religion is traded for the tacit Christian cultural imperialism imposed by supposedly secular, private, and legitimate social practices. See id. at 85 (discussing normalization as a manifestation of power).

97. 492 U.S. 573 (1989). John Hartenstein writes: "Supreme Court decisions have demonstrated that religious practice is not protected by the First Amendment unless it shares stereotypical characteristics with the generally accepted religious practices of the Christian majority." Hartenstein, supra note 24, at 994.

98. 475 U.S. 503 (1986).

99. See Morris N. Kertzer, What Is a Jew? 154–58 (1953); Joseph Telushkin, Jewish Literacy 561–65 (1991). Furthermore, when Jews and other outgroups act like Christians, even if they are not then enabled to share in some benefits with Christians, the outgroups at a minimum reduce the likelihood that they will be perceived as threatening Christian domination.

100. To go from a position of inclusion to one of exclusion resembles crossing from a "safe circle into wilderness." Williams, supra note 7, at 129. Hence, many Jews in nineteenth-century Europe were tempted to seek inclusion in the dominant social order by converting to Christianity, not because of religious faith but because, in the words of the German author Heinrich Heine, "[t]he baptismal certificate [was] the ticket of admission to European culture." Heinrich Heine, A Ticket of Admission to European Culture, reprinted in The Jew in the Modern World: A Documentary History 223, 223 (Paul R. Mendes-Flohr & Jehuda Reinharz eds., 1980).

101. See Scott, supra note 1, at 4 (arguing that social domination forces the subordinated to use or endorse the terms of the dominant group). Kimberle Crenshaw writes: "Black people do not create their oppressive worlds moment to moment but rather are coerced into living in worlds created and maintained by others. Moreover, the ideological source of this coercion is . . . racism." Kimberle Crenshaw, Race, Reform, and Retrenchment: Transformation and Legitimation in Antidiscrimination Law, 101 Harv. L. Rev. 1331, 1357 (1988); cf. Kennedy, supra note 1, at 151 (men enforce traditional identities on women in multiple ways).

102. See Scott, supra note 1, at 4–5, 25. Edward Said writes "that resistance, far from being merely a reaction to imperialism, is an alternative way of conceiving human history." Edward W. Said, Culture and Imperialism 215–17 (1993). Said offers interesting observations about cultural imperialism, but his frequent and casual references to a "Judeo-Christian" tradition disclose his unconscious antisemitism. He writes as if Jews were in the mainstream of Western history and were primarily responsible for the subjugation of non-Western people. See, e.g., id. at 243, 303, 320, 327.

103. Stereotypes of Hate, Response (the Wiesenthal Center World Report), Winter 1992, at 12, 12.

104. Marc Cooper, God and Man in Colorado Springs, The Nation, Jan. 2, 1995, at 9, 9.

105. See Richard L. Berke, White House Tries to Clarify Stand on School Prayer, New York Times, Nov. 18, 1994, at A1; Mr. Clinton's Strange Compromise, New York Times, Nov. 18, 1994, at A14; Katharine Q. Seelye, Republicans Plan Ambitious Agenda in Next Congress, New York Times, Nov. 15, 1994, at A1.

106. Cathy Lynn Grossman, Change Not Gospel to All, USA Today, Dec. 8, 1995, at 1D, 1D.

107. Pro: Putting Faith in Moral Strength, USA Today, Dec. 8, 1995, at 11D, 11D.

108. Hanna Rosin, Invasion of the Church Ladies, New Republic, Apr. 24, 1995, at 20, 21.

109. Is Newspaper Jewish Owned?, Tulsa World, Dec. 8, 1994, at 2, 2.

110. Say a Little Prayer, Wall Street Journal, Nov. 22, 1994, at A22, A22.

111. Sanford Levinson, Religious Language and the Public Square, 105 Harv. L. Rev. 2061, 2063 (1992) (quoting Andrew Rosenthal, In a Speech, President Returns to Religious Themes, New York Times, Jan. 28, 1992, at A17).

112. Barghout v. Bureau of Kosher Meats and Food Control, 66 F.3d 1337 (4th Cir. 1995) (mislabeling food as kosher); Cammack v. Waihee, 932 F.2d 765 (9th Cir. 1991), cert. denied 505 U.S. 1219 (1992) (Good Friday); Bauchman v. West High School, 900 F.Supp. 254 254 (D. Utah 1995) (public school curriculum).

113. See Dodie Smith, The 101 Dalmatians (1956).

114. Bernard Weinraub, Stereotype of Jews Is Revived, New York Times, Nov. 7, 1994, at B1, B1.

115. Hudson & Corrigan, supra note 45, at 423 (quoting Bailey Smith in 1980).

116. W.H. Martin, Dumb Bunnies, Tulsa World, Dec. 8, 1992, at A10, A10 (in section entitled "The People's Voice").

117. Football Without Prayer, Tulsa Tribune, Sept. 4, 1992, at 1A.

118. See Gary Chapman, Flamers, The New Republic, Apr. 10, 1995, at 13, 14.

119. Probably contrary to the expectations of some readers, I will not seriously recommend that the Supreme Court adopt new doctrine in religion clause cases. My preferred approach would allow the government to support and protect religious outgroups but not the religious majority. In fact, if one believes that the intentions of the constitutional framers can and should determine constitutional meaning today (and I do not believe so), then one can reasonably argue that my preferred approach would match the framers' subjective intentions. Insofar as the framers advocated the separation of church and state, they were subjectively thinking about Christian churches—not Jewish synagogues, Moslem mosques, or anything else. Nevertheless, this doctrinal recommendation deserves little discussion for three reasons. First, the Supreme Court justices generally do not listen to my (or anybody else's) recommendations. Second, even if the justices listened, they would not follow my preferred approach. Third, even if they followed my approach, the effect of such a doctrinal change on American social reality is uncertain, to say the least. For these same reasons, I will not recommend that the president appoint more non-Christians as Supreme Court justices. That is, the president is not listening, would not follow my preference even if he were listening, and even if my preference were followed, the effects on American society are uncertain. See generally Feldman, Diagnosing Power, supra note 3, at 1092–93 (discussing how postmodern legal scholars refrain from making the normative recommendations typical of modernist scholars); Schlag, Normative, supra note 40 (criticizing the urge in traditional legal scholarship to provide a normative recommendation).

Selected Bibliography

BOOKS AND ESSAYS

Abramovsky, Abraham. First Amendment Rights of Jewish Prisoners: Kosher Food, Skullcaps, and Beards, 21 Am. J. Crim. L. 241 (1994).

Ackerman, Bruce A. Constitutional Politics/Constitutional Law, 99 Yale L.J. 453 (1989).

____. Reconstructing American Law (1984).

Adair, John. Founding Fathers: The Puritans in England and America (1982).

Adams, George Burton. Constitutional History of England (1934 ed.).

Ahlstrom, Sydney E. A Religious History of the American People (1972).

Anti-Defamation League. 1992 Audit of Anti-Semitic Incidents (1993).

Antisemitism and Foundations of Christianity (Alan Davies ed., 1979).

Antisemitism in America Today (Jerome A. Chanes ed., 1995).

Aquinas, Thomas. On Kingship (Gerald B. Phelan trans., 1982 ed.).

____. Summa Contra Gentiles: Providence (Book III) (Vernon J. Bourke trans., 1956).

____. Summa Theologica (Benziger Bros., 1st complete American ed. 1946).

Aristotle. Nichomachean Ethics (I. Bywater trans.), reprinted in The Complete Works of Aristotle 1729–1867 (Jonathan Barnes ed., 1984).

____. The Politics (Carnes Lord trans., 1984).

Arkin, Marc M. "The Intractable Principle": David Hume, James Madison, Religion, and the Tenth Federalist, 39 Am. J. Legal Hist. 148 (1995).

Auerbach, Jerold S. Unequal Justice: Lawyers and Social Change in Modern America (1976).

Augustine. The City of God (Marcus Dods trans. & ed., 1948).

____. The Work of the Monks, in The Fathers of the Church 323 (Roy J. Deferrari ed., 1952).

Austin, J.L. Performative-Constative, in The Philosophy of Language 13 (John Searle ed., 1971).

Bailyn, Bernard. The Ideological Origins of the American Revolution (1967).

Balkin, J.M. Understanding Legal Understanding: The Legal Subject and the Problem of Legal Coherence, 103 Yale L.J. 105 (1993).

Bauman, Zygmunt. Intimations of Postmodernity (1992).

____. Modernity and the Holocaust (1989).

Baum, Gregory. Introduction, in Rosemary Ruether, Faith and Fratricide: The Theological Roots of Anti-Semitism 1 (1974).

Bell, Daniel. The Cultural Contradictions of Capitalism (1978).

Bell, Derrick A. Brown v. Board of Education and the Interest-Convergence Dilemma, 93 Harv. L. Rev. 518 (1980).

____. Race, Racism, and American Law (2d ed. 1980).

____. Faces At the Bottom of the Well: The Permanence of Racism (1992).

Ben-Sasson, Hayim Hillel. The Reformation in Contemporary Jewish Eyes, 4 Proceedings of the Israel Academy of Sciences & Humanities 239 (1969–1970).

Berger, Peter L. Invitation to Sociology: A Humanistic Perspective (1963).

____. The Sacred Canopy (1967).

Berman, Harold J. Law and Revolution: The Formation of the Western Legal Tradition (1983).

_____. Religion and Law: The First Amendment in Historical Perspective, 35 Emory L.J. 777 (1986).

Berns, Laurence. Thomas Hobbes, in History of Political Philosophy 396 (Leo Strauss & Joseph Cropsey eds., 3d ed. 1987).

Bernstein, Richard J. Foucault: Critique as a Philosophic Ethos, in The New Constellation 142 (1991).

_____. Incommensurability and Otherness Revisited, in The New Constellation 57 (1991).

Blitzer, Charles. Introduction, in James Harrington, The Political Writings of James Harrington (1955).

Blumenthal, Uta-Renate. The Investiture Controversy: Church and Monarch from the Ninth to the Twelfth Century (1988).

Bodin, Jean. Six Bookes of a Commonweale (Harv. Univ. Press ed. 1962, a facsimile of the English translation of 1606).

Borden, Morton. Jews, Turks, and Infidels (1984).

Bourdieu: Critical Perspectives (Craig Calhoun et al. eds., 1993).

Bourdieu, Pierre. In Other Words: Essays Towards a Reflexive Sociology (Matthew Adamson trans., 1990).

_____. Language and Symbolic Power (Gino Raymond & Matthew Adamson trans., 1991).

_____. The Logic of Practice (Richard Nice trans., 1990).

Bourdieu, Pierre, & Wacquant, Loïc. The Purpose of Reflexive Sociology, in An Invitation to Reflexive Sociology 61 (1992).

Boyne, Roy. Foucault and Derrida: The Other Side of Reason (1990).

Boyne, Roy, & Rattansi, Ali. The Theory and Politics of Postmodernism: By Way of an Introduction, in Postmodernism and Society 1 (Roy Boyne & Ali Rattansi eds., 1990).

Bradley, Gerard V. Church–State Relationships in America (1987).

Breitman, Richard D., & Kraut, Alan M. Anti-Semitism in the State Department, 1933–44: Four Case Studies, in Anti-Semitism in American History 167 (David A. Gerber ed., 1986).

Brenkman, John. Culture and Domination (1987).

Brown, Peter. Power and Persuasion in Late Antiquity: Towards a Christian Empire (1992).

Buckley, William F., Jr., In Search of Anti-Semitism (1992).

Burt, Robert A. Two Jewish Justices: Outcasts in the Promised Land (1988).

Butler, Jon. Awash in a Sea of Faith: Christianizing the American People (1990).

Bybee, Jay S. Taking Liberties With the First Amendment: Congress, Section 5, and the Religious Freedom Restoration Act, 48 Vand. L. Rev. 1539 (1995).

Calvin, Jean. Commentaries on the Catholic Epistles (John Owen trans., 1959).

_____. Commentaries on the Epistles of Paul the Apostle to the Philippians, Colossians, and Thessalonians (John Pringle trans., 1957).

_____. Commentaries on the Twelve Minor Prophets (John Owen trans., 1950).

_____. 1 Commentary on a Harmony of the Evangelists, Matthew, Mark, and Luke (William Pringle trans., 1956).

_____. Commentary on Jeremiah 30:9, in A Calvin Reader 66 (William F. Keesecker ed., 1985).

_____. Institutes of the Christian Religion (Ford Lewis Battles trans., John T. McNeill ed., 1960) (1st published 1536).

Carmody, Denise Lardner, & Carmody, John Tully. Christianity: An Introduction (1983).

Carter, Stephen L. The Culture of Disbelief (1993).

Casto, William. Oliver Ellsworth's Calvinism: A Biographical Essay on Religion and Political Psychology in the Early Republic, 36 J. Church & State 507 (1994).

Chanes, Jerome A. Antisemitism and Jewish Security in America Today: Interpreting the Data. Why Can't Jews Take "Yes" for an Answer?, in Antisemitism in America Today 3 (Jerome A. Chanes ed., 1995).

Chazan, Robert. European Jewry and the First Crusade (1987).

Church and State in American History (John F. Wilson & Donald L. Drakeman eds., 2d ed. 1987).

Church and State Through the Centuries: A Collection of Historic Documents With Commentaries (Sidney Z. Ehler & John B. Morrall trans. & eds., 1954).

Church, State, and Jew in the Middle Ages (Robert Chazan ed., 1980).

Clark, David S. The Medieval Origins of Modern Legal Education: Between Church and State, 35 Am. J. Comp. L. 653 (1987).

Cohen, Morris R. The Basis of Contract, 46 Harv. L. Rev. 553 (1933).

____. Property and Sovereignty, 13 Cornell L.Q. 8 (1927).

Cohen, Naomi W. Jews in Christian America: The Pursuit of Religious Equality (1992).

Cohen, Renae. What We Know, What We Don't Know About Antisemitism: A Research Perpsective, in Antisemitism in America Today 59 (Jerome A. Chanes ed., 1995).

Cohon, Beryl D. Judaism: In Theory and Practice (1948).

The Columbia History of the World (John A. Garraty & Peter Gay eds., 1972).

The Complete Anti-Federalist (Herbert J. Storing ed., 1981).

Congressional Quarterly, Guide to the U.S. Supreme Court (2d ed. 1990).

Conkle, Daniel O. Toward a General Theory of the Establishment Clause, 82 Nw. U. L. Rev. 1113 (1988).

Connor, Steven. Postmodernist Culture (1989).

The Constitutional Documents of the Puritan Revolution 1625–1660 (Samuel R. Gardiner ed., 3d ed. 1906).

Copleston, Frederick. 2 A History of Philosophy (1950).

Cornell, Drucilla. Beyond Accommodation (1991).

Cornell, Saul. Moving Beyond the Canon of Traditional Constitutional History: Anti-Federalists, the Bill of Rights, and the Promise of Post-Modern Historiography, 12 L. & Hist. Rev. 1 (1994).

Coulson, Margaret A., & Riddell, Carol. Approaching Sociology: A Critical Introduction (1970).

Cover, Robert M. Foreword: Nomos and Narrative, 97 Harv. L. Rev. 4 (1983).

____. Violence and the Word, 95 Yale L.J. 1601 (1986).

The Creeds of Christendom (Philip Schaff ed., 3d ed. 1877).

Crenshaw, Kimberle. Race, Reform, and Retrenchment: Transformation and Legitimation in Antidiscrimination Law, 101 Harv. L. Rev. 1331 (1988).

Crook, Stephen. The End of Radical Social Theory? Notes on Radicalism, Modernism and Postmodernism, in Postmodernism and Society 46 (Roy Boyne & Ali Rattansi eds., 1990).

Crossan, John Dominic. Who Killed Jesus? Exposing the Roots of Anti-Semitism in the Gospel Story of the Death of Jesus (1995).

Curry, Thomas J. The First Freedoms: Church and State in America to the Passage of the First Amendment (1986).

Dahl, Robert. A Preface to Democratic Theory (1956).

Davies, Brian. The Thought of Thomas Aquinas (1992).

Deanesly, Margaret. A History of the Medieval Church 590–1500 (8th ed. 1954).

The Debates in the Several State Conventions on the Adoption of the Federal Constitution (Jonathan Elliot ed., 1836).

Delgado, Richard. Words That Wound: A Tort Action for Racial Insults, Epithets, and Name-calling, 17 Harv. C.R.-C.L. L. Rev. 133 (1982).

Derrida, Jacques. Différance, in Margins of Philosophy 3 (Alan Bass trans., 1982).

____. Force of Law: The "Mystical Foundation of Authority," 11 Cardozo L. Rev. 919 (1990).

____. Of Grammatology (Gayatri Chakravorty Spivak trans., 1976).

____. Positions (Alan Bass trans., 1981).

Dewey, John. Freedom and Culture (1939).

Dickens, A.G. The English Reformation (1964).

Dinnerstein, Leonard. Antisemitism in America (1994).

Dobkowski, Michael N. A Historical Survey of Anti-Semitism in America Prior to World War II, in Persistent Prejudice: Perspectives on Anti-Semitism 63 (Hebert Hirsch & Jack D. Spiro eds., 1988).

A Documentary History of the Jews in the United States, 1654–1875 (Morris U. Schappes ed., 1950).

Documents Illustrative of English Church History (Henry Gee & William John Hardy eds., 1921).

Documents of American History (Henry Steele Commager ed., 3d ed. 1947).

Documents of the Christian Church (Henry Bettenson ed., 2d ed. 1963).

Dreyfus, Hubert L., & Rabinow, Paul. Michel Foucault: Beyond Structuralism and Hermeneutics (2d ed. 1983).

Dunn, John. The Claim to Freedom of Conscience: Freedom of Speech, Freedom of Thought, Freedom of Worship?, in From Persecution to Toleration: The Glorious Revolution and Religion in England 171 (Ole Peter Grell et al. eds., 1991).

____. The Political Thought of John Locke (1969).

Edwards, Jonathan. Doctrine of Original Sin Defended (1758), reprinted in 3 The Works of Jonathan Edwards (1970).

____. Jonathan Edwards: Representative Selections (Clarence H. Faust & Thomas H. Johnson eds., 1962).

Eichhorn, David Max. Evangelizing the American Jew (1978).

Eisenach, Eldon. Two Worlds of Liberalism: Religion and Politics in Hobbes, Locke, and Mill (1981).

Eisgruber, Christopher L. Madison's Wager: Religious Liberty in the Constitutional Order, 89 Nw. U. L. Rev. 347 (1995).

Emerson, Everett. Puritanism in America, 1620–1750 (1977).

Encyclopaedia Judaica (1971).

Epstein, Isidore. Judaism: A Historical Presentation (1959).

Erikson, Kai T. Wayward Puritans (1966).

Ewick, Patricia, & Silbey, Susan S. Conformity, Contestation, and Resistance: An Account of Legal Consciousness, 26 New Eng. L. Rev. 731 (1992).

Farber, Daniel A., & Sherry, Suzanna. A History of the American Constitution (1990).

The Federal and State Constitutions, Colonial Charters, and Other Organic Laws of the United States (Ben Perley Poore ed., 2d ed. 1924).

The Federalist (Clinton Rossiter ed. 1961).

Feldman, Stephen M. Diagnosing Power: Postmodernism in Legal Scholarship and Judicial Practice (With an Emphasis on the Teague Rule Against New Rules in Habeas Corpus Cases), 88 Nw. U. L. Rev. 1046 (1994).

____. From Modernism to Postmodernism in American Legal Thought: The Significance of the Warren Court, in The Warren Court: A Retrospective (Bernard Schwartz ed., Oxford University Press, forthcoming).

____. The New Metaphysics: The Interpretive Turn in Jurisprudence, 76 Iowa L. Rev. 661 (1991).

____. The Persistence of Power and the Struggle for Dialogic Standards in Postmodern Constitutional Jurisprudence: Michelman, Habermas, and Civic Republicanism, 81 Geo. L.J. 2243 (1993).

____. Republican Revival/Interpretive Turn, 1992 Wis. L. Rev. 679.

____. Whose Common Good? Racism in the Political Community, 80 Geo. L.J. 1835 (1992).

Feminism/Postmodernism (Linda J. Nicholson ed., 1990).

Ferguson, Everett. Backgrounds of Early Christianity (2d ed. 1993).

Field, David Dudley. The Theory of American Government, North Am. Rev. (June 1888), reprinted in 3 Speeches, Arguments, and Miscellaneous Papers of David Dudley Field 372 (Titus Munson Coan ed., 1890).

Filmer, Robert. Patriarcha, or the Natural Power of Kings (1680).

Fish, Stanley. Change, 86 S. Atlantic Q. 423 (1987).

____. Dennis Martinez and the Uses of Theory, 96 Yale L.J. 1773 (1987).

Fisher, Eugene J. Anti-Semitism and Christianity: Theories and Revisions of Theories, in Persistent Prejudice: Perspectives on Anti-Semitism 11 (Hebert Hirsch & Jack D. Spiro eds., 1988).

Flannery, Edward H. The Anguish of the Jews: Twenty-Three Centuries of Antisemitism (1985).

____. St. Thomas Aquinas, in History of Political Philosophy 248 (Leo Strauss & Joseph Cropsey eds., 3d ed. 1987).

Forrester, Duncan B. Martin Luther and John Calvin, in History of Political Philosophy 318 (Leo Strauss & Joseph Cropsey eds., 3d ed. 1987).

____. Richard Hooker, in History of Political Philosophy 356 (Leo Strauss & Joseph Cropsey eds., 3d ed. 1987).

Fortin, Ernest L. St. Augustine, in History of Political Philosophy 176 (Leo Strauss & Joseph Cropsey eds., 3d ed. 1987).

Foucault: A Critical Reader (David Couzens Hoy ed., 1986).

Foucault, Michel. Discipline and Punish (Alan Sheridan trans., 1977).

____. The History of Sexuality (Robert Hurley trans., 1978).

____. How Is Power Exercised?, reprinted in Hubert L. Dreyfus & Paul Rabinow, Michel Foucault: Beyond Structuralism and Hermeneutics 216 (2d ed. 1983).

____. Truth and Power, in The Foucault Reader 51 (Paul Rabinow ed., 1984).

____. Two Lectures, in Power/Knowledge 78 (1980).

____. Why Study Power: The Question of the Subject, reprinted in Hubert L. Dreyfus & Paul Rabinow, Michel Foucault: Beyond Structuralism and Hermeneutics 208 (2d ed. 1983).

5 The Founders' Constitution (Philip B. Kurland & Ralph Lerner eds., 1987).

Fox, Robin Lane. Pagans and Christians (1987).

Fraser, Nancy. Unruly Practices: Power, Discourse, and Gender in Contemporary Social Theory (1989).

Fricke, Weddig. The Court-Martial of Jesus (Salvator Attanasio trans., 1987).

Friedman, Lawrence M. A History of American Law (2d ed. 1985).

Gadamer, Hans-Georg. Truth and Method (Joel Weinsheimer & Donald G. Marshall trans., 2d rev. ed. 1989).

____. The Universality of the Hermeneutical Problem, in Josef Bleicher, Contemporary Hermeneutics 133 (1980).

Gerber, David A. Anti-Semitism and Jewish-Gentile Relations in American Historiography and the American Past, in Anti-Semitism in American History 3 (David A. Gerber ed., 1986).

Giddens, Anthony. Central Problems in Social Theory (1979).

____. Profiles and Critiques in Social Theory (1982).

Gilles, Susan M. "Worldly Corruptions" and "Ecclesiastical Depedations": How Bad Is an Established Church?, 42 DePaul L. Rev. 349 (1992).

Gilligan, Carol. In a Different Voice (1982).

Gilmore, Grant. The Ages of American Law (1977).

Gilson, Etienne. The Christian Philosophy of Saint Augustine (L.E.M. Lynch trans., 1960).

____. The Christian Philosophy of St. Thomas Aquinas (L.K. Shook trans., 1956).

____. History of Christian Philosophy in the Middle Ages (1955).

Ginsberg, Benjamin. The Fatal Embrace: Jews and the State (1993).

Goldwin, Robert A. John Locke, in History of Political Philosophy 476 (Leo Strauss & Joseph Cropsey eds., 3d ed. 1987).

Gordon, Robert W. Legal Thought and Legal Practice in the Age of American Enterprise, 1870–1920, in Professions and Professional Ideologies in America 70 (1983).

The Great Awakening: Documents on the Revival of Religion, 1740–1745 (Richard L. Bushman ed., 1969).

Gross, David C. How to Be Jewish (1988).

Gusfield, Joseph R. Symbolic Crusade: Status Politics and the American Temperance Movement (1966).

Halbertal, Moshe. The Scourge of Reason, New Republic, Mar. 15, 1993, at 35.

Hale, Robert. Coercion and Distribution in a Supposedly Non-Coercive State, 33 Pol. Sci. Q. 470 (1923).

Hall, Kermit L. The Magic Mirror (1989).

Hall, Timothy L. Roger Williams and the Foundations of Religious Liberty, 71 B.U. L. Rev. 455 (1991).

Hamilton, Marci A. The Belief/Conduct Paradigm in the Supreme Court's Free Exercise Jurisprudence: A Theological Account of the Failure to Protect Religious Conduct, 54 Ohio St. L.J. 713 (1993).

Hamlyn, D.W. A History of Western Philosophy (1987).

Hancock, Ralph C. Calvin and the Foundations of Modern Politics (1989).

Handy, Robert T. A Christian America (2d ed. 1984).

Haney, Craig, et al. Interpersonal Dynamics in a Simulated Prison, 1 International J. Criminology & Penology 69 (1973).

Harrington, James. The Commonwealth of Oceana (1656), in The Commonwealth of Oceana and A System of Politics 1 (J.G.A. Pocock ed., 1992).

____. A System of Politics (written around 1661 but published posthumously), in The Commonwealth of Oceana and A System of Politics 267 (J.G.A. Pocock ed., 1992).

Hartenstein, John M. Comment, A Christmas Issue: Christian Holiday Celebration in the Public Elementary Schools Is an Establishment of Religion, 80 Cal. L. Rev. 981 (1992).

Hartogensis, B.H. Denial of Equal Rights to Religious Minorities and Non-Believers in the United States, 39 Yale L.J. 659 (1930).

Hartz, Louis. The Liberal Tradition in America (1955).

Harvey, David. The Condition of Postmodernity (1989).

Hatch, Nathan O. The Democratization of American Christianity (1989).

Hay, Douglas. Property, Authority and the Criminal Law, in Albion's Fatal Tree 17 (Douglas Hay et al., eds., 1975).

Healey, Robert M. The Jew in Seventeenth-Century Protestant Thought, 46 Am. Soc'y of Church History 63 (1977).

Hebdige, Dick. Subculture: The Meaning of Style (1979).

Held, David. Introduction to Critical Theory: Horkheimer to Habermas (1980).

Hellwig, Monika K. From the Jesus of Story to the Christ of Dogma, in Antisemitism and Foundations of Christianity 118 (Alan Davies ed., 1979).

Herman, Shael. Legacy and Legend: The Continuity of Roman and English Regulation of the Jews, 66 Tul. L. Rev. 1781 (1992).

Hertzberg, Arthur. The Jews in America (1989).

Hilberg, Raul. The Destruction of the European Jews (1985).

Hill, Christopher. The Century of Revolution, 1603–1714 (1961).

____. Puritanism and Revolution (1958).

Hinsley, F.H. Sovereignty (2d ed. 1986).

Hobbes, Thomas. Leviathan (C.B. Macpherson ed., 1968) (first published 1651).

Hofstadter, Richard. The Age of Reform (1955).

Holmes, Stephen. Jean Bodin: The Paradox of Sovereignty and the Privatization of Religion, 30 Nomos 5 (1988).

____. The Secret History of Self-Interest, in Beyond Self-Interest 267 (J. Mansbridge ed. 1990).

Holy Bible (containing the Old and New Testaments) (King James Version 1611).

Holy Scriptures (Philadelphia, The Jewish Publication Society of America 1955) (according to the Masoretic Text).

Hooker, Richard. The Laws of Ecclesiastical Polity, in Hooker's Works (John Keble ed., 7th ed. 1888).

Höpfl, Harro. Luther and Calvin on Secular Authority (1991).

Horwitz, Morton J. Foreword: The Constitution of Change: Legal Fundamentality Without Fundamentalism, 107 Harv. L. Rev. 30 (1993).

____. The Transformation of American Law, 1780–1860 (1977).

Howe, Irving. World of Our Fathers (1976).

Howe, Mark DeWolfe. The Garden and the Wilderness (1965).

Hudson, Winthrop S., & Corrigan, John. Religion in America (5th ed. 1992).

Hume, David. Of Parties in General, reprinted in Essays: Moral, Political and Literary 54 (Oxford University Press ed. 1963).

Hurst, James Willard. Law and the Conditions of Freedom in the Nineteenth Century United States (1956).

Hutchinson, Allan C. Dwelling on the Threshold: Critical Essays on Modern Legal Thought (1988).

Israel, Jonathan I. European Jewry in the Age of Mercantilism 1550–1750 (2d ed. 1989).

Jacobs, Louis. The Jewish Religion (1995).

Jaher, Frederic Cople. A Scapegoat in the New Wilderness: The Origins and Rise of Anti-Semitism in America (1994).

Jameson, Fredric. Postmodernism, or, The Cultural Logic of Late Capitalism (1991).

Jay, Martin. The Dialectical Imagination: A History of the Frankfurt School and the Institute of Social Research, 1923–1950 (1973).

Jefferson, Thomas. An Act for Establishing Religious Freedom (1779), in Social and Political Philosophy 247 (John Somerville & Ronald E. Santoni eds., 1963).

____. From His "Autobiography," in Social and Political Philosophy 250 (John Somerville & Ronald E. Santoni eds., 1963).

The Jew in the Medieval World: A Source Book, 315–1791 (Jacob R. Marcus ed., 1938).

The Jew in the Modern World: A Documentary History (Paul R. Mendes-Flohr & Jehuda Reinharz eds., 1980).

The Jews of the United States, 1790–1840, A Documentary History (Joseph L. Blau & Salo W. Barron eds., 1963).

Johnson, Paul. A History of the Jews (1987).

Josephus, Flavius. Antiquities of the Jews, reprinted in 3 Complete Works of Josephus 94 (Bigelow, Brown edition, based on the Havercamp trans.).

Karst, Kenneth. Belonging to America (1989).

____. The First Amendment, The Politics of Religion and the Symbols of Government, 27 Harv. C.R.-C.L. L. Rev. 503 (1992).

Katz, David S. The Jews of England and 1688, in From Persecution to Toleration: The Glorious Revolution and Religion in England 217 (Ole Peter Grell et al. eds., 1991).

Kay, Richard S. The Canadian Constitution and the Dangers of Establishment, 42 DePaul L. Rev. 361 (1992).

Kennedy, Duncan. Sexy Dressing Etc. (1993).

____. Toward an Historical Understanding of Legal Consciousness: The Case of Classical Legal Thought in America, 1850–1940, 3 Research in Law & Sociology 3 (1980).

Kertzer, Morris N. What Is a Jew? (1953).

Knight, Janice. Orthodoxies in Massachusetts: Rereading American Puritanism (1994).

Kurland, Philip B. The Origins of the Religion Clauses of the Constitution, 27 Wm. & Mary L. Rev. 839 (1986).

Langmuir, Gavin I. History, Religion, and Antisemitism (1990).

Laslett, Peter. Introduction, in John Locke, Two Treatises of Government 15 (Peter Laslett ed., rev. ed. 1963).

Lawrence, Charles R. The Id, the Ego, and Equal Protection: Reckoning with Unconscious Racism, 39 Stan. L. Rev. 317 (1987).

____. If He Hollers Let Him Go: Regulating Racist Speech on Campus, 1990 Duke L.J. 431.

The Laws and Liberties of Massachusetts (Harvard University Press 1929) (reprint of the 1648 edition).

Lee, Robert. The Social Sources of Church Unity (1960).

Lerner, Max. Introduction, in Niccolo Machiavelli, The Prince and the Discourses (Modern Library ed. 1950).

Leuchtenberg, William E. Franklin D. Roosevelt and the New Deal (1963).

____. The Origins of Franklin D Roosevelt's Court-Packing Plan, 1966 Sup. Ct. Rev. 347.

Levinson, Sanford. Who Is a Jew(ish Justice)?, 10 Cardozo L. Rev. 2359 (1989).

Levy, Leonard W. The Establishment Clause: Religion and the First Amendment (1986).

Locke, John. A Letter Concerning Toleration (1689), in Four Letters on Toleration 2 (London 1870; reprint of 7th ed. 1758).

____. The Reasonableness of Christianity (George W. Ewing ed., 1965) (first published in 1695).

____. The Second Treatise of Government (Liberal Arts Press ed. 1952).

____. Two Treatises of Government (Peter Laslett ed., rev. ed. 1963).

Lord, Carnes. Aristotle, in History of Political Philosophy 118 (Leo Strauss & Joseph Cropsey eds., 3d ed. 1987).

Lubet, Steven. That's Funny, You Don't Look Like You Control the Government: The Sixth Circuit's Narrative on Jewish Power, 45 Hastings L.J. 1527 (1994).

Lupu, Ira C. The Lingering Death of Separationism, 62 Geo. Wash. L. Rev. 230, 231 (1994).

Luther, Martin. The Bondage of the Will (1525), in Martin Luther's Basic Theological Writings 173 (Timothy F. Lull ed., 1989).

____. Commentary on Psalm 68 (1521), in 13 Luther's Works 1 (Jaroslav Pelikan ed., 1956).

____. Commentary on Psalm 82 (1530), in 13 Luther's Works 41 (Jaroslav Pelikan ed., 1956).

____. Commentary on Psalm 101 (1535), in 13 Luther's Works 143 (Jaroslav Pelikan ed., 1956).

____. Commentary on Psalm 110 (1535), in 13 Luther's Works 225 (Jaroslav Pelikan ed., 1956).

____. Concerning the Jews and Their Lies (1543), in The Jew in the Medieval World: A Source Book, 315–1791 at 167 (Jacob R. Marcus ed., 1938).

____. Disputation Against Scholastic Theology (1517), in Martin Luther's Basic Theological Writings 13 (Timothy F. Lull ed., 1989).

____. The Freedom of a Christian (1520), in 31 Luther's Works 327 (Harold J. Grimm ed., 1957).

____. Heidelberg Disputation (1518), in Martin Luther's Basic Theological Writings 30 (Timothy F. Lull ed., 1989).

____. Lectures on Titus (1527), in 29 Luther's Works 4 (Jaroslav Pelikan & Walter A. Hansen eds., 1968).

____. The Ninety-Five Theses (1517), in Martin Luther's Basic Theological Writings 21 (Timothy F. Lull ed., 1989).

____. Temporal Authority: To What Extent It Should Be Obeyed (1523), in 45 Luther's Works 75 (Walther I. Brandt ed., 1956).

____. That Jesus Christ Was Born a Jew, reprinted in The Jew in the Medieval World: A Source Book, 315–1791 at 166 (Jacob R. Marcus ed., 1938).

____. Why the Books of the Pope and His Disciples Were Burned (1520), in 31 Luther's Works 379 (Harold J. Grimm ed., 1957).

Lyotard, Jean-François. The Postmodern Condition: A Report on Knowledge (Geoff Bennington & Brian Massumi trans., 1984).

Machiavelli, Niccolo. Discourses on the First Ten Books of Titus Livius, reprinted in The Prince and the Discourses 99 (Christian E. Detmold trans., Modern Library ed. 1950).

____. The Prince, reprinted in The Prince and the Discourses 2 (Luigi Ricci trans., Modern Library ed. 1950).

Macpherson, C.B. Introduction, in Thomas Hobbes, Leviathan (C.B. Macpherson ed., 1968).

Madison, James. To the Honorable General Assembly of the Commonwealth of Virginia: A Memorial and Remonstrance (June 20, 1785), in James Madison on Religious Liberty 55 (Robert S. Alley ed., 1985).

Maier, Pauline. Popular Uprisings and Civil Authority in Eighteenth-Century America, in American Law and the Constitutional Order 69 (Lawrence Friedman & Harry Scheiber eds., 1978).

Maitland, F.W. The Constitutional History of England (1908).

Mann, Michael. The Autonomous Power of the State, reprinted in Power in Modern Societies 314 (Marvin E. Olsen & Martin N. Marger eds., 1993).

Mansbridge, Jane. The Rise and Fall of Self-Interest in the Explanation of Political Life, in Beyond Self-Interest 3 (Jane Mansbridge ed., 1990).

Marcus, Jacob R. The Colonial American Jew, 1492–1776 (1970).

Markus, R.A. Marius Victorinus and Augustine, in The Cambridge History of Later Greek and Early Medieval Philosophy 327 (A. H. Armstrong ed., 1967).

____. Refusing to Bless the State: Prophetic Church and Secular State, reprinted in Sacred and Secular 372 (1994).

____. The Sacred and the Secular: From Augustine to Gregory the Great, reprinted in Sacred and Secular 84 (1994).

Marshall, William P. In Defense of Smith and Free Exercise Revisionism, 58 U. Chi. L. Rev. 308 (1990).

Marx, Karl. On the Jewish Question (1843), in The Marx–Engels Reader 26 (Robert C. Tucker ed., 2d ed. 1978).

Marty, Martin E. Living with Establishment and Disestablishment in Nineteenth Century Anglo-America, in Readings on Church and State 55 (James E. Wood, Jr., ed., 1989).

____. Protestantism in the United States: Righteous Empire (2d ed. 1986).

____. A Short History of Christianity (1959).

Mason, Alpheus Thomas. The Core of Free Government, 1938–1940: Mr. Justice Stone and "Preferred Freedoms," 65 Yale L.J. 597 (1956).

Matsuda, Mari. Public Response to Racist Speech: Considering the Victim's Story, 87 Mich. L. Rev. 2320 (1989).

Matthews, W.R. The Thirty-nine Articles (1961).

McConnell, Michael W. Free Exercise Revisionism and the Smith Decision, 57 U. Chi. L. Rev. 1109 (1990).

____. The Origins and Historical Understanding of Free Exercise of Religion, 103 Harv. L. Rev. 1409 (1990).

____. Religious Freedom at a Crossroads, 59 U. Chi. L. Rev. 115 (1992).

McDonald, Forrest. Novus Ordo Seclorum (1985).

McLoughlin, William G. The American Evangelicals, 1800–1900 (1968).

____. 'Enthusiasm for Liberty': The Great Awakening as the Key to the Revolution, 87 Proceedings of the Am. Antiquarian Soc. 69 (1977).

Merry, Sally Engle. Culture, Power, and the Discourse of Law, 37 N.Y.L. Sch. L. Rev. 209 (1992).
Michelman, Frank. Foreword: Traces of Self-Government, 100 Harv. L. Rev. 4 (1986).
Miller, Perry. Errand Into the Wilderness (1956).
_____. The New England Mind: From Colony to Province (1953).
_____. Orthodoxy in Massachusetts, 1630–1650 (1933).
_____. Roger Williams: His Contribution to the American Tradition (1953).
Mirsky, Yehudah. Civil Religion and the Establishment Clause, 95 Yale L.J. 1237 (1986).
Mitchell, Joshua. Not By Reason Alone (1993).
Monk, Robert C., & Stamey, Joseph D. Exploring Christianity: An Introduction (2d ed. 1990).
Morgan, Edmund S. Birth of the Republic, 1763–1789 (rev. ed. 1977).
_____. Inventing the People (1988).
Morriss, Peter. Power: A Philosophical Analysis (1987).
Muldoon, James. Popes, Lawyers, and Infidels (1979).
Myrdal, Gunnar. An American Dilemma (1944).
Nedelsky, Jennifer. Law, Boundaries, and the Bounded Self, 30 Representations 162 (1990).
Neuhaus, Richard John. The Naked Public Square (1984).
Neusner, Jacob. Jews and Christians: The Myth of a Common Tradition (1991).
Nicholls, William. Christian Antisemitism (1993).
Nicholson, Linda J. Introduction, in Feminism/Postmodernism 1 (Linda J. Nicholson ed., 1990).
Nielsen, Niels C., Jr., et al. Religions of the World (1983).
Oberman, Heiko A. The Roots of Anti-Semitism: In the Age of Renaissance and Reformation (James I. Porter trans., 1984).
Ostow, Mortimer. Myth and Madness: The Psychodynamics of Antisemitism (1996).
Pagels, Elaine. The Origin of Satan (1995).
Pangle, Thomas. The Spirit of Modern Republicanism (1988).
Parker, T.M. The English Reformation to 1558 (2d ed. 1966).
Parkes, James. The Conflict of the Church and the Synagogue (1934).
_____. Judaism and Christianity (1948).
Perlmutter, Nathan, & Perlmutter, Ruth Ann. The Real Anti-Semitism in America (1982).
Pfeffer, Leo. Church, State, and Freedom (1953).
Piper, Otto. God in History (1939).
Pocock, J.G.A. Introduction, in James Harrington, The Commonwealth of Oceana and A System of Politics (J.G.A. Pocock ed., 1992).
_____. The Machiavellian Moment (1975).
Polishook, Irwin H. Roger Williams, John Cotton and Religious Freedom: A Controversy in New and Old England (1967).
Prall, Stuart. The Bloodless Revolution: England, 1688 (1972).
Purcell, Edward A., Jr. The Crisis of Democratic Theory (1973).
Puritanism and Liberty (A.S.P. Woodhouse ed., 1938).
The Puritan Revolution: A Documentary History (Stuart E. Prall ed., 1968).
The Puritan Tradition in America, 1620–1730 (Alden T. Vaughan ed., 1972).
The Puritans (Perry Miller & Thomas H. Johnson eds., 1963 ed.).
The Puritans in America: A Narrative Anthology (Alan Heimert & Andrew Delbanco eds., 1985).
Quinley, Harold E. & Glock, Charles Y. Anti-Semitism in America (1979).
1 Records of the Colony of Rhode Island and Providence Plantations, in New England, 1636–1663 (for 1637–1638) (John Russell Bartlett ed., A. Crawford Greene and Brothers, State Printers 1856).
The Records of the First Church in Boston, 1630–1868, 39 Publications of the Colonial Society of Massachusetts (1961).
Rethinking Power (Thomas E. Wartenberg ed., 1992).
Religious Liberty in the Supreme Court (Terry Eastland ed., 1993).
Reske, Henry J. And May God Bless, 78 A.B.A. J. 47 (Feb. 1992).
Richards, David A.J. Religion, Public Morality, and Constitutional Law, 30 Nomos 152 (1988).
Riley-Smith, Jonathan. The Crusades (1987).
Roberts, J.M. The Penguin History of the World (1987).
Roth, Cecil. A History of the Jews in England (1941).

Rosen, Jeffrey. Village People, The New Republic, Apr. 11, 1994, at 11.

Rosenberg, Gerald N. The Hollow Hope: Can Courts Bring About Social Change? (1991).

Rosenberg, Roy A. The Concise Guide to Judaism (1990).

Rubenstein, Richard L. Luther and the Roots of the Holocaust, in Persistent Prejudice: Perspectives on Anti-Semitism 11 (Hebert Hirsch & Jack D. Spiro eds., 1988).

Ruether, Rosemary. Faith and Fratricide: The Theological Roots of Anti-Semitism (1974).

____. The Faith and Fratricide Discussion: Old Problems and New Dimensions, in Antisemitism and Foundations of Christianity 230 (Alan Davies ed., 1979).

Russell, Conrad. The Causes of the English Civil War (1990).

Sachar, Howard M. A History of the Jews in America (1992).

Said, Edward W. Culture and Imperialism (1993).

Sandel, Michael J. Freedom of Conscience or Freedom of Choice?, in Articles of Faith, Articles of Peace 74 (James Davison Hunter & Os Guinness eds., 1990).

Sandmel, Samuel. Anti-Semitism in the New Testament? (1978).

Sandoz, Ellis. A Government of Laws: Political Theory, Religion, and the American Founding (1990).

Sarat, Austin, & Felstiner, William L. F. Law and Social Relations: Vocabularies of Motive in Lawyer/Client Interaction, 22 Law & Soc'y Rev. 737 (1988).

Sawicki, Jana. Disciplining Foucault: Feminism, Power, and the Body (1991).

Schlag, Pierre. Normative and Nowhere to Go, 43 Stan. L. Rev. 167 (1990).

____. The Problem of the Subject, 69 Tex. L. Rev. 1627 (1991).

Schwartz, Bernard. The Roots of Freedom: A Constitutional History of England (1967).

Scott, James C. Domination and the Arts of Resistance: Hidden Transcripts (1990).

Searle, John. Introduction, in The Philosophy of Language 1 (John Searle ed., 1971).

Seaward, Paul. The Restoration (1991).

Select Documents of English Constitutional History (George Burton Adams & H. Morse Stephens eds., 1929).

Select Historical Documents of the Middle Ages (Ernest F. Henderson ed., 1892).

Shepard, Thomas. Confessions, 58 Publications of the Colonial Society of Massachusetts (George Selement & Bruce C. Woolley eds., 1981).

Silberman, Charles E. A Certain People: American Jews and Their Lives Today (1985).

Silbey, Susan. Making a Place for Cultural Analyses of Law, 17 Law & Soc. Inquiry 39 (1992).

Silver, Abba Hillel. Where Judaism Differs (1987).

Silver, Daniel Jeremy. Foreword, in Abba Hillel Silver, Where Judaism Differs (1987).

Skinner, Quentin. 1 The Foundations of Modern Political Thought: The Renaissance (1978).

Skinner, Quentin. 2 The Foundations of Modern Political Thought: The Age of Reformation (1978).

Smith, Goldwin. A Constitutional and Legal History of England (1955).

Smith, Steven D. Foreordained Failure: The Quest for a Constitutional Principle of Religious Freedom (1995).

____. The Rise and Fall of Religious Freedom in Constitutional Discourse, 140 U. Pa. L. Rev. 149 (1991).

____. Symbols, Perceptions, and Doctrinal Illusions: Establishment Neutrality and the "No Endorsement" Test, 86 Mich. L. Rev. 266 (1987).

Smith, Tom W. Anti-Semitism in Contemporary America (1994).

Spade, Paul Vincent. Medieval Philosophy, in The Oxford History of Western Philosophy 55 (Anthony Kenny ed., 1994).

Steinberg, Milton. Basic Judaism (1947).

Stevens, Robert. Two Cheers for 1870: The American Law School, 5 Persp. Am. Hist. 405 (1971).

Stokes, Anson Phelps. Church and State in the United States (1950).

Stone, Geoffrey R., et al. Constitutional Law (2d ed. 1991).

Storing, Herbert J. What the Anti-Federalists Were For (1981).

Story, Joseph. 3 Commentaries on the Constitution of the United States (1991; originally published in 1833).

Stout, Harry S. Religion, Communications, and the Ideological Origins of the American Revolution, 34 Wm. & Mary Q. 519 (1977).

Strauss, Leo. Niccolo Machiavelli, in History of Political Philosophy 296 (Leo Strauss & Joseph Cropsey ed., 3d ed. 1987).

Sullivan, Kathleen M. Religion and Liberal Democracy, 59 U. Chi. L. Rev. 195 (1992).

Sullivan, Winnifred Fallers. Paying the Words Extra: Religious Discourse in the Supreme Court of the United States (1994).

Swanson, Wayne R. The Christ Child Goes to Court (1990).

Synan, Edward A. The Popes and the Jews in the Middle Ages (1965).

The Talmud: Selected Writings (Ben Zion Bokser trans., 1989).

Tarnas, Richard. The Passion of the Western Mind (1991).

Teitel, Ruti. A Critique of Religion as Politics in the Public Sphere, 78 Cornell L. Rev. 747 (1993).

Telushkin, Joseph. Jewish Literacy (1991).

Thernstrom, Stephan. A History of the American People (2d ed. 1989).

Thompson, John B. Introduction, in Pierre Bourdieu, Language and Symbolic Power (Gino Raymond & Matthew Adamson trans., 1991).

Thurschwell, Adam. Reading the Law, in The Rhetoric of Law 275 (Austin Sarat & Thomas R. Kearns eds., 1994).

Tierney, Brian. The Crisis of Church and State 1050–1300 (1988).

____. Religion, Law, and the Growth of Constitutional Thought 1150–1650 (1982).

Tilly, Charles. Reflections on the History of European State-Making, in The Formation of National States in Western Europe 21 (Charles Tilly ed., 1975).

Tocqueville, Alexis de. Democracy in America (Henry Reeve text, revised by Francis Bowen, edited by Phillips Bradley; Alfred A. Knopf 1945).

Toon, Peter. The Question of Jewish Immigration, in Puritans, the Millennium and the Future of Israel: Puritan Eschatology 1600 to 1660, at 115 (Peter Toon ed., 1970).

Trevor-Roper, Hugh. Toleration and Religion After 1688, in From Persecution to Toleration: The Glorious Revolution and Religion in England 389 (Ole Peter Grell et al. eds., 1991).

Tribe, Laurence H. American Constitutional Law (2d ed. 1988).

Tushnet, Mark. "Of Church and State and the Supreme Court": Kurland Revisited, 1989 S. Ct. Rev. 373.

Ullmann, Walter. The Growth of Papal Government in the Middle Ages (1955).

____. A History of Political Thought: The Middle Ages (1965).

Voegelin, Eric. The New Science of Politics (1987 ed.).

Wacquant, Loïc J.D. Toward a Social Praxeology: The Structure and Logic of Bourdieu's Sociology, in Pierre Bourdieu & Loïc J.D. Wacquant, An Invitation to Reflexive Sociology 1 (1992).

Walker, Williston. The Creeds and Platforms of Congregationalism (1960).

____. A History of the Christian Church (3d ed. 1970).

Walzer, Michael. The Revolution of the Saints (1965).

Wartenberg, Thomas E. The Forms of Power (1990).

Weaver, Mary Jo. Introduction to Christianity (2d ed. 1991).

Weber, Max. The Protestant Ethic and the Spirit of Capitalism (Talcott Parsons trans., 1958).

Weinreb, Lloyd L. Natural Law and Justice (1987).

Weiss-Rosmarin, Trude. Judaism and Christianity: The Differences (1943).

West, Robin. Feminism, Critical Social Theory and Law, 1989 U. Chi. Legal F. 59.

White, G. Edward. Felix Frankfurter, the Old Boy Network, and the New Deal: The Placement of Elite Lawyers in Public Service in the 1930s, reprinted in Intervention and Detachment 149 (1994).

____. Recapturing New Deal Lawyers, 102 Harv. L. Rev. 489 (1988).

____. Revisiting the New Deal Legal Generation, reprinted in Intervention and Detachment 132 (1994).

White, Morton. The Philosophy of the American Revolution (1978).

____. Philosophy, The Federalist, and the Constitution (1987).

Wilks, Michael. The Problem of Sovereignty in the Later Middle Ages (1963).

Williams, David C., & Williams, Susan H. Volitionalism and Religious Liberty, 76 Cornell L. Rev. 769 (1991).

Williams, Patricia J. The Alchemy of Race and Rights (1991).

Williams, Robert A. The American Indian in Western Legal Thought (1990).

Williams, Roger. The Bloudy Tenent of Persecution, for Cause of Conscience, Discussed (1644), in 3 The Complete Writings of Roger Williams (1963).

Wistrich, Robert S. Antisemitism: The Longest Hatred (1991).

Wood, Gordon S. The Creation of the American Republic, 1776–1787 (1969).
____. Faux Populism, New Republic, Oct. 23, 1995, at 39.
____. The Radicalism of the American Revolution (1991).
Wood, James E., Jr. Introduction: Religion and the Constitution, in The First Freedom: Religion and the Bill of Rights 1 (James E. Wood, Jr., ed., 1990).
Wood, James E., Jr., et al. Church and State in Scripture, History, and Constitutional Law (1958).
Wright, Richard. Black Boy (1937).
Wuthnow, Robert. The Restructuring of American Religion (1988).
Young, Iris Marion. Five Faces of Oppression, in Rethinking Power 174 (Thomas E. Wartenberg ed., 1992).
Zagorin, Perez. A History of Political Thought in the English Revolution (1954).
Zinn, Howard. A People's History of the United States (1980).

CASES

Abington School District v. Schempp, 374 U.S. 203 (1963).
Aguilar v. Felton, 473 U.S. 402 (1985).
A.L.A. Schechter Poultry Corp. v. United States, 295 U.S. 495 (1935).
Barghout v. Bureau of Kosher Meats and Food Control, 66 F.3d 1337 (4th Cir. 1995).
Barron v. Baltimore, 32 U.S. (7 Pet.) 243 (1833).
Bauchman v. West High School, 900 F.Supp. 254 254 (D. Utah 1995).
Board of Education of Kiryas Joel Village School District v. Grumet, 114 S. Ct. 2481 (1994).
Board of Education v. Allen, 392 U.S. 236 (1968).
Bowen v. Roy, 476 U.S. 693 (1986).
Braunfeld v. Brown, 366 U.S. 599 (1961).
Brown v. Board of Education, 347 U.S. 483 (1954).
Cammack v. Waihee, 932 F.2d 765 (9th Cir. 1991), cert. denied 505 U.S. 1219 (1992).
Cantwell v. Connecticut, 310 U.S. 296 (1940).
Capitol Square Review and Advisory Board v. Pinette, 115 S.Ct. 2440 (1995).
Carter v. Carter Coal Co., 298 U.S. 238 (1936).
Charles River Bridge Co. v. Warren Bridge Co., 36 U.S. (11 Pet.) 420 (1837).
Church of the Holy Trinity v. United States, 143 U.S. 457 (1892).
Church of the Lukumi Babalu Aye, Inc. v. City of Hialeah, 113 S.Ct. 2217 (1993).
Committee for Public Education & Religious Liberty v. Nyquist, 413 U.S. 756 (1973).
Corporation of the Presiding Bishop of the Church of Jesus Christ of Latter-day Saints v. Amos, 483 U.S. 327 (1987).
County of Allegheny v. American Civil Liberties Union, 492 U.S. 573 (1989).
Davis v. Beason, 133 U.S. 333 (1890).
Demjanjuk v. Petrovsky, 10 F.3d 338 (6th Cir. 1993).
Edwards v. Aguillard, 482 U.S. 578 (1987).
Employment Division, Dept. of Human Resources v. Smith, 494 U.S. 872 (1990).
Engel v. Vitale, 370 U.S. 421 (1962).
Epperson v. Arkansas, 393 U.S. 97 (1968).
Everson v. Board of Education, 330 U.S. 1 (1947).
Flores v. City of Boerne, 1996 WL 23205 (5th Cir. Jan. 23, 1996).
Frazee v. Illinois Department of Employment Security, 489 U.S. 829 (1989).
Gallagher v. Crown Kosher Super Market of Massachusetts, Inc., 366 U.S. 617 (1961).
Goldman v. Weinberger, 475 U.S. 503 (1986).
Gomillion v. Lightfoot, 364 U.S. 339 (1960).
Harper v. Virginia Board of Elections, 383 U.S. 663 (1966).
Hobbie v. Unemployment Appeals Commission of Florida, 480 U.S. 136 (1987).
Lamb's Chapel v. Center Moriches Union Free School District, 113 S.Ct. 2141 (1993).
Larson v. Valente, 456 U.S. 228 (1982).
Lee v. Weisman, 112 S.Ct. 2649 (1992).
Lemon v. Kurtzman, 403 U.S. 602 (1971).

Lynch v. Donnelly, 465 U.S. 668 (1984).
Lyng v. Northwest Indian Cemetery Protective Assn., 485 U.S. 439 (1988).
Marsh v. Chambers, 463 U.S. 783 (1983).
McCollum v. Board of Education, 333 U.S. 203 (1948).
McGowan v. Maryland, 366 U.S. 420 (1961).
Mueller v. Allen, 463 U.S. 388 (1983).
Murdock v. Pennsylvania, 319 U.S. 105 (1943).
O'Lone v. Estate of Shabazz, 482 U.S. 342 (1987).
People v. Ruggles, 8 Johns. R. 290 (N.Y. 1811).
Permoli v. City of New Orleans, 44 U.S. (3 How.) 589 (1845).
R.A.V. v. City of St. Paul, 112 S. Ct. 2538 (1992).
Reynolds v. Sims, 377 U.S. 533 (1964).
Reynolds v. United States, 98 U.S. 145 (1878).
Rosenberger v. Rectors and Visitors of the University of Virginia, 115 S.Ct. 2510 (1995).
School Dist. of Grand Rapids v. Ball, 473 U.S. 373 (1985).
Sherbert v. Verner, 374 U.S. 398 (1963).
Stone v. Graham, 449 U.S. 39 (1980).
Swift v. Tyson, 41 U.S. (16 Pet.) 1 (1842), overruled by Erie R. Co. v. Tompkins, 304 U.S. 64 (1938).
Thomas v. Review Board of the Indiana Employment Security Division, 450 U.S. 707 (1981).
Thornton v. Caldor, Inc., 472 U.S. 703 (1985).
Trustees of Dartmouth College v. Woodward, 17 U.S. (4 Wheat.) 518 (1819).
Two Guys from Harrison-Allentown, Inc. v. McGinley, 366 U.S. 582 (1961).
United States v. Lee, 455 U.S. 252 (1982).
United States v. MacIntosh, 283 U.S. 605 (1931).
Vidal v. Girard's Executors, 43 U.S. (2 How.) 127 (1844).
Wallace v. Jaffree, 472 U.S. 38 (1985).
Walz v. Tax Commission, 397 U.S. 664 (1970).
West Coast Hotel Co. v. Parrish, 300 U.S. 379 (1937).
West Virginia State Board of Education v. Barnette, 319 U.S. 624 (1943), overruling Minersville v. Gobitis, 310 U.S. 586 (1940).
Widmar v. Vincent, 454 U.S. 263 (1981).
Wisconsin v. Yoder, 406 U.S. 205 (1972).
Zobrest v. Catalina Foothills School District, 113 S.Ct. 2462 (1993).
Zorach v. Clauson, 343 U.S. 306 (1952).

Index